P9-AGV-046

THE TSARIST SECRET POLICE IN RUSSIAN SOCIETY, 1880–1917

The Tsarist Secret Police in Russian Society, 1880–1917

Fredric S. Zuckerman
Senior Lecturer in History
University of Adelaide

NEW YORK UNIVERSITY PRESS
Washington Square, New York

...n Data

The tsarist secret police in Russian society, 1880–1917 / Fredric
S. Zuckerman.
p. cm.
Includes bibliographical references and index.
ISBN 0–8147–9673–7
1. Russia. Okhrannyia otdieleniia. 2. Police—Russia. 3. Secret
service—Russia. 4. Russia—History—Alexander III, 1881–1894.
5. Russia—History—Nicholas II, 1894–1917. I. Title.
HV8225.7.054Z83 1996
363.2'83'0947—dc20 95–16138
CIP

Printed in Great Britain

For Lorre, Michael and Nicola

Contents

List of Tables

Acknowledgements

This book was in the works for a long time. It began as a PhD dissertation under the guidance of Professor William L. Blackwell at New York University. Professor Blackwell's patience and suggestions especially through the early stages of preparation helped to make the dissertation better than it would have otherwise been.

Professor Jeremiah Schneiderman read the completed dissertation with the greatest care. His numerous and welcome criticisms helped me to see with greater clarity the role of the political police under the last two tsars within the panorama of Russian political and social life. Professor Schneiderman also graciously loaned me the manuscript of his subsequently published book, *Sergei Zubatov and Revolutionary Marxism: The Struggle for the Working Class in Russia.* I owe him a deep personal and intellectual debt.

My former colleague Dr Stephen Large, now of Wolfson College, Cambridge University read an early draft of the manuscript and offered several suggestions for its improvement. Mr Hugh Stretton read the manuscript in its penultimate state, offering invaluable advice and along with Professor Trevor Wilson supplied much needed encouragement during the homestretch.

I am indebted to many libraries and archives as well. The Hoover Institution on War, Revolution and Peace which was my home away from home for almost three years is certainly one of the most congenial libraries in the United States. Its librarians, archivists and staffers made my stay there both rewarding and pleasant. Of the librarians, Miss Hilja Kukk because of her help and friendship deserves special mention. In the Hoover Archives where I spent over two years digging through the wealth of primary documentation necessary for this work I made good friends who went out of their way to locate hard-to-find material for me. Some of the people are no longer at the Hoover, others are still there: Dr Franz Lassner, the former Director of Archives; Mr Charles Palm, the current Director; Mr Ronald Bulatoff, Archivist; Mrs Krone Kernke, former Archivist. At Columbia University's Boris Bakhmeteff Archive I intially received considerable help from Mr Lev Magorevsky and more recently and especially from the present Curator of the Bakhmeteff Archive, Ms Ellen Scaruffi and her staff.

The Barr-Smith Library of the University of Adelaide purchased many obscure books and manuscripts for me after they were located with skill and patience by Subject Librarian Mrs Patricia Scott and by Mrs Valerie Balagengadaran and Mrs Adrienne Jago of the Technical Services branch of the Library. Mrs Marie Robinson, Resources Librarian, always seemed to locate sufficient funds for the purchase of the material I requested.

I would also like to thank the staffs of the New York Public Library and the Sterling Memorial Library of Yale University which were my hosts at various times while I researched this book.

The Australia Research Council funded a vital summer's research in the United States.

This book has gone through many drafts, passing through the age of the electric typewriter to the desk top computer in the process. Mrs Anita Taylor, Ms Bev Arnold and Ms Marilyn Dinnis typed successive drafts of the manuscript with the utmost care while putting up with an author who always wanted to make just one more change in wording. I owe a special debt to Ms Dinnis whose friendship and kind words of support were always a welcome tonic. Mrs Marion Pearce patiently allowed the typing and retyping of my manuscript to upset the History office's routine. Ms Penelope Curtin gave the book a thorough editing just when it was required.

From its inception to its completion this work took more years than I care to remember. During these years my family's moral and financial contributions are too great to enumerate. My parents Sidney and Dorothy Bleiberg and my in-laws Louis and Judith Shapiro have contributed more to this book than they can ever imagine. About my wife, well, I could write pages. Lorre lived the book with me from the beginning. As an editor and early typist she read the drafts of the manuscript, making one useful suggestion after another. Her understanding and friendship helped me to overcome the discouragement and frustration which often plague authors who take too long to write their books.

Adelaide, South Australia FREDRIC S. ZUCKERMAN

I would like to thank the following authors, editors and publishers for granting me permission to publish several tables or parts of tables displayed in this book: G.A. Arutiunov and his publisher *Nauka* for table 7 'Stachechnoe dvizhenie v 1910–1912 gg.' (herein 12.3) and table 9 'Kolichestvo stachechnikov v Peterburge v Iiule 1914 g.' (herein 12.5) from his book *Rabochee dvizhenie v Rossii period novogo revoliutsionnogo pod"ema 1910–1914 gg.*; ('Nauka', 1975). I.P. Leiberov for Table 6 'Stachechnoe dvizhenie v Rossii (1916–1917 gg.)' (herein 13.1) taken from his book *Na shturm samoderzhaviia* ('Mysl'', 1979) ; K.F. Shatsillo for allowing me to reprint tables from his article (co-authored by B.I. Grekov and V.V Shelokhaev) 'Evolutsiia politicheskoi struktury Rossii v kontse XIX veka (1895–1913)' in *Istoriia SSSR* no. 5 (September/October 1988); and from Indiana University Press and St Martin's Press to reprint Table 3.1 (herein 9.1) from John Bushnell, *Mutiny amid Repression: Russian Soldiers in the Revolution of 1905–1906* (Bloomington: Indiana University Press, 1985) and Table 6.1 (herein 11.1) from Maureen Perrie, 'Political and Economic Terror in the Tactics of the Russian Socialist-Revolutionary Party before 1914', in *Social Protest, Violence and Terror in Nineteenth- and Twentieth-Century Europe* edited by Wolfgang Mommsen and Gerhard Herschfeld (New York: St Martin's Press, 1982). Every effort has been made to contact all the copyright-holders but if any have been inadvertently omitted the publisher will be pleased to make the necessary arrangement at the earliest opportunity.

A Note on Transliteration and Dates

I have used a modified version of the Library of Congress transliteration system. The Julian Calender used by Tsarist Russia was behind the western or Gregorian Calender by twelve days in the nineteenth century and thirteen days in the twentieth century. For domestic Russian history this is of no consequence. Tsarist police documents originating in western Europe contain both dates.

A Note on Police Terminology

The common terms used by contemporaries as well as subsequent historians to identify the Tsarist political police are *Okhrana* or *Okhranka*. Though imposing in both sound and appearance they are really meaningless and only further obscure an already confused and complexly intertwined group of organisations and bureaus. In order to help unravel the police bureaucracy I have avoided using these labels and replaced them with the proper names of the institutions which they encompassed.

A somewhat finer distinction must be drawn to the reader's attention. This is the usage of the terms 'Special Section', 'Department of Police' and its nick-name, 'Fontanka' in the text. The Special Section, as we shall see, sat atop the political police organisational pyramid and was located in Department of Police Headquarters in St Petersburg. When I use the term 'Special Section' it refers to orders, intelligence data, circulars and so on which emanated specifically from this bureau. When I refer to an opinion, circular, order and the like as having originated in the 'Department of Police' or 'Fontanka' it signifies information appearing under the general imprimatur of the Department of Police, though it was in fact issued by any one of the nine secretariats and in the case of the Weekly Intelligence Surveys, the Special Section. The reason for this awkward explanation should, I hope, become manifestly clear as the reader moves through the book.

Another point worth noting. The word *agentura* as in *Zagranichnaia agentura* has as its English equivalent 'secret service'. I found the translation of the above term, literally Foreign Secret Service, too cumbersome and not entirely accurate. I decided, therefore, to resort to some literary licence by adopting the word *agentura* into the English language, making the Russian political police abroad the 'Foreign Agentura'.

Abbreviations and Glossary

AHR	*American Historical Review*
ASEER	*American Slavic and East European Review*
ARR	*Arkhiv Russkoi Revoliutsii* (*Archive of the Russian Revolution)*
BE	Broghaus and Efron, *Entsiklopedicheskii Slovar' (Encyclopaedia)*
BO	*Boevaia Organizatsiia* (Battle Organization). The agency of Central terror for the Socialist-Revolutionary Party.
Cheka	*Chrezychainaia Komissiia* (Extraordinary Commission)
chinovnik	civil servant
CSS	*Canadian Slavic Studies*
druzhiny	Literally, detachments. In our case groups of armed men committed to acts of terrorism.
dvizhenie revoliutsionnoe	The revolutionary movement.
Extraordinary Commission	Depositions by former tsarist officials before the Extraordinary Commission investigating the illegal activities of former ministers and others. MSS Nikolaevsky Collection
FAAr	The Archive of the Foreign Agentura, located at the Hoover Institution on War, Revolution and Peace.
filer	detective
Fontanka	The nickname for the Department of Police which was located at 16 Fontanka Quai in St Petersburg.
glasnost'	openness
GM	*Golos Minuvshago* (*Voice of the Past*)
gradonachal'nik	mayor (closest but inexact equivalent)
HJ	*Historical Journal*
IR	*Istoriko – Revoliutsionnyi Sbornik* (*Historical-Revolutionary Collection*)
IV	*Istoricheskii Vestnik* (*Historical Herald*)
IZ	Istoricheskie Zapiski (*Historical Notes*)

JCH	*Journal of Contemporary History*
JG	*Jährbucher für Geschichte Osteuropas*
Kadets	Constitutional Democrats
KaS	*Katorga i ssylka* (Penal Servitude and Exile)
KGB	*Komitet Gosudarstvennoi Bezopasnosti* (Committee of State Security)
KL	*Krasnaia Letopis' (Red Chronicle)*
klichka	code name
KA	*Krasnyi Arkhiv* (*Red Archive*)
KS	*Krizis samoderzhaviia v Rossii, 1895–1917* (*The Crisis of the Autocracy in Russia, 1895–1917*)
MVD	*Ministerstvo Vnutrennikh Del* (Ministry of Internal Affairs)
NYPL	*MVD, Departament politsii, Sbornik sekretnykh Tsirkuliarov obrashchennykh k Nachal'nikam gubernskikh zhandarmskikh upravlenii, Gubernatoram i pr. v techenie 1902–1907.* (MVD, Department of Police, Secret Collection of Circulars addressed to the Chief of the provincial gendarme directorates, the Governors and others between 1902–1907). Circulars of the Nizhni Novgorod Gendarme Directorate. New York Public Library.
obshchestvennoe dvizhenie	The social movement. The politically active element of Russian society.
ordena	decorations.
OO	*Okhrannoe Otdelenie* (Security Division). These political police bureaus were located in major cities and centres of revolutionary activity.
Osobyi Otdel	The Special Section. The headquarters of the political police system, controlling all operations at home and abroad.
proizvol	arbitrariness
Protokol no. 8 (22 January 1909) *Protokol* no. 21 (7 February 1909) *Protokol* no. 22 (18 January 1909) *Protokol* no. 34 (2 March 1909)	Procurator's pre-trial statements, the A.A. Lopukhin treason case, in Russian. MSS Nikolaevsky Collection
PTsR	*Padenie Tsarskogo Rezhima* (The Collapse of the Tsarist Regime)

RH	*Russian History*
RR	*Russian Review*
RSDWP	Russian Social Democratic Workers' Party
samoderzhavie	autocracy
sanovnik	A very senior official.
SDs	social democrats
SEER	The Slavonic and East European Review
sekretnyi sotrudnik	undercover agent
Sl R	*Slavic Review*
sluzhashchii	office worker. A term to identify white collar workers in post-revolutionary Russia.
Soiuz Russkogo Naroda	Union of the Russian People
SR	*Sotsial-revoliutsioner'* (Social-revolutionary)
SRs	socialist-revolutionaries
VE	*Vestnik Evropy* (*European Herald*)
VeCheka	*Vserossiskaia Chrezychainaia Komissiia po bor'be s Kontrrevoliutsiei, Spekuliatsiei, Sabotazham i Prestupleniiam i po Dolzhnosti* (All Russian Extraordinary Commission for Combatting Counter-Revolution, Speculation, Sabotage, and Misconduct in Office)
VI	*Voprosy Istorii* (*Issues of History*)
Zagranichnaia agentura	Foreign Agentura. Also known as the Paris Office. It was the headquarters of Tsardom's political police abroad.
zakonnost'	legality
Zhandarmskie upravlenie	Gendarme Directorate. Political police bureaus located throughout Russia. Played a resentful second fiddle to the more recently constituted Security Divisions.

Part I
Setting the Stage

A Comparative Introduction

In 1908 the Sixtieth Congress of the United States debated Attorney General Charles J. Bonaparte's proposals for the establishment of a Federal Bureau of Investigation. The congressional debates and committee hearings expressed the general conclusion that the United States would not be well-served by the creation of this institution. During the debate Congressman Waldo of New York used what he hoped would be a telling argument in voicing his opposition to Bonaparte's plan. 'The only question here', Waldo declared, 'is whether we believe in a central secret-service bureau, such as there is in Russia ...'. And without the slightest hesitation he responded to his own question. 'I believe that it would be a great blow to freedom and to free institutions if there should arise in this country any such great central secret-service bureau as there is in Russia'.[1]

The reputation of the tsarist political police had indeed spread far-and-wide by 1908. Congressman Waldo's opinion of Russia's political police, although not unusual for the day, was based upon sparse data and newspaper stories more overblown than accurate.

Until recently those who studied Russia's pre-World War I political policing agencies have, like Congressman Waldo, based their opinion of the Russian political police on scattered information, filling in the factual gaps with large portions of myth. Furthermore, while popular histories of political policing and the memoirs of spymasters have proliferated, professional historians have for the most part ignored the subject. In Russian history, for example, the memoirs of tsarist political police chiefs have long been available. Yet apart from French historian Maurice La Porte's 1935 excellent study of Late Imperial Russia's political police[2] very little else has appeared.[3] None the less historians of pre-First World War Russia (as well as of Europe) with one or two notable exceptions have devoted themselves to studying those who challenged established authority rather than those who fought to preserve it. Part of the reason for this neglect lies in the difficulties accessing primary sources. Governments are reticent to share details of domestic espionage with their publics. Even in democracies, spying on one's own citizens remains an activity shrouded in mystery. It is somehow more rewarding and more reputable for scholars to concentrate on other more palatable subjects where, as it happens, archives and other sources are more readily at hand. It is just assumed that any regime with a desire to survive will resort to coercive measures to prevent its overthrow.[4] Every state develops methods of preserving internal order, identifies the threat to that order, and characterises and punishes those who wish to destabilise that order, the punishment delivered according to the complexion of its political culture. Comparing the spectrum of responses to actual and/or perceived subversion in several European states and discovering the similarities as well as the differences in their approaches to political crime supplies one of the two contexts necessary for placing political police studies within the panorama of Modern European history. The second context, the main focus of this book, examines the national historical setting within which a particular political police force operates. To understand the tsarist political police is to understand its evolution within both of these contexts.

The brief introduction that follows strives to place the development of the 'Okhrana' within the overall social and political framework that nourished the burgeoning of political police systems throughout Europe in the late nineteenth and early twentieth centuries, necessitating a brief discussion of the evolution in European attitudes toward political crime, that is: what constituted a political crime and who determined that it be considered so; how were political criminals treated by these different societies and what motivated governments, courts, and ordinary citizens to ultimately believe themselves so threatened by subversive forces that they allowed themselves to be persuaded of the need for substantial political police forces to protect them?

****

In Europe – in England, France and Germany – the character of political policing from the middle to the late nineteenth century arose from a peculiar, even a unique balance between ideology and necessity.[5] For much of the second half of the nineteenth century Victorian Liberalism dominated English politics and to a lesser though still significant degree had infiltrated itself into both French and German political thought and jurisprudence. Beginning in the 1850s and stretching almost to the last decade of the century under the influence of the humanism espoused by Victorian Liberalism the political criminal occupied the high moral ground of European politics, enjoying a reputation for courage, integrity and idealism. In England the government afforded foreign anarchists and other 'state criminals', with the exception of the Fenians, a comfortable haven from repression,[6] a restraint credited to both the rock solid stability of their nation and the liberal ideology which permeated its outlook.

In France, during the Third Republic, the Paris Prefecture despite its distaste for politicians of the Left maintained its strong apolitical stance and obeyed its republican government, a government whose liberal outlook meant that it refused to see the socialists as 'enemies of the state' and considered the working classes as integral and valuable contributors to French society. This approach to governance spread to and took firm hold of the judiciary of the Third Republic as well.[7] Even in Germany where the police brutally suppressed perceived subversion with little regard to the principles of liberalism, the forces of law and order adopted the French and British policy of treating political criminals with greater leniency than the common criminal.[8]

By the late 1880s, initiated by the spread of terrorism, confidence in a stable and tranquil future which had previously permeated both bourgeois and aristocratic life in western Europe began to erode, dissipating the generally benign attitude toward political crime. The persistence of the Irish bombing campaign in the 1880s and the first anarchist outrages in Paris during the early 1890s, including the assassination of President Carnot, unnerved the European establishment. In England the deepening concern over terrorism led to the establishment of the Special Branch in 1887, although terrorism in France and on the Continent generally far exceeded the Irish bombers in England: in 1893 a bomb in the French Chamber of Deputies and the following year the assassination of President Carnot heralding a wave of terrorism in western Europe.[9]

Both the Special Branch and the Paris Prefecture, each employing methods tailored to their needs, eventually conquered the politically motivated violence in their midst.[10] None the less, the balance between necessity and Victorian liberal ideology was shifting in favour of necessity.[11] The ruling and governing elites – the aristocracy, the gentry, the industrialists, the *haute* bourgeoisie, and the leadership of the bureaucracy – by the end of the nineteenth century confronted new and to them terrifying enemies. As a result, the definition of 'state crime' was expanded to incorporate these new horrors and the stereotype of the political criminal darkened for those who defended the status quo. No longer did the heroics of political criminals simultaneously enthral and win the admiration of law abiding citizens. By the 1890s the bravery and idealism of individual political dissenters was lost within the mist of economic depression, international rivalries, and most significantly the rise of the proletariat and the birth pangs of mass democracy which the appearance of the proletariat represented. The proudly displayed humanism and social conscience of Victorian Liberalism could not withstand the elites' fear of mass enemies whether they be classes or nations.

In England, France and Germany the masses marched with purpose toward a new European political order: Marxism. The German nation appeared to be preparing for a new, but different world order of its own. The notion of the inviolability of property and wealth – by the definition of some the same thing – were thought to be under dire threat from the possibility of both internal and external warfare. The promise of liberal capitalism to ensure the constancy of the social, political and economic orders had, even in England, been thrown fatally into doubt. On the Continent liberalism's shallow roots (at least when compared to those embedded in English soil) shrivelled before the panic of the propertied and wealthy classes and old feudal estates who held the balance of power within their nations. They declared war on the lower orders and the forces of mass democracy who fought for them. The ruling and governing elites strove to destroy every perceived challenge to their privileged position with equal gusto whether it be the suffragette movement in England, revolutionary syndicalism and anti-militarism in France, or social democracy and its union movement in Germany.

Immersed within this milieu the ruling and governing elites of Europe came to appreciate the dictum that political crime which aims at the seizure of government 'is one form of crime that is either prevented or it may never be punished'.[12] Under these conditions the political police of western Europe played a steadily greater role in preserving a tranquil and orderly world for the powers of the day. By the end of the century this reliance upon the political police became habitual and unquestioning among societies' elites as well as among less esteemed citizens.[13] In their turn, as political policing institutions matured they adopted the values of the elites they defended. It is a symbiotic though somewhat false relationship that serves both policemen and their masters well.

In England by 1914 the Special Branch of the Metropolitan Police had metamorphosised into an organisation recognisable in each of its characteristics as the fledgling post-war English internal security system. In France the Paris Prefecture of Police remained the bulwark of French society at least to 1914. But as war approached, the growth of the proletariat in provincial cities led to the establishment of a national political police force incorporating a reorganised *Sureté Generale*. The transformation of the *Sureté* from a mere skeleton bureau into a major nationwide police force gave France a national political police system, certainly not the equal of its Russian counterpart in dimensions or power, but not a trifle either.[14]

By the immediate pre-war years the *modus operandi*, the police technology, and the world view of Europe's political police were so similar to those of tsarist Russia that Italian, German, Swiss, French, Belgian, Norwegian, and English detectives and detective supervisors, for example, comfortably served in and directed Russian police operations throughout Europe.[15] In western Europe and in Russia the crisis of the old order encouraged the rise of modern political police systems whose organisation, strategy and tactics and world view led to the birth of a new, common political police culture.

****

Despite the convergence of political police cultures between western Europe and Russia, significant differences remained amongst these often allied forces of order. Within western Europe liberalism had made an indelible impression upon jurisprudence, curtailing the most unpleasant and undesirable manifestations of the police culture. Personal inviolability became the signpost of these law and order systems where the political police out of necessity strove to project the image of the protector of both state and citizen. In this environment the addition of mollifying political action (e.g. labour legislation) designed to undermine dissent preserved the status quo without 'sliding gradually or inadvertently' into a police state.[16] 'In the last analysis', as A. Fryar Calhoun discovered about the French political police in the immediate pre-First World War era, 'the politician had won out over the policeman'.[17]

In tsarist Russia things were different. The complexion of Russia's political cultural heritage, which profoundly influenced the evolution of Tsardom's forces of order, did not resemble the conglomerate of western political cultures.[18]

For example and most importantly there is the patrimonial nature of Russian governance. Tsardom despite the increasing complexity of its institutions remained a patrimony – 'where authority is primarily oriented to tradition but in its exercise makes the claim of full personal powers'[19] – even after the 1905 Revolution, as we shall see. Richard Pipes tells us that in patrimonial regimes there is no sense of reciprocity. Everything is owed to the monarchy, nothing is offered to the nation in return. In this political system no differentiation is made between state and ruler, although in reality the ruler does not govern on a day-to-day basis (except perhaps in the case of Tsar Nicholas I). Government was the province of Tsardom's bureaucratic class, the court and the gentry who together controlled both absolute political power and the majority of the nation's productive forces on behalf of the tsar. The complex of rituals and informal practices which characterised the tsar's relationship with these elites and energised and dominated the machinery of governance was a closed world[20] to the vast majority of Russians – including the new civil society arising from the Great Reforms of the 1860s.[21]

That closed world both disdained and feared the minions it governed.[22] These deeply held traditional habits of mind and behaviour, exacerbated by the elites isolation from the Russian polity, coelesced to shape Tsardom's attitude toward state (political) crime and determined the nature of the measures employed to suppress it. However, despite different perceptions of the nature of humankind Tsardom's broadly defined statutes dealing with state crime were designed to fight categories of political crime similar to those identified by western governments.

According to Ingraham political crime in western Europe fell into the categories of: acts of betrayal, challenges to political authority and legitimacy, hindrance of official functions such as the conduct of foreign relations, the coinage of money and the raising of armies, and the usurpation of those powers which concern the protection of the people from tyrannical efforts by rulers to enlarge the powers granted them and to subvert the traditional political rights enjoyed by the people.[23]

All but the last of these criteria of political criminal activity were absorbed into the tsarist state criminal statutes as we shall observe in the following chapter, but it is the absence of this criterion which significantly differentiates the West's approach to the problem. In the West political criminality was determined through the legislature and courts, a system not always perfectly just, particularly in times of crisis. Still, on a day-to-day basis, society's law-makers, and the courts which interpreted and enforced those laws did so within the framework of universally agreed parameters and against a very small minority of the population.

In the Russian socio-political environment discussed above where the ruling and governing elites suspected everyone beyond the pale of their own institutions as a potential enemy, tsarist state criminal statutes principally protected the Russian state from suspected subversion by its own people, at the expense of personal inviolability. Richard Pipes caught the flavour of this practice with his usual clarity: 'A monarchist landlord outraged by the incompetence or corruption of the bureaucracy in his district became in the eyes of the law and gendarmerie an ally of the anarchist assembling bombs to blow up the imperial palace'.[24]

Even though Tsardom tantalised society with periodic calls for cooperation, especially against terrorism, within the context of Russian political culture such appeals were meaningless. By the early 1880s it was obvious that Tsardom expected society to be nothing more than a passive observer of the struggle between itself and the forces of subversion. In pursuing this policy the Russian government threw away the support of its people, whom it did not trust, in favour of the law and order bureaucracy which it hoped could subdue the monarchy's political opponents administratively. This policy ultimately led to the imposition of draconian emergency measures negating even the veneer of liberalism which coloured the legal reforms of 1864, and subsequently caused the gap between the government and society to grow to chasmal proportions.

****

In summary then, adversarial relationships between the ruling and governing elites and the populations beneath them are marked throughout Europe (including Russia) at the end of the nineteenth century by the almost hysterical and largely unwarranted fear that the traditional societies which sustained them were frail structures, under assault by forces of social, economic and political modernisation. In the exaggerated (at least in pre-First World War Europe) opinion of these elites they were likely to be overwhelmed by these forces unless they adopted a variety of forceful counter-measures. The establishment of modern political police systems designed to withstand the rising new order became the principal weapon of those in power. In the West, however, these institutions of repression, as we have seen, operated for the most part under the control of elected legislatures and judiciaries largely influenced by the humanist principles of Victorian Liberalism until the outbreak of the First World War.

In Russia the threat to Tsardom's traditional elites by these forces of change was until the early twentieth century minimal. None the less, the upheaval caused by the Great Reforms combined with the baggage of tsarist political culture the regime carried with it forced the development of a political police system intended solely for the protection of the state from its citizenry, a system which by the end of the nineteenth century as we will discover in Chapter 2 had become independent from civil police authority: a political police system that epitomised the adversarial relationship between Tsardom and its people.[25]

The absence of a universalist political philosophy, 'a comprehensive and affirmative faith' of which both the monarchy and its defenders could boast meant that eventually only necessity and fear bound Russians to their monarchy.[26] The forces of order aggravated that fear by creating their image as an invincible, ubiquitous and effective army operating above the law largely by administrative *fiat*; striking swiftly and indiscriminately against Russia's perceived numerous internal enemies.

None the less, this image should not mask what the comparative review of European attitudes toward political crime and the evolution of political police systems to deal with it has shown us. First, the rapid evolution of modern political police systems under way *throughout* Europe by the 1880s emerged as an overblown hostile response to a nascent though exaggerated challenge to the power and authority of the ruling and governing elites. The development of the tsarist political police was part of this European-wide phenomenon. Second – and a key underlying theme of this book – the forces of order only *reflect* the complexion of a state's political character, they do not determine it.

1 Law and the Repression of Political Crime in Russia, 1826–1902

Political repression, as indicated, consists of two parts: the forces of 'law' (no matter how the statutes are conceived and invoked) and the forces of 'order' (the political police). The intertwining of these agencies of prevention and repression is obvious. However, when writing about the evolution of these guardians of political and social tranquillity within an historical context it is reasonable, for the sake of clarity, to separate them from each other. In this chapter, therefore, we will deal with the foundations of the statutory and regulatory responses to political crime in Tsarist Russia and in the succeeding chapter we will focus upon the early evolution of Tsardom's political policing institutions which benefited so substantially from them.

Law is the essential ingredient in the development of any societal organism. The type of law, that is the definition of what constitutes law, the methods of its promulgation and implementation, and official and popular attitudes toward the law determine the relationship between the rulers and the governed. In Tsarist Russia the foundation of the imperial approach to political crime is to be found in the reign of Nicholas I (1825–1856), a reign in which ironically little if any real political subversion existed. Yet, Tsardom's traditional desire to control and contain its people combined with the deeply suspicious nature of Nicholas I led to the imposition of the Criminal Code of 1845. The code, which became a milestone in the historical evolution of the Russian police state, institutionalised the long-standing custom of politics as a monopoly of the tsar and his senior officials. The Code defined what constituted political crimes and prescribed punishment for them.[1] Other countries on the continent promulgated statutes similar in nature to this one, but no other displayed such vagueness of language: the failure to distinguish deed from intent in describing state criminal activity gave Russia's political police its infamous gross latitude to harass, arrest and punish Nicholas I's subjects.[2]

This statute when combined with the absence of any restraints on arbitrary behaviour in government and society, what the Russians to this day call *proizvol*, made personal inviolability under the law only a wistful dream. *Proizvol* was a way of life for every Russian from the lowliest serf to the greatest officials (*sanovniki*) and courtiers. Russia's tsars stood above the law and they issued edicts carrying the force of law without any recognition of requirements for consistency or observance of the statutes.[3] Of course, *proizvol* was the bureaucracy's custom as much as it was the tsar's privilege. As a result, the tsarist compulsion to learn of every whiff of dissent wafting over the land placed a heavy burden on the Russian populace, a condition made worse by ignorant censors and policemen unguided by any clear regulations who applied Nicholas's orders often in a more whimsical manner than even he intended.[4]

It seemed that Russians would receive respite from this abuse, which became intense after the outbreak of the 1848 Revolution in Europe, with the implementation of the Great Reforms – especially the legal reform – under the aegis of Alexander II (1856–1881) during the first half of the 1860s. Unfortunately, this hope soon faded. The legal reforms along with the other Great Reforms, perhaps unintentionally, encouraged the growth of a civil society in Russia with rights and privileges guaranteed under the law. This civil society, small in size and politically naive, confronted ruling and governing elites who believed that the law served only one purpose: the preservation of the monarchy and through it their privileged and powerful positions. As these elites began to believe themselves threatened they strove to erode the political impact of the Great Reforms through a series of unpublished statutes dealing with political crime enacted by the government throughout the 1870s.

This contest between Tsardom and the new civil society came to a head in a group of prosecutions of alleged, even confessed, state criminals which took place in St Petersburg during the 1870s and were the first serious test of the new independent judicial system. Despite government pressure these officers of the court and jurors acquitted the overwhelming number of the accused, thereby using their recently won powers to political ends. The government was enraged by the acquittals, viewing the liberal attitudes of the courts to be themselves acts of treason.[5]

This confrontation between the government and its new courts grew into open warfare; numbers of premeditated attacks on tsarist officials by terrorists increased as did the battles between the perpetrators and the gendarmes, with society appearing to be unperturbed by the conflict. The forces of order, taking advantage of the spreading fear within official circles aroused by these incidents and ordinary society's blasé reaction to them pressured the increasingly worried and already conservative Alexander II into further distancing himself from his reforms of the 1860s, encouraging him as early as 1870 to move steadily down the road to secret and unrestrained repression.[6]

Between 1870 and 1879 Tsardom promulgated but never published for public perusal nineteen laws expanding its arbitrary authority over the Russian people.[7] The first of these edicts increased the government's authority to deal with industrial strikers by administrative means. 'Administrative authority' in this case refers to Tsardom's right to punish political criminals – those who threatened the security of the state – without due process of the law. In 1878–1879 these unpublished decrees culminated with the condemnation to 'administrative exile'[8] – the punishment of those persons adjudged a threat to the stability of society, not because of any act they necessarily committed, but merely because local law and order officials suspected them of contemplating a political crime at some time in the near future – for up to five years. Others of these edicts were worded so imprecisely that they allowed the forces of order to deal with the populations under their jurisdictions in any manner they chose. These secret decrees issued over the signature of 'Tsar Liberator' Alexander II, set the tone of Tsardom's approach toward political dissent which coloured its remaining years.

Despite these measures, the government failed to prevent the brutal murder of Alexander II in the middle of a St Petersburg street on 2 March 1881 which stunned Russian society and caused panic among the Russian ruling and govening elites.[9]

The tsar had survived several near misses, but his gruesome murder on a public thoroughfare convinced even the dullest tsarist official that a dedicated group of hardened revolutionaries existed in Russia and that something had to be done about them once-and-for-all. Yet the new tsar Alexander III (1881–1894), despite his reactionary outlook, needed at least some convincing as one Department of Police memorandum put it that 'nihilists' had driven the Russian state to the brink of dissolution.[10] Fearful of the worst, it did not take Alexander III long to agree with his law and order officials who had been assiduously encouraging him to employ harsh measures against dissent. If a wave of rebellion was beginning to break over Russia special measures must be adopted to meet it.

In response to his father's assassination a carefully coached Alexander III promulgated the Exceptional Measures (*Iskliuchitel'nye mery*) described in the Statute on Measures for the Protection of State Order and Public Tranquillity (*Polozhenie o merakh k okhraneniiu gosudarstvennago poriadka i obshchestvennago spokoistviia*). Initially the government intended that this statute combat sedition for a limited three year period, but this condition was soon forgotten and Tsardom renewed the Exceptional Measures repeatedly up to 1917. The forces of law and order implemented the Exceptional Measures in those regions of the empire declared to be under one of two forms of emergency rule: either State of Emergency (*Usilennaia okhrana*) or Extraordinary State of Emergency (*Chrezvychainaia okhrana*). In some regions of Russia a State of Emergency continued without interruption from 1881 to 1917.[11]

The authorities designed the Exceptional Measures to strengthen the powers of the political police. The provisions of the Statute empowered the police: (1) to carry out preventive arrests and to detain suspects under arrest for up to two weeks (by written order of the provincial governor this could be extended to one month) persons suspected of being involved in the commission of state crimes or of belonging to illegal associations; (2) to conduct at any time searches of any premises without exception and thereupon to seize and sequester all material related to the intent to or participation in a political crime. Even in regions not under the Emergency Statute chiefs of the police and the gendarmerie could order their subordinates to conduct preventive arrests of up to seven days duration on the same ground as granted in regions under the Exceptional Measures. And with the consent of the minister of justice, the minister of internal affairs was empowered to bring before military courts for trial and sentencing under the rules of martial law state criminal cases and cases of armed resistance to the authorities, including attacks on policemen, troops, or on other official persons in the course of performing their duties.[12]

At first, Russian society manifested indifference to the limitations imposed by this Statute on its freedom, believing that the Exceptional Measures were nothing more than a type of codification, 'highly desirable, if not necessary in the conditions of the time'.[13] It soon learned, however, that the Statute abrogated the remaining restraints against unfounded arrests.[14]

Thus Russian law even at its most unencumbered did not adequately provide for the personal inviolability of its people. The weakness of such laws in the face of the overpowering impact of the Exceptional Measures which we have just described is succinctly described by Marc Szeftel:

> The privilege normally kept by the police for the sake of the prevention of crime and temporarily given to it for the special purpose of securing political tranquillity [was] jointly of such magnitude in the Russian legislation of the absolutist period that in daily practice they greatly restricted the efficiency of the guarantees established for individual liberty by the Statute of Criminal Procedure of 1864.[15]

The erosion of personal inviolability was so widespread that it affected those segments of the Russian populace who did not live under the hammer of the Emergency Statute. The Ministry of Internal Affairs (commonly and herein often identified by its Russian initials MVD) itself expressed, to no avail, its disapproval of the growing political police habit of riding roughshod over the population at large. The MVD constantly reminded its political police chiefs to guard against making arrests which could lead to deportation of the accused without first carefully verifying the evidence, insisting that investigations be conducted in a civilised manner.[16] To field agents, who could be punished for not taking 'all necessary measures' to unmask even a scent of subversion, such restrictions were a nuisance to which only lip service was paid.[17] Political police officials became so contemptuous of the instructions they received from St Petersburg that they went so far as to employ the Exceptional Measures in non-political cases.[18] The overheated police environment created by the decrees of the 1870s and the Emergency Statute of 1881 had had their effect. In practice, the political police by the mid-1880s already operated beyond the control of the regular bureaucracy.

The capricious and high-handed behaviour of the political police mirrored the general approach to law and order taken by its superiors in the provinces who freely punished those whom the political police accused, even on the flimsiest of evidence, by applying administrative justice. The abuses of administrative justice were legion,[19] the product of a governing system which, on the one hand, encouraged its agents in the provinces to view the population under their jurisdiction with enmity and suspicion while, on the other, lacked the machinery to control those agents, who consequently employed administrative justice in a manner so sweeping and brutal that even the government in St Petersburg became embarrassed. Not once, however, after 1887 did the MVD interfere with the arbitrary infliction of administrative justice on the populace by the local authorities.[20]

The penalties most commonly invoked under the rubrics of administrative justice were exile and a procedure called 'open police surveillance' (*glasnyi politseiskii nadzor*), measures which gave the political police and the local authorities the opportunity to terrorise whomsoever they wished as well as the capability of using the system to conduct personal vendettas against innocent people. The fear of being condemned to these fates – both punishments were often inflicted together – was manifested by the victims' limited recourse to appeal. One could always petition the tsar for redress, but this in itself could be a risky business.[21]

There existed two types of administrative exile: *vyssylka* and *ssylka. Vyssylka* was the milder form of punishment, but also the more arbitrary of the two. It prohibited the 'criminal' from living within certain defined areas of the empire. The victims of this form of punishment were usually those persons suspected of being 'politically unreliable': a phrase often used to condemn people not for something they might have done, but for something they might do in the future. *Ssylka,* or deportation to a definite location, was clearly a much more severe penalty, since it condemned the convict to a particular residence, usually in Siberia for a period of up to five years, which for hardened political criminals was extended in 1897 to ten years. Provincial and local representatives of the Ministry of Internal Affairs such as governors initiated procedures for *ssylka* against individuals who actually committed political offences and against citizens thought to be too outspoken in their criticisms of the government's policies.[22]

Exile of either sort went hand in hand with 'open surveillance', a form of harassment designed to remind its victim that the slightest deviation from the pattern of normal behaviour would come to the attention of the authorities. The Ministry of Internal Affairs imposed 'open surveillance' over those already found guilty by administrative justice of threatening the tranquillity of the state; it was imposed upon persons sentenced to exile as part of their sentences and against mild offenders in their permanent place of residence as their entire sentence. Persons subjected to 'open surveillance' endured restricted freedom of movement, of profession, of action and of correspondence. The police could enter and search the premises of such individuals at any time and seize their property. This barbarous form of persecution reduced its sufferers to despair and poverty, destroying the health of innumerable exiles and driving others to suicide.

Nevertheless, the purpose of this punishment was not to murder the convicts, but to isolate political criminals from the main body of society, to break their spirit, and most important of all, through its crushing effect on its survivors, to create widespread fear of administrative punishment in the hope that such intimidation would discourage acts of subversion.[23]

It did not take long for some of the officials who administered the system to realise that administrative exile did not curtail dissident behaviour. As early as the first years of the 1880s Major General Baranov, the governor of Archangelsk province, and therefore intimately acquainted with the exile system, wrote to the minister of internal affairs warning 'that administrative exile for political reasons is much more likely to spoil the character of a man than to reform it', adding that 'if a man is infected with anti-government ideas all the circumstances of exile tend only to increase the infection, to sharpen his faculties, and to change him from a theoretical to a practical – that is [into] an extremely dangerous man'.[24] Baranov's warning and many others like it went unheeded.[25]

The application of administrative justice became Tsardom's standard practice for ridding Russian society of those it believed represented a threat, no matter how slight or tenuous, to the continued well-being of the ruling and governing elites. Certainly, during the years between 1880 and 1902 several trials of those accused of political crimes took place in Russia. But, as we have seen, the government had discovered in the 1870s that such court cases were by their very nature sensational. The forces of law and order soon realised that a convenient method of avoiding these trials with their unsure outcomes, embarrassing propaganda and consequent revolutionary agitation, was to impose administrative justice. Between 1870 and 1894 the Ministry of Justice initiated only 226 political trials. However during the following years the government drastically reduced even this small number. Between 1894 and 1902 the authorities did not turn a single political case over to the courts and during the tumultuous years of 1902 and 1903 it saw fit to commit only fifteen such cases to the court system.[26]

****

The arbitrary brutality that characterised the suppression of dissent accelerated the alienation of Russian society from its government. The ranks of revolutionary organisations began to swell and their suppression by the forces of order compelled revolutionaries to become more skilled in underground techniques, making it more difficult to dislodge them.[27]

This cycle of growing discontent and repression intensified during the mid-1890s when the effects of famine, the political obtuseness of the new tsar, Nicholas II (1894–1917) and his apparent callous disregard for human suffering combined to embarrass and frustrate educated Russians interested in moderate political reform and a return to the incipient humanism of the Great Reform era.[28]

The forces of law and order reacted to the growing distance between Tsardom and its people by accelerating the number of arrests made for political crimes between 1880 and 1903. Alexander III's forces of law and order detained and

Table 1.1 Number of Political Cases Compiled by the Ministry of Justice and Number of Persons Included in those Cases, 1894–1903

Year	*No. of formal cases brought before the Ministry of Justice*	*No. of persons included in those cases*
1894	158	919
1895	259	944
1896	309	1668
1897	289	1427
1898	257	1144
1899	338	1184
1900	384	1580
1901	520	1784
1902	1053[a]	3744[a]
1903	1988[a]	5590[a]

Source: L. Slukhotskii, 'Ocherk deiatel'nosti ministerstva iustitsii po bor'be s politicheskimi prestupleniiami', *Istoriko-Revoliutsionnyi Sbornik*, 3 (1926): 277.

[a] Between 1894 and 1901 none of the above cases was referred to the Courts for action under due process of the law. In 1902 three cases were so referred (including 38 persons) and in 1903 twelve cases were transferred to the courts (including 28 persons) as defined by part two of article 1030 of the Code of Criminal Procedure (see note 1).

interrogated 3111 persons for political offences.[29] During the decade following Alexander III's death that number grew considerably. Table 1.1 lists the number of political cases that passed through the Ministry of Justice. It is clear from this table that cases covering political crimes increased twelve fold between 1894 and 1903, while the number of suspects grew approximately six times during this decade. The substantial rise in the number of cases in 1902 and 1903 undoubtedly reflects arrests made during the peasant uprisings in Poltava and Kharkov provinces in 1902 and the massive strikes in South Russia in 1903, the growth in the revolutionary movement generally, especially the return of terror as a revolutionary tactic, and – as we shall see in Chapter 6 – the expansion and increased vigilance of the political police during V.K. Plehve's tenure as minister of internal affairs. While statistics on the number of people punished for breaches of the regulations on state security by administrative justice are inexact, the general upward trend is made explicit in Table 1.2.

It could be argued that the impact of administrative justice on the population at large should not be exaggerated here: when the number of persons prosecuted under administrative authority is compared to the size of the Russian population (which was approximately 128 000 000 in 1897) the figures presented in Tables

Table 1.2 Number of Political Criminals Sentenced by Administrative Authority, 1883–1900

	Year	*Number of Persons Sentenced*
	1883	303
	1884	402
	1885	432
	1886	440
	1887	531
	1888	503
	1889	240
	1890	380
	1891	395
	1892	332
	1893	303
	1894	679
	1895	1030
	1896	900
	1897	1984
	1898	1153
	1899	1414
	1900 (Jan.–Jun.)	832
TOTAL		12 253

Source: N.A. Troitskii, *Tsarizm pod sudom progressivnoi obshchestvennosti, 1866–1895 gg*., (Moscow: 1979), 58.

1.1 and 1.2 do not seem significant, especially by the standards of political repression we have become familiar with in the late twentieth century. However, as the Introduction indicates, within the context of late nineteenth and early twentieth century European history they are, to say the least, noteworthy. European governments, like their Russian counterpart, found that legal repression of political subversion was becoming a considerable task, potentially overtaxing their resources. Unlike the Russians, however, they confined these conflicts within the bounds of legality – except for a few revolutionary outbreaks of short duration and for Britain's interminable internal war with the Irish[30] – by developing positive political tactics, including propaganda campaigns, co-opting members of the opposition and/or its political platform or by developing reforms of their own. These tactics diffused the opposition and preserved the equilibrium of society as they saw it.

After briefly dabbling with the same principles of liberal justice during the Great Reform era the tsarist government moved to undermine the impact of its own legal reforms, particularly once Russia's elites sensed the danger to their political and social stations, resulting they believed from the implementation of this reform.

How did this happen? Tables 1.1 and 1.2 paint a sombre picture. The growing number of persons sentenced administratively in Russia and the simultaneous decline in the due process of law in political cases reveal that Tsardom rejected the path of political accommodation chosen by its neighbours, embarking instead upon a path of increasing *proizvol* against its own society. By the late 1890s the Russian forces of law and order had stood the western conception of political crime on its head. Liberalism itself became a crime akin to anarchy and revolution.[31] The implications of this fact for the future of Tsarist Russia cannot be over-estimated.

2 The Development of Modern Political Policing Institutions in Russia, 1800–1902

The growth and institutional development of the tsarist political policing system began slowly and rather haphazardly during the reign of Alexander I (1801–1825), evolved quickly under Nicholas I (1825–1856), faltered during the first, reforming, decade of Alexander II's reign (1856–1866) and then began to grow in size and institutional sophistication, eventually spreading untrammelled throughout the empire and abroad during Tsardom's remaining years.

Political policing of sorts had taken place in Russia for more than two hundred years prior to 1800.[1] However, in 1807 Alexander I, worried about public reaction to his détente with France took the first tentative steps toward preparing an institutional groundwork for a true political police system in Russia by creating the Committee for Public Safety. In 1810 he endorsed a proposal for a separate Ministry of Police, the most sophisticated effort to date at establishing a professional political police force within the empire. None the less, it failed dismally, suffering from royal neglect and populated with illiterate and venal officials concerned more with their own petty squabbles than with protecting the tsar[2] and serving as little more than his personal security force controlling those elements of society with whom the ruler was personally familiar.

Royal neglect of the political police ended with the Decembrist Rebellion in late December 1825. The Decembrist Rebellion made an indelible impression on the new Tsar Nicholas I, who thereafter, believed himself to be surrounded by subversion located within the cream of Russian society from where the Decembrists themselves had come. To protect the crown against future misguided treachery and to allay what became his perpetual fear of revolution, Nicholas I issued the *Ukaz* (Decree) of 3 July 1826, establishing the Third Section of His Imperial Majesty's Chancery. The Third Section and its subordinate military branch the Separate Corps of Gendarmes (*Otdel'nyi korpus zhandarmov*) – established on 28 April 1827 – formed the tsar's political police force.[3] Unlike its predecessors, concerned with those who composed or surrounded the court, and who for the most part lived in St Petersburg, the Third Section occupied itself with the opinions and behaviour of a much broader segment of society – Russia's educated classes: bureaucrats, officers, gentry, courtiers, and later, intellectuals.

At first glance, the Nicolaevean police system resembled the traditional police states of the eighteenth century exemplified by the administrations of Frederick II of Prussia, Joseph II of the Austrian Empire, and further refined by Fouché,

Napoleon's chief of police.[4] But this similarity was more apparent than real. Russia's political culture contributed to a remodelling of the eighteenth century *politseistaat* which stripped this system of its benevolent and developmental purposes. While both Joseph II and Nicholas I hoped to use their police systems to ensure order within their empires, vast differences in their nations' individual political cultures guaranteed different results. In western Europe the *politseistaat* amounted to a veritable charter for a society protected as well as watched by the police service, with public opinion under the continual surveillance of secret police agents. It was a system which combined paternalism, autocracy and enlightenment on the one hand, with secret police surveillance and paid informers on the other.[5] In Russia the rejection of the Enlightenment and the patrimonial nature of the autocracy gave the term 'police state' a new meaning, exemplified by the behaviour of the Third Section and the Separate Corps of Gendarmes *vis-à-vis* Russian society. In Russia the police existed for only two purposes, the maintenance of the political status quo and the enforcement of intellectual stagnation.

Ironically, the reign of Nicholas was not characterised by widespread dissent: educated society was generally compliant. By the time of Nicholas's death, however, dissatisfaction with the monarchy had grown substantially and the Third Section, whose intrusive, brutal and corrupt conduct had markedly contributed to the rising level of discontent, could no longer cope with it.

Nicholas I's police worked best against alleged critics of the regime or against those bureaucrats who failed to fulfil their assigned duties. Nicholas did not create the Third Section as a defence against a large-scale revolutionary movement. The Third Section's agents came from the ranks of Russia's army officers, non-commissioned officers, enlisted men, bureaucrats and at the lowest level the dregs of society, functioning mechanically, without thought, following the tsar's orders in slipshod fashion. Its leadership understood almost nothing of the burgeoning political and social movements erupting in contemporary Europe and floundered helplessly, unable to differentiate between harmless criticism and subversion.

By allowing policemen, governors and even local officials to decide what criteria constituted political criminal behaviour and by permitting law and order bureaucrats to determine the accuseds' degree of guilt and their appropriate punishment – as we observed in the previous chapter – Tsardom encouraged the founding of a separate police empire within the state. This empire would eventually increase its power at the expense of the crown itself. There was, however, little danger of this as long as the political police remained so inept. Even during the final six or seven years of Nicholas's rule – the time of greatest oppression during his reign – the Third Section did not undergo any significant alteration in its style or institutional development.[6]

By the mid-1860s the stagnation characteristic of both the political police system and Russian society generally between 1826 and 1856 began to dissipate.

At first, however, the revitalisation of the political police system did not appear on Alexander II's agenda. The government's awakening interest in political police reform eventually arose from three circumstances: the assassination attempt made against Alexander II by D.V. Karakozov which caused the government to become acutely aware of the potential for tragedy in the gendarmes' failings; the failure of the legal reform, at least in the government's eyes, to deal justly with even confessed political criminals; and notably, the economic, social and political dislocations wrought by the Great Reforms and Russia's steady movement into the industrial age.

After the failed attempt on the tsar's life on 4 April 1866, the government fell under the overall influence of Count P. A. Shuvalov, the Chief of Gendarmes, who undertook the expansion of the political police and increased its surveillance capacity to cover the entire empire and beyond.[7] Unfortunately, however, the Third Section possessed neither the knowledge nor the personnel to infiltrate, subvert and destroy newly formed revolutionary groups. As for the Separate Corps of Gendarmes – as a visible, repressive arm of the autocracy it cajoled and harassed those people whom it believed violated the statutes, but organised secret groups of ardent revolutionaries, in particular terrorists, were beyond the gendarmes' control.[8]

Shuvalov, who recognised the failings of these agencies, endeavoured to compensate for them by establishing a new type of police bureau in St Petersburg (becoming the prototype of the new-fashioned political police bureaus established in the 1880s in Moscow and Warsaw and between 1902 and 1914 throughout the Russian Empire), assigning it the impressive name: The Division for the Preservation of Order and Public Safety (*Otdelenie po okhrane poriadka i obshchestvennoi bezopasnosti*). Nevertheless, as a weapon against sedition it remained inert until major political police reform in the 1880s brought it to life. For more than another decade Tsardom took no further steps to create a force capable of counteracting dissent. Despite their failings the government seemed unable to decide the fate either of the Third Section or the Separate Corps of Gendarmes.

On 5 February 1880 an explosion at the Winter Palace just missed killing the tsar. A week later Alexander II decreed the convocation of a Supreme Commission for the Preservation of State Order and Social Tranquillity (*Verkhovnaia komissiia po okhrane gosudarstvennago poriadka i obshchestvennago spokoistviia*).[9] The chairman, General Mikhail Tarielovich Loris-Melikov, did not favour repression for its own sake and set about to modify some of the administrative measures of the 1870s while, at the same time, developing constructive proposals for the preservation of the autocracy.[10]

On 26 February 1880 Loris-Melikov presented a report to Alexander II which recommended the unification of the various branches of the police within a single department in order to better coordinate the campaign against sedition. In line with this recommendation Loris-Melikov subordinated the Third Section and the

Separate Corps of Gendarmes to the Supreme Commission, placing them under his direct authority.

On 6 August 1880 Loris-Melikov took the long overdue step of abolishing the Third Section altogether and establishing the new Department of State Police. At the same time, considering its usefulness to be at an end he terminated the Supreme Commission, following this action on 10 November with a report to the tsar which suggested, 'the combining of the entire higher management of the police in one establishment – the Ministry of Internal Affairs'.[11] Alexander II agreed and in an Imperial Decree of 15 November 1880 the Department of Executive Police (*Departament Ispol'nitel'noi Politsii*), the unit supervising the civil and general police throughout the empire, was amalgamated with the Department of State Police.[12]

In implementing his reform Loris-Melikov stripped the Department of State Police of all the superfluous functions which had so burdened the Third Section for the past forty-five years, transferring, 'business not having strictly a police character' to other bureaus within the Ministry of Internal Affairs.[13] Loris-Melikov streamlined the police bureaucracy still further by cutting its administrative staff by more than half and appointing civil servants of the highest calibre to posts within the Department of State Police, rewarding them with promotions commensurate with their exceptional responsibilities.[14] Loris-Melikov also set up a special Justice Department to replace the abolished Juridical Department of the Third Section. The minister of internal affairs envisioned this bureau as the focal point for the laws dealing with matters concerning political criminals. By 1883 the Justice Department had become fused with the Department of State Police.[15]

Originally the Department of State Police consisted of three secretariats (*deloproizvodstva*). The Managerial Secretariat handled general police affairs including finances. The Legislative Secretariat oversaw all police organisations throughout the empire and worked on various legal projects for the MVD. The Secret Bureau fulfilled the duties of a political police, that is, it implemented the struggle with the revolutionary movements.

The Ministry of Internal Affairs commissioned its new Department of State Police to carry out the following duties:

1. To prevent and suppress criminal activities and to guard society by maintaining safety and order.
2. To deal with matters pertaining to state crimes.
3. To organise and observe the activities of police bureaus.
4. To protect the integrity of the national border and border communications.
5. To issue passports to Russian citizens, to detain at the border crossing points those charged with being political criminals and to make sure the laws on the residence restrictions placed on the Jews were imposed.
6. To keep informed concerning all views held by cultural and educational establishments, and to affirm all the statutes of the various societies, and all other such questions of a secondary nature.

At about the same time Loris-Melikov substantially enlarged the Corp of Gendarmes to 521 officers and 6187 lower echelon personnel in the vain hope that the gendarmes would accept a position subordinate to the Department of State Police by acquiescing to what the Corps perceived as a secondary role as the backbone of the provincial police.[16]

****

The tremendous impact upon Russia's elites made by the assassination of Alexander II and the timely discovery of the plot against the life of Alexander III in 1887 created a political atmosphere laden with fear and in some quarters with panic. Under these conditions the MVD undertook an unopposed expansion of the political police administration.[17]

As we have seen in the previous chapter, the immediate response to the tsar's murder was the promulgation of the draconian Exceptional Measures, a decree which subsequently became a boon to the Department of State Police. Not only did its articles give the police wider powers than it had ever held before, but in the long run the Exceptional Measures effectively and indelibly drove the majority of Russians into varying degrees of opposition to the governing bureaucracy if not to the tsar himself. To meet the heightened demands for security produced by this phenomenon Tsardom revamped the structure of its recently renamed Department of Police.[18] Under this restructuring it began to assume the form it would maintain until the empire's demise.

By 1883 the Department of Police had grown to five secretariats, encompassing an expanded number of functions. The First Secretariat managed the Department of Police and developed the financial estimates for police projects. It handled the Department's personnel business – appointments, decorations, demotions, and the issuing of grants (from five to twenty-five rubles) to its civil servants.

The Second Secretariat, the Legislative Secretariat, occupied itself with the establishment and organisation of the police authorities in localities throughout the empire. It also investigated newly established monasteries and ecclesiastical societies, enforced the rules governing passports, especially those of foreigners, oversaw the regulation of 'relations between workers and employers' (the Factory Inspectorate), and lastly, scanned publications for articles discussing the conduct of the Department of Police. The Third Secretariat concerned itself with 'high police matters', gathering secret information on all kinds of events, 'bringing them to the attention of the government'. In less euphemistic language, the Third Secretariat searched for political crimes (until the creation of the Special Section in 1898) and mobilised general criminal investigations.[19]

The responsibility for carrying out the dispositions of the administrative exile system rested with the Fourth Secretariat. Between 1881 and 1894 this bureau processed 4295 cases and sent 5397 people into administrative exile. The 'politicals' accounted for 2250 of the total number, while 532 of these wretches had been convicted of participating in either agrarian or factory disorders. In addition the Fourth Secretariat supervised inquiries into political crimes and investigated cases of political unreliability.[20]

The Fifth Secretariat dealt mostly with political crimes, working up reports on politically unreliable persons as well as conducting open surveillance on all suspicious persons including those returned from exile and imprisonment. The heart of this bureau was its 'reference desk' (*spravochnyi stol*) which maintained an alphabetical card file containing the biographical data of 129 790 'unreliable persons'. In 1887 the Department of Police abolished the registration desk *per se,* enlarging and reconstituting it within a separate Special Registration Bureau (*Osobyi registratsionyi otdel*).

An additional unnumbered secretariat compiled the personal correspondence of the Department's director. It also issued and arranged rewards and pensions for older agents.[21]

By 1894 the demands on the Department of Police had grown to such an extent[22] that the MVD, over time, undertook a policy to devolve to newly established bureaus some of the duties previously assigned to the five secretariats, allowing for increased specialisation within each secretariat. Between 1894 and 1907 the MVD added two further secretariats which, for example, oversaw the Factory Inspectorate and supervised gendarme investigations into political crimes. In 1908 in order to reduce the strain upon existing secretariats, an Eighth Secretariat was created to direct the organs of criminal investigation.[23] In 1914, the outbreak of the First World War forced the Department of Police to append the Ninth Secretariat to all the others. This final addition to the number of secretariats coordinated police interests in the districts occupied by the army. The duties of these secretariats remained flexible with the MVD ordering them to take on additional assignments as the situation demanded. In 1907, for instance, the Department of Police expanded the brief of the Fourth Secretariat to include surveillance over the mass workers and peasant movements and over the legal associations and organisations of rural and urban self-government.[24]

This complex of bureaus resided in Department of Police headquarters, a building situated among a row of homes and offices on quiet tree-lined Fontanka Quai with the slow flowing Fontanka River moving past its windows where soon the Department of Police and the building in which it was located became so identified with each other that the forces of order commonly referred to the Department by the nickname of 'Fontanka'.

****

A crucial link in the development of the tsarist political network was the creation of the *Okhrannye Otdeleniia* or Security Divisions. The administrative structure for these OOs, as they became known – particularly after their proliferation between 1902 and 1904 (see Chapter 6) – traced its origins to the Divisions for the Preservation of Order and Public Safety. The first of these, established in St

Petersburg in 1866, as already noted, served as a model for two additional OOs set up in Moscow and Warsaw in 1880.[25] It was not until 1882, however, that they acquired any real authority. On 3 December 1882 the minister of internal affairs issued an Ordnance (*Polozhenie*) entitled 'Concerning the Structure of the Secret Police in the Empire' (*Ob ustroistve sekretnoi politsii v imperii*), which raised the status of the OOs to full-fledged political police bureaus.[26] In 1887 the MVD reiterated the OOs' responsibility, 'to carry out undercover searches and investigations into cases of state crimes with the aim of prevention and suppression'.[27] Their duties were similar to those performed by the Gendarme Directorates, with one significant difference. The OOs worked *sub rosa*, while the gendarmes were primarily occupied with official and thus external government inquiries.[28] The tsarist political police had at last become truly secret, something for which the gendarmes never forgave them.

During the 1880s the OOs remained small, managed by high-ranking and highly reliable gendarme officers with the support of a few loyal and hardworking bureaucrats. These few civil servants (*chinovniki*), however, controlled a large network of detectives and undercover agents, their authority spreading beyond the city and even the province (*guberniia*) in which they were located[29] and rightly so since the local gendarmes were completely unsuited for political police work. As one revolutionary historian who lived through the period put it, 'Gendarme Directorates ... do not have a programme to fish out the revolutionaries....'[30]

****

Despite the increased effectiveness of the political police under the new structure,[31] Loris-Melikov's goal of crushing the terrorist organisation of *Narodnaia Volia* (The People's Will) took several years even though it was given impetus by the exposure in 1887 of the plot to kill Alexander III. By 1892 the political police appeared victorious as the dream of a seizure of power by *Narodnaia Volia* or even its more modest goals of a successful campaign of terrorism had never been more remote.[32]

Nevertheless, the shock and fear reverberating through the ruling and governing elites, particularly among the forces of order as a result of the assassination of Alexander II and the attempt against the life of Alexander III resulted in a call for an expansion of the political police system. Again, the MVD temporarily resisted[33] Fontanka's suggestion for an increase in the number of OOs, establishing instead in 1898 the Special Section (*Osobyi Otdel*), a new bureau designed to oversee political police affairs throughout Russia and abroad. Additional OOs were not set up until 1902 (see Chapter 6).

The Special Section – the apex of Fontanka's political intelligence-gathering pyramid – mapped the master plan of assault against subversion. Located on Fontanka's isolated and now heavily guarded fifth floor, the Special Section was shrouded in myth evoking secrecy, its operations virtually unknown to other Department of Police employees. Entry except for its own staff and senior

Fontanka officials was forbidden. Requests for information and appointments with Special Section personnel had to be submitted in writing.[34] The Special Section's archive quickly accumulated a card file of 50 000 suspects, a total that grew steadily over the ensuing years.[35]

The Department of Police provided the Special Section with a senior staff containing both experienced civilian and gendarme officer political police specialists who were in turn supported by a chancery containing ten to twelve lower ranking *chinovniki*. Funding the Special Section and the OOs – the responsibility of Fontanka – was a sensitive and covert business.The MVD supported its political police agencies from its multi-million rouble secret fund (*sekretnyi fond*).[36] OOs, in addition to the funds they received from the Special Section garnered part of their budget from a levy placed upon the resident city.[37] This meant that even after the 1905 Revolution, the Ministry of Internal Affairs managed to exclude the funds it designated for the Special Section and its field bureaus from Fontanka's budget which it was now forced to submit to the new popularly elected legislative body, the Duma, for approval.

The administrative system to which this bureau belonged became so complex that its table of organisation proved to be overwhelmingly confusing even to its own members. (A diagram showing the lines of responsibility of the various sections of the political police network is provided at the end of the book. The Special Section directly controlled four other political police agencies: the OOs, the Foreign Agentura with its headquarters in Paris (see note 31), the Border Gendarmerie (*Pogranichnye Zhandarmerii*), and the Investigation Stations (*Rozysknye Punkty*). The Investigation Stations were first established in 1902 and though Fontanka never clearly defined their role, it seems that while exercising investigative powers of their own they mainly served as liaison between the OOs as they proliferated after 1902 and the Provincial Gendarme Directorates.[38] On numerous occasions the Special Section also issued directives to the Gendarme Directorates and the Railway Gendarmerie (*Zhandarmskoe Politseiskoe Upravlenie Zheleznoi Dorogi*) although neither of these agencies was directly subordinated to it.[39]

****

The Special Section and its subordinates became known under the popular and infamous misnomer as the 'Okhrana'.[40] With the growing dominance of these political police bureaus over Russian life A.A. Lopukhin, the Director of the Department of Police from 1902 to 1905, declared that the political police 'constitutes the entire might of the regime'.[41] Indeed, Fontanka was well aware of its privileged position within the hierarchy of Russian state institutions. 'Among the ranks of government organs', Fontanka boasted, 'the police structure always has occupied one of the most responsible places'. Accordingly, Fontanka claimed that it maintained this premier position because the establishment of 'law and order ...

and the peaceful life of its citizens is the principal duty of governmental authority', and it was this priority under the changing conditions of Russian life which 'distinguishes [us] from other state organs ...'.[42] It appeared, then, as if Russia was in the process of being transformed into a police state.[43]

However, this was not the case: political policing and political justice are functions not determinants of political culture. The brief comparative review of the impact of culture on the English, French, German and Russian forces of law and order *vis-à-vis* political crime has already confirmed this. Both Fontanka and the Separate Corps of Gendarmes were among the deepest reservoirs of Russia's political culture. Their memberships sustained a cherished belief in the monarchical principle and all of its myths and traditions. In particular, they perceived themselves to be the personal instruments of the tsar. On the one hand these beliefs made Russia's policing institutions devoted bulwarks against an increasingly disaffected populace; yet, on the other hand, they severely limited the scope and coloured the forms of political police behaviour. The dilemmas confronting the monarchy in the shape of a rising tide of political and social turmoil are reflected, therefore, in the structure and role of the tsar's political policing agencies and in their attitudes toward and interaction with the Russian people.

Yet few people at the time and fewer since have understood the intricate administrative apparatus, or the methodology of the 'Okhrana'; the personnel of the political police, its training and world view are also unknown. This book is about these people and those agencies of the political police and their struggle with Tsardom's opposition and Russian society generally which heretofore have been hidden by myth and neglect from public view.

Part II
Detectives, Secret Agents and Police Chiefs

3 Fontanka's Foot Soldiers: The Professional Lives of Russia's Political Police Detectives

At the heart of a political police are its agents – the detectives (*filery*) and undercover agents (*sekretnye sotrudniki*) who staffed the Special Section's External and Internal Agencies respectively. Under the direct order of the district and regional OO or Gendarme Directorate to which they were attached, the detectives maintained surveillance over individuals, groups or places, while undercover agents infiltrated revolutionary organisations in order to subvert or inform upon their members.[1]

The names assigned to the agencies – 'External' and 'Internal' reflected the type of police work undertaken rather than an organisational structure with a central directorate whose functions and responsibilities were clearly defined. In fact, each OO and Gendarme Directorate managed its own groups of detectives, while *sekretnye sotrudniki* were attached to every OO and some Gendarme Directorates and to the offices of a few governor-generals as well. The absence of uniform training together with a lack of operational control over the detectives and undercover agents became vexing problems never mastered by Fontanka, as we shall see, in part, in this chapter where our subjects are the detectives' training, capabilities, methods and treatment by their superiors.

****

Tsardom's first line of defence against its people had traditionally been its detective force. The centuries old practice of treating the slightest sign of dissent as political subversion is startlingly exemplified by the watching brief assigned to Russia's political police *filery*. People in all walks of life and especially those whose careers involved them in communicating ideas were regularly placed under *neglasnyi politseiskii nadzor* (secret surveillance). This large group included: known revolutionaries; persons who had completed their sentences as state criminals; students; high school and university teachers; *zemstva* workers; persons occupied in various aspects of publishing; persons working in libraries and reading rooms; agitators among the peasants; and members of the military – both officers and enlisted men. Places where suspects met and spread subversive propaganda were also kept under secret surveillance – shops, eating houses, inns and public houses.[2] The political police usually maintained surveillance over its suspects for two years, at the end of which time, if the Special Section were convinced that a person being watched did not present a threat to state security, surveillance was discontinued.[3]

The Special Section established stringent admission standards for its detective-trainees. Ideally recruits were to be chosen from the ranks of non-commissioned army officers, although in times of need they could also be recruited from low-level civil servants; applicants could not be more than thirty years old, and if they were non-commissioned officers they usually came from elite units. In addition to excellent physical health those chosen for detective duty had to display integrity and be politically and personally reliable, approaching their assignments seriously and conscientiously.[4] Before acceptance as a detective-trainee applicants had to undergo a security check, although categories of people were automatically excluded from the detective service. This policy of exclusion applied primarily to Jews and Poles.[5] Since the Special Section's list of prerequisites for detective-recruits bore little resemblance to what was actually possible in Russian conditions, it is not surprising that recruitment did not run smoothly:[6] there simply were not enough 'qualified' candidates.

Instructors did not think much of their recruits' intelligence or of their motivations for serving, noting that pecuniary considerations seemed to dominate the reasons for enlistment.[7] As for their physical and psychological inadequacies the Special Section strove to overcome them by subjecting its detective-trainees to a rigorous training programme and as early as 1894 Fontanka decided that a school for detective training should be established in Moscow as part of the Moscow OO. The initial class of thirty men had the privilege of learning their trade from Sergei Vasil'evich Zubatov, the masterful chief of the Moscow OO and his gifted assistant Evstratii Pavlovich Mednikov. At the same time other political policing agencies including the Separate Corps of Gendarmes began training their own *filery* as well, but the Department of Police relied on the better trained, more reliable, Moscow detectives in the more serious cases for as long as it could.[8] Upon the completion of their training the best of Moscow's detectives formed a 'flying detachment' (*letuchii otriad*) which had the privilege of carrying out surveillance assignments throughout the empire unhindered by local authorities. The surveillance operations conducted by this detachment proved so successful that, in January 1901, the Special Section increased its size and its budget. Eventually, probably because of its success, the Moscow detachment was broken up with its members being distributed among the OOs of the empire in the hope that this action would raise the level of detective service throughout the nation.[9]

Despite the loss of its best detectives the Moscow OO continued to produce the most able *filery* in Russia, their success attributable to the training programme developed and employed by Evstratii Mednikov and his assistant Lt Colonel von Koten who guided the Moscow OO's detective bureau and subsequently became its chief. The school itself was justly named 'Evstrakin' in honour of its founder.[10] Mednikov, a man of little formal education, began his career as one of Zubatov's recruits and soon became his close associate. He knew all the revolutionary leadership and was better informed about their activities than any other police official; this background assisted him in transforming his students into effective *filery*. Mednikov demanded that his trainees possess accurate memories and physical endurance. He took a sincere interest in the trainees, perusing their reports and issuing instructions to them personally.[11]

After passing the Special Section security check an applicant entered the Moscow detective school and came under von Koten's wing. One of von Koten's primary functions was to teach the recruits to identify their subjects in exceptional detail using precise language. The very choice of words used to describe a subject was considered vital. For instance, hair colouring was to be described as brunette, brownhaired (*shaten*), blonde, redhead (*ryzhii*) and grey. Less easily visualised words such as chestnut (*kashtanovii*), or combinations of words such as dark-redhead (*temno-ryzhii*) and light-redhead (*svetlo-ryzhii*) were not to be employed. To refine the candidates' powers of observation von Koten developed a series of exercises called 'taking distinctive marks' (*vziatie po primetam*) which progessively demanded greater powers of memory and observation from his students. He began by placing three students in a separate room and then asking them to record the distinctive physical characteristics of their comrades who remained in the classroom. The three students returned to the classroom when they finished this assignment where they described one of their colleagues who had remained behind using only the subject's distinctive physical characteristics to do so. The large group then had to identify which one of them was being described. At first von Koten's students made repeated errors, but after five or six lessons the pupils performed flawlessly. Of course once in a while, just to keep the trainees on their toes, von Koten included in this type of lesson anthropomorphic descriptions of people who were not part of the group. Von Koten also encouraged the practical training of his recruits by sending his pupils on actual surveillance operations with experienced *filery*. On these occasions the inexperienced trainees performed 'verifying exercises' to corroborate previously gathered information and practised their surveillance techniques: following subjects onto river and canal steamers without being noticed by the suspect, or the art of stepping into a courtyard in order to convince the suspect that he was not being followed. Every evening the recruits reported on their daily exercises to von Koten, their reports often being confirmed by unseen senior detectives who kept the new boys under observation.[12] Unfortunately, only the lucky few received their training at the Moscow detective school. Nevertheless, no matter where a *filer* was trained, when he successfully completed the course of instruction the Special Section assigned him to a district in his own province or a district of a province under the jurisdiction of his regional OO. Once a new detective received his assignment he was required to familiarise himself with the town or city in which he was located, especially with its saloons, beer gardens, taverns, and houses having two or more exits to the street, to memorise the tram schedules, the location of all tram stops and *drozhki* or cab stands and the arrival and departure timetables of all long-distance trains. The newly placed detective also learned the schedules of the various factory shifts in his town and needed to recognise the multiplicity of uniforms belonging to the military units billeted in his area as well as the uniforms of the local schoolboys. At the end of every day the newly assigned detective reported on his progress to his supervisor – the chief of the OO or Gendarme Directorate – who determined whether the new man had the retentive powers necessary for the job; if not, he was dismissed from the service. More experienced detectives underwent advanced training which included sending them abroad to learn foreign languages, to gather and become familiar with emigré revolutionary literature[13] and, perhaps most important of all, to identify suspected terrorists residing temporarily abroad.[14]

The ability of the senior *filer* who served as its *nadziratel′* or surveillance supervisor was essential to the success of the detective bureau. This supervisor of detectives had a huge workload, directing several detectives, instructing them in their particular assignments, gathering and collating the information they supplied and debriefing them daily. In addition to his supervisory role he was required to establish a network of hotel spies in the hostelries under his jurisdiction and maintain regular contact with people such as hotel employees – doorman, maids and room clerks, for example – engaging them in friendly conversation, asking passing questions about new registrants at the hotel or about a particularly interesting person standing in the lobby who happened to attract their curiosity.[15] The frenetic pace required by the job, its physical and mental requirements drove many prospective *nadzirateli* out of the training programme.[16] Furthermore surveillance supervisors received surprisingly little compensation for their hard work, having little but their patriotic zeal to comfort them.[17]

****

The basic function of the detective was to present a detailed account of his subject's daily life: his daily travels, from whom he received mail, where he sent his letters and to whom, who stayed in his apartment, whom he visited and who visited him and the newspapers he read,[18] information which was recorded by detectives in their diaries; the format of which was not standardised by Fontanka until 1904.[19]

Acquiring this minutely detailed information was no mean feat and could be accomplished only by the most ingenious, vigorous and talented detectives.[20] To maintain contact with their quarry *filery* had to be quick and resourceful. Detectives worked in pairs. When they were attached to a subject for surveillance they surveyed his residence making certain that it had only a single front street exit. If the building opened onto more than one street the two detectives chose their posts so they could see every possible exit. *Filery* made themselves as inconspicuous as possible. Every OO supported a wardrobe department, allowing detectives to blend into the background of the neighbourhood in which their post was located with chameleon-like expertise.[21] Once settled on their posts *filery* often found themselves in for long inactive days while their quarry remained at home. Nevertheless, they could not afford to become listless since they had to relocate their posts constantly in order to avoid detection.[22]

Once a suspect left home surveillance became hectic. The team of *filery* pursued its man separately and at a reasonable distance, always endeavouring to take advantage of the crowds on the streets, or a passing tram to make themselves as inconspicuous as possible. The pressure of split-second decisions constantly confronted political police *filery*. If an individual knew he was being followed he usually tried to lose his pursuers and decisions about how to sustain the surveillance had to be made instantly.[23]

One of the most successful weapons in the detectives' endless cat and mouse game with their subjects was the innocent looking *drozhki* and its colourful drivers. Detectives disguised as cabmen were one of the most successful methods of keeping people under surveillance. The cabby-detectives were specialists who easily slipped into the cabbies' world. As part of their training they mastered horsemanship and the accoutrements of the cabbies' *patois* and practices, making them indistinguishable from other cabbies.

Disguised as a cabby a detective could plant himself in front of the suspect's residence. He refused to carry any passengers except the individual under surveillance. When the doorman or yardkeeper approached and requested that he take a fare, the cabby-detective coldly replied, 'occupied'. Enough said. The doorman left him alone. The counterfeit-cabby fearing that he would be recognised felt even greater discomfort when forced to transport the subject of his surveillance. He would only do this when there were no other detectives available to follow his quarry, in rainy weather, in the evening when the suspect could not see his face, or, alas, when he happened to be the only drozhki available at that moment. Of course, if the person under surveillance took a drozhki on a regular basis the police arranged for his driver – always a different man – invariably to be one of their own. When circumstances forced the bogus cabby to transport his subject, he treated him exactly like any other customer, especially subjecting him to the ritual haggling over the fare. A cabby who did not bother to bicker with his passenger over the fare was bound to raise his rider's suspicion.[24] Toward the end of the tsarist era, when tramways crisscrossed many of Russia's largest cities, the political police ignominiously reduced the role of its superannuated cabmen to that of transporting detectives to their posts or chauffering OO chiefs to their destinations. Like their legitimate brethren, the cabby-detectives became victims of Russian modernisation.[25]

Detectives pursued their prey almost everywhere, especially into theatres and inns where they thought subversives carried on a good part of their business. Whenever a suspect met with other persons unknown to the surveillance team, the detectives referred to the small pocket-size picture notebook carried with them, containing the anthropomorphic descriptions of known revolutionaries.[26] If a detective recognised any of the people at the meeting from this set of pictures and anthropomorphic data he made a note of it, at the same time recording the physical descriptions of those not already in the pocketbook of photographs. In addition, the harried *filer* had to give each new face a *klichka* or code name that described an obvious physical or personal trait.[27] For example, the well-known terrorist Boris Savinkov was referred to as 'the stout one'. Other *klichka* included: 'long nose', 'the tailor' and 'the butcher'.[28] How detectives could keep their identity a secret while taking these notes will most likely remain a mystery.

When a detective team unearthed a revolutionary conference, the entire agency was thrown into turmoil as the responsible *nadziratel'* hurriedly despatched a number of detectives from less important posts to the scene of the meeting. When a conference concluded for the day the mass of detectives split up, following the gathering's participants as they exited until only the detective team originally assigned to the post remained. They then approached the yard keeper and asked him a series of questions about the premises. How many exits does it have? Can you walk in the front door without ringing the bell? Does the house have exits to the balcony? With this information in hand the political police could reduce the possibilities of escape open to the conferees if the OO decided to raid the premises.[29]

Members of the External Agency were constantly under pressure, always following their quarry and recording his every move. However, nothing upset a detective more than when his subject decided to flee the city in which the detective resided. If the trip only lasted for a short time then the detective would be only slightly inconvenienced. If, on the other hand, the trip was of lengthy duration or meant a permanent move on the part of the suspect it could then involve the same re-location for the detectives assigned to the case. The detectives' fate hung on their chief's perception of the nature of the suspect's trip. If the detectives' *nadziratel'* or his superiors did not believe the trip to be one way or nefarious in purpose, the surveillance was usually not pursued beyond uncovering the traveller's itinerary. However, if the suspect's travels aroused suspicion then the *filery* shadowed him throughout his journey. The director of security, either a chief of an OO or of a Gendarme Directorate for the town to which the suspect was travelling received notice of his impending arrival. When the shadowing *filery* arrived they were thoroughly debriefed by local detectives who then took up the surveillance while the original *filery* usually went home. Sometimes, however, Fontanka itself would order the original team to remain on the case. When this happened the detectives' morale sank since surveillance of a suspect in unfamiliar surroundings added untold pressure to their already nerve-wracking job.[30] Bypassing the local police completely the surveillance team reported their observations to their own agency – which might be hundreds of versts away.[31] Why this was done can only be surmised. Perhaps the Special Section believed that the suspect would eventually return to his place of origin necessitating, therefore, a continuous record of his subversive activities; or perhaps the group to which he belonged was based in that city and the continuous surveillance was part of an ongoing investigation.

****

Rarely did Tsardom's detectives receive adequate compensation for the physical and mental exhaustion that enveloped their lives. The average detective working within Russia earned a salary of only fifty roubles per month, though a few exceptionally hardworking *filery* were granted additional monetary compensation.[32] While Fontanka paid detectives for the expenses they incurred as part of the job, and on rare occasions awarded them special grants for particular purposes, such as the costs incurred for transferring to a new post in a distant city, these grants did not substitute for a living wage.[33] *Filery* were reduced to petty thievery, including the padding of expense accounts, in order to make ends meet.[34] Worse, Fontanka did not guarantee its retiring detectives a pension and even when retirement benefits were issued they were often inadequate as Viktor Fedorovich Borisov, whose services as a detective included taking part in the arrest of Aleksandr Ulianov in March 1887 and four years as a *nadziratel',* found out. Borisov retired from his OO at the age of fifty-seven in 1906 on a miniscule pension of 250 roubles per year. Borisov repeatedly appealed to his former superiors for additional funds, complaining that he could not support himself and his wife on this meagre allowance, but to no avail.[35]

Fontanka's refusal to adequately compensate its *filery* for their service is a reflection of the disdain in which the majority of them were held by St Petersburg. The Special Section reprimanded its detectives without respite, repeatedly questioning detectives about the accuracy of their reports and condemning them for their illiteracy, a condition for which the *filery* could hardly be blamed.[36] The Special Section exaggerated the extent of incompetence within the External Agency,[37] holding such a poor opinion of its surveillance personnel that it always made every effort to double check the authenticity of their information.[38]

Headquarters believed that the problem of shoddy detectives' reports could be solved by demanding the inclusion of minute details in the detective diaries and by enforcing strict uniformity in the format of the intelligence despatched to Petersburg. The officers of the Special Section, none of whom had ever been members of the detective service, could scarcely conceive of the difficult and long hours sustained by a detective in a normal day's work and which were chiefly responsible for the occasionally jumbled or inaccurate reports. A detective in pursuit of his quarry did not have the time to write down each of his observations neatly in his diary, scribbling his notes on any available piece of paper – a matchbook, a greeting card, hotel stationery or anything else at hand – and converting them at the end of the day into as accurate an entry into his diary as possible. If the bureaucrats of the Special Section, instead of burdening their *filery* with an avalanche of critical circulars, which served only to curtail detectives' initiative and undermine their morale, had made the effort to better understand the burdens of service placed upon them they would have been astounded at their level of achievement.[39] It is not surprising, therefore, that by 1910 the shortage in the number of recruits became so severe that OOs were recruiting men from all walks of life.[40] Indeed, many OOs accepted anyone who volunteered. An exasperated Special Section was reduced to ordering its recruiting officers to induct only healthy applicants. Still, OOs and Gendarme Directorates were forced to disregard these instructions and endure further criticisms from St Petersburg in order to employ the required number of detectives. Finally, the Special Section prevailed: it would have the final say over suitability of all applicants except for those with prior police experience.[41] Apparently, for the sake of enforcing its authority the Special Section allowed the detective service to operate severely under strength.

The problems of the detective service, therefore, were not so much the fault of the *filery* themselves as of a society which left many of them semi-literate and in poor health and of a bureaucracy that often left them under-trained and always overworked. None of this, of course, was at all clear to the detectives themselves who were abused by their chiefs in St Petersburg and the populace of Russia alike. Even some revolutionaries like the Bolshevik Shliapnikov who dodged the police daily while carrying on his smuggling activities, wrote contemptuously of the *filery* keeping him under surveillance.[42] Detectives became so disheartened that the chief of the Kharkov OO wrote that the detective-trainees must be convinced that their service was not harmful but beneficial to society.[43]

Indeed, despite the criticism levelled against them, the Russian *filery* should not be underrated. The detectives' zeal made up for their shortcomings, a consideration ignored by Fontanka's bureaucrats immersed, as they were almost entirely, in the procedures of formalism. As one revolutionary more astute than Shliapnikov wrote:

> [Although they are] little developed [intellectually] and are completely lacking in grammar, and have difficulty writing, they are physically strong, hard, and prepared to suffer cold and hunger in order to prevent the suspect from escaping surveillance.[44]

It is a measure of the detectives' success that the revolutionaries believed most large cities contained hundreds of surveillance personnel, and that in Moscow, Petersburg and Warsaw there were thousands of them.[45] In reality, there were probably no more than a thousand trained professional political police *filery* throughout Russia.[46] Yet, the average revolutionary in St Petersburg, for example, could seldom dodge the political police for more than three months.[47] Doubtless, these men despite the abuse universally heaped upon them and their low pay and long hours were among the most loyal of Tsardom's servants.[48]

4 *Sekretnye Sotrudniki*: The Lives of Russia's Undercover Agents

The External Agency supplied only superficial, although extensive, data to the Special Section. The inner life of Russia's numerous revolutionary groups was inaccessible to the Special Section's *filery*. Yet the political police believed it essential to unravel the administrative structure, programmes, tactics and internecine politics of these circles in order to develop effective counter strategies. Some of this intelligence was gleaned from the substantial variety of revolutionary publications available to Fontanka. The aspects of subversive political life that most interested the political police, however, (particularly those of the terrorists) were rarely publicised.[1] The information that the Special Section considered so vital for the success of its operations could only be obtained by a special team of undercover agents known as *sekretnye sotrudniki* (literally 'secret collaborators'). For the sake of simplicity I have shortened their title to *sotrudniki* from here onward.

Sotrudniki formed an integral part of Tsardom's political policing system and as such their service merits analysis from several perspectives: that of the agents themselves; the agents' impact on the revolutionary movement; that of changing police policy toward their use; and finally, the effect of their public unmasking on political police operations and society at large. This chapter, like the one on the *filery* that preceded it and the chapter on high-ranking political police officials that follows, concentrates on the first of these perspectives, the men (and in this case women too) who made their careers within the political police service. Here, therefore, we principally deal with the *sotrudniki* themselves. Who were these shadowy figures about whom so many stories have been told, but so little is actually known? How were they recruited? What was the relationship between *sotrudniki* and their employers and why was the quality of this relationship so important? What effect did leading double lives have upon them? How did the Special Section pay them and protect them from the comrades whom they were betraying? And what was the Special Section's attitude toward acts of provocation committed by them? These are the major questions with which this chapter is concerned. Additional perspectives on undercover agent service form part of the subject matter of later chapters.

****

Sotrudniki fell into two broad categories which together constituted the Special Section's Internal Agency[2] and although we concentrate principally upon the first category – those agents who risked their lives by infiltrating hardcore revolutionary organisations – there was another considerably less glamorous type of *sotrudniki* , those who in fact performed as little more than informers or *osvedomiteli* and never participated in deterrent action of any sort. They focused their attention on clusters of potential or known dissidents, attaching themselves to the periphery of legal associations of every sort, to society salons and educational institutions and even to the bureaucracy itself. Some were specialists who, for example, worked as 'prison agents' (*Tiuremnaia agentura*) informing on their fellow convicts or as 'agrarian agents' (*Sel'skaia agentura*) operating among the non-party peasantry. All, however, collected the intelligence data required of them from what they heard or read in their assigned area.[3]

Each OO recruited its own *sotrudniki* according to standards established by the Special Section. *Gimnazii* and universities were choice recruiting grounds for two reasons. First, *sotrudniki* needed to be clever if they hoped to survive for any length of time. And, in addition, the abilities to absorb revolutionary doctrines, to speak and to write coherently were essential requirements for most undercover agents. Second, the political police considered educational institutions as one of the most fertile environments for the spread of subversive ideas. Many student-*sotrudniki* learned their trade by informing on their fellow students and upon graduation from school joined revolutionary circles as full-fledged undercover agents.[4]

The course of recruitment within the halls of learning, however, did not always run smoothly. When a political police agency could not draw a sufficient number of volunteers to its service within a specific institution it targeted prospective recruits and pressured them into joining the Internal Agency. In these cases the recruiting officer had to possess infinite patience and the finesse of a trained psychologist.[5] Factory workers and professionals were exposed to similar forms of recruitment.[6] Yet most people recruited in this manner did not have connections with revolutionary groups and rarely possessed any knowledge of the revolutionary movement or had any desire to enter revolutionary circles.

The main body of *sotrudniki*, however, were those who participated as active members of revolutionary organisations. A *sotrudnik* of this sort first infiltrated into a revolutionary group, no easy task in itself, and then worked so assiduously on behalf of the revolution that he (or she) became a valued or perhaps indispensable member of this circle, optimally making him privy to the decisions of its inner sanctum. What motives prompted potential candidates to embark upon this dangerous profession? Money appears to have been a significant inducement[7] though by no means the only one; the satisfaction some people derive from being able to sustain their life by living perpetually on a tightrope also seems to have played a role in the decision of applicants to join; others volunteered purely out of patriotic motives. Volunteers, however, were in the minority. Most *sotrudniki* were recruited from the ranks of the revolutionary movement itself after they had been arrested for some minor offence and were, therefore, particularly susceptible to persuasion. Some of Russia's most famous political policemen spent their misbegotten youth on the fringes of Russia's subversive movements. This group includes: S.V. Zubatov, a future director of the Special Section; P.I. Rachkovskii, the first important director of the Foreign Agentura and later Russia's most powerful police official; P.S. Statkovskii, who served as an assistant chief of the Petersburg OO; M.I. Gurovich, who served in several senior posts within the political police, concluding his career as first assistant in charge of political intelligence in the capital during the first year of the 1905 Revolution; and L.P. Men'shchikov who finished his career as director of the Russian political police in Finland, before he returned to the revolutionary cause. It must be noted that the careers of these men were launched long before the edict decreeing that no *sotrudnik* could leave the Internal Agency to enter any other branch of the political police.[8]

The technique of transforming revolutionaries into agents required resourceful interrogators, displaying an ability to dissect their subjects' character. They could tell if a suspect felt a true sense of remorse for having participated in dissident behaviour, or whether the prisoner was merely distressed by the prospects of exile or imprisonment.[9] An interrogator's investigation into his subject's background often discovered other weaknesses in the prisoner, such as a desire to live beyond his means, a wish for revenge against a fellow revolutionary, or perhaps the traits of a schemer who had no qualms about betraying his comrades.[10] Once an interrogator discovered a flaw in his subject's character he utilised the weakness as a lever to pry the prisoner from his scruples and to win him over to Tsardom's cause. However, and this is a critical point, the interrogator dealing with a known revolutionary whom he hoped to convert to an undercover agent never used any kind of blackmail. The interrogator had to be positive that the converted revolutionary honestly and wholly possessed a desire to serve the Department of Police.

The master interrogator Sergei Zubatov believed that an undercover agent's loyalty could best be guaranteed by winning him over to the monarchical principle. As chief of the Moscow OO, Zubatov encouraged the young, impressionable and idealistic men and women arrested by his bureau to believe that their dreams for a better Russia could be accomplished under a new programme known as 'monarchical socialism'. Zubatov worked to convince his charges that tsarism did not oppose the economic struggle of the Russian people, especially that of the proletariat. He told them that labour can easily acquire economic betterment through the beneficence of the monarchy. The worker did not require political freedom, he argued, and noted with firm conviction that the essence 'of the monarchical idea is structured to give the country all it needs through the unleashing of society's strength without bloodshed and similar abominations'.[11]

Did this method of conversion work? Certainly, young people, many from good families, never having been arrested before, felt frightened, isolated and disassociated from reality within the walls of the Moscow OO, placing them in such a state of mental agitation and repentance that at least some of them succumbed to this primitive form of brainwashing. Zubatov boasted to Fontanka that he gave those arrested influential and even illegal books on the labour question and upon reading them the prisoners' revolutionary ardour evaporated. Their revolutionary past, he claimed, could be explained by their lack of education and he bragged that this was just fine since their education took place within the walls of the OO.[12] Perhaps, Zubatov gave too much credit to the books he supplied and not enough to the walls and atmosphere of his jail as ingredients in the formula that turned revolutionaries into *sotrudniki.* Whatever process Zubatov and other interrogators used to carry out this transformation the treason of Evno Azef (discussed in Chapter 7 and 8) and others unduly undermined the image of its effectiveness. There were undercover agents as loyal as Azef was treasonous. Zinaida Zhuchenko, for example, one of Russia's premier undercover agents, possessed the attitude Zubatov and his colleagues hoped to instil in all their subjects. After Vladimir Burtsev, who made a career of unmasking *sotrudniki,*[13] exposed her, Zhuchenko from the safety of her modest Moscow apartment defiantly wrote Burtsev, 'I serve an idea', she proclaimed, 'the highest good fortune is given to me: to remain true to my convictions to the end'.[14]

By means of the interrogation process the interrogator had to determine not only the sincerity of the conversion, but also whether the individual had the ability to exert his influence convincingly and was clever enough to make use of any discord arising in his own revolutionary circle or to exacerbate inter-party friction. In addition the *sotrudnik* had to display a capacity for understanding the various ideological facets of the group to which he belonged as well as the ideas of those who chose to follow other ideological roads.[15] Undercover agents required one further trait, a prerequisite for survival: 'Golden luck [*zolotnik schast'ia*]', remarked one police official, 'which nothing can replace'.[16]

Protecting the identity of a *sotrudnik* began as soon as he was hired. A *sotrudnik* remained under the jurisdiction of the political police agency that recruited him and it was that bureau's responsibility to shield him. After all, even under optimum conditions the average *sotrudnik* only survived for perhaps one or two years' active duty since the strain of the service usually took its toll by that time. Immediately upon an agent's appointment, therefore, his chief assigned him a *klichka* or code name and found a legitimate excuse for releasing him from detention.[17] Usually only the chief of his OO or the director of the Special Section knew the undercover agent's real name and everyone else including his case officer identified him only by his new code name.[18] OO chiefs applied special care in choosing code names for undercover agents. They were never derived from the family name of an agent, from his place of residence or his physiognomy. Whenever an undercover agent's *klichka* became well-known in police circles the bureau chief changed it. At other times the Special Section altered the *klichki* of all undercover agents as a matter of policy, usually when a turnover of personnel at the highest echelons of Fontanka demanded that it do so for reasons of security.[19] Political police bureaus were so obsessed with the security of their *sotrudniki* that they permitted opportunities to arrest some of Russia's most infamous political criminals to slip by rather than endanger their agents.[20]

Once accepted for service in the Internal Agency, an undercover agent's OO (or Gendarme Directorate) entered his name upon its role of secret agents, opening a personnel file in his name. This dossier contained a data sheet listing the agent's code name or code number (code names were much more common, but some *sotrudniki* were identified by both), the subversive organisation to which he belonged, the date he joined it, awards and honours received, positions held, his monthly allowance and the name of his case officer.[21] By maintaining these records the OOs and Gendarme Directorates were able to keep track of their agents in the field and more importantly highlight to the Special Section the numbers of *sotrudniki* secured in anti-government groups. Every OO chief knew that the more undercover agents he controlled the higher his prestige in police circles.[22] As a result of this policy each bureau attempted to outdo the others in the recruitment of *sotrudniki* and in the effort to squeeze every bit of information possible out of them.

The exact number of *sotrudniki* distributed throughout Russia's revolutionary and opposition movements at any given time is unknowable. One author, writing in 1918 from the records of the Petersburg OO, contends that there were 'several thousand provocateurs [*sotrudniki*] living in the country, reporting on and turning in their brothers'.[23] Nurit Schleifman in her research has uncovered 600 *sotrudniki* of various types operating throughout Russia and abroad.[24] Chlenov's research into the archives of the Moscow OO revealed that between 1910 and 1917 it employed 116 undercover agents,[25] and General Gerasimov claimed that he controlled between 120 and 150 agents during his close to five-year tenure as chief of the Petersburg OO.[26] Given the nature of their work and the secrecy surrounding their identities, it is unlikely that we will ever be able to uncover the number of *sotrudniki* employed by the Internal Agency over the years.

The same problem exists when trying to determine with any accuracy the number of *sotrudniki* operating within targeted groups of subversives. Popular Russian feeling on this subject was expressed by A. Volkov, one of the first historians of the Special Section, who wrote:

> [There] was not a single party, nor a single mill, factory, nor a single organisation, nor society, union, club committee, university, institute, there was not even a single newspaper editorial staff in which among its members and collaborators there would not have been several secret agents.[27]

As extreme as this statement appears, we can only judge its accuracy from the sparse available evidence. Of her 600 agents Schleifman can identify the political affiliations of 215 of them, distributing them as follows in Table 4.1. While Table 4.1 gives us a broad overview of the distribution of agents among the most

Table 4.1 Schleifman's Distribution of *Sotrudniki* among Revolutionary Parties, 1902–1914

Party	*Number*
SRs	90
SDs	82
Anarchists	43
Total	215

Source: Nurit Schleifmann, 'The Internal Agency: Linchpin of the political police in Russia', *Cahiers du monde Russe et Sovietique*, 1983, no. 1–2: 176 n. 65.

extreme parties, over a twelve year time span, we can turn to the records of the Moscow OO for a more detailed division of undercover agents by a single OO at a given point in time. The figures in Table 4.2 reveal the widespread infiltration of the Moscow OO's *sotrudniki* throughout broad sections of dissident or potentially dissident society and tentatively suggest that the seemingly exaggerated statement made by Volkov quoted above may be closer to the truth than is commonly believed.[28] This conclusion is supported by the magnitude of the financial investment Fontanka made in its Internal Agency operations. The money spent on undercover agent operations by OOs and to a much lesser extent by Gendarme Directorates grew steadily. As Table 4.3 shows, by 1914 the small Olonets

Table 4.2 Distribution of the Moscow OO's *Sotrudniki* Operating Among Revolutionary, Opposition and Suspicious Groups, beginning of 1916

Group or Institution	*Number*
RSDWP	19
Opposition Movement	11
Tramway and Electrical Workers	7
Institutions of Higher Education	5
SRs	5
Latvian SDs	3
Anarcho-Communists	2
Polish Revolutionaries	1
Total	52

Source: S.B. Chlenov, *Moskovskaia okhranka i ee sekretnye sotrudniki: Po dannym komissii po obespecheniiu novogo stroia* (Moscow: 1919), 17.

Table 4.3 Yearly Expenditure (in roubles) by OOs and Gendarme Directorates (By City or Region) on Their Undercover Operations, 1914[a]

Approximate Yearly Expenditure	*City or Region*	*Total roubles spent per year on Undercover Operations by OOs and Gendarme Directorates*
to 1000	Olonets	360
1000–2000	Archangel	2 000
2000–3000	Astrakhan, Vitebsk, Vladimir,[b] Vologda, Kaluga, Novgorod, Penza, Pskov, Riazan', Nikol'sk-Ussuriisk, Smolensk, Tver, Tula, Kholm, Blagoveshchensk, Ashkhabad, Verny, Khabarovsk	47 520
3000–4000	Kostroma, Tambov, Tobol'sk, Chernigov	13 140
4000–5000	Viatka, Kovno, Kursk, Mogilev, Omsk, Orenburg, Orel, Simbirsk, Simferopol', Ufa, Erivan, Iaroslavl'	57 360
6000–7000	Baku, Grodno, Ekaterinoslav, Enisei, Kazan, Kuban, Nizhegorod, Perm, Podolia, Poltava, Sevastapol', Kharkov, Kherson, Estliand,Turkhestan	106 920
7000–8000	Vilna, Kronshtadt, Vladimir[b]	23 400
8000–9000	Courland, Saratov	16 280
9000–10 000	The Don Region	9 120
12 000–13 000	Kiev, Odessa, Omsk	38 280
13 000–14 000	Tiflis, Finland	26 240
–	Lifland	15 200
–	Irkutsk	16 900
–	Warsaw	19 800
–	Moscow	47 320
–	St Petersburg	80 700
Total		520 540

Source: P. Pavlov, *Agenty, Zhandarmy, Palachi: Po dokumentam* (Petrograd, 1922), 1–13.

[a] This is neither a complete nor an exact set of figures. There were Gendarme Directorates not listed above, that also spent funds on undercover operations. Even the Governor General of Warsaw employed *sotrudniki.* In addition, Fontanka spent funds on rewards, pensions and other peripheral outlays which together with the list above added up to approximately 600 000 roubles.

[b] For some unexplained reason Vladimir appears twice on the list.

Gendarme Directorate costing only 360 roubles per year and the 75 000 roubles spent yearly by the powerful St Petersburg OO were the extremes encompassing dozens of other OOs and Gendarme Directorates. These sums did not include the

Foreign Agentura, however, which spent the phenomenal total of 600 000 roubles on undercover operations.

A considerable portion of the Internal Agency's budget went to pay agent salaries. Fontanka reserved the largest salaries for men and women of exceptional ability who occupied posts of major importance[29] (managers of printing presses, the guiding lights or editors of underground publications, or members of the governing bodies of various revolutionary organisations) especially among the SR's. Some of these well-placed agents worked as pieceworkers (*shtuchniki*) who received a sum of money that the Special Section based upon the value of the intelligence they supplied and upon the agents' positions within their groups. Most of the more experienced undercover agents were worth every kopek paid or lavished upon them, with several *sotrudniki* carrying out more than one assignment at a time.[30] Productive undercover agents' salaries ranged from about 100 to 200 roubles per month.[31] In contrast, the best of Russia's *sotrudniki*, most of whom lived and worked abroad in the heart of the revolutionary emigration, found themselves with a fat pay packet at the end of every month, bulging with about 400 roubles,[32] becoming wealthy in the service of the Department of Police. The Special Section permitted local OO chiefs to offer additional bonuses to their undercover agents on special occasions as well. Such largesse usually flowed after a particularly outstanding success and it did not necessarily take monetary form. If a nest of revolutionaries was uncovered and destroyed with the aid of one or more *sotrudniki* the local OO chief treated the successful agents to an extraordinary evening. He reserved a private room in the finest local restaurant and invited women to the party who were not particularly concerned with their reputations. At the appointed time the *maître de* ushered the agents, their case officers and the chief of the OO, and the gendarmes in civilian dress, into a private room. A rather exuberant party began at once. In St Petersburg these gaieties took place in either Mednikov's apartment at 40 Preobrazhenskaia Street or at the fashionable *Malyi Iaroslavets* restaurant. The Special Section honoured its most valuable *sotrudnik* Evno Azef with several such 'debauches' (*kutezhi*).[33]

This massive expenditure on the Internal Agency had one basic purpose: the collection of intelligence to be used as the Special Section saw fit. Yet procuring data from *sotrudniki* proved to be no easy matter. Political police bureaus entrusted this duty to their case officers, men who usually held the rank of captain in the Separate Corps of Gendarmes, although in some circumstances higher ranking officers, including a few OO chiefs, took this role as well. Case officers, who were generally specialists in controlling and debriefing agents within particular parties or groups,[34] on average supervised as few as five but usually twelve to twenty undercover agents, meeting their *sotrudniki* on a regular basis. Conferences between undercover agents and their controls were supposed to take place within 'conspiratorial apartments' (*konspirativnye kvartiry*). The Special Section instituted rules for the use of conspiratorial apartments and demanded that *sotrudniki* and case officers strictly obey them for their mutual safety: to protect the undercover agent's identity and thereby his life and to safeguard the case officer from his undercover agents![35]

Unfortunately, case officers did not always follow the Special Section's tight security measures, despite the fact that Zubatov himself believed the matter of undercover agent security to be of vital importance. He did not hesitate to remind some junior political police officers that they 'must look at *sotrudniki* as a beautiful woman with whom you are maintaining a secret liaison. Be careful with her as [if she] is the apple of your eye. One careless step and you disgrace her'.[36] Zubatov's vivid analogy notwithstanding, the practice of employing 'conspiratorial apartments' as secure meeting places was ignored by some case officers. Until 1906 in St Petersburg, for example, meetings took place within the local bureau's headquarters, a ridiculous practice since in every other respect the political police resorted to elaborate measures to safeguard the identities of the men and women of the Internal Agency.[37] Nevertheless, to their own detriment case officers persistently ignored the basic rules of 'conspiratorial apartment' security. The assassination of Colonel S.G. Karpov, a prominent case officer, was the most famous example of this failure to obey instructions, his death infuriating the Department of Police since he had been warned about his slipshod procedures. Furthermore, that Karpov was not entirely sure of his assassin's loyalty only served to emphasise the stupidity of his actions.[38] As a result of the Karpov assassination Fontanka issued a directive to its case officers and their superiors re-emphasising the need for security and circumspection in dealing with *sotrudniki*.

The *sotrudniki* themselves were exceptional people. It took an unusually strong personality to maintain equilibrium in a profession where severe psychological stress was often the most demanding part of the service. In order for undercover agents to be effective they had to function as revolutionaries in everything except their loyalty. In addition, *sotrudniki* developed into furtive, cunning people (if they did not possess these characteristics already), traits necessary for their self-preservation, employing them against friend and foe alike. General Viktor Russiian, a prominent political police official of the day, remembered that *sotrudniki* were extremely secretive, keeping their opinions to themselves. Unfortunately, these attributes often proved to be the *bête noire* of the Special Section and its local bureaus, because a *sotrudnik* frequently withheld all the information he held at hand if he believed his security to be threatened.[39] Faced with such closed and devious people, case officers had to throw the rulebook aside, as dangerous as this could be, in order to cultivate the flexible, relaxed, trusting relationship with their *sotrudniki* necessary to draw critical information out of them. Inevitably, the intensity of this rapport allowed disloyal *sotrudniki* to mesmerise their case officers into a lull of confidence. The murder of Colonel Karpov is just one example of what could happen to an unwary case officer.[40]

A few *sotrudniki* played a double game, supplying intelligence to both sides, while others transferred their loyalties to the revolutionaries entirely.[41] More commonly, however, and on a smaller scale, treacherous *sotrudniki* mastered a variety of techniques which they hoped would make them appear as highly valued members of the Internal Agency no matter how minor their roles within the opposition movements. Case officers were aware of the different forms of mischief their *sotrudniki* might perpetrate. Some agents, in an attempt to show their superiors that they possessed the capability of obtaining a steady flow of new intelligence titbits, never submitted all the data they held to their case officers at any single time, instead choosing to turn it over in bits and pieces. This was known as the 'piecemeal deception'. The 'piecemeal' method could be legitimately used at times when certain revelations might endanger the agent's position, but the action of keeping information to himself in order to enhance his reputation by revealing it over a period of time was not condoned.[42] Some *sotrudniki* fabricated reports to raise their reputations as well. The worst example of these were known as 'schemers' (*kombinatory*). *Kombinatory* did not have any connections with the subversive movements, they volunteered as *sotrudniki* purely for the money and did not want to take risks in acquiring it. They lied about their revolutionary connections and submitted completely fabricated reports. As we shall see, some of these so-called agents made false accusations against altogether innocent people and then offered to turn them over to the police in return for proper compensation.[43]

In order to prevent both the falsification and fabrication of intelligence and to protect the lives of their case officers, political police bureaus maintained an office that coordinated Internal Agency activity in an attempt to keep track of their *sotrudniki* and to verify the accuracy and the quality of their reports. This office collected and carefully scrutinised the agents' reports, at which point case officers often found the collated intelligence too fragmentary for use and detectives were dispatched to fill in the gaps and to ascertain the reliability of the data.[44] To minimise risk to themselves the Special Section forbade its *sotrudniki* to change their cover story, to disguise themselves through the use of make-up or to play the role of detectives.[45] The Special Section's most critical edict on *sotrudnik* life commanded them not to carry out any orders issued by the subversive organisation to which they belonged that would involve them in anti-government activity or an act of a general criminal nature such as the acquisition of weapons or explosive devices without the express (rarely given) consent of their superiors. The MVD considered any illegal behaviour by an undercover agent outside the stipulations already noted to be an act of provocation and punishable by immediate expulsion from the service and subsequent criminal prosecution.[46] General A.I. Spiridovich formally set out Fontanka's fundamental principle in this matter for young political police officers in training. 'Conformity to the law', he decreed, 'must be emphasized and explained to him [the *sotrudnik*] as the main, obligatory basis of his work'. To stress the significance of this rule he went on to elaborate:

> It must be explained to him, that the means he employs, no matter how tempting the result...are impermissible once they run contrary to the law. With his

> initiation into criminal activities or incitement to them, that is, 'provocation', the undercover agent not only ceases to be of assistance to the government in the struggle against the revolutionaries but becomes a State Criminal himself.[47]

Implicit in Spiridovich's statements is the recognition that *sotrudniki* were at best half-known agents for, as General Russiian remarked, they always maintained a degree of empathy for the revolutionary movement because of the life, the trust and the joy of working for it within a closely knit group, which it gave them.[48]

In fact, though, there was little that the Special Section could do to prevent a renegade undercover agent from acting against the government or its representatives. As a matter of policy OOs placed newly hired *sotrudniki* under surveillance until they were considered reliable, but even under the best of conditions, *filery* found this to be a frustrating assignment.[49] Since almost all of the undercover agent's working hours were spent in the revolutionary underground, a large portion of his activities went unobserved. Once regular surveillance ceased, detection of any wrongdoing would probably not be passed on to the case officer. The very secrecy surrounding the Internal Agency's membership was a distinct drawback in this situation. The average detective, while he knew of the Internal Agency's existence, never knew the identities of the *sotrudniki* who worked for it, unless a case officer specifically asked his OO to keep a particular *sotrudnik* under observation. An unsuspecting detective's observations on a *sotrudnik* were filed away in the records of the OO and the Department of Police like those of any revolutionary activist. And even if an OO carried out surveillance over a *sotrudnik* at the request of his case officer, the reported results would have been minimal because an undercover agent had an advantage over his revolutionary comrades. Since he knew that his group had been uncovered by the local OO, after all it had been his doing, he took special care not to be followed on those occasions when he broke the Internal Agency's rules.[50] Despite precautions it seemed that case officers even under the best circumstances only maintained minimal control over their *sotrudniki*. To all intents and purposes agents operated in an atmosphere of complete independence and, ironically, it was this freedom of action that allowed them to penetrate to the depths of the revolutionary underground. By disobeying the restrictions on their actions imposed by the Special Section they became valued members of the revolutionary movement. The political police found it difficult to come to terms with this paradox and, in the end, it acknowledged this anomaly by limiting the undercover agents' knowledge of other police functions and by doing its best to ensure that they knew only their case officers and no other police official.[51]

The Special Section did its best to ensure that prospective *sotrudniki* were sufficiently stable to handle the tremendous power it placed in their hands,[52] never considering that the same standard should be applied to the undercover agents' superiors. This was a mistake. The temptation of using *sotrudniki* for purposes of self-aggrandisement proved too great for many political police officers to resist. Privately, A.I. Spiridovich recognised what was happening and worried about the potential for abuse inherent within the *sotrudnik* system, admitting that the philosophy that lay behind their deployment was in itself immoral, although he argued that *sotrudniki* served an indispensable function.[53] Very few political police officials, however, felt even the slight pangs of conscience that troubled Spiridovich and the Special Section's warnings concerning the severe penalties for acts of provocation fell on deaf ears. The technique of deploying undercover agents had proven itself years before, in the 1880s during Plehve's successful campaign against the terrorist *Narodnaia Volia.*[54] To participate in a victory of this magnitude over the revolutionary movement would certainty enhance one's prestige within the MVD and particularly within Fontanka. However, Russia's political policemen soon realised that there was another, easier method of using *sotrudniki* to attract the favourable attention from St Petersburg so necessary for career advancement. The absence of any firm control by Fontanka or the Special Section over the life of its political police bureaus (a recurrent theme of this book) made abuse of the Internal Agency's powers all too easy for *sotrudniki* and their immediate superiors alike.[55]

One of the most common schemes used by *sotrudniki* and winked at by their superiors in the hope of acquiring a bit of extra money, or perhaps some other honour as well as glory for his OO or Gendarme Directorate, was the exercise known as 'the arrest of anarchists with bombs'. A typical case occurred in Warsaw in 1905. An undercover agent of the Warsaw OO named Itzhak Raikhel, who supposedly had infiltrated a local anarchist circle, actually belonged to the category of agents known as *kombinatory*. Raikhel had never bothered to gain entry to any anarchist group, choosing instead to fabricate reports. Carrying out a scheme designed to earn him a substantial reward, he picked up an itinerant labourer on the streets of Warsaw and in the course of their introductory conversation Raikhel offered him the opportunity to earn some easy money by participating in the robbery of a local merchant. The workman, in desperate need of a few extra roubles, agreed. Raikhel subsequently revealed to his OO chief, Lt Colonel Sheviakov an anarchist 'plot' involving a bomb – the bomb being planted on the unfortunate labourer by Raikhel. Raikhal supplied the details of the plot to his superior who arrested the unsuspecting labourer and the merchant he believed he was to rob as anarchists. The worker and merchant exclaimed that they had nothing to do with anarchism and although Sheviakov saw through Raikhel's cunning little plot, he took no action against him; actually rewarding him with a gift of thirty roubles. Despite their bitter protests, the two victims of the scheme were handed over to the courts for justice. The Special Section for its part showed its pleasure with the results of this 'investigation' by rewarding the Warsaw OO's director of surveillance with the Order of St Stanislav and presenting a medal to one of the OO's detectives who played a key role in the arrests.[56] Captain Martynov, the chief of the Saratov OO, succinctly expressed the general feeling among political police officers when he frankly admitted, 'that without good provocateurs it is not possible to make a career...',[57] a notion lent credibility by the preceding story.

Little provocations of this sort were merely the most common symptoms of a widely spread disease that, by Tsardom's last decade or so, was deeply imbedded in the political police system, infecting the polity of the state as well as its intended victim, the revolutionary movement. Provocation on a grand scale usually occurred when previously loyal *sotrudniki*, more at home in the world of subversion than in the world of police slowly lost their identities as they metamorphosed into enemies of the state. General Russiian vividly described this transformation. Little by little, Russiian noted, the glamorous 'false pose' of the *sotrudnik* caused him to lose his identity. *Sotrudniki* believed themselves to be beyond the control of either their fellow revolutionaries or their police employer, permitting them the independence to take matters into their own hands, whether to settle a score with a comrade or with a member of the government.[58]

A second form of full scale provocation that actually had the full support of the political police after 1906 was the strategy of planting first-class undercover agents in organisations deemed to be hostile to the well-being of the state and carefully nurturing these agents until they attained sufficient influence within their circles to paralyse them or at least to ensure that they did not present a threat to Tsardom's political stability. The famous case of *sotrudnik* Roman Malinovskii, the leading Bolshevik deputy in the Fourth Duma, is the best example of this form of provocation.[59] The considerable harm provocation caused to both its intended and unintended victims will be discussed in Chapter 12.

****

Fontanka's concern over the trustworthiness of its *sotrudniki* was matched by the undercover agents' anxiety over their security during and after their service in the Internal Agency. As we have seen, the Special Section did its best to protect its *sotrudniki* from being unmasked, even to the extent of forbidding them from doing anything that aroused their comrades' suspicions. For example, the Special Section believed that an outward appearance of poverty enhanced the undercover agents' cover stories. Therefore, headquarters forbade *sotrudniki* from spending any of the money they received from their OOs on anything at all that might give them the appearance of having suddenly acquired an unexplainable income, a circumstance that sealed the fate of several undercover agents.[60]

The vagaries of agents' lives were so great that often the Special Section could do nothing to prevent them being exposed. Even disgruntled or ex-spouses could be an undercover agent's undoing. As Spiridovich ruefully noted to fellow political police officers, 'considering the contemporary instability of family life, male married collaborators are frequently trapped by their wives after arguments and divorce'.[61] Every *sotrudnik* knew that, once unmasked, he could expect only one form of justice at the hands of his former friends in the revolutionary movement.

An SR spokesman put this ultimate plight of *sotrudniki* most succinctly. 'Death to all who act in connection with the *Okhrana* [*sic!*] Department'.[62] It is not surprising, then, that *sotrudniki* measured the quality of their bureau chief on how well he hid their identities; such a chief was likely to win the long-lasting unbreakable allegiance of his agents.[63]

An undercover agent's greatest chance of being discovered, whether he worked for a conscientious chief or not, came when he was arrested by the political police in one of their raids. An arrested agent's release needed to be arranged without raising suspicion, a costly process. Under normal circumstances, once the arresting gendarmes confirmed the identity of a jailed *sotrudnik*, he was released along with several suspects seized in the same raid, the Special Section hoping that this ruse would deflect any possible suspicion away from its *sotrudnik*.[64] Sometimes, however, when the risk to an agent's life was considered too great, his arrest, detention and imprisonment or exile became unavoidable. In this instance the local OO informed the arresting gendarmes and an OO officer was assigned to protect the agent during the period of detention and interrogation. While the agent served his term in prison or exile the Special Section held his salary and there was a good chance that he would receive a bonus for bearing his imprisonment in silence, although there were cases of *sotrudniki* who having done their duty found themselves short-changed by Fontanka.[65]

In contrast, Fontanka often exhibited an ambivalent attitude toward retired agents and in some cases toward those *sotrudniki* who were no longer useful to the Internal Agency. *Sotrudniki* who left the Internal Agency voluntarily or out of necessity were not guaranteed a pension nor protection despite their arduous service which aged them quickly and left many of them suffering from shattered nerves.[66] Sergei Zubatov, chief of the Special Section, who had once been an agent himself, sympathised with their plight. To him the retirement of an undercover agent who had given devoted service, but who could no longer stand the tension integral to his duties, was a sad event and he argued that the government had a responsibility to make a place for them in legal society and grant them a pension, reminding his superiors in the MVD, 'you lose a *sotrudnik* but you acquire a friend of the government in society, a person wholly for the State'.[67] Zubatov's advice notwithstanding, Fontanka's criteria for determining the treatment of retired *sotrudniki* depended on different, less romantic, more mundane considerations such as how much did the retiring agent know and what could he sell to the press if Fontanka rejected his supplication for funds. Fontanka would also grant pensions to agents who had performed outstanding service and were known to its chiefs. Unfortunately, the overworked and understaffed bureaucracy of Fontanka's first Secretariat, unable to handle the myriad of requests it received for benefits, simply chose to grant or deny many of them arbitrarily.[68]

Sometimes Fontanka's callousness in dealing with its former agents together with massive bureaucratic bumbling led to situations equalled only by the creations of Russia's great satirists. The fate of E.N. Shornikova, an undercover agent partly responsible for the arrest of the SD faction in the Second Duma, is a case in point. After it made these arrests, the Special Section considered her usefulness to be at an end; perhaps her SD colleagues began to suspect her loyalty. Unwanted by the political police Shornikova found herself caught in a terrible paradox. Since only her own OO knew her true loyalty and since each OO carefully guarded the names of its *sotrudniki*, the remaining OOs within the empire still pursued Shornikova as a member of the SDs! She required, therefore, a reasonable sum of money to make her escape and a general notice to all political police bureaus concerning her status as a former *sotrudnik*. She appealed directly to General Gerasimov, who denied any knowledge of her. Meanwhile the Kazan Gendarme Directorate spotted her living within its jurisdiction and reported this news to the regional OO where her former case officer must have seen this information in an Intelligence Survey. He subsequently warned her that she was about to be detained and he advised Shornikova to flee. She, however, courageously turned herself in to the gendarmes to whom she explained her situation. The Gendarme Directorate passed her story to the Special Section in good bureaucratic fashion where its authenticity was checked; the gendarmes released her and offered protection from her former comrades whom she had betrayed. None the less, the Special Section still ignored her plea for funds which would allow her to escape abroad. Shornikova's stay in Kazan eventually came to an end when she was publicly exposed as a police agent. Panic stricken, she fled to St Petersburg to plead her case first to the assistant minister of internal affairs charged with managing the police and subsequently to Colonel Eremin, chief of the Special Section. Eremin slipped her twenty-five roubles and sent her away with the promise that he would tell the director of Fontanka of her plight. After no further communication from the Department of Police, Shornikova returned to Fontanka again pleading to see the director, but another bureaucrat informed her that she could not see him, pressing fifty roubles into her hand at the same time. Shornikova begged, she needed 2000 roubles, the government must give her a chance to escape. The unexpected arrival of Shornikova on Fontanka's doorstep in Petersburg had forced Director of Fontanka Beletskii to act. Beletskii had heretofore ignored the pleas of this unknown, and minor agent, but could do so no longer, believing that the longer Shornikova's demand for protection remained unsatisfied the greater the chance that the Duma would learn of her story and through it the political police role in the subversion of the Second Duma. Beletskii's superior, Assistant Minister of Internal Affairs V.F. Dzhunkovskii, who also feared a scandal, turned to Minister of Internal Affairs Maklakov for a decision in this matter. After much bureaucratic negotiation a meeting of the Council of Ministers was called to discuss the future of an insignificant former *sotrudnik* about whom none of them really cared. Meanwhile, Shornikova awaited her fate. Finally, they decided to settle the matter by following the letter if not the intent of the law. The Council of Ministers decided to bring her to trial for political offences. She was placed under protective custody (*pokrovitel'stvo vlasti*), kindly told that she had nothing to fear, and finally brought to trial before the Senate on 26 July 1913. The Senate issued the expected verdict of not guilty of state criminal activity. Shornikova, now mollified, received 1800 roubles to begin her life anew. She departed St Petersburg on 4 September 1913 and left Russia soon afterwards, much to the relief of the Department of Police.[69]

There were glaring exceptions to these sorry episodes when the undercover agent making the request for a pension or some other substantial favour was well-known to Fontanka. In such instances, the cold-bloodedness exhibited by the Department of Police in the Shornikova case could be replaced by the generosity of a grateful government. Agent Batushanskii, for instance, had his best years as a *sotrudnik* under Plehve's ministry, though he retired during Stolypin's term in office. He immediately claimed that Plehve had personally promised him a pension of 1200 roubles per year. Stolypin politely responded that the MVD could not afford to issue pensions of that size but offered him the still generous stipend of 600 roubles per year. Batushanskii accepted Stolypin's settlement.[70] Stolypin had not been completely honest with Batushanskii since the largest pension so far awarded had been 1800 rubles.[71] A.E. Serebriakova, about whom we write below, was awarded a pension of 1200 roubles per year in 1911. In her amazing career she managed to turn in to the police hundreds of her fellow revolutionaries and was directly responsible for the collapse of scores of revolutionary circles.[72]

Money and safety were not the only rewards that were bestowed on a particularly deserving *sotrudnik*. Agent Nikulin-Mikulin received a very special reward for his outstanding service. Mikulin began his career like most other *sotrudniki* – after being arrested as a young revolutionary. After years of outstanding service Mikulin petitioned the tsar to expunge the record of his arrest as a youthful offender. The MVD considered this a most unusual request. Despite their entrance into police service, undercover agents' lives were circumscribed by their legal status as former state criminals and the record of their crimes remained in Fontanka's archives. One of the ultimate rewards, therefore, bestowed by the government on an undercover agent was to re-establish him as a citizen in good standing by erasing his police record. This could only be accomplished through a special dispensation issued by the tsar. Amazingly, Nicholas II granted Mikulin's request and pardoned *(legalizoval)* him. Mikulin received a set of documents confirming the tsar's decision and stating that he was no longer stigmatised by a criminal record.[73]

****

Unfortunately not all agents faded away gracefully or quietly at the end of their service and often their ensuing revelations became an embarassment to the MVD. There were, however, several outstanding *sotrudniki* whose careers are shining examples of why Fontanka tolerated the problems endemic in operating a vast undercover internal spy service. Zinaida Zhuchenko, Aleksandr Mass, Roman Malinovskii, Iakov Zhitomirskii, Tatiana Tsetlin were a few such agents.

One agent in particular stood out above all the others. She was Anna Egorovna Serebriakova. While Serebriakova boasted three *klichki*, her most famous one 'Mamasha' (Mother) described part of her value to the Special Section, for Serebriakova served the Moscow OO as a *sotrudnika* for about a quarter of a century. As Colonel von Koten, her last chief, wrote, Serebriakova lived and worked through a major portion of Russian revolutionary history from the repression of the 1880s to the Moscow uprising in December 1905.[74] Her career as an undercover agent began in a most peculiar, roundabout way.

Anna Serebriakova was born in Tobolsk province. By the 1870s with her education in Moscow almost completed she, like so many other students became involved in political activity. Her financial position was hopeless and the leader of her illegal circle suggested that she enter into a marriage of convenience as a means of relieving her hardship. She found a willing husband in P.A. Serebriakov, apparently another member of their group. In the early 1880s Serebriakov was arrested after purchasing some type for a clandestine press he wished to establish. He was interrogated by Chief of the Moscow OO Skandrakov, but Lt Colonel Sudeikin, Tsardom's leading political policeman, happened to be present at the time. Sudeikin soon took over Serebriakov's questioning and he used his skills as an inquisitor to force Serebriakov into betraying his cause. Once the young man took this step there was no turning back. Sudeikin released both Serebriakov and his wife, who had been detained as an accessory to the crime. Their freedom was illusory, since Sudeikin continually hounded Serebriakov to become an informer by blackmailing him. While it is unclear whether or not Serebriakov did any further work for the political police, the intense pressure led him to a nervous breakdown, forcing his wife to support them. A highly intelligent woman who had mastered several foreign languages, Serebriakova worked in the editorial offices of a Moscow newspaper as well as at other jobs considered suitable for the emancipated *intelligentka* that she was.

Sudeikin was assassinated in late 1883 and the Serebriakovs breathed more easily, since they believed that their harassment by the political police would now come to an end. It might have, if it had not been for Serebriakov's penchant for dabbling in illegal political activities. Again, he was picked up by the political police and his health began to fail under renewed interrogation. Nevertheless, Berdiaev, the chief of the Moscow OO, insisted that Serebriakov could only save himself by joining the Internal Agency or if his health did not permit this, his wife must substitute for him. Serebriakova volunteered to take her husband's place and so began the career of one of Russia's most infamous undercover agents.

Serebriakova embarked on her career as an agent by working for the semi-legal Red Cross organisation designed to aid political exiles and convicts. Her Red Cross work brought her into contact with Moscow society, especially those elements interested in politics. Serebriakova betrayed the confidences of her new friends when she believed their information worth reporting to her case officer. The Moscow OO, not satisfied with her role as an informer, insisted that Serebriakova plunge more deeply into opposition circles, which she did with enthusiasm. Serebriakova never became a classic deep cover agent burrowing into the core of a particular revolutionary party: she remained more or less above party or factional interests for most of her career, opening her home to revolutionaries and oppositionists of every political complexion. They felt completely secure in Serebriakova's presence and treated her home as a club; playing chess, drinking tea, carrying on their endless theoretical debates and even unintentionally dropping some hints about their conspiratorial business. Of course, these men and women would never have trusted a mere fellow traveller so completely. Serebriakova earned their respect by operating as a courier for illegal literature, serving as a source for collecting and distributing funds and passing on forged passports and other essential tools necessary for clandestine political life.[75]

Serebriakova listened to everything her guests said, recording the contents of each conversation, then passing them on to the OO. Her ability to collect so much valuable intelligence attracted the attention of Sergei Zubatov, who became the new chief of the Moscow OO in 1896. Indeed her role in Zubatov's liquidations of revolutionary groups, particularly the SDs in Moscow, became indispensable, though the complete record of her participation in these events is unknown.[76] Serebriakova also served as a principal source of information for Zubatov's 'flying detachment' of detectives. Her home was apparently used as a temporary sanctuary by provincial revolutionaries passing through Moscow. As a result, she was able to collect intelligence on revolutionaries intent on undermining the monarchy from as far away as Kiev, Ekaterinoslav and Kremenchug, thereby allowing the 'flying detachment' to roam successfully in provincial Russia.[77]

Given the extensiveness of her betrayals Serebriakova's longevity is a remarkable achievement. The reason for her survival involved more than 'golden luck'. In 1900, probably on Zubatov's orders, she established closer connections with the SDs than with any other party or group but maintained cordial relationships with groups as diverse as the SRs and *Osvobozhdentsy*, still possible before party lines hardened after the 1905 Revolution. While this situation permitted her to spy on a cross-section of the opposition and revolutionary movements, it also seems to have placed her above suspicion, admittedly at a time when the revolutionaries did not as yet follow up their suspicions of treachery with sufficient dedication.[78]

Consequently Serbriakova received fulsome praise from the three chiefs of the Moscow OO for whom she worked: Zubatov, and Colonels Ratko and von Koten. In addition to recognising her qualities of zeal and loyalty Zubatov remembered that 'for the functionaries of the division [OO] she was not only a deeply devoted intelligence source, but a competent advisor and sometimes an experienced teacher in security matters'.[79] No less a figure than P.A. Stolypin wrote that through her work Serebriakova managed 'to inflict quite significant damage on the revolutionary movement'.[80] Serebriakova served until the end of 1905, only retiring for the sake of her children (or so she claimed).[81]

Anna Serebriakova represented the best of Tsardom's *sotrudniki*. As far as Fontanka was concerned Serebriakova and her hundreds of colleagues within the Internal Agency served several vital purposes, supplying Fontanka with a wealth of intelligence. Modern scholarship devoted to Late Imperial Russia witnesses the vast detail that Tsardom's undercover agents amassed on innumerable facets of Russian life. This detail helped a government that stood at a great distance from the mass of its people to formulate a picture of its society, and most of this evidence was utilised toward undermining the forces of political change within Russia. As we have just seen and will see again, *sotrudniki* were themselves key weapons in the destruction of innumerable revolutionary circles. Indeed, after 1906 the Special Section employed some of its most talented agents to control, one might say defuse, radical elements within Russian society not solely by making these elements vulnerable to police harassment, but in addition by taking over the direction of those groups themselves (a policy discussed in Chapter 12). And, at least for Russia's *sanovniki*, most important of all, *sotrudniki* caused the aborting of several assassination attempts against tsarist officials, as we shall see.

Though every so often a provocateur such as Azef betrayed his employer, this was the price Fontanka grudgingly paid for the benefits the Internal Agency gave to the regime. It is clear that *sotrudniki* played a prominent role in intelligence gathering, subversion of revolutionary circles, and in the post-1905 relationship between the political police and society. For these reasons (the implications of which will be discussed later) Fontanka considered its *sotrudniki* to be the heart of Tsardom's political police system.

5 Making a Career: The Evolution of Professionalism within Fontanka

The images of the men who filled the senior and middle ranking posts within the police bureaucracy have merged over the years into a dark conglomerate, invariably seen as a brutal, corrupt band, the dregs of tsarist officialdom. This picture like most stereotypes is derived from a few glaring cases. Men such as P.G. Kurlov, M.S. Komissarov, P.I. Rachkovskii and A.A. Makarov, to be sure, fit into the mould, but Fontanka's officialdom cannot be sorted out so easily. A close look at the careers of Russia's leading police executives, especially those connected with the political police, does reveal many unsavoury aspects. Yet many police officials worked hard at their jobs, which were often so monumental that the strain ruined their health and family life. To paraphrase Gilbert and Sullivan a policeman's lot was not a happy one. Day-to-day duty was boring, unrewarding, dry and impersonal. Very few police officials enjoyed the camaraderie and close friendships usually associated with a small professional elite.[1] Any sense of comradeship wilted in an atmosphere poisoned by intrigue, where police officials were forced to expend considerable energy on advancing or preserving their careers (more on this subject later in the chapter).

The political police bureaucracy was a heterogeneous body of officials principally drawn from three distinct groups: the regular bureaucracy, the gendarmes, and from formerly 'unreliable persons' without much formal education, who, nevertheless, because of their misspent youth, had a keen instinct for political police work. These groups had little in common except their work. They often disliked and distrusted each other and approached political police business from three separate viewpoints. Whatever their differences, however, all police officials supervising bureaus engaged in political investigations were supposed to display remarkable qualities: a solid education, some knowledge of psychology, faultless logic, energy, persistence, and the purest morals.[2] Asking Imperial Russia's bureaucracy to produce a substantial number of people with such outstanding qualities who at the same time were interested in police work as a career was unreasonable.

The failings of Tsardom's political police chiefs were, on the whole, not of their own making. Most of the seventy-five higher police officials (both civilian and military), that is those who stood on the Table of Ranks between the II and VIII ranks, under review here, worked diligently at their jobs,[3] spending hours at the office on the daily routine. These men, however, like all Russians regardless of station, were products and victims of archaic traditions and whimsical impulsive leadership.

****

By inquiring into the career patterns of the three groups (civil servants, gendarmes, and unreliable persons or '*zubatovites*') who composed the upper echelons of the police bureaucracy it is possible to study the progression of a 'career' within the political police administration. The most prestigious cohort of the three was the first of these whose members occupied senior posts within Fontanka or served as assistant ministers of internal affairs, managing the police. It is with them that our discussion begins.

The *chinovniki* who managed Fontanka were quite well educated by the standards of the day. In a sample of thirty-six *chinovniki* occupying managerial positions within the police bureaucracy twenty had earned university degrees, eight others graduated from the School of Jurisprudence, one received his higher education at the Military Juridical Academy, three lacked any higher education[4] and on the four remaining *chinovniki* no information is available. The eight bureaucrats who graduated from the St Petersburg University and the eight who received their degrees from the School of Jurisprudence, of course, were born into the aristocracy or well placed families and entered the service at ranks higher than university graduates.[5] In addition, another four, one as an MVD bureaucrat and the others as procurators or their assistants, had been fortunate enough to serve in the capital. Nineteen of the thirty-six *chinovniki* under review here, therefore, either as students or as bureaucrats were familiar with the St Petersburg bureaucratic climate before being appointed to positions within Fontanka or as assistant ministers managing the police, although the remainder of the *chinovniki* appeared not to be disadvantaged since almost the entire sample held exalted ranks by February 1917, as can be seen from Table 5.1. It is clear from Table 5.1 that educational background and previous service in St Petersburg, although they would not hinder a man's career, were less important than connections made while serving in the provinces, as we shall see below.

Chinovniki could be appointed to one of several senior posts within the MVD; generally it meant exhalted rank. Starting at the top every director of Fontanka and assistant minister of internal affairs managing the police held a IV *chin* (rank) before he was appointed to the post. Directors of the Special Section if they were civilians held the title of *Statskii sovetnik* (State Councillor) the V *chin* on the Table of Ranks.[6] Excluding these powerful positions, a man could be appointed arbitrarily to senior posts within Fontanka or the Special Section by being designated as one of the many *chinovniki osobykh poruchenii* (the civil servants for special commission) who staffed the Russian bureaucracy. In this way important posts were filled with talented bureaucrats who had not achieved the requisite *chin* demanded by their new assignments.[7] Since Tsardom's rapidly

Table 5.1 Position on the Table of Ranks held by Civilian Managers of Political Police Affairs, 1917

Rank	*No.*
II	3
III	9
IV	16
V	3
VI	1
VIII	2.
Unknown	2
Total	36

Sources: See note 3.

expanding political police required bureaucrats faster than the normal procedures of the Table of Ranks could supply them, Fontanka used *chinovniki osobykh poruchenii* to fill posts in the growing number of OOs and *Rozysknye Punkty* (Investigating Stations) spreading throughout the empire (see Chapter 6).[8]

The police-related careers of the sample are charted in Table 5.2 and Table 5.3. Of the thirty-six we see in Table 5.2 that eight of these police officials during their careers held three different posts within Fontanka with a further six officials occupying two different posts. As a result, these fourteen bureaucrats presumably possessed the opportunity to familiarise themselves with Fontanka's business. As Table 5.3 clarifies, these fourteen men included six of Fontanka's thirteen directors, nine of twelve vice directors, three of four chiefs of the Special Section and two of four of the assistant ministers covered by the survey. Table 5.3 shows that, perhaps with the exception of the directorship of Fontanka, the senior posts within the police bureaucracy were generally filled with experienced personnel. Unfortunately, once these bureaucrats attained their most senior posts within the Department of Police their tenures in office were usually too brief for them to make any lasting impression, a problem discussed later in the chapter.

None the less, whether they had police experience or not, these bureaucrats were experienced men, as Table 5.4 shows, on the whole familiar with the ills of Russian society. At least twenty-three of the men listed in Table 5.4 had more than a passing acquaintance with the legal system. Eighteen of the twenty-three had first hand knowledge of police investigative procedures, they were aware of Russia's political and social conditions, and in their role as procurators came into contact (to varying degrees) with subversive society. Overall thirty-one of the thirty-six *chinovniki* surveyed in Table 5.4 (excluding the last five men)

Table 5.2 Police-Related Careers of our Civilian Sample: Number of Police Postings Occupied by Senior Police Bureaucrats and the Highest Post Attained within the Police Bureaucracy

No. of Postings	*No. of Bureaucrats*	*Civil Servants for Special Commissions*	*Chief of the Special Section*	*Vice Director*	*Director*	*Asst. Min.*	*Other* [a]
	7				x		
One	5	x					
Police	4						x
Posting	3			x			
	2					x	
	1		x				
	3	x		x			
Two	1			x	x		
Police	1				x		x
Postings	1	x					
	2			x	x		x
Three	1			x	x	x	
Police	1	x	x	x			
Postings	1	x		x			x
	1	x				x	x
	1	x	x				x
	1	x	x		x		

Sources: See note 3.

[a] Other categories included: lesser positions within Fontanka or a term as director of the Foreign Agentura.

probably understood what it meant to take up a post within the Department of Police, proudly knowing the significance of occupying a responsible *dolzhnost′* (job) within the central administration in St Petersburg. However, they also understood the value of alliances and the ability to play bureaucratic politics, an understanding which counted as much as hard work and a great deal more than integrity in making a career within the Russian bureaucracy, as we shall see. So while many of these men had served for years in the *prokurorskii nadzor*, where they ensured the integrity of police investigations,[9] and some graduated from the faculty of law at a Russian university where they were imbued 'with an idealist sense of the mission of the law', they tended to follow the lead of the graduates from the School of Jurisprudence, 'elite mediocrities, attentive to the needs of executive authority'.[10] As a result, the majority of Fontanka's bureaucrats succumbed to careerism, too often allowing ends to subsume means. Many of those police officials from the legal profession, therefore, conveniently turned a blind

Table 5.3 Number of Senior Civilian Police Officials with Multiple Job Experience within the Police Bureaucracy, as Compared to Total Number of such Officials Encompassed in this Survey

Final Position Occupied	*No. Encompassed in Survey*	*No. with multiple Job Experience within the Department of Police*
Assistant Minister	4	2
Director	13	6
Vice Director	12[a]	9
Chief of the Special Section	4	3

Sources: See endnote 3.
[a] There is some doubt as to whether I.K. Smirnov was actually a vice-director of Fontanka, although one of his colleagues testified to that fact.

Table 5.4 Careers of Senior Police *Chinovniki*: the Last Position they held before Entering Fontanka

Position	*Number*
Assistant Procurator	10
Procurator	8
Jurist	5
Career Fontanka Bureaucrats	3
MVD Bureaucrat[a]	3
Vice-Governor	2
Provincial Bureaucrat (Treasurer)	1
Zemskii Nachal'nik (Land Captain)	1
Businessman	1
Unknown	2

Sources: See note 3.
[a] Specific posts unknown.

eye toward the prevalent breaches of the statutes, including the use of provocateurs when it suited their purposes. Officials such as A.A. Lopukhin and N.A. Makarov who attempted to maintain their integrity by upholding the letter of the law in political police work found their endeavour to be very unrewarding, as we shall see (Chapters 7, 8, and 9).[11] Nevertheless, by the Russian standards of the day, these police executives were well-educated and experienced men, leaders of the Russian bureaucracy, carrying in most cases *chin* denoting exceptional personal worth in a special bureaucratic milieu that measured a man more by his position on the Table of Ranks than by any other attributes he might claim.[12]

The civilians shared their rule of Russia's police empire with men of a completely different cut – military officers, most of whom were graduates of the Separate Corps of Gendarmes and who dominated as OO executives political police operations in St Petersburg, Moscow and the provinces. How far did gendarme officers get within the political police? And what kind of men would endure the disdain of their comrades and the strains on themselves and their family lives inherent in such a thankless job, and why? These and similar questions relating to the political police will be resolved later in this chapter.[13]

Table 5.5 demonstrates that the cohort of twenty-nine gendarme officers who attained powerful positions within Fontanka were quite a select group, denoting the highest (but not the only post) held by each of these officers within Fontanka, marking the rank each achieved by 1917, after many of them *had left Fontanka* and gone on to other duties. Nevertheless, Table 5.5 illustrates the

Table 5.5 Highest Postings Held Within Fontanka by Our Cohort of Twenty-Nine Gendarme Officers Denoting Their Position on the Table of Ranks, 1917

Position	*No.*	*Final Position on Table of Ranks*			
		III	*IV*	*VI*	*VII*
Director of Fontanka	1[a]	1			
Director of the Special Section	2		1		1[b]
Attached to service within the Special Section	2			1	1
Chief of the St Petersburg OO	7[c]	1	3	2	1
Asst. Chief of the St Petersburg OO	5			3	2
Chief of the Moscow OO	2			2	
Chief of other OOs	4[d]		2	2	
Asst. Chief of other OOs	2			1	1
Officers for Special Commissions	2		2		
Inspector	1			1	
Chief of the Foreign Agentura	1[e]				1

Source: see note 3

[a] E.K. Klimovich transferred to the gendarmes in 1898, but ended his career as a Lt General of Infantry.

[b] Lt Colonel I.P. Vasil'ev was appointed Chief of Special Section in January 1917.

[c] Includes interim chiefs. [d] Includes interim chief.

[e] Served as an interim chief of the Foreign Agentura in 1909.

career attainments of successful men, especially since many gendarme officers had their careers interrupted when they left the political police to return to active duty with the regular army during the First World War, or had their careers abruptly curtailed by the February Revolution.

Both the gendarmes and the bureaucrats were, within their own professional frames of reference, elites. Although they distrusted each other, as we shall see, they despised those few men who attained influential positions within the political police through neither the army nor the bureaucracy. This small group of political police executives acquired its reputation by sheer ability, particularly through an intuitive sense of how a political police operation should be run. The most able and well known representatives of this group were: S.V. Zubatov, M.I. Gurovich, A.M. Harting, and P.S. Statkovskii. Another member of the group, P.I. Rachkovskii, became its most powerful and most infamous member. These men had in common only their shady backgrounds. Rachkovskii ended his career in disgrace after guiding the political police during the first year of the 1905 Revolution (as we shall see in Chapter 10), retiring with the rank of *Deistvitel′nyi statskii sovetnik* (Actual State Councillor) (IV *chin*) as did A.M. Harting, a converted Jew, who directed the Foreign Agentura from 1905 to 1909. Zubatov, Gurovich, and Statkovskii achieved the rank of *Statskii sovetnik* (V *chin*).[14] Gurovich, after outstanding service as an undercover agent, was made a Hereditary Esteemed Citizen (*Potomstvennyi pochetnyi grazhdanin*), no small achievement for a Jew. After successfully serving as chief of the Bucharest Agentura Gurovich returned to St Petersburg to become an inspector of OO operations throughout the empire. He retired in 1906.[15] Statkovskii's career is reviewed later on.

Policemen such as these, who earlier in their lives had shown sympathy for dissident causes, possessed the knowledge and the temperament to successfully attack Tsardom's enemies by devising new methods to subdue men and women whose motivations they clearly understood. Their experience showed them that the power of attractive social and political programmes could only be countered in like manner, by equally attractive counter-proposals and a modicum of repression. Their talent, innovative methods and the dedication (of most of them) to the monarchy made them invaluable additions to the Special Section's leadership.

As Chapter 4 has shown, Fontanka, in response to information leaks and desertions to the revolution by a few of these men, unwisely decreed that persons with a tainted political record could no longer enter the political police bureaucracy, an order which severed the supply of future political police chiefs who best understood the enemy. However, even before the 1910 edict precluding 'unreliable people' from serving in Fontanka's administration, such men were in short supply. Therefore, the Separate Corps of Gendarmes became the essential reservoir of manpower necessary to staff the executive ranks of Tsardom's rapidly expanding political police.[16]

Fontanka's unavoidable reliance on the personnel of the Separate of Corps of Gendarmes for this purpose presented it with a serious dilemma. Even those gendarme officers fortunate enough not to be contaminated by lengthy service in the gendarmerie still endured the penalties, especially in education and world view, inflicted upon them by their previous regular army duty.[17] Tables 5.6 and 5.7 show that of the twenty-five gendarme officers serving within Fontanka only four were academy trained: three at the General Staff Academy and one at the Military Juridical Academy. The remainder were the product of limited schooling. The education of the officer corps was abysmal.[18] The officers approached politics simplistically, regarding the intelligentsia as vaguely treasonous; they lacked an ethos and the government had not even bothered to imbue them with the monarchical principle. In an educational comparison with their civilian colleagues and

Table 5.6 Educational Attainments of Twenty-Five Gendarme Officers Serving in the Higher Ranks of the Political Police

Schooling	*Number*
Junker School and Military School	11
Junker School only	3
Cadet Corps, Military School and Academy	3
Realschule and Junker School	2
Cadet Corps and Cavalry School	1
Cadet Corps and Military School	1
Cadet Corps, Cavalry School and Cossack Officers' School	1
Classical *Gimnaziia* and Junker School	1
Military *Gimnaziia* and Junker School	1
Moscow Infantry School and Academy	1

Source: See note 3.

Table 5.7 Previous Military Experience of Twenty-Five Gendarme Officers Serving in the Higher Ranks of the Political Police

Branch	*Number*
Infantry	15
Cavalry	4
Grenadiers	3
Artillery	2
Household Guards	1

Source: See note 3.

superiors within the political police and Fontanka generally, the officers come off a tragically poor second.[19] To make matters worse, two-thirds of the sample of twenty-five officers, as Table 5.6 shows, came originally from the infantry, the dullest, least challenging branch of the service: the infantry, where in social background, education and potential for advancement the officers were at the bottom of the military ladder. It is no wonder, therefore, that of all branches of the military, the infantry endured the largest number of officer resignations.[20] Some of those who resigned joined the gendarmes, which appeared as a reasonable, perhaps promising alternative to the drudgery, frustration and humiliation of serving in the infantry.

Unfortunately, the Separate Corps Gendarmes did very little to educate the officers. Few gendarme officers knew anything about the world of political subversion, as future director of the Moscow OO, A.P. Martynov, found out. After serving in the gendarmes for a short time Martynov obtained permission to attend a three month course at gendarme staff school in St Petersburg where the majority of lecturers were senior adjutants on the staff of the Corps of Gendarmes. A substantial portion of the curriculum was supposed to be devoted to the techniques of political police investigation, but it was taught in a thoroughly inept manner. The instructor, who knew nothing about investigating a criminal offence, did not discuss investigative procedures at all; he merely dipped into Fontanka's archive and at random selected old gendarme reports, showing them to Martynov and his classmates in the misguided belief that his students would learn how to gather intelligence from these documents, apparently by osmosis. Not one of Martynov's lecturers attempted a clear and concise explanation of their future duties. Gendarme officers subsequently discovered the nuances of dealing with subversion only through trial-and-error.[21]

The gendarme officers worked under other handicaps too. Every officer, no matter the branch in which he had served, was imbued with a number of undesirable military traits. Even the most independent of them had been worn down by long military service, all initiative gone. Military life fostered an isolation from the reality of day-to-day life in Russia and encouraged a hostility to educated civilian society. Insulated by regular military life, ordinary officers could at least comfort themselves in their isolation with each other's company. Once they entered the world of the gendarmes, however, they confronted the most hostile elements of civilian society daily and their sudden exposure to this alien, uncomfortable and sometimes dangerous way of life intensified their insulation from society at large, and further entrenched those characteristics that made most gendarme officers inept political policemen.

In 1902 Sergei Zubatov, as chief of the Special Section, undertook a programme of recruitment designed to overcome the shortage of qualified political police officers. Zubatov hoped to train a new breed of honest, dedicated, educated men motivated by monarchist principles. He embarked on a nationwide search for talented young gendarme officers not yet tainted by the routine of the gendarmerie, not an easy task since the recruits required the fortitude necessary to escape from their backgrounds and surroundings and the courage to allow Zubatov to remould and re-educate them. Few gendarme officers were of that calibre. He intended to lure those officers who displayed these qualities with rewards for performance and promises of rapid promotions.[22]

Identifying suitable recruits was difficult although this was only one of his problems. The gendarmes considered the full-time political police duty performed by the OOs to be quite unsavoury, the majority believing that an officer who managed an OO dishonoured his uniform. Furthermore, peer pressure prevented interested candidates from enlisting in the political police.[23]

Zubatov required his recruits to undergo a basic training course that included learning the rudiments of police investigation, spying in the political milieu, methods used to liquidate terrorist groups and the history of Russia's revolutionary movements – the programmes, statutes, composition of parties, and the biographies of principal militants.[24] Perhaps of greater significance than this training for those officers who joined the Special Section between 1902 and 1903 is that they came under Zubatov's wing. This police chief's energy, fanaticism and knowledge of his opponents' programmes and the ideologies upon which they were based, deeply impressed his recruits,[25] convincing them that the monarchical principle must serve as the bulwark against the opposition.[26]

Zubatov's enthusiasms and belief in his cause thrilled his officers, influencing young gendarme officers to overcome the prejudice of their friends within the Corps of Gendarmes and to join the political police.[27] His recruits formed a close personal *cadre* that remained loyal to him even after his disgrace in 1903. Zubatov reciprocated these feelings and treated his gendarmes like younger brothers. He never demanded agreement to his point of view, rather he encouraged intelligent discussion. He greatly admired the ability of his officers and used it to the utmost. For superiors and subordinates alike Zubatov, even following his dismissal, remained Tsardom's outstanding political policeman.[28] Moreover, many of Zubatov's protegés did very well for themselves. E.I. Mednikov, the disgraced police chief's oldest colleague and friend proudly wrote Zubatov that:

> Zapyshin is already a colonel as are Spiridovich and Klimovich and Peterson moved onto the Railroad Gendarmerie [a prestigious service]. I think in the new year Vas. Vas. [Ratko] and Boris Andreevich [Gerardi] will be colonels.

Mednikov and Zubatov had every reason to be proud of their protegés. One of them, Spiridovich, for example, forced to leave the directorship of the Kiev OO after being wounded in a shoot-out with revolutionaries, became chief of the court *Okhrana* and a successful instructor to gendarme officers studying anti-revolutionary tactics. As a writer he produced still valuable studies of the Socialist-Revolutionaries and the Social Democrats that are masterpieces of objectivity, especially for one so closely involved in a life and death struggle with them.

Another, Klimovich, rose to become chief of the Special Section and briefly director of Fontanka itself. Spiridovich and Klimovich achieved the ranks of major general and lieutenant general respectively.[29]

With the departure of Sergei Zubatov from the Special Section in 1903 (Zubatov's career is discussed further in Chapters 6 and 7) an intellectual vacuum developed within Fontanka that remained unfilled until the end of the regime. While several police officials tried to fill Zubatov's shoes as an innovative strategist in Fontanka's war against subversion (and as we shall see in Chapter 10, A.V. Gerasimov partially succeeded in doing so), only one man strove to inherit Zubatov's role as a political police instructor. A.I. Spiridovich carried on the training and education of young gendarme officers in his mentor's footsteps by focusing on Zubatov's notion of a monarchical ethos as the essential ingredient in a political policeman's character. Unfortunately, his lectures lacked the innovation and break with traditional attitudes that had so inspired Zubatov's listeners.

Through his lectures Spiridovich pursued Zubatov's goal of instilling a feeling, if not an actual position, of superiority among his officers. He hoped their greater knowledge of policing techniques, on which he also lectured, a sense of absolute devotion to the monarchy, combined with a feeling of their indispensable role in preserving it, would create an *élan*, a sense of mission, forging them into the spearhead of Tsardom's campaign against subversion. This did not happen. At least a portion of the blame for this failure is to be found in Spiridovich's own teachings which incorporated the gendarme's military code of honour. Spiridovich considered this code to be the principle upon which the political police built its counter-revolutionary strategy, as he reminded his students:

> Investigatory work is secret work hidden from the eyes of society and the authorities; it is often conducted under the menace of bombs and Brownings and under conditions in which the enemy operates not in the open but underhandedly; *in most cases the entire job is a defensive struggle against the enemy* [italics mine] who is unscrupulous in his methods....
>
> These conditions are very unfavorable for the political police; they may so unfavorably influence persons who enter into its ranks that possibly young members little hardened in the revolutionary struggle, may sometimes consider the thought, with a view to benefitting the cause, of resorting to methods the permissibility of which are not clear according to the letter of existing statutes.
>
> *What is repugnant to the morale of the officer's calling [and] to the honor of the officer's uniform must not be tolerated in methods of political investigation; however inconspicuous [and] whatever be the secret revolutionary organization, these methods are not to be applied* [italics mine].

Spiridovich emotionally concluded, 'only the observance of the above mentioned conditions can place political investigation... on the high level which is appropriate to the latter as part of the Russian Army, summoned by the Monarchy to stand on guard over the existing State order.'[30]

The application of the military code of honour in Spiridovich's teachings to secret police work, was a key weakness in the OO officers' psychological armour since it forbade them from using the same effective tactics as their opponents and also because the military code of honour, though often ignored in practice, contributed to a siege mentality among OO officers. Spiridovich spoke only about defence, never about assault. He encouraged his men to study revolutionary ideologies as a defensive weapon, but he could not give them a sophisticated ethos of their own. 'Loyalty to the monarchical principle' was a call for faith, not a reasoned argument for devotion to a political system. The traditions of military service, not ideas, bound these men together. It was the only tangible and stable element in their unsure and danger filled existence.

The military code of honour contributed to the inability of the OO gendarme officers to adjust to their new civilian bureaucratic milieu within the Department of Police (a problem discussed later on in the chapter).[31] This situation bred a clannishness among OO gendarme officers of considerable proportions. OO gendarme officers when discussing a major operation were likely to bypass a superior who was not one of their own. It was likely, for example, that General Spiridovich, even though now chief of the court *Okhrana* and no longer attached to Fontanka, was better informed about political police operations and the feelings and attitudes of OO gendarme officers than either Fontanka's current director or the assistant minister of internal affairs, managing the police.[32]

****

The exclusivity and distrust that existed within the tsarist policing system were symptoms of grave problems within the socio-political structure of the Russian bureaucracy, disrupting police administration and sapping the strength of the political police in the face of ever more intimidating political unrest. The divisions between officers and civilians, between the gendarmes and men such as Zubatov and Gurevich, were irretrievably entrenched and products of ingrained political cultural patterns which divided and subdivided Fontanka's bureaucracy into often bitterly competing personal hierarchies.[33] At first glance the most obvious division is easily identified: the division between the military and civilian elites who served as Fontanka's executives. Rivalry between the military and civilian branches of governmental authority, their traditional suspicion of one another and their jealousy of each other's prerogatives were phenomena certainly not confined to Russia.[34] However, within the milieu of Fontanka, the officers' suspicion and jealousy developed, not unjustly, into a deep-seated hostility toward their civilian colleagues, as we shall see.

Less discernable, but of paramount importance, were the hierarchical subdivisions within and across Fontanka's military and bureaucratic elite structure caused by the widespread influence of patronage-clientele networks, networks certainly not unique to Fontanka, let alone to Tsarist Russia. None the less, as Daniel Orlovsky and D.C.B. Lieven confirm, clientelism was of critical importance to the functioning of Russian institutional and political life.[35] It was particularly rife in (though by no means confined to) the MVD, a ministry where the failure to distinguish between politics and administration was especially deep-seated. In order to safeguard oneself (as best as one could) against the unpredictable impact of this bureaucratic phenomenon, an official needed to belong to an ascendant patronage-clientele network that would protect him against the arbitrary intrigues of a rival or superior who belonged to a different camp. The widespread practice of clientelism so prejudiced the appointment of police officials that Minister of Internal Affairs Durnovo appointed E.I. Vuich as Fontanka's director specifically because he believed Vuich to be no one's man, thereby guaranteeing that he would be a loyal executive.[36]

Orlovsky defines clientelism as 'a form of "irrational" political behaviour involving mutual support of individuals or dyadic groups in the organizational context of the state bureaucracy'.[37] He has identified four types of clientelism operating within the tsarist institutional environment. They are: clientelism of monarchical proximity; of kinship; of geographic location and of institutional position.[38] 'Clientelism of monarchical proximity' is described by Orlovsky as 'actual physical proximity to the tsar or the preceding tsar (including the period before his or her accession to the throne)'; 'clientelism of kinship' is 'defined by mutually supportive relations based upon blood ties or marriage.' Within the confines of Fontanka clientelism of kinship and monarchical proximity did exist, though they were much less prevalent than those of 'geographic location' and 'institutional position'. The most important and solidly identifiable form of clientelism was that of 'geographic location',[39] which Orlovsky describes as:

> [P]roperly speaking...clientelism of talent and like-mindedness, since in the late imperial era it usually took the form of a high provincial official on the way to a St Petersburg career in a central ministry post or temporarily holding a provincial post or conducting a central government mission there taking along with him to the capital trusted and highly competent officials to aid his own career at the center.[40]

The linkage between OO officers and their local procurators is a vivid example of 'geographic clientelism' in operation. A.I. Spiridovich while still a young officer directing the Kiev OO was told by A.A. Lopukhin, a former procurator and now director of Fontanka, that he should not go through his professional life alone, that it was necessary to have support and he advised Spiridovich, kindly 'to find it in a procurator', noting that the procurator in Kiev was his uncle.[41] Spiridovich took Lopukhin's advice to heart and it was not long before Zubatov learned that Spiridovich's procurator was 'delighted' with his work.[42] Indeed, Lopukhin practised what he preached, choosing the obscure chief of the Kharkov Gendarme

Directorate, A.V. Gerasimov, to become chief of the powerful Petersburg OO on the basis of his acquaintance with Gerasimov's work when Lopukhin himself served as procurator in Kharkov several years before (see Chapter 8).

'Geographic clientelism' is somewhat easier to discern within Fontanka than 'clientelism of institutional position', where the personal relations between officials are formed within a 'specific bureaucratic institution'.[43] In our case, however, professional linkages of this sort developed especially in educational institutions, particularly military schools or academies. For example, General Kurlov graduated from the Nicholas Cavalry School as did his appointee as chief of the Foreign Agentura, A.A. Krasil'nikov[44] and five prominent police officers whose tenure in executive positions overlapped each other all graduated from the Polotskii Cadet School: M.S. Komissarov, Rasputin's bodyguard (1916); K.I. Globachev, chief of the St Petersburg OO (February 1915 to 27 February 1917); E.K. Klimovich, director of Fontanka (March 1916 to September 1916); M.F. von Koten, chief of the St Petersburg OO (December 1909 to February 1915); and M.N. Volkov, assistant to the chief of the St Petersburg OO (October 1914 to 27 February 1917). The placement of these officers could not possibly be a coincidence.[45] It is of critical importance, then, to keep the roles played by personal hierarchies within the Department of Police very much in mind as we investigate career developments within the upper echelons of Fontanka and their effect on the capabilities of Tsardom's political police.

St Petersburg was the place where every ambitious, upwardly mobile *chinovnik* strove to work, although appointments as chief of the Moscow and Warsaw OOs were valued equally to high ranking service in the capital by political police officers. Officers and bureaucrats who aspired to achieve a foothold in central police management in St Petersburg could do so through appointment to one of about eight respected positions: civil servant for special commissions; assistant chief of the St Petersburg OO; chief of the St Petersburg OO; chief of the Special Section; vice-director of Fontanka, managing the police; vice-director of Fontanka for general administration including finances; director of Fontanka; and assistant minister of internal affairs, managing the police. Two of these positions, director of Fontanka and assistant minister of internal affairs, managing the police, pretty well guaranteed these officeholders eventual appointment to the Senate. Civilians and soldiers made their way toward any one of these posts (including those in Moscow and Warsaw) by various means. We will discuss the career paths of three men who at the pinnacle of their careers played significant roles in Russia's political police administration: S.E. Vissarionov, P.S. Statkovksii and A.P. Martynov.

Sergei Evlampievich Vissarionov was one of those juridically trained men who came to dominate the management of Fontanka and its political police. A man of talent, Vissarionov was a bit of a *poseur*, who had an excellent command of foreign and Russian literature and adored the theatre. In his home life he was not an extravagant man, indeed he could be labelled petty-bourgeois in his habits.

Vissarionov was a good student of the revolutionary underground and an exemplary *chinovnik* in every way.[46] Fontanka could not ask for a more capable man. He began his career like so many of his colleagues in the criminal department of the *Sudebnaia Palata* (literally Chamber of Justice, the echelon of courts second in line to the Senate), beginning as a candidate then becoming an assistant secretary (*pomoshnik sekretaria*). After three and a half years he found himself transferred to a small provincial town, a considerable come-down from Moscow, where he toiled for nearly a year, until an acquaintance, a procurator in Vologda, recommended him for a post in the regional *prokurorskii nadzor*. While in Vologda, Vissarionov displayed the outstanding trademark of an up-and-coming *chinovnik*: he got on with everyone.[47]

In 1902, however, he began to look for a new assignment. His wife it seems, developed rheumatic fever and Vologda's swampy, damp climate hindered her recovery. And so Vissarionov travelled to Moscow to request a transfer to another 'modest' but drier city, otherwise he would have to resign from the service. Luckily, he found a warm reception in Moscow. The reports on him were good, more apparently because of his 'excellent relationship with everyone in Vologda', than the quality of his work. He ultimately decided the best place for him would be in Tula where his father lived or in Riazan′. Moscow told him there was no opening for him in Tula, even though his father, a *chinovnik* in the local military administration holding, 'more than a modest position' made every effort to influence the local procurator. Ultimately and luckily Vissarionov accepted a posting in Nizhni-Novgorod, a province bordering Riazan'. The procurator in Nizhni-Novgorod, I.M. Zolotarev, himself a future assistant minister of internal affairs, managing the police, ordered Vissarionov to supervise the conduct of the political cases. Many years later, after the February Revolution Vissarionov claimed that he had been troubled by the assignment and had endured his family's disapproval. Whatever pangs of guilt he may have felt in dealing out the tsarist brand of justice to the oppressed, it did not stop him from fulfilling his assignments so well that he soon came to the attention of his superiors and as a reward he found himself posted to Moscow just before the explosion of the 1905 Revolution.

Men such as Vissarionov, who could effectively cope with the administrative work load and knew how to issue arrest orders, were in short supply. As chief of the political department in the Moscow Chamber of Justice Vissarionov supervised formal investigations, immersing himself completely in political affairs. He served in Moscow as an assistant procurator from 1903 to 1906, a time when an official dealing with political matters would inevitably acquire a raw view of the state of Russian society and a first-hand look at the revolutionary movement in action. Vissarionov's superiors rewarded his excellent service by designating him a procurator in Yaroslavl, though they only allowed him to remain there for fifteen months. Fontanka could hardly permit a man of such experience and worth to slip away, and it offered him a senior post within the police system, initially being approached by an old school and university friend, who was close to Fontanka's director. Vissarionov declined this informal offer and a second offer as well. Soon, however, he discovered life in Yaroslavl was not to his taste, envisaging no future as a procurator there and finding daily life equally stifling. When a third offer from the assistant minister of internal affairs, managing the police, P.G. Kurlov, an old friend from Vologda was made, Vissarionov accepted and left sleepy Yaroslavl for St Petersburg as a *chinovnik osobykh poruchenii* and, he hoped, on a path to greater things.

Upon their transfer to St Petersburg officials discovered that they had crossed over into another world. Survival (and hopefully promotion) required administrative skills, the ability to play politics, good connections, luck, the personality to withstand the suffocating atmosphere of cloistered Petersburg bureaucratic society poisoned by an endless flow of malicious gossip,[48] and the stamina to cope with gargantuan responsibilities and never-ending tasks. Executives in every St Petersburg ministry 'were up to their necks in work', nerve-wracking work that did not let up even during holidays;[49] a burden intensified by the size and complexity of the police establishment which required new executives to undertake a considerable amount of preliminary preparation before assuming a senior post within it.[50] So, when Vissarionov arrived at Fontanka he was dumbstruck by what he found. On one side, he saw a mass of people who looked on newly arrived appointees with suspicion, as yet another factor to be considered in the game of political manoeuvering. On the other side, Vissarionov was stunned by the masses of paperwork. 'It was like a kaleidoscope', he said, 'one paper supplants another, and then a third, [as if] all Russia was papers'. He felt stunned by the magnitude of the job that lay before him. Not only were the methods new but Vissarionov had to learn as quickly as possible where the power resided in Fontanka: who could be challenged and who could not. Working conditions were so terrible that Vissarionov contemplated resigning almost as soon as he took up his appointment.[51] The fact that he remained in his post proved that ambition can overcome any discomfort.

He did not like political police work, justifying it to himself by identifying his duties as service to the state, or so he claimed, though his almost immediate appointment as vice-director of Fontanka charged with managing the Special Section (Chief of the Special Section was a separate and subordinate post) most likely swept away any misgivings he may have had. In 1912 Fontanka shortened his title to vice-director of the Department of Police, an indication that Vissarionov was no longer responsible for the Special Section[52] and he was able to concentrate on his other duties. He used his knowledge of the law to guide the work of Fontanka's Seventh Secretariat in which the Department of Police resolved its juridical problems. Then later on, he oversaw the Eighth Secretariat which carried out criminal investigations.[53] Vissarionov hoped to become Fontanka's director someday, but this was not to be, for although he appeared to be qualified for the post in every way – experienced, intelligent, energetic, affable, numbering men like Kurlov and Zolotarev, both high-ranking MVD officials, as his friends – he could not overcome the fact that he was the descendant of Jews.[54] He had gone as far as possible within Fontanka and in 1913 he left, assuming other duties within the MVD, finishing his career as a member of the ministry's council, the final appointment offered to vice-directors or senior desk officers who could be promoted no further.[55]

If Vissarionov travelled the road to influential position within the political police and Fontanka itself normally taken by most bright and affable young men, then that of P.S. Statkovskii was a stupendous aberration. Born into an undistinguished noble family, he entered the army as a non-commissioned officer like so many young men from his background, enrolling in a junker school in 1875. In other characteristics, however, he was less than typical. The school soon expelled him 'for not acting in accordance with the rank of a junker'. He returned to his old regiment and fought bravely in the ranks in the Russo-Turkish War in 1877–1878. By 1880 the army promoted Statkovskii on merit to ensign. Again, his independence of mind caused him trouble. In 1884, assigned to prison duty, he smuggled out a political prisoner's letter simply because he was asked to do so by the prisoner. Caught by his superiors, who interpreted an ordinary act of kindness in a more sinister light, he was placed under surveillance. Statkovskii wisely decided that his military career was at an end and he resigned from the army.

Not a revolutionary by any means, Statkovskii wished only to clear himself of suspicion. In 1887, although still under surveillance, he volunteered to become an undercover agent for the St Petersburg OO. In return for his services Fontanka gave him an entry certificate to St Petersburg University where he spent part of his time spying on his fellow students and the remainder studying for a degree which he received in 1893. Upon his graduation, the political police, desperately requiring educated personnel and sufficiently convinced of Statkovskii's reliability to discontinue surveillance over him, assigned him to the St Petersburg OO's chancery. Not satisfied with having convinced Fontanka of his loyalty he appealed to the tsar in 1895, petitioning for the removal from his record of the black mark for 'political unreliability'. His request granted, the loyal and hard-working Statkovskii rose steadily in Fontanka's service. In January 1900 he was named a *mladshii chinovnik osobykh poruchenii* (a junior civil servant for special commissions) within the St Petersburg OO. In June 1902 Fontanka appointed him a *starshii chinovnik* (a senior civil servant) and in 1904 and 1905 he managed the detective bureau of the same OO. During the 1905 Revolution, not the best of times for political police officials, Statkovskii became assistant director of the St Petersburg OO. As his reward for distinguished service during these turmoil filled years Statkovskii received the further appointment in 1907 of administrator of special commissions for the entire Petersburg *raion*. He retired in 1912 with a substantial pension and a chest covered with medals, rewards for long and exceptional service.[56]

The professional biographies of the civilians who managed police affairs, whether they belonged to generalists of police administration such as Vissarionov or civilian political police specialists such as Statkovskii, were strikingly different from the career portraits of OO gendarme officers. OO officers' lives were harsh, frenetic and anything but glamorous, but for the young gendarme recruits to the political police service the excitement of total dedication to their new roles masked the harsh realities they were about to face.[57] A young officer's assignment to an OO was usually arranged to the satisfaction of the OO and the new, incoming officer. Some newly appointed OO officers with independent means preferred posts in large cities, and others wanted to be close to family estates. Those whose pay and allowance were their only means for support chose distant posts since remuneration was decidedly greater the further an officer was posted from St Petersburg or Moscow.[58]

Once the new OO officers had settled into the routine of OO life any illusions about the nature of the job soon wore off, as one such officer, Captain Alexander Pavlovich Martynov, discovered. Martynov, one of the brighter lights among the junior officers in the Separate Corps of Gendarmes, volunteered for service in the political police in 1906. Fontanka appointed him director of the small Saratov OO and promoted him to Lt Colonel. The OOs housed the surveillance and undercover bureaus of the Special Section and unlike any other agency except the Foreign Agentura were in constant daily contact with the revolutionaries. The Special Section depended upon the OOs for the intelligence from which it drew up reports and determined its outlook, and the responsibility and strain of meeting the Special Section's demands sapped conscientious OO executives dry. Martynov wrote, 'I of course, did not know Sundays, holidays or timeclocks. I was on duty every day, every evening and often through the night'. Martynov rarely saw his family and was almost never home for meals. His wife complained that he was so wrapped up in his work that it was impossible to have a conversation with him. He arrived at his desk at nine o'clock in the morning and immediately perused the results of the previous day's searches. Drinking coffee as he went, Martynov next discussed the day's operations with the chief of detectives, talked over the present work in the chancery, went through the mail and perused the mass of papers requiring his signature. In the small Saratov OO Martynov was his own 'scribbler' (*pisaka*), drafting every report himself. His daily routine, in addition to the drudgery of the OO's paperwork included discussions with the local *politsmeister* concerning the life of the city and a meeting with the governor with whom he shared this information. Martynov considered his visit to the governor, not an act of subservience, but rather as a friendly filling in on the 'mood of society'. His daily tasks also included reviewing his own notes taken while interviewing his undercover agents in his role as a case officer and preparing his report to Fontanka. The evenings were taken up by meetings with his undercover agents. At times he debriefed three to four agents in one night, the sessions never lasting for less than half an hour, most were longer. Martynov often found himself rushing home after these sessions in order to work out the details for urgently required searches and arrests the next day. By ten or eleven at night and sometimes later he returned to his study to meet with his surveillance supervisor and to peruse the daily detective reports. If Martynov considered a case to be of critical importance he returned to his OO chancery where in an assembly room he met with the detectives assigned to the case to listen to their reports and arrange the surveillance assignment for the following day. Only then could Martynov return home for some sleep unless, of course, he sat up by the telephone waiting to learn the results of a midnight raid. 'My average work day', he remembered, 'began at nine o'clock in the morning and finished at nearly midnight'.[59]

In 1911 Martynov's diligence paid off when Fontanka offered him the directorship of the Moscow OO. The appointment was well-judged by Fontanka. The Department of Police had thoroughly inspected the Saratov OO, especially the effectiveness of its Internal Agency, before deciding Martynov was the man for the job.[60] In revelling in the memory of the moment Martynov reflected on how every gendarme officer interested in political police work had one goal: appointment as chief of the Moscow, St Petersburg, or Warsaw OOs. These powerful and prestigious posts paid very well, especially when the extravagant bonuses the chiefs of these OOs received on their birthdays or on special occasions are taken into account. To this income the government added an eight-room apartment, for Martynov an astonishing change from the modest hotel suite occupied by him and his family in Saratov. His family also travelled by rail for free and all of Moscow's theatres were open to the Martynovs *gratis*. Fontanka even paid for his official wardrobe.[61]

Martynov's career seems a straightforward success story, something for which his less fortunate colleagues would have been grateful. It was, nevertheless, an exhausting, taxing life which also took a toll on their families, particularly their wives.[62] It was a rare OO chief who occupied his post for more than four or five years before overwhelming fatigue forced him to step down. Often, the MVD rewarded him by making his next and final assignment a post as chief of a Gendarme Directorate in some out-of-the-way province where he could 'rest on his laurels....'[63]

Martynov's experience reflected the career of a successful OO officer in the Zubatov tradition. Unfortunately, despite the best efforts of Zubatov and his successors to fill OO executive posts with men of talent and dedication this was not always possible, since there continued to be a paucity of men of ability to fill important managerial positions. Many OO officers, therefore, remained merely regular gendarme officers seconded to Fontanka for short periods. The most noticeable quality of some OO chiefs and their deputies was their ineptitude.[64] Even General Kurlov, an arch-defender of the political police and a firm believer in the salutary effects of repression saw, 'not many distinguished Security Division chiefs'.[65] Fontanka attempted to rid itself of the worst of these officers with the establishment of inspectors general who toured Russia, reporting on minor improprieties as well as on serious cases of incompetence within the political police system. Fontanka's treatment of incompetent or irresponsible OO officers was erratic, tempered by the form of the offence and the influence an offending officer could muster in St Petersburg. It was one thing, for example, for Fontanka to treat an inveterate card-playing OO chief to no more than a slap on the wrists,[66] but it was quite another thing to allow a fool to remain in charge of one of the most important OOs in the empire. The affair of Lt Colonel Kuliabko is the case in point.

The Kuliabko case is a particularly marked example of how the overriding influence of traditional bureaucratic practice (clientelism) and an endemic social problem (lack of qualified personnel) impeded the political police in the successful fulfillment of its duties. The case stands as a stark reminder that, even by 1911, Fontanka had failed to develop within its senior administration and especially within its political police a professional ethic, that is, a rational, structured set of criteria for both entry and promotion (or demotion). Kuliabko was a classic bumbler and lazy as well, escaping transfer to a minor clerical post, however, by seeking the protection of his brother-in-law General Spiridovich and of his close friend, Vice-Director of Police M.N. Verigin, who together fended off Fontanka's sincere efforts to remove Kuliabko from his post. General Kurlov himself, though long aware of Kuliabko's failings, succumbed to the political weight of Kuliabko's influential supporters and ignored his incompetence.[67] Kurlov was apparently intimidated by the fact that Spiridovich, as chief of the court *Okhrana* was the right hand man of Court Commandant Dediulin, Kurlov's benefactor! As a result, despite Kuliabko's proven ineptitude, Kurlov relied on him for a major share of the responsibility in protecting the tsar and Stolypin during their fateful September 1911 visit to Kiev. This time Kuliabko's bungling directly caused the murder of the Prime Minister.

Clientelism within the Department of Police involved more than the one-to-one relationships we have so far described. It was an institutionalised practice which retarded the evolution of professionalism among Fontanka's executives and prevented the development of coherent long-term strategies to combat the regime's opponents. Each minister of internal affairs chose his own director of Fontanka, 'filling the important post with a man in the full enjoyment of his personal confidence'.[68] This practice saw the seemingly steady arrival and departure of Fontanka's executives. For example, between 1904 and 1917 the Department of Police welcomed eleven directors, the MVD greeted eight assistant ministers, managing the police, and between 1898 and 1917 the Special Section employed eight chiefs. These numerous and often unexpectedly sudden turnovers left their subordinates in a virtual tizzy and prevented even able men from having a significant impact on their bureaus, precluding the stability required for the development of effective counter-revolutionary programmes.[69]

As we indicated earlier in this chapter, personal hierarchies were also based on the traditional distrust between military and bureaucratic elites and they too contributed to the stultifying of professionalism within Fontanka's ranks. The careers of OO officers more often than not depended upon the beneficence of civilian superiors. As a result, the traditional suspicion that existed between the military officers and the *chinovniki* within Russia's governing institutions was inflamed within Fontanka by the bitter realisation on the part of gendarme officers that they occupied an inferior status within the Department of Police. The military men were distressed over having to deal with, and at times be subordinated to former 'criminals' such as Zubatov and Gurovich. General Spiridovich, even though an admirer and student of Zubatov's, could not avoid sniping at both him and Mikhail Gurovich in his memoirs when he indignantly wrote that Fontanka had followed the promotion of 'the former Marxist undercover agent [Zubatov]', by raising 'the *chinovnik* Mikhail Ivanovich Gurovich of the Jews', to a similar position of authority over him and his fellow gendarme officers.[70] Spiridovich would have certainly preferred that OO gendarme officers be given these posts, although OO officers themselves recognised that these low-lifes were much more adept at conducting political police affairs.[71]

However, while their humiliation was at least tempered by their grudging admiration for the talent of these 'unreliable persons', their hostility toward the generalists – those involved in administration – of Vissarionov's ilk who ruled over both officers and 'Zubatovites' was unrestrained. Even though some of the OO gendarme officers and civilian procurators formed patron–client relationships, these connections did not overcome the OO gendarme officers intense dislike, at times even hatred, for the generalists, an emotion that had its origins in their different backgrounds and the officers' realisation that they were *always* going to be in a subordinate position to these men whose professional habits they despised. When Martynov, for example, first went to work in the St Petersburg Gendarme Directorate in 1903 he found himself inundated by tasks and bureaucratic formality. It took him six months, he wryly recounts, to get used to the Petersburg way of doing things:

> Doing things slowly, not hurrying, rising in the morning...arriving at one's office fulfilling the work quota for the day and at five o'clock closing the door to the office, in order to return home and do with the evening whatever you wish, in accordance with one's taste and with comparatively modest means....[72]

Martynov's mild sarcasm was transformed into open hostility when he wrote about specific cases. He referred to N.P. Zuev in an aside as a 'typical Petersburg bureaucrat experienced in every possible [political] combination, intrigues and gossip.' Martynov accused Zuev of looking on his position as Fontanka's director, 'as an unavoidable step in the furtherance of his career'.[73] This, written in his memoirs quite some time after Tsardom's collapse, shows how deep Martynov's hostility toward the *chinovniki* within Fontanka must have been. Since Martynov knew full well that his stereotype of the St Petersburg official could be applied to many a gendarme officer – even those working within the political police – the sarcasm, the bitterness and anger which remained with him for so many years is a reflection of the frustration felt by OO gendarme officers as the perpetual junior partners to *chinovniki* at the highest administrative levels of the Department of Police. The officers believed that they did the bulk of the work and risked their lives daily, acquiring the major share of public opprobrium, and yet only very rarely did OO gendarme officers occupy a senior post within Fontanka. All of Fontanka's directors except two had been procurators or jurists, as were most of the *chinovnikov osobykh poruchenii.*[74] Most OO gendarme officers, however, finished their careers as colonels in some out of the way Gendarme Directorate, completely worn out. Those few major generals among them (with one exception) such as Spiridovich, Globachev, Popov and von Koten, never rose to be a vice-director, a director, or an assistant minister despite their rank.

Evidence to support Martynov's and his colleagues' view of their inferior status within Fontanka appears in Table 5.8 which displays the total number of military officers occupying senior posts within Fontanka, or as assistant ministers, managing the police between 1900 and 1914. Since four of the military officers represented in Table 5.8 over the span of their careers held two senior posts within Fontanka or the St Petersburg OO, only fourteen military officers in total held high ranking positions within the Department of Police between 1900 and 1917. The position worsens when chiefs of the St Petersburg OO, a powerful but quasi-independent body, are deleted and we concentrate solely on those officers who obtained appointment to the top administrative rungs of the police system – that is, to the posts of director of Fontanka and assistant minister, managing the

Table 5.8 Total Number of Senior Positions within Fontanka held by Military Officers, 1900–1917

Position	*Number*
Assistant Minister	5
Director	1
Vice-Director	1
Chief of the Special Section	4[a]
Chief of the St Petersburg OO	7[b]

Source: See note 3.

[a] One man was interim chief of the St Petersburg OO and the Special Section consecutively.

[b] Because the St Petersburg OO was the most powerful political police bureau in Tsarist Russia, its chief was a man to be reckoned with.

police. Of the six officers attaining these positions only one had been a gendarme officer. This was E.K. Klimovich, who became Fontanka's director for six months in March 1916. Even Klimovich is atypical of most of his colleagues, since he married into a family with influence at court which may very well account for his appointment to Fontanka's directorship as it most certainly did for his final rank of Lt General of Infantry.[75] The other five military men who rose to assistant minister, managing the police were not gendarmes, indeed they were cut from entirely different cloth. General of the Cavalry P.D. Sviatopolk-Mirskii, Lt General P.G. Kurlov, Majors General D.F. Trepov, V.F. Dzhunkovskii and K.N. Rydzevskii were from quite different backgrounds from the typical OO officer. Rydzevskii, Mirskii, Trepov and Dzhunkovskii were descendants from the aristocracy. The last three were graduates of the elite Corps of Pages. Rydzevskii graduated from the School of Jurisprudence. Kurlov had gone to the somewhat less distinguished Nicholas Cavalry School and received a degree from the Military Juridical Academy.[76] None of them ever served in the gendarmes.

The personnel of Fontanka and its political police were themselves the victims of the political culture they were trying to preserve. Separated by backgrounds, traditions, and rivalry, by a complex, haphazard system of promotion and reward, the gendarmes, bureaucrats, 'zubatovites' and regular military men who composed the higher administration of Fontanka and directed its OOs were incapable of forming a single standard of professionalism boasting an *esprit de corps* and the unified world view necessary for a systematic assault on the regime's enemies. These men were bound together only by their belief in the monarchical principle, embodying their undying loyalty to the tsar.[77] However, the monarchical principle, clientelism and the personal hierarchies within the bureaucracy it helped to sustain, as well as the gendarmes' military code of honour, belonged to an inflexible political culture incapable of effectively dealing with the social and political crisis confronting Russia at the beginning of this century.

Part III
The Foundations of a Modern Police State? The Political Police and the Russian People, 1902–1904

6 Spinning the Web: Plehve and the Expansion of the Political Police Network

By the end of the nineteenth century the dissident elements within Russian society were coalescing into political groups which ranged from moderate monarchist reformers to ardent, committed agrarian and marxist revolutionaries. The most prominent group became known as the Liberation Movement, under whose banner marched the entire political spectrum of the legal opposition. The Liberation Movement through its speeches, publications and actions gave respectability to the opinion that the behaviour and outlook of the regime was inappropriate for a modernising state entering the twentieth century. These men from the ranks of the professions, from the *zemstva* and from the landed gentry, in growing numbers, believed that the transformation of the autocracy by peaceful means into a constitutional regime ruled by law, not by men – a true *Rechtsstaat* – would be Russia's only salvation. For the members of this movement the remaining conceivable alternatives to a *Rechtsstaat* were a bloody left-wing revolution or a steadily increasing reaction.[1] The persistent intransigence of the regime, however, drove the Liberation Movement steadily to the Left. The founding of the *Beseda* circle – a group of prestigious *zemstva* men who met several times a year between 1902 and 1905[2] – and its increasing domination by the constitutionalists and the subsequent publication of the constitutionalist emigré journal, *Osvobozhdenie* (Liberation), infuriated and worried the MVD.[3]

Whereas the Liberation Movement signalled the birth of non-revolutionary political parties within the tsarist political spectrum, the Russian Social Democratic Workers' Party born in Minsk in 1898 and the Socialist-Revolutionary Party formed in late 1901 dominated the radical shades of this spectrum. Both of these parties had arisen out of the growing activism of the revolutionary emigration and were fed by the seething discontent on the land and in the factories.[4]

In the very early years of the twentieth century, Russia's political opposition although divided by ideological differences did not express the mutual hostility that became so entrenched after the 1905 Revolution. Rather, in these formative years of Russia's political parties the ideological groupings expressed similar views on the immediate changes they wished to impose on the tsarist system of government. Of course, for the revolutionaries among them, the establishment of a constitutional government served only as a step in a lengthy revolutionary process; while for the legal opposition this form of government was a desired end in itself. This divergence in outlook was, however, of minor significance for the Russian government. It preferred to concentrate on the terrifying image of a united opposition with sufficient strength to bring an end to almost three hundred years of absolute Romanov rule.

****

The MVD was responsible for protecting the integrity of absolute monarchical rule but unfortunately for the regime, the forces of order laboured under the guidance of men of modest ability. Between 1895 and 1899, despite growing discontent, I.L. Goremykin and I.N. Durnovo unimaginatively continued to support the policies of counter-reform established during the reigns of Alexander II and his son. In 1899, D.S. Sipiagin took charge of the MVD, exacerbating social tensions still further with his strong belief in police rule, strict censorship and his loudly proclaimed desire to restore political power to the hands of the nobility.[5] He also launched a series of measures that curtailed the activities of the *zemstva* and he suppressed the student movement with unnecessary harshness.[6] None of the measures implemented by these three ministers of internal affairs silenced dissent, although they did serve to make the ministers the focal point of popular dissatisfaction.

What better target could there be for assassination? Sipiagin became the first target of a new socialist-revolutionary terrorist campaign, but while the SRs plotted, an expelled student stole their *démarche* by murdering one of Sipiagin's colleagues. On 14 February 1901, Peter Karpovich mortally wounded N.P. Bogolepov, the reactionary minister of education, triggering mass demonstrations protesting at the government's stultifying education policies. Sipiagin attempted to limit the disturbances by quashing news about the assassination in the press.[7] When he did not succeed, further demonstrations erupted in Kharkov, Kiev, Moscow and other university towns. On 4 March the elite of St Petersburg's radical intelligentsia along with hundreds of students participated in a huge demonstration in Kazan Square. The police and cossacks used the broad latitude given them by the authorities to inflict severe beatings on many of the demonstrators and to make over 1500 arrests.

The behaviour of the cossacks and police during the Kazan Square demonstration shocked society at large and aggravated its disapproval of Sipiagin's conduct of affairs. It became clear to Russia's terrorists that the elimination of the tsar's most despised advisers by whatsoever means would have the acquiescence and perhaps approval of society. Indeed, only four days after the Bogolepov's assassination an attempt was made on the life of K.P. Pobedonostsev, the man most closely identified with Nicholas II's reactionary policies,[8] forcing Fontanka to redouble its efforts at protecting Tsardom's most senior officials, its *sanovniki*. In a report of major significance, P.I. Rachkovskii, chief of the Foreign Agentura, claimed that the revolutionary movements (in which he included the Liberation

Movement) were preparing to launch a powerful offensive against the government. Rachkovskii argued that while the revolutionaries were becoming self-assured and adventurous, the political policing agencies had become stagnant and lacked imagination and were, therefore, incapable of dealing with what Rachkovskii believed would be the forthcoming unified revolutionary action against Tsardom. 'New times – new problems', he told his superiors, 'the sooner we reorganise [the political police service] the better'.[9] Rachkovskii's recommendations fell on deaf ears. Minister of Internal Affairs Sipiagin, Director of the Department of Police Zvolianskii and Chief of the Special Section Rataev were time-serving mediocrities possessing neither the courage nor the ability to take up Rachkovskii's challenge to reorganise the political police and embark on new methods in their battle against subversion. For another eight months the MVD drifted, until in April 1902 this situation changed dramatically.

The socialist-revolutionaries had been impressed with the positive public reaction to Bogolepov's assassination, offering them encouragement in their planning of Sipiagin's murder. The man responsible for the attack against the minister of internal affairs was G.A. Gershuni, a brilliant fanatic who despised the tsarist regime with an element of personal hatred that separated him from most of his fellow terrorists. Evno Azef, the gifted undercoer agent, kept the Special Section fully informed of Gershuni's daily activities and was well aware of Gershuni's plot to assassinate Sipiagin. Fontanka, however, on Azef's advice, delayed its arrest of Gershuni, 'since he is in such close contact with our agent [Azef], his immediate arrest would leave us in the dark as to his plans and furthermore might compromise our agent', intending to arrest him and his accomplices at a later date. This turned out to be a disastrous decision.

The plan had its merits, but Gershuni as an experienced fugitive quickly discovered that he was being followed and easily managed to shake off his pursuers. As soon as he returned to Russia Gershuni met with his fellow conspirators in the plot against Sipiagin: P.P. Kraft, M.M. Melnikov and S.V. Balmashev, the man who was to carry out the murder. Sipiagin's fate was sealed. On 15 April 1902 dressed in the uniform of an officer Balmashev called on the minister of internal affairs somewhat before reception hour, announcing himself as 'the aide-de-camp of the Grand Duke Sergei'. When the minister appeared Balmashev handed him an envelope containing his death sentence and then shot Sipiagin, killing him instantly.[10] The murders of Bogolepov and Sipiagin, combined with the peasant uprisings in Kharkov and Poltava provinces completely demoralised Fontanka. Nothing could be done, however, to restore its morale or to restore order to the nation until a replacement had been found for Sipiagin.

Nicholas II chose Sipiagin's successor with uncharacteristic speed. To the overwhelming joy of Fontanka, the tsar appointed Viacheslav Konstantinovich Plehve as his new minister of internal affairs. Plehve had been Fontanka's first director and had the justly deserved reputation of an intelligent, hardworking and conservative official. Plehve also understood the intricacies of political police work. As director of Fontanka he had worked very closely with Lieutenant Colonel G.D. Sudeikin, chief of the St Petersburg OO and the ablest political policeman of his day.[11] Plehve, as one astute observer noted, had convinced himself that all of the state's creative work must be the product of cunning overlaid and skilfully accompanied by the police system,[12] considering his position as minister of internal affairs to be indistinguishable from his role as chief of police.[13]

Fully aware of the potentially explosive situation Plehve assumed command of the MVD. By early 1902 public opinion was unified in its call for a thoroughgoing alteration in the style of government. Tsarist policy in response to the call for change became increasingly repressive and contributed further to intensified civil disobedience and to a swelling of the ranks of the liberationist, socialist-revolutionary and social democratic movements, with the agitators of the latter two groups finding increasingly receptive audiences for their messages among the peasantry and the ever more numerous working class. Upon his appointment Plehve told Nicholas II exactly how serious the crisis confronting Tsardom had become over the past two decades. 'Twenty years ago when I was director of the Department of Police, if someone told me that revolution was possible in Russia I would have smiled', he told the tsar, 'but now we are on the eve of revolution'.[14] Elsewhere, he argued that in such troubled times Russia required leadership and discipline more than anything else.[15]

****

Tsardom's political police institutions were to be the spearhead of Plehve's campaign to re-establish order throughout the empire. Although the foundation of a powerful, all-pervasive political police system had been constructed during the previous century, it supported a rickety structure. Plehve inherited only three OOs, those of Moscow, St Petersburg and Warsaw, the latter two, however, virtually untapped. Political police operations, such as they were, largely rested in the hands of the Separate Corps of Gendarmes who, while they achieved major victories in the 1880s and 1890s,[16] and still supplied Fontanka with intelligence on dozens of revolutionary circles which proliferated throughout the empire,[17] were nevertheless poorly regarded by both the public and the MVD alike.

The MVD in particular scorned the Separate Corps of Gendarmes since gendarme officers who, as we have seen, were not adequately trained to carry out political police functions and to make matters worse read almost nothing, not even conservative newspapers, understanding little of the political and economic questions of the time.[18] One OO official referred to their mental output as 'intellectual squalor' (*umstvennoe ubozhestvo*).[19] The lower ranks of the gendarmerie, except for some civilian detectives, contained regular military personnel without any police training.[20]

The first official to strive toward the professionalisation of the political police was Sergei Vasilievich Zubatov, the director of the Moscow OO and the most gifted political police official in tsarist history. Not surprisingly, Zubatov had nothing good to say about the general run of gendarme officers. He found them to be incompetent, often being unable to differentiate between an indiscreet 'nincompoop' arrested in a raid or at a demonstration and an experienced agitator arrested at the same time, noting that the resultant indiscriminate mass arrests contributed to the public discontent with the regime. In 1897 in an attempt to exclude the gendarmes from political police business he denied them access to OO reports on revolutionary activity.[21] He soon discovered that he could not do this: the commanding officers of the Corp of Gendarmes possessed close and influential friends at court, including the tsar, who thought so highly of the gendarmes that he wished to re-establish the Third Section.[22] Zubatov, a rather minor official, could not overcome such influential opposition.

While it is easy to judge the gendarmes harshly, life within the Special Section was not much better. Although the Moscow OO would flourish under the inspired direction of Sergei Zubatov – as we shall see – the OOs in St Petersburg and Warsaw languished helplessly under inadequate guidance. L.A. Rataev, the man Plehve dismissed as chief of the Special Section, admitted that the structure and procedures of the political police did not inspire confidence.[23] Plehve concurred with Rataev's opinion, believing that the weakness of the police had allowed the revolutionary movements to grow in strength and that only a more vigorous police system could contain them.[24] Therefore, the restructuring and the expansion of the political police became one of his immediate goals. Yet there were circumstances that initially tempered his zeal. After years of serving within the tsarist bureaucracy, 'he came to realize', as he said, 'that the development of Russia's administrative machinery could not keep pace with the changing conditions of public life'.[25] His first visit to Fontanka, confirmed this impression, causing him to comment that Fontanka's leadership had ruined the police organisation established by Sudeikin and himself by overtaxing its limited capabilities. He condemned Fontanka's practice of keeping excessively large numbers of people under surveillance and for carrying out indiscriminate mass arrests, arguing that Fontanka should have attacked subversion by concentrating its attention on those primarily responsible for spreading disorder. It is clear that, no matter the content of his public statements, Plehve appreciated that political police measures alone could not destroy the revolutionary movement or prevent terrorism without a vast commitment of resources which he was, at least at first, not willing to make.[26] However, it would not be long before this opinion conflicted with Plehve's more deeply ingrained traditional instincts about the role of the political police in Russian society as he strove to scrub Tsardom clean of every bit of dissent passing through the land.

****

Upon his appointment, Plehve, as was the custom, had the privilege of sweeping away his predecessor's colleagues and staffing the senior posts within his bureaus with men of his own choosing who could be relied upon to carry out his policies and, more importantly, who owed their unimpeachable loyalty to their minister (an essential prerequisite in the gossip-laden atmosphere of St Petersburg).[27] Although Plehve expected unswerving loyalty from his subordinates, on the whole, he based his criteria for appointment on more objective grounds, choosing to use his broom judiciously as he sought men of talent to fill vacant posts. This does not mean that in making appointments he was immune to outside interference and considerations. As a product of the St Petersburg bureaucratic milieu he knew that 'it was impossible to accomplish anything unless one was willing to humour influential persons by granting some of their demands'. Nevertheless, subordinate officials appointed in this manner were shunted aside by Plehve and did not play any role in the MVD's decision-making process.[28] For reasons of bureaucratic politics and continuity Plehve retained Sipiagin's corps of assistant ministers almost intact, the only change being the replacement of the politically moderate Prince P.D. Sviatopolk-Mirskii as the assistant minister managing the police and serving as the titular commander of the Separate Corps of Gendarmes, with General V.K. von Wahl.[29] In fact, von Wahl functioned only as a figurehead since Plehve preferred to confer with his department heads in matters of policy. It is at this and at lower levels, what today we call 'middle management', that Plehve made the most significant changes to his ministry, surrounding himself with young, talented and ambitious men.[30]

Plehve chose Aleksei Aleksandrovich Lopukhin to be his new director of Fontanka. Aleksei Aleksandrovich, the eldest son of an ancient family, graduated from Moscow University and by 1893 had risen to the rank of assistant procurator in Moscow. In 1896 Lopukhin received a promotion to procurator and was sent briefly to Tver before returning to Moscow for a further two years.[31] In 1900 he was transferred to St Petersburg, where he established an excellent reputation with his superiors. Plehve first met Lopukhin during this period and was impressed by him, making a point of meeting him again, this time in Kharkov to where Lopukhin had subsequently been assigned in early 1902. By the time of his second meeting with Plehve, Lopukhin had witnessed the terror of the peasant *jacqueries* in Kharkov and Poltava provinces and he considered these uprisings as signalling the birth of the Russian revolution. Plehve listened carefully to what Lopukhin had to say. If Plehve had not already known that he and Lopukhin represented two disparate groups within the bureaucracy, then it must have become clear to him during the course of this conversation.

Marc Raeff labels the two groups these men represented as 'liberal reformers' and 'conservatives'. The reformers who held sway briefly during the first several years of Alexander II's reign hoped to bring about the transformation of Russia based on liberal 'bourgeois' principles. They strongly believed in the emancipation of the serfs and the validity of *zemstva* institutions and they hoped that industrial development would not be implemented at the expense of the peasant. The leadership of the second group within the bureaucracy consisted, Raeff contends, of *sanovniki* who had been educated at court and in the military. These men who revered the monarchy despised the *zemstva* and wished to curb their activities, believing that reforms had gone far enough, perhaps too far. The conservatives argued that the nation needed time to absorb the changes wrought by Alexander II before it could again move cautiously forward.

The liberals envisioned a Russia profiting from the knowledge and experience already contributing to Europe's progress. Most important, they favoured a pluralistic society, encouraging the government to place its trust in its people. These men were not rebels, however, since their proposals for reform were invariably contained within the framework of the absolute monarchy. Ironically, it was the liberals' firm belief in absolutism that frustrated their own efforts. When ruled by an unsympathetic monarch, their only support came from the liberal opposition within society, a group whom these bureaucrats dare not co-opt until the second half of 1904 when Lopukhin, and Plehve's successor, Prince Sviatopolk-Mirskii, would attempt to do so (but more of this story in Chapter 8).

The conservatives relied on the tsar for their support and used their access to the court to scheme on behalf of their ambitions. Their weakness lay in their fear of losing the monarch's favour. In order to preserve the tsar's good will, these *sanovniki* had to tailor their programmes to meet his approval.[32] While neither Lopukhin's nor Plehve's social backgrounds matched the model drawn for us by Raeff, in their political outlook and in their behaviour they fit within the patterns he has described.

Lopukhin's liberalism did not discourage Plehve, instead he used it to his own advantage. In Lopukhin, Plehve saw an outstanding young official whose dedication, integrity and administrative skills made him a perfect choice as the official to direct the reform of Russia's police system. Convincing the liberal procurator to assume command of Fontanka would not be easy since Lopukhin had already rejected an offer of a vice directorship of Fontanka made by Sipiagin. Plehve lured Lopukhin with the promise of social and political reform. The minister told him that the present system of political police investigation was inadequate and in his opinion it was necessary to abolish the OOs and to transfer political cases to the courts. In other words, to bring an end to administrative authority, thus striking a positive chord in Lopukhin who believed that the government could only survive if it acted openly and within the law. In further conversations with Lopukhin Plehve showed himself sympathetic to Lopukhin's humanist point of view, striving to prove his sincerity by asking Lopukhin to accompany him to Poltava where Plehve met with local 'social activists' representing the nobility and the *zemstva*. Plehve spoke to them about renewing the Loris-Melikov project on placing representatives of society in the State Council.[33] Lopukhin became excited by the possibilities presented by Plehve, becoming more receptive to Plehve's persuasive arguments which nurtured his dreams amd ambition:[34] at the early age of thirty-eight Lopukhin, as chief of Fontanka, would be able to advise Russia's most powerful *sanovniki* and the tsar himself. Indeed, as chief of police he would be one of the most powerful men in the empire. Eventually, the temptation proved overwhelming and he accepted the transfer from the Ministry of Justice to the MVD and Fontanka.[35]

During Lopukhin's conversation with Plehve, the discussion moved on to the distasteful subject of political repression. Lopukhin, surprisingly, had much to say on the topic. In 1893, while serving as an assistant procurator in Moscow, he struck up a friendship with Sergei Zubatov, already the chief of the Moscow OO, who willingly introduced the eager procurator to the methods of counter-revolution, just as Sudeikin had done for Plehve over a decade earlier. Zubatov outlined his plans for the development of workers' societies under the control of the political police. Lopukhin elaborated for Plehve an entire campaign against subversion based entirely on Zubatov's policies. Plehve, to Lopukhin's undoubted joy, expressed his enthusiasm for the plan.[36]

Plehve, of course, already knew of Zubatov: Zubatov's hostility towards the incompetent and amateurish Separate Corps of Gendarmes, his desire to professionalise political police work, along with his extraordinary and controversial achievements as chief of the Moscow OO, had drawn him to Plehve's attention. Zubatov, a man of medium build and ordinary appearance, with chestnut hair, a small beard and always wearing tinted glasses, looked just like any Russian intellectual and in some ways he was. After a brief dalliance with subversive circles, Zubatov discovered the fanatic monarchist within himself and abandoned his disloyal behaviour. More than that, in 1887 he offered his services to Fontanka as a *sotrudnik*. His betrayal was soon discovered and he gave up undercover work to become a *chinovnik* for the Moscow OO in 1889.[37] It was not long before Fontanka recognised Zubatov's exceptional talent and by the early 1890s we find him directing the Moscow OO. As early as 1893, Zubatov remembered, he was already 'chasing about all over Russia, fighting with the "reds" and quarrelling with the "blues" [the gendarmes], the lazybones'.[38] By 1896 Zubatov's harassment of Moscow's revolutionaries and the infiltration of his *sotrudniki* into the revolutionary movement had decimated radical circles in that city and discouraged workers from joining those that remained. By the late 1890s Moscow's professional revolutionaries were demoralised by the destructive impact of Zubatov's tactics on their movements.[39]

Zubatov must have struck Plehve as a reincarnation of Sudeikin. Plehve remembered Lt Colonel Sudeikin as a master political policeman whose innovative style, especially his use of secret agents and sophisticated interrogation techniques, destroyed the effectiveness of *Narodnaia Volia*. Now twenty years later, filling the void left by Sudeikin's assassination, Plehve at last had found a replacement in Sergei Zubatov.

Plehve's elevation to minister of internal affairs probably saved Zubatov's career, which had been placed at risk by his experimenting with techniques of social control designed to co-opt the workers' movement for the government from under the noses of the revolutionary movements. As he told his subordinates, the Moscow OO, 'is not pre-occupied with a search for the solutions to problems, [but rather], on its own, to appease [the workers] without the use of external force'.[40] The first police sponsored workers' organisation appeared in Moscow in May 1901 and proved so successful that the SDs soon recognised that they did not have an answer to the combination of police-sponsored labour organisations and police harassment that swept Moscow clear of the social-democratic movement.[41] Zubatov capped his success in Moscow by launching a commemorative march for Alexander II on the anniversary of the Tsar-Liberator's assassination. The march, involving thousands of factory workers expressing their loyalty to the regime, had a predictable, but unintended effect on governing circles. Any show of solidarity on the part of the masses, even one reflecting such firm devotion to the regime, frightened Tsardom's *sanovniki*. Neither Minister of Finance Witte nor Minister of Internal Affairs Sipiagin approved of Zubatov's methods and both ministers urged the governor general of Moscow, Grand Duke Sergei Aleksandrovich to close down Zubatov's societies. However, the Grand Duke ruled in Moscow, not Sipiagin, and he refused to do as the minister requested.

Under these precarious conditions Zubatov walked a tightrope, the continued patronage of Grand Duke Sergei Aleksandrovich being essential to his survival. Unfortunately, Zubatov possessed little political sense and soon after the incident with Sipiagin, Zubatov challenged the Grand Duke's privilege of interfering in the affairs of the Moscow OO. Zubatov's effrontery, made worse by the fact that the Grand Duke had only recently shielded him from Sipiagin's wrath, enraged Sergei Aleksandrovich, who now wished to be rid of this insolent upstart. But Zubatov worked for the MVD and the Grand Duke could not remove him without the permission of the minister of internal affairs. By this time, Sipiagin had been replaced by Plehve. The tsar intervened in the dispute and since in his mind blood was a more important factor than competence, he asked Plehve to get rid of Zubatov. In response, Plehve to his credit offered his resignation and proclaimed that, 'it will not be Grand Duke Sergei who will run the police in Moscow, but rather experienced and capable policemen, otherwise Russia will not receive the desired protection'. Nicholas II acquiesced, and in typical melodramatic fashion, he made a bundle of the Grand Duke's reports and of Plehve's letter of resignation and tore it up. Then turning to face Plehve, the tsar told his minister 'you will have a free hand'.[42] Nevertheless, freedom within the tsarist bureaucratic milieu had certain definite limits and in order to avoid offending the powerful Grand Duke Sergei any further, Plehve removed Zubatov from Moscow, allowing the Grand Duke's pride to remain intact. Zubatov found himself transferred to St Petersburg as an official for special commissions. After the short time demanded by decorum, Plehve promoted Zubatov to chief of the Special Section.[43]

In Lopukhin and Zubatov, Plehve believed that he had appointed the two men who could best give him a new political police: men who would moderate Fontanka's penchant for arbitrary repression, with a campaign of mass persuasion, implemented by an expanded, but at the same time considerably streamlined, political police system, employing well-trained and highly motivated policemen.

****

Lopukhin, Plehve's new chief of Fontanka, mistakenly believed that he shared with his minister a belief in the necessity of the decentralisation of power to Plehve's local representatives, strengthening their hand in the provinces[44] and that, with this strategy in mind, one of his first tasks was the preparation of a plan designed to increase the effectiveness of the political police without substantially increasing its size. Lopukhin wanted to simplify Russia's police structure by integrating the political police with the civil police and, to a lesser degree, with the Gendarme Directorates which he believed could be done by creating a single provincial police directorate operating under the direct authority of the provincial governor.[45] The plan eliminated the OOs as independent political police bureaus, thereby denying them their special status and the freedom of action that went along with it. Lopukhin's reform would have prevented the political police from accumulating the massive arbitrary power for which they became infamous.[46] Furthermore it would have reduced the inter-service rivalry between the OOs and the Gendarme Directorates that plagued the political police throughout its life and would have created a streamlined communications system so essential to an effective political police network.[47] Moreover, it would have placed the political police under the law and exposed its operations to public view. But Lopukhin's blueprint for police reform rubbed against his ministers' strong sympathy for an independent political police system. Plehve failed to see the benefit to be gained in an improved relationship with society that such a reform would engender; a reform that in itself would diminish the level of tension between state and society without employing a single new policeman or an additional act of repression. Instead, Plehve turned to Zubatov for advice.

Zubatov had long harboured plans for the restructuring and expansion of the political police,[48] envisioning an elite and quasi-independent political police, acting under the direct order of its own Special Section and only indirectly under the orders of Fontanka; a truly secret police expanding and operating at the behest of the MVD's edicts, circulars, and regulations and not through the statutes of the *Svod Zakonov* (Digest of Laws).

Plehve dismissed Lopukhin's plan and gave Zubatov's proposals his full support.[49] Zubatov's ideas on police reform fitted comfortably within Plehve's view of traditional tsarist bureaucratic behaviour, satisfying both his belief in Imperial power politics and his secretive nature. He conceived of political police reform in the only way his experience allowed him to: not through decentralisation of authority as Lopukhin believed, but through its deconcentration – the expansion of central authority in the provinces.[50] Indeed, this strategy would permit Plehve to swell the size of the political police to ministerial proportions. As a result Plehve would in fact hold two very powerful ministerial portfolios: minister of internal affairs and the unofficial post of minister of internal security, enhancing his power and prestige within both ministerial circles and the court, making him the most powerful man in Russia next to the tsar.

Plehve supported Zubatov's proposals for a more emotive reason as well: he was frightened. The murders of Sipiagin and Bogolepov served as terrifying object lessons to the minister. Plehve employed Aleksandr Spiridonivich Skandrakov, an experienced police official and perhaps the only man Plehve completely trusted, as his personal bodyguard. Skandrakov established a shield of personal security around his minister. For most of the year Plehve lived within Fontanka itself in apartments constructed by Sipiagin. Within his suite of rooms he enjoyed the protection not only of the regular police, but of special, muscular centurions. In the summer Plehve lived at his well-protected *dacha* at Aptekarsk Island. The shortest sojourn involved complex security precautions and on longer trips he travelled in a separate railway car, surrounded by police, that rode through towns with its shades drawn and doors locked.[51] Plehve, forced to live like a man on the run, felt a deep-seated fear and hatred for the socialist-revolutionary BO, emotions intensified by police reports informing him that the wave of terrorism was gaining momentum.[52]

Plehve's well-entrenched belief in the paramount role of the central bureaucracy, his career considerations, the knowledge that the tsar appreciated the spectacular arrest more than low key, mundane, intelligent police work, his intrinsic belief in the unsurpassed value of a modern political police network to the security of Tsardom combined with his visceral fear of assassination made Zubatov's plan for rapidly expanding, and professionalising the political police irresistably attractive.[53]

****

On 12 August 1902, Fontanka issued a circular that changed forever the nature of political police institutions in the twentieth century. Only the blandness of the bureaucratic jargon masks the significance of the document. 'In several locales of the Empire', the circular began, 'where especially large increases in the revolutionary movement have been observed, there are to be established investigation sections whose chiefs are to be entrusted with political investigations, i.e. [using] internal surveillance and secret agents in the determined *raion* [region]'.[54] In response to this circular Fontanka established OOs in Vilna, Tiflis, Kharkov, Kazan, Ekaterinoslav, Kiev, Odessa and Saratov. The Special Section decreed that additional OOs were to be established as circumstances required,[55] giving the Special Section a distinct advantage over the Separate Corps of Gendarmes, who believed themselves undermined in an indefensible way. The Special Section could ordain new OOs at will under Plehve's precedent while the proliferation of Gendarme Directorates was inhibited by law. In addition, the placement of new OOs drastically limited the authority of the Gendarme Directorates. The senior staff of the Corps saw the reform as a challenge to its authority and manpower and reacted with hostility to it. Young and ambitious gendarme officers began to transfer to the OOs, acquiring the derogatory nicknames of *'departamenskii'* and *'okhranniki'* within the Separate Corps of Gendarmes.[56] In order to assuage the Corps' irritation, the MVD allotted them a small increase in funds.[57]

Despite his gesture towards the Corps of Gendarmes, Plehve still intended to follow the plan so ardently favoured by Zubatov – that of curtailing the Corps of Gendarmes' political police functions altogether.[58] Aware, however, of the tsar's affection for the Corps of Gendarmes, Plehve realised that any drastic measures directed against the Corps would embarrass Nicholas II before his gendarme generals, possibly endangering the minister's excellent relationship with His Imperial Majesty. Rather than take this risk he chose to sacrifice what he acknowledged as one of the essential ingredients of his political police reform.[59] Plehve tried to find a way around this problem through a proliferation of new regulations restricting the Gendarme Directorates' duties, but this step only exacerbated the relationship between the Corps and the Special Section still further.[60] The appointment of Lopukhin to the post of Fontanka's director and worse, the choice of Zubatov, that former revolutionary, as chief of the Special Section when there were qualified military men available for these posts, infuriated the 'old school', whose wrath was further provoked when Plehve replaced some of the senior police bureaucrats, many of the Gendarme Directorate chiefs and lesser gendarme officers, with men more compatible with the views of Lopukhin and Zubatov.[61]

The problem for senior gendarme officers soon became obvious. Young captains or green Lt colonels as directors of OOs had the right to report independently to governors and those reports, much to the Corps of Gendarmes' chagrin, were treated on an equal basis with those originating in the Provincial Gendarme Directorates, often from the pen of a gendarme general, a practice the Corps informed Fontanka not conducive to good military discipline; furthermore the Corps demanded that Fontanka ensure that these young officers remain strictly subordinated to the 'senior and more experienced chiefs of the Gendarme Directorates'.[62] The Corps' protests were also a response to Plehve's sledgehammer tactics which eroded the Corps' authority, but neither adequately integrated nor excluded it from political police work: a problem exacerbated by Plehve's failure to resolve the important question of chain-of-command in a bureaucracy which included both military and civilian personnel.[63]

Once Plehve embarked on his political police reform he became possessed by it. Despite his initial concern over expenditure, he spared no expense. Between 1902 and 1904 the MVD spent five million roubles, the entire reserve fund of Fontanka, on building his and Zubatov's bulwark against subversion.[64] OOs were indeed expensive: 300 000 roubles on the Kiev OO alone and 100 000 roubles per year maintaining it thereafter;[65] the Moscow OOs budget averaged about 13 000 roubles per month and even the small Saratov OO received about 36 000 roubles per year from Fontanka. These amounts did not include the salaries for the OOs' gendarme officers, which were paid by the Corps of Gendarmes.[66]

The MVD spent the vast majority of its budget on the grand regional OOs of which Kiev, Warsaw, Moscow and St Petersburg were the largest. These institutions ruled over vast territory[67] and required large chanceries in order to administer their many undercover agents and detective teams. For example, within the Moscow OO the assistant chief directed the investigatory personnel and in turn each group of undercover agents and detectives had their own supervisors; the detective service was guided by supervisors who plotted their day-to-day activities (see Chapter 2), and case officers (usually gendarme officers) directing the work of the undercover agents (see Chapter 3). The ranks of OO personnel also included numerous clerks and scribes who moved from section to section within the OO as needed.

Moscow OO headquarters accommodated: an archive, offices for the different detective supervisors, the office of the director of detectives, the offices concerned with regional operations and the processing of reports from the other provinces under Moscow's jurisdiction. This OO also ran sections for the translation of foreign language periodicals and letters, the reading and clipping of newspapers, a library of revolutionary literature and other publications required for investigatory purposes, and a special office of elucidation (*vyiasnenie*) that stored numerous reference books and tables of addresses used to aid investigations. The most securely guarded room was the 'top secret office' where the OO kept those documents currently in use. The offices and cells for arrest and interrogation were within the same building, though quite separate from other sections in the OO. An integral part of any OO was its Black Cabinet (*Chernyi kabinet*). This infamous bureau for the scrutiny of the mail was situated in the local post office, and it rounds out the structure of the Moscow OO, except for one little extra. The Moscow OO maintained its own kitchen for the convenience of its employees.

The OOs were staffed by civilian bureaucrats, gendarme officers and by men whose first contact with the political police came on the other side of the fence. Sergei Zubatov is the best known example of the 'politically unreliable' person turned political police official. The Moscow OO's personnel chart contained twelve gendarme officers, about twenty-five civil servants and scribes for the chancery, nearly sixty police supervisors who determined and distributed detectives' assignments, one hundred detectives and about ninety security guards and other lower level employees used for running errands of various sorts.[68]

The well-staffed agencies, particularly of Moscow and St Petersburg, overshadowed the poorer, understaffed OOs located in provincial backwaters where subversives happened to be particularly active. For instance, the establishment in Zhitomir comprised only two gendarme officers, eight non-commissioned officers and a few secret agents.[69]

In contrast to the facilities available in the large metropolitan OOs that in Saratov, for example, operated out of a nondescript two-storey private house, with the landlord living on the lower floor. The second level of the house contained a rather large room occupied by OO Captain Fedorov, the assistant chief and supervisor of investigatory personnel, his wife and daughter. A medium sized cottage sat within the courtyard of the main house and served as the Saratov OO's chancery. A.P. Martynov, the OO's chief, and his family lived in a modest hotel suite situated two or three blocks distant from his office.[70]

The interiors of provincial OO chanceries were sparse. The Kishinev chancery contained the standard *shkaf* or cupboard, holding card files and photographs of suspects collected from a variety of sources, along with a file for intelligence gathered by detectives and undercover agents. A separate library of revolutionary publications supplied by Fontanka or seized locally, occupied another part of the room.

The staff of these chanceries were equally lean. The chief of the OO handled the secret matters including the copying of perlustrated letters.[71] The Saratov OO only employed four chancery personnel, who processed the information collected by eight or nine detective teams and the undercover agents. Two police supervisors maintained liaison with the local authorities.[72] This undermanned and underqualified staff was just not adequate for the job at hand.[73] In these out-of-the-way bureaus the poorly trained and inadequately educated scribes and clerks were barely able to cope with their clerical duties as prescribed by Fontanka. Their ineptitude is reflected in their miserable salaries of no more than twenty-five or thirty roubles per month. At a higher level, the dearth of qualified junior gendarme officers meant that incompetent assistant OO chiefs were foisted on many provincial OOs. These men did not have the slightest idea of the requirements of their position and proved to be more trouble than they were worth.[74] Some of the smaller OOs possessed terrible reputations.[75]

Provincial and city officials were blissfully unaware of conditions prevailing among these new guardians of law and order. Governors and *gradonachal'niki* were happy to have them, especially since eager OO chiefs actively sought their support.[76] Unfortunately, it was not long before they found themselves refereeing the endless disputes between the Gendarme Directorates and the OOs which prevented both agencies from effectively fulfilling their duties. Plehve's reforms bound the OOs together with the Gendarme Directorates, their antagonists, in a hopelessly complex and inefficient system of information sharing and delineation of duties,where inter-agency intelligence flowed along contorted paths, with the aim of preventing the Gendarme Directorates from conducting any investigations in depth.[77]

With the proliferation of the OOs, the Special Section dominated the field of political investigation, forcing the gendarmes to settle for less glamorous tasks. Certainly, in the regions of Russia without OOs, the local Gendarme Directorate still bore full responsibility for political investigations, though the fact that no OO had been established usually meant that there were few cases to work on. The Gendarme Directorates' reduced authority severely bruised the Corps' self-image. The gendarmes found themselves playing a peripheral role in the protection of the state order. True, the Railway Gendarmes remained a prestigious service, but on the other less shiny side of the coin, Gendarme Military Divisions, ruffians in uniform, carried out acts of repression on the order of the civil authorities.

High-ranking political policemen exacerbated the ill-feeling that existed between the Corps and the Special Section by referring to the gendarmes as brainless thugs doing the regime's dirty work, while noting with pride about themselves that, 'the *Okhrana's* job was to discover evil doers. Their punishment was not its concern...'.[78] And, 'in reality, they [the OOs] are guided not by the desire to repress the developing revolutionary mood, but by their desire to observe revolutionary circles'.[79] Thus, the OOs propagated the mythical view that they did not soil their hands with the unpleasant duty of arrests and searches,[80] these dirty tasks belonging to the menials of the Separate Corps of Gendarmes. The chiefs of the Gendarme Directorates came to hate the OOs and did their best to obstruct OO operations,[81] this hostility becoming endemic throughout the Corps. The encounter between the chief of the Saratov OO and Lt General Baron Taube, the commander of the Corps of Gendarmes is a case in point: Baron Taube sneering at Martynov, 'you are perhaps in the opinion of the Department of Police a fine gendarme officer, but in my opinion you are the worst!'[82]

The problems of dealing with OO–Gendarme Directorate relations and the damage caused to the intelligence-gathering system, though critical, are insignificant by comparison with the problems caused by the Special Section's inability to force the OOs to properly fulfil their duties. Fontanka believed that tightly regulated and strictly controlled bureaus were the only means of guaranteeing the effective collection of intelligence and the preservation of order.[83] However, it could not convince its OOs of this fact. The Special Section relied on too many political police officials who were not up to the job or who thought they knew better. For instance, OOs refused to despatch regular detailed reports to the Special Section, which meant that the Special Section could not determine the level of dissent in a given region at a particular time. It also meant that Fontanka could not determine the effectiveness of an OO nor could it evaluate the evidence on which arrests were made until it was too late to prevent miscarriages of what passed for justice in the police regulations.[84] As early as January 1903, Director of Fontanka Lopukhin issued a circular pleading with his OOs to follow the regulations covering searches, individual arrests and the liquidation of entire groups.[85] Overall, Fontanka engaged in a never-ending campaign to keep its OOs in line by means of an endless flow of new procedures, a practice which only added to the mountains of paperwork, further reducing the provincial OOs' effectiveness, without rectifying the problem.[86]

The internecine warfare between the OOs and the Gendarme Directorates, their inability to process intelligence rapidly and their failure to make the most effective use of it, the persistence of formalism and its major symptom, mountainous paperwork, all part and parcel of Russia's cumbersome bureaucratic style, became a police administrator's nightmare. That the number of OOs in operation by the regime's end was uncertain lends credibility to the enormity of the level of administrative confusion. It is virtually impossible to find two tsarist police officials who agree on the number of bureaus established by Fontanka between 1902 and 1917. Some estimates are outrageous: one former low-ranking *chinovnik* recollected that there were seventy-five OOs by 1913 while another commentator claimed there were hundreds of regional and district OOs.[87]

One fact is certain. The majority of high-ranking political police officials believed that a nationwide political police force could be established and then controlled – this had been Plehve's plan. However, it was a project that would frustrate even present-day administrators. The monolithic bureau is a myth. No one can fully control the behaviour of a large organisation and the control that does exist diminishes as the organisation grows larger. In fact, the larger an organisation becomes the poorer is the coordination among its actions.[88]

Incapable of understanding the origins of the problems inherent in enlarging the political police and unable to tackle these problems with the force of authority, Fontanka's leadership relied on the 'machine model' of human behaviour which decrees that low performance indicates a need for more detailed inspection and control over the operation of the machine.[89] This type of control requires a tremendous investment in time, money and paperwork and cannot in any sense be deemed an effective mechanism for enhancing the authority of the chain-of-command so critical to the effective operation of any bureaucracy. In 1850 Count Perovskii, in discussing procedures within the MVD's local agencies, remarked that, 'the essence of matters is choked by formalism'.[90] Apparently, the MVD had learned very little over the succeeding years.

Plehve's reforms did not lead to the development of a systematic network of well-oiled political police agencies, but rather to the development of an organisation that expanded like the famous book character Topsy who grew and grew without reason and without explanation. Fontanka's attempt to control this organisation became an end in itself, deflecting the Special Section away from its primary tasks.[91] Notwithstanding, Plehve's reform of the political police, though imperfect, was the only one of his projects to reach fruition. Despite its deficiencies, the political police under Plehve and his successors spread its tentacles throughout Russia, reaching into the core of Russia's subversive movements and making life as a revolutionary more perilous than ever before. However, the successes achieved against subversion were more the product of the talents displayed by individual political police chiefs, such as Sergei Zubatov, rather than the efficacy of a greatly expanded institutional framework whose principles of behaviour and administration, nevertheless, remained deeply rooted in the past. The establishment of every new OO reflected the growing power of the bureaucracy over the people in a most flagrant manner. In themselves, then, the OOs contributed to the growth of dissent. The joke repeated by A.S. Suvorin in his diary entry for 11 February 1902 that, 'if three [people] gather on a street they are dispersed. If more than three [people] are [seated] around a card table then the police can enter [the house] and charge the occupants with illegal gambling',[92] acquired the ring of deepening bitterness during succeeding years.

7 Time of Experiment, Time of Repression, 1902–1904

The relationship between Plehve and Zubatov was a complicated one, founded in their common desire to control and manipulate society on the one hand and their campaign to destroy the revolutionary movements on the other. These were related but very separate problems. Zubatov formulated his strategy and tactics with this distinction clearly in mind. Plehve blurred this distinction, sometimes seeing it more clearly than others but never clearly enough to allow for the sensible approach to dissent that he spoke of when he first became minister of internal affairs.

For over two generations, a debate – initially openly and subsequently more covertly – had been ongoing in the corridors of the bureaucracy. Plehve's attitude towards the role of the political police in society was unavoidably influenced by this debate over the application of *zakonnost'* (lawfulness) and *glasnost'* (publicity) to Russian politics. The two concepts embodied a wide variety of meanings. W. Bruce Lincoln has recently defined *zakonnost'* as the 'keystone' of the outlook of men who wanted 'the further rationalization of autocracy and supported the admission of responsible members of "society" into the machinery of the Imperial government to help formulate state policy'.[1] Enlightened bureaucrats saw *glasnost'* as a means of guaranteeing *zakonnost'*. *Glasnost'* was to be the means by which the most aware and loyal members of the public could 'criticize the improper or ineffective implementation of state policies, but not the content of the policies themselves'.[2] Though enlightened bureaucrats differed with their traditionalist brethren on the usefulness of *zakonnost'* and *glasnost'* in Russian conditions, the two groups did agree on the most important point of all: the preservation of both the absolute monarchy as the only appropriate form of government for Russia and the primacy of the bureaucracy as Tsardom's governing agent.

Increasingly this discussion spread from the inner sanctum of officialdom to the educated public at large, adding to the pressure on the goverment for a positive response to demands that lawfulness be introduced into Tsardom's dealing with society and that society be given at least some input into the government's decision-making process. Plehve realised that a positive reply would have to be made to these demands in order to mollify public opinion, but he was uncertain how this could be accomplished, especially given his lack of sympathy with the public's point of view. He personally believed *zakonnost'* to be a dangerous luxury in this time of crisis and he considered *glasnost'* to be anathema.

Plehve believed – and it was a belief shaped within the law and order milieu of the MVD – that in order for Tsardom to maintain its capacity to govern it needed to convince the Russian people (including its own servitors) that the traumatic events of the 1870s and 1880s combined with the ever more audible calls for alterations in the style if not the form of government were aberrations on the body politic, the causes of which were not be found in the deficiencies of tsarist policies, but elsewhere beyond the borders of Russia. Traditional xenophobia became the basis upon which the Ministry of Internal Affairs built a theory of subversion which went far beyond anything conceived of in the West at that time. The forces of law and order sought to deflect the onus of discontent away from the government toward the entire westernised element within Russian society, developing a crude model in which ideas, perhaps innocently imported from abroad, began almost at once because of their alien nature to have a corrosive effect on Russian life. The Ministry of Internal Affairs argued that high school teachers, university professors, journalists and those who hosted every day conversations within the drawing rooms of the educated elite sowed these foreign ideas throughout Russian society, where under particular conditions they took root among students, members of national minorities and other impressionable elements of society, causing them to rebel against the faith and the customs of the monarchy, becoming a major force in the internal war against Tsardom.[3]

Plehve not only accepted this viewpoint, he elaborated upon it.[4] In a conversation with the famous publicist N.K. Mikhailovskii, Plehve made plain his point of view. 'For me', he told Mikhailovskii, 'there is no doubt that this social movement is the fruit of literature. Students generally, youths, workers, peasants – they are all cannon fodder. The press is the moving force, and it must pay for the disorder and it will pay'.[5]

The men whose 'press' Plehve and his colleagues within the forces of order so intensely despised represented a broad segment of educated society: loyal monarchists calling for only the most modest reforms, moderate constitutional monarchists, and the still few men who wished to preserve the monarchy (if at all) only as window dressing for a modern, vibrant parliamentary government. Plehve acknowledged that while these men were of the highest character, the campaign they launched against the paramount role played by the bureaucracy in governing Russia served as nothing more than 'a smokescreen for society's real goal the destruction of the autocracy'.[6]

In a famous exchange with his arch-rival Minister of Finance Sergei Witte, Plehve echoed warnings expressed in hundreds of police reports when he predicted that revolution would come from the 'developing classes, the public elements and the intelligentsia', and it had only one aim: to replace the monarchy with a constitutional government. Plehve exhibited a spark of insight when he warned Witte that the revolution would not stop here. Once the progressive elements had successfully aroused society they would lose their nerve and make concession after concession until they found themselves 'at the tail of the movement' while 'the radical, criminal elements gained the upper hand'.[7]

This scenario for revolution articulated by Plehve and echoed by the members of Tsardom's internal security agencies, forced them to confront a truly horrific paradox. Harassing and arresting the few convinced revolutionaries only attacked the disease of subversion in full bloom. To eradicate the source of dissent it was necessary to start at the beginning of the cycle and silence the disseminators of unwelcome ideas and the makers of public opinion.[8] Yet Russia's professional people, her intellectuals and her students, all tainted to one degree or another by ideas foreign to Tsardom's traditional political culture, were essential for Russia's survival in the competitive arena of international economic development, and the demands of this competition forced Russian educational institutions to churn out more of these people all of the time. Swept up into this stream of knowledge were some of Russia's growing numbers of literate peasants and workers, the backbone of modern Russia's productive capacity, who in turn began to give coherent expression to the deeply felt grievances of the inarticulate majority of the population. The peasant/worker intelligentsia, as they became known, eagerly participated in the development of strategies and tactics designed to eliminate the economic and political distress of the masses. By the early twentieth century Tsardom – having rejected the moderate approach to dissent embodied in western modes of political accommodation – found itself confronted with these new transmission belts for spreading sedition throughout the lower orders.

Plehve's recognition of this paradox placed a man with his world view in a terrible quandary. He conceived of himself as a barricade preventing the erosion of the autocracy by the forces of progress and as minister of internal affairs, adopting repressive tactics he crushed all public initiative.[9] The ministry, he told a colleague A.A. Pogozhev, 'is compelled' to employ 'brutal measures' against dissent because 'historical necessity forces us to have recourse to them'.[10] Nevertheless, Plehve understood that repression and dissent were locked together in a vicious circle, a circle which could only be broken by developing innovative measures for defusing the opposition and revolutionary movements. Force would still be applied against hardened revolutionaries but the legal opposition – no matter his personal opinion of it – should not be treated so roughly. And how should he deal with the workers and peasants seduced by the irresistible utopian promises made by revolutionary agitators? Plehve believed that through a variety of methods he could convince society and the masses alike to adopt a less hostile posture toward the policies of the regime.[11] As we saw in the previous chapter, he understood that continuing mass repression only led to universal lawlessness and to the ultimate breakdown of the existing order. Thus repression would have to be used selectively, the political police defining its enemies more carefully and concentrating their forces against those well-organised groups judged to be the greatest threat to the regime. A programme of incentives and rewards combined with a modicum of repression would together recapture the loyalty of the Russian people and drain away the reservoir of support for oppositional and subversive movements.[12]

Plehve intended to accomplish these ends by embarking upon a campaign of mass persuasion. He once said that the purpose of his service as minister of internal affairs was to use 'all of my mental power to influence man'.[13] Unfortunately although he could be immensely persuasive[14] he invariably implemented no follow-up actions supporting his initial positions. The reason for his inaction derived from his ingrained experience within the MVD and his suspicious nature. To those he wished to 'persuade' Plehve claimed that he welcomed public support under the proviso that it work with the tsar and his agents for the 'gradual' and 'organic' evolution of Russian life.[15] It did not take Plehve's audience long to realise that, 'society's cooperation' meant nothing more than unequivocal obedience to the government's policies.[16] D.N. Shipov (the influential *zemstva* leader) infuriated by the dichotomy between Plehve's conciliatory words and his harsh actions wrote that 'on the face of it Plehve gives the impression of a clever man. How can one explain, therefore, that he thinks it is possible to base his whole policies on lies and hypocrisy?'.[17] It is a good question. One possible answer is that Plehve himself was floundering, not lying, unable to accept wholeheartedly the new strategies proposed to him for moulding society to the requirements of the state, even though, as we noted above, he recognised that at least some of society's demands would have to be met and even though these new methods were immensely attractive to him.

Nothing would expose the paradox faced by Plehve more clearly than his endorsement of Zubatov's police-sponsored trade union movement. At first, according to Lev Tikhomirov, Plehve expressed ambivalence toward Zubatov's achievement in Moscow, but he was soon attracted by the OO chief's ability 'to fish out revolutionaries'.[18] During subsequent discussions with Zubatov, Plehve was so impressed by Zubatov's methods of containing dissent and controlling and moulding popular opinion that he allowed his enthusiasm to overcome, at least temporarily, his traditional bureaucratic conservatism. The minister did not recognise that significant differences in perspective existed between his and Zubatov's thinking concerning the sources of Russian public opinion and between their overall strategies designed to deal with that opinion.

Plehve's views on these matters were both traditional and simplistic: he perceived public opinion as emanating from a conglomeration of well-defined groups and circles, the centres of which could be unveiled and liquidated by good police work. Once this was accomplished 'all this apparent public community will vanish like magic', he believed.[19]

Zubatov's interpretation of the social and intellectual dynamics behind the rapid growth in public opposition to government policy and his concomitant strategies were far more complex than Plehve's linear viewpoint. As Tim McDaniel writes, Zubatov's strategy combined aspects of three separate political traditions: monarchism, populism and Western liberalism. Zubatov firmly believed that the apparent incompatibility of these traditions would be overcome by the 'majesty and authority of the tsarist state, which could reconcile hierarchy and participation, traditional and modern relations'. Indeed, in describing the motivating force behind subversion Zubatov showed himself to be a sophisticated social and political analyst. For him ideas were not just the province of the elite and could not be stamped out by removing the relatively few subversives operating within Russia. Tsardom, he argued, would win over the people to its point of view only through the careful manipulation of propaganda and by the development of attractive programmes for reform. Plehve listened carefully to Zubatov, describing him half jokingly as the 'Marxist Poseur'.[20]

Plehve's description of his chief of the Special Section was more accurate than he knew. Zubatov's analysis of the role of ideology as a critical factor in western politics placed his thinking far beyond that of his minister of internal affairs, who comprehended nothing about the uses of ideology. Zubatov recognised the importance of ideology in two contexts – as a set of beliefs which drove men to make exceptional sacrifices on the one hand and as images which so effectively persuaded the masses on the other. The opposition and the revolutionaries, because they possessed clearly articulated ideologies, occupied the intellectually and morally defensible high ground.[21] Yet, Zubatov instinctively knew that the high ground must be occupied by Tsardom. Russian political culture did not possess an ideology and could not strengthen itself by developing one.[22] However, as we saw in an earlier chapter, Zubatov had something else in mind, an ethos: the monarchical principle. Zubatov placed all his faith in it. 'I believe', he proclaimed, 'that correctly understood the monarchist idea is able to give the country all it needs by freeing the social forces without bloodshed and other horrors'.[23] A Russian, Zubatov preached, should devote himself 'not so much to the status quo of the autocracy as to the dynamics'.[24] If the government wanted popular support it would have to offer its people some richly treasured benefits and protection against callous and arbitrary treatment as well. These Zubatov was prepared to concede.

Plehve apparently paid little attention to Zubatov's social theories. Quite simply, in Zubatov, Plehve mistakenly believed he had discovered a hard-headed 'practical worker' like himself, a man of action who was willing to attack the revolutionaries on their own ground. However, Zubatov was no ordinary 'practical' *chinovnik*. He was an idealist, a fanatic, with an unclouded pure image of the Russian monarchy whose continued existence he would protect with his life. He once told his friend and colleague A.I. Spiridovich, 'it is necessary to fight those who are against Russia in a fight to the finish'.[25] The new chief of the Special Section turned out to be more than Plehve had bargained for.

****

Zubatov considered the cumulative effect of social-democratic propaganda on the working masses as the greatest threat to Tsardom's future, while Plehve did not share his police chief's fears about the dangers presented by social democracy, since his primary concerns lay elsewhere.[26] Zubatov's strategy of holding the allegiance of the workers for the government by offering them the protection and advice of the political police in their struggle for better working and living conditions, struck a receptive chord in the minister of internal affairs whose ministry, including its political police, was historically sympathetic to the plight of Russian labour. As early as 1885 the gendarmes expressed their sympathy for the appalling conditions of Russia's workers. 'Having had the opportunity to examine closely the life of factory workers', wrote one gendarme officer, 'I can find very little difference between their position and that of the earlier serfs; the same want, the same need, the same rights; the same contempt for their spiritual needs'. As yet, the workers did not exhibit any interest in politics, but the gendarme warned that, 'that evil day is coming closer and closer.'[27]

Within a decade the gendarme's prediction seemed to be coming true. According to the conservative figures recorded by the Factory Inspectorate there were 68 strikes in 1895, 118 in 1896, 145 in 1897, 215 in 1898 and 189 in 1899.[28] It was the great textile strikes of 1896 and 1897 that rekindled official disquiet over the labour problem.

On 12 August 1897 Minister of Internal Affairs I.L. Goremykin dispatched a circular to provincial governors and police officials detailing the causes of the St Petersburg strikes, attributing the discipline of the strikers and the strikes' rapid spread to other cities as evidence that revolutionaries were involved. He ordered the police to embark upon 'the most strict observation of conditions' in Russian factories and that factory disorders be considered as political offences, subject to investigations by the police on the basis of the statute of state security.[29] Goremykin tempered these measures against strikers, however, by suggesting that the police should intervene in labour disputes in order to eliminate 'as far as possible, the causes for dissatisfaction in those cases where the workers have good reason to complain about the oppression or injustice of the factory owners or of the [factory] administration'[30] and in February 1899 the MVD, overcoming Minister of Finance Witte's fierce objection, established a special corps of factory police[31] which directly challenged the authority of Witte's Factory Inspectorate over managment–labour relations.

The struggle between the MVD and the Ministry of Finance over which of them should supervise labour–management relations continued into the new century, acquiring new momentum with the appointment of Plehve as the late Sipiagin's successor as minister of internal affairs. Plehve, like many of his MVD colleagues, deplored the victimisation of the workers at the hands of the industrialists. Many years before as director of the Department of Police he had expressed his compassion for the labouring masses in language that ironically became the trademark of the people he despised and spent his life pursuing:

> Before the rich capitalist, the individual factory worker is powerless and without influence, [especially] if the law, the workers' only savior, refuses to defend him. But, gathered at the factory those same workers are already a dan-

gerous force, especially when the causes for their dissatisfaction feed on bad treatment.[32]

Plehve's sympathy for the workers was undoubtedly enhanced by his distaste for the new industrial Russia in general, and his belief that the labouring masses did not present a serious danger to the regime.[33] Therefore, in Zubatov's proposals for police-sponsored labour organisations Plehve perceived a low-risk policy that might accomplish on a broad scale what it had achieved in Moscow, while at the same time, challenging Witte's already eroded authority over Russia's industrial relations. The Zubatov scheme also attracted Plehve's attention for fiscal reasons. The Special Section devoted the majority of its human and financial resources to the destruction of the SR BO at a time (1902–1904) when the MVD still managed to control the amount Fontanka spent on agents and investigations. This meant that the Special Section had difficulty keeping track of SD groups and was powerless to destroy them.[34] Zubatov's successful campaign against the SDs in Moscow showed Plehve that there appeared to be an excellent and relatively inexpensive method of defeating Russia's marxists.[35]

These factors, added to Plehve's fascination with the tactics of mass persuasion and social control, so strengthened his interest in Zubatov's police supported labour organisations that he became completely identified with it. It is clear, therefore, that Plehve was being less than honest when he repeatedly expressed the opinion that he only supported Zubatov's programme as a preliminary test, something to be replaced by a different, permanent policy later on.[36]

****

Richard Pipes remarked that Zubatov's experiment merits a special place in political police history as the first significant step taken by an internal security service away from merely a repressive role as preservers of the status quo by the negative methods of undermining revolutionary groups through arrest and/or the surveillance of their members, to the positive concept of control in which all human activity, even dissent up to a pre-determined point, is permitted, though moulded and supervised by the state.[37] Zubatov developed this tactic through a close observation of and discussion with young revolutionaries, through his study of social-democratic ideology and as a result of his personal though brief experience with underground movements. Zubatov, whose writings are laden with insights into the reasons for revolutionary ideologies being so attractive to the masses, instinctively understood that one of the first tests of strength between the state and its dissidents is who will define the basic issues of the conflict and determine what should constitute a solution.[38] We have mentioned this point before, but it is worth repeating. He believed that the autocracy was always on the defensive because it did not have a long-range programme for retaining the loyalty of its people[39] and Zubatov knew that if Tsardom failed to develop such a programme it would have a bleak future.

In mid-April 1898, while still in Moscow, Zubatov ghosted a major memorandum on the labour question for General D.F. Trepov, the *oberpolitsmeistr* of Moscow. The report discussed the workers' inherent values and their desires and how these could be satisfied. Most of all, it is unique among government studies of the time for its detailed analysis and understanding of the theory and the tactics employed by Russian social democracy to gain control of the labour movement. In this paper Zubatov argued that Tsardom needed to embark on a campaign of mass persuasion.[40] Marxist propaganda he noted, swings the masses over to its side not by sophisticated phraseology, but through appealing to the workers' every-day demands and by promising to meet their needs. Zubatov explained that this tactic often leads to mass strikes which, 'are the first school for the political education of the worker'. He elaborated on this view:

> Success in the battle brings with it to the [worker] faith in his own strength, teaches him practical methods of struggle ... [and] convinces him of the possibility of practical work and the desirability of unifying collective action in general. The excitement of the struggle makes him more receptive to the idea of socialism ...[41]

According to Zubatov the MVD could be equally persuasive among the proletariat by using the same tactics. Tsardom had to regulate in law the factory worker–industrialist relationship and at the same time remove the revolutionaries' means of plotting against the state by isolating them from the workers.

The fullest expression of the police chief's views appeared in a September 1900 report to Fontanka that specifically recommended the abolition of criminal penalties for non-political and non-violent strikes. Zubatov stressed that the concept of legality should be fostered among workers by entrusting the working class with increased rights and broad responsibility for establishing their own self-help programmes and institutions.[42] He confidently predicted that if the government allowed the working class to organise under its own leadership it would rebuff the efforts of the radical intelligentsia to control it. Zubatov did not intend to reduce the autocracy's authority. On the contrary, he saw the autocracy's role as the arbiter of society's actions as crucial to Tsardom's wellbeing, cynically arguing that 'it remains for the ... autocracy to "divide and rule"'.[43]

Zubatov's theories on social control made him the first and perhaps only monarchical revisionist among tsarist officials. His insights into the ingredients that made for a dynamic society left other law and order officials far behind. Zubatov's discussion of the worker-intelligentsia who began to appear in Russia's factories revealed the orderly and sophisticated style of his thought. He called the worker-intelligentsia 'the connecting link between [the intelligentsia] and the workers' milieu'. They were the key to controlling the labouring masses and he believed he could turn these people to the government's advantage, by convincing as many of them as possible that the workers' interests could best be served by the state.[44] Zubatov thought he could achieve this end by playing upon what

George Rudé calls the 'popular ideology' of the masses. This system of beliefs is made up of two elements. The first of these is their inherent beliefs formed by experiences which *do not* come from listening to lectures, seminars or reading books and pamphlets. When these inherent beliefs combine with the second element, the stock of ideas that are 'derived' from the expressions of the intelligentsia, a 'popular ideology' is formed.[45] One thing can be said for certain, that the stubbornness of the original inherent beliefs held by the worker-intelligentsia alter the new 'derived' ideas so much, that those ideas that are absorbed by the worker-intelligentsia will have undergone considerable reshaping before they are passed on to its audiences.[46] Now, this notion of 'popular ideology' makes the worker-intelligentsia's contribution to the dynamics of subversion of vital, paramount importance. As numbers of worker-intelligentsia increase, the professional revolutionary-intelligentsia find themselves isolated from the working class and, though by no means extraneous to the worker and peasant movements, certainly of diminished importance to them.

For Zubatov the key to winning over the workers to the moderate path of the worker-intelligentsia was education. Zubatov insisted that Russia's industrial workers must eradicate their 'cultural backwardness' by attending night school and other cultural-enlightenment organisations. There, they will expose themselves to the lectures 'of the peaceful and serious' liberal intelligentsia who will acquaint them with the history and practice of foreign trade union movements, making them aware of the indispensable necessity of legal behaviour.[47]

Of course, Zubatov himself played a key role in the process of indoctrination. At interrogation after isolating the revolutionary-intelligentsia from the worker-intelligentsia among his prisoners, Zubatov impressed upon the latter group his sympathy for the workers' movement', alleging that the government was preparing generous labour measures.[48] He went on to maintain a close if autocratic relationship with those members of the worker-inteliigentsia he won over.[49] 'Everything must be directed toward the authorities and through the authorities', he warned them.[50]

****

Zubatov's courage and genius allowed him to transform his social theories into a highly imaginative programme of social control. Underlying his scheme was the belief that ideas cannot be destroyed, all that the government can do is to keep abreast of the revolutionary movements, attacking only the core of the revolutionary groups.[51] Infiltration of revolutionary circles by *sotrudniki* and the frequent arrest of their leadership became the foundation upon which he built his investigative apparatus. That apparatus employed a modern intelligence processing system. In order to strike effectively at the centre of revolutionary organisations, the resourceful Zubatov, in 1900 while still chief of the Moscow OO, imported the Bertillon identification system from France .[52] The Bertillon cataloging procedure permitted the Special Section to register and to identify almost any intelligent person who at some time or other was overheard to utter what an agent of the political police interpreted as seditious statements.[53] Zubatov also used synoptic tables, a tool long employed by the political police, to determine the relationship between a principal suspect or suspects in a case and his associates and friends.[54] The synoptic table is a prime example of guilt by association, but it nevertheless helped Zubatov separate the fellow travellers, innocent bystanders and hardcore revolutionaries from each other. The Special Section expanded the process of identification and differentiation of subversives and their groups by devising organisation charts for each revolutionary group. The chain-of-command diagrams helped Zubatov fathom the usually complex organisational structures and relationships that masked the leadership of Russia's subversive movements, the *pisaki* of the registration bureau regularly revising the synoptic tables and chain-of-command diagrams to reflect fresh intelligence so they could serve as the basis for the Special Section's long-term assault on its quarry. He believed that his system would be able to isolate the SDs from the masses, crushing their organisations at the same time.

Zubatov's programme struck a sympathetic chord among the Separate Corps of Gendarmes' most enlightened officers, who responded to Zubatov's claim that 'all the oppressed and insulted will find in the Okhrana Department paternal attention, advice, support, and help in word and in deed'.[55] Zubatov's words appealed to the gendarmes traditional hostility toward capitalism and several chiefs of Gendarme Directorates threw themselves enthusiastically behind the labour organisation experiment by vociferously supporting workers in their disputes with their employers. One of Zubatov's most ardent supporters, Colonel N.V. Vasil′ev, chief of the Minsk Gendarme Directorate, took it upon himself to act as an advisor to the local proletariat. He suggested that those workers dissatisfied with their working conditions should form a representative committee to present their grievances to him. He listened to their complaints and offered them the following advice:

> Gentlemen... You are gathered to discuss your needs. You are employees. You must defend your rights, but to take each [case] separately will not turn out well. You must join together..., and then your employers will take your demands into account. I am ready to help you. I am a representative of tsarist authority and therefore nothing is as dear [to me] as the happiness of the working class. But you will be sorry if you take it into your heads to oppose the state order. Then you can expect no help. I will be implacable.[56]

Vasil′ev supported his speeches with tangible evidence of the government's goodwill. In May 1901 as the strike of the Minsk metal workers threatened to get out of hand, Vasil′ev intervened, and his no-nonsense arbitration won the worker's the legal twelve-hour workday rather than their accustomed fourteen. His stand on behalf of the metal workers encouraged artisans in other professions to seek his intercession on their behalf. Colonel Vasil′ev's intervention in labour relations went beyond the enforcement of the law. At times he functioned as the workers' advocate, presenting their demands to the employers and extracting concessions from the bosses under duress. Vasil′ev's tactics weakened the influence of the *Bund* in Minsk and were an outstanding example of Zubatov's labour programme in action.[57] Zubatov's own confidence in his strategy was undoubtedly buoyed by his successful experience in Moscow and the results achieved by sympathetic gendarme officers like Vasil′ev.

In his naive enthusiasm for his police sponsored labour organisations Zubatov remained unaware that he, his ideas and operations were also pawns in Plehve's rivalry with Witte and served his minister's dreams of self-aggrandisement. Plehve, above all, evaluated every one of his programmes for its capacity to improve his position within the government; those that didn't were abandoned and Zubatov's experiment contained a serious flaw that would cause Plehve to become bitterly disenchanted with it. The police chief's philosophy was infused with the belief that , 'workers are not capable of being independent; they immediately fall under alien influences',[58] which led him to create an atmosphere of encouragement for the working class in south Russia who consequently came to believe that the government supported their demands and actions for a better life.[59] This situation would lead to his undoing.

Not all of Russia's gendarme officers were in favour of Zubatov's labour policy. General Novitskii, chief of the powerful Kiev Gendarme Directorate refused to participate in the experiment. Novitskii, despite his reputation as an old-time gendarme officer, foreshadowed the long term benefits Zubatov's labour organisation would have on the spread of the revolutionary movement amongst the workers.[60] Plehve and Lopukhin were committed to Zubatov's plan, neither perceiving the danger envisioned by Novitskii. Nevertheless, Novitskii began to arrest members of Zubatov's Jewish Independent Labour Party, declaring that there was little difference in purpose between the Independents and the revolutionary parties. Lopukhin responded to Novitskii's action by notifying the general that the Independents worked with the full knowledge and approval of Fontanka and that their goals were completely in line with government policy.[61]

It was not long, however, before Novitskii's arguments against Zubatov's labour organisations began to ring true. Lopukhin started to receive reports from the field describing the Independents' apparent role in recent labour unrest in south Russia. In April 1903, he invited some of the party's leaders to St Petersburg to warn them that further breaches of the law would not be tolerated.[62] Plehve remained unconcerned. The countryside appeared calm, and Zubatov seemingly controlled the labour movement.[63] This was anything but the case. In early July a strike erupted in Odessa and it spread like a wildfire across southern Russia. Strikes were reported in Odessa, Kiev, Nikolaev, Baku, Tiflis, Elizavetgrad, Batum, Ekaterinoslav, Kerch and several smaller cities. The labour question, which Plehve had believed to be of relatively little importance, now seized centre stage. As the strike movement spread, information suggesting possible causes for the monumental size of the strikes flowed into St Petersburg from a variety of sources. Lopukhin, as Fontanka's director, received his reports from Colonel Vasil´ev and these moderate descriptions of the workers' protests, combined with Lopukhin's rather liberal world-view, encouraged him to call for concessions to the strikers as the most sensible means of defusing the unrest.[64] He wrote to Lt General D.G. Arsen´ev, the Odessa city governor, suggesting a policy of appeasement.[65] Lopukhin's advice, however, was unlikely to have any effect on Arsen´ev, who at the same time was dispatching reports to Plehve emphasising the likelihood of violence between the strikers and the authorities. Arsen´ev's reports convinced Plehve that the strikers were using force to compel an alteration in their working conditions, information which infuriated the minister. Worse, these strikes embarrassed him before the tsar and supplied Witte with considerable ammunition in the two men's competition for power. Given these conditions, Plehve could adopt only one course of action. He ordered that resolute measures be taken against the strikers.[66] It was an angry and shaken minister of internal affairs who wrote to the Odessa authorities that 'we must show concern not about the workers but for the maintenance of order.... I approve in advance all drastic measures'.[67] General Arsen´ev obeyed Plehve's orders.

The strike and the government's response to it confused and enraged Zubatov. Upon learning of the Odessa strike he reportedly exclaimed, 'kill them all [the workers], the scoundrels!'[68] On discovering that Plehve had decided to use force to put down the strikes, however, he became equally furious with his minister, rashly declaring that 'the sooner he [Plehve] would leave or be dismissed the better it would be for the tsar and for Russia...'.[69] The parting of the ways between minister and political police chief had come. Zubatov plotted openly with Witte and Prince Meshcherskii for Plehve's removal in the vain hope that the then all powerful and grateful minister of finance would support his labour programme.[70] Such was the political naiveté of Zubatov that he believed Witte would suddenly support a policy to which he had been opposed for almost a decade.

Meanwhile, Lopukhin responded to the plight of his friend by visiting Odessa, Kiev and Nikolaev to investigate the economic conditions of the workers in these cities and evaluate the role subversive parties played in stirring up worker discontent. Lopukhin reported that the blame for these events did not lay with Zubatov's 'Independents', and that the police chief's organisation acted as a brake on revolutionary agitation by making the government's point of view known to the workers. Propaganda aside, working conditions in the strikers' trades and the intransigent attitude of the employers towards improving those conditions gave the labourers 'some justification to strike'. And, he noted, irrespective of any role the 'independents' might have played in instigating the Odessa strike, 'a strike, would have arisen sooner or later', in any case.[71]

Lopukhin's report could not save Zubatov. On 19 August the chief of the Special Section confronted his minister at Plehve's summer residence on Aptekarsk Island. During the heated conversation between the two men Zubatov defended his labour policy as best he could. Plehve abruptly ended the interview by firing Zubatov on the spot and ordering his departure from St Petersburg forthwith. The available evidence indicates that Plehve staged his performance for Zubatov after he learned of the police chief's negotiations with Witte and Meshcherskii. Zubatov's duplicity could not go unpunished and the Odessa strike may have served Plehve as a convenient excuse to rid himself of this disloyal subordinate, with a minimum of embarrassment.[72]

Zubatov's career, his relationship with Plehve and the probable reasons for his dismissal, tell a sad tale about the all-pervasive power of Russian political culture in the tsarist government's decision-making process. To Zubatov, a single-minded optimist, the solution to the government's paralysis over the issue of regulating industrial worker–management relations was to create a police-sponsored trade union movement.[73] However, the extra-legal nature of the Zubatov unions removed them from the mainstream of Russian political, economic and social institutions. Therefore, in both political and institutional terms his police union movement was nothing more than an elaborate laboratory experiment conducted under highly controlled conditions. As long as the hothouse atmosphere of a laboratory was preserved the experiment seemed to have a reasonable chance of success. In Moscow, where these laboratory conditions were enhanced by a depression between 1899 and 1902 that encouraged workers to seek relief against obdurate factory owners from any available source, including the police, and where many workers were still little more than peasants incapable of absorbing SD propaganda, the movement proved to be an outstanding success.[74] When some of the ingredients were missing, especially Zubatov's energy and the complete cooperation of the local authorities, the experiment did poorly.[75]

In addition, Zubatov's insights into the *mentalités* of Russia's revolutionaries and her workers unfortunately did not extend to the thinking of his superiors, nor to the machinations of bureaucratic politics. Though Zubatov failed to recognise it, the support for his strategy was founded in traditional bureaucratic practices and outlook and relied upon a smooth-functioning patronage–clientele network, a basic ingredient of bureaucratic politics. Zubatov had acquired the friendship of D.F. Trepov, who as *oberpolitsmeistr* of Moscow used his influence with Grand Duke Sergei Aleksandrovich to convince him of the value of Zubatov's labour programme, as we have seen. Later on the patronage of the Grand Duke waned, but by then Zubatov had acquired the support of Plehve which was buttressed in turn by the appointment of his old friend A.A. Lopukhin as Fontanka's director. Like many of his colleagues within the political police, Zubatov's successful career was built as much by playing the game of leapfrog with patrons, moving from one powerful friend to another while maintaining equilibrium, as it was by his undeniable talent. In Zubatov's case, however, he played this game awkwardly, alienating first the Grand Duke Sergei and then Plehve, his fatal error being his attempt to switch to Witte's camp. When Zubatov crossed over to Witte's camp in July 1903, he did so unthinkingly, in a moment of self-righteous indignation. Zubatov's betrayal of Plehve was almost public knowledge and although there are several versions of Zubatov's involvement with Witte in a plot against Plehve, one thing is clear: the police chief talked about it to too many people.[76] The chief of the Special Section stood alone. Plehve was far too powerful to be challenged over Zubatov's future, a future made considerably less rosy, at any rate, by the strikes in south Russia. No senior official raised a hand to save Zubatov, who was officially dismissed for behaviour detrimental to the well-being of the autocracy and for plotting to have Plehve removed from his post as minister of internal affairs.[77] Zubatov believed that his fanatic commitment to the autocracy and the inestimable value to the regime of his labour organisations automatically safeguarded his position. He never realised that his career actually hung by a thread.[78]

Zubatov's dismissal harmed Tsardom's prospects for the future. As far as Zubatov's labour experiment was concerned, Plehve managed to destroy the laboratory and to remove the experiment's guiding light, so to speak, without terminating the experiment itself. Government-sponsored labour organisations lingered on within a political framework that forced these organisations to pursue a course of action, as we shall discover in Chapter 8, that could only represent a risk to state security of considerable proportions.[79]

Plehve's response to the strikes in south Russia established the limits beyond which political police intervention in Russian life could not go. Painfully, Zubatov discovered that a political police agency's goals are bound by the values and practices of the political system it protects. In the case of Tsarist Russia this meant that Zubatov's plan for instituting a policy of mass-control based on devotion to the monarchical principal could not be realised. The history of labour management–state relations of which Zubatov's police labour organisations were a part, shows us why this was so. The battle between the Ministry of Finance and the MVD and between Witte and Plehve in particular reinforces the view that Tsardom was unable to formulate its policies in clear theoretical terms: an essential ingredient in the development of a modern police state.[80] The tsarist political system encouraged ministers to compete with each other for the tsar's ear and his approval. Each knew that the slightest sign of disapproval by the monarch was often enough to sidetrack, sometimes permanently derail, a valued ministerial project. The minister who managed to attain the role of principal adviser to the tsar, therefore, held tremendous power in his hands. Even so, this position did not guarantee that such a minister would be able to secure his policies in the face of the tsar's opposition. As Plehve's career amply confirms, in order to maintain royal patronage, policies and programmes often had to be sacrificed. Under the monarchical principle, therefore, the development of policies and their defence often depended upon the personal ambitions of the minister and the whim of the tsar rather than the long-range needs of the state. As a result, the ethos of the monarchical principle which Zubatov considered the essential ingredient in his programme for social control was unsuited for the task since it became nothing more than a symbol for inertia.

****

Even in their halcyon days in Moscow and Odessa Zubatov's police-supported trade union organisations were not intended to replace the use of repression as a method of social and political control in the MVD's arsenal. Lopukhin, Zubatov and Plehve (at least at first) believed, however, that *only* persons who represented a clear and present danger to the stability of the regime should be arrested; this, Zubatov made clear was 'the duty of the state police'.[81] In order to achieve this goal Lopukin and Zubatov, in particular, required the cooperation and restraint of their subordinates throughout the empire. The question was: could Tsardom's political policemen alter their traditional behaviour at a time when the MVD was embarking upon the largest campaign against subversion yet seen?

The Special Section, which had always operated on a war footing,[82] began to hum with even greater activity than usual as Plehve undertook to thoroughly prepare himself for the MVD's confrontation with Russia's subversives. Within a month of his appointment Plehve had gathered every piece of intelligence, all the statistics, graphs and descriptive charts he could find on subversive organisations.[83] These documents painted a worrying picture. Reports received from eighteen chiefs of provincial Gendarme Directorates, for instance, emphasised their disquiet over what they perceived as growing dissident activity in their regions.[84] Socialist-revolutionary and social-democratic propaganda spread steadily in 1901 and 1902 not only among the peasants and workers, but among students and soldiers as well. In response Fontanka announced that an 'intensive development of the Russian revolutionary and opposition movements' was taking place.[85] Clearly, there was no time to lose.

On 1 October 1902 Plehve launched his assault against Tsardom's enemies, using the data he had collated to carry out a stunning series of arrests. While these arrests cut across each of the revolutionary and opposition groups,[86] the SRs and their peasant allies became the Special Section's principal targets. In particular, Fontanka feared the 'classlessness' (*bezsoslovnyi*) of the SRs who, 'invited to its ranks all classes of the population more simply and clearly than did the social democrats...'.[87] Fontanka worried that this broad-based, terrorist oriented party would be particularly attractive to the ordinary Russian because, 'there exists within [every Russian] man a belief in the positive creative role of terror. For by such extreme measures they think it is possible to curtail the authority of the government'.[88]

Fontanka's concern that successful terrorist actions would inevitably draw thousands of young Russians to the SR Party, combined with Plehve's justified fear about his own safety (as we saw earlier in Chapter 6) induced the minister to declare the destruction of the SR's terrorist arm, its Battle Organisation (BO), to be his first priority. Plehve made the arrest of G.A. Gershuni, the leader of the BO, a test of Zubatov's skill and an affirmation that he had chosen the best man for the job as chief of his political police. Zubatov found this to be a slow and frustrating task. He knew, however, that Evno Azef, one of the Special Section's top *sotrudniki* had infiltrated the BO. With Azef's help the political police had already forced the BO to abandon plans to assassinate both Plehve and Zubatov and to short-circuit other SR ventures as well. Zubatov placed his complete confidence in Azef's information in his campaign to track down Gershuni, but this was a mistake. Azef's instinct for survival and his primitive cunning made him a master of deceit which he used against friend and foe alike and since he relied on Gershuni, who was his strongest supporter within SR Party ranks,[89] Azef could not possibly divulge Gershuni's leading role within the BO to Zubatov. Instead, in his reports to the Special Section Azef identified P.P. Kraft and M.M. Mel′nikov as the coordinators of the BO's actions, contending that Gershuni played only a secondary role.[90] By the winter of 1903 both Lopukhin and Zubatov began to doubt the accuracy of Azef's reports and the confessions of two recently arrested SR terrorists convinced the police chiefs that it was Gershuni not Mel′nikov and Kraft who led the BO. Plehve flew into a rage when he learned that the Special Section had been duped. He taunted Lopukhin and Zubatov by placing a framed picture of Gershuni on his desk and each time he met with either of his police chiefs he pointed to the photograph and enquired about the terrorist's health.[91] Nicholas II supported his minister's sense of urgency by promising a reward for Gershuni's arrest.[92]

On 6 May Gershuni murdered Ufa Governor Bogdanovich. From then on it seemed as if the Special Section devoted its full attention to the pursuit of the elusive Gershuni until on the evening of 18 May he was captured in Kiev by Captain Spiridovich, chief of the local OO and one of Zubatov's most able officers.[93]

Spiridovich bathed in fulsome praise as congratulatory letters and telegrams poured into his office from colleagues and superiors. The Corps of Gendarmes promoted Spiridovich to Lt Colonel and he never looked back. Mednikov in his typical prosaic style admonished his friend, 'do not yawn at the reward, for they want to pay you twenty thousand .... It is necessary to strike while the iron is hot ....'[94] And the iron was indeed hot. The SR's promotion of Azef as Gershuni's replacement as chief of the BO gave a particularly sweet flavour to Plehve's victory. By mid-1903 the Special Section had demolished the BO, leaving it with only three experienced members: Azef, Dora Brilliant and Boris Savinkov.[95] Plehve believed that for the second time in his career he had defeated the terrorists and he thought himself relatively safe from assassination.[96]

The destruction of the BO was only one of the tasks Plehve assigned to his political police. The Kharkov and Poltava uprisings also focused Plehve's attention on those revolutionaries who subverted the peasants' loyalty to the regime.[97] The peasant *jacquerie* in these provinces was ignited by both economic and political causes. While recently there has been some uncertainty expressed concerning the extent of the agrarian crisis existing in Russia at the end of the nineteenth century,[98] there is no doubt that the vast majority of contemporaries, the political police among them, believed that such a crisis existed. By the spring of 1902 peasant food supply had dwindled and in a desperation fuelled by rumours that the tsar had authorised their seizure of grain, the peasants took matters into their own hands, with approximately five thousand peasants participating in riots which ravaged twenty-six estates in Kharkov and seventy-nine in Poltava. In both provinces the governors employed troops to quell the riots; after its savage repression of the disturbances, the government summoned a thousand peasants to trial.[99]

Though economic hardship had been the principal cause of the Poltava and Kharkov risings, it was not the only cause. By the early twentieth century the peasants' lives and consequently their outlook was beginning to change. The agrarian policies of Alexander III, especially the creation of the *zemskii nachal'niki* (land captains), caused the peasants to despise the local authorities and landlords more than ever before. A decline in religious fervour reduced the Orthodox church's hold on them as well. Growing literacy among the peasantry, combined with the urban experiences of those who worked in factories to supplement their incomes, exposed them to a totally new environment: the world of ideas. These changes promoted the development of a rural intelligentsia who included among their membership teachers, *fel'dshery* (doctors' assistants) and other professional and semi-professional people who, although still free agents, felt comfortable with the SR's arguments. The rural intelligentsia worked assiduously in the villages in the years before the Poltava and Kharkov risings. Their efforts, largely uncoordinated but attuned to the needs of the peasantry and featuring the messages of social and agrarian reform, made a notable impact on the peasants' psyche.[100] All of these factors gave impetus to the unrest in the black-earth provinces in 1902

While A.I. Spiridovich, the former chief of the Kiev OO, attributed the anarchy in the countryside primarily to the alliance between the rural intelligentsia and the SR party,[101] Lopukhin's analysis of the crisis placed Spiridovich's argument within a broader, more sophisticated perspective. Lopukhin blamed the rural disturbances primarily on economic conditions and on the ineptitude of the local administration to ferret out the simmering unrest. Lopukhin also noted the widespread use of revolutionary propaganda which the SRs employed so effectively, taking advantage of the popular heroism of their terrorists, and giving the SR party a romantic hue resulting in a surge of membership.[102]

The Special Section unleashed its forces against the SRs and their rural intelligentsia allies. The campaign began with the disruption of the contraband in smuggled literature and extended into intensive searches for typographies and stores of pamphlets and other propaganda, no easy task in south Russia where illegal meetings were often held in the open air in the countryside and in Kiev on boats in the Dnieper River, which made police surveillance difficult. The fact that so many cities in southern Russia had large Jewish quarters made the Special Section's task that much harder. The Jewish quarter, generally, provided lecture halls and conspiratorial apartments for revolutionaries that guaranteed their safety.[103] In the long run though, the protection of the Jewish quarter where everyone knew everyone else, where alert sentries could spot *filery* at a glance, was not enough to protect the revolutionaries from the nationwide onslaught of the political police who achieved one success after another, the impact of raids seriously crippling and demoralising the SRs.[104]

In 1903 more arrests of SRs continued in Kiev, Odessa, Petrograd, Kozlov, Ekaterinoslav, Kursk, Saratov, Moscow and elsewhere. These arrests and seizures of typographies and propaganda, along with the discovery of conspiratorial apartments and secret addresses used for mail drops and serving as the domestic groups' links with the party leadership living abroad, wreaked havoc on the SRs. The police action drove many SR groups into inactivity and made others extremely cautious.[105]

****

Raids on the SRs, and on other groups as well, certainly obtained the immediate benefits Plehve desired, though their lasting effects were almost entirely negative. The widespread harassment of the populace at large, an inherent by-product of the Special Section's campaign, caused the spread of dissent rather than its subsidence and this, in turn, further increased the pressure on the forces of order who, succumbing to the deeply ingrained habit of preserving order at all costs, found it impossible to follow Zubatov's standing order to avoid mass arrests.[106] In making arrests Zubatov and Lopukhin had expected the political police to surgically remove the dedicated revolutionaries from the main body of society with a scalpel. Instead, the OOs and Gendarme Directorates proceeded to use an axe.

Lopukhin recognised that the brutish manner employed by the political police enraged the populace and contributed to the unravelling of the fabric of society.[107] In a lengthy circular dispatched to his political police agencies he pleaded with them to modify their ways. He explained that the character and size of the revolutionary movements were changing. Growing numbers of people were enlisting in revolutionary circles and although the majority of these people did not present any danger to the regime they were coming under the scrutiny of the political police. The habit of indiscriminate searches and arrests drained the Special Section and procurators' offices of their resources, while the real activists escaped detection. Ironically, Lopukhin warned, many of those innocent or trivial offenders who were incarcerated in prison for long periods of time awaiting the resolution of their cases became so embittered by the experience that it transformed them into hardcore revolutionaries. In order to bring this spiral of violence and reprisal to an end, Lopukhin ordered his political police to use their common sense and practice self-restraint in making these arrests.[108]

Lopukhin's exhortations made little headway against the stubbornness of his police who themselves were confused by the chaotic conglomeration of criminal statutes and administrative edicts. With the proliferation of repressive laws[109] the boundaries of legislation became less and less clear: the muddle being made worse by the application of the archaic Criminal Code of 1845 to twentieth century requirements. The political police circumvented this problem by resorting to administrative justice, which they had come to see as having no boundaries at all. V.M. Gessen wrote that one of the major reasons for the persistent application of administrative justice was the overall incompetence of the police.[110] While this is certainly true, a significant source of that incompetence must be blamed upon the clumsiness of the law; a dilemma that bedevilled every commission that attempted to revise Tsardom's laws on internal security.[111]

Under the combination of these conditions, lawlessness and mass arrests abounded during Plehve's years as minister of internal affair, as Table 7.1 shows. During Plehve's first two years as minister of internal affairs the number of state criminal cases recorded by the Ministry of Justice expanded four-fold and there were six times as many political cases treated administratively by the Ministry in 1903 as there were in 1901. What did this intensive and arbitrary campaign of repression accomplish? According to Spiridovich not very much at all. Despite the pressure placed upon the revolutionary groups in 1902 and 1903, throwing them into confusion, new groups proliferated, with the dissident movement continuing to spread among the *intelligentsia*.[112] To make matters worse, disgust

Table 7.1 Number of State Criminal Cases (excluding those under military justice) Compiled by the Ministry of Justice, 1901–1903[a]

Year	*No. of Formal Cases brought before the M.J.*	*No. of persons included in these cases*	*No. of cases resolved by Imperial Command*	*No. of persons included in these cases*
1901	520	1784	250	1238
1902	1053	3744	347	1678
1903	1988	5590	1522	6405

Source: L. Slukhotskii, 'Ocherk deiatel'nosti ministerstva iustitsii po bor'be s politicheskimi prestupleniiami', *Istoriko-Revoliutsionnyi Sbornik*, vol. 3. Extract from the table on p. 277.

[a] Data for 1904 is unavailable.

with the regime's behaviour debased the value society placed upon the law as a guardian of justice. In Russia, where the concept of an organic body of law did not thrive in the absence of the veneration accorded to judicial authority in the West, educated people began to see the law as nothing more than an instrument of repression necessary to prop up the existing order.[113] This sense of collusion between the forces of order and the law was reinforced by the recognition that there existed an intimate relationship between the MVD and the Ministry of Justice in the investigation and prosecution of state crimes.[114]

In order to overcome some of these problems described above the government had been working on a new criminal code since the late 1890s. Finally, a revised criminal code was approved by Nicholas II on 22 March 1903. This code was devised to transfer the burden of political cases away from administrative justice by processing them through the courts. The revised code, however, like its predecessor again emphasised the preservation of law and order rather than civil rights.[115] The government reasoned that the maximum punishments that could be imposed under administrative justice were far too mild and unwieldy to deal effectively with the rapidly growing opposition to the government and that by returning the political cases to the courts they would be processed more rapidly and the convicted condemned to more severe punishment than under administrative justice.

The new chapters within the Criminal Code of 1903 dealing with state crimes broadened the government's description of what constituted a political offence. As a result, the Criminal Code of 1903 built upon the foundations of its predecessor in moving Tsardom a little closer to the realisation of a modern police state.[116]

On 7 June 1904, the State Council ordered that the collaboration between the MVD and the Ministry of Justice over the adjudication of administrative justice be brought to an end. From that point onward the MVD alone would have the entire responsibility for administrative justice.[117] The law of 7 June 1904, when combined with the provisions for state crime in the criminal code reform of 1903, institutionalised the extra-legal procedures of administrative justice within a systematic judicial framework in order to legitimise and give official permanence to Tsardom's methods for repressing dissent. The Russian government had promulgated a legal fiction, a clever device that masked the continuing perversion of justice that so humiliated and angered Russian society. Fictions of this sort are an essential part of a successful police state's arsenal, for they allow the government to piously proclaim that the political police system is operating within the law and for the good of society, thereby acquiring the acquiescence, even the support of the majority of the population. In Russia, however, where the law and order bureaucracy enforced the traditional practice of unquestioning obedience to the autocracy, Tsardom was prevented from fulfilling its desire to reinforce its legitimacy and respectability: an achievement which would have had long-term political benefits for the regime.[118] Instead, as Lopukhin wrote at the end of 1904, 'the revolutionary movement grew and grew ... [becoming] wider and deeper'.[119]

****

Zubatov's and Plehve's search for solutions to Russia's political problems had left the first man embittered and the second deeply distressed and confused. In explaining why he refused the invitation of Prince Sviatopolk-Mirskii – Plehve's successor – to return to political police service, Zubatov bitterly remarked, 'if I returned to the business, I would again concentrate on repression and this can satisfy me still less than before, for the essence of the matter is not found in it. Plehve rendered me a service by flinging me out'.[120] By mid-1904 Plehve too realised that 'the essence of the matter' was not found in repression, though he was unsure where it could be discovered. In a despondent mood in July 1904, the last month of his life, Plehve despairingly told the new Minister of Finance V.N. Kokovtsov, 'you do not know much, nor do I, perhaps, of what is going on around us'.[121]

The reaction to Plehve's assassination by the Russian people illustrates the contempt and loathing felt for him and his policy of repression. Plehve succumbed to the wiles of his own agent, Evno Azef who as a Jew, wished to avenge the slaughter of his co-religionists during the Kishinev Pogrom for which he held Plehve responsible.[122] On 22 July 1904 the minister of internal affairs set out in his carriage for his daily appointment with Nicholas II. As the carriage trundled along the Izmailovskii Prospekt it slowed down in front of Egor Sazonov one of the terrorists. As Sazonov approached the carriage, Plehve caught sight of him and shrank away from the assassin, but there was no place for him to go. Sazonov threw his bomb, killing Plehve instantly.[123]

In the aftermath of Plehve's murder the British journalist E.J. Dillon wrote:

> Plehve's end was received with semi-public rejoicings. I met nobody who regretted his assassination or condemned the author. This attitude towards crime, although by no means new, struck me as one of the most sinister features of the situation.[124]

Sazonov's father, an ordinary peasant travelling by train from his home in Ufa Province to be with his imprisoned, seriously wounded son encountered a similar situation, when he was recognised by a fellow passenger. Soon, the entire train learned that Egor Sazonov's father was on board. The shamefaced elder Sazonov was stunned as people approached him to shake his hand merely because he was the father of Plehve's assassin. In the buffet an officer drank to his health.[125] The regime was rapidly losing control over its people and something had to be done about it.

Part IV
Revolution, Counter-Revolution and Collapse: The Tsarist Political Police and Russian Society, 1904–1917

8 P.D. Sviatopolk-Mirskii and A.A. Lopukhin: The Political Police and Mirskii's 'Spring'

Plehve's assassination created serious problems for Lopukhin. His failure to protect Plehve had seriously damaged his reputation; furthermore, once Lopukhin had accepted the job as Plehve's police chief he implicitly joined his ministers' patronage–clientele network and this automatically made him some very powerful enemies. With the disintegration of Plehve's network Lopukhin became vulnerable to their machinations and unless he could find another patron to protect him from them, and from the charge of ineptitude in the handling of Plehve's security, his career would probably be at an end. Lopukhin's immediate concern, however, was his obligation to discover the causes in the breakdown of security which led to Plehve's assassination. Lopukhin did not embark on an official investigation into the role of the political police in the Plehve assassination, launching instead an informal enquiry into the affair, questioning L.A. Rataev, the chief of the Foreign Agentura and Azef's immediate superior, about how such a plot could go undiscovered. Although Rataev looked into the matter and reported to Lopukhin that he did not find any evidence of Azef's involvement in Plehve's death,[1] Lopukhin was not satisfied with Rataev's cursory investigation and he turned the enquiry over to E.P. Mednikov. Mednikov recalled Rataev to St Petersburg for further questioning. Mednikov, like Lopukhin, was dissatisfied with Rataev's explanations. 'Well if Raskin [one of Azef's *klichki*] knows nothing ... [about the plot to kill Plehve]', exclaimed Mednikov, 'it signifies a bad business'.[2] Nevertheless, Mednikov did nothing more than chastise Rataev for failing to elicit the proper information from Azef,[3] and he was allowed to return to his post as if nothing had happened. In September, Lopukhin received Rataev's reports on the Paris Conference of revolutionary and opposition groups convened to discuss the unification of their forces. The raw intelligence on this important gathering was supplied by Azef. This confirmed Lopukhin's suspicions about his principal *sotrudnik.* 'This circumstance,' Lopukhin remembered, 'indicated to me that Azef undoubtedly belonged to the central committee of the [SR] party' where, according to Lopukhin's reasoning, he must have learned the details of the plot to kill Plehve. Azef had obviously lied to Rataev about his role in the revolutionary movement and perhaps worse. Lopukhin, now deeply suspicious of Azef, decided to dismiss him from the service; however, nothing came of his intention.[4]

Mikhail Bakai, a one-time political police *chinovnik* who opted for the revolutionary cause, claimed that Azef was just too valuable to discredit since he played a central role in SR affairs, particularly those pertaining to the BO. Bakai's reasoning here is less likely than his second explanation for Fontanka's failure to act against Azef: that prominent police officials M.I. Trusevich, P.I. Rachkovskii and A.G. Gerasimov knew of Azef's provocation, but in order to preserve calm in the highest circles they chose not to pursue the matter.[5] Public opinion frightened the Special Section and Lopukhin, though he himself had repeatedly expressed the need for openness in police work, could not allow any of Fontanka's suspicions to leak out if he hoped to protect his career. These factors, combined with the general antipathy felt toward Plehve by Zubatov's Special Section colleagues and friends and the deep hatred for the assassinated minister of internal affairs felt by most Russians, probably contributed to the relative ease with which Fontanka covered up the entire mess. Lopukhin, therefore, escaped the public humiliation, certain dismissal and official disgrace that would have befallen him if the story of Plehve's assassination had become known. Although he survived this crisis, doubts about Lopukhin's future remained as he awaited the tsar's decision on Plehve's replacement.

One thing had become clear to the few remaining liberal bureaucrats such as Lopukhin and to Russian society as a whole. Bureaucratic conservatism characterised by a pathological distrust of society and an ability to deal only with the most immediate, short term problems, had dominated the outlook of Russia's *sanovniki* since the 1870s.[6] While Lopukhin worked for Plehve, conducting his professional life under his minister's wing, he followed the time-worn Russian bureaucratic practice of pleasing one's superior by presenting a facade of solidarity with him. In spite of this behaviour, he never fully developed the sceptical, indifferent attitude and the inclination to compromise which Vladimir Gurko attributed to Russia's well-worn bureaucrats.[7] It was probably his integrity, as soiled as it was, that saved his career. Lopukhin was deeply disappointed by Plehve's failure to fulfil his promise to implement major reforms.[8] Privately, he wrote to S.N. Trubetskoi, a leading gentry liberal, about his pessimistic view of Tsardom's future under the present political system.[9] Publicly, his appeals to the political police on behalf of *zakonnost'*, his outspoken support for Zubatov after the Odessa strikes and his honest reporting of the causes of these strikes distanced him from Plehve's policies in the eyes of liberal society.[10] In retrospect, then, it is clear that even while Plehve's police chief, Lopukhin, had been harbouring and sporadically expressing views based on his belief that *obhchestvennoe dvizhenie* (the social movement) and *dvizhenie revoliutsionnoe* (the revolutionary movement) were fundamentally different: the latter must be destroyed, the former, however, must be encouraged to participate in Tsardom's political processes.[11] This point of view separated him from the vast majority of his colleagues within the law and order bureaucracy.

Lopukhin systematically presented his views in reports and pamphlets he wrote between 1903 and 1907. He consistently argued for political reform based primarily on Tsardom's response to society's needs through the legislative process, which he believed would help bridge the gap between Russian society and its government.[12] For Lopukhin the *zemstva* movement played a key role in reducing this gap. He felt so strongly about preserving the rights of the *zemstva*, that he courageously opposed Plehve's mistreatment of some of their liberal and outspoken members, though to no avail.[13] He argued that the elimination of the bureaucracy's rule over society would not lead to the anarchy predicted by the vast majority of Tsardom's bureaucrats, but rather to the foundations of democracy. He firmly believed that the best means of preventing political crime was the equitable application of the law, not arbitrary rule by bureaucratic edict.[14] The abuses, he argued, resulted from the absence of a proper codification of Russia's police regulations. Lopukhin suggested that only a new and carefully conceived police statute, precisely defining the duties and privileges of the police could remedy this anarchic situation.[15] Although Lopukhin abhorred extra-legal action of any sort, he was not naive. If Tsardom required a political police, and by the end of Plehve's tenure in office, no one wishing to preserve the monarchy could deny that it did, the police must appear as society's policemen, not the government's.[16]

Given these views, Lopukhin must have been overjoyed to learn that the tsar had appointed Prince P.D. Sviatopolk-Mirskii as Plehve's successor. Nicholas II had admired Plehve and as his replacement he wished to appoint someone of the same political mould. However, he was prevailed upon – perhaps by his mother – to appoint a different sort of man, one who displayed greater sympathy toward public initiative and less tolerance for arbitrary police behaviour.[17] In Mirskii, Lopukhin knew he had an ally. For the only time in the history of Imperial Russia, Tsardom could boast of liberal officials simultaneously occupying the post of minister of internal affairs and the directorship of the Department of Police. When Nicholas II offered Mirskii the MVD, Mirskii made it crystal clear to the tsar that he did not share the views of either Sipiagin or Plehve. He warned Nicholas II that if the political situation in Russia continued to deteriorate Russia would soon be divided between those under surveillance and those carrying it out 'and then what?' Mirskii believed that there must be widespread tolerance for local self-government and that only terrorists and regicides should be treated and punished as political criminals, and he insisted on giving increased rights to the press. Nicholas agreed with all of this, and Mirskii went on, telling the tsar that he called himself 'a *zemstvo* man' and that a *zemstvo* congress would be a goal of his administration.[18] The new appointee publicised his views in two announcements. In the first he declared that his policy would be based on religious tolerance and close collaboration with the *zemstva* and in his second statement, made during a speech to MVD department chiefs, the new minister declared that he placed his full confidence in society. Mirskii immediately, as confirmation of his sincerity, relaxed press censorship and restored full rights to many prominent members of the opposition.[19] These speeches and others like them caused widespread rejoicing.[20]

The question is, could a minister of internal affairs successfully divorce himself from the nasty business of political policing when his internal security agencies formed such a large and essential part of the institutions of law and order? Remember that the Special Section and its agencies and the Separate Corps of Gendarmes were key sources of information on political activism within Russia, supplying data required by the minister of internal affairs in his development of policies and strategies. This type of intelligence was especially valuable to a progressive, reforming minister who must carefully evaluate the effect of his policy of political liberalisation on the attitudes and ambitions of the populace at large. After all, it is a truism that the most dangerous period in the life of a traditional regime is when it undertakes major political and social reform.

Unfortunately, Mirskii's immediate actions as minister led to his isolation from this vitally important branch of his ministry. An early decision to co-opt Lopukhin as one of his principal political advisers on the proposed reforms distracted Lopukhin's attention away from the daily operations of Fontanka. Immediately after Mirskii's designation as minister of internal affairs, he invited Lopukhin to visit him in Vil′na where he still awaited confirmation of his appointment. Mirskii discussed his ideas for reform with the police chief, requesting his overview of the political situation. Lopukhin reported his pessimistic view: 'In essence', Lopukhin commented, 'the revolution is already beginning'. Nevertheless, Mirskii informed Lopukhin that he had decided to persist with his broadbased reforms which included the curtailment of the political police.[21]

Though warned by Lopukhin of impending trouble, Mirskii still wished as a step toward establishing a new image of the minister of internal affairs in the public eye to disassociate himself from the unsavoury internal security functions of his ministry. He isolated himself from Tsardom's police apparatus by asking Nicholas II to issue an Imperial Decree expanding the authority of the assistant minister of internal affairs, who commanded the Corps of Gendarmes, to encompass 'the general management of affairs for the prevention and combating of crime and for the preservation of general peace and order, and with the resolution of nearly all problems pertaining to the Department of Police which fell within the competence of the Minister of the Interior'.[22] Mirskii gave this job to General K.N. Rydzevskii, a man wholly unsuited for the task.[23] Lopukhin was horrified by the effect of this decree on the classification of his job as director of Fontanka. He considered himself a generalist, responsible for the overall administration of the Department of Police; these duties now were being given to a courtier, while he was expected to take charge of the overall operations of Russia's political police. In effect he had become Zubatov's replacement! Lopukhin confessed to his new minister that he was not the man for the job. He found the responsibility of holding the lives of the Imperial Family and other High Personages in his hands an overwhelming burden. He argued that such a responsibility must fall on the shoulders of an 'especially able' political police specialist. Lopukhin requested permission to retire from the post as director of the Department of Police. Mirskii reported this conversation to Nicholas II and they agreed to free him from the post as soon as they found a replacement – but no such search was undertaken during Mirskii's ministry. Lopukhin continually petitioned Mirskii for a change of post[24] while at the same time having as little to do with political police work as was possible for a man in his position. As a result, during Mirskii's five months in office the political police were without any significant leadership, causing a decline in morale and a decrease in the accuracy of intelligence that would soon have disastrous consequences for Tsardom.

These difficult circumstances were magnified by the strained relationships Mirskii and Lopukhin endured with the tsar and with their colleagues. Mirskii's and Lopukhin's opponents did not hide their distrust of them and their hostility to Mirskii's reforms.[25] The diary kept by Mirskii's wife and Lopukhin's memoirs also reveal that Mirskii never believed that he held Nicholas II's confidence.[26] Lopukhin also came under attack from conservative court circles, because they deemed that Fontanka had become soft and inactive under his guidance.[27]

****

It was now time to confront Plehve's terrible legacy. His assassination served as a catalyst releasing the tensions of Russian society. The widespread discontent manifested itself in a variety of ways. Incidents of factory unrest and the strike movement, though not as frightening as the year before, still featured in the dispatches that the OOs, gendarmes and procurators sent to St Petersburg.[28] The peasant movement, however, was a greater threat to Tsardom in the second half of 1904. The stunning success of Plehve's assassination made heroes of its perpetrators, winning recruits both for the SR Party and its BO.[29] The public admired the terrorists' courage and fell under the romantic spell which acompanied acts of violence perpetrated in the name of freedom. The SR party became synonymous with terrorism in both popular and police opinion. In the countryside SR propaganda and agitation made an impact on a peasantry suffering from growing economic deprivation and government neglect. Rural disturbances continued to increase in number and intensity. In many districts of Saratov, Tambov, Kherson, Penza and Kiev provinces the peasants became increasingly violent, setting fire to estates throughout the region.[30]

The Special Section's deepest fear was that the worker and peasant movements would unify with Russia's disgruntled liberal intelligentsia under a single revolutionary banner. The burgeoning Liberation Movement, the *zemstva* and the newly forming professional unions were seen as the focal point of any unified movement. By early Autumn 1904 the Liberation Movement appeared to be moving in that direction, with opposition and revolutionary groups holding a conference in Paris in order to coordinate the opposition to Tsardom. Eighteen organisations were invited to participate and even though ten declined the invitation (including the six SD parties) it was an impressive gathering. The Special Section received a full report on the conference from Evno Azef, who attended it as a member of the SR delegation. Azef reported that the conference decided upon two principles. First, the participants agreed that they were united in their desire to destroy the autocracy and would combine their efforts in order to hasten the fall of Tsardom. Second, they agreed that the new regime should be based on democratic principles. The delegates to the conference declared that, 'the Conference after ascertaining that all its participants are striving to establish a democratic regime in Russia, has agreed on the following formula accepted by all participating parties: that the popular representatives [of such a government] must be elected by universal suffrage'.[31]

The Special Section in its interpretation of Azef's reports left no doubt about what this conference meant to the future of the subversive movement in Russia. Spiridovich summed up the Special Section's opinion when he wrote that as a result of the Paris Conference the Union of Liberation, the leftwing *zemstva* men and the radical elements of the professions had united with the representatives of the revolutionary parties to develop a general programme for 'extinguishing the monarchical structure and replacing it with a free democratic regime'.[32]

Lopukhin read Azef's report and discussed the Special Section's analysis of the decisions drawn by the Paris Conference with Mirskii.[33] They decided to respond to them not by repression but through negotiations which had serious implications for the future of political police behaviour. Mirskii was playing a very dangerous game as he offered the olive branch to his wary and cynical adversaries. On the one hand he had to convince the opposition movement that his platform for political reform offered a viable alternative to the goals expressed at the Paris Conference; on the other hand he had to deal with Nicholas II, an inveterate reactionary who made even the mildest political concession only under extreme duress. To make matters more difficult for Mirskii, the leadership of the *zemstva* movement was falling into the hands of the fervent constitutionalists. Although the moderate-monarchist D.N. Shipov still led the movement, radicals such as I.I. Petrunkevich and N.N. L′vov began to supplant the monarchists among them, Shipov's influence becoming more nominal than real. The political police noted this fact;[34] none the less Mirskii persisted in the belief that the constitutionalists did not represent a danger to the monarchy[35] and decided to fulfil his promise made upon his appointment by allowing the *zemstva* conference to take place. Mirskii and Lopukhin permitted considerable latitude during the conference which convened on 6 November[36] and although the police apparently knew the location of the meetings, they did not interfere with them. Amazingly, telegrams from the provinces addressed only 'St Petersburg, Conference of *zemstva* activists' or to the '*Zemskii* Conference', many of which expressed constitutionalist sentiments, were duly delivered to the private residences serving as the conference's venues. The MVD even forwarded a telegram from political exiles in Archangelsk to the Conference.[37]

Enthusiasm for the conference and its outcomes was conveyed to Mirskii by Lopukhin's friend S.N. Trubetskoi, who presented a summary of the proceedings to the minister. Trubetskoi's report echoed Mirskii's own view on the deterioration of Russian political life and it concluded that, 'the government must advance and not fall behind society and actively organise Russia's political freedom on the basis of popular representation'.[38] Mirskii, energetically and courageously attempted to impress upon Nicholas II the urgent need for a new approach to society and to governing Russia generally. As early as 1 November he told the tsar that the critical situation in Russia demanded positive action and 'that 99% of thinking Russia wants' to participate in the political process. The tsar remained unmoved.[39] Again in mid-November, he implored the tsar to liberalise his views.[40] The expectation created by the decisions of the conference and Mirskii's positive response to them were ultimately, however, bound to come into conflict with the rigid stance of the tsar and that of the majority of his bureaucracy.[41]

Mirskii foolishly did not convey the content of his discussions with the tsar to Shipov. As a result, the new political atmosphere remained untrammelled by reality and it was in this circumstance that the famous banquet campaign began. The 'banquets' were a guise behind which serious political discussions took place, and demands for reform were made,[42] causing a sensation in Russia. None the less, Lopukhin's political police, bitterly following the will of their chief, remained passive, thereby allowing public opinion to become increasingly bold, expressing previously forbidden opinions with temerity. The buoyant atmosphere encouraged the Union of Liberation to embark upon the establishment of professional unions to serve as a political base for the constitutional movement. The moderate journal *Osvobozhdenie* was pushed aside as the mouthpiece of the Liberation Movement and D.N. Shipov and his moderate faction were overwhelmed by the support given to I.I. Petrunkevich and Prince L′vov and their radical constitutionalist following in the *zemstva* movement.[43] The political situation was getting out of hand.

On 16 November, Mirskii spent the entire evening meeting with Lopukhin and with S.E. Kryzhanovskii, a like-minded MVD functionary, to finalise a memorandum to the tsar which he hoped would serve as the basis for far-reaching political and social reform thereby defusing the crisis. Kryzhanovskii was the principal author of the memorandum, which he began writing on 4 November in line with detailed instructions supplied to him by Mirskii. Andrew Verner in a recent dissertation has thoroughly analysed this document.[44] The memorandum, which ran to 110 pages, embodied the ethos of Russia's liberal bureaucrats. Mirskii, Kryzhanovskii and Lopukhin argued that legality (*zakonnost′*) and autocracy (*samoderzhavie*) were compatible and that the union of *zakonnost′* with *samoderzhavie* was the product of the natural course of Russian history. The era of unbridled bureaucratic decision-making and arbitrary police repression was over. The emergence of public interest and public opinion were powerful forces which the government had to take into account. The memorandum noted that, 'the societal development of the country has outgrown the administrative forms and modes employed till now and society no longer submits to their influence to a sufficient degree'. Therefore, the 'time has come to change these methods and to adapt them to the changed conditions'.[45]

Mirskii, unlike his predecessor Plehve, believed that the vast majority of Russians wanted to preserve the structure and main principles of the autocracy. Within this framework these people wished to implant mechanisms that, as Andrew Verner states:

> Guarantee each person the right to develop his talents and personality, to observe the inviolability of the law, to eliminate administrative arbitrariness, and to allow the population to make its needs known to the tsar directly....[46]

Among the most significant of the reforms proposed by Mirskii were the restoration of the Senate as the supreme guardian of the law; altering the laws on censorship; a thoroughgoing investigation into the usage of the Exceptional Measures; and the necessity of placing popularly elected representatives within the State Council (one of Lopukhin's pet projects) in order to allow society direct access to the tsar without the interference of the bureaucracy. 'These measures', Mirskii affirmed, 'ensure more than the most decisive police measures, the internal tranquillity so necessary right now...'.[47] To A.A. Mosolov, the chief of the Imperial Chancery, Mirskii used different language when describing why he fought so vigorously for these reforms. 'These measures', he told Mosolov, 'will quiet public opinion and avert the introduction from below of more radical political institutions' which represented a greater danger to the monarchy than the political changes he was proposing. Mirskii added that these reforms had to be introduced by the throne before 15 December, when the *zemskii* associations were to meet.[48] Mirskii perhaps naively believed that his political programme would not infringe on the tsar's supreme authority, at least in the immediate future.[49]

Lopukhin advised Mirskii to present Nicholas II with a report surveying the deplorable political conditions within Russia in order to buttress his case for urgent political reform. Mirskii responded that his relationship with the tsar was so cool that such a report could only do their cause harm. After some thought, Lopukhin suggested a little ruse. He would write this report and present it to Mirskii in the course of his duty as director of Fontanka. Mirskii could then present the report to the tsar in the line of duty, as the latest information on the state of society. The fact that it arrived at about the same time as his memorandum on reform could be interpreted as mere coincidence.[50] Lopukhin did not mince his words in describing the volatility of the revolutionary situation, nor did he do so in his attacks on the exile system and the evils of censorship, both of which he suggested had to be eradicated at once. Mirskii presented his memorandum to Nicholas II on 24 November and Lopukhin's report followed almost two weeks later. The depth of Mirskii's desperation is recorded in his wife's diary. He told her that if nothing came of his initiative he would resign.

Nicholas II, with Mirskii's approval, appointed a special committee to study the proposals. The question of popular representation, as limited as it was, became the major bone of contention during the debate over Mirskii's proposals.[51] The tsar, in his usual style, vacillated over what course to follow. Finally, on 11 December, largely on the advice of Witte, Nicholas decided to delete this clause.[52] The next day the tsar promulgated the Decree which was perceived by Nicholas and his advisers as a major concession to public opinion and they were not prepared to retreat any further.[53] Moreover Nicholas II ordered the cessation of all illegal meetings (e.g. the 'banquets'). The shallowness of the reform offered by the Decree of 12 December stunned the Liberation Movement and infuriated Mirskii and for the second time (the first was on 21 November),[54] Mirskii offered Nicholas his resignation; this time the monarch did not protest. He only asked Mirskii to stay on perhaps for a month or so while he chose a replacement. Mirskii could not control his tongue. 'I hope to God, that I am mistaken', he told Nicholas, 'but I am convinced that within 6 months you will regret [your decision] to delete the point on the election [from the Decree]'.[55] Mirskii's comment was prophetic. The tsar's actions played right into the hands of the radical *zemstva* men, and the Union of Liberation, the very people Mirskii wished to disarm through his project. Lopukhin, who had been deeply involved in the negotiations with the moderate *zemstva* leadership,[56] was profoundly disappointed by the tsar's rejection of the clause on popular representation. He also realised that his frank criticism of the government's behaviour *vis-à-vis* society in his 6 December report had discredited him with the majority of his colleagues in the MVD, who at best wrote him off as someone whose career was coming to an end or at worst considered him to be in league with the revolutionaries. As for the tsar, Nicholas II's cursory perusal of the report meant that Lopukhin had lost the monarch's confidence as well.[57] His hopes for major political police reforms were also dashed. The feelings of both Mirskii and Lopukhin are best summed up by the dispirited minister of internal affairs when he told one of his aides, 'everything has failed. Let us build jails'.[58]

****

Mirskii's first four months in office had been an unmitigated disaster. He had bolstered the expectations of the Liberation Movement and had been unable to fulfil his promises. His false 'Spring' had shown the Union of Liberation, and the *zemstva* movement generally, that Plehve's administration was not an aberration, but actually mirrored Nicholas II's attitude toward society. Realising that only a considerable diminution of the autocrat's power and that of his bureaucracy could bring political and social justice to Russia, the Liberation Movement moved steadily to the left.

By the end of December the stage was set for the confrontation between state and society; a confrontation for which the Russian government was ill-prepared. Unwisely Nicholas permitted Mirskii, a lame duck minister of internal affairs who had lost his and society's confidence, and Lopukhin, a disgraced liberal police chief who for several months had tried to escape the job and who did not command the respect of his subordinates, to linger on as masters of Tsardom's internal security forces. Lopukhin's rule over the political police undermined its confidence and paralysed its operations.[59] Neither Mirskii nor Lopukhin had much use for the political police and while concentrating on their negotiations with the Liberation Movement and the tsar in late November and early December 1904, they had ignored its operations, which had become sloppy: A.V. Gerasimov, the chief of the Kharkov Gendarme Directorate, remembered that agents in the field were not informed of the MVD's strategy during Mirskii's ministership and were not asked their opinions about much of anything. 'We were doomed to remain almost silent witnesses to a tableau of universal disintegration', a disintegration which also enveloped the political police.[60]

Under these disintegrating conditions the forces of order actually supported the campaign of a man who would set revolutionary events in motion. This man was Father Grigorii Gapon and his vehicle for change was his Workers' Assembly (*Sobranie*) which was a legacy of Zubatov's experiments in social control. After Zubatov's dismissal, Gapon remembered the lessons his master had taught him and he decided to turn them to legitimate use.[61] He broke off his relationship with the police, then in February 1904, he successfully applied to Plehve for permission to establish his Workers' Assembly.

While the Zubatov and Gapon movements were historically connected, as Solomon Schwartz points out, they differed in several respects and these differences made the latter organisation palatable to the authorities.[62] The Gapon movement was quite small, centred around a few tea rooms located in Petersburg's factory districts. It preached traditional Russian values, avoiding the dangerous rhetoric of the Zubatov movement which had offered the illusory and, to the MVD, radical hope of a social monarchy. The political police kept an eye on the Workers' Assembly and was satisfied that it was a positive influence on the capital's workers.[63] The Special Section and the St Petersburg OO were so certain of the beneficial effect of Gapon's influence that they granted him a small sum of money to help him establish additional tea-rooms.[64]

In June 1904, Gapon attempted to spread his still insignificant influence beyond St Petersburg to other cities. His campaign amongst the workers of Moscow, his first stop, infuriated Grand Duke Sergei Alekandrovich, who wrote Plehve a long letter of complaint detailing Gapon's activities in Moscow. Plehve apologised to the Grand Duke and instructed General Fullon, the *gradonachal'nik* of St Petersburg to call on Gapon and warn him that if he continued to agitate among the workers he would lose his church posting and be subject to administrative exile. Plehve issued this order on 10 July, only one week before his assassination.[65]

Gapon continued on his travels unaware of the official reaction to his meddling among Moscow's workers. While his further endeavours to spread his influence beyond the capital were on the whole unsuccessful, he had considerable hope that he would be able to achieve some headway in south Russia. In his bid to establish branches of his assembly in Kharkov he planned to approach General Kleigels, governor general of Kiev. In order to smooth his way with Kleigels, Gapon visited Colonel Spiridovich, the chief of the Kiev OO, an old acquaintance whom he was certain would support his submission to Kleigels. In fact, after listening to Gapon, Spiridovich decided to oppose the priest's plan and told Kleigels so. He found Kleigels' assurance that Gapon's organisation would not be permitted to establish itself in Kharkov less than convincing. This was especially so since Gapon had told Spiridovich that his plan had the support of Lopukhin. The sceptical OO chief decided to meet with Lopukhin in Petersburg in order to confirm Gapon's assertion that he had the chief of Fontanka's approval. As Lopukhin listened to Spiridovich's report he became indignant, clearly the priest had lied. The chief of police asked his secretary to bring him Gapon's dossier from which he read about the Moscow incident and saw Plehve's instructions to Fullon. Although he had every reason to act against Gapon, Lopukhin praised Spiridovich for his diligence and then did nothing.[66]

Walter Sablinsky, the American historian of the Gapon movement, believes that Plehve's assassination made all the difference to the future of Gapon's Assembly. Sablinsky contends that in the weeks following Plehve's death the Assembly 'was eclipsed by long-range, complicated decisions on national policy .... The atmosphere of relative political freedom made it difficult if not impossible to take repressive measures against Gapon'.[67] Yet, while these factors were important, it is Lopukhin's attitude toward Gapon that is crucial. Lopukhin's liberalism dominated his very weak policeman's instincts and his sympathies, as we have seen, were with those who wished to improve the condition of life throughout Russia by non-violent means. Gapon's unprincipled behaviour was mitigated by his cause, of which Lopukhin's retired mentor, Sergei Zubatov, approved.[68] Still, given the evidence presented by Spiridovich, it is unforgivable that Lopukhin allowed Gapon to carry on his activities without close and constant police supervision. As Spiridovich wrote:

> By permitting Gapon to work widely throughout Petersburg, the authorities forgot that this was not a man who could be looked after by them, could be guided by them, [whose] movement could be held in one's hands, as was done by Zubatov.[69]

Instead of turning control of Gapon over to the Special Section, which would have been the proper course of action, Mirskii gave the job to General Fullon, a man totally naive in political police matters. Gapon convinced Fullon that neither he nor the workers belonging to his Assembly were revolutionaries. Fullon's conversations with Gapon seemed to confuse the general: 'I am a military man', he told Gapon, 'and I do not understand anything about politics. To me by what you have said, it seems that you are preparing a revolution. You say altogether something else. Who is right, I do not know. Swear to me on the sacred gospel, that you will not go against the Tsar – and I will trust you'.[70] This was a recipe for disaster.

As Mirskii and Lopukhin immersed themselves in their campaign for significant political reform Gapon faded from their view, a phenomenon aided by political police reports that continued to be full of praise for Gapon and his Assembly.[71] Without harassment Gapon's Assembly grew in strength throughout the autumn of 1904. Its branches flourished within the factory districts of the capital. Gapon's influence over the labouring populous of St Petersburg proved so magnetic that it drew off potential recruits from the SD movement as well. 'It is better to go to the Gapon organization', an SD weaver argued, 'because thousands of people go there, people believe in it and have hopes for it'.[72]

It was only a matter of time before Gapon would exercise the power given to him by massive worker support on their behalf. By the end of 1904 Gapon had established contact with representatives of the Union of Liberation and though the relationship between Gapon and the liberals was not a smooth one, liberal newspapers such as *Nasha Zhizn (Our Life)* which were distributed to the branches of the Assembly, gave the workers some insight into the generalised condition of discontent and excitement over Mirskii's policies within society at large.[73] The priest, despite his oath to Fullon, began to synthesise a mixture of monarchist, liberal and radical ideas into a plan for popular government, not through revolution, but rather by direct appeal to Nicholas II. The OO issued no forewarning of Gapon's latest plans, the reasons for this lapse were incompetence and its assumption about Gapon's official status: as V.I. Gurko observed, 'they considered Gapon their own agent and one who enjoyed the special confidence of the governor; consequently they did not supervise his activity. They trusted his reports of the events among the workers and were generally of the opinion that Gapon was carrying on his activities with the knowledge and approval of his superiors'.[74]

By the last days of December, Gapon's conception of his role in the St Petersburg labour movement and the temperament of his organisation had altered to the point where he decided to place his prestige and the power of his Assembly behind the striking workers of the Putilov works. Still Mirskii and Lopukhin remained unconcerned. However, within a few days, by early January 1905, the MVD and the *gradonachal'nik* had lost control of the political situation in Petersburg. The capital's *sanovniki*, sensing the impending crisis, were already in a panic.[75] The atmosphere was not improved any by the resignations of Grand Duke Sergei Aleksandrovich and of General Trepov who relinquished their posts in Moscow on 1 January 1905, in protest against Mirskii's policies.[76] Mirskii and Lopukhin, however, continued to be disconcertingly calm, accepting the reassuring reports of the St Petersburg OO about the peaceful demeanour of the workers and the loyalty of Gapon and his followers to the regime.[77] For his part, General Fullon defended his benevolent attitude toward Gapon as official policy.[78]

While the forces of order remained unmoved, the strike spread beyond the Putilov factory to encompass most of St Petersburg's working class. On

4 January Gapon received a telephone call from General Fullon, who appeared to be acting as an intermediary between Gapon and the Putilov factory management. The priest responded that a compromise no longer sufficed; that the entire working class of St Petersburg might go on strike, although he believed that he could control them. Gapon asked Fullon to trust him and to avoid using force. 'Perhaps the workers will want to submit a petition to the tsar', he told the *gradonachal'nik*, 'don't be alarmed; everything will be orderly and peaceful. The workers only want to be heard'. Finally, he extracted a promise from Fullon that neither he nor his assistants would be arrested. None the less, the next day the branches of the Assembly came under the intense scrutiny of the Petersburg OO for the first time.

Mirskii defended his attitude toward Gapon before Nicholas II, claiming that he was doing all that was possible within the limits of the law. Mirskii did not elaborate on the situation in the capital since to do so would have risked decisive action on the part of the tsar and this Mirskii apparently wished to avoid. He was playing a dangerous game, hoping to resolve the crisis by legal and peaceful means. Nicholas, however, was not concerned with legality; he ordered Mirskii to bring an end to the workers' meetings and public discussion about them.[79]

The next day Kokovtsov, the worried minister of finance, informed the tsar in detail about the deteriorating situation in the capital. He pointed out the harmful nature of the Gapon movement, the illegality of the strike and the ineptitude and culpability of the Ministry of Internal Affairs.[80] Kokovtsov's fears were justified. On that very day, 5 January, Gapon appeared before a huge meeting of workers and students where he openly discussed the possibility of submitting a petition to the tsar. Some of the more prudent workers suggested that a small deputation be chosen to present their grievances to Nicholas II. The majority, however, stirred by Gapon's speech shouted, 'we will all go [to the tsar] with the petition'. The rousing mood of the meeting and its desire to present the tsar with a petition *en masse*, was a clear warning sign to the government of impending confrontation. Unfortunately, the political police did not report it. For despite its orders to augment surveillance over the Gapon movement no political police agent attended this meeting.[81]

Two days later the strike expanded into the general work stoppage that Gapon had been agitating for. Since it was now an act of political protest the government had a legitimate excuse to employ punitive measures. The chief of staff of the St Petersburg Military District, General N.F. Meshetich, went to see General Fullon to report that the tsar had placed the capital under martial law and as a result of this decree, Prince Vasil'chikov, the commander of the Guards, was to assume responsibility for governing the city and for maintaining order. But, as we shall see, martial law was apparently never imposed and Mirskii continued to be responsible for the security of Petersburg.[82]

While the meeting between Meshetich and Fullon was taking place, Gapon was handing a copy of the petition he intended to present to the tsar to Minister of

Justice Murav′ev. As he perused the document Murav'ev exclaimed in amazement, 'but you wish to limit the autocracy!' Murav′ev passed a copy of the petition on to the ill-informed[83] Lopukhin who finally awakened to the crisis confronting Tsardom. A popular manifesto limiting the autocracy could not be permitted. Gapon unknowingly had crossed that line which separated even the best intentioned bureaucratic liberal from the constitutionalists within Russian society. Lopukhin, now clearly unnerved, ordered that any meeting or demonstration was to be dispersed by the army. In this moment of crisis and panic the MVD closed its shutters; from now on decisions concerning Gapon would be made in the cloistered atmosphere of the MVD's chancery, uninfluenced by public advice.[84]

Gapon was the key to defusing the crisis. Minister of Justice Murav′ev decided that the priest was 'clearly a revolutionary'.[85] None the less, Mirskii did not want to arrest Gapon, at least not yet.[86] He still hoped to resolve the crisis without bloodshed. The arrest of the renegade priest and his chief assistants almost certainly would have led to disorders, and any action closing the branches of the Assembly was equally out of the question.[87] Mirskii only went so far as to order troops to protect private and government property.[88]

By Saturday 8 January the crisis confronting the government was apparent to St Petersburg society and to Gapon as well.[89] Gapon had requested and was denied an interview with Mirskii as early as 6 January,[90] now he tried again. Mirskii again refused to see the priest and directed him to Lopukhin. Gapon, probably fearing a trap, refused to go. In retrospect it is difficult to understand why Mirskii failed to take advantage of his last opportunity to defuse the oncoming confrontation. Perhaps Mirskii did not wish to confront the man who had made a mockery of his faith in the people. When Lopukhin learned of Mirskii's refusal to see Gapon, he realised that the minister had made a serious error of judgement and strove to undo the damage by asking the Metropolitan of St Petersburg to serve as an intermediary in negotiations with the priest. Gapon, still suspicious, declined the Metropolitan's summons.[91]

Mirskii with advice from Fullon and Meshetich decided to follow Lopukhin's call for the military to break up any demonstrations, basing this decision on their evaluation of Gapon's petition which they interpreted as a political, that is to say, a subversive document. While Lopukhin and Fullon were instructed to report the decision to the Petersburg OO and to local and political police officials within the capital, it appears that their failure to do so contributed to the likelihood of confusion on the following day. Lt Colonel L.N. Kremenetskii, chief of the OO, wrote to Lopukhin complaining about this lack of up-to-date information. He feared that the revolutionaries would take advantage of Gapon's demonstration, using it for their own purposes and he wanted Lopukhin's advice.[92] As far as we know Kremenetskii did not receive any response to his note. The political police appeared to be completely cut off from events. Mirskii and Lopukhin, though they may have felt aggrieved by what they perceived as the OO's inaccurate and inadequate reporting, should, nevertheless, have taken advantage of its services. If they had done so, they might have discovered the implacable determination of the strikers to fulfil their mission of delivering the petition to the tsar in front of the Winter Palace the following day.

Military preparations for the defence of the capital went ahead. Still, Mirskii hoped to avoid trouble by maintaining control of the situation in his hands, and, whatever his fears, he presented a calm facade to his colleagues during their final meeting that evening which he convened at 8:30. The senior officials who had been directly involved in the events of the past two weeks were in attendance: Minister of Finance Kokovtsov; his Assistant Minister Timiriazev; Minister of Justice Murav′ev; Mirskii's Assistant Ministers Durnovo and Rydzevskii; Generals Fullon, Meshetich and Vasil′chikov; and Lopukhin also attended the session, but strangely did not participate in the discussion. Lopukhin's silence is perplexing. He had seen the determination of the workers in southern Russia the year before, men stirred up by the same grievances as those festering among the workers of Petersburg and led by agitators who were less charismatic than Gapon. Why didn't he speak up? He alone of all the men in that room must have known that the workers would not retreat before the troops. As a staunch friend and confidant of Mirskii, perhaps he could have convinced the minister of internal affairs that he was on a collision course. In any case after considerable debate they decided not to admit the workers to Palace Square and ordered the arrest of Gapon and nineteen of his top assistants.[93] Unfortunately, the Petersburg OO failed again. Given specific instructions to keep Gapon under close surveillance, it had lost him, a terrible mistake for which OO Chief Kremenetskii would lose his post.[94]

Through all of this Mirskii's sang-froid stands out, especially since he could not have avoided the foreboding felt by other senior bureaucrats observing the unfolding of events. E.I. Vuich, procurator of the St Petersburg Chamber of Justice, who was keeping an eye on the Gapon movement for his ministry, wrote to the minister of justice, expressing his misgivings that the confrontation on the morrow would lead to 'a bloodbath' driving over a hundred thousand workers toward revolution. He suggested that someone close to the tsar arrange to receive the workers. A.A. Klopov, the tsar's personal adviser, appealed to Nicholas himself to treat the petitioners with compassion.[95] Even the tsar was becoming anxious. Early on Saturday evening, before Mirskii met with his colleagues, Count Fredericks visited him at the behest of Nicholas II. Fredericks told Mirskii that the tsar realised that his imperial command placing Petersburg under military control had not been implemented and the displeased monarch wanted his command invoked.[96] Mirskii brought this issue before the assembled meeting but convinced them that the tsar should revoke his order to impose martial law since the regular authorities were capable of controlling the situation, a decision that allowed Mirskii to remain in charge of preparations for defusing the crisis.[97] Again, it is important to remember that martial law represented arbitrary repression at its worst, the evil that Mirskii and Lopukhin so heartily despised.

His meeting with his colleagues concluded, Mirskii travelled to Tsarskoe-Selo to report to Nicholas II on the status of the crisis. He convinced the tsar that he had the situation under control. However, he failed to mention the decision of the meeting not to employ martial law. Most likely, he believed that if he could lull the tsar into a false sense of security, the issue of martial law might not arise. If this was his tactic it succeeded, the tsar did not mention it.[98] None the less, Mirskii admitted to his secretary that despite the absence of martial law, the maintenance of order on the following day would be the responsibility of the military authorities. It is clear that Mirskii did not envision the potential for violent confrontation created by this circumstance.[99]

Meanwhile members of the liberal intelligentsia who had placed so much faith in Mirskii attempted to make an appointment with him in an effort to avoid the onrushing catastrophe. Mirskii claimed that he was too busy to see them and instructed General Rydzevskii to receive them in his place. The liberals subsequently pleaded with Rydzevskii not to use force. The General told them that the government was in control of the situation and nothing came of the meeting.[100] The delegation proceeded to Witte's residence. He listened to them attentively and with apparent sympathy, but did not offer them assistance, although he did telephone Mirskii, who received him coldly, as his wife's diary records. 'He [Mirskii] knows what they want, that Rydzevskii had conveyed [the information] to them, and what they wanted was unfeasible'.[101] Mirskii's refusal to meet with the group of liberals was a traditional tsarist bureaucratic response to interfering members of society and must have stunned these men who had come to expect something different from Mirskii's administration. All avenues for compromise were now closed. At nearly midnight the minister of internal affairs met one last time with Vasil'chikov, Meshetich, Fullon, Rydzevskii and Lopukhin in order to finalise the disposition of troops throughout the capital ordered to take place within a few hours.[102]

The chaos and bloodshed of the next day made a mockery of all that Mirskii and Lopukhin believed in. The confusion and panic among troops and marchers alike led to the shooting of hundreds of loyal Russian subjects. The exact number of casualties has never been determined, though a reasonable estimate appears to be between 800 and 1000 victims, of whom between 150 and 200 were killed.[103] The shock of the slaughter extended to the MVD and to Fontanka itself. According to his wife, Mirskii was devastated by the tragedy.[104] The political police blamed itself for the disaster, not because it had failed to supply Lopukhin with adequate intelligence, but rather because it thought of itself as responsible for Gapon's Assembly.[105] The post-mortem of the causes for Bloody Sunday took a more official form as well. On Sunday evening, for about two and a half hours Mirskii met with the men who in one form or another held some share of the responsibility for the horrific events of the day.[106]

The recriminations which characterised the meeting were pointless since the primary causes of this tragedy were to be found not in men, but in archaic political institutions and traditional practices which were unable to cope with the pressures placed on Tsardom by a politically maturing populace. Both the Plehve-Zubatov and Mirskii-Lopukhin combinations had hoped to develop policies which would preserve the monarchy in the face of this pressure. The police reforms intended to expand the OO network implemented by Plehve and Zubatov fitted within the already established administrative structure of the MVD and thrived as a result. In contrast, Zubatov's innovative approach to mass social control, which was designed to enhance the role of the political police within Russian society foundered, ironically, on the same shoal that wrecked the Mirskii-Lopukhin strategy intended to substantially reduce the role of political police and *proizvol* within society. The Plehve-Zubatov and Mirskii-Lopukhin strategies were derailed by a common problem: they were principally the endeavours of a few men attempting to impose their goals on ill-prepared institutional and ideological foundations. Without these vital supports both the Plehve-Zubatov and Mirskii-Lopukhin initiatives were bound to fail as soon as they challenged the traditional political structure. This was especially true, of course, for our latter pair of MVD officials. In September 1904, Prince Meshcherskii prophetically wrote that it was not easy to be a liberal police chief or minister of internal affairs in conflict-ridden Russian society.[107] Mirskii and Lopukhin proved that by 1904 it was not merely difficult, it was impossible. As we have seen, the views of both men alienated them from the tsar and their bureaucratic colleagues and by November 1904, they were supported only by the moderates in the *zemstva* movement, a group in the process of losing its authority to the radical constitutionalists. Trapped by circumstances during the first days of January 1905, and unable to resist the well-established methods of preserving order Mirskii did his best to keep the reins of authority over these methods in his own hands in the hope of avoiding bloodshed. General Meshetich, however, bluntly told Mirskii and the others assembled for the post-mortem that this had been an idle dream:

> Concerning the shootings, these are unavoidable when troops are summoned. Did you summon them for a parade? There are definite regulations concerning this matter. If the crowd, despite three warnings, does not wish to disperse and continues to press against the troops, the designated signals are given and then the troops open fire.[108]

The Bloody Sunday fiasco and the failure of Mirskii's policies generally significantly influenced the type of men selected to direct the forces of order for the next twelve years. The events of the past six months also convinced the government that despite the reorganisation and expansion of the political police undertaken by Plehve, the political police was only as effective as the ability of its managers and the policies of the government allowed it to be. Clearly men such as Mirskii and Lopukhin could not do the job. Since Zubatov's departure over a year before Fontanka had lacked a hardnosed political policeman as chief of the Special Section. As far as Mirskii was concerned, the political police in Russia believed he was a disaster as minister of internal affairs and as their titular chief. 'A man of the highest quality', Spiridovich wrote of him, but 'by intellect and by character [he] was completely unsuited for the post to which he was named'.[109] Mirskii's policies were condemned as 'chaos' by the political police who argued that they encouraged the development of widespread opposition to the autocracy.[110]

The forces of order wanted and needed conservative leadership within the MVD which would firmly support the political police and establish goals for it within the realm of the possible. After Bloody Sunday the appointment of those officials who would be affiliated with the political police, albeit too often influenced by the manipulations of the patronage-clientele system, was based upon the principle of assigning tough political police specialists to critical posts within the internal security agencies and appointing staunchly conservative officials as directors of Fontanka.

****

The appointment of D.F. Trepov as governor-general of St Petersburg set the pattern for these changes. The sudden elevation of Trepov to this exceptionally powerful post was so hasty that it ignored the etiquette that usually accompanied a notable appointment. Trepov had interrupted the official post-mortem of Bloody Sunday with the surprising announcement that the tsar had just re-established the post of Governor-General of St Petersburg and had named him to it. For Mirskii, Trepov's news meant that the events of Bloody Sunday were no longer his official concern and he adjourned the meeting.[111] Trepov's appointment signalled a significant alteration in the methods, administration (chain-of-command) and outlook of the managerial personnel of the political police.

The resignations began at once: first General Fullon who was replaced by Adjutant General V.A. Deduilin[112] and several days later, on 18 January, the tsar finally allowed Mirskii to resign and he did so in disgrace. Nicholas refused to appoint him to any further posts, not even granting Mirskii the formal courtesy of appointing him to the State Council. His replacement, A.G. Bulygin, was excluded from police business, as we shall see.[113] Surprisingly, Lopukhin remained in his post. Moreover Trepov evinced so much confidence in Lopukhin that he allowed him to choose a replacement for Colonel Kremenitskii, former chief of the St Petersburg OO, the next victim of the bungling leading up to Bloody Sunday. Why Lopukhin was immune to this mass changing of the guard can only be surmised. Perhaps Lopukhin's close relationship with Zubatov and the staunch defence he made on behalf of the former chief of the Special Section in the face of Plehve's wrath, impressed Trepov, who still considered Zubatov one of his closest friends. No matter, keeping Lopukhin as director of Fontanka was clearly inappropriate because of his general political stance, his isolation from the bureaucrats and police officers within the MVD, his desperate desire to leave the post and his general weariness caused by occupying one of the most stressful offices within the tsarist bureaucracy.[114] Certainly any one of these reasons warranted his replacement; nevertheless, he remained, a decision Trepov would soon deeply regret.

In late January, when Trepov asked Lopukhin to suggest a replacement for Kremenitskii at the Petersburg OO, Lopukhin recommended an unknown gendarme officer, Aleksandr Vasil'evich Gerasimov, whom he had met while serving as a procurator in Kharkov. By the winter of 1905 Gerasimov had risen to become chief of the Kharkov Gendarme Directorate. Gerasimov, after being summoned to St Petersburg, arrived on 2 February, knowing only that Lopukhin wished to consult with him about an urgent matter. Lopukhin opened this interview by telling Gerasimov, 'you know that General Trepov has been designated St Petersburg Governor-General by His Majesty with almost unlimited powers. The extraordinary events of the past days demand extraordinary measures'. Lopukhin continued, 'Trepov found the Petersburg *Okhrannoe otdelenie* in a state which absolutely displeased him'. Gerasimov learned that Trepov wanted the OO to undergo a thorough shakeup and Lopukhin told him that of all the gendarme officers he knew, he believed that Gerasimov was the best man for the job. The choice of Gerasimov for such a senior post appeared on the surface to be completely unreasonable. By his own description, he was a country bumpkin who possessed neither the training (he was not a member of the Zubatov trained OO elite) nor the inclination to assume such a vital post.[115] Other officers with far greater reputations such as A.I. Spiridovich, the chief of the Kiev OO, were available for selection. None the less, Gerasimov repaid Lopukhin's confidence in him. He was one of those fortuitous appointments occurring every so often within Fontanka, quickly showing himself to be an intelligent and innovative police chief. He eventually became an intimate of P.A. Stolypin and by mid-1906 Gerasimov controlled political police operations throughout Russia, as we shall see.

Gerasimov's introduction to political police work in the capital was much more stressful than even he imagined it would be. General Trepov asked Lopukhin to assign a special bodyguard to protect the Grand Duke Sergei Aleksandrovich, whose assassination was high on the BO's list of priorities. Lopukhin refused, probably because of manpower shortages.[116] On 4 February in Moscow the BO succeeded in adding Grand Duke Sergei Aleksandrovich to its inventory of victims. This was the first assassination of a member of the Imperial Family since the murder of Alexander II in 1881. When Trepov learned that his friend and patron had been murdered he fell into a rage, blaming Lopukhin for the Grand Duke's death and proclaiming him a murderer.[117] Shortly afterwards the tsar expressed his dissatisfaction with the work of Fontanka, leaving Lopukhin no other choice but to resign.[118]

Nicholas II did not consult the experts within Fontanka in his search for a new director. Instead he sought out Trepov's advice. Trepov advised Nicholas to replace Lopukhin with the disgraced former chief of the Foreign Agentura P.I. Rachkovskii, one of the most clever and disreputable members of the political police fraternity.[119] It appears that Trepov had known Rachkovskii for quite some time. How and exactly when the two men met is not exactly clear, although it may have been through Prince Meshcherskii or Sergei Zubatov. However, not even Trepov could convince the tsar to make this appointment, instead he bypassed the tsar's decision by having Rachkovskii assigned to Fontanka in the special capacity of police chief for the St Petersburg region. Essentially, Rachkovskii became Gerasimov's adviser.[120]

Lopukhin's successor as director of Fontanka was S.G. Kovalenskii, a nonentity, excluded from political police business.[121] It was Trepov, Rachkovskii and Gerasimov, then, who as Tsardom's senior political police officials felt the full brunt of the 1905 Revolution. These men were of a completely different sort from their predecessors and the campaign they launched against the Revolution and against society itself reflected these differences.

9 The Political Police and the 1905 Revolution, I: The Descent into Chaos, January–November

Colonel Gerasimov, the newly appointed chief of the St Petersburg OO, wrote that Bloody Sunday 'opened a new epoch in the history of Russia'.[1] For Tsardom's political police this statement held special meaning. Bloody Sunday and the events that followed upon it forever altered the tsarist political police's relationship with Russian society. During the revolution the political police witnessed the alliance of almost the entire population against the monarchy[2] – against them personally[3] – and as the revolution progressed the forces of order came to recognise that they were not capable of subduing the swelling unrest. The sudden awareness of their powerlessness before this greatest threat to the autocracy's existence in the three hundred year history of the dynasty demoralised them.[4]

In the face of this crisis Fontanka at the very least required calm, firm, decisive leadership. This basic need was not met. During 1905 the political police system suffered under the indecisive and inept guidance of two men: Dmitrii Fedorovich Trepov and Peter Ivanovich Rachkovskii.

Nicholas II turned to Trepov immediately after the debacle of Bloody Sunday, appointing him to the post of St Petersburg Governor-General with the privilege of reporting directly to the tsar. Within several weeks of his appointment Trepov's power extended far beyond St Petersburg, as we shall see, as he, not the mediocre A.G. Bulygin, Mirskii's replacement as minister of internal affairs, came to direct the MVD.[5] A close relationship soon blossomed between Nicholas II and his new strong man and the tsar frequently took Trepov's advice on sensitive and critically important matters of political policy.[6] The public image of Trepov is best captured by Prince Urusov's famous description of him: 'by education a sergeant, by vocation a pogrom-maker', Urusov sneered.[7] Despite this prevalent contemporary opinion Trepov was not a stupid man, displaying a greater political awareness and social conscience than was commonly attributed to him. Trepov had willingly allowed himself to become Sergei Zubatov's intellectual disciple and became a wholehearted supporter of Zubatov's methods, defending his mentor in the face of considerable opposition.[8] 'For me', Zubatov affectionately wrote years after the two men had worked together, 'he is very dear. He is my political disciple, my alter ego, my staunch ally and friend (in the business with Plehve)'.[9] Nevertheless, though not the fool and thug of Urusov's slur, neither was he the man for the moment. The rapidly changing political complexion of Russia had transformed Trepov into a man of the recent past unsuited for the responsibility placed upon him by the tsar. P.P. Mendeleev, an official who knew Trepov well, claimed that he was 'not dumb' but a man 'without any preparation for government affairs'.[10] No one questioned his unbounded devotion to the tsar and the monarchy, but, as Gerasimov wrote, 'he did not understand what it was necessary to do for their protection'.[11]

The first clear example of Trepov's unsuitability for the post was his handling immediately after his appointment of the workers' response to the Bloody Sunday massacre. The industrial labouring population of Russia reacted with amazing speed, expressing its bitterness over the events of 9 January by going out on strike, the one means of protest readily available to the worker. The strikes began in Moscow on 10 January 1905, the day after Bloody Sunday, and within ten days spread to: Warsaw, Kharkov, Vilna, Kovno, Helsingfors, Riga, Kiev, Voronezh, Mogilev, Libau, Saratov, Lodz, Mitau, Perm, Minsk, Smorgon, the Moscow-to-Brest Railroad, Borisov, Batum, Ekaterinoslav, Brest, Grodno, Bialystok, Tiflis, Samara, Narva, Czestochowa and Kazan. In all nearly 500 000 workers went on strike in January, a greater number of workers than the total over the previous decade.[12]

Trepov's response to this vast expression of anger revealed how little he understood the character and meaning of the workers' distress. He believed that a demonstration of goodwill by the tsar might succeed in defusing the wave of strikes overtaking the country,[13] suggesting to Nicholas II that a group of selected local workers be brought before the monarch. During the meeting the tsar would inform these men and through them Russia's entire working class of his distress over the events of Bloody Sunday and reassure them that the monarchy had their best interests at heart. In preparing the first draft of the speech for Nicholas II Trepov applied everything Zubatov taught him about winning over the workingman. His draft, laden with emotion and significantly different in character from the finished speech,[14] reflected (or so he believed) the tsar's deep regret over the bloodshed caused by his subordinates. This more than any other available document encapsulates in a nutshell the St Petersburg Governor-General's inept political style and archaic world view.[15] Soon a broad mass movement already gaining momentum would supplant the myth of tsarist paternalism among Russia's factory workers. Trepov, whose concern for the workers' plight was sincere, did not understand that the MVD's traditional paternalism which reached its apogee under Zubatov's guidance, would no longer placate the workers. The factory labourer's traditional belief that 'the tsar would provide justice and defend us against [our] enemies',[16] though supposedly anchored deeply in tradition disappeared seemingly overnight as the news of Bloody Sunday spread throughout the empire. It was as if all of Russia had awakened from a deep, timeless dream, confronting a reality in which the monarch was the emblem only of a harsh, arbitrarily brutal, bureaucratic state, not the mystical father image who 'as anointed by God without whom the state could not exist, as no household could exist without a master'.[17] By the time of the October Manifesto, as Victoria Bonnell claims, perhaps most of Russia's workers had abandoned their faith in tsarist paternalism.[18]

By the end of February the deeply distressed and confused monarch turned steadily more to Trepov for advice, so that by late April Minister of Internal Affairs Bulygin believed that Trepov's growing influence with Nicholas II seriously challenged his authority over the MVD.[19] On 24 May Trepov received official affirmation of the tsar's reliance upon him. On that date Nicholas appointed Trepov to the dual posts of assistant minister of internal affairs, managing the police and chief of the Separate Corps of Gendarmes, thereby confirming Trepov as his new favourite and making him the most powerful *sanovnik* within the empire. The appointments stunned public opinion for it placed Tsardom's entire police machinery under the control of this despised figure.[20] The Russian public came to think of Trepov as a dictator, but in reality his influence over tsarist politics suffered severely from his habit of equivocation. According to Gerasimov, who came to know his chief well, Trepov was 'indecisive' and 'unsteady' and 'liable to fall under another's influence'.

Indeed, with his traditional paternalism rebuffed by the workers Trepov was at a loss, again requiring the guidance of an innovative and imaginative police chief – someone like Zubatov – to help him to resolve the crisis. Since, as we shall see, no such person was forthcoming he relied instead on his own instincts and on poor advice to lead the counter-attack of the forces of order against the burgeoning revolution. By the end of January, Tsardom confronted half a million striking workers, and signs of peasant unrest began to appear in the countryside.[21] Tens of thousands of students, members of the professions – professors, lawyers, journalists, doctors – as well as merchants, and manufacturers vociferously and sometimes violently, expressed their opposition to the recent course of events.[22] To make matters worse, Russia's police forces, particularly its political police, were in disarray. Gerasimov, still an unknown quantity who had yet to prove his worth, found the St Petersburg OO to be in complete disorder. Even those OOs which remained calm during the early stages of the revolution and which endeavoured to take swift action against dissidents were demoralised by cautious or frightened superiors who refused to permit them to do so.[23]

Overwhelmed, Trepov sought the counsel of his old mentor Zubatov,[24] but Trepov must have had as little success as Mirskii in luring Zubatov back to work since he began to look elsewhere for a new 'expert' who could help him fulfil his duty to Nicholas II by developing a strategy to bring the nationwide unrest to an end. Trepov chose Peter Ivanovich Rachkovskii to be Zubatov's successor as his guide in police affairs; a more disreputable police official than Rachkovskii it would have been difficult to unearth. He was a devious, even sinister man, completely amoral in his dealings with colleagues and Russian society alike;

Lopukhin considered him to be 'the most malicious provocateur'.[25] Rachkovskii had spent twenty years as director of the Special Section's Foreign Agentura and during his years abroad he made powerful friends – Witte, Prince Meshcherskii, Court Commandant Hesse, and Zubatov – and even more powerful enemies – Plehve, Lopukhin, and most importantly the previous and current tsars, Alexander III and Nicholas II. Fired from his job as chief of the Foreign Agentura and banished from both his beloved Paris and St Petersburg by his bitter enemy Plehve, he settled in 1902 in Warsaw where he became the manager of a friend's factory.[26] This was late in 1902. By early 1905 Plehve was dead, Lopukhin had been dismissed and Nicholas II's hostility toward Rachkovskii had abated, though it had not completely disappeared. Meanwhile the former police chief's close friends Witte and Trepov were in the ascendant. Rachkovskii's chance to revive his career and to acquire the status in Petersburg society he so longed for had come.

Nicholas II, in his search for Lopukhin's replacement as director of the Department of Police, did not consult the experts within Fontanka, seeking instead Trepov's advice. Although – as we saw in Chapter 8 – Trepov did not succeed in having Rachkovskii appointed to this post, he nevertheless overcame the tsar's objections by a quick sleight of hand. The nonentity S.G. Kovalenskii became the nominal chief of Fontanka, while Trepov retained the power associated with this office for himself, appointing Rachkovskii to a new post specifically invented for him: police chief of the St Petersburg region. Unfortunately for Trepov, Rachkovskii was incapable of serving as a reliable adviser to anyone; he was an adventurer, nothing more, nothing less.

Was Trepov so lacking in intelligence, such a bad judge of human character that he could not perceive the difference between a man like Zubatov and one such as Rachkovskii? This question is not as straightforward as it initially appears. There were many striking parallels between the two men; both came to political police service after dabbling in the revolutionary movement; both were exceptionally intelligent and cunning, using these attributes to good advantage in their assault upon subversion; both men acquired a reasonably clear understanding of the finer points of the ideologies that dominated the revolutionary movement and both men could see beyond the propaganda of the revolutionary press and their own prejudices to offer valuable, realistic judgements on the potential dangers these subversive organisations presented to Tsardom's future. Rachkovskii and Zubatov possessed the same police instincts. Like Zubatov, for example, Rachkovskii was less interested in mass assaults than in the tactics of surveillance and limited, selected arrests. He valued the use of skilled *sotrudniki* and as chief of the Foreign Agentura he proved that he could recruit talented undercover agents into the Internal Agency and control them. Superficially at least, the philosophies of these two police chiefs appeared similar: the purpose of the political police was to control and manipulate the basically loyal population, while at the same time using *sotrudniki* to infiltrate and undermine the hardcore revolutionary movement, especially the terrorists, and root them out of Russian society.

The fundamental differences between Zubatov and Rachkovskii resided in their attitude toward service and their ability to contribute to the development of counter-revolutionary strategy. Zubatov was a selfless man, devoted unwaveringly to the preservation of the monarchy. Rachkovskii was devoted only to his own self-aggrandisement. As we have seen, in order to defeat the revolutionary movement Zubatov developed a system of social control – though crudely formulated and to at least some degree, ill-conceived. Rachkovskii did not have any strategy and never formulated one.

Rachkovskii did not share Zubatov's inclination to experiment with new strategies: he was as much at sea as Trepov in the new post-Bloody Sunday political environment. Despite the altered circumstances he persisted in his tactics of limited arrests and close surveillance – the moderate approach – so inapplicable to a nationwide, broadly based, full-fledged revolution in which the organised professional revolutionary movement took so little part. Gerasimov, who was instructed to work closely with Rachkovskii by Trepov,[27] did not take very long to become disenchanted with his immediate superior, to the extent that he offered to take the operational guidance of the OO's External and Internal agencies out of his hands, an opportunity quickly seized upon by Rachkovskii who was only too pleased to divest himself of day-to-day administrative duties.[28]

Rachkovskii preferred to devote his time to the thrill of petty intrigue and the acquisition of political influence, becoming 'close personal adviser' to Trepov who required a stabilising influence to guide him, a man capable of formulating a consistent policy of counter-revolution while at the same time restraining his impulsive behaviour.[29] Rachkovskii did not play these roles and the indecisiveness of Trepov and his adviser and their pursuit of contradictory policies 'well-nigh paralysed authority'.[30]

Rachkovskii in fact had nothing to offer Trepov as chief of police, nothing at all. None the less, as Trepov's power increased so did Rachkovskii's and on 27 July 1905, Rachkovskii became chief of political investigations for the Russian Empire, another post specifically devised for him. This new appointment placed him outside the organisational framework of the Department of Police with responsibility only to Trepov. The two men were inseparable,[31] a situation which perfectly suited Rachkovskii, a man who built his entire career solely by taking advantage of the traditional characteristics of the Russian bureaucracy's patronage–clientele system. The progress of his career depended on the goodwill of powerful friends. He was a creature of interest groups and the patronage networks he served and was hardly known within the regular bureaucracy.[32]

The new post of director of political investigations throughout the empire created for Rachkovskii was in theory an excellent idea since in times of crisis a government often creates extraordinary agencies which are unencumbered by bureaucratic formalities. The concept of creating a chief of political police investigations to coordinate Fontanka's counter-revolutionary campaign during the revolution was easily defensible in the face of the chaos and demoralisation which overtook Fontanka and its Special Section in 1905. Whether a well-led coordinating political policing agency would have made any difference to the outcome of the Revolution is immaterial. When such bodies are created they should be staffed by the most able and intelligently decisive officials available. The post so inadequately filled by Rachkovskii could have been filled if not by Zubatov, Tsardom's most talented political policeman, then by any one of his experienced and capable associates who were well known and respected within Fontanka for their skill and experience. Rachkovskii did not even attempt to win the respect and loyalty of his subordinates. Instead, during the height of the 1905 Revolution he contributed to the incapacity of the Special Section and its field bureaus by embarking on the development of his own patronage–clientele network within the political police system. He dispatched those police officials he suspected of disloyalty to distant posts and promoted new men, sometimes just simple gendarme officers, untrained in the intricacies of political police work to posts within the Special Section merely because he believed that they would be loyal servants.[33] The two directors of Fontanka with whom he dealt, S.G. Kovalenskii and N.P. Garin, became mere figureheads and N.P. Zuev, the long-serving vice-director of the Department of Police, was reduced to functioning as a glorified clerk.[34] E.P. Mednikov, the grand old man of political investigations in his ongoing correspondence with Zubatov, expressed his own feelings as well as those of his fellow political policemen toward Rachkovskii, when he wrote:

> P.I. [Rachkovskii] is not a bureau man, he understands little about this bureau [the workings of the Special Section]. He, of course prospers in the first place because of intrigue.
>
> . . . .
>
> But Dimitrii Fedorovich [Trepov] is completely under Peter Ivanovich's influence and the latter twists him around.[35]

Of course, for the ambitious Rachkovskii things could not have worked out better. The chief of political investigations had always dreamed of holding immense power in his hands, an aim he had achieved by the summer of 1905. The placement of Trepov and himself above the confines of the bureaucracy to which he had never really belonged and his special relationship with the assistant minister brought him close to the imperial presence, a proximity that he believed would provide the status and power he craved.[36] Not even Minister of Internal Affairs Bulygin was able to interfere in Rachkovskii's operations. The special *ukaz* appointing Trepov to the post of assistant minister of the MVD had stipulated his independence from Bulygin, stripping the minister of any vestiges of the control he had maintained over the political police.[37]

The diminished role of Bulygin in the affairs of his own ministry and the elevation of Trepov and his protegé Rachkovskii to positions of authority dependent upon the goodwill of Nicholas II introduced a particularly backward step in the development of the tsarist political police system. It signified the beginning of Fontanka's removal from the control of the MVD and its decline into the murky, phantasmagorical milieu of the court camarilla.[38] Of course, the intertwined relationship between the court camarilla and the bureaucracy was not new. However, during the final twelve years of Nicholas II's reign the involvement of the camarilla with the management of the political police system grew both in intensity and complexity.[39] Trepov brought Fontanka directly into the court for the first time and it would never really leave (see the discussions in Chapters 11 and 12). Trepov, recommended to Nicholas II by Count Frederiks for the post of St Petersburg Governor-General, became an intimate of the tsar's practically from the day of his appointment. His social background, the illustrious service record of his family[40] and his impressive military bearing eased his way into the court, placing him in a unique position as a powerful assistant minister who was also a courtier. Usually, assistant ministers, managing the police and directors of Fontanka had very limited, strictly regulated personal access to the monarch. Their minister spoke to the tsar on their behalf. However, Trepov with his feet firmly planted in the court environs gave Fontanka the ear of the tsar through its own chief in a voice the tsar trusted.

Unfortunately for the political police system Trepov and Rachkovskii held sway at 16 Fontanka during the critical period between February and October 1905. The two men failed to implement any policy for the restoration of order at Fontanka and their vacillation between repression and concession, as we shall observe shortly, contributed to the political police's sinking morale. Only one political police official within the capital possessed any leadership qualities at all: A.V. Gerasimov.

The appointment of A.V. Gerasimov to the position of chief of the St Petersburg OO was no more reasoned than those of Trepov and Rachkovskii, though it proved to be considerably more fortuitous. Despite his apparently unimpressive credentials, Gerasimov – an untutored gendarme colonel – was destined to become Tsardom's last outstanding political policeman. As soon as he took command at 32 Moika, the home of the St Petersburg OO, Gerasimov showed himself to be a no-nonsense officer, who believed in the destruction of subversive activity wherever he found it. Soon, however, as revolution spread and the impossibility of this task became clear to him, he altered his strategy, as we shall see in Chapter 11. But for now – January to March 1905 – he had three immediate chores in front of him: crushing unrest in St Petersburg, protecting the capital's *sanovniki* against acts of terrorisms, and reorganising his demoralised OO. All of these tasks required that he work hand-in-hand with Trepov and Rachkovskii, men whom he did not respect. His constant struggle with his chiefs over his desire to impose hard-line tactics against dissent frustrated Gerasimov, but not nearly so much as the disorder he discovered within the capital's OO, the largest and most important political police bureau in the land.

Gerasimov bore the responsibility for the performance and security of between 600 and 700 Petersburg OO employees. He discovered that despite its size, his OO did not operate effectively. His staff lacked the rigorous discipline required by the demands of political police work. His OO did not even maintain a system for managing and protecting its undercover agents. 'These defects of organisation, this chaos', Gerasimov lamented, 'were caricatures of a secret political police'. He could not believe that he was expected to protect the capital and in particular its most important citizens with this force.[41]

Yet, Gerasimov understood that Governor-General Trepov meant him to do just that. The reform of the Petersburg OO would have to be delayed until he had placed himself in a more secure position *vis-à-vis* Trepov and Rachkovskii by at least partially alleviating his superiors' fears of terrorism. As we described in the previous chapter, the murder of Grand Duke Sergei Aleksandrovich enraged Trepov, bringing Lopukhin's tenure at Fontanka to an ignominious end. Gerasimov witnessed the outburst of rage Trepov had unleashed against Lopukhin at that time, an incident that certainly impressed upon him the fate of police officials who failed to protect Russia's *sanovniki*. As if the object lesson of Lopukhin's fate was not incentive enough, Gerasimov found himself called before the governor-general to be told:

> It emerges that a new terrorist group, recently arrived from abroad, is operating in St Petersburg. The group is plotting to assassinate the Grand Duke Vladimir and who knows else. Now listen! Your primary task is to liquidate this group! Do not worry about large expenses – seize these people at any cost. Do you hear: at any cost![42]

The government could ill-afford too many more of these murders. While a coordinated campaign of assassination directed against prominent personages and government officials may not be the primary cause for the downfall of a regime, such a campaign invariably disorients the government and contributes to the destruction of the moral underpinnings of law and order upon which both the population and government rely.[43] As Gerasimov wrote in his memoirs, 'with the horrific end to Plehve began the process of the rapid disintegration of the central authority within the Empire which then greatly intensified further.'[44] It was primarily for this reason that organised terror had to be brought to a halt. Of course, though Gerasimov and his colleagues would not have admitted it, the successful suppression of terrorism was the benchmark against which the talents of political police chiefs were invariably measured.

For Gerasimov, as for his colleagues, the SR Party was the source of the terrorist campaign against the lives of Russia's officials and as a consequence they focused their attention upon this revolutionary party above all others.[45] During the 1905 Revolution the political police confronted two forms of terrorism organised by the SR Party: the terrorism of its Central Battle Organisation (BO) and the terrorism of local groups known as *boevoi druzhiny* or battle detachments. In 1905 only four of the fifty-one terrorist acts committed by the SRs were carried out by the BO.[46] Yet it was the BO's focus on the Royal Family and Russia's *sanovniki* – it had murdered Plehve and the Grand Duke Sergei Aleksandrovich – many of whom lived and worked within Gerasimov's jurisdiction that so worried him and Trepov.

In March 1905, however, in what became known as the Bristol Hotel case Gerasimov achieved a resounding victory over the BO that secured his position as Russia's outstanding political policeman. The story of the Bristol Hotel explosion begins two months earlier on Bloody Sunday itself. During that tumultuous day the St Petersburg OO, still under the guidance of Gerasimov's predecessor arrested one Boris Markov. While searching his person the police discovered a letter that identified him as a member of the BO. Other evidence collected from among Markov's personal effects convinced the authorities that he was in the capital on terrorist business. When Gerasimov took command of the OO he pursued Markov's colleagues whom he was certain were planning to murder the Grand Duke Vladimir Aleksandrovich.

Despite his intense investigations Gerasimov discovered nothing. Nevertheless, his instincts were correct, a plot on a grand scale was indeed in the making, with multiple simultaneous targets. The BO planned to ignite a massive explosion on 1 March after the government's commemoration service for Alexander II in the Peter and Paul Cathedral. The terrorists intended to explode the bomb just as the BO's illustrious targets were leaving the Cathedral. Four more important targets would be difficult to name: Governor-General Trepov, Minister of Internal Affairs Bulygin, his assistant minister, the soon to be infamous P.N. Durnovo and Grand Duke Vladimir Aleksandrovich.

Ironically, the plot became unstuck not as the result of Gerasimov's investigative skill, but rather as the result of bad luck. Mark Schweitzer, the terrorist responsible for the manufacture of the bombs, was blown to smithereens in his hotel room by one of his own infernal machines. The horrific scene of the explosion stunned even Gerasimov who discovered from his interrogation of the Bristol Hotel staff that the victim had registered himself under the name of 'McCullough'. Gerasimov, convinced that this 'McCullough' had been a terrorist, ordered a desperate search to locate his accomplices. A few weeks later with the help of Nikolai Tatarov – a young revolutionary turned *sotrudnik* recruited by Rachkovskii a few weeks before the Hotel Bristol explosion – Gerasimov discovered the names of other terrorists connected to the BO, and shortly thereafter the OO chief struck, arresting twenty suspects in the plot; only terrorist Dora Brilliant managing to escape the police dragnet.[47] Gerasimov's arrests severely crippled the BO on the eve of the greatest opportunity for centrally directed terror that Russia had ever seen.[48]

The chief of the St Petersburg OO considered this case and his successful handling of it, 'the turning point in the activities of the Security Division: it signified in itself the beginning of firm-handed policies. And for me personally, it had a decisive significance. I began to feel firm ground under me ...'.[49] He had won Trepov's respect with this sensational victory over terrorism and now both men agreed that, of 'first and foremost importance', was the fundamental reorganisation of the St Petersburg OO.[50] Gerasimov began to develop the radically new idea of making the St Petersburg OO the centre of political investigations conducted throughout Russia. He would, however, have to wait for another year before he would be able to embark seriously on this ambition.

****

By the end of March 1905 the complexion of Tsardom's political police leadership had completely altered from only ninety days before. To the public at large Rachkovskii and Gerasimov remained, unsurprisingly, unknown. Trepov came to epitomise the counter-revolution as the hard, brutal, arbitrary defender of tsarism. Yet, in fact, he was the pawn of the other two, vacillating between the indecisive and, at first, seemingly moderate Rachkovskii and the hard-line Gerasimov.[51]

For the next nine months this threesome lived under immense pressure. The revolutionary conflagration placed unbearable strain on the political police system for at least two reasons. First of all, the outbreak of such widespread disturbances was a major embarrassment, since, correctly or not, political police chiefs are forced to assume a considerable share of the responsibility for not having prevented such outbreaks in the first place. And second, as if such a burden were not already demoralising, the tsarist political police understood almost from the outset of the revolution (as we noted earlier in the chapter) that they would not be able to physically subdue the troubles without the aid of the army. The chief of the Moscow OO perceptively advised Trepov in early February 1905 that only compromise with the moderate elements of society, with Russia's tertiary institutions and with the press over censorship, combined with a revision of the cumbersome and inadequate statutes dealing with state crimes, would permit the government to peacefully defuse the crisis.[52]

Trepov, deeply affected by the murder of Grand Duke Sergei Aleksandrovich and the rapid spread of urban unrest, ignored the advice of the Moscow OO and during the winter and spring of 1905 fought determinedly against political compromise. He ordered the arrests of the leaders of the Liberation Movement, considering them to be the instigators of the rebellion,[53] and of the SDs and SRs throughout the empire – in Riga, Baku, Tiflis, Kharkov, in the Urals, and many other industrial centres as well.[54]

Even though the uprising continued to spread, encompassing continually wider bands of the economic, social and political spectrums of Russian life, Trepov stubbornly persisted in his opposition to compromise. In a memorandum dated 16 February 1905 he pleaded with Nicholas II to withhold concessions of any sort for the time being, at least until the conclusion of the Russo-Japanese War, warning that new concessions would only lead to further demands.[55]

Initially, the tsar listened to wiser counsels and on 18 February 1905, issued a rescript to Bulygin foreshadowing the convocation of a representative consultative assembly. An accompanying *ukaz* to the Senate reaffirmed the right of everyone of the tsar's subjects 'to be heard by the monarch' and instructed the Council of Ministers to examine proposals made by the public at large for the betterment of the general welfare.[56] There was a considerable sense of foreboding in official circles over the promulgation of the rescript and its accompanying *ukaz*.[57] Trepov, horror stricken, attempted to neutralise the tsar's decision, ultimately suggesting as a substitute a particularly conservative form of electoral system.[58] In addition, Trepov attacked the press, condemning them, for instance, for publicising the events of the spreading revolution and thereby possibly adding to the restive condition of society. He asked Bulygin to censure Russia's newspapers, purging stories of strikes, strikers' petitions, school closings and assassinations from its pages.[59]

Nicholas II had confidently believed that the rescript and the imperial manifesto which accompanied it would dampen popular enthusiasm for further political reform. However, public and private petitions demanding further concessions and offering advice poured into the government. On 11 March Bulygin warned Nicholas that society had overstepped what he considered the limits of permissible expression. Public discussion of the proposed reforms was becoming commonplace and worse, revolutionary agitators were using these public forums for their own ends. The popular reaction to the rescript of 18 February 1905 stunned the tsar and his *sanovniki*. Throughout the spring of 1905 educated society unleashed its pent up frustrations over the inept course of tsarist politics through a torrent of words and actions,[60] all of which had, as Vasilii Maklakov the moderate liberal recognised, one common theme: '*that to continue as before was impossible* [italics in the original]'.[61]

During the spring and summer of 1905 opposition to the regime grew. The number of strikes increased steadily between February and September 1905 as Table 9.1 reflects. The spreading unrest was equally apparent among the peasantry, who increasingly resorted to *jacqueries* to express their overwhelming discontent with the conditions of their lives. The number of peasant disturbances also increased more or less steadily between February and June (before the false relative calm of August and September) as Table 9.2 indicates. Although they undoubtedly struck terror into the landlords who were victimised by them, the peasants were not well organised or ably led in the months prior to October and did not produce any serious alarm within the government, although the authorities recognised the potential danger they represented.[62]

Despite the industrial and rural unrest, the government focused its attention on the educated elements of Russian society whom it believed to be responsible for arousing popular discontent. Trepov appeared to possess particular antipathy for the professionals employed by the *zemstva* – the so-called third element – writing the tsar that no concessions would satisfy them. The *zemstva* men went so far as to hold, in April 1905, a national convention during which they voted for a 'four-tail' franchise for elections to the national assembly promised by the rescript of 18 February 1905. The April *Zemstva* Congress also insisted on broad functions for this assembly that would have converted it into something akin to a constituent assembly; a decision which gave no comfort to the government, even though it provoked a split in the *zemstva* movement between the constitutionalists and the moderate monarchists led by D.N. Shipov.[63] The *zemstva* movement's jousting with the government and with the tsar himself continued throughout the spring and summer of 1905. Nicholas II's duplicitous behaviour in his dealings with the movement infuriated the *zemstva* men and exacerbated their already substantial frustration with the tsar's recalcitrance.[64]

The government's mood was not helped by the creation of the Union of Unions in late spring 1905. The Union of Unions represented the beginning of a common, though not ideologically united front against social injustice and political inequality. To Gerasimov the newly arisen professional union movement under the *aegis* of the Union of Unions seemed a far greater danger to the regime than the familiar opposition of the *zemstva* movement and the Union of Unions leadership would eventually suffer for the Petersburg OO chief's hostile opinion of it.[65]

However, by the spring of 1905 Tsardom's political police network no longer appeared capable of neutralising the growing popular dissent. In a law and order system as highly centralised as the tsarist one, where initiative is neutralised by an endless flow of instructions contained within a plethora of circulars, a drying up of orders often led to paralysis as OOs and Gendarme Directorates waited in vain for instructions from the capital. A typical case was that of Captain Zavarzin, who in Rostov-on-Don waited for months before he received a directive from St Petersburg to crush the local rebellion. He recalled that by then it was too late, all the rebels were 'on the barricades',[66] and no longer a police matter. It was now a military problem.

The instructions political police did receive from Fontanka during 1905 were not at all helpful, since these circulars solely took the form of harsh criticisms of their performance. No doubt, the Special Section was stunned by the incompetence of so many of its political police officers during this crisis, though there were exceptions.[67] However, the Special Section based its criticism of their performance on the erroneous belief that its field bureaus were still only confronting isolated revolutionary groups within an otherwise stable environment. This was not at all the case and it is clear that Rachkovskii did not have the slightest notion of the size or character of the movement his bureaus now confronted.[68] Those OOs and Gendarme Directorates that continued to function seemed to spend every minute of their time occupied with smashing printing presses, uncovering bomb factories, and especially searching out the terrorist groups in their midst.[69] As early as April 1905, Tsardom's political police received notice of a coming terrorist onslaught, but the political police in the field could do little about it. When

Table 9.1 Workers on Strike, February–September 1905

Month	*Workers on Strike*	*Percentage on Strike for Political Reasons*
February	293 152	39.7
March	73 081	27.3
April	104 646	75.2
May	220 523	50.4
June	155 741	64.6
July	152 474	42.6
August	104 133	68.3
September	37 851	38.5

Source: John Bushnell, *Mutiny amid Repression: Russian Soldiers in the Revolution of 1905–1906* (Bloomington: Indiana University Press, 1985), 46; S.M. Dubrovskii, *Krest'ianskoe dvizhenie v revoliutsii 1905–1907 gg.* (Moscow: 1956), 42.

Table 9.2 Peasant Disorders, January–September 1905

January	17
February	109
March	103
April	144
May	299
June	492
July	248
August	155
September	71

Source: S.M. Dubrovskii, *Krest'ianskoe dvizhenie v revoliutsii 1905–1907 gg.* (Moscow: 1956), 42.

an OO or Gendarme Directorate eradicated one terrorist group another one soon arose to replace it.[70]

This frustration of being unable to subdue their traditional opponents, their fear of the mass movement and the absence of constructive leadership from Fontanka drove gendarme officers to extremes. They relieved their anxiety by striking out in unauthorised[71] assaults against Jews, *zemstva* employees such as doctors and teachers and against students as well – all of them traditional stereotypes of Tsardom's enemies – while at the same time encouraging gangs of hooligans, the 'black hundreds', to attack and make 'citizen's' arrests of whomever they chose, turning the lucky ones over to the police. Fontanka apparently recognised that the behaviour of these thugs and their police patrons only served to stoke the revolution further, ordering its political police field bureaus not take any further part in the physical repression of demonstrations, and confine themselves to preventive investigations.[72] None the less, those detained by OOs and Gendarme Directorates were not safe. Nothing stopped the political police from venting their anger during interrogations when beatings of detainees sometimes took place.[73]

The chaos enveloping the tsarist political police did not escape the notice of the tsar. The numerous intelligence summaries Nicholas II received from Bulygin informing him of the spreading turmoil throughout Russia inflamed the tsar's anger still further.[74] Trepov needed to strike down the *zemstva* movement and the Union of Unions, if for no other reason than to maintain the tsar's confidence in him. In attempting to do so, however, he confirmed what some contemporaries already suspected, that his 'dictatorship' suffered from the fatal disease of inept half-measures.[75] Gerasimov, already frustrated by Trepov's incapacity to crush the *zemstva* movement, approached both him and Rachkovskii about the need to crush the Union of Unions – the focus of Gerasimov's concerns. Rachkovskii vacillated, worrying about the outcry that such an operation would most likely raise within society. But finally, he and Trepov agreed with Gerasimov that it was at least necessary to arrest the central bureau of the Union of Unions. Nevertheless, Trepov imposed two conditions on Gerasimov: that only the leaders of the Union of Unions be detained and that proof of criminal activities must be collected against these persons. With Trepov's rubrics in mind Gerasimov ordered the arrest of 10–12 persons. The evidence collected, according to Gerasimov, was sufficient to permit Trepov to hand the members of the central bureau over to the courts. To Gerasimov's chagrin this did not happen. Instead, Trepov under pressure from hostile public opinion and probably with Rachkovskii's urging, released the recently arrested union officials.[76] This was hardly the decisive action required of a government endeavouring to neutralise dissent; indeed, the arbitrary harassment of these men only exacerbated popular hostility toward the regime.

The dismissal of the charges against the unionists did not immediately signal an alteration in the government's course;[77] however this situation soon changed as Trepov suddenly replaced the failing policy of repression of dissent with a policy of compromise with its perpetrators. Gerasimov blamed the new strategy on Rachkovskii whom the OO chief claimed stood for compromise and reform.[78] In fact, as we shall see, Rachkovskii supported any position he could sense on the prevailing winds: a man without any principles, or policies of his own, he operated as a free agent capable of following any course of action that would benefit his career. Although Vladimir Gurko is considerably less certain than Gerasimov of the reasons behind Trepov's change in attitude, he appears no less disdainful of it. 'For some unknown reason – perhaps it was the quiet season – the government, which had wavered between repression and concession to the public, began to favor the latter procedure'.[79] By late August, 1905, Trepov had gone so far toward concession that he forbade the arrests of anyone but terrorists.[80] None the less, the political police still fulfilled their routine tasks such as ferreting out illegal typographies and while Gurko contends that they limited themselves to confiscating the machinery, there is evidence that at least some arrests were still made, though sufficiently distant from the capital so that neither Trepov nor Rachkovskii were likely to notice.[81]

At the end of August, Trepov decided to grant autonomy to the universities. Again Gerasimov claims that decision also belonged to Rachkovskii who expressed the logic behind it to the incredulous St Petersburg OO chief. Rachkovskii argued that university autonomy would pacify the intelligentsia. No doubt it meant the beginning of an endless number of meetings, Rachkovskii admitted, yet he contended that even this development could be considered a good thing. For Rachkovskii believed that once the government met the students' demands for university autonomy many of them would at once abandon the revolution and as a result the police will have an easier time in its struggle with the revolutionary movement. Gerasimov rebutted that the universities would become 'an open forum for revolutionaries, helping them win over the entire student population'. Rachkovskii simply responded, 'Well, you are a known pessimist. You see everything in sombre colours'.[82]

Indeed, Rachkovskii's sense of student politics may very well have been fairly accurate, as recent research has shown.[83] Gerasimov's perspective, however, also proved to be correct. University lecture theatres under the newly granted autonomy served the interests not only of students, but of the public at large. Revolutionary students allotted lecture halls to meetings for soldiers, officers, clerks, domestic servants, even policemen and political police agents![84] These assemblies contributed to unifying the classes for a major and seemingly victorious assault on the autocracy. The radicalisation of public opinion grew steadily throughout September. In the words of one witness:

> The [Moscow] resident had formerly been indifferent or even hostile to the revolution. Now sympathy for the revolution began to infect the broad mass of the intelligentsia, white-collar employees, residents. It became easier to find apartments for assemblies, secret meetings, storage places, printing presses. Sympathy for the revolution even began to penetrate the milieu of the concierges, doormen [many doormen and concierges worked for the political police] and the police themselves. Their enthusiasm for espionage and denunciation diminished, and occasionally they even co-operated in illegal activity.[85]

Under these conditions the demoralisation of the police steadily deepened throughout September. The ineptitude of Trepov and Rachkovskii left the police only with their crude and typically indiscriminate methods of dispersing crowds which, of course, enraged the population still further.[86]

The political crisis of early to mid-October is neatly – though not entirely accurately – summed up from the government's perspective by Vladimir Gurko:

> At first the revolutionary movement did not appear in the street; it was concentrated in different official and private buildings, chiefly the universities; but there it raged ....
>
> The stimulus to open revolutionary acts was the announcement on October 3, of the ratification of the Portsmouth Treaty. The war was over. The population, which had unconsciously realized that internal strife was not to be indulged in when the country was at war no longer felt this moral restraint. Beginning with October 4, strikes of an openly political character broke out in St. Petersburg and very quickly spread through all the factories and embraced ever widening groups of the people. Slowly but surely they affected nearly every public utility service such as the streetcars, the power station, and the water works .... By October 10 nearly all the working population of St. Petersburg was on strike. Some of the railroads near St. Petersburg had gone on strike on October 7. During the nights the city was plunged in darkness and was usually in a state of siege .... The Cossack patrols and the mounted police were powerless to prevent ... gatherings of the rebellious crowd. Party workers went among the people and inflamed their passions with lengthy harangues.... In some streets barricades appeared .... agitators even tried to penetrate into military barracks ....
>
> News from the guberniias told tales of similar occurrences in many other cities. At Kharkov, Odessa, and Ekaterinoslav the strike turned into an armed uprising, beginning October 10. Barricades erected by the insurgents were taken by the troops only after considerable fighting.
>
> The railroad strike, in accordance with orders from St. Petersburg spread, beginning October 12, over the entire network and paralyzed the economic life of the country. This railway strike originated in an agreement between the revolutionary parties and the extreme leftwing of public circles embodied in the Union of Unions.
>
> In Moscow the strike movement progressed more slowly than in St. Petersburg; but by October 15, all the Moscow factories were on strike and the normal life of the city was disrupted. There was no electricity, no transportation. The *zemstvo* and city employees were on strike; some of the government institutions suspended operations; actors of the Imperial Theatre, druggists, physicians and the students of secondary schools all joined the strike.[87]

Law and order crumbled throughout the empire. In the first two and a half weeks of October 1 500 000 workers employed by almost 3000 industries of all sorts and sizes including mines and railways went on strike with the firm support of thousands of urban *intelligentsii*, white collar workers and merchants. While, at the same time, the countryside endured the ravages of 219 peasant disorders.[88]

The political police in particular found the tumultuous decline in order thoroughly frightening. Understaffed, they could not successfully disrupt or even maintain adequate surveillance over the political gatherings Trepov ordered them to disband. As the fabric of society unravelled, they themselves became the victims of the people's wrath.[89] At the beginning of October one of Gerasimov's detectives was murdered. This incident nearly caused a strike to erupt among his own *filery*, who refused to pursue their quarries within Petersburg's working class precincts.[90] Worse was the hysteria that overtook the OO's *sotrudniki*. The chaotic conditions caused by the revolution resulted in the exposure of hundreds of *sotrudniki*.[91]

Trepov kept himself well-informed about the chaos enveloping town and countryside by means of twice daily meetings with St Petersburg *Gradonachal'nik*, Dediulin and daily conferences with Gerasimov, who repeatedly requested instructions.[92] At first he received only one response. 'Wait, wait', Trepov told him, 'all will clear itself up in a few days'.[93] The crisis did not resolve itself in a few days. Particularly disturbing to Trepov, as he informed Nicholas II, was the news that as many as 6000 of St Petersburg's workers had armed themselves and nearly 300 of these had formed self-defence groups, divided into patrols each of between eight to ten members. They patrolled the streets from 8.00 pm to 6.00 am ostensibly, Trepov claimed, 'protecting merchants and peaceful citizens from the pogroms of hooligans, but in reality their aim is to protect the revolutionaries from arrest by the police or the military'. Trepov called these workers' behaviour 'the symptoms of the times'.[94] Equally a symptom of the times were the monarchist thugs – the so-called 'black hundreds', whom it is likely Rachkovskii with Trepov's approval helped to organise. These gangs roamed the streets of Russia's towns and cities attacking often at random and at other times in organised pogroms individuals or groups they considered disloyal to the monarchy – Jews, students, striking workers – and adding to the urban chaos. It would not be long before the forces of order came to value the 'black hundreds' as their strongest if not only ally amongst the people, as we shall see in the following chapter. As sections of the population began to take the law into their own hands, the authority of the state evaporated, creating a political vacuum which on the left at least was partially filled by the spontaneous spread of workers' soviets.[95]

On 12 October 1905 Trepov finally decided on action. He enforced unification of command among the forces of order by placing the capital's military units under his control: the control of an assistant minister of internal affairs. This meant that for the first time the regular army, the Separate Corps of Gendarmes and the Special Section and its OOs had the potential capacity to share a chain-of-command and communication network that would maximise the effectiveness of their forces against the revolution. While the paucity of forces available to

Trepov did not permit the immediate implementation of this administrative tactic to quell the turmoil in the capital, it facilitated regular conferences, arranged by Gerasimov between the St Petersburg garrison commander and police representatives. It was the cooperation among the forces of order fostered by these conferences which ultimately contributed to the crushing of armed insurrections such as the December uprising in Moscow.[96] Had the government pursued this policy on a national scale the effectiveness of the tsarist political police system would have been immeasurably enhanced. Unfortunately, as William C. Fuller has shown, such consistently systematic cooperation between political police and regular army eluded the government. At any rate, in October 1905, Tsardom's impotence is reflected in Trepov's hysterical and hollow blustering to the army and police forces to quickly and decisively crush 'any attempt at massive disorders' and by his infamous advice to them. 'If necessary', he decreed, 'do not fire blank salvos and do not spare the cartridges'.[97] The ludicrousness of this sanguine directive under the conditions confronting the forces of order only emphasised the governments' hopeless position. Tsardom must retreat.

Sergei Witte, just returned from Portsmouth, New Hampshire where he had acquired an honourable peace for his nation, sized up the situation in Russia and instantaneously wrote Nicholas II that the government's precarious position demanded that the tsar grant a constitution encompassing civil liberties for the people and a unified ministerial cabinet to lead them. Reluctantly, the tsar's closest advisers – even Trepov – convinced Nicholas II that Witte's solution was the only viable one.[98]

On 17 October 1905, Nicholas II announced in a document written by Witte and known as the October Manifesto his major political concessions to the Russian people. The provisions of the Manifesto and Witte's *vsepoddanneiskii doklad* (most humble report) which accompanied it gave expression to his image of post-reform Russia; an image that had a traumatic impact on the *mentalité* of Tsardom's political police. It is therefore worth spending some time elaborating on the contents of the Manifesto and the accompanying *doklad*. The Manifesto's three main articles announced by the monarch were:

1. To grant the population the unshakable foundations of civil liberty based on real personal inviolability, freedom of conscience, speech, assembly and association.
2. Without halting the scheduled elections to the State Duma, to admit now to participation in the Duma, as far as is possible in the short time remaining before its convocation, those classes of the population who at present are totally deprived of the franchise, leaving the further development of the principle of a universal electoral law to the newly established legislative order.
3. To establish as an unbreakable rule that no law can become effective without the approval of the State Duma, and that the elected representa-

tives of the people be guaranteed the opportunity for actual participation in supervising the legality of the actions of the authorities established by Us.[99]

In addition, Witte instructed the tsar in his *doklad* that the government must design a Duma – a popularly elected national legislature – that met the demands of a majority of society. He also insisted that the State Council (proposed as the upper house) reflect popular sentiment by including elected members within its ranks. Witte argued that the government must be bound by the following principles:

1. Frankness and sincerity in the establishment of all the newly granted blessings of civil liberty and guarantees for this liberty.
2. A desire to eliminate extraordinary regulations.
3. Coordination of the activities of all Government organs.
4. Avoidance of repressive measures against actions that do not threaten society and the state.
5. Opposition to all actions clearly threatening society and state, operating according to law and in spiritual union with the moderate majority of society.[100]

Together the October Manifesto and Witte's *doklad* through the creation of new political institutions buttressed by an organic concept of law derived in part from constitutional legislative enactment heralded fundamental alterations to Tsardom's political culture. In both proclamations Witte, as Andrew Verner points out, had gone as close to appealing for a *Rechtsstaat* as he could. Witte's ideal was that of a '"legal order" of depersonalised, institutionalised bureaucratic authority separate from that of the sovereign, of the modern bureaucratic state headed by someone other than the ruler'. However, Verner recognises a critical, perhaps ultimately fatal contradiction in the goals expressed by Witte and the method necessary to implement them. In contradiction to his desire, Witte's plan for a Russia ruled by law, not by men, was undermined by the continued demands placed on the monarch's unlimited power to remodel Russia's institutions and create new ones as Witte and his colleagues desired. To quote Verner again, 'consciously or not, October 17 ... marked a superficial compromise between conflicting conceptions [of governance] which was to be sorely tested in the days and months to come – with far-reaching political consequences'.[101] The inherent contradictions between Witte's proposals and the means of implementing them would eventually lead to a state fixed in permanent transition – neither constitutional nor autocratic – with advocates for one political system or the other battling tooth and nail for a favourable outcome. Fontanka's intimate involvement in this battle did much to shape its post-1905 character.

However, none of this was apparent to Tsardom's law and order officials at the time. The less perspicacious among them expressed relief that the crisis was at last at an end. D.F. Trepov, though initially deeply suspicious of the October Manifesto's provisions[102] quickly changed his mind as he delightedly announced to Gerasimov, 'tomorrow the whole country will celebrate the great patriotic national holiday of the birth of a new, free Russia'.[103] Rachkovskii, in his usual place at Trepov's side, was even more effusive. 'Thank God, Thank God. Tomorrow in the streets of St Petersburg people will be kissing each other in memory of Christ's resurrection [*khristosavat'sia*]'. The following day V.A. Dediulin, the governor-general of St Petersburg read the Manifesto aloud before an assemblage of his city's highest police officials and kissed it![104]

To the forces of order such expressions were meaningless. They had more pressing matters on their minds and the weeks after 17 October were to be amongst the worst of their lives. The convictions of Trepov, Rachkovskii and Dediulin that such a generous manifesto emanating from the tsar himself would overawe the masses into a state of obedience proved nothing more than an act of self-delusion. The Manifesto had descended upon Russia without any preparation, causing overwhelming confusion, a situation made worse by the ongoing transportation and communication strikes. But when the basic tenets of the October Manifesto became known to the population at large their reaction proved to be anything but tranquil. Revolutionary fervour, including attacks on the police, increased as did the violence of pro-monarchist demonstrators which often exploded into the most horrific pogroms, particularly against the Jews.[105]

Within a few days of the Manifesto's publication, the course of events reduced the MVD to confusion, bewilderment and fear.[106] 'It was as if something had cracked in our life, which was being filled by an avalanche, moved by an intangible outside force', wrote a senior ministry of internal affairs bureaucrat.[107] That 'intangible outside force' initially pressed most heavily upon the forces of order. The Separate Corps of Gendarmes had only recently – 7 June 1904 – acquired enhanced power over the investigation of political crimes, dispensing with the remaining, but by 1904, mostly pro forma guarantees against arbitrary arrest.[108] Now suddenly, seemingly overnight, the steady trend of increasing political police power over society had not only collapsed, but had been reversed by the tsar himself. Rachkovskii's circulars signalled this reversal to political policemen throughout the empire. Only the day before the appearance of the October Manifesto, Rachkovskii instructed both his political police bureaus and Russia's governors to take resolute measures against disorders within their jurisdictions.[109] Four days later, however, he did a sudden volte-face, commanding his subordinates throughout the empire to restrain their zeal and follow the requirements on personal inviolability embodied within the October Manifesto and the *doklad*.[110] A political policeman trained to consider the most minor expression of dissent as worthy of investigation and prosecution found these new orders confusing. Even more disheartening was Rachkovskii's circular of 26 October 1905, ordering his political police to apply a limited amnesty to certain categories of political detainees.[111] It is no wonder that the majority of Gerasimov's men believed that the OOs would be dismantled and many of them asked Gerasimov to protect them, while others requested transfers to different branches of the police service. Gerasimov calmed them: 'Quiet gentlemen', he ordered, 'they cannot manage without us. Police have a place even in the French Republic. Who wishes can leave, but work will be found for us'.[112] He was right of course.[113]

But only the densest of political policemen would not have understood that the reformist bureaucrats' desire to at last impose *zakonnost'* on Russian life meant a significant diminution of political police power within the empire. The rules governing arrest, detention, searches and perlustration of the mail prior to 17 October 1905 were rooted deeply in the past.[114] The October Manifesto undermined these officials' ingrained belief in the nature and sources of the law as 'instructions from above.'[115] It is not surprising then, that political police officials condemned Witte's appeal to *zakonnost'* as the 'first indication of a subversive mind'.[116] Nor is it surprising that, subsequently, the political police reduced the effect of the October Manifesto to a confrontation between their practice of rule by secret ministerial circular[117] and imperial edict on the one hand, and the principle of thoughtfully constructed published statutes, defensible in a court of law, on the other hand. Daniel Orlovsky has suggested that circulars which regulated all aspects of Russian life 'should be viewed as one of the underpinnings of the Russian ministerial form of government and one of the primary factors inhibiting the development of separation of powers or the rule of law.'[118] This situation appeared to be particularly true within the political police bureaucracy, where some bureau chiefs were completely ignorant of established laws of any sort.[119] Such men cannot be left to their own devices; tragically this is what happened. New laws were slow in coming. The five months separating the October Manifesto from the publication in April 1906 of the new Fundamental Law were an unforgivable interlude in Russian legal history: a period of lawlessness, after the pre-October Manifesto juridical system had been disavowed, but before the new legal system was established.[120] As we shall see in the following chapter, the forces of order took advantage of this lacuna to undo as much of the intent of the October Manifesto and Witte's *doklad* as possible.

The situation deteriorated even further – at least from the police point of view – with Trepov's resignation from his dual posts of assistant minister of internal affairs managing the police and commander of the Separate Corps of Gendarmes.[121] Nicholas II, reluctant to part with the valued Trepov, appointed him at once as his new court commandant.[122] Trepov's departure, at least from the overt leadership of the forces of order meant, to the horror of Russia's political policemen, that their new chief would be none other than P.I. Rachkovskii.

Earlier in this chapter we described the hostile opinion of Rachkovskii held by senior political policemen such as Gerasimov and Mednikov. Rachkovskii for his part had attempted to fulfil the role expected of him. And it should be noted that it was he who had supervised the brutal suppression of the Moscow uprising in December 1905, as we shall see in the following chapter.[123] None the less, he did not project a firm policy of his own; and now, forced to develop one, failed dismally.[124] His inability to offer the Department of Police strong, decisive leadership further undermined the confidence of Fontanka and its political police.[125] As one important MVD official sadly concluded, within Fontanka 'nothing whatever could be undertaken and nothing could be decided...'.[126] The story was the same in the OOs and Gendarme Directorates throughout the empire: paralysis had seized the political police.[127]

10 The Political Police and the 1905 Revolution, II: Durnovo, Rachkovskii and Internal Warfare

The near hysterical reaction of the political police to the events of late October was natural and understandable: Fontanka's men would have required nerves of steel to behave otherwise. Over the next several months in both the countryside and the cities they became embroiled in a bloody internal war – a civil war – in which, as one contemporary observer remarked, labels such as '"sedition", "political crime" and "disorders" lost any meaning'.[1]

The character and intensity of the conflict between the political police and the revolutionaries during the months of the counter-revolution were to critically affect political police attitudes, behaviour and strategy for the remaining years of the regime – mostly to the detriment of the dynasty.

By November 1905, it became clear to officialdom that the sense of relief it had experienced with the promulgation of the October Manifesto had been premature. As the grass roots revolution burgeoned, the optimism of late October was replaced by anger and disillusionment. The massive growth in peasant disorders – 796 in November, more than tripling the October number – and the 130 military mutinies in November as compared to only 17 the previous month more than overshadowed the news that 193 218 fewer workers went on strike in November than did in October.[2]

The increase in dissent and the continued decay of the forces of order terrified the government.[3] The tsar's patience with Witte, indeed with all of his servitors, grew thin. 'Everybody is afraid of taking courageous action: I keep on trying to force them – even Witte himself – to behave more energetically', he complained. Nicholas II noted sagaciously for once that the inaction of his servitors reinforced the impression that the government was afraid to 'state openly what is permitted and what is not'.[4] Clearly, Nicholas II believed the situation required the services of a ruthless, courageous and intelligent man – another Plehve – with the ability to lead the Romanov dynasty out of this revolution without any further sacrifices of the imperial prerogative.

The tsar, not without some misgivings, chose P.N. Durnovo for this arduous role. However, the announcement of Durnovo's appointment as acting minister of internal affairs inspired Tsardom's political policemen with confidence. 'Everyone started to work, the machinery went into high gear'. Colonel Martynov remembered. 'Arrests began ... and as never [before we] plunged into instituting a gigantic number of investigations'.[5] Durnovo, a highly intelligent man, grew to maturity within the MVD as a former director of the Department of Police and assistant minister of internal affairs, managing the police under Plehve. To view Durnovo as a simple brute no different from the generals engaged in crushing the rural rebellion is a mistake.[6] As recently as January 1905 he attacked the arbitrary application of the Exceptional Measures and rule by decree before the Council of Ministers, arguing that these forms of repression caused bitterness among the populace and fomented unrest against the government without any reciprocal benefit.[7] Durnovo, at least until the burdens of office altered his reasoning, defended the October Manifesto as a fact of life and he saw the implementation of its principles as one of his duties.

Yet, Durnovo's interpretation of the course of events in 1905 relied upon a world view largely determined by his life within the bureaucracy, and the MVD in particular. As a typical long serving MVD *chinovnik* Durnovo held the liberal intelligentsia who were in the forefront of the constitutional movement in disdain. Echoing his predecessor, V.K. Plehve, Durnovo told P.P. Zavarzin, a ranking political police officer, 'that the radical intelligentsia [the constitutionalists] is so weak, that it will not possibly hold power in its own hands [for long]. It will be transferred immediately into the hands of the extreme revolutionary elements'.[8] Durnovo like most law and order officials had even less faith in the masses than he did in the intelligentsia. He believed they were easily swayed by the revolutionaries in their midst. The new minister contended that Tsardom must display a firm hand and preserve its supervisory and tutelage roles over the masses if it hoped to survive. To dismantle Russia's authoritarian machinery before the evolving capitalist development of the country could produce rock solid, conservative vested interests to serve as the pillars on which Tsardom could safely rest, would cause Russia's fragmented society to crumble before the onslaught of the revolutionary masses.[9] So, while he respected the law, his primary purpose – the preservation of the dynasty – drove him to stretch the law to its limits and beyond. Realising that the legal system was incapable of repressing the opposition and that a police force restrained by being held strictly accountable to the courts would be too demoralised to act effectively against the revolution, Durnovo resorted in order to achieve his ends to employing the Exceptional Measures and rule by circular.[10] He became a harsh taskmaster to subordinates and a brutal hated destroyer of rebellion to the Russian people – an example, in the popular mind, of the savagery of which tsarism was capable. Still, as D.C.B. Lieven concludes, Durnovo's intelligence and decisiveness, his toughness, as minister of internal affairs, saved the state from collapse in the winter of 1905–1906.[11]

However, the singleminded brutality for which Durnovo became famous was not immediately apparent. First of all, as we have shown, he was not a tyrant by nature. Secondly, he was in a somewhat precarious political position. His reputation as a womaniser clung to him long after it had almost ruined his career and ceased to be true. Both Nicholas II and Witte persisted in thinking of Durnovo as an unsavoury character who was only worthy of appointment as *acting* minister of internal affairs. Nicholas II appointed him minister in his own right only in January 1906 after Durnovo had proved his inestimable value to the dynasty. These factors combined with Durnovo's understandable fear of a possible popular reaction to any attempt to stem the tide of revolution undoubtedly caused the minister of internal affairs to act with caution.

Even though Durnovo made sweeping changes to his ministry's personnel, including its governorships and brought in E.I. Vuich as his director of Fontanka to replace N.P. Garin, he left Rachkovskii, a close friend of both Trepov and Witte, and his political police chiefs in place. Neither did Durnovo interfere directly with the day-to-day operations of the Special Section and its bureaus, at least at first.[12]

The minister of internal affairs faced a daunting task. Durnovo in reality confronted two revolutions: an urban one which was an unfamiliar experience for the forces of order and the more traditional rural *jacqueries* that periodically threatened the stability of the dynasty throughout its history. Naturally enough, Durnovo emphasised the primacy of the rural revolt over the urban one.[13] The minister's view came from his long years within the MVD where tradition and experience decreed that peasant rebellion represented the greatest danger to the stability of the monarchy and, as we shall see in Chapter 13, despite evidence to the contrary the MVD persisted in this belief practically to the final days of the regime.

Yet, it had become impossible to ignore the pernicious influence of the largely urban-based soviet movement spreading throughout Russia which had come to threaten the regime. The soviets, often formed from strike organising committees, spread rapidly, making their presence felt also in the army and in villages.[14] Toward the end of 1905 soviets appeared in 55 cities and workers settlements throughout Russia. The largest urban soviets are listed in Table 10.1.

By November 1905 the St Petersburg Soviet had become the symbol of the national workers' movement and, seeing itself as 'a second government' it demanded that government offices treat it accordingly. Its perceived jurisdiction covered even the political police whose detention cells it arrogantly inspected. The Soviet also openly collected arms, supplying them to its own militia which, as we have seen, occupied the streets of the city interfering with the duties of the police.[15] St Petersburg, the city that personified the empire, its wealth and power, was slipping out of the government's control into the hands of the Soviet. This informal transfer of authority had not escaped the attention of Nicholas II who considered the forces of law and order in the capital 'to have less courage than anywhere else...'.[16] The tsar's concern was not misplaced.

Durnovo, who dealt with Nicholas II directly, could not have missed the significance to him personally of the tsar's dissatisfaction. The minister of inter-

Table 10.1 Largest Urban Soviets

Location	*Number of Delegates (approximate membership)*
St Petersburg	562
Rostov	400
Moscow	200
Voronezh	200
Tver	200
Kostroma	135
Novorossiiske	72
Samara	40

Source: K.F. Shatsillo, *1905-i god* (Moscow: 1980), 155.

nal affairs asked Gerasimov for a solution. The political police chief responded that, 'it would be my decision to shut down the typographies printing revolutionary publications and to arrest 700–800 people'. Durnovo was astounded. 'Well of course', he wryly responded, 'to arrest half of St Petersburg would be better still'. To Gerasimov's proposal the minister commented that neither he nor Witte could agree, informing the chief of the Petersburg OO, 'we are a constitutional government. The October Manifesto will not be withdrawn and this must be faced'.[17] Gerasimov hoped Durnovo would change his mind and he did his best to persuade him.[18] Throughout November, the OO chief met almost daily with his minister, meetings attended from the outset by Rachkovskii as well. Durnovo and Rachkovskii rejected Gerasimov's repeated request that he be allowed to make mass arrests, especially of the delegates to the Soviet. The MVD permitted the St Petersburg OO to arrest only specific individuals and to confiscate clearly offensive publications. Even these decisions – whom to arrest or whether or not to confiscate a particular publication – had to be painstakingly determined by a committee composed of Rachkovskii, Director of Fontanka Vuich, a representative from the procurator's office, and, one supposes, the chief of the Petersburg OO himself.

If Witte, Durnovo, and Rachkovskii were waiting for the urban revolution to lose steam of its own accord while the provincial authorities and the army under the tsar's personally appointed adjutant generals crushed the rebellion in the countryside they were to be deeply disappointed. The urban revolution continued to swell. At first the November strikes concentrated on preserving the rights won in October and resolving issues of social injustice. However, both white collar professional unions and soviets joined together in calling for civil disobedience when they learned of injustices perpetrated by officialdom or struck in sympathy with strikes in other localities.[19]

By mid-November the government began to react to the growing conservatism of the propertied elements of Russian society by becoming slowly less tentative in its dealings with the urban revolution and began to issue edicts establishing the 'legal' basis for the mass repression to follow.[20] In this environment Durnovo took his first steps against the urban revolt.[21] On 26 November the government arrested the president of the St Petersburg Soviet, G.S. Khrustalev-Nosar and several of its delegates. Abraham Ascher notes that the decision to embark upon this action probably grew from a conference at Tsarskoe Selo of unnamed 'influential people' who decided that society, tired of the political turmoil, would not oppose these arrests. However, no firm policy toward the soviets or the urban revolt they represented arose from the Tsarskoe-Selo conference.[22] According to Gerasimov, Durnovo decided to arrange a second conference specifically to consider the question of dismantling the Petersburg Soviet. Vuich, the Director of the Department of Police and Rachkovskii, along with Gerasimov and spokesmen from the procurator's office attended the meeting, chaired by the Assistant Minister of Justice I.G. Shcheglovitov. All but one of the participants (a procurator) opposed Gerasimov's proposed tough stand against the Soviet.[23]

However, just at that moment the Petersburg Soviet responded to the arrest of its chairman – they issued a manifesto declaring economic war on the government – inadvertantly strengthening Gerasimov's position.[24] The Soviet's precipitous behaviour did not influence Durnovo who still remained reluctant to act. Minister of Justice Akimov – Durnovo's brother-in-law – however, threw vociferous support behind Gerasimov's hard line tactics, promptly ordering the arrest of the delegates to the Soviet,[25] thereby forcing Durnovo's hand. Gerasimov's scheme did not go as smoothly as he would have hoped and the planned arrests became an open secret, allowing several delegates to avoid arrest when Gerasimov struck on the evening of 3 December. The Soviet, under the guidance of its surviving members, did its best to reconstitute itself,[26] but the tide of the revolution had turned against it. The eight newspapers that published the Soviet's financial manifesto were suppressed as well. Nicholas II was ecstatic.[27]

The arrest of the St Petersburg Soviet opened the floodgates of counter-revolution. On 6 December 1905 Durnovo, clearly impressed by the ease of Gerasimov's victory over the Soviet and the tsar's appreciative reaction to it, admitted to Gerasimov that he had been right after all.[28] Durnovo now abandoned his policy, disregarding the principles of the October Manifesto which he had only recently defended.[29] On 7 December 1905 Durnovo composed and dispatched a telegram to all Gendarme Directorates ordering them to arrest the leading revolutionaries in their jurisdictions and to suppress every subversive action.[30] In addition he gave Gerasimov *carte blanche* to clean up the capital. In one evening Gerasimov, already prepared for such an order, coordinated nearly 350 searches and arrests, confiscated 3 dynamite producing laboratories, nearly 500 bombs, a large store of arms, and several illegal printing presses. In four or five places where the police met armed resistance the rebels were shot on the spot. The following day Gerasimov supervised another 400 searches and arrests.[31] This campaign against subversion guaranteed the St Petersburg OO chief's future, as an impressed and grateful Durnovo showed his appreciation in every way.[32]

****

The same could not be said of V.V. Ratko, Gerasimov's counterpart in Moscow. On 7 December 1905, the city of Moscow burst into insurrection. The uprising had its origins in a strike precipitated by the arrest of the delegates to the St Petersburg Soviet, though trouble had been brewing for several weeks. As early as 20 November Witte informed the tsar that anarchy reigned in Moscow and he recommended the immediate appointment of a new governor-general to take charge of the chaotic situation. The tsar appointed Admiral F.V. Dubasov who came to Moscow from his post as commander of the punitive expedition in Chernigov.

Although Durnovo instructed Dubasov to employ the draconian provisions provided by the Exceptional Measures in order to restore order,[33] the admiral quickly found himself in the midst of total anarchy with the forces of order under his command in complete disarray. Finally on 12 December Dubasov telegraphed Petersburg:

> The situation is becoming very serious: the ring of barricades around the city is steadily tightening; the troops have clearly become inadequate for the counteraction. It is absolutely necessary to send at least temporarily a brigade of infantry from St Petersburg.[34]

Durnovo responded to Dubasov's pleas for assistance by dispatching Rachkovskii to Moscow to coordinate the suppression of the rebellion and by sending Colonel Min's Semenovskii regiment (with additional military units) along with him to carry out the police chief's orders. Rachkovskii, always anxious to please his superiors, fulfilled his assignment with brutal gusto. The Semenovskii regiment became in effect the troops of the MVD and the success of placing well-armed regular military units under the control of the political police was not lost on the Romanov's Bolshevik successors.

Colonel Min's soldiers literally pounded the workers into submission. The destruction of the Presnaia district, the locus of the uprising, by incessant artillery shelling, combined with the ruthlessness with which Min dealt with prisoners, especially those captured with arms – shooting them on the spot – forced the Moscow Soviet to conclude that all was lost and it declared 19 December 1905 as the date the strike, that is the rebellion, would end. The time of year – Christmas season – also contributed to the erosion of resolve as peasant workers abandoned their barricades to return to the countryside to be with their families for the holiday season.[35] The rebellion was over.

The government's victory over the working-class populations of Russia's two capitals is considered by most historians the turning point in the revolution. Certainly, despite the continued urban and rural disorders, the balance of power between the contending forces had shifted to the government. However, the impact of these horrific months echoed within the collective consciousness of the political police far longer than Min's artillery or the snap of rebel rifle fire: that echo reverberated to the end of the regime, as we shall see. The unique political chemistry of 1905 that drove Tsardom to grant the concessions contained within the October Manifesto, although short-lived, remained as a memory fixed in the political police *mentalité*, colouring the Special Section's perceptions of Russian political life and determining its tactics and strategies for another decade (discussed in Chapters 11, 12 and 13). Most notably, the intermingling of intelligentsia and workers as an essential ingredient in the making of revolution congealed as an *idée fixe* within the police mind.[36]

****

During the autumn strikes large numbers of workers attended the mass meetings often held by unionists of various political stripes, all of whom demanded similar popular reform: a call for a democratic republic; the guarantee of broadly based civil liberties; and economic benefits such as the eight-hour work day. These emotionally charged meetings conducted in densely packed university or hired halls, considerably reduced class antagonisms, and created a bond of common political purpose. To be sure, the workers themselves did not rush to join one political organisation or another, but beginning in mid-October and for the following two months more than eighty trade union meetings were convened in St Petersburg and more than two hundred in Moscow, exposing thousands of workers to radical ideas of which they had little if any previous knowledge. The enthusiasm of the workers was contagious and a sense of solidarity arose within the working class of Russia's two capitals, expressing itself in an enthusiasm for unionisation which in turn generated a phenomenal growth in the number of unions. By the spring of 1907 thirty-seven of them had appeared in Petersburg alone.[37]

As 1905 drew to a close the workers had not yet wholeheartedly committed themselves to one or another revolutionary party. They remained somewhat suspicious of the intelligentsia whatever its political coloration. None the less, as the new year approached, substantial sections of Russia's working class had been transformed into politically sensitive elements. Not even the defeats they endured in Moscow and St Petersburg could dim the realisation that they themselves through their own collective efforts could bring real change into their lives.[38]

Meanwhile, in the countryside the peasant uprising took a particularly destructive complexion. In the period between the promulgation of the October Manifesto and the end of the year rampaging peasants destroyed between 1900 and 2000 estates. In the ten provinces most ravaged by the peasant rebellion during that time – Saratov, Samara, Kursk, Chernigov, Tambov, Kherson, Voronezh, Ekaterinoslav, Orel, and Poltava – property damage amounted to more than 25 000 000 rubles.[39] Fontanka saw in all of this – urban and rural – only what it chose to see: an intelligentsia-led revolution incorporating diverse political views and constituting a cross-section of the Russian polity, all with the single common aim, 'of changing the existing governmental structure in Russia'.[40]

By the end of 1905, therefore, despite the government's victories in Moscow and St Petersburg, the forces of order perceived themselves to be engaged in a struggle for the regime's very survival. In late December Durnovo launched a counter-offensive against the revolution which in its merciless quality reflected Tsardom's sense of desperation. Throughout the winter of 1906 Durnovo blanketed the provincial outposts of his ministry with countless secret circulars urging his minions to strike decisively and pitilessly against the revolution.[41] And he left his subordinates in no doubt about where they would stand if they failed or refused to carry out his orders.[42]

The Exceptional Measures contained the mechanisms whereby repression could be imposed. Up to 1 March 1906, sixty provinces and regions (thirty in their entirety and thirty partially) or nearly 69 per cent of all the provinces and regions of Russia, suffered under the provisions of strengthened or extraordinary security.[43] These measures, however, did not sufficiently satisfy Durnovo's requirement for rapidly crushing the revolution. The minister of internal affairs ordered 'that all those detained ... be unconditionally held under arrest', even if insufficient evidence had been gathered to convict them under the normal disposition of their cases. Simultaneously, Durnovo and Minister of Justice Akimov, despite the provisions of the October Manifesto, continued the practice of issuing *ukazy* designed to gradually limit the peoples' right to protest to the point where no political opinion whatsoever could be expressed – a policy continued by Durnovo's and Akimov's successors.[44]

None the less, while these laws, no matter how unpalatable, were at least openly published for all to see, rule by secret circular, an even more odious form of control condemned by the October Manifesto, underwent rejuvenation, becoming one of Durnovo's most powerful weapons against the revolution. As we discussed in Chapter 9, its common use before 17 October 1905 represented the most blatant example of *proizvol*. The steady flow of secret circulars emerging from Fontanka added immeasurably to the powers of the political police. The very vagueness of the instructions that characterised rule by circular suited it. The Special Section's field bureaus and the Gendarme Directorates interpreted the contents of the circulars as they saw fit – treating them as laws to be obeyed or choosing to think of them only as advice, or ignoring them entirely.[45] In particular, rule by secret circular released the political police from the restraints briefly imposed upon them by the growing pressure of popular opinion and by the October Manifesto, Tsardom's political police chiefs quickly taking advantage of the arbitrary powers granted to them by their minister and making it extremely difficult for such organisations as the professional unions and the Peasant Union to continue operations.[46] Meanwhile Gerasimov, allowed a free hand by Durnovo, wreaked havoc on the revolutionary movement in St Petersburg.[47] One estimate claims that from 25 December 1905 to 25 January 1906, 1716 people were arrested in the capital, many seemingly without cause.[48]

Often the arresting authorities[49] did not concern themselves with evidence. For example, the police arrested fathers and brothers of the accused simply because guilt by family association became commonplace. Peasants who for one legitimate reason or another annoyed local landowners became the victims of false charges designed to remove them from their communities.[50] Frequently, the police did not charge arrested suspects or only charged them under general headings such as: 'Taken at the barricades'; arrested for 'bearing arms'; or 'for participating in a peasant conference'.[51] This lawless practice, which went far beyond the generous provisions for arrest provided by the Exceptional Measures led to the incarceration of so many persons that the population of Russia's prisons reached bursting point.[52] The tsarist prison system was not designed to cope with arrests of this magnitude. At least 70 000 people were imprisoned by Durnovo between 17 October 1905 and May 1906.[53] Lopukhin claims that 45 000 of them were arrested between mid-October 1905 and mid-January 1906.[54]

It is impossible to know how many law and order officials understood the implications of Durnovo's practice of repression by circular and how many of these displayed the courage to speak out against it. One who did was Governor Osorgin of Tula province who fearing their tragic outcome fiercely objected to Durnovo's methods. Osorgin proclaimed to his minister: 'I dutifully carry it out [Durnovo's instructions for the ruthless suppression of the rebellion], since any expression of the Imperial Will in the normal course, is law which we are obligated to implement'. Osorgin then struck at the heart of the matter. '[However,] if this instruction originates from your immediate authority as minister ... then I do not acknowledge it as law and therefore am obligated to abstain from carrying it out'. The October Manifesto, Osorgin reminded Durnovo, permitted 'arrest only by a decree of judicial authority'. The governor noted that even under the Exceptional Measures officials were obligated to follow procedures by establishing guilt before they could take action. 'Mass arrests ... without observing the recognised necessary public formalities and guarantees, doubtlessly call forth explosive passions, the consequences of which can be extraordinarily dangerous ...'. If therefore, the order for ruthless and arbitrary repression originated with Durnovo and not the tsar and if the minister insisted it be carried out Osorgin said he had no choice but to resign. Durnovo removed him from office.[55]

The concerns that drove the conscionable Osorgin to sacrifice his career were substantiated on at least two related counts. First, the secretive nature of these circulars gave the political police system the means for by-passing the renovation of Russia's institutions set in train over the next seven years. Indeed, the continued use of the circular system of instruction and regulation mightily contributed to placing the political police beyond the constraints of the post-1906 government. Second, the broad latitude given to Russia's political policemen to brutalise public life as described above had a disturbing effect upon them: the development of the callous disdain for the wellbeing of their countrymen at large. Witness the callousness displayed by a young gendarme officer when asked about the vast number of innocent people victimised by Durnovo's policies: 'If measures that are undertaken turn out to be inefficient', then he said, '[they are] doubtlessly ... undertaken against innocent people'.[56]

Such an attitude toward innocent suffering was nothing new; it was embedded within the political police system before the 1905 Revolution. But along with it there had been a strong traditional moderating strain of paternalism that caused Zubatov's police trade union movement to be so popular with many gendarme officers and made sympathy for the plight of the peasantry commonplace amongst them. It is this strong traditional ethos of paternalism that disappeared during the 1905 Revolution. For beneath their ruthless behaviour every political policeman and police bureaucrat felt a burgeoning fear of their own people. By late 1905 and for the following two years Russia's political policemen lived in unmitigated terror as targets of both organised assassination plots and spontaneous lynch mobs. Indeed, it became customary to reward gendarme officers, particularly those serving in OOs, wounded by terrorists with orders or promotions as a means of preserving their morale.[57] As for the gendarme officers themselves they developed an air of fatalism about them[58] as P.A. Stolypin recounts in a speech glorifying their sacrifice during the 1905 Revolution:

> There is a high sense of honour, an oath of loyalty within the police. [For instance,] I am familiar with the service of a local Security Division and of its ranking officers' scornful attitude toward deadly danger. I remember two chiefs of the Security Division serving with me in Saratov and I remember how coolly they asked me to attend to their families when they are killed. And they are both dead and they consciously died for the Tsar and their country.[59]

This speech made before the Duma in defence of the political police system may have reflected Stolypin's sincere feelings toward the courage and sacrifice he considered the political police officers he worked with in Saratov to have made on behalf of the monarchy. But oozing from Stolypin's flowery and melodramatic phraseology is the diabolical brutality of a life and death struggle between police and people.[60] The SRs for instance, openly declared partisan warfare against government officials, particularly the police. They encouraged the rural population, 'to beat [and] choke the lackeys of the tsarist government. [To] beat them without mercy, just as they have no mercy on you the defenseless ones'.[61]

The exact number of political policemen killed during the 1905 Revolution is unknown,[62] but the number was enough to create panic among them. During the

Moscow December uprising one morning an SR terrorist flung two bombs through a window of the Moscow OO,[63] killing two of its employees who had taken to sleeping within what they believed to be secure surroundings since living at home had become too dangerous for OO personnel and their families.[64] The incident shattered the OO chief's nerves. He wrote that some of his colleagues were frightened out of their wits, while 'the frequency of suicide has already increased [among them]'.[65] Gerasimov himself in St Petersburg lived under a pseudonym and kept his residential address secret.[66]

The brutality the political police inflicted upon the population and the reverse – the violence against the guardians of order inflicted by the Russian populace – combined to make an indelible impression on the collective *mentalité* of Tsardom's political policemen. In the aftermath of the 1905 Revolution, the Russian people were uniformly perceived by the political police as united in their intent to destroy the monarchy and with it them. This belief created a hatred for all forms of opposition to the monarchy no matter its political coloration and – to the detriment of the empire – blurred the Special Section's ability to distinguish adequately between the intensity and type of dissent abroad in Russia, a phenomenon discussed in the following chapters.

****

The 1905 Revolution and its aftermath exposed in bold relief the inadequacies of Tsardom's traditional police culture by forcing its agencies to face unfamiliar, daunting and disorienting situations caused both by the dynamics of the 1905 Revolution itself and the new institutions and new values that arose from it. The Revolution introduced into Russia a new pattern of politics common in the West, but completely alien and largely incomprehensible to the forces of order.[67] The political police found itself in the forefront of an internal war, in a sense a civil war where its ethos 'reaffirm the monarchical principal when it weakened, defend it when it was attacked' proved totally inadequate in the face of the tidal wave of violence and alien political concepts sweeping over the nation. Fontanka was never to recover from this experience.

The MVD's most astute officials understood that Russian society and politics had irrevocably changed for the worse. D.N. Liubimov wrote of his impressions on the promulgation of the new Fundamental Law of 1906 and the convocation of the Duma. 'One thing seemed clear to me', he remembered, 'old Russia, willing to us its entire past, the Russia in which we were born, grew up ... which we so loved', had departed, 'yielding its place to something new, mysterious, incomprehensible to us ...'.[68] A.I. Spiridovich shared this view and he argued with his mentor and friend Sergei Zubatov that the political police could no longer afford to distinguish between Russia's revolutionary movement on the one hand and the opposition movement of society on the other, reminding Zubatov that the 1905 Revolution was called to life not by the revolutionary parties, but by Russia's 'social activists'. Spiridovich called for a change in political police strategy.[69]

But what could this new strategy be? One thing is certain, returning to the past was impossible and the development of a new strategy that took present socio-political circumstances into account, but underpinned by the monarchical principle required the services of an imaginative strategist. However, in early 1906 the man charged with the overall management of political police affairs, whose responsibility it was to develop a strategy, was none other than P.I. Rachkovskii: a man predisposed to adventurism and intrigue, not the development of strategy. No successful scheme of social control could be developed until someone removed Rachkovskii from his post and replaced him with a suitable successor. This does not mean, however, that Rachkovskii was idle. Rachkovskii, whose response to the need for a new strategy suited his undisciplined and venal character, employed guerilla tactics, which although damaging to individuals promoted rather than contained popular dissent. Yet, Rachkovskii's operations symbolised a good deal more than the thuggery for which they are commonly known. A man of keen intuition, Rachkovskii's tactics expressed the elemental hatred festering within the police, court and other reactionary circles for the new order. His campaign against what the defenders of the *ancien régime* considered to be the protagonists of change – groups such as the Jews, institutions such as the Duma – laid the groundwork for the final stage in the evolution of the Russian political police system.

Rachkovskii's schemes, though intended primarily to enhance his own reputation in court circles, received their impetus from the bitter isolation felt by Russia's senior police executives and field officers. These men considered themselves to be doubly besieged. While the masses and the intelligentsia struck at them from below, as we have seen, bureaucratic reformers within their own ministry struck at them from above. Witte, and most significantly Stolypin, as we shall see, and their reform-minded colleagues within the bureaucracy as enemies of the status quo ante were anathema to most senior law and order officials. These reform-minded bureaucrats practised albeit with considerable modifications necessitated by the times what Daniel Orlovsky has called 'conservative renovation'. The common goal of conservative renovators, 'was to permit necessary innovations in political, economic, and social life without inviting the destruction of the regime by internal revolution'.[70] The 1905 Revolution somewhat ironically served as a catalyst for conservative renovation on a grand scale, a renovation with which the political police did not sympathise and within which they found it increasingly difficult to operate.

The guerilla warfare begun by Rachkovskii reflected the siege mentality now characteristic of Fontanka and since a political police can ill-afford such an attitude, Rachkovskii, in order to reduce Fontanka's sense of isolation, searched for allies outside his own ministry and the government who could bolster Fontanka's flagging morale. Rachkovskii's endeavours in this direction led him to secretly activate a pogrom-baiting campaign through the machinery of the Department of Police and to develop a semi-official[71] relationship with extremist monarchist groups. These groups distributed in their names the circulars he produced and responded to the calls for bloodshed contained within them. In all probability Rachkovskii himself was a founder of the most famous of these groups: *Souiz Russkogo Naroda* (the Union of the Russian People, hereafter SRN). Rachkovskii became convinced that he had uncovered the monarchy's true friends amongst the artisans, small merchants and *lumpenproletariat* of Russia's cities. These people, many of whom were victimised by the state's economic modernisation and embittered by the dislocation it caused them were ripe for membership in a reactionary organisation such as the SRN.

Paradoxically, Fontanka's regulations forbade police sponsored pogrom-baiting and equally frowned on the SRN which it deemed to be dangerous and subversive.[72] None of this inhibited Rachkovskii, who carried his rabble-rousing still further after the publication of the October Manifesto when he launched a massive propaganda campaign designed to stir up reactionary elements within society against the growing constitutional movement by printing inflammatory pamphlets – with the aid of a few gendarme officers – on a typography seized from some revolutionary publicists. Rachkovskii's agents soon found this press inadequate for their task and in December 1905 moved their operation into the bowels of the Department of Police, using one of Fontanka's own presses capable of turning out a thousand copies an hour. When Chief of the Special Section N.A. Makarov returned to his post – he had taken sick leave between August 1905 and January 1906 – he discovered Rachkovskii's pogrom-baiting operation. In a fury, he dispatched a report detailing Rachkovskii's publishing venture to Minister of Internal Affairs Durnovo. The chief of the Special Section demanded that charges be brought against Rachkovskii and his associates. Durnovo rewarded Makarov for his integrity by dismissing him, and Trepov, who approved of Rachkovskii's activities, suppressed his report![73] Poor Makarov must have been taken aback by the hostile reaction of his superiors to his charges against Rachkovskii. Not only did his dismissal fly in the face of Fontanka's own policy concerning right-wing organisations, but it directly contradicted the recent government reaction to the Gomel pogrom in which the MVD dealt swiftly and harshly with those political police officials whom it considered culpable.[74]

In fact, Makarov fell victim to the evolving struggle between the court circles and the mainstream MVD bureaucracy, a struggle where loyalties were unclear and in flux and where battle lines were not yet well defined. The political police found themselves, thanks to Rachkovskii and his like-minded successors, in the forefront of this power struggle and the SRN became one of the reactionary movement's most vicious weapons. The connection between the formation and functions of the SRN and the political police is still unclear. It seems likely that at the beginning of 1906 Rachkovskii impressed General V.F. von der Launitz, the newly appointed *Gradonachal'nik* of St Petersburg, with his idea for an officially sponsored patriotic union to serve as an auxiliary of the political police. Von der Launitz soon became the SRN's unofficial and secret patron and protector while Rachkovskii organised *druzhiny* (battle detachments) within the SRN and these maintained liaison with the political police through a member of Gerasimov's staff, more than likely Rachkovskii's close ally M.S. Kommisarov, who passed information about particularly troublesome members of all but the most extreme right-wing parties on to the SRN. The sources of funding for these *druzhiny* remains a mystery, though it is most likely that their funds came from the Ministry of Internal Affairs, Fontanka and the St Petersburg OO.[75] Although Rachkovskii became a victim of P.A. Stolypin's housecleaning in late spring 1906 (see below), the *druzhiny* he had initiated continued in other hands. The SRN *druzhiny* compiled a list of forty-three persons marked for death. They attempted to murder at least five of these people during the period of the first two Dumas and succeeding in four of those attempts.[76] The involvement of the political police in the SRN's murder of two Jewish deputies to the Second Duma and an aborted SRN plot to assassinate Sergei Witte is likely, though available evidence is circumstantial.[77] Law and order officials openly joined the SRN; some of them believed in the aims of the organisation, others did not, but joined anyway to enhance (so they believed) their chances for promotion.

Of critical importance is that this alliance between powerful elements of the police system and the SRN symbolised a breach in the relationship between the forces of order within the MVD and the mainstream bureaucrats of their own ministry, a breach which would steadily widen over time. Tsardom's police leadership was abandoning its place within the chain-of-command of the regular bureaucracy for an alliance with the most reactionary elements of Russia's governing circles, an alliance that placed the Department of Police alongside strongly traditional elements of Russian life, particularly the court, who opposed all that was modern in Russia: capitalism, individualism, proletarianism and the political economic and social institutions upon which this new modern world was built. The experience of the police system during the 1905 Revolution, combined with the traditional ethos of that system made such an alliance seem almost inevitable. Ironically, only Gerasimov, as we shall see, stood in the way of the realisation of this alliance.

****

The freewheeling style of adventurism and thuggery fostered by Rachkovskii – which involved besides the SRN and pogrom-baiting ventures considerable time devoted to plotting with the infamous *sotrudnik* Evno Azef as well as Father Gapon and his assassin P. Rutenburg – contributed to the deterioration of Russian life. However, the replacement of P.N. Durnovo by P.A. Stolypin in late April 1906 appeared to signal the beginning of the end of Rachkovskii's exploits. To society Rachkovskii remained an unknown figure, truly a secret policemen, but not to Stolypin, and the likely confrontation between the two men became a certainty with the public exposure of Rachkovskii's publishing venture located in Fontanka's basement.

At first the notoriety he received did not unduly concern Rachkovskii, who believed himself to be secure under the patronage of Trepov and Witte.[78] Rachkovskii hoped to win over Stolypin by publicly announcing that, 'to me is promised the honourable post of tutor [to Stolypin]'. But he found his new minister unreceptive to this offer. Stolypin did not intend to take on an alter ego and the first meeting between the two men became a coldly formal affair. Stolypin understood that the Rachkovskii affair was the first test of his ability to wrest the Russian political policing system from the grasp of the court camarilla, returning it to its place within the ministry's chain-of-command, responsible to, if not directly under the guidance of, the minister of internal affairs and he acted accordingly. Unceremoniously, Stolypin, using his ministerial prerogative, stripped Rachkovskii of his police powers[79]; forcing him into retirement a few weeks later.[80]

Ridding Fontanka and the MVD of Rachkovskii proved to be only a successful minor skirmish in Stolypin's campaign to re-acquire ministerial control over the political police system and made almost no impression on conservative and court circles. Rachkovskii's enforced retirement and the scandal which surrounded it did not affect his status or prestige within the court. The former police chief remained influential, though unofficially so. Despite his notorious lack of achievement as a political police chief, his close relationship to the court garnered him emoluments of office including *ordena* and special financial rewards which ordinarily were emblems of a respected bureaucratic career! Nicholas II himself demonstrated his esteem for Rachkovskii by presenting him with a gift of 72 000 rubles upon his departure from the civil service and bestowed upon him the most significant honour of them all: the privilege of reporting directly to the tsar when he awarded Rachkovskii the Order of St Stanislav First Class.[81] This right was not granted merely as window dressing. Rachkovskii employed this privilege in his capacity as the SRN's liaison with the tsar.[82] Stolypin was aware of the court's treatment of the man he dismissed from the directorship of the political police system for gross misconduct, but he felt powerless to do anything about it.[83]

The beneficence, protection, and status the court bestowed upon Rachkovskii became an object lesson which impressed the less responsible and more reactionary elements managing the police in the years to come, thereby contributing to Stolypin's inability to subdue them. Eventually, it was such men who came to rule the MVD's forces of order (discussed in Chapters 11 and 12).

The antipathy that grew up between Stolypin and Fontanka arose primarily for reasons which at first glance are not all that easy to discern. This is especially so since Stolypin insisted that he believed in the essential role the political police played within the framework of Russian government, 'because without it', he said of the Special Section, 'without its methods of investigation, without its espionage, no government would be able to foresee and prevent'.[84] Actually his philosophy of law and order was quite confused. Stolypin understood that 'new forms of political organisation are beginning to enter [Russian] life'.[85] But his infamous formula for a renewed and permanent stability for Russia – called by one unsympathetic contemporary 'repression for reform' – satisfied neither the concept of law and order envisioned by the new politics nor the traditional one preserved by the political police. The fact that this formula did not satisfy constitutionalists is not surprising,[86] but that it did not satisfy Fontanka is.

The Department of Police must have been disgruntled with something other than the willingness and ability of its new minister to extinguish the embers of the 1905 Revolution. Stolypin's achievements in the name of repression went far beyond those even contemplated by Plehve,[87] especially his reliance upon martial law and field court martials. During the eight months between 19 August 1906 and 21 April 1907 in which they operated these special court martials terrorised the countryside. In fact during the first three years of Stolypin's tenure in office 26 000 persons were sentenced to death, hard labour, or prison.[88]

The disagreement between minister and police is therefore not to be found in the mechanisms and intensity of the counter-revolution employed by the former, but in the end it was hoped they would achieve. Put simply, the polity Stolypin defended so resolutely was not the one Fontanka's leadership fought to preserve. Despite the imposition of the Fundamental Law of 1906 and its creation of an elected legislative system, the police system's unshakable faith in the myth of the tsar's personal rule was maintained.[89] The forces of order quixotically fought to retain the old Russia, the absolute monarchy unimpeded by a representative legislative chamber, in which they continued staunchly to believe.[90] At the same time Stolypin strove to foster conservative renovation. In a handwritten note he made this point emphatically clear to its readers:

> Reform at a time of revolution is necessary because largely the shortcomings of the domestic order have spawned revolution. If we exclusively struggle with revolution at best we eliminate the consequences and not the cause: we lance the boil but the infected blood spawns new ones. Moreover, this path of reform has been proclaimed, the State Duma has been created and there is no turning back. This would be a critical mistake – where a government suppressed revolution (Prussia, Austria) it succeeded not exclusively with physical force, but relying on strength, by boldly standing in the forefront of reform. To reduce the creativity of the government to police measures is to acknowledge the powerlessness of the ruling authority.[91]

The divergence in political outlook between Stolypin and his police is reflected most in their perceptions of whom constituted the enemies of order. The political police (as we have seen) made no secret of their hatred of most elements of

Russian life residing beyond the walls of Tsardom's traditional institutions and even of the reform-minded officials working within them. Stolypin projected a different view. To be sure, the law and order messages he dispatched to his provincial governors and police chiefs constantly admonished them to act with vigour against subversion in order to re-establish the government's authority before the population. None the less, unlike P.N. Durnovo, Stolypin couched his tough language in measured tones.[92] 'The struggle [the counter-revolution] is being waged not against society, but against the enemies of society', he told his subordinates. 'Therefore' he warned them, 'indiscriminate repression cannot be approved.... A strong government ... will undoubtedly find support in the best part of society'.[93] Scarred by the events of 1905 to 1907, most of Russia's political policemen could not accept this logic.

Stolypin's relationship with the political police system reflects, as Roberta Manning observed, 'the ambiguities and contradictions of the transitional social-political order over which he presided as prime minister in the key 1906–1911 period'.[94] Luckily for Stolypin, during the first three years of his tenure in office he successfully kept his enemies within Fontanka at bay with the indispensable aid and firm support of A.V. Gerasimov, who had decided to hitch his career to Stolypin's.

11 Stolypin and the Russian Political Police, 1906–1911

Between 1905 and 1907 a 'participation explosion' occurred in the empire.[1] Russians abandoned their parochial concerns to strike out against the tsarist regime in an effort to secure a better life. The subsequent confrontation re-aligned political structures and allegiances between the masses and tsarist authority. The traditional axiom, the governor of Simbirsk told Durnovo, that 'the people know us, they will follow us, they trust us', no longer held true. The patriarchical attitude of the government and the upper classes no longer corresponded to the way people felt.[2]

In 1906 and 1907 this process of political evolution spurred the population on to seeking redress of its grievances through a variety of legal and semi-legal outlets on the one hand and through membership within the revolutionary parties on the other. From early 1906 to the *coup d'état* of 3 June 1907 – and despite the *ukaz* of 4 March 1906, which circumscribed their activities – the unions defended labours' legal rights and publicised the workers' cause through the establishment of a legal press and by throwing themselves into electoral politics. Meanwhile the SDs and the SRs were bursting at the seams with new members. The SDs boasted 150 000 members within 143 party organisations while the SRs, enlisted 50 000 members by 1906 who were supported by approximately 300 000 sympathisers spread throughout 126 party organisations.[3] In addition the SRs, whose influence expanded in the countryside and cities alike, organised 415 peasant brotherhoods or *bratsva*. These *bratstva* exchanged and spread SR propaganda from village to village, organising the peasants to do battle with the landlords and with the local authorities.[4]

The most powerful political party, however, was the Constitutional Democratic Party (the Kadets). At the height of its power during late 1906 and early 1907 the Kadets counted between 70 000 and 100 000 members working within nearly 300 party organisations.[5] Most importantly, unlike the revolutionary parties the Kadets controlled one of the levers of power within the post-1905 constitutional system: the new Duma.[6]

Non-party organisations in particular flourished during 1906 and 1907. The locus of the non-party rural movement resided within the Peasant Union although little is known of its size, geographic distribution and composition.[7] Similarly, the influence of the rural intelligentsia is unknown, though the Peasant Union projected the long-term desires of the peasant estate rather than the platform of any political party and its programme avoided appeals to spontaneous *buntarstvo* and agrarian violence.[8] Trade unions and self-help organisations remained non-party in the first years following the 1905 Revolution, although this condition did not inhibit the development of their popularity. In Petersburg alone by the spring of 1907 several legal cultural-educational organisations had sprung up. The largest of these was the Petersburg Society of People's Universities where for example in 1906, 10 329 people attended its lectures, the number more than doubling the following year. Though it was ostensibly legal, the political police looked upon the society's lecture series with a jaundiced eye. According to the *gradonachal'nik* of the capital the lectures contained political themes interspersed within the educational commentary and the police regularly interrupted lectures they deemed suspiciously political.[9]

Not all 'educational' groups were legal of course. Some clandestine groups served principally as schools for the propagation of Marxism under the sponsorship of local SD committees. However, such circles seemed to fade in importance with the spread of the legal trade union movement.[10] In 1907 during the height of trade union activity in Russia an estimated 1096 unions offered their services to Russia's workers.[11]

The pressure of this 'participation explosion' had a particularly telling effect on the ability of Fontanka and its Special Section to process and evaluate the intelligence it collected. Fontanka designed its intelligence retrieval and analysis system upon the premise of leisurely research and reporting, and prior to 1905 appeared to function adequately during times of relative tranquillity. An OO, for example, submitted a report which in turn was reviewed by an official within the Special Section who often requested further information, while at the same time berating the OO chief for vague, partial or if he noticed, inaccurate reporting. This created a morass of paperwork clogging communication channels. The ordinary way of dealing with this problem in most bureaucracies is merely to slow down the handling of messages without changing either the design or capacity of their communication network structures or transmission rules.[12] This is how the Special Section functioned.

A bureaucracy that operates in a highly uncertain environment and which like Tsardom's political police is expected to operate effectively during crises cannot permit itself this luxury. It must be able to handle high-volume information flows efficiently.[13] To Fontanka this meant employing more chancery staff throughout its political police network, a measure which would add considerably to the cost of political police operations, though this would not have been the principal obstacle to any such proposal; it was rather the paucity of trained and able chancery personnel which precluded this option. As things stood, the ability of the clerks and scribes who did the bulk of the collation and processing of intelligence for the OOs and Fontanka was questionable. Many were elderly men with such limited training, that they had difficulty understanding Fontanka's increasingly complex instructions for the filing and reference of intelligence items.[14]

As a result, the 1905 Revolution and its aftermath stretched the Special Section's intelligence processing system beyond its capacity to fulfil the *immediate* demands of the MVD for some coherent picture of what was going on in the countryside. OOs and Gendarme Directorates were forced to dispatch their intelligence to St Petersburg by telegraph and the ordinary post. Nevertheless, information arrived in waves and there was insufficient staff to cope with it. Fontanka's and the Special Section's chancery staffs were so undermanned that senior police officials, including the man charged with managing the political police, were forced to read and comment on incoming dispatches.[15] For the entire year of 1906 Russia's political police chiefs, who usually carried out other tasks, 'wrote, wrote and wrote', and did little else.[16]

By the end of 1906 the intelligence system was in disarray. It had not been constructed to keep track of a mass movement. The Bertillon system, for example, which Zubatov had introduced for registering suspicious persons, and which is described in Chapter 6, instead of aiding in the identification of state criminals became an unwieldy and unreliable tool: its cumbersome system of photographs, and compilation of suspects' anthropomorphic and dactylographic data proved too much for the OOs.[17]

The failure of the intelligence processing system placed Gerasimov in an especially unenviable position. Considered by the capital's *sanovniki* and the members of the Royal Family as their protector, Gerasimov increasingly found intelligence concerning assassination plots hard to come by or poorly evaluated. He chose therefore to place Russia's most powerful men within a protective cocoon, forcing them to live a caged existence. D.F. Trepov lived in a secret residence, Stolypin resided in the Winter Palace and Gerasimov confined Nicholas II to the grounds at Peterhof.[18] Stolypin himself adopted a fatalist tone, suggesting to the tsar that he appoint 'reserve ministers' capable of instantly replacing any assassinated minister.[19] Nicholas II himself in August 1906 commented that 'the incessant murdering of officials and attempts to murder them, as well as the audacious acts of looting that occur daily, are bringing the country to a state of anarchy ...'.[20] Both the tsar and Stolypin assessed the situation accurately. The majority of the terror's victims were tsarist officials.[21]

****

It was within this chaotic milieu that Tsardom's political police, with the unqualified support of Prime Minister Stolypin, undertook administrative and personnel reforms and developed a new strategy designed to allow it to cope more effectively with the political environment which it confronted in 1906.

Change came to the political police as soon as Stolypin became minister of internal affairs on 27 April 1906. He removed Rachkovskii from his post and swept Fontanka clean of the former political police chief's cronies. Since their replacements were men little acquainted with political police work[22] the new minister was forced to rely solely on advice from Gerasimov about whom he had received an exceptional report from Durnovo.[23] Summoning Gerasimov to his office soon after his appointment as minister, Stolypin asked the OO chief to become in effect his personal political police chief, reporting to him daily on the state of political subversion within the empire. 'For you', Stolypin told Gerasimov, 'if there is something urgent, I am at home any time day and night'.[24] Very rapidly the chief of the St. Petersburg OO became an exceptionally powerful figure.[25]

In his memoirs Gerasimov claimed that Stolypin wished to install him as assistant minister of internal affairs.[26] Although this did not happen, Gerasimov unofficially played the role of assistant minister with Stolypin's blessing.[27] As the Petersburg OO chief boasted, 'the Department of Police found itself under my control in those areas of its work which were of special interest to me'.[28] It was not long before the provincial OOs and Gendarme Directorates along with the smaller field bureaus began to consider the Petersburg OO the centre of political investigations throughout the empire and opted to follow the orders of Gerasimov, a gendarme officer like themselves and Russia's outstanding political policeman between 1906 and 1909, rather than the generalist officials charged with the official management of police affairs. This circumstance *de facto* transferred the management of political investigation away from the Special Section to the St Petersburg OO. Stolypin had thereby stripped Fontanka of its control over the single most important duty performed at 16 Fontanka Quai, the resultant bitterness stirring up considerable animosity toward the minister within the regular police bureaucracy which festered throughout his tenure in office.[29]

Gerasimov's close relationship with Stolypin gave the OO chief the opportunity to devise and implement a new political policing strategy designed to contain the effects of the political participation explosion that marked Russian politics in the post-1905 era. The OO chief rejected out of hand the Special Section's standard methods of dealing with subversion first introduced by his illustrious predecessor Sergei Zubatov. Gerasimov condemned Zubatov's strategy of focusing only on what had been in his day the relatively few hardcore revolutionaries by arresting the ringleaders of revolutionary organisations or cells, leaving the majority of less committed dissidents and fellow travellers unscathed.

Gerasimov's strategy was premised on an analysis of the political character of post-1905 Russia. He argued that the opposition and revolutionary movements could no longer be defeated, they could only be contained. Gerasimov perceived that the widespread nature and sophisticated character of the opposition to the regime currently confronting the political police could not be subdued by Zubatov's strategy.[30] The strategy, one in which the Internal Agency was a key player, called for Gerasimov and his colleagues to encourage their undercover agents to acquire control of the subversive groups to which they belonged, then to manipulate them into directions least harmful to the state. At the same time these *sotrudniki* would inform their case officers about their organisation's plans and activities such as the printing and dissemination of revolutionary propaganda. The OOs (and to a lesser degree the Gendarme Directorates) would then use this intelligence to repeatedly frustrate their actions. Gerasimov hoped his strategy would dishearten the membership of these organisations, driving them out of the subversive movement or at least into a state of inertia. He believed that it would take several undercover agents unknown to each other boring into each organisation to accomplish this end. The Petersburg OO chief argued that this approach would be particularly useful against Russia's feared and hated terrorists.[31]

Gerasimov clearly understood the risks inherent in his strategy. The OOs left the revolutionary executive committees unmolested in order to protect the identities of the Internal Agency's finest *sotrudniki* who otherwise could have been implicated in the arrests. OOs still ordered arrests, but these were usually confined to those revolutionaries caught red-handed – propagandists, bombmakers, terrorists and the like. To be sure, the political police could detain important leaders of any movement if the investigators considered them a threat to the regime. In addition, Gerasimov taught that revolutionaries on good terms with undercover agents were wherever possible to be left alone, while those whom the *sotrudniki* perceived to be their enemies were to be arrested. The police should arrest the entire executive of any organisation only during a revolutionary crisis or when the field bureau believed the organisation had decided to mount a major offensive against the government.

Gerasimov's strategy demanded a dramatic alteration in the policy – though by no means always in the practice – which regulated the parameters of undercover agent activity. Under the guidelines for Internal Agency operations *previously* established by Fontanka a *sotrudnik* must never permit himself to become intimately involved in revolutionary duties. Ideally, he was to be no more than a human sponge soaking up information supplied to him by trusting co-conspirators. The regulations stipulated, as we know, that undercover agents must never play more than a secondary role in any subversive organisation to which they belonged. Unofficially, of course, case officers had informally permitted their *sotrudniki* to flaunt these rules for the sake of uncovering worthwhile intelligence (discussed in Chapter 4). Now, Gerasimov transformed unofficial behaviour into official policy. Provocation became an officially sanctioned tactic in the campaign against subversion.[32] In a directive to every political police bureau throughout the empire and abroad Stolypin proclaimed, 'it is the duty of all [political police bureaus] to acquire provocateurs and increase investigations in every direction'.[33]

The central place Stolypin and Gerasimov gave to provocation in police strategy demanded two things of them. Firstly, that Russia's undercover agents be made to feel sufficiently secure so that they could carry out their assignments with confidence bred by the knowledge that their chiefs would quickly and safely extract them from precarious situations. Secondly, that the Duma be kept completely in the dark over every aspect of political police business, particularly provocation. We discussed the exceptional security measures Gerasimov implemented for his own *sotrudniki* in Chapter 4. Unfortunately, as powerful as Gerasimov became he could never do the same for every undercover agent operating within Russia and abroad. Indeed, in the end, the unmasking of Evno Azef, Gerasimov's own premier undercover agent and provocateur *extraordinaire*, terminated the police chief's career, as we shall discover later in this chapter.[34] Stolypin fulfilled his obligation to shield the political police from the interference of the Duma with confidence instilled by the knowledge that the Dumas knew almost nothing either about the identities of political police personnel or about its chain of command[35] and Stolypin refused point blank to enlighten any of the three Dumas with which he dealt about political police affairs.[36]

****

Although in the long-run Gerasimov's strategy of containment and immobilisation would be most assiduously employed against the social democrats by S.P. Beletskii (discussed in Chapter 12), it was the SR Party which initially became the focal point of Gerasimov's new methods.[37] There really could have been no other choice. Fontanka held the SRs responsible for the deaths of several *sanovniki* and the terrorisation of many others. The litmus test of Gerasimov's strategy would be its ability to safeguard Tsardom's High Personages. M.I. Trusevich, the newly appointed Director of the Department of Police, wholeheartedly supported him in this endeavour.[38]

Gerasimov, who apparently knew nothing concrete about Azef's part in the murders of Plehve and Grand Duke Sergei Aleksandrovich, though he probably had his suspicions that Azef might at one time have played a double game,[39] decided (in any case) to employ Azef, the chief of the BO, to lead his terrorist organisation into one blind alley after another, demoralising and paralysing its membership.[40] After all, this was not the BO of 1902 to 1905. Though the BO's membership had risen to thirty, these were not the 'artists of terror' with whom Zubatov had parried a few years before. The BO had suffered considerable attrition in its struggle with Tsardom and the replacements were journeymen filled with fanatic devotion to their task at hand, but lacking the imagination of their mythologised predecessors. Their *modus operandi* remained unchanged and the stale methods they employed made their exposure a relatively easy task.[41]

Yet, the strategy deployed by Gerasimov against the SRs proved far from infallible. It concentrated upon the neutralisation of the central BO. In a sense, he succeeded too well. In the autumn of 1906 the BO under the joint leadership of Azef and Savinkov disbanded, with both leaders pleading exhaustion. In place of the BO there arose decentralised terrorism under the guidance of new men. Each of these freshly created groups followed its own path, maintaining only the faintest connections with the SR Central Committee. In St Petersburg three such terrorist cells used new modes of operation, thereby making it extremely difficult for Gerasimov to keep track of them. They could be caught only with the help of inside information, but the essential source of intelligence dried up when Azef went into 'retirement' abroad.

Gerasimov's inability to hunt down these particular groups before they could strike led to tragic consequences. On 15 December 1906, a terrorist cell attempted to murder Admiral Dubasov; General von der Launitz succumbed to assassination on 3 January 1907, and on 8 January General Pavlov, the chief military procurator, followed von der Launitz to the grave. A few weeks later the governor of the St Petersburg temporary holding prison (for political prisoners) also fell prey to SR assassins. The St Petersburg OO cannot be blamed entirely for this slaughter since Gerasimov actually discovered that both Launitz and Stolypin were targeted for the attack on 3 January at the same official function. The OO chief succeeded in convincing Stolypin to remain at home, but Launitz and Gerasimov were to say the least not on good terms and the St Petersburg Governor-General ignored the OO chief's warning.

Nevertheless, while saving Stolypin's life and ultimately arresting those responsible for Launitz's murder[42] most certainly saved Gerasimov's career, it could not compensate for the horrific bloodletting caused by SR terrorists in 1906 and 1907. Table 11.1 details the pattern of terrorism conducted by the SR Party between 1902 and 1911 in which 205 assassinations were attempted, of which the vast majority (140) were carried out in 1906–1907.

Indeed as the large number of victims of terrorism listed in Table 11.2 reveals, the majority of terrorist style acts directed against tsarist officials were not initi-

Table 11.1 SR Terrorist Acts, 1902–1911

Year	*Number of Acts*
1902	2
1903	3
1904	1
1905	51
1906	78
1907	62
1908	3
1909	2
1910	1
1911	2
Total	205

Source: Maureen Perrie, 'Political and Economic Terror in the Tactics of the Russian Socialist-Revolutionary Party before 1914', in *Social Protest, Violence and Terror in Nineteenth-and-Twentieth-century Europe*, ed. by Wolfgang Mommsen and Gerhard Herschfeld (New York: St Martin's Press, 1982), 67.

Table 11.2 Victims of Terrorism, 1905–1 May 1909

Year	*Killed*	*Wounded*	*Total*
1905	233	358	591
1906	768	820	1588
1907	1231	1312	2543
1908	394	615	1009
1 January–1 May 1909	65	117	182
Total	2691	3222	5913

Source: 'V gody reaktsii', *KA* 8 (1925) : 242.

ated by the SRs – 205 compared to an overall number of 5913 – the intense object of political police attention between 1906 and 1907[43] at all, but by hundreds of ordinary individuals or groups who used the chaotic conditions arising from the 1905 Revolution to seek their own vengeance against both their real and perceived oppressors. The exact number of officials who came under attack during these years is unknown, though various estimates exist.[44] Generally, the massive size of the terrorist campaign against officialdom and other persons associated by the masses with the oppressiveness of the state indicated by the slaughter revealed in Table 11.2 placed the containment of terrorism beyond the capacity of the political police.[45]

Gerasimov knew that under these conditions the political police could in reality only protect very few of Tsardom's men and even in this endeavour he had been anything but successful. Gerasimov recognised that his salvation lay in persuading Azef to return to the service – even in his self-imposed retirement Azef had supplied the key information in solving the Launitz case. Azef, already bored by his retirement, readily accepted Gerasimov's offer to return to work, the short-term benefit to the political police of his re-employment being considerable. He supplied his chief with information that allowed Gerasimov to arrest twenty-eight members of a group plotting to assassinate the tsar, resulting in a grateful Nicholas II rewarding Gerasimov with promotion to the rank of Major General.[46] Azef continued his work well into 1908 undermining SR terrorists at every opportunity. The chief of the St Petersburg OO through a combination of skill and luck – after all Azef chose not to betray him as he did other police chiefs before Gerasimov – succeeded despite the general carnage in helping to restore official confidence in the political police and established his reputation as Russia's outstanding political policeman.[47]

Actually, a closer look at the causes leading to the decline in the popularity of terrorism as a weapon against the regime reveals that Gerasimov and his methods can at best only claim partial credit for this achievement. Maureen Perrie argues that SR terrorism was more effective in the years between 1902 and 1904 than during the post-1905 era for reasons other than those ascribed to Gerasimov's methods. The murders of Sipiagin and Bogolepov in 1902 rekindled the romantic aura of the old *Narodnaia Volia*, bringing the SR Party considerable prestige and new members (discussed in Chapter 7). As Perrie points out, the even more spectacular assassinations of Plehve and the Grand Duke Sergei Aleksandrovich drove Tsardom into granting dramatic though often ephemeral concessions to its people. During the 1905 Revolution itself SR terrorists carried out several murderous attempts against some of the most despised men in the empire: Dubasov, von der Launitz and Min are just three that come to mind.[48] Yet with their two major targets, the tsar and Stolypin, the SRs were unsuccessful, in part thanks to the work of Azef. However, by 1906 the political environment had changed and within this new milieu the romanticism and heroism associated with the terrorist movement faded. With mass participation in the revolutionary movement and an increasingly enlightened population, political change came to be seen as a more sophisticated process than it had previously. By 1906 the people understood that political terror had become counter-productive, and gave Stolypin and Gerasimov an excuse to introduce draconian counter-revolutionary measures.[49]

****

One assassination attempt stands out above all the others and deserves special attention. This is the Maximalist bombing of Stolypin's summer residence on Aptekarsk Island. It is an event worth discussing not so much because of its value as evidence that groups other than the SRs, poorly infiltrated and relatively unknown to the police, could strike at even the best protected *sanovniki* within the empire with horrific results – this is more or less common knowledge – but because of its importance in the context of the professional relationship between Director of the Department of Police Trusevich and Chief of the St Petersburg OO Gerasimov.

The 'Maximalists' broke away from the SRs in order to conduct their own terrorist campaign based on a new tactic. They planned to strike down their intended victims swiftly without the lengthy, often laborious and lately clumsy planning that characterised the SR Battle Organisation and which made SR terrorists so vulnerable to police investigation.

M.I. Trusevich, the new director of Fontanka, took it upon himself to neutralise the Maximalists by employing one of their numbers as a *sotrudnik*. The police in Kiev had arrested a young Maximalist named Solomon Ryss for participating in an 'expropriation' or robbery designed to replenish the coffers of his group. Ryss and his fellow 'expropriators' committed a murder in the course of the robbery and in order to save himself from the dire straits in which the robbery and murder had placed him Ryss decided to play the double game. He offered his services to the political police as a *sotrudnik* amongst the Maximalists, an organisation relatively unknown to the Special Section. When Ryss met Trusevich he found him to be an easy prey for his disingenuous intentions. Trusevich, a recent appointment to Fontanka, displayed exceptional ability, although he had a reputation for stubbornness and arrogance.[50] This self-important man, judging the recruitment of Ryss to be a great personal *coup*, uncritically and on his own accepted Ryss's rather wishy-washy offer of his services. The appointment of Ryss lulled Fontanka into a false sense of security concerning any possible attempt by the Maximalists on Stolypin's life. Gerasimov himself did not have any *sotrudniki* among the Maximalists[51] and when he discovered their existence he suggested to Trusevich that extraordinary protection for Stolypin be arranged at the minister's summer residence on Aptekarsk Island. Trusevich responded to Gerasimov by ordering the OO chief to abandon his investigation of the Maximalists, informing the OO through the Special Section that everything was under control. The Maximalists, he said, were in his pocket.[52]

They were not. On 12 August 1906 two men disguised as policemen entered the grounds surrounding Stolypin's *dacha*. They rushed into the foyer of the house where they ignited a deafening explosion which immediately spread carnage throughout the grounds. The explosion struck down nearly 100 persons and of these at least 27 died. Stolypin, who had been in his study located some distance from the epicentre of the explosion and protected by the structure of the house, though severely shaken, remained unharmed. Sadly, one of his daughters was not so fortunate, sustaining serious injuries.[53]

The reverberations within the Department of Police caused by the Ryss case made inevitable the alienation of Fontanka from Stolypin. Trusevich when confronted by Gerasimov over the Apterkarsk Island bombing commented that it was Gerasimov not he who held primary responsibility for Stolypin's security. Trusevich's transferring the blame for the disaster to Gerasimov hardly endeared him to the OO chief. It must have given Gerasimov great satisfaction, then, to expose Solomon Ryss for what he was: a confidence man using Trusevich's vanity for his own ends.[54] The exposure of Ryss and with it his own incompetence in political police matters traumatised Trusevich, who permanently terminated his involvement with the Internal Agency.[55] Trusevich never forgave Gerasimov for exposing his foolishness.[56] Trusevich, fearful of another embarassing and career endangering incident, reversed his previous stance, now condemning the use of provocation by his political police, and despite his recent strong support for it, ordered that the practice be brought to an end. In 1907 the Department of Police produced a set of rules for undercover operations entitled *Instruktsiei po organizatsii i vedeniui vnutrennago nabliudeniia* (Instructions for the Organisation and Conduct of Internal Surveillance) in which Fontanka laid out the principles of Internal Agency operations, strictly forbidding 'provocation' – the carrying out of an assignment on behalf of a revolutionary organisation which involved the *sotrudnik* in the commission of a crime. Trusevich's *Instruktsiia* contained one critical modification to similar previous documents.

Significantly, while this document contained the same loopholes as past instructions, it transferred the onus of any future disasters caused by provocation to the shoulders of the political police by declaring that the conduct of their *sotrudniki* was the sole responsibility of the gendarme officers.[57] This provision safely distanced Trusevich and the Department of Police administration from any future imbroglios. It also directly disavowed the strategy Gerasimov and Stolypin had chosen to pursue. It goes without saying, that Trusevich's *Instruktsiia* drove Russia's political police officers into Gerasimov's arms.

There can be no doubt that Trusevich considered Gerasimov his principal rival for the control of the Russian political police system. The director of Fontanka could not, however, challenge Gerasimov's skill as a political policeman nor could he rival the OO chief's close personal relationship with Stolypin. Trusevich decided to compete with Gerasimov at another level, by refurbishing the tarnished image of the Special Section. He raised the standards of professionalism within it by appointing gendarme officers to the Special Section who were well-experienced in the art of political investigation.[58] For example, it would be difficult to identify officers more experienced in political police affairs than Colonel E.K. Klimovich, his new chief of the Special Section or than Lt Colonel V.A. Beklemishev and Captain A.M. Eremin, two of Klimovich's immediate subordinates.[59]

As we have seen, two of the major problems with the political police exposed by the 1905 Revolution were its inability to control the behaviour of its field bureaus and the incompetence of many of its OO chiefs. Trusevich sought to overcome these dilemmas in part by somewhat decentralising political police authority. As a result of his prodding, the MVD divided the empire into *okhrannye okrugi* (security districts). Each *okrug* contained several Gendarme Directorates[60] subject to the authority of a regional OO. Trusevich intended that each one of these regional OOs should come under the command of an exceptionally capable and experienced political police officer. However such men were not easily found since officers trained by Zubatov and Mednikov were held in contempt by the new men of the political police bureaucracy.[61] Trusevich, in his search for able gendarme officers untainted by Zubatov's influence, was forced, therefore, to appoint junior and relatively inexperienced officers to his regional OO postings, ironically just as Zubatov had done only five and six years before. Gendarme generals found themselves again subordinated to freshly promoted lieutenant colonels and even to captains. To make matters worse, Trusevich bestowed special treatment upon his recruits, obviously wishing in time-honoured fashion to buy their gratitude and thus deprive Gerasimov and his all powerful St Petersburg OO of their support.[62] Unfortunately, Trusevich did not possess the opportunity to experiment with police reforms for very long. Fontanka was about to undergo yet another upheaval, Trusevich himself, as we shall see below, becoming a victim of the patronage-clientele system set in motion by the appointment of new superiors.[63]

****

Stolypin appointed many officials to the MVD during his tenure as minister. However, none were more fateful to his own future and that of Fontanka than those of S.P. Beletskii and P.G. Kurlov. Stolypin selected Beletskii, then the vice-governor of Samara, for a vice-directorship of police in July 1909 because he knew him well from his services in Grodno and 'considered him a remarkable worker'.[64] This means of selecting new executives possibly had some merit especially since as Stolypin himself complained he had too few capable people to choose from, but it often did not work out as planned. As we shall see in Chapter 12, Beletskii was not the wisest of choices.

Why Stolypin chose P.G. Kurlov to be one of his vice-directors of police in April 1907 is somewhat of a mystery. Kurlov certainly fitted Stolypin's requirement of a man with 'a bent' for political police work and was blessed with a sufficiently strong personality and with the ability to supervise the enthusiastic, 'gifted' but amateurish Trusevich in matters of political investigation. None the less, Stolypin knew that Kurlov's negative characteristics far outweighed his attributes. He was an unmitigated reactionary who hated constitutional government and the feeling was mutual. Even moderate members of the Third Duma despised this odious man whom they saw merely as a creature of Court Commandant V.A. Dediulin.[65]

It is probable that Kurlov's court connections influenced Stolypin's decision to appoint him against his better judgement as a means of appeasing hostile reactionary circles. Stolypin certainly knew of Kurlov's excessively brutal repression of political unrest in Minsk where he served as governor in 1905–1906 and which resulted in his removal from that post and led to an investigation into his alleged misconduct by the Senate. However, Kurlov came under the protection of sympathetic friends. The investigation into the Minsk incident was discontinued. Shortly thereafter he received successive prestigious postings within the MVD. In April 1907, as noted above, he became vice-director of the Department of Police, initiating a meteoric rise within the MVD. In the summer of 1907 Kurlov became acting director of Fontanka (Trusevich was on leave), followed a few months later by his appointment as chief of the Main Prison Administration. On 1 January 1909 he attained the pinnacle of his career as assistant minister of internal affairs, managing the police. Two months later he received the rarely granted honour of also being designated commandant of the Separate Corps of Gendarmes.[66]

Kurlov achieved his promotions within the MVD despite blatant disloyalty to the man who initially appointed him. He besmirched the reputations of Stolypin and Gerasimov before the tsar's courtiers. He intercepted Stolypin's correspondence and openly countermanded his orders.[67] Why didn't Stolypin rid himself of this insubordinate functionary and potentially dangerous opponent? At first the minister undoubtedly tolerated Kurlov's behaviour in order to appease the court, although it would not have taken Stolypin very long to realise that Dediulin and his ilk could not be bought off so cheaply. The explanation for Stolypin's behaviour *vis-à-vis* Kurlov is to be found in his sadly mistaken belief that Gerasimov's control of Russia's political police system made Fontanka and Kurlov irrelevant to Tsardom's and Stolypin's own requirements and in his renowned lackadaisical management of subordinate departments.[68] After Kurlov's dual promotion to assistant minister and commandant of the Separate Corps of Gendarmes had placed considerable power in his hands, Stolypin tried to convince himself that Kurlov 'has begun to recognise my authority and has become more devoted to me.'[69] He fooled no one. Though the relationship between the two men appeared correct, Kurlov consistently refused to inform his minister of Fontanka's operations and Stolypin for his part finally looked for an opportunity to rid himself of Kurlov, a situation of which the assistant minister was well aware.[70]

Kurlov's appointment and rapid promotion through the law and order bureaucracy is best understood by placing the assistant minister's good fortune within the context of the realignment of bureaucratic forces in the post-1905 era. Stolypin stood at the forefront of the developmental sector of the bureaucracy. He aimed to sustain Russia's economic growth, while at the same time preserving the nation's political stability by creating an alliance between the entrepreneurial elements of the peasantry, the developmental sector of the bureaucracy and moderate circles within the Third Duma. The Prime Minister's plans met with increasing opposition from the landed gentry, elements of the law and order bureaucracy and the court.[71] Within the law and order bureaucracy itself senior and middle ranking officials openly took sides, choosing to support or obstruct Stolypin's policies of conservative renovation. Alongside Stolypin stood Gerasimov and A.A. Makarov[72] while Kurlov and his allies – including men such as Colonel S.G. Karpov who replaced Gerasimov in 1909 and E.K. Klimovich, Chief of the Special Section – aligned against him. Beletskii though never one of Kurlov's cronies also associated himself with the traditionalists when he became a vice-director of police in 1909. Director of Fontanka Trusevich remained a free agent in this struggle, failing to endear himself to either side, a position which made him exceptionally vulnerable to the machinations of Kurlov.

Assistant Minister of Internal Affairs Kurlov set about removing Trusevich and Gerasimov from their posts, the two men who blocked his absolute control of police affairs throughout the empire. The removal of Trusevich from his post was effected with relative ease. Trusevich and Kurlov did not get along[73] and the director of Fontanka – passed over in favour of his subordinate Kurlov for the coveted post of assistant minister, managing the police – must have realised his days at 16 Fontanka were numbered. As soon as Kurlov assumed his new post as assistant minister he implemented the traditional prerogative that went along with it of naming his own chief of Fontanka, thereby ridding himself of the bright and stubbornly independent Trusevich. It goes without saying that the serious and long overdue reform of the political police administration launched by Trusevich during his tenure as director of the Department of Police came to an abrupt halt with his dismissal.

Kurlov knew that shedding Gerasimov would be a much more difficult assignment. In fact it was Gerasimov's ill-luck that forced Stolypin to part with him, not the assistant minister's intrigues. In 1908 while still a vice-director of police, Kurlov made it clear that he wished to replace Gerasimov with Colonel Karpov. Gerasimov contends that under these circumstances he requested Stolypin's permission to resign, claiming that Makarov and Stolypin refused to let him go.[74] While the bare facts of this scenario are probably true, the cause prompting Gerasimov's proffered resignation – pressure from Kurlov – is probably not. The chief of the St Petersburg OO, a tough, thick-skinned man, protected by the patronage of Stolypin and bolstered by the gratitude of Nicholas II whose life he had saved, would not have succumbed to the pressure applied by a mere vice-director of police. It is probable that this exercise of submitting his resignation and then being 'persuaded' to withdraw it by Stolypin and his ally Makarov was in fact nothing more than a snub at Kurlov, an exercise in the drawing of battle lines between adversaries within the MVD.

In a sense as strange as it might seem, Gerasimov's devotion to Stolypin not only represented the minister's control over Russia's political police system, but to some degree symbolised the ascendancy of the renovators within the MVD itself. Gerasimov had become a pawn in a game he did not understand and was certainly ill-equipped to play. A cunning, experienced political police specialist, Gerasimov built his reputation, as we have shown, on hard-nosed police work and the ability to take decisive action. This man of peasant background did not possess the polished veneer or style to ingratiate himself at court, and despite Nicholas II's appreciation of his services to the dynasty, court circles treated this country bumpkin upstart with disdain[75] and was hated by them as a symbol of Stolypin's power.

By late 1908 Gerasimov's luck began to run out. The St Petersburg OO chief's best efforts could not prevent leaks concerning the nefarious activity of the Internal Agency from escaping into the press. *Pravo (The Law)*, Russia's foremost legal journal began in its 12 August 1907 issue a debate which lasted for several years over the criminality of 'provocation' under the Russian statutes. In 1908, on a lower but more effective level, Vladimir Burtsev began his public exposures of *sotrudniki* in his Paris journal *Byloe (The Past)*.[76] During the final months of 1908 accumulated publicity of this sort began to have an effect on public opinion. In the autumn of 1908 the Third Duma undertook an investigation into cases of provocation and challenged the right of the MVD to employ criminal types as undercover agents. The Duma could not understand how Fontanka could hire proven, though supposedly repentant, revolutionaries as guardians of state security. During the course of the Duma's debate on this matter A.A. Makarov appeared before it to explain police policy toward acts of provocation. He unequivocably announced, 'provocation is intolerable', reminding the Duma that, 'any provocational act is criminal and must sicken the disposition of any orderly man and diverts the members of the *Okhrana [sic!]* from the serious problem of the struggle with the revolution'.[77] Although the content of Makarov's statement seemed plausible, the assistant minister knew it was a boldfaced lie.[78]

The Third Duma, however, did not bother to verify Makarov's statement. Instead, it gave the MVD a vote of confidence in its ability to cleanse itself of provocateurs![79] Gerasimov just barely had time to breath a sigh of relief when an open letter addressed to Prime Minister Stolypin appeared in *The Times* of London. This letter written by former Director of Fontanka Lopukhin 'informed' Stolypin of Evno Azef's dual life. The same letter appeared in the 25 January 1909 issue of *Pravo*.[80] In *Pravo*, Vladimir Nabokov, one of Russia's most respected jurists, summed up the rising tide of public opinion against provocation when he wrote that, 'provocation ... is not only a gross moral evil, but to institute [provocation] in a cultured, legal state is absolutely intolerable and inadmissible'.[81] To make matters still worse for Gerasimov and Stolypin, the SRs themselves confirmed Azef's double life in early January 1909.[82] Finally, the Duma had sufficient ammunition to initiate an inquiry into Azef's career and his relationship with Fontanka. The Duma and the public opinion it represented demanded to know how a renowned terrorist could be employed by the government to protect officials whose colleagues he had been murdering on a regular basis for years! Stolypin did his best to contain the scandal[83] and managed to keep the operations of the Special Section and its OOs shrouded in secrecy, convincing the Duma to leave the elimination of provocation in the hands of the political police, the very people who supported it so enthusiastically in the first place![84]

During the autumn of 1908 the rumours of Gerasimov's central role in the proliferation of provocation intensified. Finally, Stolypin had no other choice but to place Gerasimov on long-term leave until the politically charged environment had time to cool down. Unfortunately for Gerasimov, Trusevich made certain that this did not happen. The director of Fontanka had been waiting for over two years for just such an opportunity to avenge himself upon the Internal Agency and Gerasimov after his humiliation in the Solomon Ryss affair. After Azef's exposure Trusevich publicly condemned provocation,[85] supporting his rhetoric with action. He cut back funding for the Internal Agency, forcing the OOs and the Foreign Agentura to release many *sotrudniki* from the service.[86] Trusevich told the large number of undercover agents who remained in service that, 'any provocational activities will be exposed without fail by the bureau and the breach of his [the undercover agent's] duty not to break the law will result in his being handed over for justice without any hope of mercy'. In the next breath Trusevich almost parenthetically added, 'of course we will undertake all measures to defend them in those cases where the charge of provocation is false'.[87] Trusevich's lukewarm support for the innocent offered little solace to Tsardom's undercover agents. It seemed unlikely to them that in the future any *sotrudnik* charged with provocation would be defended with any degree of conviction by the government. In addition, most undercover agents believed that the Special Section would do nothing to help them as long as such action involved the slightest risk.[88] Zinaida Zhuchenko, one of Tsardom's premier undercover agents, bitterly exclaimed to E.K. Klimovich, her former chief in Moscow, that while traitorous police officials who defected to the Revolution (she meant L.P. Men′shchikov and M.I. Bakai) and exposed *sotrudniki* as a matter of course went unpunished, loyal and hard-working undercover agents suffered the slur of being labelled 'provocateurs'.[89]

Gerasimov could not hope to survive a scandal of this magnitude when even the Director of the Department of Police almost with relish condemned the operations of the Internal Agency and sapped the morale of its *sotrudniki* who lived on the razor's edge in any case. After four months of imposed leave Gerasimov returned to his post only to discover that many things had changed. Stolypin's appointment of Kurlov to the post of assistant minister of internal affairs deeply hurt Gerasimov[90] and served to make life even more difficult for the Director of the St Petersburg OO. There was nothing Gerasimov could do. The Azef Affair forced Stolypin to part with him. General Gerasimov retired from the St. Petersburg OO and Kurlov ensured that he would never interfere in political police work again.[91]

The OO chief's dream of controlling dissent within the empire by planting a massive secret network of undercover agents throughout the subversive and opposition movements who would place the control of these organisations into the hands of the government never came to fruition. Nevertheless, his strategy on a much smaller scale persisted. Authority over this network of *sotrudniki*, however, passed from Gerasimov and his headquarters on the Moika Canal to the men at 16 Fontanka Quai. Stolypin had lost control of the political police system.

The balance of power within the MVD was shifting away from those who favoured the policies of conservative renovation within a limited constitutional system to those who stubbornly refused to accept the outcome of the 1905 Revolution and gloried in the routinised charisma of the monarchy. The battle for control of the political police network reflected in microcosm this irreconcilable polarisation of opinion over the fate of the Russian polity within the government.

As for Kurlov, his control of Fontanka remained tantalisingly incomplete. The assassination of Karpov, Gerasimov's successor at the Moika, prevented Kurlov from completely subordinating the Petersburg OO to his will[92] and Kurlov still confronted the possibility of a Stolypin inspired overhaul of the Department of Police embodied in the Makarov Commission's recommendations.

****

The pressure to launch a major overhaul of the *entire* tsarist police system originated years before with Lopukhin's suggestions for the consolidation of all civil, political and military (gendarme) police forces within a unified command at the provincial level. At the same time Lopukhin condemned those traditional Russian cultural patterns and the institutional behaviour that led to widespread *proizvol*, calling for its abolition (discussed in Chapter 6). In early 1905 a commission under Count A.P. Ignat′ev, though ultra-conservative in composition, echoed and elaborated upon Lopukhin's criticisms of Tsardom's policing system.[93] As we have seen, P.N. Durnovo launched a programme of police reform and while he managed to implement some desirable modifications to the police system, overall it remained unchanged.

Although Stolypin knew much less about police business than his predecessor Durnovo, he also recognised the need for a thorough revamping of the entire police system. In September 1906, the prime minister issued a circular which suggested methods of increasing political police efficiency. At about the same time he appointed an inter-departmental commission under the chairmanship of A.A. Makarov (as we have already noted) for the purpose of developing a plan designed to improve the overall performance of all branches of the police with the exception of the Special Section and its field bureaus. Nevertheless, two of the Makarov Commission's conclusions directly affected political police operations. The Commission resolved that the broad spectrum of Fontanka's duties must be placed under the law and that the entire police force, including the political police, operating within a given *guberniia* must be subordinated to a single chief embodied in a new office to be designated as the assistant governor for police affairs.[94]

The exceedingly slow headway of the Makarov Commission must be laid at the doorstep of Assistant Minister of Internal Affairs Kurlov. He justified his reticence to act by explaining 'restructuring the whole system of political investigation demanded time', and he was too busy to develop a new system. Under Kurlov, Fontanka continued its time-worn method of quick fix alterations in the political police network's operation through the steady flow of often contradictory *instruktsii*. Kurlov refused to reduce the number of OOs or to introduce any other significant modifications in the structure of the political police.[95] The Makarov Commission struggled against Kurlov's obstruction while the Third Duma patiently awaited the outcome of its deliberations until Stolypin's assassination in early September, 1911. His death, caused by the indifference and ineptitude of General Kurlov and the Kiev OO (discussed below) catapulted the Duma into pressing for immediate police reform.[96] The Duma demanded that Fontanka be completely reorganised and subordinated to the governors, the *gradonachal'niki* and the law.[97] Nicholas II himself agreed that Kurlov's methods of directing the police required revision[98] and finally when Makarov's report appeared it called for a fundamental reform of Fontanka.[99]

Unfortunately, Kurlov's considerable influence over the proceedings of the Commission had prevented it from coming to terms with those 'liberal' issues that had so concerned Lopukhin and the vast majority of Duma deputies, such as the question of a police code of ethics, an essential ingredient in bringing Fontanka and the Separate Corps of Gendarmes under the rule of law.[100] However, it would be 1913 before the Fourth Duma would even debate this or any other issue related to police reform. By early 1912, the unsavoury S.P. Beletskii directed the Department of Police. As reactionary as Kurlov (who claims he chose Beletskii for this post before his enforced retirement),[101] Beletskii was equally uninterested in a thoroughgoing renovation of the Department of Police.[102] Only in 1913, with active support from N.A. Maklakov, the new minister of internal affairs, who expressed a pronounced interest in police affairs did the MVD review the proposals of the Makarov Commission for revamping the police. The MVD dropped the suggested new office of assistant governor for police affairs at the behest of both the gendarmes and the governors[103] and at the same time issued under the imprimatur of the Department of Police its reply to the Makarov Commission's findings and recommendations as a whole.

With refreshing frankness Fontanka admitted some of its major failings. Although the Department of Police did not specifically mention the agencies of the political police in its reply, its words apply equally to the Special Section and its branches. Fontanka confessed that:

1. Its administrative structure urgently required modification.
2. Its bureaus wasted a good deal of money.
3. The absence of a unified command was a serious problem.
4. There were too many chiefs holding a wide variety of disparate views on the duties of the police.
5. Its structure was too complex, and confused, failing to clearly delineate functions among its executives at all levels of command.
6. The professional qualifications of those serving within the Department of Police were inadequate and needed to be raised.
7. The Department employed too few policemen for the quantity of work they were required to undertake and for the density of the population.
8. Policemen were underpaid.
9. Duties not related to police business weighed heavily on the police.
10. And, most important, the absence of a general police statute prevented the regulation and unification of the complex and diverse duties associated with police service.[104]

Fontanka's recognition of its failings and the Makarov Commission's desire to rectify them did not satisfy the Fourth Duma. The Duma bitterly noted the omission from the Makarov Commission's recommendations of a statute guaranteeing the personal inviolability of the Russian people, considering such a provision a *sine qua non* of the reform. In addition, the failure of the Commission to recommend the disbanding of the Separate Corps of Gendarmes deeply disappointed the Duma.[105] These omissions combined with the staggering cost of the projected reform[106] led to a lengthy debate over the proposed legislation drawn up by the Commission[107] which continued to the outbreak of the First World War. With the onset of mobilisation the proposed legislation on police reform paled into insignificance. The police reform bill never came before the Duma for final consideration.

****

The victory of Kurlov, Beletskii and their ilk over police reform and their conquest of Fontanka on behalf of the court and reactionary bureaucratic circles formed the context within which the assassination of P.A. Stolypin and the government's and tsar's response to it must be seen. The story of Stolypin's murder is often repeated and an aura of mysterious conspiracy still hangs over the assassination. What is clear in this case is that the policemen assigned to protect Stolypin were unconcerned about his welfare and ill-prepared for their complicated assignment. The protection of *sanovniki en route* required the expertise of a specialist in matters of travel security.[108] Kurlov did not provide such an expert for this trip. Indeed, it seems likely that Kurlov and his hand-picked Vice Director of Police M.N. Verigin took advantage of the notorious incompetence of Lt Colonel Kuliabko, chief of the Kiev OO (see Chapter 5) to place Stolypin's life at great risk, but this is only educated speculation.

The First Department of the State Council concluded its investigation into the assassination of Stolypin by finding that Kurlov, Kuliabko, Verigin and Chief of the Court *Okhrana* Spiridovich were guilty only of gross negligence. Before the proceedings recommended that these men be brought to trial under this charge Nicholas II intervened to bring the process to an abrupt halt, saving the four police chiefs from public humiliation. The tsar told Chairman of the Council of Ministers Kokovtsov, for example, that he knew Spiridovich particularly well and could not believe that this 'unfortunate man' would want to do anything 'evil and culpable'. His *only* crime, the tsar told the startled Kokovtsov, was that 'he did not take every precautionary measure.' Kokovtsov appealed to the tsar that such a decision would simply affirm the popular conviction that Stolypin had been murdered by the political police.[109] His warning may have had some impact on the fate of at least three of the four men held responsible by the State Council for Stolypin's death. While Spiridovich remained in his post as chief of the court *Okhrana* Nicholas II more or less gently sacrificed Kurlov, Verigin and Kuliabko to public opinion.[110]

The gentle treatment of these four men emphasised the tsar's key role in the ascendency of the extreme right within Russia's governing circles and also reflected the relief of these circles that Stolypin, though not nearly so influential as he had once been,[111] was now absent from the political scene.[112] For the political police, however, the mild punishments doled out to Kurlov and his associates possessed considerable significance. Fontanka's men in one form or another had participated in assassination plots directed against *sanovniki* before. Witte, for example, had barely escaped an attempt against his life most certainly involving the Moscow OO. The Stolypin case was different, however, because it involved at the least the criminal negligence of three of Tsardom's most senior police officials who were saved from prosecution by the high-handed abuse of Imperial Authority. These men had escaped from their crime with impunity.[113] As a consequence, the outcome of the Stolypin murder, therefore, bound the court circles and the upper echelons of the law and order bureaucracy closer together than ever before.[114] The men who controlled Fontanka and Tsardom's political police system, with one rather ineffectual exception (see Chapter 12) between 1911 and 1917, abandoned any pretence of moulding Fontanka to the conditions of post-1905 Russian society. In 1913 from the floor of the Fourth Duma V.A. Maklakov angrily complained about this situation. He attacked the government for abandoning Stolypin's 'platonic' invitation to legality 'in favour of a cynical call to lawlessness'.[115] Ironically, the victory of the forces of reaction within the law and order segment of the bureaucracy led to behaviour which weakened the surviving pillars of the traditional regime still further.

12 S.P. Beletskii and V.F. Dzhunkovskii and the Forces of Modernity within Russian Society

Stolypin's assassination capped an exceptionally tumultuous period in MVD politics. The tsar himself hoped that the new minister of internal affairs, A.A. Makarov, would be able to terminate the energy-wasting internecine warfare within the MVD.[1] The turmoil created by Stolypin's policies, the Azef Affair, the persistent calls for police reform and the work of the Makarov Commission and ultimately by the scandal surrounding Stolypin's assassination confirmed that the tsar's concern was not misplaced. Yet the OOs and Gendarme Directorates alike misjudged the significance of such adversities upon the future of the political police, so busy were they in revelling in the apparent magnitude of *their* victory over the opponents of the regime on the battlefield of revolution.[2] Between 1908 and 1912 the exhausted and defeated dissident movements allowed Fontanka to bask in this illusion.

The effectiveness of the political police grew as the subsidence of the 1905 Revolution led to a restoration of their confidence. Throughout 1906 and 1907 the tsarist political police rounded up Russia's revolutionaries, a chore made relatively easy by the openness of the revolutionary movements whose hundreds of new members and fellow travellers did not understand the essential requirement for security demanded by the revolution. The political police triumphantly recorded the hardships they had inflicted upon the revolutionary movements.[3] The SRs especially suffered from the effects of police repression. By 1909 they had been thoroughly routed (along with the Maximalists and the Anarchists).[4] Indeed, the demoralisation caused by the Azef Affair and by Stolypin's agrarian reforms which overshadowed their own proposals for an agrarian revolution caused the SRs to spend the remainder of the pre-war years sinking ever deeper into enervating squabbles and endless recriminations over the practice of political terror which had sustained the party for so long.[5]

The SDs, though they were often victimised by the police, suffered less violent although no less effective repression than the SRs.[6] The widespread penetration of SD groups by Internal Agency *sotrudniki* in particular destroyed their morale and comradeship. As one social democrat in the Ukraine ruefully complained, 'the spreading of hundreds of provocateurs, who have succeeded in penetrating the very centre of the organisation, temporarily makes [party] work completely impossible'.[7] The knowledge that one's best mate could be a police agent 'made everyone suspect everyone else ...'. One SD leaflet described this fear as 'an extremely noxious poison which seeps into all the pores of the organization, kills all its tissues, and eventually paralyzes its activities'.[8]

These conditions were not confined to a particular locale within the empire[9] nor to Russia itself. The post-1905 SD emigrés like their SR colleagues had retreated to western Europe hardened by bitter disillusionment. Lenin seemed overwhelmed by the disaster. 'Tsarism was victorious', he wrote. 'All the revolution and opposition parties were smashed. Depression, demoralization, dispersion, discord, desertion [and] pornography took the place of politics'.[10] SD Party membership declined to miniscule proportions and in some areas of Russia the party ceased to exist altogether.[11] It appeared that the link established between the intelligentsia and the working class – so important the Special Section believed for the success of any revolutionary movement – was broken.[12] It is no wonder that Assistant Minister of Internal Affairs Gurko remembered that 'the successful suppression of the 1905–1906 [revolutionary] movement had given an assurance of the stability of the regime and deprived the newly awakened workers' movement of any dangerous aspect'.[13] Russia's workers were further deflated by their apparently unconditional defeat at the hands of Stolypin's *coup d'état* of 3 June 1907, which stripped the labouring masses of a legal public platform for the expression of their grievances. These tragic events were capped by an economic depression that blanketed Russian industry during the years following the 1905 Revolution, smothering any remaining rebelliousness within the working class.

Both Gerasimov in the capital and Martynov in Moscow agreed that 1909 was the quietest year they could remember during their lengthy careers.[14] The underground movement hardly existed.[15] Chief of the Moscow OO Martynov noted that although SD underground cells were scattered through most large cities they survived only by the grace of the political police, he boasted and 'only in the interest of political investigation'.[16] Martynov and his colleagues had lulled themselves into a false sense of security.

****

Despite the apparent victory of the forces of order, in reality Tsardom's efforts to stem the increasing power of public opinion – the *bête noir* of the political policing system – failed. The voicing of public opinion continued to grow in sophistication and spread itself more deeply through and across the layers of Russian society. In particular, public opinion generated by opposition and legal radical newspapers and by the debates and speeches from the floor especially of the Fourth Duma combined to stimulate and protect the revitalised workers' movement in the critical sixteen months between the Lena goldfield massacre in April 1912, and the mobilisation of the Russian army for war.

The beacon of public opinion within Russia was the new Duma. It is no wonder then that Fontanka focused its hatred upon this institution. Forays against the Duma as an institution were rarely undertaken by the political police. Initially, the Special Section did its best to subvert the elections to the First Duma and when this tactic failed Rachkovskii attempted to infiltrate the Duma chamber. These crude plots and others like them miscarried.[17] The following year Gerasimov had greater success when the Petersburg OO manufactured the provocation that gave Stolypin his excuse for launching his famed *coup d'état* of 3 June 1907.[18] But for the majority of the police leadership Stolypin's *coup* was nothing more than a pyrrhic victory. The Special Section considered the liberal intelligentsia the backbone of the revolutionary movement and while the Third and Fourth Dumas were considerably more conservative than their predecessors, thanks to Stolypin's revision of the electoral law, they still represented in the eyes of the police two of liberalism's most powerful weapons deployed against Tsardom: legality and public opinion.

The struggle over police reform which we described in the previous chapter showed that even the Third Duma could challenge the ascendency of the forces of order from the floor of the Tauride Palace. The Fourth Duma increasingly began to resemble a modern western legislative body. The public opinion aroused by its debates drove the political police to distraction. In particular the escape of the liberals into the Duma, and escape is exactly how the police viewed it, appeared to be a masterful tactical stroke that placed them beyond the reach of the forces of order. K.I. Globachev, chief of the Petrograd OO from 1915 to the end of the regime, clearly remembered his frustration. He claimed that his OO was geared to battle revolutionaries, but not the liberal intelligentsia, and he placed the blame for the collapse of Tsardom squarely on its shoulders and on the Duma which served as its fortress.[19]

While Globachev's bitter memories were coloured by his highly prejudiced perspective they nevertheless reflect the impact of the strengthening alliance between public opinion and the new political institutions upon the Russian political process. Indeed, each of these elements of renovated Russia protected and served the interests of the other.[20] For example, the moderate and opposition press in particular developed a symbiotic relationship, with the Duma fighting for the freedom of the press on the one hand, while the press reported on Duma business on the other. As Casper Ferenczi recently wrote, 'to a certain extent, the skilfully organized co-operation between press and parliament balanced the deficiencies of the political system'.

Despite intensifying harassment by the political police – the St Petersburg OO created a new corps of *sotrudniki* who specialised in infiltrating editorial offices[21] – the moderate and opposition press remained relatively unscathed between 1907 and 1914. During the Third of June regime the press enjoyed a substantial growth in reading public: over a third of the Russian population prior to the First World War maintained regular contact with newspapers and through them with the

Duma itself. By 1914 the massive growth in print media overwhelmed the government's limited capacity to censor it. In particular, the political police quickly grasped the problem the new working-class newspapers presented to the government:[22] they were distinguished by their cheapness and thanks to large printings they reached a substantial section of the population. However, as A.A. Makarov told a group of factory owners protesting against the appearance of the new legal Bolshevik paper *Pravda*, 'it is no longer as in the past, when the Ministry had almost unlimited power in relation to the daily press'.[23] Indeed, by August 1913, the political police reported that the radical press had become so popular among the workers that mere rumours of its suppression aroused intense hostility from the working class.[24]

The statistics presented in Table 12.1 must be evaluated cautiously, none the less they indicate the ebb and flow of the ongoing skirmishing between the Russian government and the press. In terms of the ratio of openings versus forced closings, generally, of Russia's newspapers presented in Table 12.1, it appears

Table 12.1 Number of New Publications Versus Number of those Ceasing Publication, 1905–1913[a]

Year	*Opening*	*Closing*
1905	166	156
1906	706	435
1907	337	313
1908	278	259
1909	299	189
1910	282	193
1911	247	239
1912	308	256
1913	367	243

Source: B.I. Grekov, K.F. Shatsillo, V.V. Shelokhaev, 'Evoliutsiia politicheskoi struktury Rossii v kontse XIX–nachale XX veka (1895–1913)', *Istoriia SSSR* no. 5 (September/October 1988): 43–44.

[a] Some periodic journals such as *Pravda* closed under one name would shortly reopen under a slight variance in the name. The source does not indicate if this consideration is taken into account in the authors' calculations. Logic would tell the reader that it had not been, since to the police the opening and closing of *Pravda, Rabochaia Pravda, Severnaia Pravda, Pravda Truda, Za Pravdy, Proletarskaia Pravda, Put' Pravdy* and *Trudovaia Pravda,* for example, would have been recorded as statistically independent events.

that the press was gaining the upper hand as the forces of order became more sensitive to the pressures applied against them by a public opinion which held them accountable to the law.[25] As a result, late Tsarist Russia 'possessed a relatively free press of high quality which in its freedom of criticism was not substantially different from the western press'.[26]

The labour movement, too, continued to evolve under the Third of June system. Recent writers on labour have challenged the Special Section's view of the Russian labour movement in the post-revolutionary years as more or less inert.[27] For quite some time the magnitude of the defeat of the working class at the hands of the counter-revolution obscured exactly how much the revolutionary struggle between 1905 and 1907 had tempered it: how much the labouring masses had learned about themselves, their government and the society of which they were now a part. They learned that their suffering derived from the actions of men and was not a function of an inevitable pre-ordained order. And they developed tactics to alter this state of affairs. During the revolutionary years their suspicion of the radical intelligentsia declined and they began to absorb and respond to political ideas.[28] As Geoffrey Swain so succinctly put it, 'the labour movement after the "years of freedom" could never be led by an orthodox priest like Gapon'.[29]

This is not to say that the years between 1907 and 1912 were notable for a booming labour movement; clearly they were not. However, the form of self-improvement adopted by Russia's workers in their trade unionism and enlightenment circles boded well for the future of moderate social democracy (or so at least it seemed at the time). The law of 6 March 1906 that decreed the legality of trade union organisation, albeit in a restricted and intensely controlled environment, had a seemingly instantaneous effect on the development of unions and other worker self-help organisations which proved so popular with the masses. From March 1906 to March 1912 between 600 and 900 unions of all sorts were established.[30] Despite the interminable importunity they endured, legal and semi-legal trade unions became the single most important outlet for worker expression and a mechanism for the learning of practical labour politics.

The MVD under Stolypin made every effort to contain the influence and size of the union movement, arguing that it still favoured a not-so-benign form of paternalism. However, despite the overall hostility of the forces of order to the union movement, the Special Section initially favoured their continued existence for two reasons. First, the legal operations of unions considerably eased the problem of *filery* surveillance over the worker movement. Second, the Special Section also recognised the salutary effect of the trade unions on the workers 'who were sobering up from the revolutionary hangover [1905] and beginning to develop a consciousness of their purely professional needs'.[31]

Unfortunately after toying with these notions the MVD soon abandoned them, as Fontanka witnessed the attempt of the SDs working within the major unions to link the roles of these legal organisations with underground 'illegal' activities.[32]

As a result, police attacks against trade unions intensified. Between 1907 and 1910 Fontanka reported that a total of 214 unions had been closed by the authorities and many other unions ceased to exist under the pressures induced by political and economic circumstances,[33] a situation which worsened after Stolypin's death in September 1911. In 1911 and 1912 the MVD closed unions throughout the empire and the political police demanded membership lists from those unions that survived.[34] Table 12.2 clearly illustrates the impact of the MVD's assault against the trade union movement although a closer look reveals that, despite their harsh treatment by the government, the number of unions extant never dropped below 200. After falling to a low of 208 in 1912 the number of unions in Russia *rose* to 234 in 1913. As Geoffrey Swain wrote, although Tsardom was most uncomfortable with the principle of freedom of association, it did cope with its union problem within the framework of the law. The government's refusal to reject the provisional regulations of March 1906 on trade union formation in order to return to the blatant arbitrariness of the pre-1905 period allowed unionism to survive.[35]

However, it would be naive to assume that the government's decision not to wipe out unionism altogether was based solely on a growing respect for the law. That respect, such as it was, received considerable reinforcement from the power of public opinion. Thus, when the political police – who continued to harass the trade unions at every turn[36] – wanted to go still further by liquidating them altogether, it found that Fontanka would not permit them to do this. Why? Because, as Fontanka warned them in an October 1913 memorandum, the mood of the working class had taken on 'the character of a style of psychosis'. Therefore, Fontanka argued the liquidation of professional organisations such as trade unions would 'only hasten an outburst of the strike movement'.[37]

****

This new Russia of vociferous public opinion and political activism fuelled by the demands of a population growing in political sophistication and sustained by now firmly entrenched semi-constitutional institutions drove the forces of order to

Table 12.2 Number of Trade Unions in Russia, 1905–1913

Year	*1905*	*1906*	*1907*	*1908*	*1909*	*1910*	*1911*	*1912*	*1913*
No. of Unions	465	836	1096	419	304	242	216	208	234

Source: B.I. Grekov, K.F. Shatsillo, V.K. Shelokhaev, 'Evoliutsiia politicheskoi struktury Rossii v kontse XIX – nachale XX veka (1895–1913)', *Istoriia SSSR*, 1988, No. 5: 44–5.

choose between one of two directions: either to ignore the political transformation of the Russian polity in the post-1905 era or to attempt to come to terms with it. Between 1912 and 1915 Fontanka would initially choose the first path under the guidance of S.P. Beletskii and then reluctantly and briefly trod the second road under the persistent prodding of V.F. Dzhunkovskii.

Public opinion, legality and the re-invigoration of the working class became the dominant problems confronting S.P. Beletskii when he became director of the Department of Police in late February 1912. Beletskii first appeared in St Petersburg when chosen by Stolypin for the post of vice-director of the Department of Police managing finances.[38] Beletskii's associates and acquaintances universally proclaimed him to be a remarkable worker with the ability to quickly unravel exceptionally complex problems and they remembered that he often worked through the night while serving as chief of Fontanka. He also boasted the reputation of possessing a talent, one might even say a special gift, for police affairs. Most of his acquaintances found him to be extraordinarily ambitious, cunning and overweening; a keen observer of all that went on around him. A.A. Makarov, who as minister of internal affairs appointed Beletskii to direct Fontanka, went so far as to call him an 'honest worker' who stuck to his task and scrupulously avoided interfering in the affairs of MVD departments other than his own.[39] However, Makarov's glowing description of Beletskii does not ring true since ambition and cunning, not integrity, appear to have been Beletskii's most prominent attributes. He wasted his ability on satiating his ambition for power and toward this end allied himself with the most unscrupulous courtiers.[40]

Once installed as vice-director responsible for finances, Beletskii found Fontanka to be in fiscal chaos. He immediately set out to initiate a new regime of much tighter budgetary controls on Russia's OOs and its Foreign Agentura, only to be told that this sensitive aspect of their operation was not within his province. General Kurlov, by now assistant minister of internal affairs managing the police, had placed the reform of regional budgetary processes in the hands of his own men, Vice-Director S.E. Vissarionov and Chief of the Special Section E.K. Klimovich. The new vice-director Beletskii was ordered to confine his role to accounting procedures at police headquarters. Not satisfied with this duty Beletskii insinuated his fiscal agents into Kurlov's inspection groups, thereby ensuring access to valuable information detailing the operational expenses of the Special Section's field bureaus as well as gaining an insight into their *modus operandi*.[41] When he became director of Fontanka in 1912 Beletskii used this information to curb what he considered to be the excessive, wasteful activities of the tsarist political police at home and abroad. Yet, despite his keen interest in making the Department of Police a financially responsible institution, Beletskii did not exhibit any desire to undertake a thoroughgoing overhaul of Department of Police procedures. When as director of Fontanka he encountered V.F. Dzhunkovskii, the newly appointed assistant minister of internal affairs, managing the police, who wished to embark on a major renovation of the Special Section,

Beletskii's deep-seated bureaucratic conservatism and sense of self-preservation came to the fore: he believed that improved police work could be realised by Fontanka's present structure and personnel.

Upon assuming the directorship of Fontanka, Beletskii ordered a massive penetration of Russian society by his field bureaus especially among the peasantry, railway workers, high school students and Russia's military and naval forces 'without delay' and he warned his field bureaus that 'the availability or absence of intelligence [*agenturnogo osveshcheniia*] serving as the basis for reports to the minister of internal affairs' would determine an OO or Gendarme Directorate chief's future in the service.[42] Like Plehve, he wished no nook nor cranny of possible dissent to escape his attention. However, Beletskii was not satisfied with simply spying on society, he wanted to control it as well. The relationship between public opinion (the Duma and the press) and the workers' movement became the focus of Beletskii's experiment in social control. The sudden upsurge in widespread opposition at all levels of society to the government after the Lena goldfield massacre[43] discussed below gave Beletskii the opportunity to display his skill as the leading defender of the regime. Beletskii concentrated his efforts against the labour movement as he attempted, by becoming the *bête noire* of the revolutionary movement, to smooth the path to ministerial appointment.[44]

Beletskii's previous experience within the Department of Police had not introduced him to the subterranean world of the political police. He relied entirely on his experienced assistant S.E. Vissarionov, who himself had little new to contribute to political police strategy or tactics. Instead, Beletskii, Vissarionov and Chief of the Special Section Eremin reworked two earlier counter-revolutionary strategies which they believed would totally demoralise the social democrats, the one revolutionary movement they perceived as having the capacity to take advantage of the 'muted dissatisfaction accumulating among the population during recent years'.[45]

First, Beletskii employed the strategy of 'divide and conquer' for which he is renowned,[46] though it had long been a weapon within the political police arsenal. He merely refined the technique and expanded its application. Second, he took a page from Gerasimov's book by ordering the Internal Agency to penetrate the SD movement so deeply that its *sotrudniki* would be able to acquire control of the SD's grass roots leadership on the one hand and the SD-controlled unions on the other hand. This strategy allowed Beletskii to circumvent the law and public opinion which proved particularly irksome to him.[47] Beletskii believed that through this strategy of infiltration and control he would be able to frustrate and discourage the membership of these organisations, driving them into a state of inertia, or perhaps as Victoria Bonnell suggests, driving them underground. This latter option appealed to the political police since the Special Section felt much less restrained in its handling of the illegal revolutionary movement than it did in dealing with the legal trade unions.

To this end Fontanka devised a stategy to manipulate the Bolshevik movement into disrupting moderate social democracy. Bolshevism by its very nature offered the perfect vehicle for this strategy.[48] Historians have noted that the decision to adopt this strategy was a grossly ill-considered one. After all what did Beletskii and the Special Section accomplish? As Laura Engelstein and Victoria Bonnell (among others) have pointed out, Fontanka's strategy ensured the demise of moderate social democracy in Russia by producing frustration and anger amongst young workers, the potential leaders of their class. Beletskii's strategy drove these young men and women into the arms of the radical intelligentsia, who promised that by rejecting moderation in favour of extremism the workers would attain the economic and political goals they so desired.[49] The end result contributed, therefore, to placing Lenin and his Bolsheviks at the forefront of the labour movement.

Yet, strange as it may seem – since Bolsheviks were the enemy of Tsardom – Beletskii apparently supported and fostered a movement and its leader for whom he and the analysts of the Special Section had considerable respect.[50] Certainly, there must have been more to the Special Section's and Beletskii's rationale than the discovery that Bolshevism could be easily penetrated by their *sotrudniki* (a circumstance not unique to Bolshevism in any case) and the belief that Lenin's fractious personality was not conducive to party unity. Why did these characteristics of Bolshevism outweigh what in retrospect appear to be the obvious dangers of this strategy.

The answer to this question is to be found in an analysis of the political police mind sets which universally influence political police attitudes toward dissent, a full discussion of which is undertaken in the following chapter. Here, it is only necessary to discuss three of them narrowly, *vis-à-vis* Bolshevism. First, the political police habit of distorting its analyses of intelligence by fixating on the substance of subversive and opposition statements instead of analysing them only for indications of possible strategies;[51] focusing on the opponents' propaganda at the expense of a careful analysis of programmes and activities, the Special Section exaggerated the danger and impact of those groups which, although making the most outrageous claims posed little or no threat to the regime. On the other hand, the political damage of the less shrill groups including the Bolsheviks was often underestimated. Political policing systems are bound to fall into this trap since they evaluate the potentiality of a revolutionary party based on evidence of specific action, rarely taking the general mould and structure of the party into account.[52]

In the case of Bolshevism Lenin's strategy was crystal clear, expressed without obfuscating bombast, and based on assumptions about the dynamics of the Russian polity which the Special Section not only understood but with which it agreed! Klara Klebovna, a Maximalist who resided in Paris between 1909 and 1914, after attending a debate between Lenin and Viktor Chernov, the acknowledged spokesman of the SR Party, observed that 'Chernov was eloquent, but he seemed uncertain as to what he wanted. Lenin on the other hand was not at all eloquent, but his logic was flawless and he knew exactly what he wanted'.[53]

What Lenin wanted and how he intended to get it reflected the second characteristic of a political police mind set which affected the Special Section's attitude toward Bolshevism. Lenin's clearly delineated authoritarian and elitist posture matched Fontanka's own bureaucratic sentiments and psychological landscape. For, although Fontanka and Bolshevism represented, as Marc Raeff has put it, the 'two opposite poles of Russian society' – the monarchy and the radical intelligentsia – they held critical attitudes in common concerning the process and form of Russian political development. As Raeff has explained:

> In fact, neither the intelligentsia nor bureaucracy wished to see the country develop without its aid. Neither wished to see progress and organic development based on rising productivity and increased prosperity. Paradoxically, those two sworn enemies, the radical intelligentsia and the imperial bureaucracy were linked together by hostility to the real civil society, to pluralism, administrative autonomy, common law, and liberalism in politics and culture.... After 1861, a constant concern of both the intelligentsia and the government was the need to regiment the Russian people, out of fear for its anarchic and destructive potential.[54]

Fontanka and the Bolsheviks were the most vociferous advocates of this 'unconscious alliance'. Both Lenin and his political police opponents argued that the political, social and economic characteristics of the Russian polity pre-ordained that revolution could only succeed when the masses placed themselves under the guidance of a well-organised, disciplined elite party drawn from elements of the intelligentsia.

Finally, to the third characteristic – that of evaluating the present in terms of the past – and perhaps the most commonly employed of all, which influenced the Special Section's attitude toward Bolshevism and, indeed, social democracy generally. The social democrats had always been considered to be a relatively easily managed group of political subversives. By the measurements of police chronology the Marxists were a new group which first came to the attention of the Department of Police in the 1890s. They did not have a long history of revolutionary campaigning behind them and unlike the SRs contained few diehards of the type who so frightened the Special Section.[55] So, while Fontanka considered the newly formed (in 1901) SR Party to be composed of a gang of bloodthirsty cut-throats, the social democrats, it believed, approached their combat with Tsardom armed primarily with books and knowledge.[56]

It was especially these phenomena that lulled the Special Section into a false sense of security. To a political police, an enemy whose strategy and organisational *raison d'être* can be deciphered and, more than that, clearly understood, appears much less fearsome and is thought to be more easily managed than even ineffectual opponents, such as the post-Azef emasculated SRs, who often quite unintentionally kept the Special Section guessing as to their strategy and organisational structure, who bombarded it with vague though threatening propaganda, and who by past action had shown themselves once to have been a serious threat to the survival of the regime. These factors buttressed the opinion that the strategy of manipulating the Bolshevik movement for its own ends involved Fontanka in little risk, while the rewards would be substantial.

By 1911 the political dynamics of the labour movement within Russia justified the implementation of this strategy to Fontanka. During that year unease over the possibility of the SDs taking advantage of growing labour unrest permeated throughout Fontanka.[57] At the same time, despite the Special Section's disdain for the Mensheviks, it was Menshevism, not Bolshevism that had the greatest influence on the working class prior to the Lena goldfield massacre.[58] Moderate Menshevik dominance of the working class movement was unlikely to lead to the internecine warfare within the working class that Fontanka had wished to encourage ever since the 1905 Revolution.[59] This would never do. In order to ensure that events transpired according to its plan the Special Section decided to acquire sufficient influence within the SD movement to control the course of events. It was at this point that Fontanka decided to disrupt working class organisations.

Late in 1911 Fontanka took the first significant step toward implementing its strategy of disruption. The political police set up the forthcoming Prague Conference (it met in early January 1912) to suit the Bolsheviks by preventing the majority of Lenin's opponents from attending the gathering, therefore making it possible for the Bolsheviks to establish themselves as Tsardom's principal social democratic opponents.[60] As General Spiridovich wrote in his police manual on the SDs, 'Lenin and his friends, henchmen in revolutionary work, henchmen in centralism and firm authority in party organisation, are placed at the head of the party so that he could not, not have an effect on the further life of the party'.[61] Six months after the Prague Conference the Foreign Agentura reported exactly what Fontanka wished to hear: under present conditions the unity of the SD party is not possible.[62] The disorganisation of the working class political movement was in the police mind well underway.

****

Beletskii became director of Fontanka only on 21 February 1912. He, therefore, inherited a strategy already operating successfully and which appeared to benefit the MVD – a strategy worth pursuing and claiming as one's own. He was a traditionalist whose self-assurance and firm commitment to the political police practices he employed arose from his static image of Russian socio-political life. Within the space of twenty-three months, however, this director of Fontanka found himself completely out of his depth, his confidence shattered by the failure of his methods in the face of the new forces of political modernity: public opinion and legality which spurred on, reinforced and protected the burgeoning labour movement from his machinations.

Of course, upon assuming command of Fontanka, Beletskii had no inkling of what the future held in store for him. By the barometers employed by political police analysts to determine the level of political unrest in Russia it appeared as if 1912 was going to be a quiet year. Indeed, the relative tranquillity of the labour movement during the first three months of 1912, as Table 12.3 reveals, did much to sustain this belief. The Lena goldfield massacre suddenly demolished that expectation.

The horror of the massacre at Lena in April 1912 in which troops shot into a peaceful demonstration of miners and their families, killing or wounding more than a hundred of them, was compounded by the callous response to the bloodshed by Minister of Internal Affairs Makarov. His coldblooded and now infamous comment on the incident before the Duma – 'so it was, and so it shall be in the future' – perhaps more than the massacre itself precipitated a massive wave of strikes.[63] Fontanka compared the shooting of the Lena miners with Bloody Sunday as a catalyst capable of mobilising the popular discontent that had been simmering over the past three or four years against the government.[64] On May Day demonstrations erupted in fifty provinces, compared to only seventeen on the same date the year before. According to police records nearly one million workers went out on strike that day.[65] No wonder Fontanka was stunned by this sudden explosion of labour unrest.[66] Moreover, the post-Lena massacre strikes impressed the Special Section with the new sense of unity and the developing political consciousness within the working class manifested in them.[67]

Despite his concerns Beletskii did not consider the burgeoning strike movement to be a symptom of a major shift in attitude toward the government by the working class and primarily blamed poor police work for the outburst of these strikes. He was angry with his field bureaus for their lack of penetration into workers' circles, sure that Fontanka had not received even from comparatively large bureaus any intelligence relating the preparation of strikes and demonstrations. Beletskii seemed particularly perturbed about being unable to discover who was behind the strikes, though he personally believed that elements of the intelligentsia were responsible for the most recent industrial turmoil. The chief of Fontanka made it clear to his subordinates that he was not going to be all that patient awaiting the results of their investigations into exactly who caused these disturbances. Beletskii ordered that *sotrudniki* be placed as close to the leadership of workers' organisations as possible so that they could unmask the leadership of the strike movement and determine its causes.[68]

Fontanka eventually reported to Beletskii on the findings of the political police, which had determined that while the social democrats did not create the new and steadily billowing wave of labour unrest, they quickly took advantage of it – especially the Bolsheviks.[69] The Special Section reported that the Bolsheviks were making a significant impression on the proletariat, particularly in the capital.

Table 12.3 The Strike Movement, 1910–1912, from the Data of the Factory Inspectorate[a]

Year	*Economic Strikes*		*Political Strikes*		*Total*	
	Number of Strikes	*Number of Strikers*	*Number of Strikes*	*Number of Strikers*	*Number of Strikes*	*Number of Strikers*
1910	214	42 846	8	3777	222	46 628
1911	442	96 730	24	8380	466	105 110
1912	732	175 678	1300	549 813	2032	725 491
1912 per month						
January–March	69	18 167	1	1622	70	19 789
April	68	14 913	591	231 459	659	246 372
May	132	46 089	492	170 897	624	216 986
June	109	30 801	No information available	No information available	109	30 801
July	76	19 880	2	859	78	20 739
August	115	10 501	No information available	No information available	115	10 501
September	26	10 784	30	8734	56	19 518
October	70	6329	72	52 470	142	58 799
November	46	9796	99	65 853	145	75 649
December	21	8418	13	17 919	34	26 337

Source: G.A. Arutiunov, *Rabochee dvizhenie v Rossii v period novogo revoliutsionnogo pod"ema 1910–1914gg.* (Moscow: 1975), 197

[a] Arutiunov presents two additional tables as well, portraying statistics supplied in the first case from the records of the Society of Manufacturers of the Moscow industrial region and in the second case those he compiled himself from the records of the factory inspectorate, the popular press of the time and archival sources. However, as far as Fontanka was concerned the data supplied by the factory inspectorate would have been its principal guide to the intensity of the strike movement and that is all that concerns us here.

Even Sergei Zubatov, far away on his estate, acknowledged that the Bolsheviks attracted deepening support from the proletariat, he noted with perverse satisfaction, by adopting his methods of co-opting the legal workers' movement.[70]

Beletskii responded to this situation by ordering large numbers of *sotrudniki* to be placed amongst the Bolsheviks to frustrate their plans, thereby containing and disheartening the workers' movement. Beletskii proclaimed to his OOs that they must not fail 'to take all measures agreed upon by Fontanka' to preserve social calm and order at that significant moment.[71] Russia's political police chiefs responded accordingly. OOs, particularly those in Moscow and St Petersburg, thoroughly infiltrated the local Menshevik and Bolshevik organisations, and major unions in these cities were also targeted by well-placed *sotrudniki* representing each major SD faction.[72] Increasingly though, Beletskii's men concentrated their attention on the Bolsheviks, particularly in the light of police reports which advised Fontanka that the Mensheviks were steadily losing the support of the workers. The Bolsheviks, on the other hand, whom the police had already aided in Prague the previous January (discussed above) established themselves as the principal SD faction with several newspapers under their control and considerable financial resources.[73] It is important to note that the political police, at first, were not perturbed by this state of affairs, since Bolshevik organisations had been so thoroughly infiltrated that OO chiefs considered them to be merely extensions of OO chanceries. Martynov, chief of the Moscow OO, boasted that he did not have any trouble implementing Fontanka's tactic of infiltration against the Bolsheviks:

> Thanks to this enlightenment [supplied by my agents] the Moscow Security Division not only could give the Department of Police absolutely exact information on all phases of the activities of bolshevik organisations, but at the same time could liquidate their activities while allowing the bolshevik underground to remain intact, or wholly break it up, or [leave them] undisturbed, vainly making the effort to set things right.[74]

Significantly, Beletskii chose to elaborate on this strategy of containment through infiltration still further. In a gamble of considerable proportions the director of Fontanka believed that he could control the workers' movement by employing the very forces of democracy which sprouted from the 1905 Revolution to his own advantage: the Duma, the union movement and the legal radical press. This gamble led to Beletskii's audacious plan to penetrate the Bolshevik Duma faction with Roman Malinovskii – his Azef – the most notorious provocateur during Tsardom's final years and a charismatic figure whose penetrating oratory and apparently sterling record as a Leninist ensured his selection as leader of the Bolshevik faction within the Fourth Duma. From the floor of the Duma, speeches given by Malinovskii, approved and sometimes written by Beletskii, would appear in both the liberal and radical press.[75] His influence was also felt throughout the trade union movement.[76]

Beletskii's proposal to place a top *sotrudnik*[77] within the Duma among the Bolsheviks did not elicit instantaneous approval from his subordinates. Beletskii's and Vissarionov's plan was that Malinovskii would enter the Bolshevik Duma faction and from his prestigious position sow dissension among social democratic organisations and paralyse their activities. Some MVD officials were cautious about the plan, fearing that its exposure would cause the government terrible humiliation which it could ill-afford.[78] In the end, however, Beletskii got his way.

At this point Beletskii conducted a major campaign to ensure Malinovskii's eligibility as a candidate for the Fourth Duma soon to be convened, and his subsequent election to it. He removed Malinovskii's file from Fontanka's records, literally erasing his criminal record, and conducted more or less open warfare against his rival candidates. The Special Section spent the considerable sum of 14 505 roubles on Malinovskii's campaign, paying for such things as press releases, bulletins and political tracts to ensure that all went smoothly.[79]

Once established within the Duma, Malinovskii performed for Beletskii, but it soon became apparent that earlier concerns over security were well-justified. Like Trusevich before him Beletskii, a mere *chinovnik,* did not know how to handle such men. Indeed, who worked for whom? Vissarionov and other political police officials worried about this problem. The discussion over whether or not Malinovskii should be retained in the Duma continued after his election and into 1913. Vissarionov, though he supported Beletskii at the outset of this project now warned Beletskii that he did not trust Malinovskii, believing him to be a free agent, recognising neither Beletskii's nor the Bolshevik party's leadership. Beletskii defended his decision and initially Vissarionov was placated, but when he began to read of Malinovskii's behaviour in the Duma he concluded that Fontanka must disassociate itself from him.[80] Perhaps he had seen a letter written by Malinovskii to an acquaintance which had been intercepted and in which he stated:

> The single merit of the Duma is that from its tribune we can openly defend the demands of the working class, and by doing so we can contribute to the dissemination of our idea to the broad masses.[81]

While Beletskii persisted in his support of Malinovskii, Vissarionov and Martynov (who was admittedly no friend to Beletskii) came to believe that Malinovskii's usefulness to the Bolsheviks outweighed the harm he did to the labour movement.[82] Malinovskii helped to implement the Bolshevik's Prague Conference resolutions. He assisted in the establishment of two workers' newspapers, often spoke publicly on workers' issues, and urged his listeners to participate in union and other legal organisations. Malinovskii's charismatic personality, his excellent public oratory, the fact that he was a worker himself (a lathe operator) allowed him more than any other social democratic deputy to promote workers' interests and most significantly, he did so as a Bolshevik.[83]

Still, Malinovskii's position remained secure as long as Beletskii remained Director of the Department of Police, despite the fact that Beletskii's subordinates were becoming increasingly uncomfortable with reports detailing the growing influence of the Bolsheviks among elements of the working class.

Field reports had been warning of the impending crisis within urban Russia for some time. The political police in the field had discovered that Bolshevik circles, cells, and organisations were spreading rapidly.[84] The Kiev OO with a sense of urgency as early as April 1913 warned of Lenin's growing popularity and the effectiveness of his propaganda. This same OO analyst concluded:

> The contemporary situation of the Russian Social Democratic Workers' Party can be put [as follows:] out of all the revolutionary organisations existing in Russia and abroad, the sole one which did not remain in the rear of the contemporary ascent of the workers' movement and which had sufficient success in combining its slogans and theory with practice and which does not remain behind the revitalisation of common society is the Bolshevik fraction of the Russian Social Democratic Workers' Party.[85]

Further, the Special Section reported that the Leninists wished to alter the nature of economic strikes, 'which have a rather weak political bent', striving to transform the strike movement into a campaign with serious political overtones. To the Special Section this meant changing, 'the peaceful course' of economic strikes and 'taking them onto the streets transmuting them into noisy street demonstrations and meetings'. The Special Section ordered every one of its agencies, 'to turn most serious attention to the growing membership of the Russian social-democratic workers' party of the Bolshevik-Leninist direction ...'.[86]

Still, Beletskii did not appear particularly concerned. His relaxed attitude to the field bureaus' reports, which had so disturbed Vissarionov and Martynov, is attributable to his belief that, unlike his worried colleagues, he possessed from his position as director of the Department of Police a view of the entire political panorama. General Spiridovich, the most astute police observer of the revolutionary scene, expressed similar sentiments when he remembered that, 'the social democrats generally and the bolsheviks in particular were not sufficiently dangerous' to concern Fontanka.[87] Indeed, the broad panorama of Russian life for most of 1912 and 1913 provoked no anxiety within the forces of order. After all, the countryside was tranquil and though the strike movement was certainly worrisome it only caused Fontanka to moderately qualify its claim that 'there are no grounds to expect that a massive revolutionary movement will arise in the near future'.[88] Indeed, Fontanka communicated this sense of wellbeing to the highest levels of government, as we can see from the content of the Special Journals of the Council of Ministers. In Table 12.4 we see that in 1913, in absolute numbers there were fewer discussions devoted to the struggle with subversion than at any other time during the previous seven years, and statistically only one year listed within Table 12.4 was significantly smaller. Since the standard practice of police reporting was to exaggerate not downplay political dissent abroad in the land,[89] we can only assume that despite the spreading strike movement Fontanka must have been supremely confident in its capacity to contain what it considered to be limited dissent. After all, two of the main criteria established by Fontanka for identifying 'a revolutionary situation' – rural unrest and heavy reliance on the army to restore order [90] – had not made an appearance.

As early as the summer of 1913, however, Beletskii's superiors within the MVD decided that the problems of labour unrest could not be resolved principally by police methods.[91] Both Minister of Internal Affairs N.A. Maklakov and his much more enlightened Assistant Minister of Internal Affairs V.F. Dzhunkovskii decided that factory management–labour relations must be conducted within the framework of the law. Although Maklakov demanded that the full weight of the police fall on those responsible for 'initiating and instigating' strikes intended to threaten the tranquillity of the state or to create social calamity *(bedstvie)*, he did not recommend the use of administrative authority as a means of ridding society of these troublemakers, fearing the negative effect of its application upon public opinion. Instead, Maklakov appealed for new criminal statutes that would prevent agitators and other undesirables from slipping through justice's net.[92] Even an arch-reactionary such as N.A. Maklakov had begun to succumb to the pressure of public opinion.

Table 12.4 Number of Journals of the Council of Ministers having to do with the Struggle against the Revolutionary Movement, 1906–1913

Year	*Overall No. of Journals*	*No. of Journals concerned with the Struggle against the Revolutionary Movement*	*% of Total to (nearest 0.00%)*
1906	135	84	62
1907	143	58	41
1908	394	87	22
1909	405	100	25
1910	352	43	12
1911	393	25	06
1912	234	25	11
1913	226	24	11

Source: Adopted from B.I. Grekov, K.F. Shatsillo, V.V. Shelokhaev, 'Evoliutsiia politicheskoi struktury Rossii v kontse XIX – nachala XX veka (1895–1913)', *Istoriia SSSR*, 1988, no. 5: 44–5.

Beletskii succumbed to political reality more grudgingly than did his minister. By the end of 1913, however, the spreading strike movement eroded Fontanka's confidence in its ability to safeguard the political stability of Russia and Beletskii's sang-froid evaporated. He now ordered his political police to drive its *sotrudniki* harder and to process the intelligence gathered from them and elsewhere with greater speed.[93] Mass arrests had begun in earnest several months before, but from early February 1914 it became clear to any sensible observer that repression by itself could not subdue the burgeoning industrial turmoil.[94] The breadth and intensity of the strike movement grew exponentially in the spring of 1914 (more than 500 000 workers struck all over Russia on May Day alone). For, while the big picture appeared relatively tranquil, the evolution of the political process begun in 1905 had gathered momentum during the years of reaction (1907–12). The increasingly robust workers' movement supported by public opinion expressed through the institutions of the Duma and the liberal, and especially the workers' press, was an element of this phenomenon. As we have seen, political police efforts to squelch the sources of that opinion generally, and the workers' movement in particular, confronted new safeguards – especially respect for the law – against arbitrary harassment of the individual by the forces of order. No doubt, the process of protecting society from *proizvol* was still in its infancy, but it was maturing. Fontanka's capacity to contain and control life in the traditional manner was diminishing. For example, even factory owners interfered with Fontanka's campaign against the ringleaders of the strike movement. The owners feared that such action by the Department of Police would invariably cause a fresh outburst of industrial disruptions.[95] In addition, the much respected General Spiridovich argued that crushing demonstrations gave a propaganda advantage to the social democrats.[96]

In June 1914, the Department of Police officially terminated Beletskii's strategy of containment and control when it ordered the political police to take every possible measure to prevent the revolutionary parties from manipulating legally constituted workers' organisations toward their own ends. Fontanka now reverted to Plehve's policies of more than a decade earlier. It recommended that its OOs attack the revolutionary organisations themselves through periodic liquidations 'that would paralyse them, preventing these groups from carrying out their criminal activities'.[97] Political police tactics had come full circle. Nevertheless, in early July a massive wave of strikes spread through Russia, its epicentre located in St Petersburg. Fontanka struck back fiercely. Using the threat of impending war as an excuse for sweeping legality aside[98] Minister of Internal Affairs Maklakov took the sternest measures possible against the strikers, their unions and their radical intelligentsia allies. All unions were closed, *Pravda*'s editorial offices were smashed up, the Menshevik paper *Luch* was closed and arrests were made.[99] However, as Table 12.5 demonstrates, the wave of repression did not appear to make much difference as the strike movement continued to grow for several more days.

Table 12.5 Number of Strikers in St Petersburg, July 1914, according to St Petersburg OO Statistics

Date	*Number of Strikers*
July 1	1 069
2	2 800
3	no data
4	70 937
5	48 450
6 (Sunday)	–
7	111 000
8	78 595
9	117 000
10	111 000
11	111 000
12	no data
13 (Sunday)	–
14	87 166
15	50 000

Source: G.A. Arutiunov, *Rabochee dvizhenie v Rossii v period novogo revoliutsionnogo pod"ema 1910–1914 gg.* (Moscow: 1975), 373.

The forces of order expected the worst.[100] But calm returned to Russia's cities before it did within the halls of Tsardom's OOs and Gendarme Directorates, with Fontanka still expecting revolution. In a circular issued on 2 September 1914 to all OOs and Gendarme Directorates, the Department of Police pleaded for a united front against revolution, warning ominously that 'we must be ready to meet further revolutionary excesses'.[101]

****

Beletskii's strategies had failed. The political milieu in which his scheme operated, had evolved beyond his comprehension and his control. V.F. Dzhunkovskii, who was designated assistant minister of internal affairs and commandant of the Separate Corps of Gendarmes at the end of January 1913, was, however, more attuned to that political milieu than his subordinate. Dzhunkovskii wanted to revamp political police administration and strip it of its most nefarious practices in order to make the institution acceptable to the politically moderate society with which he associated.

Dzhunkovskii received his appointment at the specific request of Minister of Internal Affairs N.A. Maklakov, apparently because, like the minister,

Dzhunkovskii despised the Separate Corps of Gendarmes.[102] Moreover, Nicholas II was only too happy to approve the appointment of his long-time close acquaintance. Dzhunkovskii had spent much of his career in the Moscow Governor's office, rising rapidly to the rank of major-general and to the governorship of Moscow in 1905. As a consequence of his service he possessed a thorough background in administration, but no direct experience with police affairs, knowing little about political police methods. Dzhunkovskii shone as an adroit, worldly, hard-working bureaucrat who boasted a reputation as an honest man who hid his feelings behind a mask of cold politeness. Moscow society thought highly of him.

Dzhunkovskii, with close friends in moderate circles such as the Octobrist Guchkov, got on well with the Duma which found Minister of Internal Affairs Maklakov difficult to deal with. It was Guchkov and his friends who encouraged Dzhunkovskii to embark upon political police reform.[103] Dzhunkovskii responded positively to the Duma's desire to make Fontanka, especially its political police, responsible for its actions, deploring the independence of the Department of Police from the MVD's chain of command and he blamed the most nefarious aspects of political police work on this absence of control by higher ministerial authorities.

There could not have been two more dissimilar men than Dzhunkovskii and Beletskii and they became bitter enemies. As soon as Dzhunkovskii assumed his post as assistant minister, Beletskii discovered what was in store for him. Though Dzhunkovskii could not muster sufficient political leverage to oust the powerful Beletskii from his post, he was sufficiently powerful to crack down on wayward underlings[104] by subordinating them to persons who would be held accountable for the actions of the OOs and Gendarme Directorates. The second aspect of Dzhunkovskii's reform, and the one that brought him into direct conflict with Beletskii, was his firm commitment to the eradication of provocation and other unsavoury features of the Internal Agency's operations. Basically, the new assistant minister's proposed reforms would prevent Beletskii from achieving his ambition of becoming minister of internal affairs by dismantling the political police apparatus Beletskii employed as a means of acquiring the reputation necessary to attain this goal.

Though he was powerless to tamper with the Warsaw, Moscow and St Petersburg OOs, all of which had been constituted under the law, this was not the case with the Regional OOs. Dzhunkovskii considered these field bureaus – which had been created outside of the law – to be impossible to control, serving as the fertile soil where 'provocation flourished'.[105] He began to close them. So by 1914, twelve years after Plehve had set in motion the process which spread OOs of various sizes and *Rozysknye Punkty* throughout the empire, Dzhunkovskii brought a halt to the 'knee jerk' growth of Tsardom's political police and began to rationalise the system.

In Dzhunkovskii's boldest alteration to the political police structure the Special Section was subsumed by Fontanka's Sixth Secretariat, where it remained throughout his tenure as assistant minister. The title 'Special Section' disappeared from police circulars and dispatches to be replaced by the designation 'Sixth Secretariat'. At first glance not much more than cosmetic surgery seemed to have taken place. The content of the circulars remained unchanged, appearing over the name of M.E. Broetskii, the same *chinovnik* who directed the formerly independent Special Section. The difference significantly resided in Broetskii's new title: as chief of the Sixth Secretariat he functioned merely as one of nine secretariat chiefs. Dzhunkovskii claimed his actions eliminated those police agencies operating *ad hoc* outside the law and forced political police operations back into legally constituted institutions.

Unfortunately, the course of reform did not run as smoothly as Dzhunkovskii implied. Despite his best efforts the assistant minister did not acquire control over the still vast and complex policing machine;[106] Beletskii also did everything in his power to subvert Dzhunkovskii's authority, enjoying the complete support of Russia's political police officers who cooperated with Dzhunkovskii as little as possible during the assistant minister's tenure in office.[107] Beletskii himself often refused to carry out Dzhunkovskii's orders, indeed at times acting in direct opposition to them.[108]

The Special Section had survived reformers before – Lopukhin and Sviatopolk-Mirskii in particular come to mind – but it had never encountered one so well-connected at court. Worse, as far as the Special Section was concerned, Dzhunkovskii combined an antideluvian military code of honour with a very modern recognition that provocation corrupted those involved with it and brought the legal system and the government itself into disrepute. These attitudes led the assistant minister to conclude that undercover agents should have strictly limited and closely supervised uses within Russia's political police system. More than any other issue the question of the future of the Internal Agency brought Dzhunkovskii into conflict with Beletskii.[109]

While perusing a list of undercover agents Dzhunkovskii noticed that many of them were *gimnazia* students. This observation infuriated him and he ordered the dismantling of this crucial branch of political police operations. Even more damaging to the Special Section was Dzhunkovskii's hatred for stool pigeons among the tsar's soldiers[110] and again, Dzhunkovskii ordered these undercover operations to cease at once.[111] This decision met stiff opposition from Colonel von Koten, chief of the St Petersburg OO, Beletskii and Vissarionov since they considered spying on the officer corps essential to the survivial of the regime. Paradoxically, by taking this stance against the army these men made a fatal blunder: they challenged the honour of the officer corps and paid for this posture with the loss of their posts![112]

Worse was yet to come for the Internal Agency. In early 1914 Dzhunkovskii, now with Beletskii out of the way, forced Roman Malinovskii, the Internal Agency's outstanding *sotrudnik,* to resign from the Duma, terminating his undercover career. The question of when Dzhunkovskii learned of Malinovskii's double role in the Duma could be asked. Beletskii contends that Dzhunkovskii not only knew of it from the outset of the venture, but supported it.[113] What, then, caused him to change his mind? R.C. Elwood, Malinovskii's most recent biographer, argues that Dzhunkovskii may have sensed a change in the political wind, which Beletskii did not notice. Certainly, as we have already discussed, this was possible. In 1912 the Bolsheviks were not nearly so successful as they appeared to be in 1914. By the latter date, Elwood suggests, perhaps Dzhunkovskii would have employed any means to discredit the spreading Leninist movement and what better means 'than by removing its most eloquent spokesmen from the Duma and by allowing it to be discreetly known that a leading member of their [the Bolsheviks'] Central Committee was in fact an agent provocateur?' Elwood continues, 'in the ensuing internecine struggle, only the tsarist regime and the police could profit .... If this was indeed Dzhunkovskii's reasoning, he very nearly achieved his objective'.[114]

Elwood's scenario appears to make good sense, but upon close examination there are still several problems with it. Dzhunkovskii undoubtedly knew about Malinovskii's double role by early 1913 when he told Vissarionov that he wished to be rid of Malinovskii.[115] But other reasons for Dzhunkovskii's decision to jetison Beletskii's outstanding *sotrudnik* can be identified. After all, early in 1913 when Dzhunkovskii first made his view known, Fontanka's confidence *vis-à-vis* its control over Russian society could not have been higher. It is more likely that there were other more compelling reasons for Dzhunkovskii's decision to expose Malinovskii. Dzhunkovskii truly hated undercover operations and had little sympathy for even the most loyal *sotrudniki*[116] and in 1913 informed a flabbergasted A.A. Krasil′nikov, director of the Foreign Agentura, that he wished to discontinue the use of undercover agents as political police weapons entirely.[117] At the same time Vladimir Burtsev was wreaking havoc within the Internal Agency by unmasking a large number of *sotrudniki.*[118] Apparently the assistant minister had good reason to fear that Burtsev was about to print an exposé of Malinovskii's double life in the former's journal *Budushchee (The Future)*,[119] creating another Azef-like scandal at Fontanka's expense. It seems likely, therefore, that he would have distanced Fontanka from Malinovskii months earlier than he did had it not been for Beletskii's influence. Beletskii, like Dzhunkovskii, was very well-connected at court and until the end of 1913 when his refusal to terminate the Internal Agency's infiltration of the Army caused his dismissal he had done nothing to jeopardise that position. Dzhunkovskii could now appoint a director of the Department of Police who sympathised with the hostile stance he had taken toward the Internal Agency. He found such a man in V.A. Briun-de-Sent-Ippolit.[120] It was then and only then that Malinovskii suffered the fate Dzhunkovskii believed he so richly deserved. It seems, therefore that the vagaries of MVD–court politics, not practical political considerations, determined the timing of Malinovskii's disposal by the assistant minister.

Dzhunkovskii sought to bring the political police system into tune, as it were, with the rhythm of the moderate society he represented. Yet, his was only an ephemeral success, except in the domain of political police penetration into the army, where the subsequent absence of *sotrudniki* did the regime considerable harm. The problem in part is to be found in the nature of Dzhunkovskii's actions which were ironically not any different from those of Plehve taken a dozen years before and to opposite purpose. The reduction in the number of OOs and the constraints placed on the Internal Agency came about through administrative *fiat* not legislative process. Dzhunkovskii's circulars, like those of his predecessor Plehve, gave the impression that little forethought and certainly no lingering afterthoughts had been spent on how best to implement his instructions or on the effects these decisions might have on future political police operations.

This meant that his influence as with that of his predecessors lasted only more or less as long as he did. As far as the average political police official was concerned, the eighteen month period between January 1914 (the date of Beletskii's dismissal) and September 1915 when Dzhunkovskii himself left office was a somewhat damaging, but temporary interlude in traditional practice. Dzhunkovskii was a man who was well thought of in the Duma and at the same time boasted the type of support that Nicholas II offered only his closest personal friends. None the less, he could not take advantage of this situation. His reforms succeeded only where the tsar personally insisted that they be implemented. For example, Dzhunkovskii was most successful in eliminating Internal Agency penetration within high schools and the Army: operations that Nicholas himself found distasteful. Police reform would only be successful from beyond the walls of Fontanka and only pressure from society backed up with the force of law could ever have hoped to transform the culture upon which Fontanka fed. A grudging respect for the law based on fear of public opinion had begun to take root within the MVD and Fontanka itself. But this process had been too slow to advance and had arrived far too late in the life of the monarchy. The deeply imbedded traditions of Russia's police culture and of supervisory 'state control' over Russian life generally, meant that the arduous transformation of police *mentalité* required more time than Tsardom had to spare.

13 Illusion and Reality: Into the Abyss, 1915–1917

The First World War placed the political police system of Russia on alert. The forces of order like so many other institutions in Russia believed that the outbreak of war had merely granted Russia a reprieve from revolution, that its conclusion (with the inevitable victory of course) would bring on the long expected second revolution in the new century, challenging the last bits of authority the Romanov dynasty possessed over its people.[1] In the face of this bleak prospect, the forces of order assigned Fontanka's political police essential roles in the defence of the monarchy.

During the war the political police had access to vast resources[2] allowing it to spread its tentacles more widely and deeply into Russian life than it ever had before. Tasks assigned to it beyond its standard brief to contain and control Russia's opposition and revolutionary forces included: uncovering profiteers; vigilance over the masonic movement; stirring up loyalty for the dynasty by supporting the patriotic right-wing press and making payments to reactionary members of the State Council; supplying skilled political police officers to the army for counter-intelligence purposes and training military and particularly naval officers in the art of counter-espionage; unmasking pro-German sympathisers and defeatists; maintaining surveillance over foreign diplomatic staff including those of Russia's own allies and the establishment of surveillance over an entire range of civilians and officers it considered unreliable.[3]

Despite this effort the political police system was remarkably ineffective in sustaining even the traditional role it perceived for itself: as the bulwark of the dynasty. Why was this so? In part, as we shall discover, Fontanka was itself victimised by the Byzantine politics that came to dominate the milieu of the MVD during the First World War and in part the political police succumbed to its own traditions and mind set.

****

The dismissal of V.F. Dzhunkovskii in September 1915 removed the last voice advocating reform at 16 Fontanka Quai to the end of the regime. With Dzhunkovskii's departure to the regular army, Fontanka restored the Special Section to its former independence[4] and re-established the Internal Agency to its former pre-eminent position.[5] Meanwhile the MVD re-instated most normal pre-Dzhunkovskii practices including the policy of placing undercover agents within the high schools and generally releasing its *sotrudniki* from the restrictions imposed upon them by Dzhunkovskii and Director of Fontanka Briun-de-Sent-Ippolit (who was dismissed a few days after his mentor).[6]

The man behind the revitalisation (at least as Fontanka saw it) of the political police was none other than S.P. Beletskii who returned to 16 Fontanka Quai in late September 1915 as assistant minister of internal affairs managing the police. Almost immediately Beletskii acquired control over every aspect of Fontanka's affairs. This task was made easy by the inexperience of his immediate subordinates, successive interim directors of Fontanka R.G. Mollov and K.D. Kafafov, and the indecisiveness and prevarication of Minister of Internal Affairs A.N. Khvostov.[7] Beletskii restaffed the Department of Police with experienced men upon whom he could rely and placed within the Special Section itself experts knowledgeable about the opposition and revolutionary movements. Beletskii worked long hours, rarely seeing his family. His wife repeatedly asked him to resign, without success. Notwithstanding the public excuses he made later for staying on, he remained in office to fulfil his consuming ambition to build a ministry of police.[8]

Although available evidence does not incontrovertibly link Beletskii to proposals for creating a modern police state, it is clear from Beletskii's memoirs that he was in all probability involved with the development of such a plan, ostensibly proposed by B.V. Shturmer, Khvostov's successor as minister of internal affairs. Shturmer suggested the creation of a super police: a completely conspiratorial organisation hidden from even the most powerful *sanovniki.* This new force would employ a huge network of secret agents programmed to penetrate into every aspect of Russian life. The information they collected would be reported directly to Shturmer. Beletskii's claim that this proposal was Shturmer's idea and failed to be implemented only because Shturmer fell from his post is not convincing.[9] Much of this programme was in fact already part of Fontanka's *modus operandi* devised under Beletskii's own auspices before Shturmer became minister of internal affairs. None the less, if these functions had been located within a truly independent, highly secret police institution and then combined with General Alekseev's proposal of a dictatorship under what he called a Supreme Minister of Defence, the foundations of a modern police state would have been laid.

Indeed, there is little doubt that there had arisen an awareness in right-wing circles that an alternative form of government to the traditional monarchy – a modern dictatorial police state – could better dispose of the constitutional and revolutionary forces assailing the government.[10] Beletskii, however, lived and worked in a milieu where the establishment of such a state was no longer (if it had ever been) possible. Shturmer, although given 'dictatorial powers' by Nicholas II, was incompetent and just bumbled along without encouragement from either the court or the bureaucracy both of which felt, in any case, exceptionally uncomfortable with these proposals.[11]

In reality, the incompetence, professional insecurity and corruption which permeated the tsarist government during the First World War condemned the political police to an embittering isolation, dashing even Beletskii's pipe dreams of creating an all-pervasive institution of 'state control'. Beletskii, himself, along with Tsardom's other senior law and order officials became enmeshed within this milieu, an environment characterised by the infamous and longstanding practise of 'ministerial leapfrog': the sarcastic label given to the rapid, sudden and arbitrary replacement of ministers and the internecine politics which accompanied it.

Between 1915 and 1917 the MVD endured six ministers of internal affairs (N.A. Maklakov, N.B. Shcherbatov, A.N. Khvostov, B.V. Shturmer, A.A. Khvostov, and A.D. Protopopov) who in turn were served by five directors of the Department of Police (V.A. Bruin-de-Sent-Ippolit, R.G. Mollov, K.D. Kafafov. E.K. Klimovich and A.T. Vasil'ev). These five men ruled over a Special Section consecutively guided by two nonentities, M.E. Broetskii, a run-of-the-mill *chinovnik* who was succeeded in January 1917 by I.P. Vasil'ev, an alcoholic. This constant reshuffling meant that the perpetually new men had little time to learn their jobs and consequently were indecisive and incapable of developing any policies. Under such conditions none of these hapless ministers could win the respect of their subordinates within the political police. As Prince V.M. Volkonskii, who served five of the ministers listed above, recalled, the MVD sank into chaos.[12]

The tenures of three of Tsardom's wartime ministers of internal affairs – A.N. Khvostov, B.V. Shturmer, and A.D. Protopopov – were particularly notable for their apalling relations with the police system. The appointment of Khvostov, a man with a well-deserved unsavoury reputation, was universally ridiculed. When L.V. Kochebei, for example, learned of Khvostov's appointment he raged 'Goremykin [chairman of the Council of Ministers] has gone completely off his rocker' if 'at such a difficult moment in the country' he appoints 'the well-known troublemaker and wise guy Khvostov to the MVD'.[13] General Spiridovich, the then current *doyen* of Russia's political police chiefs, characterised Khvostov as 'an ignoramus in both politics and police'.[14] Goremykin, however, in appointing Khvostov was just carrying out the tsaritsa's wishes.[15]

Khvostov appointed long-time personal friend K.D. Kafafov director of Fontanka, in the knowledge that he would be an obedient and loyal subordinate. Beletskii, Khvostov's assistant minister, managing the police, showed himself to be an entirely different sort of man and, as we shall see, it was not long before the two inordinately ambitious and notoriously short-tempered men fell out.[16] Beletskii expended considerable energy in his new post in enhancing his own interests which many believed would lead ultimately to his appointment as the next minister of internal affairs.[17]

The Khvostov–Beletskii intrigues over Rasputin are infamous[18] and brought both men nothing but discredit[19] and served only to increase the animosity between the two men.[20] Khvostov appeared especially agitated by Beletskii's complete domination of Fontanka; Beletskii had even gone as far as placing his minister under surveillance.[21] Finally the relationship became marked by such a level of hostility that when Khvostov was asked by an acquaintance if Beletskii would succeed him as minister of internal affairs, he emphatically replied, 'no ... I, of course, am very dissatisfied with Beletskii, because as you see, he has not preserved my interests'.[22] At that point Khvostov became a serious, perhaps fatal, obstacle to Beletskii's ambitions.

Finally, Beletskii had the opportunity to cut the ground from under his minister, thereby preserving his chances of fulfilling his ambitions. Beletskii, who knew or had the means to discover everything of significance in the capital, soon discovered another grossly ill-conceived plot by Khvostov to murder Rasputin on behalf of far right-wing circles and he obtained corroborating evidence to this affect. Armed with his evidence he rushed off like a schoolboy telling tales to show it to Rasputin, Shturmer who was the new Chairman of the Council of Ministers, Metropolitan Pitirim, and the tsaritsa's confidant, Anna Vyrobova. As Beletskii had hoped, Khvostov was dismissed but unfortunately for the assistant minister, in a strange twist of justice, the tsar delayed Khvostov's dismissal for some weeks after the scandal broke. The disgraced minister took advantage of this fortuitous circumstance to dismiss Beletskii and witness his assistant minister's departure, one could imagine, with bitter glee.[23]

The antics of Khvostov and Beletskii inflicted considerable harm upon the reputation of the government. What is less known, however, is the damage their behaviour caused to the political police system. The Khvostov–Beletskii affair deepened the alienation of the political police from its own superiors – a process which had begun earlier during Stolypin's tenure. For instance, Globachev, the chief of the Petrograd OO, told Khvostov outright that he believed that the minister did not have any faith in him, in fact, that Khvostov was conspiring against him,[24] as indeed he was since Globachev's most important task was the protection of Rasputin.[25] It is no wonder that Globachev despised Khvostov.[26] Considerably worse, however, was to come for Globachev and his colleagues who had still to endure the ministries of Shturmer and Protopopov.

Shturmer, like his predecessor was a self-serving schemer, who regularly quarrelled with his colleagues, and used his office for petty matters and personal vendettas. The minister launched one such vendetta against E.K. Klimovich, appointed by Shturmer's predecessor to the directorship of the Department of Police. The public bickering between the minister and his police chief went on for several months – from March to September 1916 – further demoralising Fontanka. Klimovich declared that Shturmer failed to offer any leadership to the forces of order, leaving the Department of Police to flounder. It seemed to him that the MVD 'was completely without a rudder, without a sail, not knowing what to do'. These troubled times demanded some kind of policy, but no instructions came from Shturmer and the absence of direction undermined Klimovich's ability to fulfil his duty. Things were so bad that the frustrated police chief 'asked God above to give me some kind of general directives'.[27] Shturmer's vendetta against his police chief culminated in the unjustified dismissal of

Klimovich from his post.[28] Shturmer, for nothing more than personal pique, had removed an experienced and relatively competent director of Fontanka (though by no means a paragon of virtue) at a time when the police system could least afford the turmoil that the dismissal of its chief invariably caused.

Under Protopopov, Tsardom's last and most incompetent minister of internal affairs and a man who inspired only ridicule,[29] the crisis of confidence between the political police and the law and order bureaucrats within the ministry reached its peak. In matters of internal security Protopopov deferred to P.G. Kurlov – his 'best friend and pal'.[30] Kurlov, a corrupt and venal man – as we discovered in Chapter 11 – carried the well deserved reputation of an intriguer *par excellence*. The first and most damaging instance of Kurlov's influence came with the appointment of A.T. Vasil′ev as director of the Department of Police. To be sure, Vasil′ev received the post after a lengthy career within Fontanka, including a stint as chief of the Special Section. Yet in the final crisis of the Romanov dynasty his political police found him wanting, as we shall see. Vasil′ev's contact with Protopopov can only be described as sporadic and it was generally recognised that he did not have sufficient authority with Protopopov to influence or advise him on the broad spectrum of Russian politics with which a minister of internal affairs was required to deal. The combination of a nonentity as director of Fontanka and Protopopov's reliance on Kurlov erased any remaining confidence that political police chiefs such as General Globachev in Petrograd and Colonel Martynov in Moscow may have had in their superiors.[31]

By the autumn of 1916, then, just as the political police awakened to the depth and nature of the crisis before it, this lack of confidence and the animosity between police chiefs and ministers had shredded the remnants of the MVD's chain-of-command – the sinew of the forces of order. The failure of police chiefs and their superiors within Fontanka to communicate had become endemic, as ministers and assistant ministers lost themselves in the machinations of the court and their own petty intrigues.

****

Within the maelstrom of the MVD's internal disintegration the Special Section and its field bureaus struggled to fulfil their primary duty: to forewarn the government of impending disaster. From the autumn of 1914 the Special Section, in preparation for the anticipated revolutionary onslaught, relied more than ever before upon the interpretive skills of its intelligence assembling and processing personnel. These people – including those operating within the OOs – served as Tsardom's early warning system, making certain that neither Fontanka nor its masters would ever be caught by surprise again and held to ransom by the panic and chaos that dominated Russian politics between 1905 and 1907.

The responsibility for intelligence assembly fell most heavily upon the shoulders of General K.I. Globachev and Colonel A.P. Martynov, the political police chiefs of the Petrograd and Moscow OOs respectively. Since those who held these posts carried special status in the eyes of their superiors, their analyses of events and the advice they imparted, at least until the war years, were especially valued by the MVD. For this reason an understanding of Globachev's and Martynov's world view is important – their capacity to make sense out of the socio-economic and political forces they encountered, how they evaluated the danger these forces presented to the stability of the state and their ability to communicate these views to their superiors.

The content of the political intelligence transmitted to the capital by Globachev, Martynov and their colleagues throughout Russia and abroad depended upon a variety of institutional and traditional factors which gave their reports, and those of the Special Section, a complexion not always justified by events. The accuracy of political intelligence suffered from the pitfalls which police reporting has in common with the processing of data within other types of organisations,[32] the mind set common to all political policemen[33] and the physical limitations forced upon the Special Section and its field bureaus by the exigencies of war.

Political intelligence arrived at the Special Section where its chief and chancery staff parcelled the data out to appropriate specialist departments. Organisations such as the Socialist-Revolutionary Party, the Social Democrats, non-Russian organisations such as the Jewish *Bund*, the Anarchists, and the legal–social and political movements including the *zemstva*, professional unions and the Constitutional Democrats (the Kadets) were each allotted such specialist departments where the relevant data were collated, analysed and then forwarded to the department for current investigations.[34] Periodically the intelligence information was synthesised into the different types of circulars required by the Special Section, Fontanka, the MVD or by the tsar himself.[35] The most useful circular format, the 'Intelligence Surveys' (*Obzory*), reviewed developments in Russia's social, political and economic life and discussed strategic plans for counter-revolutionary action.[36]

By its very nature, tsarist political police intelligence was biased, a most common failing of networks specialising in the processing of information and which can never be completely eliminated.[37] In information retrieval and processing networks, bias is often an unintentional ingredient in reports and it occurs automatically as information flows through the communication channel, encountering several levels of analysts each of whom brings his own outlook to the process of evaluating the intelligence placed before him.[38] The explosive growth enjoyed by Department of Police and its Special Section between 1902 and 1914 exacerbated this problem. The rapid injection of new and relatively untrained staff caused by this expansion meant that police officials found it difficult to judge the accuracy of information supplied to them by little-known subordinates. As we have seen, the rapid turnover in the highest executive positions within the police hierarchy during the First World War compounded this situation by often preventing the persons at the top of the communication pyramid from knowing the abilities and outlooks of those who selected and evaluated the intelligence for them.

At times careless administrative practices also contributed to the unintentional distortion of political police intelligence. So when Assistant Minister of Internal Affairs Beletskii found himself pressed for time and unable to read and comment on the thousands of neatly typed pages placed before him, he struck on a solution in desperation. Why not sign blank sheets of paper and have chancery personnel read incoming reports and respond to them over his signature?[39] While this was an extraordinary case, it was not unusual to have lengthy reports prepared for high-ranking officials not by specialists, but by ordinary chancery workers whose lack of expertise may have contributed considerable bias in the reports they produced.[40] Of course, idiosyncratic behaviour by political police officials added to the problem of biased political police intelligence as well. For example, the political police generally reported on aspects of behaviour which it considered illegal, subversive, or merely sensational: in other words, subjects which aroused the MVD's interest and paid its agents' salaries. Therefore, the views that field bureaus portrayed were often exaggerated or one-sided.

Most important of all, the ability of the Special Section and of its bureaus to divine the signs of oncoming revolutionary turmoil was critically harmed by the mind set to which political police analysts universally succumb.[41] As we have already seen, the most significant and dangerous practice followed by a political police is the inclination to extrapolate from the past actions of its opponents in order to predict the future. In this practice tsarist policemen were no different from colleagues in other times and other places searching Fontanka's archives in order to discover what to expect next from the population under surveillance. At best, therefore, the Special Section's analysts were a step behind events. In particular, the overwhelming foreboding that came to dominate Fontanka's surveys of the moods of Russian society during the First World War was deeply coloured by its experiences in the 1905 Revolution. During the war years most significant intelligence reports reflected this phenomenon in one way or another.[42]

To its credit, the Department of Police tried to be precise in its memory of 1905 by constructing an etiology of the 1905 Revolution, intending this etiology to serve as an alarm system to help the Special Section to identify the warning signals of an oncoming catastrophe. Nevertheless, the Special Section's analysts understood that the dynamics of one revolution were unlikely to be exactly duplicated in a subsequent uprising. 'It is not possible to conjecture on the form of new revolutionary struggles', Fontanka told the readers of the 2 September 1914 circular which offered this etiology, 'but none the less we must be ready to meet further revolutionary excesses'. The author of this circular warned that 1905 was merely a preparatory event and worse was yet to come.The Special Section's analysis of the dynamics of the 1905 Revolution confirmed one of the most common of political policemen's beliefs: that only an elite spearhead incorporating the united opposition and revolutionary movements could arouse the masses to revolution. The police concluded from the events of 1905 that it was the Union of Unions and the St Petersburg Soviet of Workers' Deputies that unified and guided the workers and peasants 'with the goal of forcibly attaining a constitution'.[43] This is a credible though overly simple explanation for what transpired in 1905. However, it would have been impossible for the Special Section to draw any other conclusion.

The leadership syndrome has always appealed to the police mind, while belief in spontaneous discontent has not.[44] Indeed, in the Russian case, by emphasising the role of political agitators real or imagined,[45] the forces of order in their own minds made the discontent rumbling through Russia appear manageable. Also, by shifting responsibility for the unrest and discontent to a small minority of malcontents within the empire, Tsardom hoped to maintain its credibility and legitimacy in the eyes of the public.[46] Thus, popular protest as an expression of deeply felt grievances was misunderstood by the political police, who believed instead that agitators had been hard at work driving the ordinarily placid masses into challenging the authority of the government.[47]

The political police also persisted, as we saw in the previous chapter, with the unfortunate habit of calculating the calibre of the opposition to the regime by over-valuing their opponents' propaganda points, including the public utterances some of them made from the floor of the Duma, at the expense of careful analyses of both their programmes and capacity to achieve their goals. Thus, the Special Section often exaggerated the danger to the regime posed by those groups, paricularly the Kadets (at least to the late summer of 1916) whose rhetoric far outstripped their skill as revolutionaries.

The integrity of political police intelligence was further reduced by the natural desire of political police analysts, especially OO chiefs, to guard against the worst possible outcomes by passing unverified alarm signals up through Fontanka's communication channels. This common, though informal, practice created a dichotomy between duty and behaviour openly acknowledged by police officials. For instance, a prominent police chief when instructing fledgling officers on the proper procedure for processing intelligence told them:

> To whatever degree the information received seemed to him to be dreadful, sensational or improbable rumors he is obligated to treat it thoughtfully, without bias; he must verify it and immediately after that assess the case and take any necessary measures.[48]

In practice, however, the same chief noted:

> The system of the Department of Police consisted precisely in giving nothing concrete – but in contenting itself with scaring people. To produce another document in order to say later, 'but we warned you'.[49]

This 'but we warned you' reaction often occurred when an analyst, after digesting the information on his desk, communicated the inference rather than the evidence on which his inferences were based, as a consequence communicating to the exclusion of all else his own unfounded fears and personal bias to his superiors.[50] This failure to analyse intelligence objectively arose particularly in time of crisis or when a potentially de-stabilising event occurred unexpectedly, allowing the Special Section's analytic machinery too little time to discover its causes, or when the truth was too difficult to face or contradicted long-held beliefs. In all likelihood the analyst sincerely believed in his conclusions. Lopukhin's explanation for Bloody Sunday is one outstanding example[51] of this phenomenon. We will shortly observe how this failing affected the integrity of Globachev's analysis of events during the war years.

And finally, the quality of political police intelligence suffered from the impact of the First World War upon the staffing of Fontanka's political police chanceries. The quality of intelligence gathered from the field depended in large part on the ability and placement of undercover agents within groups targeted by the Special Section or by its OOs; their number and the competence of these people diminished considerably between 1914 and 1917 as the government drafted undercover agents into the army. At the same time field bureaus found it increasingly difficult to recruit new undercover agents.[52]

In a foolhardy attempt to compensate for this critical shortage of agents the Special Section demanded ever more intelligence from its OOs, instructing them to collect it by all possible means. As we shall discover below, most of the material collected in this manner was of dubious, and at times overstated, value and its influx overwhelmed political police chanceries deprived by the war of their staff.[53] It became impossible for large OOs to process intelligence adequately or to retrieve information from its files quickly;[54] the situation at Fontanka itself was no better.[55] No wonder Director of Fontanka E.K. Klimovich pleaded in 1916 for leaner, more concise reporting. 'The less you write the better!' he proclaimed.[56] Vasil′ev, Klimovich's successor at Fontanka, appealed to the tsaritsa for permission to recruit wounded and shell-shocked officers who were unable to return to active military service, but would in Vasil′ev's opinion make excellent police officials.[57] By then, however, this crisis had become insurmountable as the drain on manpower caused by the battlefield carnage of the First World War stripped the political police bureaus of their administrative staffs.[58]

****

Constrained by these limitations on their intelligence gathering and processing machinery and operating within an unreliable and untrustworthy chain-of-command, Globachev, Martynov and their fellow OO chiefs confronted a society undergoing a socio-economic and political transformation whose values the forces of order either rejected or did not understand. The combination of these factors frightened the political police. Their fears and uncertainties were projected as hatred for the people and institutions considered by the regime responsible for the turmoil that shook the monarchy during the war years.

Against the revolutionaries, whom they held partially to blame for this circumstance, their response – permitted by the outbreak of the First World War – was a fullscale repression which decimated SD and SR ranks. The remnants of these parties found the working class distracted and becalmed by an ephemeral surge of patriotism through the first half of 1915.[59] During the war years the SRs recorded statistically insignificant gains in membership[60] while the SDs were reduced to recruiting inexperienced teenagers, training them to carry out several vital functions previously in the hands of veterans of the struggle currently under arrest or in exile – such as operating illegal workers' societies, spreading propaganda and inciting confrontations with the police.[61]

In the short term the workers' new-found patriotism, the mass arrests of party activists, and the problems of recruitment left the SRs and the SDs in disarray. In the longer term, ironically, some of these factors contributed to the re-emergence of the labour movement under conditions which befuddled the forces of order, as we shall see below. For example, out of necessity SRs and SDs blurred party alliances further than ever before, allying with each other on the basis of the stance taken toward the war: patriotic, defensist, or defeatist.[62] These new alliances enhanced the impact of the remaining professional revolutionaries on the factory floor. Worse, at least for the political police, the Special Section discovered that since Bolshevism's new recruits maintained such a low profile in the revolutionary movement – usually working within factory party cells and never having been arrested (at least up to that point) – they could not be identified by the Special Section's Registration Desk. Nevertheless, the political police, bound to a firm belief in the 'leadership syndrome', insisted that, though unknown, these people were leading the labour movement which began to revitalise in the second half of 1915. Actually instead of leading the labour movement from the factory floor they were now just one element of it.

In fact, by mid-1915 Russia's working class began to endure deprivation induced stresses introduced or exacerbated by the demands made upon Russian life by the war, all of which contributed to the revitalisation of strike action. The number of workers grew substantially in Russia's industrial centres, particularly in the two capitals, fulfilling the requirements of expanding manufacturing capacity in defence industries including: metallurgy, chemicals, ordnance and textiles. By late 1916, for example, nine-tenths of Moscow's labour force worked in defence related industries.[63] The urban overcrowding produced by the influx of labour into the industrial centres was made worse by those who serviced collateral industries and ballooning government departments. The pressure on housing, feeding and transporting such a sudden increase in population caused a steady deterioration in living conditions which frayed the nerves of workers already enduring long working hours, speeded-up production, the learning of new production methods – often, as a result, with diminished safety – and perhaps worst of all, as the war dragged on, hyper-inflation. Indeed, prices inflated to heights that placed everyday necessities beyond the grasp of workers and Russians generally. In Petrograd between 1913 and 1917, for instance, the cost of rye flour rose 269 per cent, buckwheat 320 per cent, wheat 308 per cent, salt 500 per cent, butter 845 per cent, and granulated sugar 457 per cent. At the same time the cost of shoes and clothing rose between 400 and 500 per cent![64]

To one degree or another industrial labour resident in each of the major combatant nations suffered considerable discomfort from at least some of the same factors which plagued Russia's proletariat during the war. However, in Russia (where strikes were often substitutes for other forms of mass politics available in other nations but not in Tsardom and where the ineptititude of the Russian government and of its military appeared to the population to be infinitely worse than elsewhere) strikes, whether officially labelled 'political' or 'economic',[65] were in fact political protests against overall government callousness in the face of the workers' needs and reflected a growing hostility to the war. Therefore, in their intensity and number they reflected Russia's deteriorating economic, political and military positions.

Thus, by the second half of 1915 the strike movement began to recover from its stupor as 539 528 workers went on strike during the year.[66] Fontanka labelled two-thirds of these strikes as 'economic' and the remaining one-third as 'political', noting that the 'economic' strikers were demanding a shortened work day and increased wages while the 'political' strikers were expressing their dissatisfaction with the continuation of the war, demanding freedom from arrrest of their fellow strikers and an official holiday in memory of Bloody Sunday.[67] The forces of order often attacked 'political' strikers, beating and shooting them indiscriminantly. The strikes protesting against the war in Kostromo and Ivanovo-Vosnesensk in the summer of 1915 were according to Fontanka's own report accompanied by violent, armed disorders leaving many workers dead or wounded.[68] By the autumn of 1915 strikes were breaking out in many parts of the country. The political police responded to these by widespread arrests[69] which, however, as we shall see below, did not impede the increasing intensity and number of labour protests. However, at least until early summer 1916 the political police did not focus its primary attention on the strike movement probably, as we shall see, because the Special Section did not understand the new form of dynamics driving it and thus they believed the truly dangerous sources of dissent were at least for the time being not to be found on the factory floor.

The political police rather focused its suspicion and hatred upon the Duma system in particular and the wartime organisations which arose from the new political culture that the Duma represented. To Globachev, the Duma system came into its own during the war when it drove the government into retreat before the wave of opposition aroused by its deputies against the regime.[70] Globachev like most of his colleagues became mesmerised by the emotional, hyperbolic attacks on the regime from the Duma's rostrum, the themes of which echoed in the press. Globachev heard the moderate and liberal deputies decry the deteriorating state of Russian society, question the credibility of the government, ridicule the diminishing authority of the monarchy, and worst of all advocate taking 'part in a revolution in order to organise a new "healthy" government, which would finish off the existing system', replacing it with a democratic republic.[71] Mistaking opposition rhetoric for programmes of action, the Special Section did not evaluate the capacity of these groups to implement their threats – it just assumed that they would.

As a result, Globachev and his colleagues, through glasses tinted by the 1905 Revolution, believed that they were witnessing the rejuvenation of liberal 'revolutionary' politics with the creation in 1915 of the Progressive Bloc[72] and the so-called public organisations – the Union of Zemstvos and Towns (known by the acronym *Zemgor*).[73] While the political police considered these institutions nothing less than successors to the Union of Unions and the St Petersburg Soviet, they feared that the Progressive Bloc and the public organisations would be ideally placed to rectify two of the flaws in the revolutionary formula brewed so haphazardly in 1905 and which had condemned the 1905 Revolution to defeat: the absence of a unified, pre-meditated plan of action and, once the revolution appeared victorious, the victors' inability to reconcile the differences between their competing political programmes. The Department of Police warned the government that these public organisations under the *aegis* of the Progressive Bloc, itself guided by the liberal intelligentsia 'who like in 1904–1905 are the leaders of the revolutionary movement' will 'bring about an onslaught [against the government] at the triumphant conclusion of the war' hand-in-hand with the Russian masses.[74]

As for Globachev, he believed that the Duma had declared revolutionary war on the nation and by 1916 had formed 'a definite revolutionary centre' with the silent blessing of M.V. Rodzianko, the Duma's President. Accordingly, Globachev claimed that this 'revolutionary centre' was closely associated with the Progressive Bloc, the public organisations and especially with the Central War Industries Committee (CWIC).[75] The Chief of the Petrograd OO reserved his greatest suspicion for the Workers' Group of the CWIC, which he insisted linked the labouring masses to the Duma, giving 'the revolutionary centre' the ability to lead the proletariat in whatever direction it chose. To the Petrograd political police chief the CWIC was nothing more than 'a political organisation that served the exclusive aim of laying the groundwork for revolution'. Globachev's opinion was shared by other police chiefs as well.[76]

Their fear and hatred of the Duma system was exacerbated by the knowledge that the dramatic leftward swing of public opinion in recent years would prevent the MVD from fashioning a Duma more 'suitable' to the aims of monarchy than the present Fourth Duma.[77] Anyway, Globachev reasoned, it was too late to return to the past, legality (*zakonnost'*) and public opinion (*glasnost'*), the Duma's most powerful weapons, had stripped the government of its decisiveness.[78]

A. P. Martynov, the Chief of the Moscow OO, though a more level-headed and more intelligent observer of Russian society than his Petrograd colleague, none the less believed that the liberals were only a step, maybe less, away from being revolutionaries themselves. To Martynov, the legal opposition served as an introduction to the delights of rebellion and he imagined a symbiotic relationship growing up among the opposition parties, the revolutionaries and the Russian people.[79] The Department of Police elaborated on how this relationship would function, concluding that while the public organisations under the guidance of the liberal intelligentsia strove to direct the life of the country in wartime, members of the currently atomised and ineffectual revolutionary parties poured into these organisations, using them to spread their own propaganda through their skills as agitators. Fontanka claimed that this propaganda crystallised 'the amorphous mass' of the population by whipping up the sedition 'the constitutionalists had sown'. Clearly the police believed that the next stages on the road to revolution according to its etiology of 1905 – armed demonstrations, terrorism directed against officialdom, partisan crimes, and agrarian and industrial economic terror – were about to be realised.[80] By employing this interpretation of events the Special Section's analysts concluded that the situation in the early summer of 1916 paralleled 1904–1905 so closely that 'the present moment is extremely dangerous'.[81]

In this case at least the political police had not fallen prone to overstatement. As Table 13.1 reveals, the first six months of 1916 had witnessed a massive increase in the number of strikes which approached the levels of the late pre-war period.[82] However, Table 13.1 also shows us that the vast majority of these

Table 13.1 The Strike Movement in Russia, 1916–1917

	Total No. of Strikes and Strikers		*No. of Political Strikes and Strikers*		*No. of Economic Strikes and Strikers*	
	No. of Strikes	*No. of Strikers*	*No. of Strikes*	*No. of Strikers*	*No. of Strikes*	*No. of Strikers*
January–June 1916	816	620 675	101	140 349	715	480 326
July–September 1916	248	134 212	8	20 543	240	113 669
October–December 1916	311	258 643	134	149 408	177	109 235
January 1917	382	249 315	229	162 978	153	86 337
Total	1 757	1 262 845	472	473 278	1 285	789 567

Source: I. P. Leiberov, *Na shturm samoderzhaviia: Petrogradskii proletariat v gody pervoi mirovoi voiny i Fevral'skoi revoliutsii, (Iiul' 1914–Mart 1917 g.)*, (Moscow: 1979), 114.

strikes were still concerned with factory floor issues, rather than national or political concerns. Certainly, the Progressive Bloc, rather than fomenting such strikes, was deeply ill-disposed toward any such action which undermined the war effort. No one, including the Workers' Group of the CWIC, wished to encourage that.

Indeed, the reality of political life within the Progressive Bloc – Globachev's imagined 'revolutionary centre' – was quite different from the partial truths and hyperbole of the political police. As early as the spring of 1916, several months before the police made their prediction of events reviewed above, the liberals themselves recognised what should have been apparent to the political police – that their efforts to organise the masses under bourgeois leadership through the wartime public organisations could not succeed. Progressive Bloc members of every political stripe feared the workers' movement and therefore never seriously encouraged it to join the opposition's harassment of the government.[83]

However, a few political police analysts did not totally subscribe to the image of popular discontent formulated by the majority of their brethren. For example, as early as 1915, worrying unorthodox observations began to creep into Martynov's reports, indicating his growing sensitivity to the changing political chemistry of society at large and of the factory in particular. Martynov expressed growing discomfort with the outdated Special Section axiom that the masses were little more than a collective *tabula rasa*, naturally imbued only with traditional loyalties and burning patriotism[84] and he attempted to disabuse his superiors of this notion.[85]

As the political crisis intensified, Martynov became bolder.[86] During the winter of 1916, he warned that 'the prestige of the supreme authority has palled', courageously conveying the unadulterated truth – something he would do with increasing frequency over the next several months – by placing the responsibility for this state of affairs squarely on the ineptitude of the government and the scandalous behaviour of the court.[87]

The inability of Martynov and those of his colleagues who shared his point of view to impress their unorthodox views upon their superiors did not – at least for them – become a matter of urgency, however, until the disaster of the Brusilov offensive. The last desperate hopes for victory faded with the collapse of Brusilov's daring and initially successful assault against the Austrians and the rout of his army. In particular, the bitterness caused by defeat in a campaign which only a few weeks before had begun with such promise combined with skyrocketing prices to enrage the workers, especially of the Vyborg district of Petrograd who struck repeatedly against the government's mismanagement of both the consumer economy and the war.[88] Table 13.1 tells that after a comparatively quiet July–September period in which only eight out of a total of 248 strikes throughout Russia were classified as 'political' the following October–December period showed that the number of strikes motivated by non-factory floor issues had increased to 134 (out of a total of 311) strikes. As early as 19 October 75 400 workers at 63 plants were on strike in Petrograd.[89]

Jolted by the magnitude of the Brusilov defeat and the popular rage it stirred against the regime, the political police awoke from its stupor. Yet, as the OO chiefs' message began to change and as an air of desperation crept into their phrases, Russia's political police chiefs found their superiors still stubbornly unwilling to listen to the reformulated analyses and forecasts emanating from Russia's OOs.

Let us look at two reports on the state of Russian society prepared in October 1916, one by Martynov and the other by the more traditional Globachev, in order to corroborate this last point. By October 1916, Martynov had completely altered the analytical structure in which he had begun to discuss Russia's political crisis. Martynov held nothing back from Headquarters. 'It is difficult to name a class of society which would stand solidly with the government', Martynov wrote, commenting that the entire political spectrum from right to left, from the gentry to the large industrialists, and most of all the average man in the street, blamed its economic hardship, the terrible military defeats and the equally distressing demoralisation of the home front on the government. The hatred of the liberal intelligentsia for the government had never been more intense, Martynov warned. The chief of the Moscow OO went so far as to question the continued loyalty of Russia's civil servants whose lives were being ruined by inflation.

Most notably in this report Martynov transferred the onus for the crisis from the opposition and the subversive elements of society to the government itself, something, as we have seen, he had begun to do more tentatively and unsystematically several months before. Of equal significance was his elaboration upon his previous comments concerning the evolution of class consciousness and the division of society by class interest and, for the first time, an insight into the chemistry that would soon ignite and drive the coming revolution. Martynov stood the traditional police formula for revolution – a *sine qua non* of Special Section philosophy – on its head by proclaiming to the Department of Police that a revolutionary elite is not necessarily the impetus for rebellion, though revolutionaries will certainly take advantage of this situation once given the opportunity.[90]

Globachev, not nearly so astute as Martynov, came to understand this last critical point only in retrospect when writing his memoirs.[91] But even he began to modify his opinion concerning the nature of dissent spreading throughout Russia. His October 1916 intelligence summary was less sophisticated and not as frank as Martynov's report and he cautiously cloaked his opinions in the words of the opposition and legal Bolshevik press, a common political police method of self-preservation. None the less, like Martynov in Moscow, Globachev was struck by the independence of the masses from revolutionary organisations, and by the resilience of the workers in the face of ruthless repression. Agreeing with Martynov, he blamed the obdurate behaviour of the factory workers on economic misery, announcing that 'every kind of strike has blazed up purely by chance'.[92] General Globachev seemed amazed that the strikes taking place under his jurisdiction did not appear to exhibit 'any clear political programme', but once set in motion became 'unconditionally and clearly political'. Unlike his Muscovite counterpart, however, Globachev refused to accept the conclusions of his own analysis, falling back on time-worn traditional explanations. He insisted that the bitterness of the masses was directed only against the government's 'forgetting' its needs and the responsibility for the discontent spreading throughout the capital remained with the people. With a lack of sensitivity and with a crudity of expression unusual even for a gendarme, he chastised not the government, but the people themselves for their 'wearying craving for the rapid satisfaction of their "immediate" needs...'. Globachev warned that the masses would follow any party 'which is the first to satisfy the demands of their stomachs...'. He prophesied that this party was more likely to be a revolutionary party than an oppositional one.[93]

These intelligence surveys contain much the same information, but despite their similarity they are fundamentally different. Globachev's reporting was self-contradictory, drawing outdated, familiar conclusions from observations that described an unfamiliar reality. Consequently his advice on the appropriate action to be taken by the government was often useless or worse, counter-productive. None the less, Globachev's superiors took comfort from his reports, which blamed the familiar traditional enemies – the press, the Duma, the radical and oppositionist intelligentsia, the impatience of the population – for the widespread discontent. Clearly, under such conditions a fresh analysis of the dynamics of mass dissent could not penetrate beyond the outer offices of the Department of Police. As the official who read Martynov's report noted:

> A report composed with excessive caution, apparently the most critical moments are not reflected in it. Order the Chief of the Moscow Otd. po okhr. [OO] that especially on these [vital] questions he should not be afraid to get closer to the truth.[94]

How much closer to the truth could an OO chief get? It seems that the official who read this report felt deeply uncomfortable with Martynov's turnabout, though a perceptive reader of his reports would have seen it coming for a long time. Except for the government itself there is a distinct absence of villains in Martynov's survey. Where were the Lenins, Martovs, Chernovs, Savinkovs, Miliukovs, and Guchkovs? Where were the Workers' Group of the CWIC and other organisations, legal and illegal that had dominated police reporting for the past thirty-six years (at least)? This is what the police official who appended the above comment to the Moscow OO chief's October report missed. Martynov is describing a mass movement that had gone beyond the bounds of the MVD's understanding – it had entered the realm of culture.[95]

****

A movement generated by a societal transformation of this magnitude could not be contained by police measures. As P.G. Kurlov remarked in his memoirs, his acquaintance with the affairs of the Department of Police in October 1916 forced him to conclude that Tsardom confronted a threat against which it 'was extremely difficult to contemplate undertaking [any sort of] police measures which would possibly restore order'.[96] But if this was his contemporary opinion, not even he, Protopopov's 'pal' could convince the MVD of this fact. Globachev too, in spite of his limitations, was awakening to the intensity – if not as yet to the dynamics – of the crisis. As the autumn passed he reported his concern to every official in Petrograd responsible for law and order within the capital[97] but found no one who would listen to the warning that the police had been issuing since the end of October: 'that an unavoidable rapidly approaching catastrophe was clear'.[98] The political police were whistling into the wind.

By January 1917 workers in both capitals had reached the end of their tether. On 9 January 1917 – the anniversay of Bloody Sunday – 137 000 workers in Petrograd and 31 780 in Moscow embarked upon a commemorative strike.[99] Table 13.1 show us the extent of this explosion in labour unrest. In January alone the total number of strikes far exceeded the total for the previous three months with 'political' strikes making up 60 per cent of the total. Once this movement took on such massive proportions the remnants of Russia's revolutionary parties, slowly rebuilding at the grass roots and often working together, became increasingly involved in what clearly had become a revolutionary situation, just as Martynov had predicted they would.[100]

Under these conditions Globachev found both Vasil′ev's and Protopopov's indifference extremely frustrating. Despite all the evidence supplied to him Vasil′ev, commenting that the peasantry appeared not merely tranquil but content while the liberal and the radical elements of society had so far failed to unite in their opposition to the monarchy, persisted in the view that 'a revolutionary action in the near future is not practicable'.[101] Unfortunately for Globachev, Vasil'ev was not the worst of his problems. How much did Protopopov know about the perilous state of Tsardom and what exactly did he tell the Imperial Couple about the massive discontent abroad in Russia? According to Globachev, Protopopov 'saw nothing and understood nothing and confused everything'.[102]

As for Nicholas II, he had not been accessible to first hand political police opinion for some time. Globachev, as chief of security in the capital during turbulent times, should have received at least occasional access to the tsar as did his predecessor during and immediately following the 1905 Revolution. Instead Nicholas perused the bi-weekly 'newspaper', the *Okhrana Gazette,* of which he received the only copy and to which he only paid cursory attention.[103] A major potential source of political intelligence also available to the tsar came from a special department within the court commandant's office which operated under the direction of former Chief of the Moscow OO Colonel V.V. Ratko. Ratko's special department synthesised the political intelligence the court commandant received from various sources throughout Russia, and of course from Fontanka itself. Ratko then prepared an overview on the internal state of Russia for

Nicholas II.[104] While officials like Ratko structured their intelligence surveys with the tsar's limited ability to digest sophisticated analyses in mind[105] Ratko's reports were still worthy of the monarch's serious attention, which unfortunately they were not given. The political police had long known that even the starkest horrors, including the events of the 1905 Revolution, could not undermine the tsar's endless capacity for self-delusion which within the obscurantism of the court became more pronounced during the monarchy's last years.[106] The tsar's mind was closed and neither ministers of internal affairs such as Maklakov and Protopopov, nor all of the intelligence surveys compiled by the various branches of the political police and gendarmes could pry it open. Nicholas II knew his real enemies, and no one could tell him otherwise, as he told the French ambassador, 'the miasma of Petrograd, you can feel it even here at Tsarskoe Selo twenty versts away. And it is not from the peoples' neighbourhoods that these odours come; it is from the salons. What a shame! What wretchedness!'[107]

Globachev, Martynov and their colleagues having to one degree or another finally thrown off their own blinkers observed with trepidation this growing chasm between illusion and reality within Tsardom's governing circles. Frightened and leaderless, these men did not possess the luxury of simple, passive self-delusion enjoyed by their superiors. The signs of impending catastrophe in the intelligence gathered by their bureaus were unmistakable. Russia's political police chiefs found themselves in an untenable position. On the one hand they were unable to alert their superiors to the warning signals and on the other hand they were forced to confront their own impotence *vis-à-vis* the deepening political crisis. These circumstances became too much for them to bear. They could not face the fact that the police system no longer practised its traditional role as the bulwark of the regime which, at least in the minds of the police, had given Fontanka paramount status within the panoply of Russia's governing institutions. As a consequence Russia's political policemen, despite the evidence of their growing impotence, continued to fulfil the requirements of their ethos – to reaffirm the monarchical principal when it weakened, to defend it when it was attacked – by the usual means of surveillance and repression to which they had long been accustomed.

Globachev, in particular, became the victim of what Karl Mannheim labelled 'utopian thinking' which condemns its sufferers to be 'not at all concerned with what really exists, rather in their thinking they seek to change the situation that exists'.[108] Globachev's 'utopian thinking' not only led him to strike out against those whom he perceived to be the opponents of the regime, but paradoxically, despite the weight of evidence before him and his own dire warnings to his superiors, convinced him that the employment of traditional methods of harassment and arrest against specific groups would actually save the regime.[109] These time-worn methods of combating sedition, however, only spread anti-government sentiment further[110] and that sentiment, as the police themselves discovered, became more not less difficult to root out.[111] In a classic example of this entire syndrome we see Globachev convinced that the crisis could still be defused if only Protopopov would dissolve the Duma, thereby 'liquidating the "revolutionary centre"' and with it, as Globachev imagined, the influence of its ringleaders located in the CWIC, the public organisations and the Progressive Bloc.[112] So when Protopopov asked the exasperated Globachev for advice, the Petrograd OO chief claimed that he did not mince words. He presumptuously offered his minister two choices: dissolve the Duma or retire![113]

Globachev made his arrests throughout January and February 1917, but they mattered little.[114] By mid-February the entire apparat of the Department of Police, the Corps of Gendarmes and the Petrograd *gradonachal'nik* was girding itself for revolution.[115]

Yet in the surreal world of the MVD self-delusion persisted. Vasil'ev informed the tsaritsa 'that revolution as such was quite impossible'. The Director of Fontanka admitted to Alexandra that, 'there certainly existed among the people a certain nervous tension due to the prolonged duration of the war and to the heavy burdens it entailed'. Nevertheless, Vasil'ev reassured the tsaritsa, 'that the people trusted the tsar and were not thinking of rebellion'.[116] Protopopov himself, despite being shown evidence to the contrary[117] persisted in his belief in the loyalty of the army and professed his ignorance of the strength of the workers' movement.[118] It is no wonder then that on 10 February 1917, in response to Rodzianko's expressed fear of revolution, the tsar calmly countered, 'my information indicates a completely different picture'.[119]

Finally, such illusions had their limits. On the morning of 23 February 1917 Vasil'ev warned a surprised Protopopov that the workers' movement displayed a massive character in which neither discipline nor leadership could be discerned. By noon 50 000 Petrograd workers had walked off their jobs to commemorate International Women's Day; that number would double before the end of the day.[120] None the less, Vasil'ev expressed his hope that the strikers would get up and go to work in the morning[121] and when they did not he informed Protopopov that 'the situation was more confused than it had [previously] seemed'. He then turned to Globachev, ordering him to collect fresh intelligence in order to sort things out. 'Everyone', Vasil'ev prayed, 'hoped that the masses can still be calmed'. The chief of the Petrograd OO less optimistically expressed the opinion that order might have to be restored by force of arms.[122]

Fresh intelligence poured in from Globachev's bureau and other sources, indicating a mass movement taking on nightmarish proportions.[123] The Petrograd OO were particualrly anxious about the news that the police were arresting people who had never been arrested before. Gradually the impact of the forces of order became less effective – perhaps it was the size of the crowds or the aura of power which emanated from them. When the police did disperse the crowds Globachev reported, they did so 'without special heart'.[124] By Sunday, 26 February about 78 per cent of Petrograd's proletariat were on strike.[125] There was little left Globachev's men could do. Globachev held nothing back from his chief. 'The uprising has risen into a blaze without any party preparation and without preliminary discussion of plans of action'. He continued:

> Now everything depends on the line of conduct of the military, if at last, it does not come down on the side of the proletariat then the movement will quickly wane, but if the military rejects the government then nothing will save the country any longer from the revolutionary turmoil. Only decisive and immediate action can weaken and halt the rising movement.[126]

On 28 February with Petrograd in chaos and his own OO overrun by the revolutionary crowd (see the Epilogue) Globachev fled to Tsarskoe Selo where to his amazement he failed to convince the chief of the court police or anyone else for that matter of the chaos and panic in the capital.[127]

Moscow soon followed Petrograd's example where Martynov suffered an equally bitter experience. 0n 3 March the Moscow OO was set alight. With angry crowds invading the building, throwing archives and current records onto a growing bonfire, the old regime in Moscow came to an end.

****

The glacially slow transformation of Russian society begun with the Great Reforms had finally driven the political police system – a symbol of the entire old regime – into a *cul-de-sac* from where both Globachev and Martynov conceded they were powerless to retrieve the situation.[128]

The forces of order, rendered ineffectual by their mind set and traditional prejudices and further debilitated by the exigencies of war and the disappearance of collegial respect and trust, were unable to make the transition from the no-longer real political and social context of traditional Russia which they had for so long inhabited to the harsh reality of an increasingly modern socio-political environment. As a result, their value to the faltering regime was reduced to nil.

Certainly a political police force, no matter how able cannot by itself save a declining regime. It does not have the physical resources to subdue large scale popular unrest let alone the capacity to restore the corroded authority of its government. On the contrary, as our observations have shown, the political dynamics of a tottering regime forces its political police despite its best intentions to contribute to the collapse of the government it has sworn to defend.

Epilogue

Despite the growing awareness that the Romanov Dynasty's hours were numbered, the bureaucrats, detectives and undercover agents of the political police exhibited remarkable sang-froid in sticking to their posts and continuing to supply the Petrograd OO with telephoned reports until midday 27 February. Even when the OO's contacts with Fontanka and with the commander of the Petrograd military district had been cut, Globachev remained at his post in touch with the Petrograd *gradonachal'nik*, the Winter Palace, the MVD and Tsarskoe Selo.[1]

By two o'clock on the afternoon of 27 February the revolutionary crowd had surrounded Fontanka and although it was not captured until the next morning, Globachev, at his OO headquarters, realised that further resistance was pointless.[2] At 3:00 p.m., in his last communication with Protopopov, the Petrograd OO chief advised his minister of his opinion.[3]

While some diehard defenders of the old regime armed with rifles and machine guns fought a useless and subsequently infamous rearguard action against the rebellious population of the capital,[4] Globachev remained ensconced in his OO until 5:00 p.m. when he learned that a large crowd was moving toward his headquarters on the Moika. He immediately ordered most of his personnel home. The OO chief and his closest associates stayed behind and in an astoundingly futile gesture locked all the entrances![5] Only then did he slip out of Petrograd.

Unlike Globachev, some political policemen chose suicide; others tried to escape but were captured and summarily executed on the embankment of the Neva River. By and large, a policeman's survival depended upon the speed with which he shed his uniform and surrendered to the new government; police queued at the Tauride Palace to be arrested and face their uncertain fate.[6]

The Provisional Government imprisoned senior police officials in the Fortress of Peter and Paul, but this did not guarantee their safety.[7] The Prime Minister of the Provisional Government, Prince G.E. L'vov and Minister of Justice A.F. Kerensky did their best to defuse the popular desire for vengeance directed against the guardians of the former regime. Kerensky strove to calm the nerves of incarcerated tsarist officials by announcing that the new government would deal with them strictly according to the due process of the law. It is doubtful whether such a promise would have assuaged the misgivings of the prisoners detained in the capitals. In any case, L'vov's and Kerensky's appeals for calm, generosity and for acceptance of the due process of the law most certainly did not penetrate the provinces, where hundreds of arrested policemen filled the old regime's prisons.[8]

The official death knell of the tsarist political police tolled in the first weeks of March 1917, when the Provisional Government abolished Tsardom's OOs, the

Separate Corps of Gendarmes, the Railway Gendarmerie and the Foreign Agentura. The government transferred officers and enlisted men who had served in the gendarmes to the regular military authorities for the purpose of their reassignment to the army. Indeed, most of these men would gladly take their chances at the front rather than face the wrath of the local populace. At about the same time the Provisional Government ordered the release of all persons convicted of or under investigation for political crimes, while Kerensky ordered the immediate liberation of any person previously condemned to exile for political crimes by the deposed monarchy's administrative order.[9]

The dismantling of the institutions of the Imperial police (the Department of Police itself was also abolished in March 1917) created a void throughout Russia which was, at best, inadequately filled by the new government's commissars whom it dispatched to the countryside. The Provisional Government commanded these men 'to introduce the new order at all levels of life.... To place everywhere people embued with the new ideals loyal to the new regime'. The commissars were told to accomplish this task quickly and legally. 'The main thing', the government instructed them, 'is not to think or act in the old manner'.[10]

With the Provisional Government's desire to implement a complete break with the police tradition of the previous regime, any suggestion for a reconstituted higher political police apparatus was rejected. Instead, throughout provincial Russia law and order were overseen by a newly created institution that incorporated the nests of vigilantes which had spontaneously arisen in the countryside upon the collapse of the monarchy. This militia – so named to avoid comparison and association with its odious predecessors – was established by two decrees, the first issued on 22 March 1917 and the second on 17 April 1917. These decrees placed the militia under the immediate control of provincial and district authorities in a decentralised chain-of-command reminiscent of Lopukhin's disregarded recommendations to Plehve. The preservation of state security was devolved to Russia's disintegrating Army.[11]

The Provisional Government, anxious to sweep away the remnants of Tsardom's political police, decided to rid itself of the old regime's political policemen as quickly as possible, not by executing them, but by setting them free. Those who volunteered for service at the front were the first to be liberated. Globachev, a bitter enemy of the liberal and moderate socialist forces then ruling Russia, remained in prison only until July 1917. Upon his release, despite his former career and his open hostility to the new regime, he served on active duty as an officer of the reserve attached to the staff of the Petrograd Military District until December 1917 when by the order of the victorious Bolsheviks, he was dismissed from the service.[12]

Globachev, along with an unknown number of his former colleagues, remained in Russia into 1918, long after the Bolshevik Revolution. For some, including S.P. Beletskii and V.E. Vissarionov, this decision proved to be fatal. The Bolshevik regime treated former tsarist law and order officials severely, disenfranchising them under the Soviet Constitution of July 1918, subjecting them to automatic arrest and exclusion from any subsequent amnesties. The Bolsheviks often took former political policemen and their superiors as hostages – summarily executing many of them.[13] It is surprising, therefore, that Globachev remained at large in the capital until his escape from Petrograd in September 1918, the time that many of his former colleagues were being shot in the onset of the Red Terror.[14] Globachev was not the only important tsarist law and order official to escape the Bolsheviks' clutches. It would appear that the Bolsheviks attempts at revenge were as inefficient as they were indiscriminate. Kurlov, Vasil′ev, Martynov, Komissarov, Russiian, Spiridovich and Zavarzin, to name a few, escaped the Bolsheviks' grasp and survived the Civil War to live out their lives in exile.

****

The fate of Globachev, Kurlov, Beletskii and their ilk, however, is less important to Russian political police history than the destiny of the hundreds of lesser, even minor officials who functioned more or less anonymously within the chanceries of the political police. It is likely that the professional lives of these men and women became integral to the evolution of Bolshevik political police institutions.

The number of white-collar personnel who transferred from the tsarist political police system to the VeCheka – established by a resolution of The Council of People's Commissars on 20 December 1917 – is unknown. Gary Waxmonsky has told us that published Soviet archives indicate that by the summer of 1918 'the VeCheka retained on its staff the second lowest percentage of white-collar employees from the old regime among all branches of the central state apparatus'.[15] But this body counting misses the point. How then do we respond to the question: how did the VeCheka with limited talent and inadequate training of personnel[16] manage to build a successful administrative structure and to develop the techniques of investigation and repression which, by the 1920s, culminated in a massive institution that successfully combined the administrative and investigative traditions of the Special Section and its OOs with the ruthless nature of the new regime?

There is no doubt that the Bolsheviks were less forgiving in dealing with the personnel of the Imperial Ministry of Internal Affairs than they were with the servitors of other ministries.[17] However, circumstantial evidence supports the speculation that the Bolsheviks' hatred for the praetorian guard of the old regime was tempered by the practical and urgent political policing requirements of Lenin's government and may not have extended to what Daniel Orlovsky describes as the 'lower-middle strata' of employees at all. For example, the services of the Special Section's brilliant cryptographer, Zybin, were retained by the Bolsheviks despite the central role he played in disrupting the revolutionary movement during Tsardom's last decades.[18]

It would be surprising if the VeCheka had not taken advantage of the dozens of detectives, clerks, and detective supervisors whom the Provisional Government's investigators found innocent of any wrongdoing – 'an unskilled workforce fulfilling their duties mechanically',[19] it said – and who, at the same time, possessed the expertise and institutional continuity required by the VeCheka organisation as it grew.[20]

Indeed, there is a piece of tantalising evidence in the memoirs of General Globachev which gives credence to this supposition. According to Globachev, who knew political policing as well as anyone, and witnessed the early development of the VeCheka, the Bolshevik political police arose from inauspicious beginnings:

> As investigative organs they [the Chekas] were highly unsatisfactory. That is, on the one hand the composition of the personnel was [chosen] by chance, from highly unreliable elements, without specialised knowledge and experience, and on the other hand, the technical work left much to be desired.[21]

None the less, Globachev's observations, especially after taking his obvious bias into account, are surprisingly mild and unintentionally revealing. His criticism that 'the technical work [of the Chekas] left much to be desired', is typical of the condescending comments made by high-and middle-ranking tsarist police officials, particularly gendarme officers, of their civilian chancery personnel or *sluzhashchie,* as such white-collar workers became known in post-revolutionary parlance. It seems that it is exactly these people whom Globachev is criticising, except now they are in the service of the Bolsheviks. Lenin needed them. The men (and women?) who populated Tsardom's chanceries were equipped to carry out the every day administrative functions which lay at the core of an institution's operations, but to which the Bolshevik intelligentsia itself was not intellectually predisposed. It is, therefore, reasonable to assume that it was these *sluzhashchie* who provided the VeCheka and especially its successors with the institutional framework which was to become the bulwark of the Bolshevik and Soviet states. The traditions they conveyed across the October Revolution remain ingrained within the Russian political police system to this day.[22]

****

While it is probable that police *sluzhashchie* inherited from Tsardom made available to Feliks Dzerzhinskii, chairman of the VeCheka, the bureaucratic infrastructure and police methodology necessary to build an intimidating political police force, they did not supply the VeCheka or its successor agencies with those characteristics which have given the Soviet political police its notorious reputation.

It is likely that the complexion of the VeCheka and its successors was determined by the complex linkage between revolutionary dynamics on the one hand

and the catalyst of events on the other hand. In this sense the VeCheka was, as Sheila Fitzpatrick claims, a new institution with no direct line of descent from its tsarist predecessor.[23]

For more than a century those Russians who battled to construct a normative legal order confronted two major obstacles that interfered with the fulfillment of their goal. First, they could not reconcile their desire to reform and rationalise the political system with the government's continued reliance on law and order agencies whose brutal arbitrariness – characterised by their absence of concern for personal inviolability – undermined these very efforts. Second, a normative legal order can thrive only in a rule compliance culture and unfortunately, Russia possessed a deeply imbedded task achievement culture.[24] Task achievement cultures are ruled by men not laws. In the decade between 1905 and 1915 the Russian polity was *beginning* to overcome these political and cultural roadblocks as it struggled to develop a *Rechtsstaat*. The impact of the First World War brought this process to a halt. The Bolsheviks, after their victory in October 1917, rejected the philosophy upon which a *Rechtsstaat* is based altogether, relying instead, as Amy Knight has suggested, on an extra-legal charismatic culture whose mechanisms for getting things done arose from both tsarist administrative practice – the practice of supervisory control – and the nature of Bolshevism itself.

With the demise of the monarchy the countryside lost any semblance of law and order. The Provisional Government published a panoply of laws, circulars and regulations designed to restore order to provincial Russia and generally to get things done and appointed local and provincial commissars to implement them, but to little effect. As George Yaney wrote, 'it was left to the Bolsheviks to carry out their plans for mobilisation by finding all-powerful monitors and hurling them broadside at the population'.[25] Traditionally, Russia's police forces have ranked high amongst these monitors of state control.[26]

As time went by Lenin, faced with widespread bureaucratic corruption and administrative inefficiency, turned repeatedly to the Cheka to investigate and resolve particular problems of governance and management. Indeed, by 1921 the Cheka had become indispensable as a branch of bureaucratic administration.[27] So wrote Martin Latsis, a prominent chekist, when he boasted that, 'it [the Cheka] must watch everything: military, life, food, education, positively all economic organs, health, outbreaks of fire, communication etc.'[28]

This untrammelled supervisory role of the Cheka as the 'vanguard of the revolution' was frighteningly and bloodily enhanced by the impact of Bolshevik rhetoric. The dynamic of revolution is stimulated by the rhetoric of its leadership and although that rhetoric, as Carl Friedrich has said, may only be the garb in which the political culture is dressed, it makes all the difference. 'For the garbs of tradition are the words in which it is expressed'.[29] And it is the new language of policing Russia – the rhetoric of Leninism – that establishes the tone adopted by the Cheka during the Civil War. Lenin, particularly, in his *The State and*

Revolution, invented it, but his disciples gladly carried it on. The condemnation of class opponents to oblivion by whatever means necessary, may initially have served as a rhetorical mechanism for the release of frustration by an anxious and impotent revolutionary emigré, but ultimately it was this brutal language of Bolshevism which aroused the Bolsheviks' audience into a frenzy of violence.

Rhetoric of this sort was employed, for instance, by Iakov Peters, Dzerzhinskii's well-known associate, when he explained the difference between the tsarist Special Section and the Cheka to critics of the latter organisation who saw in it uncomfortable similarities to the former:

> The deeds of the Tsarist secret agents who had fought against the proletariat, searched them, and sent them to Siberia, imprisoned them, sent them to the gallows – all this remained fresh in the memory of every communist. And here a new power was being organized, the power of the workers and peasants and once again there were searches, arrests and violence.
>
> To many there was no clear difference between the repression of the past and present.... Many did not understand that the October days did not solve the question of the class struggle, that this struggle had only begun, that the enemy was not asleep, but only in hiding, gaining strength; that therefore there was no time for sentimental dreaming – the enemy had to be finished off. They did not understand that the situation was extremely grave – the country devastated and hungry and that the proletariat and workers as a whole could not immediately understand the revolution completely. All these factors inclined many to be so sentimental that they only reluctantly entered the service of the VeCheka and only reluctantly took part in searches, arrests, and the conduct of investigations. A long period of struggle and defeat was needed before every revolutionary clearly recognized that revolution is not made in silk gloves, that where there is war there are casualties.[30]

Peters' message is a clarion call to destroy unspecified villains whose cunning and capacity for deceit masked their nefarious behaviour from the view of the goodhearted and naive masses. It is an excuse for murder.

Martin Latsis, when serving as chairman of the Eastern Front Cheka, took this form of rhetoric to the edge of hysteria when in a November 1918 article he wrote for the Cheka's own organ *Krasnyi Terror* (Red Terror), he proclaimed:

> We are not waging war against individual persons. We are exterminating the bourgeoisie as a class. During the investigation, do not look for evidence that the accused acted in deed or word against Soviet power. The first questions that you ought to put are: to what class does he belong? What is his origin? What is his education or profession? And it is these questions that ought to determine the fate of the accused. In this lies the significance and essence of the Red Terror.[31]

This bloodcurdling rhetoric fell on particularly receptive ears. When the great revolutions of the modern age released the human spirit from bondage they unleashed 'the vagaries and villainies of people, as well as their virtues'.[32] During the white heat of revolution those 'villainies' include the indiscriminate and conscienceless assault by the newly free masses against both their real and perceived former oppressors as well as against anyone considered to be a threat to the revolution. In the Russian case this phenomenon was magnified by what Moshe Lewin calls the 'geological shift' backward taken by Russian society caused by the Civil War where civilisation at first disintegrated and then regressed into neo-barbarism. Mankind was dehumanised – isolated from human affection where the only loyalty was to the tribal group – the Cheka, the Red Army, The Bolshevik Party – everything and everyone beyond the pale of the tribe was suspect and a potential enemy and therefore subject to the most conscienceless brutality.[33] The Cheka came to resemble 'an armed charismatic community'[34] fostering an 'elitism and dedication analogous to that exhibited by Hitler's SS troops'.[35] This *mentalité* extended itself to the Cheka's *sluzhashchie* who laid plans for the system of concentration camps for political prisoners at the end of 1918 and participated in the organisation of the forced labour camps in early 1919.[36] The men and women of the Cheka became enemies not only of tradition, but also of revolution.

The Bolsheviks' lack of vision, their almost willful ignorance of bureaucratic interest and behaviour allowed their political police to avoid integration within the regime's network of governing institutions, thereby escaping the real, although informal, constraints such a process would have placed on its actions.[37] Except for the years of the NEP when the political police were brought under the supervision of the Commissariat of Justice[38] it remained an institution beyond the authority of the state apparatus and from the mid-1930s until Stalin's death in 1953 beyond the control of the Communist Party itself.

****

Stalin's passing brought an end to his police state. The extra-legal charismatic culture of Stalinism disappeared with surprising speed, to be replaced by the beginnings of a legal bureaucratic system[39] which appeared as the new Soviet leadership strove to acquire the stability and certainty which had been absent from their lives under Stalin. The Soviet government reorganised the political police in March 1953, as one of its first steps in moving toward this goal. The Soviets created the KGB whose principal domestic function is the maintenance of tranquillity and order – the same brief as its tsarist predecessor.

To accomplish this end the KGB turned – how consciously remains a matter for speculation – to the precepts of the most astute of their Imperial predecessors. Sergei Zubatov and A.A. Lopukhin would have been proud of the recent KGB. Over the past decade or so the KGB moved steadily away from repression to prevention of dissent through the manipulation of the popular mind. The KGB began to portray itself as society's protector, seeking to enlist the help of the population in its campaign to persuade misguided individuals to return to the fold and to safeguard society against those dissidents who refused to comply with this 'request'. Lopukhin, as director of Fontanka, implored his OOs to adopt just this strategy more than seventy years before. The professionalisation of the KGB and the methods of interrogation employed by this agency are reminiscent of Zubatov's ideals: intelligent, well-educated investigators, familiar with the world view of their opponents, who during interrogation undermined the resolve of their bitterest enemies with politeness, even with empathy and kindness. 'The old KGB officer', wrote Valentyn Moroz:

> [W]as a sadist, who killed people or had them killed.... Young KGB officers achieve more through cunning than through brutality. A beating in prison is not such an effective instrument as one may think. It closes up a person and mobilizes his powers of resistance. Today's KGB officer knows this. Therefore as a rule he employs the following tactics: there is brutality all around. The guards are brutal; the surroundings are brutal. Only the investigative officer is a normal human being. He is polite. He might even bring the prisoner some butter or items from home. And there develops an involuntary attachment to him. These psychological details, insignificant at first glance, are highly dangerous. More than one prisoner has relaxed and weakened, without himself noting this, before a "civilized" KGB officer, although he most likely would not fear Stalin himself.[40]

Zubatov would have been proud of these men. The professionalism, elitism, public image and the methodology of the KGB[41] – as far as its domestic operations are concerned – are achievements of which the Special Section's brilliant chief could only have dreamed.

It is these attributes which may see the KGB through the turmoil of the August 1991 Revolution. Despite the less malevolent facade that has evolved from its apparently reduced power we should not forget that this is a political police more influential and powerful than its Imperial and perhaps, still, its Soviet predecessors. It is far too soon to predict the likely role of the remoulded police force in a revamped Russian state. One thing is certain, however; if the new state hopes to contain its internal security system, it must overcome Russia's historic inability to develop a normative legal culture. Only *zakonnost'* and the legal–rational juridical philosophy which sustains it will permit the new Russia to escape the overwhelming burden of its past.[42]

Notes and References

A Comparative Introduction

1. Max Lowenthal, *The Federal Bureau of Investigation* (New York: Harcourt Brace Jovanovich, 1950), 3–4.
2. Maurice La Porte, *Histoire de l'Okhrana la police secrète de tsars*, 1880–1917 (Paris: Payot, 1935).
3. Richard J. Johnson, 'Zagranichnaia Agentura: the Tsarist Political Police in Europe', *JCH* 7 (January–April 1972); D.C.B. Lieven, 'The Security Police, Civil Rights, and the Fate of the Russian Empire, 1855–1917', in *Civil Rights in Imperial Russia*, ed. Olga Crisp and Linda Edmondson (Oxford: Clarendon Press, 1989), 235–262; Nurit Schleifman, 'The Internal Agency: Linchpin of the Political Police in Russia', *Cahiers du monde Russe et Sovietique* 24 (1983): 151–77: Nurit Schleifman, *Undercover Agents in the Russian Revolutionary Movement: The SR Party, 1902–1914* (Basingstoke: Macmillan, 1988); Fredric S. Zuckerman, 'Vladimir Burtsev and the Tsarist Politial Police in Conflict, 1907–1914', *JCH* 12 (January 1977), 193–219: F.S. Zuckerman, 'Self-Imagery and the Art of Propaganda: V.K. von Plehve as Propagandist', *The Australian Journal of Politics and History* 28 (1982): 68–82: Fredric S. Zuckerman, 'Political Police and Revolution: The Impact of the 1905 Revolution on the Tsarist Secret Police', *JCH* 27 (1992): 279–300.
4. A. Fryar Calhoun, 'The Politics of Internal Order: French Government and Revolutionary Labor, 1898–1914' (PhD diss., Princeton University, 1973), 4.
5. Barton L. Ingraham, *Political Crime in Europe: A Comparative Study of France, Germany and England* (Berkeley and Los Angeles: University of California Press, 1979), 26.
6. Ingraham, *Political Crime in Europe*, 115–16, 218–19, 318.
7. Calhoun, 'The Politics of Internal Order', vii, 25, 114–15, 603; Brian Chapman, *Police State* (Basingstoke: Macmillan, 1970), 45.
8. Ingraham, *Political Crime in Europe*, 120, 199.
9. Calhoun, 'The Politics of Internal Order', 69; Chapman, *Police State* , 87–8.
10. Calhoun, 'The Politics of Internal Order', 70; Bernard Porter, *The Origins of the Vigilant State: The London Metropolitan Police Special Branch Before the First World War* (London: Weidenfeld & Nicolson, 1987), 125–6.
11. Ingraham, *Political Crime in Europe*, 169.
12. Ibid., 26.
13. Calhoun, 'The Politics of Internal Order', 63–4; Alf Lüdtke, *Police and State in Prussia, 1815–1850*, trans. Pete Burgess (Cambridge: Cambridge University Press, 1989), xvii.
14. Calhoun, 'The Politics of Internal Order', 17, 119–20, 122–3; Raymond Fosdick, *European Police Systems* (New York: Century Co., 1915), 142–3; Porter, *The Origins of the Vigilant State*, xiii, 176–7; Bernard Porter, *Plots and Paranoia: A History of Political Espionage in Britain 1790–1988* (London: Unwin Hyman, 1989), 232.
15. Fredric Scott Zuckerman, 'The Russian Political Police at Home and Abroad (1880–1917): Its Structure, Functions, and Method, and Its Struggle with the

Organized Opposition', (PhD diss., New York University, 1973), especially chapters 10–11.

16. Ingraham, *Political Crime in Europe*, 319; Calhoun, 'The Politics of Internal Order', 6, 19, 606; Porter, *Origins of the Vigilant State*, 116.
17. Calhoun, 'The Politics of Internal Order', 601.
18. Discussions on the nature of that culture are readily available. For example, Edward L. Keenan, 'Muscovite Political Folkways', *RR* 45 (April 1986): 115–81; Richard Pipes, *Russia Under the Old Regime* (London: Weidenfeld & Nicolson, 1974; Penguin Books, 1977).
19. Pipes, *Russia Under the Old Regime*, 22.
20. Keenan, 'Muscovite Political Folkways', 143, 147, 159; Arno Mayer, *The Persistence of the Old Regime: Europe to the Great War* (New York: Pantheon Books, 1981), 120; Pipes, *Russia Under the Old Regime*, 24, 68, 71, 94; Hans Rogger, *Russia in the Age of Modernization and Revolution 1881–1917* (London and New York: Longman, 1983), 7, 15, 29.

    The complexity of these rituals and the difficulty present-day scholars have had in understanding their roles is exemplified by the following studies: Hilju Bennet, 'The *Chin* System and the Raznochintsy in the Government of Alexander III, 1881–1894' (PhD diss., University of California, Berkeley, 1971); Hilju A. Bennet, 'Evolution of the Meanings of *Chin*: An Introduction to the Russian Institution of Rank Ordering and Niche Assignment from the Time of Peter the Great's Table of Ranks to the Bolshevik Revolution', *California Slavic Studies* 10 (1977): 1–43; L.E. Shepelev, *Otmenennye istoriei chiny, zvaniia i tituly v Rossiiskoi Imperii* (Leningrad: 1977).
21. W. Bruce Lincoln, *The Great Reforms* (DeKalb: Northern Illinois University Press, 1990).
22. Keenan, 'Muscovite Political Folkways', 126, 162; Robert F. Byrnes, 'Pobedonostsev on the Instruments of Russian Government', in *Continuity and Change in Russian and Soviet Thought*, ed. Ernest J. Simmons (Cambridge: Harvard University Press, 1955), 115.
23. Ingraham, *Political Crime in Europe*, 19–22.
24. Pipes, *Russia Under the Old Regime*, 315.
25. Ibid., 302; Mayer, *The Persistence of the Old Regime*, 304–5.
26. Rogger, *Russia in the Age of Modernization*, 11–12.

Chapter 1

1. The phrases 'state crime' and 'state criminal' appear repeatedly throughout this work in their Russian context. In that context these phrases refer to so-called political crimes described most thoroughly in Articles 1030 and 1031 of the Code of Criminal Procedure (*Ustav Ugolovnogo Sudoproizvodstva*) covering the following important political offences: (a) acts directed against the life, personal welfare, liberty and general inviolability of the persons of the tsar, tsaritsa and heir and attempts to dethrone the reigning tsar and to limit the content of his supreme authority; (b) forceful attempts to alter the succession to the throne, change the form of government, or alienate Russian territory; (c) insulting or threatening the persons, or violating the images of the tsar, tsaritsa and heir; (d) state treason including such acts as serving in hostile armies, espionage, unauthorised revelations of vital secrets, sabotage of defence installations or supplies, incitement of desertion to the enemy; (e) sedition including participation in a public gathering deliberately organised to

express disrespect for the reigning monarch or to censure the form of government or to demonstrate sympathy with mutiny and treason.

Article 1031 lists the following acts construed as state crimes: (a) the failure of officials to prevent or suppress political crimes; (b) the failure to report such crimes; (c) the suppression or tampering with evidence; (d) harbouring state criminals; (e) counterfeiting the state or other Imperial seals.

Compare these criteria for identifying political criminal acts with those listed by Ingraham for western Europe and repeated in the preceding Introduction. The comparison is noteworthy, particularly for the different emphases.

2. Richard Pipes, *Russia Under the Old Regime* (London: Weidenfeld & Nicolson, 1974: Penguin Books, 1977), 293–5.
3. Heidi Whelan, *Alexander III & the State Council: Bureaucracy & Counter-Reform in Late Imperial Russia* (New Brunswick: Rutgers University Press, 1981), 47–8.
4. I.V. Orzhekhovskii, *Samoderzhavie protiv Revoliutsionnoi Rossii* (Moscow: 1982), 61, 66, 78, 81.
5. Ibid., 123–4; Pipes, *Russia Under the Old Regime* 290, 296–7.
6. Orzhekhovskii, *Samoderzhavie protiv Revoliutsionnoi Rossii*, 172–3; Pipes, *Russia Under the Old Regime*, 304.
7. N.I. Falaev, 'Rossiia pod okhranoi', *Byloe*, no. 10 (22): 9.
8. The Ministry of Internal Affairs provided a Special Commission under the chairmanship of the assistant minister managing the Department of Police to adjudicate cases of administrative exile. The composition of the Commission changed regularly, but it always included four civil servants, two from the Ministry of Internal Affairs and two from the Ministry of Justice. The minister of internal affairs confirmed the decisions made by the Special Commission.
9. A.S. Suvorin, *Dnevnik A.S. Suvorina* (Moscow: 1923), 232.
10. Astrid von Borcke, 'Violence and Terror in Revolutionary Populism: The *Narodnaya Volya* 1879–1883', in *Social Protest, Violence and Terror in Nineteenth and Twentieth Century Europe*, ed. Wolfgang Mommsen and Gerhard Hershfeld (New York: St Martin's Press, 1982), 48.
11. Jacob Walkin, *The Rise of Democracy in Pre-Revolutionary Russia: Political and Social Institutions Under the Last Three Tsars* (New York: Frederick A. Praeger, 1962), 55–7.
12. Ernest V. Hollis Jr, 'Police Systems of Imperial and Soviet Russia'. MS Bakhmeteff Archive, Columbia University, 207. For a thorough analysis of the Emergency Statute see V.M. Gessen, *Iskliuchitel'noe polozhenie* (St Petersburg: 1908). For the legislative background leading up to the promulgation of the Statute see Falaev, 'Rossiia pod okhranoi', 1–43. P.A. Zaionchkovskii offers a masterful discussion of the Emergency Statute within the context of Alexander III's reign in P.A. Zaionchkovskii, *Rossiiskoe samoderzhavie v kontse XIX stoletiia, (politicheskiaia reaktsiia 80 -X – nachala 90 -X godov* (Moscow: 1970).
13. Falaev, 'Rossiia pod okhranoi', 24.
14. A.I. Spiridovich, 'Pri tsarskom rezhime', *ARR* 15 (1924): 137–8. While the gendarmes may have equated some of the more humane prosecutors with defence attornies, defence attornies themselves were frustrated by their lack of access to the evidence unearthed during the gendarmes' preliminary investigations. The tsarist government established several successive commissions (in 1894, 1901 and 1908) to tackle this problem, but nothing came of their efforts. N.A. Troitskii, *Tsarizm pod sudom progressivnoi obshchestvennosti, 1866–1895gg*. (Moscow: 1979), 200.
15. Marc Szeftel, 'Personal Inviolability in the Legislation of the Russian Absolute Monarchy', *ASEER* 17 (February 1958): 23–4.
16 Hollis, 'Police Systems', 147–8.

17. Ibid., 145; A.A. Lopukhin, *Nastoiashchee i budushchee russkoi politsii* (Moscow: 1907), 41.
18. Walkin, *The Rise of Social Democracy in Pre-Revolutionary Russia*, 56.
19. For example see, George Frost Kennan, *Siberia and the Exile System* 2 vols. (1891; reprint New York: Russell & Russell, 1970); N.A. Troitskii, *Bezumstvo khrabrykh: Russkie revoliutsionery i karatel'naia politika tsarizma, 1866–1882gg* (Moscow: 1978); A.V. Bogdanovich, *Tri poslednikh samoderztsa*: *Dnevnik A.V. Bogdanovich[a]* (Moscow: 1924), 33.
20. Falaev, 'Rossiia pod okhranoi', 36–7.
21. Szeftel, 'Personal Inviolability', 9; Kennan, *Siberia and the Exile System*, 1:248–9.
22. Szeftel, 'Personal Inviolability', 9.
23. How many people did the police keep under 'open surveillance'? Available statistics are unreliable. One thing is certain, however, the number of persons actually kept under 'open surveillance' was much smaller than the number that the public believed to be under surveillance. For example, in 1880 the government claimed that it kept 6790 individuals under 'open surveillance'. In the same year Madame Bogdanovich in her diary referred to comments made by a reliable source that, 'now there are 400 thousand people under police surveillence throughout Russia'. Troitskii, *Tsarizm pod sudom*, 32; Bogdanovich. *Tri poslednikh samoderzhtsa*, 33.
24. Kennan, *Siberia and the Exile System*, 1:277.
25. Troitskii, *Tsarizm pod sudom* 121–70 passim.; Troitskii, *Bezumstvo khrabrykh* 64–5.
26. Troitskii, *Tsarizm pod sudom,* 118; L. Slukhotskii, 'Ocherk deiatel'nosti ministerstva iustitsii po bor'be s politicheskimi prestupleniiami', *IR 3* (1926): 277.
27. Harry Ekstein, 'On the Etiology of Internal Wars', *History and Theory* 4 (1965): 154.
28. Quoted in Michael T. Florinsky, *Russia: A History and An Interpretation* (New York: Macmillan, 1953), 2: 1147.
29. Zaionchkovskii, *Rossiiskoe samoderzhavie,* 166–7.
30. Otto Kirkheimer, *Political Justice: The Use of Legal Procedure for Political Ends*, (Princeton: Princeton University Press, 1961), 132.
31. Whelan, *Alexander III & the State Council*, 78.

Chapter 2

1. Tsarist Russia's first political police was Ivan the Terrible's *Oprichnina* under the direction of the brutal Malyuta Skuratov. Abolished in 1572 it was not replaced until 1656 when Tsar Alexei established the *Prikaz*. Peter the Great replaced the *Prikaz* with his own *Preobrazhenskii Prikaz*. The Preobrazhenskii Chancery (changed from *Prikaz* in 1726) ceased in 1729. The police of Anna Ivanovna which followed was named the Chancery for Secret Investigation. Although officially liquidated by Peter III, it continued its work under Catherine the Great with the new name Secret Office (*Taina Ekspeditsiia*); carrying on its work through the reign of Paul I (1796–1801).

   For studies of the Russian political police prior to 1880 see: M.K. Lemke, *Nikolaevskye Zhandarmy i literatura, 1826–1855gg*. (St Petersburg: 1909); Sidney Monas, *The Third Section: Police and Society under Nicholas I* (Cambridge: Harvard University Press, 1961); I.V. Orzhekhovskii, 'Trete otdelenie', *VI*, 1972, no. 2: 102–9; I.V. Orzhekhovskii, *Samoderzhavie protiv revoliutsionnoi Rossii* (Moscow: 1982): P.S. Squire, *The Third Department: The Political Police in the Russia of Nicholas I* (Cambridge: Cambridge University Press, 1968).
2. Orzhekhovskii, *Samoderzhavie protiv revoliutsionnoi Rossii*, 11–12, 14–16.

3. Ibid., 40, 45–6. The Separate Corps of Gendarmes was officially attached to the Third Section in 1839 when the post of chief of staff of the Corps of the Gendarmes was combined with the post of director of the Third Section.
4. Brian Chapman defines a traditional police state as 'an organized state devoted to mobilisation and development with extensive police powers concentrated in a civil service under a single directing will, with a police apparat enjoying a national watching brief over the safety of the state, the integrity of public officers and the morale of the population'. Brian Chapman, *Police State* (London: Macmillan, 1970), 33, 127.
5. Ibid., 26–7.
6. Orzhekhovskii, *Samoderzhavie protiv Revoliutsionnoi*, 168.
7. Ibid., 104, 124; Ernest V. Hollis Jr, 'Police Systems of Imperial and Soviet Russia'. MS Bakhmeteff Archive, Columbia University, 273–4, 302.
8. Orzhekhovskii, *Samoderzhavie protiv Revoliutsionnoi*, 168.
9. N.P. Eroshkin, *Istoriia gosudarstvennikh uchrezhdenii dorevoliutsionnoi Rossii*, 2nd ed. (Moscow: 1968), 208.
10. Ibid., 208–9.
11. Ibid., 164–5, 244.
12. Hollis, 'Police Systems', 307–8.
13. P.A. Zaionchkovskii, *Krizis samoderzhaviia narubezne 1870–1880 godov* (Moscow: 1964), 244.
14. Ibid., 245; 'Istoricheskii ocherk organizatsii i deiatel′nosti Departamenta politsii (materiali k obzoru deiatel′nosti Ministerstva vnutrennikh del s 1802 po 1902 g.)', TsGAOR (The Central State Archive of the October Revolution). I would like to thank Professor Terence Emmons of Stanford University for loaning me his notes on this document.
15. Zaionchkovskii, *Krizis samoderzhaviia*, 246–8; P.A. Zaionchkovskii, *Rossiiskoe samoderzhavie v kontse XIX stoletiia, (politicheskaia reaktsiia 80-X – nachala 90-X godov)* (Moscow: 1970), 158.
16. Zaionchkovskii, *Rossiiskoe samoderzhavie*, 162.
17. Chapman, *Police State*, 137–8.
18. Zaionchkovskii, *Rossiiskoe samoderzhavie*, 158.
19. Ibid., 158–60; *Sovetskaia Istoricheskaia Entsiklopediia* (Moscow: 1964), 5: 122.
20. Gessen, *Iskliuchitel′noe polozhenie* (St Petersburg: 1908), 372–4.
21. Zaionchkovskii, *Rossiiskoe samoderzhavie*, 158–63; Eroshkin, *Istoriia goudarstvennikh uchrezhdenii*, 215.
22. Zaionchkovskii, *Rossiiskoe samoderzhavie*, 166–7.
23. Eroshkin, *Istoriia gosudarstvennikh uchrezhdenii*, 215–82.
24. Ibid., see the diagram at the end of his book.
25. Ibid., 236.
26. Zaionchkovskii, *Rossiiskoe samoderzhavie*, 164. The *Polozhenie* also created the short-lived post of inspector of political police affairs. The first and only inspector of political police affairs was G.P. Sudeikin, the talented and infamous chief of the Petersburg OO. As inspector of political police affairs Sudeikin worked under rules presented in the guideline 'Instructions to the inspector of the secret police' issued on 29 January 1883 which gave him control of political police operations throughout the empire. Though the post disappeared with Sudeikin's demise, two of his successors in the early twentieth century, S.V. Zubatov and A.V. Gerasimov, would *de facto* hold the positions as we shall see in Chapters 7, 12.
27. Zaionchkovskii, *Rossiiskoe samoderzhavie*, 165.
28. Ibid., 165.
29. Ibid., 165.
30. I.V. Alekseev, *Provokator Anna Serebriakova* (Moscow: 1932), 9.
31. Another major link in the tsarist political police security system was the Foreign Agentura, established in Paris in 1883. At first, the Department of Police considered

this bureau to be of rather little value, but with the growth of the revolutionary emigration in the twentieth century it assumed a critically important role. The history of the Foreign Agentura's war with the revolutionary emigration and its relationship with European police forces is beyond the scope of this study and is the subject of a separate monograph now underway.

32. Norman Naimark, *Terrorists and Social Democrats: The Russian Revolutionary Movement under Alexander III* (Cambridge: Harvard University Press, 1983), 235.
33. Alekseev, *Provokator*, 6.
34. Ellis Tenant, 'The Department of Police 1911–1913: From the Recollections of Nikolai Vladmirovich Veselogo', MS Hoover Institution Archives.
35. Emmons' notes. The Special Section's organisation and operating procedures underwent periodic modifications suitable it was thought to the conditions it confronted. L.I. Tiutiunik, 'Istochniki po istorii Departamenta politsii (1880–1904 gg.)', *Sovetskie Arkhivy*, 1984, no. 3: 53.
36. 'Dopros gen. E.K. Klimovicha', *PTsR*, 1:66. Klimovich claimed that the 'secret fund' contained five million rubles.
37. A. Volkov, *Petrogradskoe okhrannoe otdelenie* (Petrograd: 1917), 3–4.
38. Eroshkin, *Istoriia gosudarstvennikh uchrezhdenii*, 236, 299 and Eroshkin's schematic of Fontanka's organisation at the back of the book; Department of Police Circular no. 109050, issued by the Special Section, 24 August FAAr, 158, XIIId (1); From the Director of the Department of Police, Weekly Intelligence Survey no. 127/3566, 13 March 1905, FAAr, 154, XIIIc (2), 6A.
39. FAAr. 158, XIIId (1), contains hundreds of circulars issued to each of these agencies. These missives, except for those concerned with military espionage, emanated from the Special Section.
40. The label 'Okhrana' is appropriately applied only to the Court *Okhrana* which served as the bodyguard to the Imperial Family at home and when they travelled abroad. Although it liaised with the Department of Police it was not under Fontanka's jurisdiction and played no role in formulating its policies, nor did it implement its orders. The Court *Okhrana* boasted a contingent of 280 men, including four officers and its chief. The rank-and-file members of the bodyguard were chosen from the ranks of the non-commissioned officers serving in St Petersburg Guards Regiments. V.K. Agafonov, *Zagranichnaia okhranka* (Petrograd: 1918), 120–1; Tenant, 'The Department of Police 1911–1913', 15.
41. Quoted in Richard Pipes, *Russia under the Old Regime* (London: Weidenfeld & Nicolson, 1974; Penguin, 1977), 307.
42. Ministerstva Vnutrennikh Del. Departament Politsii. Po 2 Deloproizvodstvu, O *preobrazovanii politsii v Imperii*, 1 Sentiabria 1913g. no 20.083, 1–2.
43. Chapman, *Police State*, 78–80.

Chapter 3

1. A.T. Vasilyev, *The Okhrana: The Russian Secret Police*, trans. René Fülöp-Miller (London: George Harrap, 1930), 59.
2. 'Rossiia pod nadzorom politsii', *Osvobzhdenie*, 1903, no. 5 (29): 87 and no. 11 (35): 185; V.M. Gessen, *Iskliuchitel'noe polozhenie* (St Petersburg: 1908), 12.
3. 'Rossiia pod nadzorom politsii', *Osvobvozhdenie*, 1903, no. 11 (35): 187.
4. 'Instruktsiia no. 298 po organizatsii naruzhnago (filerskogo) nabliudeniia', FAAr, 41, VIf.
5. 'Instruktsiia no. 298'
6. MVD, Department of Police circular no. 438, issued by the Third Secretariat, 28 June, FAAr, 158, XIIId (1), 8.

7. 'Shkola filerov', *Byloe* n.s., 1917, no. 3 (25): 49.
8. L.P. Men′shchikov, *Okhrana i revoliutsiia: k istorii tainykh politicheskikh organizatsii sushchestvovavshikh vo vremena samoderzhaviia* (Moscow: 1928).
9. 'Shkola filerov', 41. The great success of the Moscow 'flying Squad' caused the innovator Sergei Zubatov to establish a similar unit of experienced detectives in St Petersburg when he became director of the Special Section. Zubatov dispatched detectives from this unit throughout Russia and it reported its findings directly to him. P.P. Zavarzin, *Rabota tainoi politsii* (Paris: 1924), 70–1.
10. A.I. Spiridovich, 'Pri tsarskom rezhime', *ARR*, 1924, 15: 125.
11. A.T. Vasilyev, *The Ochrana: The Russian Secret Police*, trans. René Fülöp-Miller, American edition (Philadelphia: J.P. Lippincott, 1930), 51, 125; Maurice La Porte, *Histoire de l′Okhrana la police secrète des Tsars, 1880–1917* (Paris: Payot, 1935), 94.
12. 'Shkola filerov', 43–7.
13. Dispatch no. 611, Paris, 18 November/1 December 1909, FAAr, 41, Vle, 2.
14. MVD, Department of Police Circular no. 134136, issued by the Special Section, FAAr, 41, Vle, 2.
15. 'Shkola filerov', 48.
16. Ibid., 49.
17. The average salary of a *nadzirateli* ranged from 40 to 75 roubles per month before the First World War and 100 to 120 roubles during the war; much of the difference merely reflected inflation rather than a real increase in wages. As a sympathetic police official stated in arguing for a raise on behalf of these underpaid men, 'apartments have long since not been inexpensive'. Ibid., 51; S.B. Chlenov, *Moskovskaia okhranka i ee sekretnye sotrudniki: Po dannym komissii po obespecheniiu novogo stroia* (Moscow: 1919), 37.
18. Ibid., 48.
19. From the Director of the Department of Police, Intelligence Survey no. 86, 20 May 1904, FAAr, 153, XIIIc (2), 4.
20. Samples of Fontanka's mania for time-wasting detail are to be found in its instructions on how to construct diaries and how to summarise them. Fontanka told its detectives that their diaries must be constructed in the following manner:

    1. At the heading of the diary it is necessary to have the name of the suspect's revolutionary group. The diarist must record the names of all the suspect's acquaintances, noting their revolutionary group.
    2. In the text of the diary the first step is to list the suspect's family name, patronymic, age, rank, class, title, place of residence, occupation and *klichka*.
    3. The reason that the surveillance has been undertaken must also be listed. In the diary the person suspected must be designated by his family name, not his *klichka*.
    4. All places visited by the suspect must be reported; designations must be specific.
    5. If one cannot establish the location visited by the suspect enter a question mark.
    6. Give a physical description of the suspect.

    And their weekly *svodka* must include:

    1. Under the column labelled *klichki* list all the *klichki* of those persons mentioned in the body of the diary and arrange them [the *klichki*] in alphabetical order.
    2. In the column labelled Setting (*Ustanovka*) list all persons mentioned in the text of the diary by surname, given name, patronymic, age, title or rank and occupation. In the absence of this data leave a blank space.
    3. In the columns labelled Visited (*Posetil*) and With Whom Seen (*S kem videlsia*) one must give the *klichki* and family name, of the person visited or seen.

4. In the column Visited one must, if possible, list the apartment number and the house in which the meeting took place.
5. In the column entitled Residence (*Mestozhitel′stvo*) one must indicate all addresses and note any change of address.
6. In the column labelled Location (*Mesto*) all houses listed in the diary must be placed in numerical order, or in alphabetical order according to the family name of the owner.
7. In the column labelled Setting it is necessary to note the physical description of all people the suspect visited. If any suspect should take a trip one should indicate in this column when and where the person went. If the information is not readily available place a question mark [in the appropriate space]. See, from the Director of the Department of Police, Intelligence Summary no. 86, 20 May 1904, FAAr, 153, XIIIc (2), 4.

21. Vasilyev, *The Ochrana*, 42.
22. 'Instruktsiia no. 298'. The description of detective activities is derived from this seventeen page document on the operational procedures to be used by surveillance agents.
23. Ibid.
24. Ibid.
25. Chlenov, *Moskovskaia okhranka*, 41.
26. V. Zhilinskii, 'Organizatsiia i zhizn′ okhrannago otdeleniia vo vremena tsarskoi vlasti', *GM*, 1917, nos. 9/10: 259.
27. 'Instruktsiia no. 298.'
28. Maurice La Porte, *Histoire de l′Okhrana* , 96–8.
29. 'Instruktsiia no. 298'.
30. If their chief believed the assignment to be a lengthy one, in order to bolster the detectives' morale, he often encouraged the *filery* team to move their families to the place of surveillance. How the *filery* were to accomplish this chore in the midst of their official duties is impossible to fathom. 'Instruktsiia no. 298'.
31. Ibid.
32. Report issued by the Special Section, 1913, FAAr 8, IId, 3; MVD, From the Director of the Department of Police, Weekly Intelligence Survey no. 44/7222, FAAr, 152, XIIIc (2), 2c; *Moskovskoe okhrannoe otdelenie* (1917), 7.
33. MVD, Department of Police Circular no. 115350, issued by the Special Section, FAAr, 158, XXIIId (1), 10; MVD, Department of Police Circular no. 167410 issued by the office of the Vice-Director of Police, 24 February 1914, FAAr, 158, XIIId (1), II; Report issued by the Special Section 1913, FAAr, 8, IId, 3.
34. MVD, Department of Police Circular no. 115350, issued by the Special Section, FAAr, 158, XXIIId (1), 10.
35. 'Okhrannik ob areste uchastnikov l marta 1887 goda', *KA*, 1925, no. 2 (9): 299.
36. MVD, Department of Police Circular no. 108379, issued by the Special Section, 15 November 1910, FAAr, 158, XIIId (1), 10.
37. MVD, Department of Police Circular, issued by the Special Section, 31 August 1911, FAAr, 98, Xe, 59g.
38. MVD Department of Police Circular no. 117938, issued by the Special Section, 15 November 1910, FAAr, 158, XIIId (1), 10.
39. MVD, Department of Police Circular no. 127461, 18 November 1910, FAAr, 185, XVb, 2c.
40. Ibid.
41. MVD, From the Director of the Department of Police, Weekly Intelligence Survey no 30/4043, 24 April 1903, FAAr, 152, XIIIc (2), 2B.

42. Michael Futrell, *The Northern Underground: Episodes of Russian Revolutionary Transport and Communications Through Scandinavia and Finland, 1863–1917* (London: Faber & Faber, 1963), 103.
43. 'Shkola filerov', 50.
44. Zhilinskii, 'Organizatsiia i zhizn', 252–3.
45. M.E. Bakai, 'Iz vospominanii M.E. Bakaia: Provokatory i provokatsiia', *Byloe*, Paris, 1908, no. 8: 109.
46. The number of *filery* attached to any one Gendarme Directorate or OO ranged from six to forty depending upon the size of the city. In the capital cities there were about fifty to one hundred *filery* on duty from day-to-day. This number did not include those assigned to protect the tsar and his ministers. If, however, you count all sorts of informers there may have been as many as 700 people in the political police's employ in Moscow alone. Zhilinskii, 'Organizatsiia i zhizn', 258. Mikhail Bakai, the long-time political police official, offered a more exact though similar set of figures for the distribution of political police *filery* throughout the empire. Bakai, 'Iz vospominanii', 109.

    A recent writer offers a modest figure for the number of detectives serving at any one time within the political police. Z.I. Peregudova claims that there were about 700 of them. She notes that most detectives served in Russia's large cities and those towns with worker and student populations. Others were spread throughout the empire: Baku – 12; Vil′no – 15; Ekaterinoslav – 15; Eniseisk – 12; Irkutsk – 30; Kiev – 25; Lifland – 24; Minsk – 12; Nizhegorod – 12; Odessa – 15; Perm – 12; Saratov – 15; Tiflis – 30; Tomsk – 20; Finland – 20; Kharkov – 15; Estliand – 16. Z.I. Peregudova, 'Istochnik izucheniia sotsial-demokraticheskogo dvizheniia v Rossii (materialy fonda departamenta politsii)', *VI*, 1988, no.9: 97.
47. Michael Futrell, *The Northern Underground*, 112.
48. A good example of the loyalty of men employed as detectives is the statistic revealing that the large majority of detectives served for more than twenty years. Zhilinskii, 'Organizatsiia i zhizn′, 42.

Chapter 4

1. After 1905 reduced censorship of the press made the newspapers a better source of information, although they still had to be read with care. The most valuable information came from the legal newspapers and journals with either a left-wing or right-wing stance. 'From the files of the Moscow Gendarme Corps: A Lecture on Combatting Revolution', *CSS*, 1968, no. 1: 98.
2. The Gendarme Directorates, Railway Gendarmes and Border Gendarmes also employed undercover agents. They were few in number and, on the whole, of considerably less value than those of the OOs. Chlenov, *Moskovskaia okhranka i ee sekretnye sotrudniki: Po dannym komissii po obespecheniiu novogo stroia* (Moscow: 1919), 51–9.

    Also, some *sotrudniki* served more than one master by carrying out espionage duty for military intelligence in addition to their work for the Special Section. Often such agents found that their dual loyalty created serious communication problems between them and their rival superiors. See the personnel file of Minas Stepanovich Sanvelov, FAAr, 21, IIIF, 1B.
3. P. Pavlov, *Agenty, zhandarmy, palachi: Po dokumentam* (Petrograd: 1922), 7.
4. V.K. Agafonov, *Zagranichnaia okhranka* (Petrograd: 1918), 210–11.
5. 'Psikhologia predatel′stva (Iz vospominanii sotrudniki)', *Byloe*, 1924, n.s., nos. 27/28: 230.

6. *Izoblichennye provokatory* (Petrograd: [1917]), passim.
7. Evno Azef is a principal example of this form of recruitment. For studies of Azef's career see: Boris Nikolaejewskii, *Aseff the Spy, Russian Terrorist and Police Stool* (New York: Doubleday, Doran, 1934); Agafonov, *Zagranichnaia okhranka*.
8. MVD, Department of Police Circular no. 116818, issued by the Special Section, 19 October 1910, FAAr, 158, Xllld (1), 10.
9. For a detailed account of interrogation procedures, see V.P. Makhonovets, *Kak derzhat′ sebia na doprosakh* (Geneva: 1902).
10. M.E. Bakai, 'Iz vospominanii M.E. Bakaia: Provokatory i provokatsiia', *Byloe* 8 (1908): 124–34.
11. N.A. Bukhbinder, *Zubatovshchina i rabochee dvizhenie v Rossii* (Moscow: 1926), 4.
12. Jeremiah Schneiderman, 'Sergei Zubatov and Revolutionary Marxism: The Struggle for the Working Class in Tsarist Russia', MS loaned by the author, 103.
13. Fredric S. Zuckerman, 'Vladimir Burtsev and the Tsarist Political Police in Conflict, 1907–14,' *JCH* 12 (1977): 193–219.
14. Pavlov, *Agenty, zhandarmy*, 35–6.
15. V. Zhilinskii, 'Organizatsiia i zhizn′ okhrannago otdeleniia vo vremena tsarskoi vlasti', *GM* 1917, nos. 9/10: 282.
16. A.P. Martynov, *Moia sluzhba v Otdel′nom Korpuse Zhandarmov: Vospominaniia* (Stanford: Hoover Institution Press, 1972), 151.
17. A.A. Kulakov, 'O trekh predatel︠i︡akh (El′ko Ostrouman, Geir)', *KaS*, 1930, no. 6 (67): 79–88; Zhilinskii, 'Organizatsiia i zhizn^', 282, 285.
18. Agafonov, *Zagranichnaia okhranka*, 173.
19. A.T. Vasilyev, *The Okhrana: The Russian Secret Police*, trans. René Fülöp-Miller (London: George G. Harrap, 1930), 55–6.
20. Martynov, *Moia sluzhba*, 70.
21. A.N. Cherkunov, 'Provokator Vladislav Feliksovich Gabel′: (Iz vospominanii smolenskogo katorzhanina)', *KaS*, 1926, no. 1 (22): 203–4.
22. Zhilinskii, 'Organizatsiia i zhizn^', 297.
23. A. Volkov, *Petrogradskoe okhrannoe otdelenie* (Petrograd: 1917), 15.
24. Nurit Schleifmann, 'The Internal Agency: Linchpin of the political police in Russia', *Cahiers du monde Russe et Sovietique* 24 (1983): 164.
25. S.B. Chlenov, *Moskovskaia okhranka*, 13–30.
26. A.V. Gerasimov, *Na lezvii s terroristami* (Paris: YMCA Press, 1985), 58.
27. Volkov, *Petrogradskoe okhrannoe otdelenie*, 14.
28. *Izoblichennye provokatory*, another source of information on the widespread infiltration of *sotrudniki* into the opposition and revolutionary camps, though too vague to rely upon without reservation, seems to confirm this view.
29. It should be noted that many of the piece workers were persons who chose to inform on others out of allegiance to the regime, for personal reasons, or quite plainly for the recompense paid to them by a grateful political police. Some of these people, who could hardly be called professional agents, earned very small rewards of between three and five rubles for their information. The political police garnered this gossip from people of every class and rank including: bishops, professors, students, civil servants, and domestic servants. As we have seen, students who worked for the political police were paid considerably larger sums and tuition for their information. The best piece workers were professional *sotrudniki* who earned anywhere from fifteen to one hundred rubles for each bit of intelligence they supplied, the price being determined by the usefulness of the data to the Special Section. Zhilinskii, 'Organizatsiia i zhizn^', 302; *Izoblichennye provokatory*, see the section on undercover agents among the students; Agafonov, *Zagranichnaia okhranka*, 189; M.E. Bakai, 'Iz vospominanii M.E. Bakaia', *Byloe*, 1909, nos.11/12: 165–6; MVD

Department of Police Circular no. 13437, issued by the Sixth Secretariat, FAAr, 38, Vlb, 2.

30. Agafonov, *Zagranichnaia okhranka*, 128.
31. Bakai, 'Iz vospominanii', 166.
32. Agafonov, *Zagranichnaia okhranka*, 189. Nurit Schleifmann claims that agents in the SR Party earned three times what their Social Democrat counterparts earned. She states that in 1907 agents within the SRs averaged 160 roubles per month, among the anarchists 90 roubles per month and those placed among the SDs only 50 roubles per month. Schleifmann, 'The Internal Agency', 165, 176.
33. Bakai, 'Iz vospominanii', 166.
34. For example, the Moscow OO during the First World War, divided up its undercover agents among its case officers as follows:

Case Officer	*Number of Undercover Agents*	*Movements Infiltrated*
Col. Martynov (Chief of the OO)	8	General social movement
Lt Col. Znamenskii	9	SRs, Anarchists
Captain Gan'ko	11	RSDWP
Captain Zubkovskii	7	student movement, anarchists
Captain Belikov	5	tramway employees
Captain Mishin	6	RSDWP, workers' movement
Nadvornyi sovetnik Kulsynskii	6	General social movement

Note that one of the case officers was a civilian. This was not an uncommon posting. Chlenov, *Moskovskaia okhranka*, 21, 24.

A second source claims that in 1915 the Moscow OO controlled 48 *sotrudniki*. It apportioned 34 of them the following way, the remaining 14 having been called to military service:

SRs	5	student movement	5
Anarchists	2	Polish revolutionaries	1
RSDWP	3	tramway and power station workers	7
General social movement	11		

'Moskovskaia okhranka v 1915g.', *GM*, 1918, nos 1–3: 253–4. If these statistics are accurate then at least ten *sotrudniki* working among the SDs and two among the SRs had been lost to military service, diminishing the quantity and perhaps the quality of intelligence collected on these groups. For St Petersburg see Gerasimov, *Na lezvii*, 58.

35. A.T. Vasilyev, *The Ochrana: The Russian Secret Police*, trans. René Fülöp-Miller (Philadelphia J.P. Lippencott, 1930), 58–9; Zhilinskii, 'Organizatsii i zhizn'', 285.
36. Martynov, *Moia sluzhba*, 302.
37. Ronald Hingley, *The Russian Secret Police: Muscovite, Imperial Russian and Soviet Political Security Operations* (New York: Simon & Schuster, 1970), 99. In Moscow

in 1916, there were four or five such apartments and because of the size of the city this was probably close to the maximum number of conspiratorial apartments any single OO possessed. See, Chlenov, *Moskovskaia okhranka*, 25; Vasilyev, *The Okhrana*, 58–9.

38. Vasilyev, *The Ochrana*, 80–3.
39. V.N. Russiian, 'Rabota okhrannykh otdelenii v Rossii', MS Moravsky Collection, Hoover Institution, n.p.
40. Vasilyev, *The Okhrana,* 395–6; Zhilinskii, 'Organizatsiia i zhizn^283.
41. See the personnel files of *sotrudniki* Boleslav Brodsky and Vladimir Edelstein, FAAr 21, IIIf, 1a.
42. Bakai, 'Iz vospominanii M.E. Bakaia', 124–8.
43. Ibid., 131.
44. Volkov, *Petrogradskoe okhrannoe otdelenie*, 9; 'From the files of', 97.
45. Zhilinskii, 'Organizatsiia i zhizn^, 284–5.
46. Ibid., 285; Agafonov, *Zagranichnaia*, 190.
47. 'From the files of', 94–5.
48. Russiian, 'Rabota okhrannykh otdelenii', n.p..
49. Kulakov, 'O trekh predatel'iakh', 88.
50. Fredric Scott Zuckerman, 'The Russian Political Police at Home and Abroad (1880–1917): Its Structure, Functions, and Methods, and its struggle with the Organized Opposition', (PhD diss., New York University, 1973), 468–95.
51. Apparently, Azef was the exception to the rule for he was acquainted with both Gerasimov, who served as Azef's case officer, and Stolypin.
52. Russiian, 'Rabota okhrannykh otdelenii', n.p.
53. Spiridovich, 'Pri tsarskom rezhime', *ARR* 15 (1924): 124–5.
54. Edward H. Judge, 'The Russia of Plehve: Programs and Policies of the Ministry of Internal Affairs, 1902–1904', (PhD diss., University of Michigan, 1975), 49.
55. Testimony of A.I. Spiridovich before the Extraordinary Commission, 43.
56. Bakai, Iz vospominanii M.E. Bakaia', 134.
57. Zhilinskii, 'Organizatsiia i zhizn^, 297.
58. Russiian, 'Rabota okhrannykh otdelenii', n.p..
59. Boris Nikolaejewsky, *Aseff*, 174–5. The case of Roman Malinovskii is also well-known to historians of Russia. For example, see Ralph Carter Elwood, *Roman Malinovsky: A Life Without A Cause*, Russian Biography Series no. 2 (Newtonville MA: Oriental Research Partners, 1977).
60. Zuckerman, 'The Russian Political Police at Home and Abroad', 468–95.
61. 'From the files of', 94.
62. Dispatch no. 55, Paris, 18/31 January, 1910, FAAr, 192, XVId (3).
63. Aleksandr Guerassimov, *Tsarisme et Terrorisme: Souvenirs du Général Guerassimov* (Paris, Plon: 1934), 22
64. Zhilinskii, 'Organizatsiia i zhizn^, 285.
65. 'Sekretnye sotrudniki v avtobiografiiakh', *Byloe*, n.s., 1917, no. 2 (24): 238–9: Agafonov, *Zagranichnaia okhranka*, 197.
66. Vasilyev, *The Okhrana*, 55–6.
67. Spiridovich, 'Pri tsarskom rezhime', 124.
68. 'Sekretnye sotrudniki', 232.
69. 'K istorii aresta i suda nad sotsial demokraticheskoi fraktsiei II Gosudarstvennoi Dumy,' *KA*, 1926, no. 3 (16): 95–7; Alfred Levin, 'The Shornikova Affair', *SEER*, 21 (November, 1943): 11–15; 'Dopros N.A. Maklakova'; 'Dopros S.P. Beletskogo'; 'Dopros grafa V.N. Kokovtsova', *PTsR*, 3:122, 3:412–30, 7: 107–12.
70. 'Sekretnye sotrdniki', 236.
71. Alekseev, *Istoriia odnogo provokatora. Obvinitel'noe zakliuchenie i materialy k protsessu A.E. Serebriakovoi* (Moscow: 1925), 37.

72. Agafonov, *Zagranichnaia okhranka,* 221.
73. A. Lipkin, 'Provokator Nikulin – Mikulin', *KaS*, 1926, no. 2 (23): 113–15.
74. I.V. Alekseev, *Provokator Anna Serebriakova* (Moscow: 1932), 67.
75. Ibid., 18–36.
76. Alekseev, *Istoriia odnogo provokatora*, 44–8.
77. Alekseev, *Provokator*, 121–22.
78. Serebriakova performed additional services for Zubatov out of the realm of espionage, but invaluable none the less. She supplied him with literature on the labour movements in the West, translating this material into Russian for him and she served him as a sometime secretary, helping him to draft his reports and position papers. Ibid., 135.
79. Ibid., 63.
80. Ibid., 73.
81. Serebriakova received a massive lump sum retirement payment of 5000 roubles in 1908, a huge sum for an undercover agent. In November 1909 her luck began to sour. She was exposed by Vladimir Burtsev as having been a *sotrudnika* and, simultaneously, her health began to fail. The bookstore she had purchased with part of the lump sum payment from Fontanka had to be sold to help her pay for an operation that would remove the cataracts that were destroying her vision. In January 1910 Fontanka paid her another 200 roubles out of its secret fund to help her out. Finally, in 1911, she applied for a pension and with the full support of P.A. Stolypin received 1200 roubles per year. For the full correspondence dealing with Serebriakova's finances in retirement see: Ibid., 61–74; Alekseev, *Istoriia odnogo provokatora*, 29–44.

Chapter 5

1. Ellis Tennant, 'The Department of Police, 1911–1912: From the Recollections of Nikolai Vladimirovich Veselago', MS Hoover Institution, 21.
2. V.N. Russiian, 'Rabota okhrannykh otdelenii v Rossii' MS Moravsky Collection, Hoover Institution, n.p.
3. The biographical data used for both the police bureaucrats and gendarme officers on which the statistics are based can be found in 'Ukazatel' Imen', *PTsR*, 7: 299–443. This data is supplemented by career information elicited in the testimony of tsarist officials before the Investigating Commission of the Provisional Government (*PTsR*, 7 vols.).

   There are other sources for career data on my subjects in official tsarist *spisok* such as: *Obshchii Sostav, Upravlenie i chinov, Otdel'nago Korpusa Zhandarmov*, printed twice a year. For the career histories of K.N. Rydzevskii and I.D. Bologovskoi, I used: *Spisok Vysshikh Chinov Tsentral'nykh Ustanovlenii Ministerstva Vnutrennikh Del*, (St Petersburg: 1905). I found, however, the 'Ukazatel' Imen', though it contained some ambiguity and a few minor errors, to be more compact, more thorough and therefore more suited to my needs.

   Police officials, especially political policemen (OO gendarme officers) preferred not to identify themselves as such in official publications. Indeed some of them were only uncovered through their titles and signature on police documents and through the testimony of their colleagues in *PTsR*.

   Therefore, no other footnote will be required which specifically relates to material taken from the 'Ukazatel' Imen' used herein as a basis for statistical calculations.
4. Although I.A. Bologovskoi lacked higher education his career is unique within the civilian sample because he was a graduate of the Corps of Pages. He served in the Household Guards from 1882 to 1888 when he transferred to the civil service by

joining the MVD in the Department of General Affairs. He attained the IV rank in 1904 immediately before his appointment as a vice-director of the Department of Police.

5. Richard S. Wortman, *The Development of a Russian Legal Consciousness* (Chicago: University of Chicago Press, 1976), 206, 287.
6. If a military man held this post he was either a *podpolkovnik* (a Lt colonel) with a VII *chin*, or a *polkovnik* (colonel) with a VI *chin*. The military equivalent of the civilian Table of Ranks no longer possessed a V *chin*. My research did not reveal any Special Section chiefs holding lower ranks from those listed in the text.
7. Hilju Bennett, 'The Chin System and the Raznochintsy in the Goverment of Alexander III, 1881–1894' (PhD diss., University of California, Berkeley, 1971), 82. Bennett's discussion must be modified somewhat by the more recent and detailed research of D.C.B. Lieven. Lieven argues that the *chin* rules were frequently evaded after 1860, so much so that in his research he did not find 'a single example of a man failing to be appointed to a job because of his lack of correct rank'. Lieven writes that he discovered ministers and desk officers holding the same rank and jobs at the level of V *chin* being held by officials holding a X *chin*. I did not locate any such extreme cases of flaunting the *chin* rules, within Fontanka. Dominic C.B. Lieven, 'Russian Senior officialdom under Nicholas II: Careers and Mentalities', *JG* 32 (1984): 208.
8. Dopros S.P. Beletskogo', *PTsR*, 3: 259.
9. 'Dopros S.E. Vissarionova', *PTsR*, 3: 441. The *Prokurorskii nadzor* served as the honest brokers of the police investigating system, making certain, at least in theory, that no one breached the law right up to the carrying out of sentence. The *prokurorskii nadzor* existed as part of the legal system throughout the empire.
10 Wortman, *The Development*, 387.
11. *Pravo*, 14 May 1906; V.L. Burtsev, *Protokoly 'Sionskikh mudretsov': dokazannyi podlog* (Paris: 1923), 74; B.P. Koz′min, *S.V. Zubatov i ego korrespondenty* (Moscow: 1928) 123; and 'Dopros A.A. Reinbota', *PTsR*, 6: 122.
12. Bennett, 'The *Chin* System', 62–3.
13. That is officers who were: assistants to OO chiefs, OO chiefs, worked for the Foreign Agentura, worked in the Special Section or directed it. 'Ukazatel′ Imen', 299–443.
14. Ibid., 322, 331, 343;
15. Gurovich joined the Special Section as an administrator in 1903 and in 1904 he was made an inspector general for OOs. In this capacity he travelled throughout the empire, giving advice and issuing directions to the Special Section's OOs as well as determining their shortcomings. While his inspection tours frightened some gendarme officers, on the whole, he acquired many admirers among them. For many political police officers Gurovich was the ideal counter-intelligence officer, a teacher and example to inexperienced personnel. Gurovich continued to be promoted and during the first year of the 1905 Revolution he served General Trepov and then P.I. Rachkovskii as first assistant in charge of intelligence in the capital. He retired in 1906. 'File on M.I. Gurovich', FAAr, 21, IIIf, 1a.
16. *Svod Zakonov Rossiiskoi Imperii* (St Petersburg: 1892), 2: 186.
17. P.P. Zavarzin, *Zhandarmy i revoliutsionery: Vospominaniia* (Paris: 1930), 62.
18. For the best study of Russian military education in the late nineteenth century and the early twentieth century see P.A. Zaionchkovskii, *Samoderzhavie i russkaia armiia na rubezhe XIX–XX stoletii* (Moscow: 1973), 297–337.
19. Comparing ranks to length of service between bureaucrats and officers is useless since there were a variety of different promotion schedules and varying standards for qualifying for offices. Bennett, 'The *Chin* System', 80.

20. Peter Kenez, 'A Profile of the Pre-revolutionary Officer Corps', *California Slavic Studies* 7 (1973): 129, 136.
21. Gendarme officers who graduated from the staff school were eligible to become officers of the reserve – the officers assigned by Gendarme Directorates to investigate political crimes. The officers who performed this role formed an elite within the Gendarme Directorate administration. Martynov claims that there were only sixteen of them at any one time in the Corps of Gendarmes. Five of these worked in the St Petersburg Gendarme Directorate, two or three in Moscow and the others were spread among the large directorates in Kiev, Riga, Warsaw, Kharkov and perhaps Tiflis. Martynov claims that the officers of the reserve were sufficiently intelligent to unravel complex political cases and were aware of the world about them. A.P. Martynov, *Moia sluzhba v Otdel'nom Korpuse Zhandarmov: Vospominanii* (Stanford: Hoover Institution Press, 1972), 26–7.
22. A.P., 'Departament politsii v 1892–1902 gg.. (Iz vospominanii chinovnika)', *Byloe*, n.s., 1917, nos. 5/6 (27/28): 19; Vladimir I. Gurko, *Features and Figures of the Past: Government and Opinion in the Reign of Nicholas II*, The Hoover Library on War Revolution and Peace Publication no. 14 (Stanford: Stanford Univetrsity Press, 1939), 11, 20.
23. Aleksandr Gerasimov, 'Rukopis' vospominanii', MS Nikolaevsky Collection, 2.
24. Maurice La Porte, *Histoire de l'Okhrana, la police secrete des tsars, 1880–1917* (Paris: Payot, 1935), 51.
25. Zavarzin, *Zhandarmy*, 55.
26. Ibid., 56.
27. Martynov, *Moia sluzhba*, 28.
28. Ibid., 127; A.I. Spiridovich, 'Peter Ivanovich Rachkovskii', MS Spiridovich Collection, Sterling Memorial Library, Yale University, 4.
29. 'Ukazatel' Imen', 323, 354.
30. 'From the Files of the Moscow Gendarme Corps: A Lecture on Combatting Revolution', *CSS* 2 (1968): 88–9.
31. Zavarzin, *Zhandarmy*, 51.
32. Tennant, 'The Department of Police', 8.
33. George L. Yaney, 'Law, Society and the Domestic Regime in Russia in Historical Perspective', *American Political Science Review* 59 (1965): 385.
34. John A. Armstrong, 'Old Regime Governors: Bureaucrats and Patrimonial Attributes', *Comparative Studies in Society and History* 14 (January, 1972): 4.
35. Daniel T. Orlovsky, 'Political Clientelism in Russia: the Historical Perspective', in *Leadership Selection and Patron–Client Relations in the USSR and Yugolsavia*, ed. T.H. Rigby and Bohdan Harasmiw (London: George Allen & Unwin, 1983); and Dominic C.B. Lieven, 'Russian Senior Officialdom'.
36. Wayne D. Santoni, 'P.N. Durnovo as Minister of Internal Affairs in the Witte Cabinet: A Study in Suppression', (PhD diss., University of Kansas, 1968), 56–7.
37. Orlovsky, 'Political Clientelism in Russia', 175.
38. Ibid., 177–9.
39. Jean Longuet and George Silber, *Terroristy i Okhranka* (Moscow: 1924), 170.
40. Orlovsky, 'Political Clientelism in Russia', 178.
41. A.I. Spiridovich, 'Pri tsarskom rezhime', *ARR* 15 (1924): 158; Martynov, *Moia sluzhba*, 274.
42. 'Pis'ma Mednikova Spiridovichy', *KA*, 1926, no. 4 (17): 200, Martynov, *Moia sluzhba*, 26–7; 'Ukazatel' Imen', *PTsR*.
43. Orlovsky, 'Political Clientelism in Russia', 179.
44. 'Ukazatel' Imen,' 339, 359.
45. Ibid., 318, 326, 354, 356, 359.

46. Martynov, *Moia sluzhba*, 54–5.
47. Vissarionov's own testimony is supported by Martynov, who as chief of the Moscow OO witnessed his superior in action. Ibid., 55.
48. Lieven, 'Russian Senior Officialdom', 216.
49. Gurko, *Feature and Figures*, 199.
50. P.G. Kurlov *Gibel′ imperatorskoi Rossii* (Berlin: 1923), 81.
51. 'Dopros S.E. Vissarionova', *PTsR*, 5: 230.
52. Ibid., 5: 227–32; 'Ukazatel′Imen', *PTsR*, 7: 317.
53. 'Dopros S.E. Vissarionova', *PTsR*, 3: 440.
54. Martynov, *Moia sluzhba*, 54–5.
55. 'Ukazatel′Imen', *PTsR*, 317; Lieven, 'Russian Senior Officialdom', 213.
56. 'S. – Petersburgskoe okhrannoe otdelenie v 1895–1901 g.g.. (Trud chinovnika otdeleniia P. Statkovskogo)', *Byloe* n.s., 1921, no. 16: 108–11.
57. V. Zhilinskii, 'Organizatsiia i zhizn′ okhrannago otdeleniia vo vremena tsarskoi vlasti', *GM*, 1917, nos. 9/10: 266.
58. Ibid., 267.
59. Martynov, *Moia sluzhba*, 128–31.
60 Ibid., 213–14, 219.
61. Colonels earned 300 roubles per month. Fontanka issued Martynov another 100 roubles per month travelling expenses and free railway transportation. This was very nice but not so grand. The significant benefits came with the system of bonuses. For example, the government paid Martynov 2000 roubles on his birthday and 2000 roubles at Easter came from the Moscow *gradonachal′nik* and an additional 1000 roubles came from the Department of Police. Ibid., 46, 216–17.
62. V.S. Novitskii, *Iz vospominanii zhandarma* (Leningrad: 1929), 25.
63. Russiian, 'Rabota okhrannykh', n.p.
64. MVD, Department of Police Circular no. 10950, issued by the Special Section, 24 August 1905, NYPL.
65. L. Gan, 'Ubiistvo P.A. Stolypina', *IV* 136 (April 1914): 210.
66. P. Pavlov, *Agenty, zhandarmy, palachi: Po dokumentam.* (Petrograd: 1922), 13–14.
67. *Zhurnaly I Departamenta Gosudarstvennago Soveta*, no. 5, 20 March 1912 (St. Petersburg: 1912), 5.
68. A.T. Vasilyev, *The Ochrana: The Russian Secret Police* (Philadelphia: J.P. Lippincott, 1930), 191.
69. For example, factional strife in the Moscow OO between Martynov's favourite with whom he had served in Saratov and another officer, caused a lack of communication between the two men which seriously hampered undercover operations. 'Moskovskaia okhranka v 1915', *GM*, 1918, nos 1–3: 284–6.
70. Spiridovich, 'Pri tsarskom rezhime', 180.
71. Zavarzin, *Zhandarmy*, 62.
72. Martynov, *Moia sluzhba*, 45–6.
73. Ibid., 175.
74. 'Dopros S.P. Beletskogo', *PTsR*, 3: 375.
75. It never hurt to have a vivacious wife with a famous and respected maiden name. The intelligent Ekaterina Petrovna Klimovich used her descent from the famous conservative poet Fedor Tiutchev to gain *entré* to the court, where she used her influence to her husband's best advantage. Martynov, *Moia sluzhba*, 273, 277.
76. 'Ukazatel′Imen', *PTsR*, 7: 326, 334, 347, 364, 399, 416, 420, 425; *Spisok Vysshikh*, 5.
77. Allen A. Sinel, 'The Socialisation of the Russian Bureaucratic Elite, 1881–1917: Life at the Tsarskoe-Selo Lyceum and the School of Jurisprudence', *Russian History* 3 part 1 (1976): 11–12.

Chapter 6

1. Terence Emmons, *The Formation of Political Parties and the First National Elections in Russia* (Cambridge: Harvard University Press, 1983), 22.
2 To quote Terence Emmons, 'The circle was originally set up as a sort of clearing-house and lobby for zemstvo affairs *vis-à-vis* the government and, more specifically, to facilitate coordinated zemstvo responses to what was generally seen as a new government offensive against the independence and competence of the zemstvo institutions'. Ibid., 28.
3. Shmuel Galai, *The Liberation Movement in Russia* (Cambridge: Cambridge University Press, 1973), 133.
4. Norman M. Naimark, *Terrorists and Social Democrats: The Russian Revolutionary Movement Under Alexander III* (Cambridge: Harvard University Press, 1983), 171; *Russkii politicheskii sysk za granitsei*, ed. L.P. Men'shchikov, pt. one (Paris: 1914), 28, 38, 70–1, 81, 123; Jeremiah Schneiderman, 'Sergei Zubatov and Revolutionary Marxism. The Struggle for the Working Class in Tsarist Russia'. MS loaned by the author, 97; 'Doklad P. Rachkovskago zavedyiushchego zagranichnoi agentury', *IR* 2 (1924): 248.
5. A.A. Kizevetter, *Na rubezhe dvukh stoletii: Vospominaniia (1881–1914)* (Prague: 1929), 338.
6. Galai, *The Liberation Movement*, 109; Jeremiah Schneiderman, *Sergei Zubatov and Revolutionary Marxism: The Struggle for the Working Class in Tsarist Russia* (Ithaca: Cornell University Press, 1976), 99.
7. A.S. Suvorin, *Dnevnik A.S. Suvorina* (Moscow: 1923), 290.
8. Galai, *The Liberation Movement*, 113–15.
9. Rachkovskii to Fontanka, Paris, 20 July/2 August 1901. FAAr, 189, XVIa, 2.
10. Boris Nikolaejewsky, *Aseff the Spy: Russian Terrorist and Police Stool,* (1934; reprint, Hattiesburg Miss.: Academic International, Russian Series vol. 14, 1969), 48–50.
11. Edward H. Judge, *Plehve: Repression and Reform in Imperial Russia 1902–1904* (Syracuse: Syracuse University Press, 1983), 20.
12. Kizevetter, *Na rubezhe dvukh stoletii,* 338.
13. A. Pogozhev, 'Iz vospominanii o V.K. von-Pleve', *VE* 7 (July 1911): 265.
14. Lopukhin's testimony to the Extraordinary Investigation Commission, 8 Oct. 1917, Nikolaevsky Collection, Hoover Institution, 39.
15. A.A. Polovtsov, 'Dnevnik A.A. Polovtsova', *KA* 3 (3) (1929): 169.
16. *Tekhnika bol'shevistskogo podpol'ia: Sbornik statei i vospominanii,* 2d ed. (Moscow: 1925), 98–9.
17. For example see the large collection of gendarme directorate reports held at the Hoover Institution entitled, 'Obzor: vazhneishikh doznanii, proizvodivshikhsia v Zhandarmskikh Upravleniiakh Imperii, po gosudarstvennym prestupleniiam', 1892–1901. They are rather extensively used by Norman Naimark in *Terrorists and Social Democrats.*
18. Ellis Tenant, 'The Department of Police 1911–1913: From the Recollections of Nikolai Vladimirovich Veselago', MS Hoover Institution, 18–20.
19. M.E. Bakai, 'Iz vospominanii M.E. Bakaia: Provokatory i provokatsiia', *Byloe* 8 (1908): 109.
20. A.P., 'Departament politsii v 1892–1908' (Iz vospominanii chinovnika), *Byloe* n.s., 1917, nos. 5/6 (27/28): 20; Vladimir I. Gurko, *Features and Figures of the Past: Government and Opinion in the Reign of Nicholas II*, trans. Laura Matveev The Hoover Library on War, Revolution and Peace Publication no. 14 (Stanford: Stanford University Press, 1939); 639–40; Wayne D. Santoni, 'P.N. Durnovo as Minister of

Internal Affairs in the Witte Cabinet: A Study in Suppression', (PhD diss., University of Kansas, 1968), 72, 399; Bakai, 'Iz vospominanii', 109.

21. 'Zapiska Generala Novitskogo', *SR* 2 (Paris, 1910): 88.
22. A.V. Bogdanovich, *Tri poslednikh samoderzhtsa: Dnevnik A.V. Bogdanovich[a]* (Moscow: 1925), 233–4.
23. The St Petersburg OO, for example, languished helplessly under inadequate guidance. See L. Rataev, 'Evno Azef: Istoriia ego predatel'stva', *Byloe*, n.s., 1917, no. 2 (24): 194, 200.
24. *The Times,* 2 June 1902.
25. Gurko, *Features and Figures,* 109.
26. Ibid., 112–13.
27. Dominic C.B. Lieven, 'Russian Senior Officialdom under Nicholas II: Careers and Mentalities', *JG* 32, 1984, no. 2: 214–15.
28. Gurko, *Features and Figures,* 111.
29. Judge, *Plehve,* 48–9.
30. Ibid., 49.
31. Nikolaejewsky, *Azef,* reprint, 6–7.
32. Marc Raeff, *Understanding Imperial Russia: State and Society in the Old Regime* (New York: Columbia University Press, 1984), 197–201.
33. Lopukhin testimony to the Extraordinary Investigation Commission, Nikolaevskii Collection, Hoover Institution, 3–4; *Delo A.A. Lopukhina v osobom prisutsvii pravitel'stvuiushchago senata: Stenograficheskii otchet* (Petersburg: 1910), 113–14.
34. Lieven, 'Russian Senior Officialdom', 215.
35. Nikolaejewsky, *Azef,* reprint, 9.
36. Ibid., 8–9.
37. Ibid., 33–4; N.A. Troitskii, *Tsarizm pod sudom progressivnoi obshchestvennosti, 1866–1895 gg*. (Moscow: 1979), 35.
38. Schneiderman, 'Sergei Zubatov', 64.
39. *Na zare rabochego dvizheniia v Moskve: Materialy po istorii Proletarskoi Revoliutsii,* ed. N.N. Ovsiannikov, collection no. 2 (Moscow: 1919), 39, 93–4, 131–2.
40. S.V. Zubatov, 'Zubatovshchina', *Byloe,* n.s., 1917, no. 4 (26): 173.
41. N.A. Bukhbinder *Zubatovshchina i rabochee dvizhenie v Rossii* (Moscow, 1926), 20; 'Tainyi Doklad I.d. Moskovskogo Ober-politsmeistera (po okhrannomy otdeleniiu) 8 Aprelia 1898g.', *Rabochee Delo,* 1899, no. 1: 36.
42. Bukhbinder, *Zubatovshchina,* 21–3.
43. 'Politika tsarizma v rabochem voprose', in *KS,* 88.
44. 'Samoderzhavie nakanune revoliutsii. Vnutripoliticheskii kurs V.K. Pleve', in *KS,* 147–8.
45. Ibid., 147–8.
46. 'Protokol no. 22', 43; A.A. Lopukhin, *Nastoiashchee i budushchee* (Moscow: 1907), 67–9.
47. Anthony Downs, *Inside Bureaucracy* (Boston: Little, Brown & Co, 1967), 130; Herbert A. Simon, *Administrative Behavior: A Study of Decision-making Processes in Administrative Organization* (New York: John Wiley & Sons, 1958), 236–40.
48. A. Gerasimov 'Rukopis' vospominanii', MS Nikolaevsky Collection, Hoover Institution, 22–22A; V.I. Novikov, 'Leninskaia "Iskra" v bor'be s Zubatovshchinoi', *VI* 8 (1974); 26.
49. *Delo A.A. Lopukhina,* 114.
50. Neil Weissman, *Reform in Tsarist Russia. The State Bureaucracy and Local Government, 1900–1914* (New Brunswick: Rutgers University Press, 1981), 43–60.
51. 'Samoderzhavie nakanune revoliutsii', 152; Judge, *Plehve,* 232–3.

52. Department of Police, *Doklad,* 4 June 1902, FAAr, 189, XV1a, 2.
53. General Spiridovich related the rapid increase in the number of OOs directly to growing SR activity. A.I. Spiridovich, *Revoliutsionnoe dvizhenie v Rossii: Partiia Sotsialistov–Revoliutsionerov i eia predshestvenniki* pt. 2 (Petrograd: 1916), 134.
54. MVD, Department of Police Circular, issued by the Special Section, 12 August 1902, FAAr, 158, XIIId(1), 9.
55. MVD, Department of Police Circular, no. 5200, issued by the Special Section, 13 August 1902, FAAr, 158, XIIId(1), 8.
56. A.I. Spiridovich, 'Pri tsarskom rezhime', *ARR 25* (1924): 156–7.
57. MVD, Department of Police Circular no. 5200, issued by the Special Section, 13 August 1902, FAAr, 158, XIIId(1), 8.
58. A.A. Lopukhin, *Nastoiashchee i budushchee,* 34.
59. MVD, Department of Police Circular no. 5800, issued by the Special Section, 16 September 1902, FAAr, 158, XIIId(1), 8.
60. A.P. Martynov, *Moia sluzhba v Otdel′nom korpuse zhandarmov: Vospominaniia* (Stanford: Hoover Institution Press, 1972), 77.
61. Ibid., 273–4; Rataev, 'Evno Azef', 200–3.
62. A. Gerasimov, 'Rukopis′ vospominanii', 22A.
63. P.P. Zavarzin, *Zhandarmy i revoliutsionary*: Vospominaniia (Paris: 1930), 51.
64. Galai, *The Liberation Movement,* 206.
65. A. Mushin, *Dmitri Bogrov i ubiistvo Stolypina* (Paris: 1914) 189–201.
66. Martynov, *Moia sluzhba,* 92.
67. N.P. Eroshkin, *Istoriia gosudarstvennikh uchrezhdenii dorevoliutsionnoi Rossii* (Moscow: 1968), 288.
68. Martynov, *Moia sluzhba,* 239.
69. *Pravo,* no. 25, 20 June 1904.
70. Martynov, *Moia sluzhba,* 71.
71. Zavarzin, *Zhandarmy,* 71.
72. Martynov, *Moia sluzhba,* 79, 92.
73. Ibid., 134.
74. Ibid., 135, 156.
75. *Pravo,* 12 March, 1906.
76. Spiridovich, 'Pri tsarskom rezhime', 156.
77. 'Svod pravil vyrabotannykh v razvitie utverzhdennago Gospodinom Ministrom Vnutrennikh Del, 12 avgusta tekushchago goda [1902]. Polozheniia o Nachal′nikakh Rozysknykh Otdelenii', *Byloe,* Paris, 1908, no. 8: 54–67.
78. A.T. Vasilyev, The Ochrana: The Russian Secret Police, trans. René Fülöp-Miller (Philadelphia: J.P. Lippincott, 1930), 39.
79. V.N. Russiian, 'Rabota okhrannykh v otdelenii v Rossii', MS Moravsky Collection, Hoover Institution, n.p..
80. 'Vremennoe polozhenie ob okhrannykh', issued by the Department of Police, 30 June 1904, FAAr, 158, 12F (1) 9.
81. Martynov, *Moia sluzhba,* 72, 103.
82. Ibid., 119.
83. 'Svod pravil'; 'Vremennoe polozhenie ob okhrannykh', 30 June 1904.
84. Martynov, *Moia sluzhba,* 89–90.
85. MVD, From the Director of the Department of Police, Circular no. 15/378, 10 January 1903, FAAr, 152, XIIIc (2), 2a.
86. Martynov, *Moia sluzhba,* 89–91. As soon as the 1905 Revolution subsided Fontanka's director chaired a conference of regional OOs called to impress upon them the need for obeying the Special Section's instructions and regulations. A perusal of the Special Section's circulars to its OOs and to the Foreign Agentura

between 1910 and 1914 reflects St Petersburg's increasingly strong call to these bureaus that in administrative and in financial matters they follow the letter of the regulations. See 'Pravila i formy: Raskhodovaniia i predstavleniia otchetnosti po agenturnym kreditam, otpuskaemym Departamentoi Politsii na Soderzhanie Okhrannykh otdelenii i rozysknykh punktov, 14 dekabr′ 1912 g.', issued by the MVD, FAAr, 26, IVa, lb; 'O preobrazovanii politsii v Imperii', 1 September 1913, no. 20.083, issued by the MVD, Departament politsii, po 2 deloproizvodstvu, Sterling Memorial Library, Yale University, 71.

87. Tennant, 'The Department of Police', 17; Maurice La Porte, *Histoire de l'Okhrana la police secrète des tsars* (Paris: Payot, 1935), 29; *Martynov, Moia sluzhba*, 324 n. 10; Russiian, 'Rabota okhrannykh otdelenii', n.p..
88. Downs, *Inside Bureaucracy,* 143, 270–1.
89. Herbert A. Simon and James G. March, *Organizations* (New York: John Wiley & Sons, 1958), 43–5.
90. S. Frederick Starr, *Decentralization and Self-Government in Russia, 1830–1870* (Princeton: Princeton University Press, 1972), 26.
91. In 1904 the cost of the Russo-Japanese War forced the financially embarrassed government to temporarily reduce the funds devoted to the expansion and maintenance of its political police. In that year the political police suffered a 10 per cent cut in funding which necessitated the temporary closing of some of the smaller OOs. The law and order bureaucracy held the cut in funding responsible for the police's failure to shield Plehve from his assassins. After Plehve's murder and the soon-to-follow 1905 Revolution efforts to control the budget of the political police met with very little success. 'Protokol no. 22'.
92. Suvorin, *Dnevnik,* 284.

Chapter 7

1. W. Bruce Lincoln, *In the Vanguard of Reform: Russia's Enlightened Bureaucrats 1825–1861* (Dekalb: Northern Illinois University Press, 1982), 183.
2. Ibid., 183, 204.
3. Rachkovskii to Fragnan, 1887 FAAr, 4, IIa, 3; N.A. Troitskii, *Bezumstvo khrabrykh: Russkie revoliutsionery i karatel′naia politika tsarizma, 1866–1882gg.* (Moscow: 1978), 145.
4. *Pamiati Viacheslava Konstantinovich Pleve (Sbornik)* (St Petersburg: 1904), 11.
5. N.K. Mikhailovskii, *Vospominaniia* (Berlin: 1906), 25.
6. D.N. Liubimov, 'Russkaia smuta nachala deviatisotykh godov 1902–1906: Po vospominaniiam, lichnym zapiskam i dokumentam', MS Bakhmeteff Archive Columbia University, 19, 23.
7. Ibid., 51–3.
8. IU. Delevskii, *Protokoly sionskikh mudretsov: Istoriia odnogo podloga* (Berlin: 1923), 124–5.
9. D.N. Shipov, *Vospominaniia i dumy o perezhitom* (Moscow: 1918), 182.
10. A. Pogozhev, 'Iz vospominanii o V.K. von-Pleve', *VE* 7 (July 1911): 263.
11. Plehve's overall plans for political reform are thoroughly discussed in two recent books: Edward H. Judge, *Plehve: Repression and Reform in Imperial Russia 1902–1904* (Syracuse: Syracuse University Press, 1983); Neil B. Weisman, *Reform in Tsarist Russia: The State Bureaucracy and Local Government, 1900–1914* (New Brunswick: Rutgers University Press, 1981). My concern is only with those of Plehve's ideas which focused on renovating the structure and methods of the political police.

12. Jeremiah Schneiderman, *Sergei Zubatov and Revolutionary Marxism: The Struggle for the Working Class in Tsarist Russia* (Ithaca: Cornell University Press, 1976), 66.
13. *Pamiati Viacheslava Konstantinovicha Pleve*, 20.
14. F.S. Zuckerman, 'Self-imagery and the Art of Propaganda: V.K. von Plehve as Propagandist', *The Australian Journal of Politics and History* 28 (June, 1982): passim.
15. Edward H. Judge, 'The Russia of Plehve: Programs and Policies of Minister of Internal Affairs, 1902–1904', (PhD diss., University of Michigan, 1975), 257.
16. Liubimov, 'Russkaia smuta nachala deviatisotykh godov 1902–1906', 43–5; Kathleen Prevo, 'The Revolution of 1905 in Voronezh', (PhD diss., Indiana University, 1975), 44–5; 'Samoderzhavie nakanune revoliutsii: Vnutripoliticheskii kurs V.K. Pleve', in *KS*, 124–5.
17. Quoted in Shmuel Galai, *The Liberation Movement in Russia* (Cambridge: Cambridge University Press, 1973), 151.
18. A.P. Korelin, 'Krakh Ideologii "Politicheskogo sotsializma" v Tsarskoi Rossii', *IZ* 92 (1973): 134.
19. A.P. Korelin, 'Russkii "Politseiskii sotsializm" (Zubatovshchina)', *VI*, 1968, no. 10: 57.
20. S.V. Zubatov, 'Iz nedavniago proshlago: g. Zubatov "Zubatovshchine"', *VE* 3 (March, 1906): 435; Korelin, 'Russkii "Politseiskii sotsializm"', 57; Korelin, 'Krakh Ideologii "Politseiskogo sotsializma"', 113.
21. Lucian W. Pye, 'The Roots of Insurgency and the Commencement of Rebellions', in *Internal Wars: Problems and Perspectives*, ed. Harry Eckstein (London: Free Press, 1964), 168.
22. Marc Raeff, *Understanding Imperial Russia; State and Society in the Old Regime* (New York: Columbia University Press, 1984), 148.
23. B.P. Koz′min, *S.V. Zubatov i ego korrespondenty* (Moscow: 1928), 64–5; Korelin, 'Krakh Ideologii "Politseiskogo sotsializma"', 110.
24. A.I. Spiridovich, 'Pri tsarskom rezhime', *ARR* 15 (1924): 123.
25. Ibid., 123.
26. A.I. Spiridovich, *Revoliutsionnoe dvizhenie v Rossii: Partiia Sotsialistov-Revoliutsionerov i eia predshestvenniki* , pt. 2 (Petrograd: 1916), 134.
27. Norman M. Naimark, *Terrorists and Social Democrats: The Russian Revolutionary Movement under Alexander III* (Cambridge: Harvard University Press, 1983), 33–4.
28. Walter Sablinsky, *The Road to Bloody Sunday: Father Gapon and the St Petersburg Massacre of 1905* (Princeton: Princeton University Press, 1976), 29.
29. 'Politika tsarizma v rabochem voprose', in *KS*, 76; Schneiderman, *Sergei Zubatov*, 33.
30. Quoted in Schneiderman, *Sergei Zubatov*, 33–4.
31. Judge, 'The Russia of Plehve', 256.
32. Naimark, *Terrorists, and Social Democrats*, 34–5.
33. A.V. Bogdanovich, *Tri poslednikh samoderzhtsa: Dnevnik A.V. Bogdanovich[a]* (Moscow: 1924), 290.
34. Spiridovich, 'Pri tsarskom rezhime', 133.
35. Schneiderman, *Sergei Zubatov*, 197–9.
36. Walter Sablinsky, *The Road*, 63.
37. Richard Pipes, *Russia Under the Old Regime* (London: Weidenfeld & Nicolson, 1974; Penguin Books, 1977), 312.
38. Lucien W. Pye, 'The Roots of Insurgency',168.
39. Jeremiah Schneiderman, 'Sergei Zubatov and Revolutionary Marxism: The Struggle for the Working Class in Tsarist Russia', MS loaned by the author, 497.
40. Ibid., 97.

41. 'Tainyi doklad I.d. Moskovskogo Ober-politsmeistera (po okhrannomy otdeleniiu), 8 Aprelia 1898g.', *Rabochee Delo*, 1899, no.1: 26–7.
42. Schneiderman, *Sergei Zubatov*, 96.
43. Quoted in Ibid., 97; Korelin, 'Krakh Ideologii "Politseiskogo sotsializma"', 110, 113.
44. Schneiderman, *Sergei Zubatov*, 77–78; Korelin, 'Krakh Ideologii "Politseiskogo sotsializma"', 117.
45 George Rudé, *Ideology and Popular Protest* (London: Lawrence and Wishart, 1980), 28–9.
46. Ibid., 36.
47. Korelin, 'Krakh Ideologii "Politseiskogo sotsializma"', 117, 134. Lev Tikhomrov suggested a significant change in the type of education which should be imparted to Russia's factory workers which Zubatov fatefully adopted. By the end of 1901 the place of the liberal intelligentsia in the Zubatov movement was by degrees occupied by the clergy. Increasingly, the emphasis was placed on the moral and religious cultivation of the workers. Zubatov's turn to disseminating religion and Zionism would have disastrous outcomes.
48 *Schneiderman, Sergei Zubatov*, 81–2.
49. B. Erenfel'd, *Tiazhely front: Iz istorii bor'by bol'shevikov s tsarskoi tainoi politsiei* (Moscow: 1983), 86.
50. Sablinsky, *The Road*, 60.
51. P.P. Zavarzin, *Zhandarmy i revoliutsionery: Vospominaniia* (Paris: 1930), 56–7.
52. Maurice La Porte, *Histoire de l'Okhrana la police secrète des tsars, 1880–1917* (Paris, Payot, 1935), 54.
53. V. Zhilinskii, 'Organizatsiia i zhizn' okhrannago otdeleniia vo vremena tsarskoi vlasti', *GM*, 1917, nos. 9/10: 259–60.
54. La Porte, *Histoire*, 33.
55. Tim McDaniel, *Autocracy, Capitalism and Revolution in Russia* (Berkeley and Los Angeles: University of California Press, 1988), 68.
56. 'Rabochee dvizhenie i zhandarmskaia politika', *Revoliutsionnaia Rossiia* 1902, no. 4: 12.
57. Schneiderman, *Sergei Zubatov*, 238–40.
58. Sablinsky, *The Road*, 61.
59. Victoria E. Bonnell, *Roots of Rebellion: Workers' Politics and Organizations in St. Petersburg and Moscow, 1900–1914* (Berkeley: University of California Press, 1983), 186.
60. 'Zapiska Generala Novitskogo', *SR*, 1910, no. 2: 96.
61. Schneiderman, 'Sergei Zubatov and Revolutionary Marxism', 411.
62. Schneiderman, *Sergei Zubatov*, 277.
63. Edward H. Judge, *Plehve*, 122.
64. N.A. Bukhbinder, *Zubatovshchina i rabochee dvizhenie v Rossii* (Moscow: 1926) 36; Schneiderman, *Sergei Zubatov*, 312, 339.
65. Quoted in Schneiderman, *Sergei Zubatov*, 339–40.
66. Bukhbinder, *Zubatovshchina i rabochee dvizhenie*, 36.
67. Schneiderman, *Sergei Zubatov*, 339.
68. Ibid., 340.
69. V.I. Novikov, 'Leninskaia "Iskra" v bor'be s Zubatovshchinoi', *VI*, 1974, no. 8: 25–6; Spiridovich, 'Pri tsarskom rezhime', 149.
70. A.A. Lopukhin, *Otryvki iz vospominanii (Po povodu 'Vospominanii gr. S. IU. Witte'*) (Moscow: 1923), 71.
71. 'Zapiska directora depart. pol. Lopukhina o stachkakh v iiule 1903g. v Odesse, Kieve, Nikolaeve', *KL*, 1922, no. 4: 388–9.

72. Schneiderman, *Sergei Zubatov*, 350, 357.
73. Korelin, 'Krakh Ideologii "Politseiskogo sotsializma"', 122–3.
74. Bukhbinder, *Zubatovshchina i rabochee dvizhenie v Rossii*, 21–2.
75. Schneiderman, *Sergei Zubatov*, 180–1, 190; Korelin, 'Russkii "Politseiskii sotsializm"', 58.
76. Different perspectives on Zubatov's betrayal of Plehve are to be found in: Vladimir Gurko, *Features and Figures of the Past: Government and Opinion in the Reign of Nicholas II*, trans. Laura Matveev, The Hoover Library on War, Revolution, and Peace, no. 14 (Stanford: Stanford University Press, 1939), 120; A.N. Kuropatkin, 'Dnevnik A.N. Kuropatkina', *KA*, 1922, no. 1: 82; Lopukhin, *Otryvki iz vospominanii*, 71; Sergei Witte, *Vospominaniia*, 2: 218–219; 'Prikliucheniia I.F. Manuilova: Po arkhivnym materialam', *Byloe* n.s., 1917, nos 5/6 (27/28): 270; Schneiderman, *Sergei Zubatov*, 352–4.
77. Spiridovich, 'Pri tsarskom rezhime', 153.
78. After Zubatov's banishment from Petersburg by Plehve, the former police chief took up residence in Moscow where he attempted to interfere in the affairs of his former bureau, the Moscow OO. This indiscretion gave Plehve the opportunity to banish Zubatov to Vladimir, his home province, with an interdiction against his participating in any form of political activity.

    Of course, disloyalty was an ephemeral condition in the world of the Russian bureaucracy, sustaining an impact only as long as the offended party possessed influence. As for the charge of behaviour detrimental to the security of the state, well, it seems no one, not even the tsar, took this accusation against Zubatov too seriously. A few months after Plehve's death, his successor, Prince Sviatopolk-Mirskii, removed the restrictions placed on Zubatov's lifestyle and movements imposed by his predecessor and rewarded him with a pension commensurate with his outstanding service to the state, in place of the insultingly small one granted to him by Plehve. Mirskii also asked Zubatov if he would like to direct the powerful Foreign Agentura with the broad rights and exceptional privileges that had been possessed by P.I. Rachkovskii, who had been dismissed from the post in 1902. Zubatov again would have the opportunity to work for Lopukhin, who remained director of Fontanka, and for a minister who was well-disposed toward him. He took almost two months to make up his mind, before rejecting Sviatopolk-Mirskii's offer. Korelin, 'Russkii "Politseiskii sotsializm"', 58; 'Pis′ma Mednikova Spiridovichy', *KA*, 1926, no. 4 (17): 210; '25 let nazad (Iz dnevnikov L. Tikhomirova)', *KA*, 1922, no. 1 (38): 24.
79. Schneiderman, *Sergei Zubatov*, 192.
80. For similar points of view see: Brian Chapman, *Police State* (London: Macmillan, 1970), 78; Marc Raeff, *Understanding Imperial Russia*, 148.
81. 'Politika tsarizma', 79.
82. Erenfel′d, *Tiazhelyi front*, 38.
83. La Porte, *Histoire de l′Okhrana*, 57.
84. Erenfel′d, *Tiazhelyi front*, 82–3.
85. Ibid., 84. What such statements actually meant in numerical terms is impossible to determine with any exactitude. David Lane estimates that in 1903 SD Party membership, excluding the *Bund* 'could not be more than a few thousand'. In 1904 he comes up with a suspiciously exact membership of 3255, while by 1905 SDs numbered 16 800. Guesses at SR membership in the pre-1905 period are even more inexact. Michael Melancon tells us that out of sample of a thousand pre-1917 SRs '13.5 percent joined [the Party] in the year before or the year after 1905–1907'. David Lane, *The Roots of Russian Communism: A Social and Historical Study of Russian Social-Democracy 1898–1907* (Assen: Van Gorcum, 1968), 12; Michael

Melancon, *The Socialist Revolutionaries and the Russian Anti-War Movement, 1914–1917* (Columbus: Ohio State University Press, 1990), 104.

86. La Porte, *Histoire de l'Okhrana*, 57.
87. Spiridovich, *Revoliutsionnoe dvizhenie v Rossii*, pt. 2, 96.
88. MVD, from the Director of the Department of Police, Intelligence Summary No. 8/7394, 18 November 1902, FAAr, 152, XIIIc (2), 1.
89. Boris Nikolaejewsky, *Aseff the Spy: Russian Terrorist and Police Stool* (1934; reprint, Hattiesburg Miss.: Academic International, Russian Series vol. 14, 1969), 55–6.
90. Ibid., 57.
91. D.N. Liubimov, 'Russkaia smuta nachala deviatisotykh godov 1902–1906', 116.
92. Nikolaejewsky, *Aseff the Spy*, reprint, 62–3.
93. 'Pis'ma Mednikova Spiridovichy', 197–9; MVD, From the Department of Police, Memorandum no. 4933, 25 May 1903, FAAr, 200 XVIIn, 214.
94. 'Pis'ma Mednikova', 200–1.
95. Boris Savinkov, *Memoirs of a Terrorist*, trans. Joseph Shaplen (New York: Albert & Charles Boni, 1933), 137.
96. Ibid., 36; Edward H. Judge, *Plehve,* 224.
97. Plehve listed the resolution of the crisis in the countryside as his first priority. See: A.V. Bogdanovich, *Tri poslednikh samoderzhtsa: Dnevnik A.V. Bogdanovich[a]* (Moscow: 1924), 290.'
98. James Y. Sims Jr, 'The Crisis in Russian Agriculture at the End of the Nineteenth Century: A Different View', *Sl R* 36 (September 1977): 377–98.
99. Ibid., 41; 'Politika tsarizma', 60.
100. Maureen Perrie, *The Agrarian Policy of the Russian Socialist-Revolutionary Party: From its origins through the revolution of 1905–1907* (Cambridge: Cambridge University Press, 1976), 54–51, 61; Oliver Radkey, *The Agrarian Foes of Bolshevism: Promise and Default of the Russian Socialist Revolutionaries February to October 1917* (New York: Columbia University Press, 1958), 57, 59; Spiridovich, *Revoliutsionnoe dvizhenie v Rossii*: pt. 2, 89.
101. Spiridovich, *Revoluitsionnoe dvizhenie v Rossi*: pt. 2, 118.
102 'Zapiska A.A. Lopukhina o razvitii revoliutsionnago dvizheniia v Rossii (1904g.)', *Byloe*, Paris, 1909, nos. 9/10: 74–5; Spiridovich, *Revoliutsionnoe dvizhenie v Rossii*, pt. 2, 109–110, 149; Manfred Hildermeir, 'The Terrorist Strategies of the Socialist-Revolutionary Party in Russia, 1900–1914', *in Social Protest, Violence and Terror in Nineteenth and Twentieth century Europe* ed. Wolfgang Mommsen and Gerhard Herschfeld (New York: St. Martin's Press, 1982), 82–83.
103. Spiridovich, *Revoliutsionnoe dvizhenie v Rossii*, pt. 2, 102–3.
104. Ibid., 134–5.
105. Ibid., 135.
106. P.P. Zavarzin, *Zhandarmy i revoliutsionery* , 56–7; Jeremiah Schneiderman, Sergei Zubatov, 54.
107. V.M. Gessen, *Iskliuchitel'noe polozhenie* (St. Petersburg: 1908), 245–6.
108. MVD, From the Director of the Department of Police, Circular no. 15/378, 10 January 1903, FAAr, 152, XIIIc(2), 2a.
109. N.I. Falaev, 'Rossiia pod okhranoi', Byloe, St. Petersburg, 1907, no. 10 (22): 2–3; N.F. Efremova, *Ministerstva iustitsii rossiiskoi imperii 1802–1917 gg*. (Moscow: 1983), 126.
110. Gessen, *Iskliuchitel'noe polozhenie*, 70.
111. Falaev, 'Rossiia pod okhranoi', 3.
112. Spiridovich, *Revoliutsionnoe dvizhenie v Rossii,* pt. 2, 136.
113. Richard S. Wortman, *The Development of a Russian Legal Consciousness* (Chicago: University of Chicago Press, 1976), 3.

114. L. Slukhotskii, 'Ocherk deiatel'nosti ministerstva iustitsii po bor'be s politicheskimi prestupleniiami', *IR* 3 (1926): 269, 271–2.
115 Marc Szeftel, *The Russian Constitution of April 23, 1906 : Political Institutions of the Duma Monarchy*, (Brussels: 1976), 243.
116. Slukhotskii, 'Ocherk deiatel'nosti', 280; E.P. Brovtsnova, 'Karatel'noe zakonodatel'stvo tsarizma v bor'be s Revoliutsiei 1905–1907 godov', *Istoriia SSSR*, 1975, no. 5: 111–113.
117. Slukhotskii, 'Ocherk deiatel'nosti', 279.
118. Otto Kirchheimer, *Political Justice: The Use of Legal Procedure for Political Ends* (Princeton: Princeton University Press, 1961), 218.
119. Spiridovich, *Revoliutsionnoe dvizhenie v Rossii*: pt. 2, 107, 166; 'Zapiska A.A. Lopukhina', 77–8.
120. Koz'min, *S.V. Zubatov i ego korrespondenty*, 65.
121. Vladimir N. Kokovtsov, *Out of My Past: The Memoirs of Count Kokovtsov*, trans. Laura Matveev, Hoover War Library Publications, no. 6 (Stanford: Stanford University Press, 1935), 29.
122. This story is told best by Boris Nikolaevskii in his classic, *Aseff the Spy*, reprint, 67–88 and most recently by Judge, *Plehve*, 238–247.
123. Nikolaejewsky, *Aseff the Spy*, reprint, 88; Judge, *Plehve*, 235.
124. E.J. Dillon, *The Eclipse of Russia* (New York: George M. Doran, 1918), 133.
125. 'Samoderzhavie nakanune revoliutsii', 153.

Chapter 8

1. 'Protokol no. 34', 2 March 1909.
2. M.E. Bakai, 'Iz zapisok M.E. Bakaia', *Byloe*, Paris, no. 9/10: 206; *Za kulisami okhrannago otdeleniia. S dnevnikom provokatora pis'mami okhrannikov, tainymi instruktsiiami* (Berlin: 1910), 27.
3. Ibid, 27.
4. 'Protokol no. 8', 22 January 1909.
5. Bakai, 'Iz zapisok', 206.
6. Richard Pipes, *Russia Under the Old Regime* (London: Weidenfeld & Nicolson, 1974; Penguin Books, 1977) 128; Karl Mannheim, *Ideology and Utopia: An Introduction to the Sociology of Knowledge* (London: Routledge & Kegan Paul, 1960), 106.
7. Quoted in Dominic C.B. Lieven, 'Russian Senior Officialdom under Nicholas II: Careers and Mentalities', *JG* 32, no 2 (1984): 221.
8. A.A. Lopukhin's testimony to the Extraordinary Commission, 8 October 1917, Nikolaevsky Collection, Hoover Instituision, 3–4.
9. A.A. Lopukhin, *Otryvki iz vospominanii: (Po povodu 'Vospominanii gr.s. IU.Vitte'* (Moscow: 1923), 13.
10. Lopukhin apperently maintained his 'liberal' image even after the events of Bloody Sunday. Several months later when Witte was searching for a new minister of internal affairs the social activists Witte was negotiating with suggested Lopukhin as a candidate for minister of internal affairs. Witte rejected Lopukhin, claiming that he was dissatisfied with his governorship of Estliand province. Lopukhin, *Otryvki iz vospominanii*, 94.
11. Mary E. Schaeffer, 'The Political Policies of P.A. Stolypin' (PhD diss., Indiana University, 1964), 73.
12. *Poslednii samoderzhets: Ocherki zhizni i tsarstvovaniia Imperatora Rossii Nikolaia 11-go* (Berlin: n.d.), 68.
13. Sergei D. Urussov, *Memoirs of a Russian Governor*, trans. Herman Rosenthal (London: Harper & Brothers, 1908), 171.

14. A.A. Lopukhin, *Nastoiaschchee i budushchee russkoi politsii* (Moscow: 1907), 52–8.
15. Ibid., 12–13.
16. Urussov, *Memoirs*, 171.
17. 'Dnevnik E.A. Sviatopolk-Mirskoi', ed. A.L. Sidorov *IZ* 77 (1965): 236–7.
18. Ibid., 241–2.
19. Shmuel Galai, *The Liberation Movement in Russia* (Cambridge: Cambridge University Press, 1973), 208.
20. Vladimir Gurko, *Features and Figures of the Past: Government and Opinion*, trans. Laura Matveev, The Hoover Library on War, Revolution, and Peace, no. 14 (Stanford: Stanford University Press, 1939), 299.
21. Lopukhin, *Otryvki iz vospominanii*, 43–4; Daniel Turnbull, 'The Defeat of Popular Representation, December 1904: Prince Mirskii, Witte and the Imperial Family', *SlR* 48 (Spring 1989): 60-61.
22. Gurko, *Features and Figures*, 300.
23. For a summary of Rydzevskii's career see, *Spisok vyshikh chinov: Tsentral′nykh i mestnykh ustanovlenii ministerstva vnutrennikh del′* (St Petersburg: 1905), 5.
24. 'Protokol no. 22', 18 January 1909.
25. Vladimir N. Kokovtsov, *Out of My Past: The Memoirs of Count Kokovtsov*, ed. H.H. Fisher, trans. Laura Matveev, Hoover War Library Publications no. 6 (Stanford: Stanford University Press, 1935), 31.
26. Lopukhin, *Otryvki iz vospominanii*, 43; 'Dnevnik E.A. Sviatopolk-Mirskoi', passim.
27. Boris Nikolaejewsky, *Aseff the Spy: Russian Terrorist and Police Stool* (1934; reprint, Hattiesburg Miss.. Academic International, Russian Series vol. 14, 1969), 14.
28. For a sample of some of the documents and a calendar of strikes during this period see, *Rabochee dvizhenie v Rossii v 1901–1904gg.: Sbornik dokumentov* (Leningrad: 1975), 305–44, 508–39.
29. A.I. Spiridovich, *Revoliutsionnoe dvizhenie v Rossii: Partiia Sotsialistov–Revoliutsionerov i eia predshestvenniki*, pt. 2 (Petrograd: 1916), 149.
30. Lopukhin to the Committee of Ministers, 6 December 1904.
31. Galai, *The Liberation Movement*, 215–17.
32. A.I. Spiridovich, *Revoliutsionnoe dvizhenie v Rossii: Rossiiskaia Sotsial-Demokraticheskaia Rabochaia Partiia* pt. 1 (St Petersburg, 1914), 71–2.
33. 'Protokol no. 21', 7 February 1909; 'Protokol no. 34', 2 March 1909.
34. A.I. Spiridovich, 'Pri tsarskom rezhime', *ARR* 25 (1924): 184.
35. 'Dnevnik E.A. Sviatopolk-Mirskoi', 245.
36. Galai, *The Liberation Movement*, 226–7.
37. D.N. Shipov, *Vospominaniia i dumy o perezhitom* (Moscow: 1918), 258–9.
38. E.D. Chermenskii, *Burzhuaziia i tsarism v pervoi russkoi revoliutsii* (Moscow: 1970), 37.
39. 'Dnevnik E.A. Sviatopolk-Mirskoi', 251–2.
40. Ibid., 259.
41. Shipov, *Vospominaniia*, 282.
42. V.R. Leikina-Svirskaia, *Russkaia intelligentsiia v 1900–1917 godakh* (Moscow: 1981), 219.
43. Ibid., 220; Galai, *The Liberation Movement*, 234.
44. Andrew Marshal Verner, 'Nicholas II and the Role of the Autocrat During the First Russian Revolution, 1904–1907' (PhD diss., Columbia University, 1986), 179, 192–6.
45. Ibid., 194.
46. Ibid., 195.

47. 'Nachalo pervoi russkoi revoliutsii i vnutripoliticheskii kurs tsarizma', in *KS*, 164; Lopukhin, *Otryvki iz vospominanii*, 44–5.
48. Chermenskii, *Burzhuaziia i tsarizm*, 41.
49. Verner, 'Nicholas II and the Role of the Autocrat', 197.
50. Lopukhin, *Otryvki iz vospominanii* 54.
51. Shipov, *Vospominaniia*, 286–9; Chermenskii, *Burzhuaziia i tsarizm*, 42–3; Galai, *The Liberation Movement*, 237–8.
52. Shipov, *Vospominaniia*, 290.
53. Sidney Harcave, *First Blood: The Russian Revolution of 1905* (New York: Macmillan, 1964), 61–2.
54. 'Dnevnik E.A. Sviatopolk-Mirskoi', 256.
55. Ibid., 260–6.
56. In addition, Lopukhin acted as an intermediary between Shipov and Mirskii. Harcave, *First Blood*, 53.
57. Lopukhin, *Otryvki iz vospominanii*, 55.
58. Gurko, *Features and Figures*, 304.
59. Spiridovich, 'Pri tsarskom rezhime', 187.
60. A.V. Gerasimov, *Na lezvii s terroristami* (Paris: YMCA Press, 1985), 15, 17.
61. Gapon and Zubatov continued to correspond with each other on the friendliest terms after Zubatov's dismissal. Solomon M. Schwarz, *The Russian Revolution of 1905: The Workers' Movement and the Formation of Bolshevism and Menshevism*, trans. Gertrude Vakar (Chicago: University of Chicago Press, 1967), 272.
62. Ibid., 59.
63. N.A. Bukhbinder, *Zubatovshchina i rabochee dvizhenie v Rossii* (Moscow: 1926), 52, 54; 'K istorii "Sobraniia Russkikh Fabrichno–Zavodskikh Rabochikh g.s. Peterburga": Arkhivyne dokumenty', *KL* 1922, no. 1: 298–9.
64. 'K istorii "Sobraniia"', 299.
65. Ibid., 300–1.
66. Spiridovich, 'Pri tsarskom rezhime', 186–7.
67. Walter Sablinsky, *The Road to Bloody Sunday: Father Gapon and the St Petersburg Massacre of 1905* (Princeton: Princeton University Press, 1976), 117–18.
68. Schwarz, *The Russian Revolution*, 272.
69. Spiridovich, 'Pri Tsarskom rezhime', 187.
70. Gerasimov, *Na lezvii*, 25.
71. Harcave, *First Blood*, 65–6.
72. Victoria E. Bonnell, *Roots of Rebellion: Workers' Politics and Organization in St. Petersburg and Moscow, 1900–1914* (Berkeley: University of California Press, 1983), 100.
73. Sablinsky, *The Road*, 133; Galai, *The Liberation Movement*, 237.
74. Gurko, *Features and Figures*, 344.
75. Lopukhin, *Otryvki iz vospominanii*, 55.
76. 'D.F. Trepov v bor'be s obshchestvennost'', *Russkoe Proshloe*, 1923, no. 4: 43; 'Nachalo pervoi russkoi revoliutsii', 167.
77. Sablinsky, *The Road*, 164; 'Nachalo pervoi russkoi revoliutsii', 168–9.
78. 'Vsepoddaneiskii otchet S. Peterburgskogo gradonachal'nika za 1904g.' quoted in Sablinsky, *The Road*, 201–2.
79. 'Dnevnik E.A. Sviatopolk-Mirskoi', 271.
80. Harcave, *First Blood*, 77–8; '9-e Ianvaria 1905g.', 3–4.
81. D.N. Liubimov, 'Gapon i 9 Ianvaria,' *VI* 1965, no. 8: 125–6.
82. 'Nachalo pervoi russkoi revoliutsii', 169
83. D.N. Liubimov stated that Fontanka knew nothing about the rapidly unfolding events of 7 and 8 January. D.N. Liubimov, 'Gapon i 9 Ianvaria', 124.

84. 'Nachalo pervoi russkoi revoliutsii', 170–1.
85. Ibid., 169.
86. Ibid., 170.
87. 'Dnevnik E.A. Sviatopolk-Mirskoi', 277.
88. Ibid., 273.
89. Ibid., 273.
90. Sablinsky, *The Road*, 170.
91. Spiridovich, 'Pri tsarskom rezhime', 188.
92. 'Nachalo pervoi russkoi revoliutsii', 171–2.
93. G. Gapon, *Istoriia moei zhizni*, ed. A.A. Shilov (Leningrad: 1925), 169; Sablinsky, *The Road*, 207–8.
94. 'Doklad direktora departamenta politsii Lopukhina ministru vnutrennikh del o sobytiiakh 9-go Ianvaria', *KL* 1922, no. 1: 335; Spiridovich, 'Pri tsarskom rezhime', 189; Sablinsky, *The Road*, 225–6.
95. 'Nachalo pervoi russkoi revoliutsii', 172; 'K istorii 'Krovavogo voskresen'ia' v Peterburge: Doklady prokurora Peterburgskoi sudebnoi palaty E.I. Vuicha ministru iustititsii', *KA* 68, no. 1 (1935): 48.
96. 'Nachalo pervoi russkoi revoliutsii', 173; D.N. Liubimov 'Russkaia smuta nachala deviatisotykh godov 1902–1906: Po vospominaniiam lichnym zapiskam i dokumentam', MS Bakhmeteff Archive, Columbia University, 184.
97. Sablinsky, *The Road*, 207.
98. Spiridovich, 'Pri tsarskom rezhime', 190; 'Dnevnik E.A. Sviatopolk-Mirskoi', 273.
99. D.N. Liubimov, 'Gapon i 9 Ianvaria', 129.
100. This incident has been subjected to slightly different interpretations. Nevertheless, the general conclusions of scholars and witnesses are consistent. See for example, Spiridovich, 'Pri tsarskom rezhime', 189; 'Nachalo pervoi russkoi revoliutsii', 172; Sablinsky, *The Road*, 223–4.
101. 'Dnevnik E.A. Sviatopolk-Mirskoi', 274.
102. 'Nachalo pervoi russkoi revoliutsii', 172.
103. Sablinsky, *The Road*, 267.
104. 'Dnevnik E.A. Sviatopolk-Mirskoi', 277.
105. Gerasimov, *Na lezvii*, 23.
106. 'Nachalo pervoi russkoi revoliutsii', 173; Sablinsky, *The Road*, 260–1.
107. D.C.B. Lieven, 'Stereotyping an Elite: The Appointed Members of the State Council, 1894-1914', *SEER* 63 (April, 1985): 264.
108. 'Nachalo pervoi russkoi revoliutsii', 173.
109. Spiridovich, 'Pri tsarskom rezhime', 183.
110. Ibid., 183; 'Nachalo pervoi russkoi revoliutsii', 167; Spiridovich, *Revoliutsionnoe dvizhenie v Rossii*, pt. 2, 254.
111. Sablinsky, *The Road*, 261.
112. 'Ukazatel′Imen', *PTsR* 7: 332–3; 'Dnevnik E.A. Sviatopolk-Mirskoi', 293, n.163.
113. Gurko, *Features and Figures*, 335–6.
114. 'Protokol no. 22', 18 January 1909.
115. Gerasimov, *Na lezvii*, 5–6.
116. Spiridovich, 'Pri tsarkom rezhime', 192–4.
117. Gerasimov, *Na lezvii*, 8.
118. Nikolaejewsky, *Aseff the Spy*, 117.
119. 'Kar′era P.I. Rachkovskago: Dokumenty', *Byloe*, n.s. 1918, no. 2: 78–87.
120. Gerasimov, 'Rukopis′ vospominanii', MS Nikolaevsky Collection, Hoover Institution, 39; Gerasimov, *Na lezvii*, 30.
121. A.A. Lopukhin's testimony on the Azef affair to the Extraordinary Commission, 15.

Chapter 9

1. Aleksandr Gerasimov, 'Rukopis′ vospominanii', MS Nikolaevsky Collection, Hoover Institution, 1.
2. Leonid Men′shchikov, *Okhrana i revoliutsiia. K istorii tainykh politicheskikh organizatsii sushchestvovavshikh vo vremena samoderzhaviia*, 3 vols in 2 (Moscow: 1925–1932), 172.
3. A.V. Gerasimov, *Na lezvii s terroristami* (Paris: YMCA Press, 1985), 55; A.I. Spiridovich, *Revoliutsionnoe dvizhenie v Rossii: Rossiiskaia Sotsial–Demokraticheskaia Rabochaie Partiia*, pt. 1 (St Petersburg: 1914), 82; B.P. Koz′min, *S.V. Zubatov i ego korrespondenty* (Moscow: 1928), 64–5; Richard Pipes, *Russia Under the Old Regime* (London: Weidenfeld & Nicolson, 1974; Penguin Books, 1977), 315–16.
4. Men′shchikov, *Okhrana i revoliutsiia*, 172.
5. 'D.F. Trepov v bor′be s obshchestvennost′iu', *Russkoe Proshloe*, 1925, no. 4: 48; Vladimir I. Gurko, *Features and Figures of the Past: Government and Opinion in the Reign of Nicholas II*, trans. Laura Matveev, The Hoover Library on War, Revolution and Peace, Publication no. 14 (Stanford: Stanford University Press, 1939), 355; Gilbert S. Doctorow, 'The Introduction of Parliamentary Institutions in Russia During the Revolution of 1905–1907', (PhD diss., Columbia University, 1975), 64–5.
6. Solomon M. Schwarz, *The Russian Revolution of 1905: The Workers' Movement and the Formation of Bolshevism and Menshevism*, trans. Gertrude Vakar (Chicago: University of Chicago Press, 1967), 77; 'D.F. Trepov', 43.
7. Gurko, *Features and Figures of the Past*, 336.
8. B. Erenfel′d, *Tiazhelyi front: Iz istorii bor′by bol′shevikov s tsarskoi tainoi politsiei* (Moscow: 1983), 81.
9. Koz′min, *S.V. Zubatov i ego korrespondenty*, 69.
10. Quoted in: Andrew Marshall Verner, 'Nicholas II and the Role of the Autocrat During the first Russian Revolution, 1904–1907', (PhD diss., Columbia University, 1986), 450.
11. Gerasimov, *Na lezvii*, 29; Gurko, *Features and Figures of the Past*, 335–6, 360.
12. Sidney Harcave, *First Blood: The Russian Revolution of 1905* (New York: Macmillan, 1964), 104.
13. Ibid., 121–2; John Bushnell, *Mutiny amid Repression: Russian Soldiers in the Revolution of 1905-1906* (Bloomington: Indiana University Press, 1985), 46.
14. Schwarz, *The Russian Revolution of 1905*, 81.
15. 'Trepovskii proekt rechi: Nikolaia II k rabochim posle 9 ianvaria 1905g.', *KA*, 20 (1927): 241.
16. Victoria E. Bonnell, *Roots of Rebellion: Workers' Politics and Organizations in St. Petersburg and Moscow, 1900–1914* (Berkeley and Los Angeles: University of California Press, 1983), 102.
17. D.N. Liubimov, 'Russkaia smuta nachala deviatisotykh godov 1902–1906: Po vospominaniiam, lichnym zapiskam i dokumentam', MS Bakhmeteff Archive, Columbia University, 211.
18. Bonnell, *Roots of Rebellion*, 189–90.
19. Doctorow, 'The Introduction of Parliamentary Institutions', 64–5.
20. 'D.F. Trepov', 45. Within the MVD chain-of-command, it was the assistant minister, managing police affairs who had the power (though it was not always exercised) of coordinating questions of political police investigations and organisations throughout the empire. He issued circulars and instructions, conducted discussions with governor-generals, governors, *gradonachal′niki*, and *ober-politsmeistery*. He

presided over the Special Board that was responsible for all state criminal matters which came under the jurisdiction of the Department of Police.

It was, however, Trepov's simultaneous appointment as chief of the Separate Corps of Gendarmes that gave him the rare opportunity to coordinate the operations of Tsardom's entire political police machinery. See: *Pravo*, 26 September 1904; Gurko, *Features and Figures of the Past*, 299–300; 'Dopros I.M. Zolotareva', *PTsR*, 5:66, 129.

21. Roberta Thompson Manning, *The Crisis of the Old Order in Russia: Gentry and Government* (Princeton: Princeton University Press, 1982), 141; Harcave, *First Blood*, 108–9.
22. Ibid., 104.
23. P.P. Zavarzin, *Zhandarmy i revoluitsionery: Vospominaniia* (Paris: 1930), 98.
24. Koz′min, *Zubatov i ego korrespondenty*, 60.
25. V.L. Burtsev, *Protokoly sionskikh mudretsov: dokazannyi podlog* (Paris: 1938), 75.
26. Jean Longuet and George Silber, *Terroristy i Okhranka* (Moscow: 1924), 122.
27. Gerasimov, *Na lezvii*, 7.
28. Ibid., 13, 30.
29. Gurko, *Features and Figures of the Past*, 335.
30. Gerasimov, *Na lezvii*, 30.
31. Gerasimov, 'Rukopis^', 40.
32. Gurko, *Features and Figures of the Past*, 360.
33. Maurice La Porte, *Histoire de l'Okhrana la police secrète des tsars, 1880–1917* (Paris: Payot, 1935), 119–20
34. Liubimov, 'Russkaia smuta', 298–9.
35. Koz′min, *Zubatov i ego korrespondenty*, 112.
36. Gurko, *Features and Figures of the Past*, 336; Gerasimov, 'Rukopis^', 3.
37. Gurko, *Features and Figures of the Past*, 355–60.
38. Ann K. Erickson Healy, 'The Russian Autocracy in Crisis: Tsarism and the Opposition from 1905 to 1907', (PhD diss., University of Wisconsin, 1972), 27.
39. L.G. Zakharova, 'Krizis samoderzhaviia nakanune revoliutsii 1905 goda', *VI*, 1972, no. 8: 139.
40. 'Ukazatel′Imen', *PTsR* 7:425.
41. Ibid., 56.
42. Nurit Schleifmann, 'The Internal Agency: Linchpin of the political police in Russia', *Cahiers du monde Russe et Sovietique* 24 (1983):165.
43. Thomas Perry Thornton, 'Terror as a Weapon of Political Agitation', in *Internal Wars: Problems and Approaches*, ed. Harry Eckstein (London: Free Press, 1969), 83.
44. Gerasimov, *Na lezvii*, 16.
45. Gerasimov, 'Rukopis^', 86.

    As for the SDs, the political police expressed no particular concern over their 'expropriations' at first, but as the 1905 Revolution progressed the Special Section became disturbed by the SDs, particularly the Bolsheviks' growing disposition toward 'personal terror' which they labelled 'partisan actions'. MVD, Department of Police, Circular no. 8500 issued by the Special Section, 4 June 1906, FAAr, 158, XVIId (1), 9; John Keep, *The Rise of Social Democracy in Russia* (Oxford: Oxford University Press, 1963), 289; Spiridovich, Revoluitsionnoe dvizhenie v Rossii, pt. 1, 133–4.
46. Allison Blakely, 'The Socialist-Revolutionary Party, 1901–1907: The Populist Response to the Industrialization of Russia', (PhD diss., University of California Berkeley, 1971), 135; Maureen Perrie, 'Political and Economic Terror in the Tactics

of the Russia Socialist-Revolutionary Party', *in Social Protest, Violence and Terror in Nineteenth and Twentieth-century Europe*, eds Wolfgang J. Mommsen and Gerhard Herschfeld (New York: St Martin's Press, 1982), 67.

47. Gerasimov, *Na lezvii*, 10–13; Ronald Hingley, *The Russian Secret Police: Muscovite, Imperial Russian and Soviet Political Security Operations* (New York: Simon and Schuster, 1970), 96–7; Boris Nikolaejewsky; *Aseff the Spy: Russian Terrorist and Police Stool* (New York: Doubleday, Doran & Co., 1934), 107–11, A.I. Spiridovich, Revoliutsionnoe dvizhenie v Rossii: Partiia Sotsialistov-Revoliutsionerov i eia predshestvenniki, pt. 2, (Petrograd: 1916), 190–1.
48. Boris Savinkov, *Memoirs of a Terrorist*, trans. Joseph Shaplen (New York; Albert & Charles Boni, 1931), 130–1.
49. Gerasimov, *Na lezvii*, 14.
50. Ibid., 15.
51. Ibid., 30.
52. Men'shchikov, *Okhrana i revoliutsiia*, 172–3.
53. Shmuel Galai, *The Liberation Movement in Russia* (Cambridge: Cambridge University Press, 1973), 243.
54. V.I. Bovykin *et al.*, *Pervyi shturm tsarizma* (Moscow: 1986), 50.
55. E.D. Chermenskii, *Burzhuaziia i tsarizm v pervoi russkoi revoliutsii* (Moscow: 1970), 60; Verner, 'Nicholas II', 293–5.
56. Michael T. Florinsky, *Russia: A History and An Interpretation* (Macmillan: 1953), 2: 1172–3.
57. Liubimov, 'Russkaia smuta', 233.
58. Although Trepov did not directly author this decree, it is clear that it expressed his views and he most certainly had a hand in its drafting. Manning, *The Crisis of the Old Order*, 90; Chermenskii, *Burzhuaziia i tsarizm*, 60.
59. 'Iz bymagy D.F. Trepova', *KA*, 11/12 (1925): 451.
60. Verner, 'Nicholas II', 312.
61. Quoted in Harcave, *First Blood*, 116–17.
62. Ibid., 140.
63. Manning, *The Crisis of the Old Order*, 98–9.
64. Ibid., 108–11; Chermenskii, *Burzhuaziia i tsarizm*, 91.
65. For a brief but intensive review of the history of the Union of Unions see: V.R. Leikina-Svirskaia, *Russkaia intelligentsiia v 1900–1917 godakh* (Moscow: 1981), 218–45.
66. Zavarzin, *Zhandarmy*, 102-3.
67. Wayne D. Santoni, 'P.N. Durnovo as Minister of Internal Affairs in the Witte Cabinet: A Study in Suppression', (PhD diss., University of Kansas, 1968), 476–7; *Revoliutsiia 1905 goda i samoderzhavie*, ed. V.P. Semennikov (Leningrad: 1928), 38, 130, 133.
68. For example see MVD, Department of Police Circular no. 10950, 24 August 1905, NYPL.
69. For example see P.P. Zavarzin, *Rabota tainoi politsii* (Paris: 1924), 73-97.
70. MVD, From the Director of the Department of Police, Intelligence Summary no. 135/6209, 28 April 1905, FAAr, 154, XIIIc (2), 6B; MVD, Department of Police Circular no. 9776, issued by the Special Section, 25 June 1906, FAAr, XIIId (1); Spiridovich, *Revoliutsionnoe dvizhenie v Rossii*, pt.2, 159; Zavarzin, *Rabota tainoi politsii*, 78.
71. F. Dan, 'Obshchaia politika pravitel'stva i izmeneniia v gosudarstvennoi organizatsii v period 1905–1907 g.g.', in *Obshchestvennoe dvizhenie v Rossii v nachale xx-go veka*, ed. L. Martov *et al.* (St Petersburg: 1912), 4:316.

72. MVD, From the Director of the Department of Police, Weekly Intelligence Summary no. 24/2729, FAAr, XIIIc (2), 2a; T. Asin, 'K statistike arestovannykh i ssyl′nykh', *Russkoe Bogatstvo*, 1906, pt.2: 17.
73. Ibid., 18. In at least one reported case the interrogating officer used torture to extract a confession from four suspected assassins. Unable to hold out they confessed to crimes they did not commit and were duly executed. E.J. Dillon, *The Eclipse of Russia* (New York: George N. Doran, 1918), 183.
74. Andrew Verner claims that there were at least forty such reports between 18 February 1905 and 31 March 1905. Verner, 'Nicholas II', 317, 409 n.113.
75. U.A. Shuster, *Peterburgskie rabochie v 1905–1907* (Leningrad: 1976), 136; Chermenskii, *Burzhuaziia i tsarizm* 91; F. Dan, 'Obshchaia politika pravitel'stva', 4: 313–14, 318.
76. Gerasimov, 'Rukopis^, 44; Gerasimov, *Na lezvii*, 32.
77 Laura Engelstein, *Moscow 1905: Working-class organizations and political conflict* (Stanford: Stanford University Press, 1982), 70.
78. Gerasimov, *Na lezvii*, 33.
79. Gurko, *Features and Figures of the Past*, 391.
80. Gerasimov, 'Rukopis^, 49.
81. *Tekhnika bol′shevistskogo podpol′ia: Sbornik statei i vospominanii*, 2nd ed. (Moscow: 1925), 269–70; Gurko, *Features and Figures of the Past*, 391–2.
82. Gerasimov, *Na lezvii*, 34.
83. Abraham Ascher, *The Revolution of 1905: Russia in Disarray* (Stanford: Stanford University Press, 1988) 198.
84. Gurko, *Features and Figures of the Past*, 392.
85. Quoted in Engelstein, *Moscow 1905*, 69.
86. Ibid., 73.
87. Gurko, *Features and Figures of the Past*, 393–4.
88. K.F. Shatsillo, *1905-i god* (Moscow: 1980), 126–7; Chermenskii, *Burzhuaziia i tsarizm*, 128–9, 151; Engelstein, *Moscow 1905*, 120; Manning, *The Crisis of the Old Order*, 139–40.
89. At a meeting of the Institute of Civil Engineers, for instance, the assembly discussed the question of arming the people and how to go about conducting an uprising, including the liquidation of police and gendarmes. Shuster, *Peterburgskie rabochie*, 150.
90. Gerasimov, *Na lezvii*, 38, 56.
91. La Porte, *Histoire*, 125–6.
92. Verner, 'Nicholas II', 368; Shuster, *Peterburgskie rabochie*, 147.
93. Gerasimov, *Na lezvii*, 38.
94. Shuster, *Peterburgskie rabochie*, 173.
95. Manning, *The Crisis of the Old Order*, 139–40.
96. Hingley, *The Russian Secret Police*, 97.
97. Quoted repeatedly by authors on the 1905 Revolution. For example, F. Dan, 'Obshchaia politika pravitel'stva', 4:3 42; Shatsillo, *1905-i god*, 128, Gurko, *Features and Figures of the Past*, 394–5.
98. Bushnell, *Mutiny amid Repression*, 71; Chermenskii, *Burzhuaziia i tsarizm*, 143–5; Harcave, *First Blood*, 194–5.
99. Quoted in Verner, 'Nicholas II', 388.
100. Ibid., 390–1.
101. Ibid., 432–3.
102. 'D.F. Trepov', 52.
103. Gerasimov, *Na lezvii*, 38; Gurko, *Features and Figures of the Past*, 401.
104. Ibid., 401.
105. Bushnell, *Mutiny amid Repression*, 78–9; Harcave, *First Blood*, 199–206; Healy 'The Russian Autocracy', 5-6, 9; P.G. Kurlov, *Gibel′ imperatorskoi Rossii* (Berlin:

1923), 48–9; Howard Mehlinger and John M. Thompson, *Count Witte and the Tsarist Government in the 1905 Revolution* (Bloomington: Indiana University Press, 1972), 51; Robert Weinberg, 'Workers, Pogroms and the 1905 Revolution in Odessa', *RR* 46 (January, 1987): 60–3.

106. For example see, Liubimov, 'Russkaia smuta', 343.
107. Quoted in Healy, 'The Russian Autocracy', 8.
108. Daniel C. Dussel, 'Russian Judicial Reforms and Counter-reforms 1864–1914', (PhD Diss., University of Missouri, 1981), 118.
109. *Revoliutsionnoe dvizhenie v Rossii Vesnoi i Letom 1905 goda, Aprel'–Sentiabr'* (Leningrad: 1957) 1: 709; *Vserossiiskaia politicheskaia stachka v Oktiabria 1905 goda* (Moscow: 1955), 2: 61.
110. MVD, Department of Police, Circular no. 5025, 20 October, 1905, issued by the Fifth Secretariat, NYPL.
111. MVD, Department of Police, Circular no. 7430, issued by the Fifth Secretariat, 26 October 1905, NYPL.
112. Gerasimov, *Na lezvii*, 38–9.
113. Gerasimov himself claimed that despite the facade he put on for his men, he was so demoralised by the October Manifesto that he enlisted in the extreme right-wing organisation the Union of the Russian People which he abandoned a year later. Gerasimov, 'Rukopis', 223.
114. Marc Szeftel, 'Personal Inviolability in the Legislation of Russian Absolute Monarchy', *ASEER* 17 (February 1958), 22.
115. Marc Szeftel, *The Russian Constitution of April 23, 1906: Political Institutions of the Duma Monarchy* (Brussells: 1976), 239.
116. Richard S. Wortman, *The Development of a Russian Legal Consciousness* (Chicago: University of Chicago Press, 1976) 287; Szeftel, *The Russian Constitution*, 239.
117. 'Rossiia pod nadzoram politsii', *Ozvobozhdenie*, 1903, nos. 20/21: 357.
118. Daniel T. Orlovsky, *The Limits of Reform: The Ministry of Internal Affairs in Imperial Russia, 1802–1881* (Cambridge: Harvard University Press, 1981), 37.

    The situation was made even more complicated by the ruler's power to overrule and to nullify any law or procedure. Indeed, only the desire of a ruler to do so, even if expressed through one of his *sanovniki,* had the same effect. As Richard Wortman explained:

    > Down to the end of the empire it remained impossible to distinguish a law (*zakon*) from an administrative ruling (*razporiazhenie*), which had the force and often the scope of law. The tsar could make the recommendation of a subordinate law by issuing an imperial command (*vysochaishchee povelenie*). Repeated efforts to distinguish between laws and administrative rulings failed, as the monarch's decree (*ukaz*) could give any ruling he chose legislative force, whether or not it had gone through prescribed channels or conflicted with earlier laws. (Wortman, *The Development of a Russian Legal Consciousness*, 16.)

119. *Pravo*, 19 March 1906, 1030–1035. The rule of law actually unnerved the police to the point of paralysis. Loris-Melikov in the early 1880s, for instance, demoralised the forces of order by his insistence that the police should always act legally. 'One can with truth say', A.N. Kulomzin, a senior MVD *chinovnik,* wrote, 'that he [Loris-Melikov] caused its [the police's] collapse: this is a strange statement but its true. Our police never knew anything about laws and when threatened with responsibility for infringing the law it becomes lost and prefers to sit and do nothing'. D.C.B. Lieven, 'Bureaucratic Authoritarianism in Late Imperial Russia: The Personality, Career and Opinions of P.N. Durnovo', *HJ* 26 (1983): 399, note 47.

120. Ben Cion Pinchuk, *The Octobrists in the Third Duma 1907–1912* (Seattle: University of Washington Press: 1974), 51.
121. Trepov explained his resignation in a letter that he wrote to Witte on 25 October. He wrote to Witte that present circumstances demanded his retirement. Overwhelming hostility to Trepov throughout the land made appeasement of the population impossible as long as he remained in office. Therefore, for the good of the state he decided to resign, 'D.F. Trepov', 53.
122. Chermenskii, *Burzhuaziia i tsarizm*, 151.
123. MVD, Department of Police, Circular no. 10950, issued by the Special Section, 24 August 1905, FAAr, 158, XIIId (1), 9; MVD, Department of Police, Circular no. 12900, issued by the Special Section, 8 October 1905, FAAr, XIIId (1), 9.
124. *Vserossiiskia politicheskaia stachka v Oktiabriia 1905 goda*, passim.; FAAr, 154, XIIIe (2), 6b and c.
125. Gerasimov, 'Rukopis', 45.
126. Liubimov, 'Russkaia smuta', 298–9.
127. A.P. Martynov, *Moia sluzhba v Otdel'nom Korpuse zhandarmov: Vospominaniia* (Stanford: Hoover Institution Press, 1972), 59; Santoni, 'P.N. Durnovo', 467.

Chapter 10

1. T. Asin, 'K statistike arestovannykh i ssyl'nykh', *Russkoe Bogatstvo*, 1906, pt. 2: 2.
2. John Bushnell, *Mutiny amid Repression: Russian Soldiers in the Revolution of 1905–1906* (Bloomington, Indiana University Press, 1985), 76.
3. For example see Kathleen Prevo, 'The Revolution of 1905 in Voronezh: The Labor Movement and Political Consciousness in a Russian Provincial City', (PhD diss., Indiana University, 1979), 220. John Bushnell argues that by late November the mutinies gravely weakened the government and that 'the soldiers' revolution posed the single greatest threat to the continued existence of the Tsarist regime'. Ibid., 105.
4. Anne K. Erickson Healy, 'The Russian Autocracy in Crisis: Tsarism and the Opposition from 1905 to 1907', (PhD diss., University of Wisconsin, 1972), 49–50.
5. A.P. Martynov, *Moia sluzhba v Otdel'nom korpuse zhandarmov: Vospominaniia* (Stanford: Hoover Institution Press, 1972), 59; The St Petersburg OO and the Special Section shared Martynov's relief and renewed enthusiasm upon Durnovo's appointment. These two agencies compared Durnovo to Plehve: the greatest compliment they could pay Durnovo. *Soiuz Russkogo Naroda: Po materialam chrezvychainoi sledstvennoi komissii vremennogo pravitel'stva 1917g.*, ed. V.P. Viktorov (Moscow: 1929), 81.
6. For a brief biographical sketch of Durnovo see Dominic Lieven, 'Bureaucratic Authoritarianism in Late Imperial Russia: The Personality, Career and Opinions of P.N. Durnovo', *HJ* 26 (1983): 393; Wayne D. Santoni, 'P.N. Durnovo as Minister of Internal Affairs in the Witte Cabinet: A Study in Suppression', (PhD diss., University of Kansas, 1968), 33. For a typically hostile contemporary opinion of Durnovo by those who opposed his methods, but were of course not in his position, see A.P. Izvolsky's character sketch of the minister of internal affairs in his memoirs. Alexander Isvolsky, *Recollections of a Foreign Minister (Memoirs of Alexander Isvolsky)* trans. Louis Seeger (New York: Doubleday, Page and Co., 1921), 18.
7. Jacob Walkin, *The Rise of Democracy in Pre-Revolutionary Russia: Political and Social Institutions Under the Last Three Tsars* (New York: Frederick A. Praeger, 1962), 56.

8. P.P. Zavarzin, *Zhandarmy i revoliutsionery: Vospominaniia* (Paris: 1930), 107–8.
9. Vladimir I. Gurko, *Features and Figures of the Past: Government and Opinion in the Reign of Nicholas II*, trans. Laura Matveev, The Hoover Library on War, Revolution, and Peace, Publication no. 14 (Stanford: Stanford University Press, 1939) 182; Lieven, 'The Personality', 397; D.C.B. Lieven, 'Stereotyping an Elite: The Appointed Members of the State Council, 1894–1914', *SEER* 63 (April, 1985): 264–5.
10. Ibid., 398–9.
11. Ibid., 394.
12. Andrew Marshall Verner, 'Nicholas II and the Role of the Autocrat During the First Russian Revolution, 1904–1907', (PhD diss., Columbia University, 1986), 463–4; D.N. Liubimov, 'Russkaia smuta nachala deviatisotykh godov 1902–1906. Po vospominaniiam, lichnym zapiskam i dokumentam', MS Bakhmeteff Archive, Columbia University, 353.
13. Walter Sablinsky, *The Road to Bloody Sunday: Father Gapon and the St Petersburg Massacre of 1905* (Princeton: Princeton University Press, 1976), 177
14. Healy, 'The Russian Autocracy', 18.
15. A.V. Gerasimov, *Na lezvii s terroristami* (Paris: YMCA Press, 1985.) These were not isolated incidents. For example, see: U.A. Shuster, *Peterburgskie rabochie v 1905–1907* (Leningrad: 1976), 182.
16. Healy, 'The Russian Autocracy', 50.
17. Gerasimov, *Na lezvii*, 43.
18. Gerasimov, 'Rukopis′ vospominanii', MS Nikolaevsky Collection, Hoover Institution, 58.
19. Sidney Harcave, *First Blood: The Russian Revolution of 1905* (New York: Macmillan, 1964), 226–7; Laura Engelstein, *Moscow 1905: Working-class Organizations and Political Conflict* (Stanford: Stanford University Press, 1982), 224.
20. F. Dan, 'Obshchaia politika pravitel′stva i izmenenia v gosudarstvennoi organizatsii v period 1905–1907 g.g.', in *Obshchestvennoe dvizhenie v Rossii v nachale xx-go veka*, ed. L. Martov *et al.* (St Petersburg: 1912), 4: 362–3.
21. Ibid., 4: 364; Harcave, *First Blood*, 231; E.D. Chermenskii, *Burzhuaziia i tsarizm v pervoi russkoi revoliutsii* (Moscow: 1970), 215.
22. Abraham Ascher, *The Revolution of 1905: Russia in Disarray* (Stanford: Stanford University Press, 1988), 298.
23. Gerasimov, *Na lezvii*, 48–9.
24. Shuster, *Petersburgskie rabochie*, 198.
25. Gerasimov, *Na lezvii*, 49; Gerasimov, 'Rukopis^', 65. Gerasimov's account differs from Gurko's in which Durnovo takes the responsiblity before Witte for arresting the Soviet. It is clear that once the decision was made, Durnovo decided to claim it as his own and sink or swim with it. See: Gurko, *Features and Figures of the Past*, 443–4.
26. Shuster, *Petersburgskie rabochie*, 199.
27. K.F. Shatsillo, *1905-i god* (Moscow: 1980), 158.
28. Gurko, *Features and Figures of the Past*, 50.
29. Witte, too, had begun to alter his outlook. As early as 1 December 1905 he told the tsar that he would 'put down the revolution decisively' by arresting 'the principal leaders of the insurrection'. On 3 December, however, when Durnovo informed him of the arrest of the Petersburg Soviet, he announced to the session of the Council of Ministers he was chairing, 'All is lost. Durnovo has just placed the entire Soviet of Workers' Deputies under arrest'. Forty-eight hours later when it appeared there would be no repercussion from the arrests, Witte told a group of *sanovniki* that the

country was calmer and that 'in his soul everyone rejoiced'. His elation was premature. *Gerasimov, Na lezvii*, 443–4; Healy, 'The Russian Autocracy', 55; Verner, 'Nicholas II', 469–70.

30. The provincial response to Durnovo's directive was practically instantaneous. Russia's governors ordered the swift identification of all leaders and instigators of the anti-government movement, imprisoned them in local jails and treated them according to the directives of the minister of internal affairs. Durnovo ordered the forces of order to make a still greater effort to collect incriminating data against those arrested, too many were only being detained briefly. Soon Durnovo would order that suspects be detained without any evidence at all. Prevo, 'The Revolution of 1905', 242; *Dekabr'skoe vosstanie v Moskve 1905g.: Materialy po istorii Proletarskoi Revoliutsii*, collection no. 3, ed. N.N. Ovsiannikov (Moscow: 1920), 88–9.
31. Gerasimov, *Na lezvii*, 51–2; Ronald Hingley, *The Russian Secret Police: Muscovite, Imperial Russian and Soviet Political Security Operations* (New York: Simon and Shuster, 1970), 97.
32. Boris Nicolaejewsky, *Aseff the Spy: Russian Terrorist and Police Stool* (1934; reprint, Hattiesburg Miss.: Academic International, Russian series, vol. 14, 1969), 170.
33. *Revoliutsiia 1905 goda*, 225.
34. Shatsillo, *1905-i god*, 168.
35. Engelstein, *Moscow 1905*, 202–4, 206, 210–11, 215, 218–19; Harcave, *First Blood*, 237–38; Gurko, *Features and Figures of the Past*, 444–5.
36. *Burzhuaziia nakanune Fevral'skoi Revoliutsii*, ed. B.B. Grave (Moscow, 1927), 33–8.
37. Shuster, *Peterburgskie rabochie*, 271.
38. Engelstein, *Moscow 1905*, 6, 14–15, 43, 54, 69–70, 161; Victoria E. Bonnell, *Roots of Rebellion: Workers' Politics and Organizations in St. Petersburg and Moscow, 1900–1914* (Berkeley and Los Angeles: University of California Press, 1983), 124–5, 133, 136, 164, 168–71, 192.

    The Revolution of 1905 made an impression, though perhaps less deeply on workers in the provinces. A crude form of political consciousness began to develop, an awareness of their own power, an awareness that they belonged to a national movement that when united could influence national politics. Prevo, 'The Revolution of 1905', 323–8.
39. Roberta Thompson Manning, *The Crisis of the Old Order, in Russia: Gentry and Government* (Princeton: Princeton University Press, 1982) 141–2.
40. 'Krest'ianskoe dvizhenie 1905 goda: Dokladnaia zapiska departamenta politsii predsedatel'iu soveta ministrov S.IU.Vitte', *KA* 9 (1925): 68.
41. Santoni, 'P.N. Durnovo', 220–3, 474, 228–9; *Agrarnoe dvizhenie v 1905–1907 g.g. Materialy Departamenta politsii*, comp. S.M. Dubrovskii (Leningrad: 1925), 248.
42. Manning, *The Crisis of the Old Order*, 174; Howard Mehlinger and John M. Thompson, *Count Witte and the Tsarist Government in the 1905 Revolution* (Bloomington: Indiana University Press, 1972), 131, 371 note 71.
43. By January 1912, out of a population of 157 million only 5 million persons lived in locales which were free of martial law, or the provisions of the Exceptional Measures. F. Dan, 'Obshchaia politika pravitel'stva', 4:367–8; 'Borba techenii v praviashchikh verkhakh po voprosam vnutrennei politiki (1907–1909 g.g.)', *KS*, 448–9.
44. E.D. Brovtsnova, 'Karatel'noe zakonodatel'stvo tsarizma v bor'ba s Revoliutsiei 1905–1907 godov', *Istoriia SSSR*, 1975, no. 5: 114–16; 'Tsarizm v bor'be s revoliutsionnoi pechat'iu v 1905g.: Vvodnaia stat'ia I. Kovaleva', *KA* 105 (1941): 154; V.

Levitskii, 'Sotsial'naia kharakteristika kontr-revoliutsionnoe dvizheniia nachala XX veka', in *Obshchestvennoe dvizhenie v Rossii v nachale XX-go veka*, ed. Iu. Martov et al., 4 vols, (St Petersburg 1909–1914), 3: 370–1; F. Dan,' Obshchaia politika pravitel'stva', pt. 2, ibid., 4:66. These pages contain a sample of the edicts and temporary regulations promulgated by the government in 1906.

45. MVD, Department of Police, Circular no. 8107, issued by the Seventh Secretariat, 18 November 1906, NYPL; MVD, Department of Police, Circular no. 8108, issued by the Seventh Secretariat, 18 November 1906, NYPL; MVD, Department of Police, Circular no. 11617, issued by the Seventh Secretariat, 23 June 1907, NYPL; Ernest V. Hollis Jr, 'Police Systems of Imperial and Soviet Russia', MS Bakhmeteff Archive, 146–7.
46. V.P. Leikina-Svirskaia, *Russkaia intelligentsiia v 1900–1917 godakh* (Moscow: 1981), 228; Shuster, *Peterburgskie rabochie*, 219.
47. Ibid., 209.
48. Mehlinger and Thompson, *Count Witte*, 171.
49. The 'arresting authorities' were composed from a variety of 'law and order' groups – some legitimate and others purely vigilantes. For example one sample of arrests made in a single town show the arresting parties to have been: city police – 18; *uezd* police – 12; 'Flying detachments' (usually Black Hundreds led by OO officers in plain clothes) – 22; 'hooligans' – 3; a peasant – 1; gendarmes with or without the help of cossacks – 96. Asin, 'K statistike', 17–18.
50. Ibid., 16.
51. Ibid., 36–7.
52. *Revoliutsionnoe 1905 goda*, 205.
53. Manning, *The Crisis of the Old Order*, 173.
54. A.A. Lopukhin, *Otryvki iz vospominanii (Po povodu 'Vospominanii gr. S.IU. Vitte')* (Moscow: 1923), 93.
55. *Agrarnoe dvizhenie*, 135–6.
56. Dan, 'Obshchaia politika pravitel'stva', 4: 363–4. Compare the view expressed therein with that expressed by A.I. Spiridovich, who had left the political police before the 1905 Revolution. Spiridovich remembered that Fontanka's political investigations were motivated by one aim, 'to know about the preparation of revolutionary undertakings, to acquire advance notice and to suppress them in the bud'. Spiridovich Testimony, 8 October 1917, Extraordinary Commission.
57. It finally occurred to the new Director of the Department of Police, M.I. Trusevich, in 1907 that the best political policemen were not necessarily the ones wounded by terrorists, but those whose jurisdictions were notable for the absence of revolutionary activity. None the less, OO and Gendarme Directorate officers were rarely rewarded for quiet achievement. Fontanka appeared oblivious to the administrative and investigatory talent and the capacity to manage *sotrudniki* that it took to free a region of subversive elements. Martynov, *Moia sluzhba*, 274–5.
58. Gerasimov, *Na lezvii*, 143, 145–6. The SRs actually developed an elaborate plot to blow up the St Petersburg OO. The date chosen was 6 January 1907. The plot was uncovered in late December 1906. Spiridovich, *Revoliutsionnoe dvizhenie v Rossii*, pt. 2, 282.
59. Russia, Gosudarstvennaia Duma 3d 1909, *Zapros ob Azefe v Gosudarstvennoi dume (zasedaniia 50 i 51 oe): Po stenograficheskomu otchetu* (St Petersburg: 1909), 57.
60. MVD, Department of Police, Circular no. 17273, issued by the Special Section, FAAr, 158, XIIId (1), 9.
61. G.T. Robinson, *Rural Russia Under the Old Regime* (Berkeley and Los Angeles, University of California Press, 1967), 195.

62. Spiridovich, *Revoliutsionnoe dvizhenie v Rossii*, pt. 2, 158–9; 272; *Boevyia predpriiatiia sotsialistov-revoliutsionerov v osveshchenii okhranki* (Moscow: 1918), 102–7; P.P. Zavarzin, *Rabota tainoi politsii* (Paris: 1924), 73, 126, 130; A.I. Spiridovich, 'Pri tsarskom rezhime', *ARR* 15 (1924): 201, 203–4; M.E. Bakai, 'Iz zapisok M.E. Bakaia', *Byloe*, Paris, 1909, nos 9/10: 199.
63. Spiridovich, *Revoliutsionnoe dvizhenie v Rossii*, pt. 2, 207; M.A. Osorgin, 'Dekabr′skoe vozstanie 1905 g. v Moskve v opisanii zhandarma', *GM*, 1917, nos 7/8: 357–8.
64. Ibid., 359.
65. Ibid., 360.
66. Gerasimov, *Na lezvii*, 143, 145–6.
67. Michel Crozier, *The Bureaucratic Phenomenon* (Chicago: The University of Chicago Press, 1964), 237–8; Daniel T. Orlovsky, *The Limits of Reform: The Ministry of Internal Affairs in Imperial Russia 1802-1881* (Cambridge: Harvard University Press, 1981), 4, 12.
68. Liubimov, 'Russkaia smuta', 478–9.
69. A.I. Spiridovich, 'Poslednie gody Tsarskosel′skogo Dvora', MS Box 15, Spiridovich Collection, Sterling Memorial Library, Yale University, 2:845.
70. Orlovsky, *Limits of Reform*, 202.
71. *Soiuz Russkogo Naroda*, 77; Asin, 'K statistike', 17. There is little doubt, although conclusive evidence is unavailable, that Rachkovskii encouraged his police officials to organise counter-revolutionary pogroms even before 17 October 1917.
72. MVD, Department of Police, Circular no. 4863, issued by the Special Section, 15 April 1905, NYPL.
73. 'Deposition of A.A. Lopukhin', 6 November 1917, untitled and in Russian, Extraordinary Commission, Nikolaevsky Collection, Hoover Institution; *Pravo*, no. 19, 14 May 1906; 'Dopros A.A. Reinbota', *PTsR*, 7: 372; *Sovetskaia Istoricheskaia Entsiklopediia* (Moscow: 1964), 5:123.
74. *Revoliutsiia 1905 goda*, 60-61.
75. The testimony of G.F. Veber, which we tend to believe, is not supported by Gerasimov who writes of the creation of these 'battle detachments', in the passive voice, not mentioning Rachkovskii at all and trying at the same time to distance himself from them. None the less, at first glance one would assume that if Rachkovskii had been guilty of establishing these detachments Gerasimov, who despised his chief, would have been only too happy to blame him. Instead he places the responsibility for the SRN's thugs squarely on Launitz's shoulders. However, given Rachkovskii's history within the political police it is reasonable to assume that Gerasimov was attempting to protect his beloved political police – not Rachkovskii – by shifting much of the blame from Rachkovskii where we believe it belongs to the culpable, but not organiser of these groups – Launitz. Gerasimov, *Na lezvii*, 150, 152; *Soiuz Russkogo Naroda*, 84–5.
76. Ibid., 85–7.
77. Ibid., 75–7, 108; Gerasimov, *Na lezvii*, 150, 152–3; Gerasimov, 'Rukopis^', 225; 'Dopros I.F. Manasevich-Manuilova', *PTsR*, 2: 43–4.
78. A.V. Gerasimov, 'Azef i Lopukhin', MS Nikolaevsky Collection, Hoover Institution, 3.
79. *Vechernee Vremia*, 21 May 1906.
80. Russia, Gosudarstvennaia Duma 1st 1906, *Stenograficheskii otchety* (St. Petersburg: 1906), 2: 1128, 1132, 1134, 1140.
81. Russia, Inspektorskii Otdela Sobstvennoi E.I.V. Kantseliarii, *Spisok Grazhdanskim Chinam: Chertvertago Klassa* (St Petersburg: 1906), 915.
82. *Za kulisami okhrannago otdeleniia: S dnevnikom provokatora pis′mami okhrannikov, tainymi instruktsiiami* (Berlin: 1910), 58; Jean Longuet and George Silber,

Terroristy i Okhranka (Moscow: 1924), 167–8. Rachkovskii also used his meetings with Nicholas II to report to him on foreign affairs and on the Franco-Russian Alliance in particular (on which he was considered to be expert). A.S. Suvorin, *Dnevnik A.S. Suvorina* (Moscow: 1923), 357.

83. Dan, 'Obshchaia politika pravitel′stva', pt. 2, 4: 44.
84. Maurice La Porte, *Histoire de l'Okhrana la police secrète des tsars* (Paris: Payot, 1935), 213.
85. 'Mobilizatsiia reaktsii v 1906g.', *KA* 32 (1929): 181.
86. Dan, 'Obshchaia politika pravitel′stva', pt. 2, 4: 104–5.
87. In his first year in office Stolypin promulgated several restrictive decrees, for example: doubling the penalty for distribution of anti-governmental propaganda within the armed forces and prohibiting persons under surveillance from being recruited into the army. He also urged that the regulation allowing police to use arms only in self-defence be abolished and that they be allowed to follow army crowd control regulations. And finally in 1907 he exempted the gendarmes and – although unmentioned – by implication the political police as a whole from the regulations stipulating the prosecution of officials who had committed criminal acts while on duty. Mary Schaeffer Conroy, *Peter Arkad′evich Stolypin: Practical Politics in Late Imperial Russia* (Boulder: Westview Press, 1976), 93, 104.
88. 'Bor′ba techenii v praviashchikh verkhakh', 448.
89. Geoffrey A. Hosking, *The Russian Constitutional Experiment: Government and Duma, 1907–1914* (Cambridge: Cambridge University Press, 1973), 54–5, 243–4; Manning, *The Crisis of the Old Order*, 113, 328; Rogger *Jewish and Rightwing Politics in Imperial Russia* (Berkeley and Los Angeles: University of California Press, 1986), 231; Marc Szeftel, *The Russian Constitution of the Duma Monarchy* (Brussells: 1976) 236–7.
90. Gilbert S. Doctorow, 'The Introduction of Parliamentary Institutions in Russia During the Revolution of 1905–1907', (PhD diss. Columbian University, 1975), 574; Terence Emmons, *The Formation of Political Parties and the First National Elections in Russia* (Cambridge: Harvard University Press, 1983), 184–90, 192–3, 223, 283, 363; Gerasimov, *Na lezvii*, 76, 97; Spiridovich, 'Poslednie gody Tsarskosel′skogo Dvora', Spiridovich Collection, Sterling Memorial Library, Yale University, 2: 559.
91. Quoted in Francis W. Wcislo, 'Soslovia or Class? Bureaucratic Reformers and Provincial Gentry in Conflict, 1906–1908', *RR* 47 (January, 1988): 23.
92. *Agrarnoe dvizhenie v 1905–1907 gg.*, 252, 306, 482, 531–2; 'Mobilizatsiia reaktsii v 1906 g.', 158–82; Predsedatel′ Soveta Ministrov, Ministra Vnutrennikn Del, 'General-Gubernatoram, Gubernatoram i Gradonachal'nikam', 1906, Nikolaevsky Collection.
93. Hosking, *The Russian Constitutional Experiment*, 23–4.
94. Conroy, *Peter Arkad′evich Stolypin*, 105; Manning, *The Crisis of the Old Order*.

Chapter 11

1. Sidney Verba and Gabriel A. Almond, 'National Revolutions and Political Commitment', in *Internal Wars: Problems and Approaches*, ed. Harry Eckstein (London: The Free Press, 1969), 207.
2. Howard D. Mehlinger and John M. Thompson, *Count Witte and the Tsarist Government in the 1905 Revolution* (Bloomington: Indiana University Press, 1972), 283.'
3. Allison Blakely, 'The Socialist Revolutionary Party, 1901–1907: The Populist Response to the Industrialization of Russia', (PhD Diss., University of California, Berkeley, 1971), 94; E. SH. Khaziakhmetov, 'Organizatsiia pobedov politicheskikh

ssyl'nyka iz Sibiri v 1906–1917 godakh', in *Ssylka i obshchestvenno-politicheskaia zhizn' v sibiri* (xviii-nachalo xx v) ed. L.M. Goriushkin (Novosibirsk: 1978), 60.

4. V.N. Ginev, *Bor'ba za krest'ianstvo i krizis russkogo neonarodnichestva 1902–1914 gg.* (Leningrad: 1983), 138–9; A.I. Spiridovich, *Revoliutsionnoe dvizhenie v Rossii: Partiia Sotsialistov-Revoliutsionerov i eia predshestvenniki*, pt. 2 (Petrograd: 1916), 159, 168–9, 173, 180–2.
5. V.P. Leikina-Svirskaia, *Intelligentsiia v 1900–1917 godakh* (Moscow: 1981), 246.
6. The police were not alone in this fear. The upper echelons of the administration generally feared the constitutional movement more than it did the revolutionary one because they believed that 'the constitutional movement ... would have brought about the next and inevitable change in the form of government'. Vladimir I Gurko, *Features and Figures of the Past: Government and Opinion in the Reign of Nicholas II*, trans. Laura Matveev, The Hoover Library on War, Revolution, and Peace, Publication no. 14 (Stanford: Stanford University Press, 1939), 120.
7. The only scholarly estimate suggests that it was widespread containing 470 branches with a membership of 200 000. Scott J. Seregny, 'A Different Type of Peasant Movement: The Peasant Unions in the Russian Revolution of 1905', *Sl R* 47 (Spring, 1988): 65; Teodor Shanin, *Russia, 1905–07: Revolution as a Moment of Truth* (New Haven: Yale University Press, 1986), 114–17.
8. Ibid., 99–101.
9. U.A. Shuster, *Peterburgskie rabochie v 1905–1907* (Leningrad: 1976), 273–4.
10. Ralph Carter Elwood, *Russian Social Democracy in the Underground: A Study of the RSDRP in the Ukraine, 1907–1914*, Publications on Social History, issued by the International Institute of Social History, no. 8 (Assen: Van Gorcum & Comp., 1974), 154–7.
11. B.I. Grekov, K.F. Shatsillo, V.V. Shelokaev, 'Evoliutsiia politichesikoi struktury Rossii v kontse xix–xx veka (1895–1913)', *Istoriia SSSR*, 1988, no. 5: 44–5.
12. Anthony Downs, *Inside Bureaucracy* (Boston: Little, Brown: 1967), 270.
13. Ibid., 129, 139.
14. A.P. Martynov, *Moia sluzhba v Otdel'nom korpuse zhandarmov: Vospominaniia* (Stanford: Hoover Institution Press, 1972), 156.
15. MVD, Department of Police, Circular no. 12900, issued by the Special Section, 8 October 1905, NYPL; *Dekabr'skoe vosstanie v Moskve 1905g.: Materialy po istorii Proletarskoi Revoliutsii*, collection no. 3, ed. N.N. Ovsiannikov (Moscow: 1920).
16. B.P. Koz'min *S.V. Zubatov i ego korrespondenty* (Moscow: 1928), 123.
17. MVD, Department of Police, Circular no. 1, issued by the Registration Bureau, December 1906, NYPL, MVD, Department of Police, Circular no. 150326, issued by the Registration Bureau, 23 November 1907, NYPL; MVD, Department of Police, Circular no. 125693, issued by the Special Section, 11 May 1907, NYPL. Fontanka never overcame this problem. See 'Dopros S.P. Beletskogo', *PTsR*, 3: 292–3; Ernest V. Hollis, Jr., 'Police Systems of Imperial and Soviet Russia', MS Bakhmeteff Archive, 361–2.
18. M.E. Bakai, 'Iz vospominani M.E. Bakaia: Provokatory i provokatsiia', *Byloe*, Paris, 1909, no. 8: 112; Maria Petrovna von Bock, *Reminiscences of My Father, Peter A. Stolypin*, trans. and ed. Margaret Potoski (Metuchen, N.J.: The Scarecrow Press, 1970), 162; E.D. Chermenskii, *Burzhuaziia i tsarizm v pervoi russkoi revoliutsii* (Moscow: 1970), 287; Anne Erickson Healy, 'The Russian Autocracy in Crisis: Tsarism and the Opposition from 1905 to 1907', (PhD Diss., University of Wisconson, 1972), 242.
19. Mary Schaeffer Conroy, *Peter Arkad'evich Stolypin: Practical Politics in Late Tsarist Russia* (Boulder: Westview Press, 1976), 91.
20. Donald Rawson, 'The Death Penalty in Late Tsarist Russia: An Investigation of Judicial Procedures', *RH* 11 (September, 1984): 47–8.

21. Conroy, *Peter Arkad'evich Stolypin*, 91; Hollis, 'Police Systems', 385–6; Marc Szeftel, *The Russian Constitution of April 23, 1906: Political Institutions of the Duma Monarchy* (Brussells: 1976), 103.
22. Martynov, *Moia Sluzhba*, 128; Boris Nikolaejewsky *Aseff the Spy: Russian Terrorist and Police Stool* (New York: Doubleday, Doran and Co., 1934), 168.
    M.I. Trusevich, Stolypin's choice as director of Fontanka, and A.A. Makarov his selection as assistant minister, managing the police, as was the tradition, had both been procurators. From 1903 until his appointment as director of Fontanka, Trusevich served as an assistant procurator in the St. Petersburg Chamber of Justice. Since 1901 Makarov had worked as a procurator in the Saratov Chamber of Justice. His tenure coincided with Stolypin's governorship of Saratov province. 'Ukazatel' Imen', *PTsR*, 7: 372, 426.
23. A.V. Gerasimov, *Na lezvii s terroristami* (Paris: YMCA Press, 1985), 65, 75.
24. Ibid., 75.
25. 'Dopros E.K. Klimovicha', *PTsR*, 1: 108.
26. A.V. Gerasimov, 'Rukopis' vospominanii', MS Nikolaevsky Collection, Hoover Institution, 222.
27. Gerasimov, *Na lezvii*, 58–9.
28. Boris Nikolaejewsky, *Aseff the Spy: Russian Terrorist and Police Stool* (1934, reprint, Hattiesburg Miss.: Academic International, The Russian Series vol. 14, 1969), 171.
29. 'Dopros E.K. Klimovicha', *PTsR*, 1: 109.
30. Gerasimov contends that he never thought very much of Zubatov's strategy. As chief of the Kharkov OO he obstructed its implementation and eventually argued with Zubatov over its use. Finally, relations between Zubatov and Gerasimov became strained. Gerasimov, 'Rukopis^', 55–6; Gerasimov, *Na lezvii*, 17–18.
31. Gerasimov, *Na lezvii*, 59–60.
32. Nikolaejewsky, *Aseff the Spy*, reprint, 172–5.
33. Stolypin included student groups, book and journal publishers, societies and professional unions as ripe for infiltration. He wanted at least one, but preferably more than one agent in every subversive group. M.E. Bakai, *'Iz vospominanii: Provokatory'*, 106–7; V.K. Agafonov, *Zagranichnaia okhranka* (Petrograd: 1918), 190.
34. Nikolaejewskii, *Aseff the Spy*, reprint, 185.
35. Even the designation 'Special Section' seemed unknown to the Duma. Russia, *Gosudarstvennaia Duma 1st 1906, Stenograficheskii otchety* (St Petersburg: 1906), 2: 1133–34, 1140.
36. M.E. Bakai, 'Iz zapisok M.E. Bakaia', *Byloe*, Paris, 1909, nos. 9/10: 205; Bock, *Reminiscences*, 195–196; Maurice La Porte, *Histoire de l'Okhrana la police secrète des tsars, 1880–1917* (Paris: Payot, 1935), 213.
37. In a very cautious sample, Nurit Schleifman, the expert on undercover agents within the SR Party, has shown the political police emphasis on SRs through tentative but nevertheless indicative calculations. Her sample of 215 agents is distributed through the revolutionary movement thus: SRs-90; SDs-82; and Anarchists-43. Schleifman has calculated the ratio of *sotrudniki* to the number of party members as follows:

PARTY	RATIO OF AGENTS TO MEMBERS
Anarchists	1:142
SRs	1:750
SDs	1:1266

Nurit Schleifmann, 'The Internal Agency: Linchpin of the political police in Russia', *Cahiers du monde Russe et Sovietique 24* (1983): 176.

38. Bakai, 'Iz vospominanii M.E. Bakaia Provakotory', 101–3; V.N. Russiian, 'Rabota okhrannykh otdelenii v Rossii', MS Moravsky Collection, The Hoover Institution, n.p..
39. Nikolaejewsky, *Aseff the Spy*, reprint, 162–3; 'Pokazaniia V.L. Burtseva', *PTsR*, 1: 303.
40. Ibid., 184–8; Bock, *Reminiscences*, 178. Gerasimov had employed the same tactics a short while before to save Durnovo's life.
41. Nikolaejewsky, *Aseff the Spy*, reprint, 136.
42. Gerasimov, *Na lezvii*, 99–101.
43. Essentially the story of SR terrorism ends in 1907. General Spiridovich painted a black picture of SR decimation at police hands. Spiridovich, *Revoliutsionnoe dvizhenie v Rossii*, pt. 2, 383, 492.
44. For example see: Conroy, 'Peter Arkad'evich Stolypin', 91; Healy 'The Russian Autocracy', 241; Hollis, 'Police Systems', 385–6.
45. This crisis was intensified by the haphazard nature of some of the attacks. Single acts of terror perpetrated by completely unknown people without organisational affiliation did not help the police or the nerves of the officials who were the main targets of assassination either. *Revoliutsiia 1905 goda i samoderzhavie* ed. V.P. Semennikov (Leningrad: 1928), 193.
46. Nikolaejewsky, *Aseff the Spy*, reprint, 214–3.
47. Ibid., 225–45. Nurit Schleifman's recent book, *Undercover Agents in the Russian Revolutionary Movement: The SR Party 1902–1914* (Basingstoke: Macmillan, 1988), arrived too late to be used as a source for this chapter. It adds much to the story of political police infiltration of the SR Party and I refer readers interested in the operations of the Internal Agency within the SR Party to her work.
48. Boris Savinkov claimed that Azef had participated in the assassinations of Governor of Ufa Province Bogdanovich; Minister of Internal Affairs Plehve; Grand Duke Sergei Aleksandrovich; attempts on the lives of General D.F. Trepov, Governor-General of St Petersburg, General Kleigels, Governor-General of Kiev, Baron Unterberg, Governor-General of Moscow, General Min, P.I. Rachkovskii, Admiral Cherchnin and Prime Minister Stolypin; the murder of Father Gapon; and three attempts to kill the tsar. In addition, Azef knew in advance of plots against the lives of several *sanovniki*, including General von der Launitz and Grand Duke Nikolai Nikolaevich about which he did not tell the police. Boris Savinkov, *Memoirs of a Terrorist*, trans. Joseph Shaplen (New York: Albert and Charles Boni, 1931), 316–17.
49. Maureen Perrie, 'Political and Economic Terror in the Tactics of the Russian Socialist-Revolutionary Party before 1914', in *Social Protest, Violence and Terror in Nineteenth and Twentieth-century Europe*, ed. Wolfgang Mommsen and Gerhard Herschfeld (New York: St Martin's Press, 1982), 68; Manfred Hildermeier, 'The Terrorist Strategies of the Socialist-Revolutionary Party in Russia, 1900–14', in Ibid., 83–4; Russia, Gosudarstvennaia Duma 3d 1909, *Zapros ob Azefe v Gosudarstvennoi dume (zasedaniia 50 i 51oe): Po stenograficheskomu otchetu* (St Petersburg: 1909), 56.
50. Gerasimov, *Na lezvii*, 89–90; P.G. Kurlov, *Gibel' imperatorskoi Rossii* (Berlin: 1923), 79, Martynov, *Moia sluzhba*, 39, 60.
51. Gerasimov, *Na lezvii*, 91; 'Dopros A.A. Makarova', *PTsR*, 2: 99.
52. Ibid., 88; 'Pokazaniia V.L. Burtseva', *PTsR*, 1: 311.
53. Ibid., 88–89; Bock, *Reminiscences*, 155–6; Gurko, *Features and Figures of the Past*, 497–8; Nikolaejewsky, *Azeff the Spy*, reprint, 188–9.
54. Gerasimov, *Na lezvii*, 88–93; 'Pokazaniia V.L. Burtseva', *PTsR*, 1: 310–311. Ryss escaped custody and continued to involve himself in 'expropriations'. Finally he

was arrested in 1907 and transferred to the authority of the field court martials. He was hanged in 1908.

55. Gerasimov, *Na lezvii*, 93.
56. 'Dopros M.I. Trusevicha', *PTsR*, 3: 214.
57. 'Dopros S.E. Vissarionova', *PTsR*, 3: 447–9. Despite this regulation the general belief among Fontanka's senior officials remained that provocation was a necessary evil. When challenged by the chairman of the Provisional Government's Extraordinary Commission about the legality of the use of provocateurs, Kurlov responded coolly, 'legal – no, but necessary – yes'. 'Dopros P.G. Kurlova'. *PTsR*, 3: 204. Trusevich himself argued before the same body that the 'motivation' of the undercover agent was a critical factor in determining whether he behaved as a state criminal or not, 'there can be no crime without a motive', he proclaimed to his perplexed interrogator. 'Dopros M.I. Trusevicha', *PTsR*, 3: 212.
58. Martynov, *Moia sluzhba*, 128; A.P. 'Departament politsii v 1892–1908 (Iz vospominanii chinovnika)', *Byloe*, n.s. 1917, nos. 5/6 (27/28): 22.
59. 'Ukazatel′Imen', *PTsR*, 7: 307, 339, 354.
60. At the same time Gendarme Directorates were supplied with increased funds. 'Mobilizatsiia reaktsii v 1906g.', 166.
61. Koz′min, *S.V. Zubatov i ego korrespondenty*, 130.
62. N.P. Eroshkin, *Istoriia gosudarstvennikh uchrezhdenii dorevoliutsionnoi Rossii*, 2d. ed. (Moscow: 1968), 288; Kurlov, *Gibel'*, 79–80.
63. 'Dopros gen. E.K. Klimovicha', *PTsR*, 1: 81–2.
64. Kurlov, *Gibel′*, 107; Szeftel, *The Russian Constitution*, 434.
65. Ibid., 66; A. IA. Avrek, *Stolypin i Tret′ia duma* (Moscow: 1968), 396-7.
66. 'Ukazatel′Imen', *PTsR*, 7: 364.
67. 'Dopros A.V. Gerasimova', *PTsR*, 3: 11; Mary E. Schaeffer, 'The Political Policies of P.A. Stolypin', (PhD Diss., Indiana University, 1964), 68.
68. Gurko, *Features and Figures of the Past*, 464.
69. Bock, *Reminiscences*, 242; Vassilyev, *The Ochrana*, 396–7.
70. Ibid., 397.
71. Manning, *The Crisis of the Old Order*, 233; Geoffrey A. Hosking and Roberta Thompson Manning, 'What Was the United Nobility?' in *The Politics of Rural Russia 1905–1914*, ed. L. Haimson (Bloomington, Indiana University Press, 1979), 142–83; Roberta Thompson Manning, 'Zemstvo and Revolution: The Onset of the Gentry Reaction, 1905–1907', in Ibid., 30–66; Werner E. Mosse, 'Russian Bureaucracy at the End of the *Ancien* Regime: The Imperial State Council, 1897–1915', *Sl R* 39 (December, 1980): 632.
72. Gerasimov, *Na lezvii*, 151, 156.
73. For Kurlov's opinion of Trusevich see *Kurlov, Gibel′*, 78.
74. 'Dopros A.V. Gerasimova', *PTsR*, 3: 12.
75. Gerasimov, *Na lezvii*, 99.
76. Fredric S. Zuckerman, 'Vladimir Burtsev and the Tsarist Political Police in Conflict, 1907–14', *JCH* 12 (1977): 193–219.
77. M.E. Bakai, 'Iz zapisok', 191.
78. Ibid., 200.
79. Ibid., 191.
80. John Bohon, 'Reactionary Politics in Russia 1905–1909', (PhD Diss., University of North Carolina, 1967), 183. Lopukhin's letter appeared in *Humanité* as well. Jean Longuet and George Silber, *Terroristy i Okhranka* (Moscow: 1924), 175–6.
81. *Pravo*, 15 February 1909, 432.
82. Agafonov, *Zagranichnaia okhranka*, 228.
83. *Zapros ob Azefe*, passim.; Bakaia, 'Iz zapisok', 202–3, 205.

84. Ibid., 148, 151.
85. I.V. Alekseev, *Provokator Anna Serebriakova* (Moscow: 1932), 16.
86. MVD, Department of Police Circular no. 130947, issued by the Special Section, 7 June, 1909, FAAr, 185, XVb, 1d.
87. V. Zhilinskii, 'Organizatsiia i zhizn′ okhrannago otdeleniia vo vremena tsarskoi vlasti', *GM*, 1917, nos. 9/10: 246–306.
88 Stolypin wanted Azef forgotten as rapidly as possible. He hoped to make the *Azefshchina* no more than an unpleasant memory by preventing the occurance of similar episodes. He reaffirmed Trusevich's warning to *sotrudniki* that any agent arrested for committing a criminal act would have to face the legal consequences, that is when no safe method could be found to release him or her from detention. He offered his undercover agents, with whom – unlike Trusevich – he clearly sympathised, little solace when he noted that imprisonment protected them from discovery and probably enhanced their reputations in revolutionary circles. In addition convicted *sotrudniki* would be paid for the time they spent in prison. Agafanov, *Zagranichnaia okhranka*, 198.
89. P. Pavlov, *Agenty, zhandarmy, palachi: Po dokumentam* (Petrograd: 1922), 45–6.
90. Gerasimov, 'Rukopis^', 257.
91. Boris Nikolaevski has left us with the standard, but somewhat garbled account of Gerasimov's plight. Nikolaejewsky, *Aseff the Spy*, reprint, 283–5. For Gerasimov's own explanation see Gerasimov, 'Rukopis^', 257–8, 267 (2), 268 (3); Gerasimov *Na lezvii*, 173–6; 'Ukazatel′Imen', *PTsR*, 7: 323.
92. MVD, Department of Police, Circular No. 98952, issued by the Special Section, 30 March 1912, FAAr, 158, XIIId (1), 11; Karpov's replacement Colonel M.F. von Koten, like Gerasimov also kept his distance from Fontanka. 'Dopros S.E. Vissarionova', *PTsR*, 3: 457.
93. Neil B. Weissman, *Reform in Tsarist Russia: The State Bureaucracy and Local Government, 1900–1914* (New Brunswick: Rutgers University Press, 1981), 205–6.
94. Ibid., 213; Russia, MVD, Departament Politsii. Po 2 Deloproizvodstvu, 'O preobrazovanii politsii v Imperii', I Sentiabria 1913 g., No. 20.083, Sterling Memorial Library, Yale University, 95–6, 101.
95. Kurlov, *Gibel′*, 100, 117. To be sure Kurlov's deepseated opposition to major police reform was not the only reason for the Makarov Commission's slow progress. General von Taube, the reactionary Commander of the Separate Corps of Gendarmes, for example, was another law and order official who did his best to hinder the process of reform. Weissman, *Reform in Tsarist Russia*, 213.
96. Ben Cion Pinchuk, *The Octobrists in the Third Duma 1907–1912* (Seattle: University of Washington Press, 1974), 97–9.
97. A. Mushin, *Dmitrii Bogrov i ubiistvo Stolypina* (Paris: 1914), 206, 266.
98. A.I. Spiridovich, 'Poslednie gody Tsarskosel′skogo Dvora', MS Spiridovich Collection Sterling Memorial Library, Yale University, 2: 597.
99. Schaeffer, 'The Political Policies of P.A. Stolypin', 70.
100. Weissman, *Reform in Tsarist Russia*, 209, 225.
101. Kurlov, *Gibel′*, 107.
102. Spiridovich, 'Poslednie gody Tsarskosel′skogo Dvora', 2: 597–9, 668–9.
103. Weissman, *Reform in Tsarist Russia*, 215–16.
104. 'O preobrazovanii politsii v Imperii', 2, 10–11.
105. In November 1911, Baron A. Meyerendorff after having collected material for a bill on personal inviolability asked representatives of the law and order bureaucracy whether they were principally concerned with the protection of the individual from police *proizvol* or with the opposite, broadening the powers of Fontanka? He did not receive any response whatsoever. Tsardom failed to promulgate any law on personal inviolability to the end of the regime. Szeftel, *The Russian Constitution*, 251.

106. Weissman, *Reform in Tsarist Russia*, 217.
107. 'O preobrazovanii politsii v Imperii', 110.
108. 'Pokazaniia S.P. Beletskogo', *PTsR*, 4: 340–3.
109. *Ubiistvo Stolypina: Sviditel'stva i dokumenty*, comp. A. Serebrennikov (New York: Telex, 1986), 285; Avrekh, *Stolypin i Tret'ia duma*, 405.
110. *Ubiistvo Stolypina*, 283; 'Ukazatel' Imen', *PTsR*, 7: 316, 363, 364, 420.
111. By the late summer of 1911 Dediulin and Kurlov treated Stolypin with unmitigated disdain. Avrekh, *Stolypin i Tret'ia duma*, 399.
112. Ibid., 406.
113. The Kiev OO was forced to arrange its own escape from a proper investigation which most certainly would have condemned the OO to ridicule and humiliation. Lt. Colonel Ivanov, Kuliabko's deputy, extracted a confession from Bogrov, Stolypin's assassin which preserved the honour of the OO more-or-less intact. Then Bogrov was executed before Senator Trusevich (the former director of Fontanka and no friend of Kurlov's) in charge of the investigation into the incident could interview him. Avrekh claims that the order for the rapid execution of Bogrov could only have come from the highest circles. He suggests that Dediulin may have played a role in taking this decision. Ibid., 404; B.Iu. Maiskii, 'Stolypinshchina i konets Stolypina', *VI*, 1966, no. 2: 129–30, 132, 133–5.
114. Gerasimov, *Na lezvii*. Though Kurlov's clients controlled Fontanka to the end of the regime giving him considerable unofficial influence, he never achieved the official position he desired. Though the tsar said he bore Kurlov no ill-will over the Stolypin assassination and even felt quite close to him through his performance at Stavka during the war, he refused to appoint him Commander of Separate Corps of Gendarmes, a post Kurlov desperately wanted. Rasputin told Kurlov that even he could not help him. Kurlov was not popular 'up on high'. 'Pokazaniia A.D. Protopopova', *PTsR*, 4: 30.
115. Weissman, *Reform in Tsarist Russia*, 217.

Chapter 12

1. V.N. Kokovtsov, *Out of My Past: The Memoirs of Count Kokovtsov*, ed. H.H. Fisher, trans. Laura Matveev, The Hoover Library on War, Revolution, and Peace, Publication no. 6 (Stanford: Stanford University Press, 1935), 277.
2. Maurice La Porte, *Histoire de l'Okhrana la police secrète des tsars, 1880–1917* (Paris: Payot, 1935), 154; 'Uchet departamentom politsii opyta 1905 goda', *KA* 18 (1926): 216–17, 225.
3. For example: Dispatch no. 414, Paris, 5 October/22 September 1907, FAAr, XVIa, 2; Dispatch no. 99, Paris, 10/23 March 1908, FAAr 194, XVIb(6) (a), 1; Dispatch no. 554, Paris, 3/16 November 1909, FAAr, 191, XVIb (3); Dispatch no. 1387, Bordeaux, 6/19 September 1914, FAAr, 198, XVIIg, 1; Dispatch no. 1344, Paris, 22 October/4 November 1912, FAAr, 195, XIIIc, 2; A.I. Spiridovich, *Revoliutsionnoe dvizhenie v Rossii: Rossiiskaia Sotsial-Demokraticheskaia Rabochaia Partiia*, pt. 1 (St Petersburg: 1914), 175, 194; A.I. Spiridovich, *Revoliutsionnoe dvizhenie v Rossii: Partiia Sotsialistov-Revoliutsionerov i eia predshestvenniki*, pt. 2 (Petrograd: 1916), 383, 385; A.P. Martynov, *Moia sluzhba v Otdel'nom korpuse zhandarmov: Vospominaniia* (Stanford: Hoover Institution Press, 1972), 229.
4. Martynov, *Moia sluzhba*, 261; Kathleen Prevo, 'The Revolution of 1905 in Voronezh: The Labor Movement and Political Consciousness in a Russian Provincial City', (PhD diss., Indiana University, 1979), 272–6; 303–5.
5. Maureen Perrie, *The Agrarian Policy of the Russian Socialist-Revolutionary Party: From its origins through the revolution of 1905–1907* (Cambridge: Cambridge University Press, 1976), 195.

6. La Porte, *Histoire*, 205; R.C. Elwood, *Russian Social Democracy in the Underground: A Study of the R.S.D.R.P. in the Ukraine 1907–1914*, Publications on Social History issued by the International Institute of Social History, no. 8 (Assen: Van Gorcam and Comp., 1974), 51–2; B. Erenfel′d, *Tiazhelyi front: Iz istorii bor′by bol′shevikov s tsarskoi tainoi politsiei* (Moscow: 1983), 110–14.
7. Quoted in Elwood, *Russian Social Democracy*, 52.
8. Quoted in Ibid., 52.
9. Ibid., 52, note 6.
10. Quoted in Ibid., 25.
11. Ibid., 35-37; Spiridovich, *Revoliutsionnoe dvizhenie v Rossii*, pt. 1, 175.
12. Laura Engelstein, *Moscow 1905: Working-class Organizations and Political Conflict* (Stanford: Stanford University Press, 1982), 122; Elwood, *Russian Social Democracy*, 64.
13. Vladimir Gurko, *Features and Figures of the Past: Government and Opinion in the Reign of Nicholas II*, trans. Laura Matveev, The Hoover Library on War, Revolution, and Peace, Publication no. 14 (Stanford: Stanford University Press, 1939), 534.
14. A.V. Gerasimov, *Na lezvii s terroristami* (Paris: YMCA Press, 1985), 145; Martynov, *Moia sluzhba*, 264–5.
15. Geoffrey Swain, *Russian Social Democracy and the Legal Labour Movement, 1906–1914* (London: Macmillan, 1983), 57, 61–2.
16. Martynov, *Moia sluzhba*, 261.
17. Gilbert S. Doctorow, 'The Introduction of Parliamentary Institutions in Russia During the Revolution of 1905–1907', (PhD diss., Columbia University, 1975), 574; Terence Emmons, *The Formation of Political Parties and the First National Elections in Russia* (Cambridge: Harvard University Press, 1983), 184–90, 192–3, 223, 283, 363; Gerasimov, *Na lezvii*, 76.
18. Alfred Levin, *The Second Duma: A Study of the Social Democratic Party and the Russian Constitutional Experiment* (New Haven: Yale University Press, 1940), 307–39.
19. K.I. Globachev, 'Pravda O Russkoi Revoliutsii: Vospominaniia byvshago Nachal′nika Petrogradskago Okhrannago Otdeleniia', MS Bakhmeteff Archive, 3–4,14.
20. G.R. Swain, 'Freedom of Association and the Trade Unions, 1906–14', in *Civil Rights in Imperial Russia*, eds Olga Crisp and Linda Edmondson (Oxford: Clarenden Press, 1989), 190; Caspar Ferenczi, 'Freedom of the Press under the Old Regime, 1905–1914', in Ibid., 213; Howard Mehlinger and John M. Thompson, *Count Witte and the Tsarist Government in the 1905 Revolution* (Bloomington: Indiana University Press, 1972), 172.
21. P. Pavlov, *Agenty, zhandarmy, palachi: Po dokumentam* (Petrograd: 1922), 27.
22. *Partiia Bol′shevikov v gody pervoi mirovoi voiny i sverzhenie monarkhii v Rossii* ed. S.I. Murashov (Moscow: 1963), 129.
23. Quoted in Victoria E. Bonnell, *Roots of Rebellion: Workers' Politics and Organizations in St. Petersburg and Moscow, 1900–1914* (Berkeley and Los Angeles: University of California Press, 1983), 372–3.
24. 'Uchet Departamentom politsii opyta 1905 goda', *KA* 5 [18] (1926): 221.
25. Ibid., 226–7; MVD, Department of Police, Circular no. 100368, issued by the Sixth Secretariat, 13 January 1916, FAAr, 158, XIIId (2), 12.
26. MVD, Department of Police, Circular no. 99787, issued by the Special Section, 15 May 1913, FAAr, 158, XIIId (1), 11; Ferenczi, 'Freedom of the Press', 192, 197–8, 201, 213–14.
27. Indeed, a close look at the political police record reveals that at least some Special Section analysts were not so sanguine over the depressed state of Russian labour

politics. Dispatch No. 6, Paris, 3/16 January 1909, FAAr, 196, XVIIa, 2R; Dispatch No. 375, Paris, 3/16 July 1909, FAAr, 193, XVIb (6), 1a.

28. Victoria E.Bonnell, *Roots of Rebellion: Workers' Politics and Organizations in St. Petersburg and Moscow, 1990–1914* (Berkeley and Los Angeles: University of California Press, 1983), 446–7; Prevo, 'The Revolution of 1905 in Voronezh', 321–2.
29. Swain, *Russian Social Democracy*, 185.
30. Elwood, *Russian Social Democracy*, 193. Undoubtedly the large number of registrants reflects the constant requirements of unions harassed by the police to reconstitute themselves – in some cases repeatedly – and then re-register.
31. Bonnell, *Roots of Rebellion*, 277.
32. Swain, *Russian Social Democracy*, 91.
33. Bonnell, *Roots of Rebellion*, 323.
34. G.A. Arutiunov, *Rabochee dvizhenie v Rossii period novogo revoliutsionnogo pod"ema 1910–1914* (Moscow: 1925), 97; Swain, *Russian Social Democracy*, 123–5.
35. Swain, 'Freedom of Association', 190.
36. Bonnell, *Roots of Rebellion*, 374–5.
37. 'Uchet departamentom politsii', 224.
38. 'Dopros S.P. Beletskogo', *PTsR*, 3: 256–7. Beletskii's tenure as vice-director apparently began in July 1909. He claimed that he was appointed to the post only on 1 March 1910. If this was the case, it is clear that his first six months in office was a trial period devoted primarily to training and to observing Beletskii's ability to cope with the job.
39. A.N. Naumov, *Iz utselevshikh vospominanii 1868–1917*, 2 vols (New York: 1954), 2: 189–90; P.G. Kurlov, *Gibel' imperatorskoi Rossii* (Berlin: 1923), 141; Martynov, *Moia sluzhba*, 218; 'Pokazaniia kn. V.M. Volkonskogo', *PTsR*, 6: 137; 'Dopros K.D. Kafafova', *PTsR*, 2: 137; 'Dopros Makarova', *PTsR*, 2: 119–20.
40. N.P. Kharlamov, who knew Beletskii well from his service within the MVD, believed him to be 'altogether worthless in the state service sense'. A. IA. Avrekh, *Tsarizm nakanune sverzheniia* (Moscow: 1989), 111.
41. 'Pokazaniia S.P. Beletskogo', *PTsR*, 4: 430–1.
42. 'Dopros S.P. Beletskogo', *PTsR*, 3: 342–3.
43. Swain, 'Freedom of Association', 189.
44. Beletskii never considered Fontanka more than a stepping stone in furthering his career. Martynov, *Moia sluzhba*, 218.
45. Arutiunov, *Rabochee dvizhenie v Rossii*, 153.
46. 'Dopros S.P. Beletskogo', *PTsR*, 3: 286; Bonnell, *Roots of Rebellion*, 425; Leonard Schapiro, *The Communist Party of the Soviet Union* (New York: Random House, Vintage Books, 1960), 136; Swain, *Russian Social Democracy*, 185.
47. For example, the Office for Trade Union Affairs cognisant of the power of public opinion and acting in accordance with the law refused to accede to the demands of the MVD for increased harassment and closure of trade unions. Swain, 'Freedom of Association', 189.
48. For example, Schapiro, *History of the Communist Party*, 136.
49. Laura Engelstein, *Moscow* 1905, 225; Bonnell, *Roots of Rebellion*, 317.
50. 'Dopros S.P. Beletskogo', *PTsR*, 3:344; Dispatch No. 422, Paris, 6/19 November 1908, FAAr, 196, XVld, 1; Dispatch no. 375, Paris, 3/16 July 1909, FAAr, 193, XVlb(6), 1a; Foreign Agentura Report on the Second Party Conference of the RSDWP, FAAr, 190.
51. Lucien W. Pye, 'The Roots of Insurgency and the Commencement of Rebellions', in *Internal Wars: Problems and Approaches*, ed. Harry Eckstein (London: Free Press, 1964), 172.

52. Otto Kirchheimer, *Political Justice: The Use of Legal Procedure for Political Ends* (Princeton: Princeton University Press, 1961), 148.
53. Allison Blakely, 'The Socialist Revolutionary Party 1901–1907: The Populist Response to the Industrialization of Russia', (PhD diss., The University of California, Berkeley, 1971), 238.
54. Marc Raeff, *Understanding Imperial Russia: State and Society in the Old Regime* (New York: Columbia University Press, 1984), 170–1.
55. 'Doklad Rachkovskago', 20 July/2 August 1901, FAAr, 189, XV1a, 2; Spiridovich, *Revoliutsionnoe dvizhenie v Rossii*, pt. 2, 19–23, 50–2.
56. Spiridovich, *Revoliutsionnoe dvizhenie v Rossii*, pt. 1, 11–12.

    An excellent example of the impact of these habits of mind on Beletskii appeared in his testimony to the Provisional government's investigation commission that he feared the SRs more than the SDs because his infiltration of the SD movement was superior to that of the SRs and that the SDs communicated with each other through the mail more frequently than did the SRs. As a result, Fontanka's perlustration of the mail gave them access to more intelligence on the SDs than on the SRs. Not knowing or understanding the course of party activity apparently worried the political police more than any other consideration. 'Dopros S.P. Beletskogo', *PTsR*, 3: 286.
57. MVD, From the Vice Director of the Department of Police, Circular no. 104760, 7 July 1911, FAAr, 185, XVB, 2C; 'Iz istorii Ural'skikh zavodov', *KA* 74 (1936): 72.
58. Leopold Haimson, 'The Problem of Social Stability in Urban Russia 1905–1917', *Sl R* 23 (December, 1964): 625.
59. Director of the Department of Police, Weekly Intelligence Summary no. 132/5728, 7 April 1905, FAAr, 154, XIIIc (2), 6A.
60. Israel Getzler, *Martov: A Political Biography of a Russian Social Democrat* (Cambridge: Cambridge University Press, 1967), 134; V. Zhilinskii, 'Organizatsiia i zhizn′okhrannago otdeleniia vo vremena tsarskoi vlasti', *GM*, 1917, nos 9/10: 278; Dispatch no. 228, Paris, 18 February/2March 1912, FAAr, 193, XVIb(6), 1b.
61. Spiridovich, *Revoliutsionnoe dvizhenie v Rossii*, pt. 1, 162.
62. Dispatch no. 967, Paris, 25 July/7 August 1912, FAAr, 193, XV1b (6), 1b.
63. For example, SD meetings and hideouts were usually raided without gunfire from either side. Elwood, *Russian Social Democracy*, 56–7.
64. MVD, From the Office of the Vice Director of the Department of Police, 30 September 1912, Circular no. 106452, FAAr, 34, IVe, 2.
65. Arutiunov, *Rabochee dvizhenie v Rossii*, 159, 161.
66. Ibid., 153, 179.
67. MVD, From the Office of the Vice-Director of the Department of Police, 30 September 1912, Circular no. 106452, FAAr, 34, IVe, 2.
68. V.K. Agafonov, *Zagranichnaia okhranka* (Petrograd: 1918), 208; The Special Section ultimately concluded that the April–May 1912 strikes were the responsibility of a variety of political groups. 'Utchet departamentom politsii', 208, 224.
69. MVD, Department of Police, Circular no. 103537, issued by the Special Section, 25 August 1913, FAAr, 194, XV1b (6) (c), 2.
70. S.V. Zubatov, 'Zubatovshchina', *Byloe*, n.s., 1917, no. 26: 177–8.
71. Agafonov, *Zagranichnaia okhranka*, 208.
72. Bonnell, *Roots of Rebellion*, 423.
73. MVD, Department of Police, *Spravka*, 5/18 July 1912, FAAr, 196, XV1d, 1.
74. Martynov, *Moia sluzhba*, 225–6.
75. Ferenczi, 'Freedom of the Press', 212.
76. For example: R.C. Elwood, *Roman Malinovsky: A Life Without a Cause*, Russian Biography Series, no. 2 (Newton Mass.: Oriental Research Partners, 1977); B.K.

Erenfel'd, '"Delo Malinovskogo",' *VI*, 1965, no. 7: 106–15; Bertram D. Wolfe, *Three Who Made a Revolution*, 4th rev. ed. (New York: Dell Publishing Co., 1964).

77. La Porte, *Histoire*, 169; Erenfel′d, '"Delo Malinovskogo"', 108.
78. 'Dopros S.E. Vissarionov', *PTsR*, 5: 219.
79. La Porte, *Histoire*, 173–4.
80. 'Dopros Vissarionov', *PTsR*, 5: 218–19.
81. Quoted in: Bonnell, *Roots of Rebellion*, 419.
82. Martynov, *Moia sluzhba*, 233; Vladimir Burtsev, 'Lenine and Malinovsky', *Struggling Russia* 1 (May, 1919): 139.
83. Bonnell, *Roots of Rebellion*, 419.
84. Arutiunov, *Rabochee dvizhenie v Rossii*, 392.
85. Dispatch no. 589, Kiev, April 1913, FAAr, 193, XVlb (6), lb.
86. MVD, Department of Police Circular no. 103537, issued by the Special Section, 25 August 1913, FAAr, 194, XVlb (6), (c), 2.
87. Spiridovich, 'Poslednie gody Tsarskosel′skogo Dvora', 2 vols, MS Spiridovich Collection, Sterling Memorial Library, 2:821. Spiridovich had just completed his superb manual on the RSDWP written to instruct young gendarme officers on the history of the social democratic movement. Lack of interest in the SDs made publication difficult, though it finally was published by the press of the staff of the Separate Corps of Gendarmes. The manual is a first-rate piece of work and can be read with considerable profit today.
88. William C. Fuller, Jr, *Civil-Military Conflict in Imperial Russia 1881–1914* (Princeton: Princeton University Press, 1985), 257.
89. Aleksandr I. Spiridovich, *Les dernières anneès de la cour de Tsarskoe-Sélo*, trans. M. Jeanson, 2 vols. (Paris: 1928), 1:279.
90. Fuller, *Civil-Military Conflict*, 257.
91. 'Tsarizm v bor′be s rabochim dvizheniem v gody pod″ema: S predisloviem M. Lur'e', *KA* 74 (1936): 50.
92. Ibid., 56–7; Arutiunov, *Rabochee dvizhenie v Rossii*, 312–13; Bonnell, *Roots of Rebellion*, 379.
93. 'Uchet departamentom politsii', 226–7.
94. Arutiunov, *Rabochee dvizhenie v Rossii*, 272–3,338–9, 341.
95. A.I. Spiridovich, *Istoriia bol′shevizma v Rossii: Ot vozniknoveniia do zakhvata vlasti 1883–1903–1917* (Paris: 1922), 65.
96. Spiridovich, *Revoliutsionnoe dvizhenie v Rossii*, pt. 1, 41–2.
97. MVD, Department of Police, Circular no. 172874, issued by the Ninth Secretariat, 14 June 1914, FAAr, 158, X111d (1) 11.
98. A. Badayev, *The Bolsheviks in the Tsarist Duma* (New York: International Publishers, 1932), 183; *Partiia bol′shevikov v gody mirovoi imperialisticheskoi voiny*, 391.
99. Arutiunov, *Rabochee dvizhenie v Rossii*, 368.
100. Lt Colonel Martynov remembered that by 1914–1915 the political police was clearly on the defensive in its relationship to Russian society. Martynov, *Moia sluzhba*, 153–4.
101. MVD, Department of Police, Circular no. 175641, 2 September 1914, FAAr, 158, X111d (1), 11.
102. 'Dopros V.F. Dzhunkovskogo', *PTsR*, 5:69; 'Dopros N.A. Maklakova', *PTsR*, 3: 114.
103. Spiridovich, 'Poslednie gody Tsarskosel'skogo Dvora', 2: 735; 'Pokazaniia kn. V.M. Volkonskogo', *PTsR*, 6:131; Martin Kilcoyne, 'The Political Influence of Rasputin', (PhD diss., University of Washington, 1961), 252.
104. Beletskii was very popular in high court circles. Avrekh, *Tsarizm*, 111.

105. 'Dopros V.F. Dzhunkovskogo', *PTsR*, 5: 72.
106. 'Dopros kniazia N.B. Shcherbatova', *PTsR*, 7: 225.
107. Kurlov, *Gibel'*, 142–3; Martynov, *Moia sluzhba*, 243.
108. 'Dopros V.F. Dzhunkovskogo', *PTsR*, 5: 75.
109. 'Dopros kn. M.M. Andronnikova', *PTsR*, 1: 392–3.
110. Fuller, *Civil-Military Conflict*, 189, 211–18.
111. Apparently, Dzhunkovskii conveyed this order to each OO and Gendarme Directorate chief directly. 'Dopros N.A. Maklakova', *PTsR*, 3: 116–18.
112. 'Dopros Dzhunkovskogo', *PTsR*, 5:70; Fuller, *Civil-Military Conflict*, 211–18.
113. 'Dopros S.E. Vissarionova', *PTsR*, 5: 220; Erenfel'd, '"Delo Malinovskogo"', 110–12.
114. Elwood, *Roman Malinovsky*, 41–4.
115. 'Dopros S.E. Vissarionova', *PTsR*, 5: 220.
116. The case of Shornikova related to the reader in Chapter 4 herein is a good example of Dzhunkovskii's attitude toward *sotrudniki*. He decided that despite Shornikova's loyal service to the political police she must undergo a public trial. Although the trial was a mere formality and Shornikova was found innocent by the Senate the fact that an assistant minister of internal affairs, managing the police would have put a former *sotrudnik* who had loyally served police interests through such an ordeal emphasises how little he thought of these people. Alfred Levin, 'The Shornikova Affair', *SEER*, 21 (November, 1943), 11–15.
117. Spiridovich, 'Poslednie gody Tsarskosel'kogo Dvora', 2: 743.
118. Fredric S. Zuckerman, 'Vladimir Burtsev and the Tsarist Political Police in Conflict, 1907–14', *JCH* 12 (1977): 193–219.
119. Elwood, *Roman Malinovskii*, 41.
120. Briun-de-Sent-Ippolit had neither the experience nor the talent of Beletskii, as former Minister of Internal Affairs N.A. Maklakov noted. 'Dopros N.A. Maklakova', *PTsR*, 3: 115; 'Ukazatel' Imen', *PTsR*, 7: 311.

Chapter 13

1. Spiridovich, though proud of the official festivities celebrating the Jubilee Year of 1913, was clearly disturbed at the same time by the loss of prestige of the monarchy across the entire spectrum of Russian society. A.I. Spiridovich. 'Poslednie gody Tsarskoesel'skogo Dvora', 2 vols, MS Spiridovich Collection, Sterling Memorial Library, Yale University, 2:813.
2. A.A. Miroliubov, 'Dokumenty po istorii Departamenta politsii perioda pervoi mirovoi voiny', *Sovetskie Arkhivy* 3 (1988): 81.
3. MVD, Department of Police Circular no. 171902, issued by the Ninth Secretariat, 24 May 1914, FAAr, XIIId(1), 11; 'Pokazaniia A.D. Protopopova', *PTsR*, 4: 85–6; 'Dopros gen. E.K. Klimovicha', *PTsR*, 1:57; 'Pokazaniia S.P. Beleskogo', *PTsR*, 4: 132–4.
4. 'Dopros S.P. Beletskogo', *PTsR*, 3: 331; Ernest V. Hollis Jr., 'Police Systems of Imperial and Soviet Russia', MS Bakhmeteff Archive, 374.
5. Miroliubov, 'Dokumenty po istorii Departamenta politsii', 83.
6. 'Dopros S.P. Beletskogo', *PTsR*, 3: 330–1; K.I. Globachev, 'Pravda O Russkoi Revoliutsii. Vospominaniia byvshago Nachal'nika Petrogradskago Okhrannago Otdeleniia', MS Bakhmeteff Archive, 52–3.
7. 'Dopros Kafafova', *PTsR*, 2: 137–8, 144.
8. Beletskii made extravagant use of Fontanka's *reptil'nyi fond* for these purposes. *Soiuz Russkogo Naroda: Po materialam chrezvychainoi sledstvennoi komissii vremennogo pravitel'stva 1917g.*, ed. V.P. Victorov (Moscow: 1929), 138–40; 'Dopros

A.N. Khvostova', *PTsR*, 6: 101; 'Dopros K.D. Kafafova', *PTsR*, 2: 137–9; 'Pokazaniia S.P. Beletskogo', *PTsR*, 4: 120–1, 130–1, 359–60.

9. Ibid., 4: 514.
10. 'Dopros S.P. Beletskogo', Ibid., 5: 245–7.
11. V.S. Diakin, 'The Leadership Crisis in Russia on the Eve of the February Revolution', trans. Michael S. Melanson, *Soviet Studies in History* 23 (Summer, 1984): 15; Tsuyoshi Hasegawa, *The February Revolution: Petrograd 1917* (Seattle: University of Washington Press, 1981), 47–8.
12. 'Pokazaniia kn. Volkonskogo', *PTsR*, 6:138.
13. Diakin, 'The Leadership Crisis', 20.
14. A. IA. Avrekh, *Tsarizm nakanune sverzheniia* (Moscow: 1989), 110.
15. For the unsavoury machinations that helped give Khvostov and Beletskii their posts see Martin Kilcoyne, 'The Political Influence of Rasputin', (PhD Diss., University of Washington, 1961), 214–32.
16. 'Dopros K.D. Kafafova', *PTsR*, 2: 137.
17. A.N. Naumov, *Iz utselevshikh vospominanii 1868–1917*, 2 vols (New York: 1954), 2: 191.
18. For studies dealing with the *Rasputinshchina* see the old classic René Fülöp-Miller, *Rasputin: The Holy Devil*, trans. F.S. Flint and D.F. Tait (London: G.P. Putnam's Sons, 1928) M.K. Kasvinov, *Dvadsat tri stupeni vniz*, 2 ed. (Moscow: 1988); Kilcoyne, 'The Political Influence of Rasputin'; and Avrekh, *Tsarizm*.
19. Naumov, *Iz utselevshikh vospominanii*, 2: 191.
20. Kilcoyne, 'The Political Influence of Rasputin', 233–5.
21. 'Dopros kn. M.M. Andronnikova', PTsR, 1: 315; 'Dopros A.N. Khvostova', *PTsR*, 1: 26, 40.
22. M. Suborin, 'Iz nedavniago proshlago: Beseda s ministrem vnutrennikh del A.N. Khvostovym', *Byloe*, n.s. no. 1 [23] (July, 1917): 62.
23. Fülöp-Miller, *Rasputin*, 271.
24. 'Dopros A.N. Khvostova,' *PTsR*, 1: 26.
25. Shturmer ordered Globachev to protect Rasputin as if he were a member of the Royal Family. 'This is the express wish of the Emperor and Empress', he said. Fülöp-Miller, *Rasputin*, 147.
26. Globachev, 'Pravda O Russkoi Revoliutsii', 61; 'Dopros gen. E.K. Klimovicha', *PTsR*, 1: 67. The mire of intrigue into which Klimovich sank is described and probably somewhat exaggerated in Ibid., 67–75.
27. 'Dopros gen. E.D. Klimovicha', *PTsR*, 1:72.
28. 'Pokazaniia S.P. Beletskogo', *PTsR*, 4: 514–15; 'Dopros B.V. Shturmer', *PTsR*, 268–72.
29. Diakin, 'The Leadership Crisis', 18.
30. Globachev, 'Pravda O Russkoi Revoliutsii', 68, 71.
31. Ibid., 69; 'Dopros kn. M.M. Andronnikova', *PTsR*, 1: 400; 'Pis′mennyi obiasneniia A.T. Vasil′eva', *PTsR*, 1: 423.
32. Herbert A. Simon and James G. March, *Organizations* (New York: John Wiley & Sons, 1958), 167.
33. For the classic discussion of political police reporting see Richard Cobb, *The Police and the People: French Popular Protest 1789–1820* (Oxford: Oxford University Press, 1970), 3–81.
34. Each group considered inimical to the wellbeing of the regime and kept under surveillance had a number assigned to it which made the collation and cross-referencing of intelligence relatively easy. For example, the RSDWP was number, 5; the SRs 9; trade unions, 17; the Octobrists, 147; and the Union of Russian People, 244. Miroliubov, 'Dokumenty po istorii', 82.

35. Ellis Tennant [Edward Ellis Smith], 'The Department of Police 1911–1912: From the Recollections of Nikolai Vladimirovich Veselago', MS Hoover Institution, 10–13; V. Zhilinskii, 'Organizatsiia i zhizn′ okhrannago otdeleniia vo vremena tsarskoi vlasti', *GM*, nos. 9/10 (September/ October 1917): 304–5.
36. *Russkii politicheskii sysk zagranitsei*, ed. Leonid Men′shchikov (Paris: 1914), 12; FAAr, 158, XIIld (1), 8–12.
37. Ideally, experienced analysts should have been able to develop a counter-biased attitude to the reports they received from their subordinates. In practice, however, error remains since it is impossible for each superior to infallibly estimate the nature of his subordinates' biases. Anthony Downs, *Inside Bureaucracy* (Boston: Little, Brown and Co., 1967), 120–2.
38. Simon and March, *Organizations*, 164–5; Graham T. Allison, *The Essence of Decision: Explaining the Cuban Missile Crisis* (Boston: Little, Brown and Co., 1971), 120.
39. 'Dopros S.P. Beletskogo', *PTsR*, 3: 374.
40. A. Pogozhev, 'Iz vospominanii o V.K. von-Pleve', *VE* 7 (July, 1911): 264.
41. Cobb, *The Police and the People*, 45, 78.
42. For example, *Burzhuaziia nakanune Fevral′skoi Revoliutsii*, ed. B.B. Grave (Moscow: 1927), 45; 'Politicheskoe polozhenie Rossii nakanune Fevral′skoi revoliutsii v zhandarmskom osveshchenii', *KA* 17 (1926): 6; 'V nachale 1916 goda (Iz dokumentov)', *KL*, 1923, no. 7: 208.
43. 'Uchet departamentom politsii opyta 1905 goda', *KA* 18 (1926): 224.
44. Cobb, *The Police and the People*, 3–81.
45. As one political police chief remarked, 'the habitual persistent attention devoted by the Department of Police to the dangers of our underground revolutionary organisations are created by departmental investigative routine'. A.P. Martynov, *Moia sluzhba v Otdel′nom korpuse zhandarmov: Vospominaniia* (Stanford: Hoover Institution Press, 1972), 283.
46. During the 1905 Revolution, for example, Fontanka received hundreds of reports on the cases of peasant unrest. While many of them naturally enough placed the blame for disaffection on propaganda and agitation by the SRs amongst others, there were other officials such as the chief of the Kazan Gendarme Directorate who categorically stated that the unrest was founded in economic causes. The chief of the Riazan′ Gendarme Directorate actually pleaded on behalf of the peasants living under his jurisdiction. None the less, in a detailed analysis presented to Chairman of the Council of Ministers Witte, Fontanka placed unwarranted emphasis on the roles of SR agitation and propaganda in stirring up the peasants. 'Krestianskoe dvizhenie 1905g. Dokladnaia zapiska departamenta politsii predsedatel'iu soveta ministrov S.IU. Vitte', KA 9 (1925): 66–93.
47. William Kornhauser, 'Rebellion and Political Development', in *Internal Wars: Problems and Approaches*, ed. Harry Eckstein (London: Free Press, 1964), 150.
48. 'From the Files of the Moscow Gendarme Corps: A Lecture on Combatting Revolution', *CSS* 2 (1968): 99.
49. Aleksandr I. Spiridovich, *Les dernières années de la cour de Tsarskoe-Sélo*, 2 vols, (Paris: 1928), 1: 279.
50. Simon and March, *Organizations*, 167; Allison, *The Essence of Decision*, 120.
51. 'Doklad Direktora Departamenta Politsii Lopukhina Ministru Vnutrennikh Delo Sobytiiakh 9-go Ianvaria', *KL*, 1922, no. 1: 334–5.
52. Fredric S. Zuckerman, 'Vladimir Burtsev and the Tsarist Political Police in Conflict, 1907–14', *JCH* 12 (1977): 193–219.
53. 'Dopros K.D. Kafafova', *PTsR*, 2: 138; P.G. Kurlov, *Gibel′ imperatorskoi Rossii* (Berlin: 1923), 30.

54. S.B.Chlenov, *Moskovskaia okhranka i ee sekretnye sotrudniki: Po dannym komissii po obespecheniiu novogo stroia* (Moscow: 1919), 10; 'Moskovskaia okhranka v 1915g.', *GM*, 1918, nos. 1–3: 283.
55. In 1915 the Sixth Secretariat (the Special Section) received 60 000 documents and issued 27 000 of them alone. The chief of the Sixth Secretariat expected that the quantity of this paper would grow significantly. At the same time, this Secretariat had lost thirty-four *chinovniki* to the army and, as a result, was unable to fulfil its duties. Fontanka secunded thirteen new men to it. Miroliubov, 'Dokumenty po istorii Departamenta politsii', 81.
56. Nurit Schleifmann, 'The Internal Agency: Linchpin of the Political Police in Russia', *Cahiers du monde Russe et Sovietique* 24 (1983): 158–9.
57. Kurlov, *Gibel'*, 30.
58. 'Obshchee polozhenie k iiuliu 1916g.: Zapiska departamenta politsii', *Byloe*, n.s., 1918, no. 3 (31): 30.
59. A. Badayev, *The Bolsheviks in the Tsarist Duma* (New York: International Publishers, 1932), 61; Michael Melancon, *The Socialist Revolutionaries and the Russian Anti-War Movement, 1914–1917* (Columbus: Ohio State University Press, 1990), 82–3; Leopold Haimson, 'The Problem of Social Stability in Urban Russia 1905–1914', *Slavic Review* 23 (December 1964): 637.
60. Melancon, *The Socialist Revolutionaries*, 104.
61. Martynov, *Moia sluzhba*, 279–80.
62. Melancon, *The Socialist Revolutionaries*, 3, 37–8, 90, 166.
63. Diane Koenker, *Moscow Workers and the 1917 Revolution* (Princeton: Princeton University Press, 1981), 25.
64. I.P. Leiberov, *Na shturm samoderzhaviia: Petrograskii proletariat v gody pervoi mirovoi voiny i Fevral'skoi revoliutsii (Iiul' 1914-Mart 1917g.)* (Moscow: 1979), 13, 15, 20, 22; Diane P. Koenker and William G. Rosenburg, *Strikes and Revolution in Russia, 1917* (Princeton: Princeton University Press, 1989), 29, 42–3, 46–9, 54–55, 56.
65. For a concise discussion of the factors constituting 'political' and 'economic' strikes see: Koenker and Rosenberg, *Strikes and Revolution*, 16.
66. Ibid., 58.
67. MVD, Department of Police, *Obshchii Ocherk*, 5 April 1916, FAAr, 189, XVIa, 2.
68. MVD, Department of Police, No, 412, *Obzor deiatel'nosti Rossiiskoi sotsial-demokraticheskoi...*, FAAr, 194, XVIb (6), 1.
69. Chlenov, *Moskovskaia okhranka;* Melancon, *The Socialist Revolutionaries*, 104–5.
70. Globachev, 'Pravda O Russkoi Revoliutsii', 49.
71. Quoted in: Hasegawa, *The February Revolution*, 178.
72. 'The Progressive Bloc was composed of six Duma caucuses, comprising about 241 of the 407 deputies in the Duma in August 1915. The Kadets, Progressists, and Left Octobrists formed the 'liberal' segment of the Bloc, at least on most issues, while the Centrists, Zemstvo Octobrists, and Progressive Nationalists comprised the more conservative wing. Michael F. Hamm, 'Liberal Politics in Wartime Russia: An Analysis of the Progressive Bloc', *Sl R* 33 (September, 1974): 453.
73. The principal public organisations were the All-Russian Union of Zemstvos for the relief of Sick and Wounded Soldiers and the Union of Towns. At first the two unions limited themselves to the relief of the sick and wounded. They established hospitals, and maintained hospital trains, canteens and medical stores. In 1915 the two unions began to participate in the process of military supply. A joint committee for the supply of the army united the two unions in this endeavour. This organisation, known as *Zemgor,* placed war orders, assisted in the establishment of factories, the shipment of supplies to the front and so on. Though not without major shortcom-

ings *Zemgor* enjoyed great popularity and commanded the allegience of thousands of employees. Michael T. Florinsky, *Russia: A History and An Interpretation* (New York: Macmillan, 1953), 2: 1366–67.

74. *Burzhuaziia*, 33–8; 'Obshchee polozhenie k iiuliu, 1916g.', 26–27.
75. The Central War Industries Committee controlled smaller war industries committees located throughout provincial Russia. The establishment of these committees, whose purpose was the self-mobilisation of industry for national defence, was due to the initiative of business circles. Florinsky, *Russia*, 2: 1370.
76. Globachev, 'Pravda O Revoliutsii', 23–5; P.P. Zavarzin, *Zhandarmy i revoliutsionery: Vospominaniia* (Paris: 1930), 201–3; 'Pokazaniia S.P. Beletskogo', *PTsR*, 4: 139–42.
77. Raymond Pearson, *The Russian Moderates and the Crisis of Tsarism 1914–1917* (London: Macmillan, 1977), 103.
78. Globachev, 'Pravda O Russkoi Revoliutsii', 11–12.
79. *Burzhuaziia*, 33–8.
80. MVD, Department of Police Circular no. 175641, 2 September 1914.
81. 'Obshchee polozhenie k iiuliu 1916g.', 25.
82. Koenker and Rosenberg, *Strikes and Revolution*, 26.
83. Hamm, 'Liberal Politics', 463, 465–6, 468.
84. Globachev, 'Pravda O Revoliutsii', 49.
85. MVD, Department of Police, no. 412, 'Obzor deiatel′nosti Rossiiskoi sotsial-demokraticheskoi ...', FAAr, 194, XV1b (6), 1; MVD, Department of Police, 'Obshchii Ocherk', 5 April 1916, FAAr, 189, XV1a, 2; B. Grave, *K istorii klassovoi bor′by v Rossii v gody imperialisticheskoi voiny: Iiul′ 1914g.–Fevral′ 1917g.* (Moscow: 1926), 129, 181; Martynov, *Moia sluzhba*, 279–80.
86. *Burzhuaziia*, 65.
87. Martynov though courageous was not foolhardy. He valued his career far too much to express these criticisms as personal opinion. He enumerated the following reasons for his conclusion as expressions of the Duma rather than of himself. He condemned: the Imperial Couple's relationship with Rasputin; the unsatisfactory explanation given for the dismissal of Procurator of the Holy Synod Samarin; and the tsar's refusal to grant a general amnesty. Ibid., 75-81.
88. Diane Koenker, *Moscow Workers*, 59, 87.
89. Melancon, *The Socialist-Revolutionaries*, 219.
90. 'Tsarskaia okhranka o politicheskom polozhenii v strane v kontse 1916g.', *Istoricheskii arkhiv*, 1960, no. 1: 204–8.
91. Globachev, 'Pravda O Russkoi Revoliutsii', 14–16.
92. Even ordinary gendarme officers commented on the backwardness of the economy and its inability to fulfil the demands placed upon it by the war. Grave, *K istorii klassovoi bor′by*, 47.
93. 'Politicheskoe polozhenie Rossii', 4–35.
94. 'Tsarskaia okhranka', 204.
95. Diane Koenker writes that the evolution of an urban working class culture which although still shared by 'a relative minority of Moscow workers had assumed a distinctive form, characterised by self-improvement, sobriety, collegiality, and pride in class identity'. Koenker, *Moscow Workers*, 93.
96. Kurlov, *Gibel′*, 211.
97. Globachev, 'Pravda O Russkoi Revoliutsii', 13–14.
98. Ibid., 14, 77.
99. Koenker, *Moscow Workers,* 96; Koenker and Rosenberg, *Strikes and Revolution*, 66.
100. Leiberov, *Na shturm samoderzhaviia*, 72, 74, 82; Melancon, *The Socialist Revolutionaries*, 212, 275.

101. *Burzhuaziia*, 136–9.
102. Globachev, 'Pravda O Russkoi Revoliutsii', 71–2.
103. Mary E. Schaeffer, 'The Political Policies of P.A. Stolypin', (PhD diss., Indiana University, 1964), 76; A.T. Vasilyev, *The Ochrana: The Russian Secret Police* (Philadelphia: J.P. Lipincott, 1930), 91.
104. 'Dopros A.I. Spiridovicha', *PTsR*, 3: 47–8.
105. Durnovo, for example, made certain that his reports to Nicholas II were highly descriptive rather than analytical in character. Wayne D. Santoni, 'P.N. Durnovo as Minister of Internal Affairs in the Witte Cabinet: A Study in Suppression', (PhD diss., University of Kansas, 1968), 118.
106. V.N. Kokovtsov quoted in Marc Szeftel, *The Russian Constitution of April 23, 1906: Political Institutions of the Duma Monarchy* (Brussels: 1976), 407. For an example of the distorted image the court held of the world beyond Tsarskoe-Selo see A.A. Mosolov's description of 'the wall' separating the tsar from the world about him. A.A. Mossolov, *At the Court of the Last Tsar*, trans. E.W. Dickes (London: Methuen and Co., 1935), 127–30; Francis W. Wcislo, 'Soslovia or Class? Bureaucratic Reformers and Provincial Gentry in Conflict, 1906–1908', *RR* 47 (January, 1988), 24.
107. Kilcoyne, 'The Political Influence of Rasputin', 68.
108. Karl Mannheim, *Ideology and Utopia: An Introduction to the Sociology of Knowledge* (London: Routledge & Kegan Paul, 1960), 36.
109. Globachev, 'Pravda O Russkoi Revoliutsii', 14–16.
110. Koenker, *Moscow Workers*, 89.
111. *Partiia bol'shevikov v gody mirovoi imperialisticheskoi voiny: Vtoraia revoliutsiia v Rossii 1914 god–Fevral' 1917 goda* (Moscow: 1963), 117–18: *Burzhuaziia*, 131–2; Hasegawa, *The February Revolution*, 84.
112. Globachev, 'Pravda O Russkoi Revoliutsii', 25, 73.
113. Ibid., 70. Hasegawa credits Protopopov with the ruthless assault against the opposition in January and February 1917. It seems to me that this decisiveness was completely alien to the man. Clearly it was Globachev, Kurlov and Beletskii who forced these actions upon him. Hasegawa, *The February Revolution*, 150–1, 205.
114. I.P. Leiberov, *Na shturm samoderzhaviia*, 86–7; Globachev, 'Pravda O Russkoi Revoliutsii', 72. Protopopov claims A.I. Guchkov was not arrested because Fontanka believed that such an arrest would only increase his popularity. 'Pokazaniia A.D. Protopopova', *PTsR*, 4: 86–7, 89; 'Pis'mennye obiasneniia A.T. Vasil'eva', *PTsR*, 1: 424–5.
115. Leiberov, *Na shturm samoderzhaviia*, 132–3.
116. Vasilyev, *The Ochrana*, 199.
117. Grave, *K istorii klassovoi bor'by v Rossii*, 219–25.
118. 'Pokazaniia A.D. Protopopova', *PTsR*, 4: 95.
119. Quoted in Hasegawa, *The February Revolution*, 155.
120. Koenker and Rosenberg, *Strikes and Revolution*, 23. For a slightly different set of strike statistics see: Leiberov, *Na shturm samoderzhaviia*, 131.
121. 'Pokazaniia A.D. Protopopova', *PTsR*, 4: 96.
122. Ibid., 4: 98; Zavarzin, *Zhandarmy*, 236.
123. Although political police reports discussing the participation of the two members of Workers' Group remaining at large were true, these people did not represent a threat to the forces of order and were soon dealt with. Intelligence concerning the involvement of professional revolutionaries contribution to popular unrest in the capital was also true, but grossly exaggerated as both habit and fear dictated. Hasegawa, *The February Revolution*, 262–3.
124. 'Fevral'skaia revoliutsiia', 161–2.
125. Leiberov, *Na shturm samoderzhaviia*, 242.

126. 'Fevral'skaia revoliutsiia', 173–4.
127. Globachev, 'Pravda O Russkoi Revoliutsii.'
128. Hasegawa, *The February Revolution*, 229–30; Martynov, *Moia sluzhba*, 297; 'Fevrals'skaia revoliutsii', 169.

Epilogue

1. K.I. Globachev, 'Pravda O Russkoi Revoliutsii. Vospominaniia byvshago Nachal'nika Petrogradskago Okhrannago Otdeleniia', MS Bakhmeteff Archive, 82–3; 'Fevral'skaia revoliutsiia i okhrannoe otdelenie', *Byloe*, n.s., no. 1 [29] (January, 1918): 170.
2. Tsuyoshi Hasegawa, *The February Revolution: Petrograd, 1917* (Seattle: University of Washington Press, 1981), 304.
3. Globachev, 'Pravda O Russkoi Revoliutsii', 83.
4. I.P. Leiberov, *Na shturm samoderzhaviia: Petrogradskii proletariat v gody pervoi mirovoi voiny i Fevral'skoi Revoliutsii (iiul' 1914–mart 1917g.)* (Moscow: 1979), 252.
5. Globachev, 'Pravda O Russkoi Revoliutsii', 84. That evening the insurgents ransacked the Petrograd OO along with several conspiratorial apartments. On 3 March a fire broke out at the Moscow OO probably begun by police officials hoping to destroy the bureau's records. A mob prevented firemen from dousing the blaze while others stoked the bonfire with the OO's archives. *The Russian Provisional Government: Documents*, eds Robert Paul Browder and Alexander F. Kerensky, 3 vols (Stanford: Stanford University Press, 1961), 1: 215–16; Diane Koenker, *Moscow Workers and the 1917 Revolution* (Princeton: Princeton University Press, 1981), 99; Leiberov, *Na shturm samoderzhaviia*, 247.
6. P.P. Zavarzin, *Zhandarmy i revoliutsionery: Vospominaniia* (Paris: 1930), 244–5, 248–9; Globachev, 'Pravda O Russkoi Revoliutsii', 91.
7. Ibid., 91; George Leggett, *The Cheka: Lenin's Political Police* (Oxford: Clarendon Press, 1981), xxv.
8. *The Russian Provisional Government*, 1: 159; Zavarzin, *Zhandarmy i revoliutsionery*, 251–2.
9. *The Russian Provisional Government*, 1: 192, 196, 215–18; Richard S. Wortman, *The Development of a Russian Legal Consciousness* (Chicago: University of Chicago Press, 1976), 63.
10. George Yaney, 'Bureaucracy as Culture: A Comment', *Sl R* 41 (Spring, 1982): 110; *The Russian Provisional Government*, 1: 159.
11. Ibid., 1: 154, 218–19, 243, 249, 309; Leggett, *The Cheka*, xxv; Gary Richard Waxmonsky, "Police and Politics in Soviet Society, 1921–1929', (PhD diss., Princeton University, 1982), 63.
12. Globachev, 'Pravda O Russkoi Revoliutsii', 110, 113, 115–18, 126, 129, 130–1, 134–5.
13. Leggett, *The Cheka*, 191–2.
14. Globachev, 'Pravda O Russkoi Revoliutsii', 134–5.
15. Waxmonsky, 'Police and Politics', 51.
16. Frank James McDaniel, 'Political Assassination and Mass Execution: Terrorism in Revolutionary Russia, 1878–1938', (PhD Diss., University of Michigan, 1976), 246, 296; Waxmonsky, 'Police and Politics', 335.
17. Daniel T. Orlovsky, 'State Building in the Civil War Era: The Role of the Lower-Middle Strata', in *Party, State, and Society in the Russian Civil War: Explorations*

in Social History, eds Diane P. Koenker, William G. Rosenberg, and Ronald Grigor Suny (Bloomington: Indiana University Press, 1989), 192.

18. A.T. Vasilyev, *The Okhrana: The Russian Secret Police*, trans. René Fülöp-Miller (London: George C. Harrop, 1930), 93–5.
19. S.B. Chlenov, *Moskovskaia okhranka i ee sekretnye sotrudniki: Po dannym komissii po obespecheniiu novogo stroia* (Moscow: 1919), 36.
20. Ronald Grigor Suny, 'Commentary: Administration and State Building', in *Party, State, and Society in the Russian Civil War*, 234; Orlovsky, 'State Building in the Civil War Era', in Ibid., 202.
21. Globachev, 'Pravda O Russkoi Revoliutsii', 136.
22. Amy W. Knight, *The KGB: Police and Politics in the Soviet Union*, rev. ed. (Boston: Unwin Hyman, 1990) 9; Waxmonsky, 'Police and Politics', 57; Leggett, *The Cheka*, 32, 37, 194, 302, 358; Lennard D. Gerson, *The Secret Police in Lenin's Russia*, (Philadelphia: Temple University Press, 1976), 167–70.
23. Sheila Fitzpatrick, 'The Civil War as a Formative Experience', in *Bolshevik Culture*, eds Abbott Gleason, Peter Kenez, and Richard Stites (Bloomington: Indiana University Press, 1985), 66.
24. Knight, *The KGB*, xviii–xix.
25. Yaney, 'Bureaucracy as Culture', 110.
26. David Christian, 'The Supervisory Function in Russian and Soviet History', *SIR* 41 (Spring, 1982): 75; Waxmonsky, 'Police and Politics', 321–2, 325–6.
27. Ibid., 341.
28. E.J. Scott, 'The Cheka', *St. Antony's Papers*, 1956, no. 1: 23.
29. Carl J. Friedrich, *Tradition and Authority* (London: Macmillan, 1972), 114.
30. Gerson, *The Secret Police*, 59.
31. Leggett, *The Cheka*, 114.
32. Brian Chapman, *Police State* (London: Macmillan, 1970), 136.
33. Moshe Lewin, 'The Civil War: Dynamics and Legacy', in *Party, State, and Society in the Russian Civil War*, 403, 417.
34. Waxmonsky, 'Police and Politics', 57.
35. McDaniel, 'Political Assassination and Mass Execution', 251.
36. Scott, 'The Cheka', 5.
37. Waxmonsky, 'Police and Politics', 318–19.
38. Ibid., 89, 100; George H. Leggett, Lenin, 'Terror and Political Police', *Survey* 21 (August, 1975): 176–9.
39. Waxmonsky, 'Police and Politics', 359.
40. Knight, *The KGB*, 195.
41. Leggett, *The Cheka*, 194. Indeed, at training school KGB candidates study Special Section records and are amazed by the close parallel between Special Section and KGB *modus operandi*.
42. The information and insights which appear in the final pages of this Epilogue dealing with the KGB are largely derived from Amy Knight's excellent book. See especially pages: xviii–xix, 9–10, 119, 160, 162, 173–4, 176–7, 192, 194, 196, 211, 310–12.

Bibliography

Note on Archival Sources

This book is based on the information located within the Archive of the Russian Political Police Abroad deposited at the Hoover Institution, Stanford, California. The Archive is made up of over 100 000 documents divided into several subsections explained by a detailed but often misleading index. The Archive contains: the complete history of the Foreign Agentura's organisational and methodological development; thousands of despatches detailing the activities of revolutionary individuals and groups; and hundreds of memorandums, instructions and circulars dealing with every phase of political police activity within the empire. This last group of documents is the essential ingredient, when combined with published documents, memoirs and secondary sources, which gives the historian the capability of reconstructing the development of late Tsarist political police institutions.

Four other Archives supplied valuable data. Two of these, the Nikolaevsky Collection and Moravsky Collection are also located at the Hoover Institution. The Nikolaevsky Collection is one of the great archives on Russian History located outside of Russia.

The Moravsky Collection is mostly concerned with the affairs of emigrés in the post-revolutionary period who for the most part resided in China.

The Spiridovich Collection, located within the Sterling Memorial Library at Yale University, holds the papers, manuscripts and assorted paraphernalia of General A.I. Spiridovich, one of Tsardom's most renowned political policemen. It also holds some of P.I. Rachkovskii's papers and those of Rachkovskii's son. It is a valuable collection more for what it tells us about Spiridovich and to a lesser extent about Rachkovskii themselves than it does about political police affairs.

The Fourth archive which held valuable material is the Boris Bakhmeteff Archive at Columbia University, which owns both the invaluable Liubimov and Globachev manuscripts and the very useful draft PhD dissertation by Ernest V. Hollis Jr.

One final bibliographic comment; the reader should be aware of the differences between the journals commonly called *Byloe.* There were in fact three such journals, two of which contributed much to this work. The first is entitled *Byloe: Sbornik po istorii russkogo osvoboditel'nogo dvizheniia*, published by Vladimir Burtsev which appeared in fifteen numbers from: 1900–1904, 1907–1913. Burtsev published his *Byloe* in Paris and London. In 1933 he published another, and less valuable *Byloe* under the title, *Byloe: Sbornik po noveishei russkoi istorii.* This second journal, also published in London and Paris, appeared in only two numbers in 1933 and it was marked by a rabidly anti-Soviet bias. The third journal, *Byloe: zhurnal posviashchenyi istorii osvoboditel'nogo dvizheniia*, was first published in Russia during the 1905 Revolution (January 1906–October 1907) until the censor forced its closure. This invaluable journal reappeared in July 1917 and ran until 1926 (nos 1–35). In the following bibliography this last series is designated with the abbreviation n.s. (*novaia seriia*).

In order to avoid confusion I have described articles from these three journals in more bibliographic detail than is customary in current academic bibliographies.

I UNPUBLISHED SOURCES

(a) Archives

The Hoover Institution, Stanford, California
The Records of the Foreign Agentura of the Russian Political Police
The Boris Nikolaevsky Collection
The Moravsky Collection
Yale University, Sterling Memorial Library
The Spiridovich Collection
Columbia University, New York
The Boris Bakhmeteff Archive

(b) Manuscripts, Reports and Depositions

'Attachment [*sic!*] to Bulletin No. 7 of the Executive Committee of the Paris Council of Representative Political Organizations (received for publication from the Special Commission engaged in investigating the Archives of the Paris Okhrana).' [English translation], 10 October 1917. The Records of the Foreign Agentura...(FAAr), (Folder) IIa, (Box) 4.

Deposition of A.A. Lopukhin before the Extraordinary Investigating Commission investigating the illegal activities of former ministers and others, 6 November 1917 (in Russian). Untitled MS, Nikolaevsky Collection.

Director of the Department of Police Lopukhin to the Committee of Ministers, 6 December 1904 (in Russian). Untitled MS, Nikolaevsky Collection.

'Dopros D.S.S. A.A. Krasil'nikova. Protokoly: No. 3 7/20 Iiunia; No. 5 9/22 Iiunia 1917; No. 7 27 Iiunia/10 Iiulia 1917', FAAr 9, IIf, 10.

Gerasimov A. 'Rukopis' vospominanii'. Nikolaevsky Collection.

Globachev, Konstantin Ivanovich. 'Pravda O Russkoi Revoliutsii. Vospominaniia byvshago Nachal'nika Petrogradskago Okhrannago Otdeleniia'. Boris Bakhmeteff Archive, Columbia University.

Hollis, Ernest V. Jr 'Police Systems of Imperial and Soviet Russia.' Boris Bakhmeteff Archive, Columbia University.

Liubimov, D.N. 'Russkaia smuta nachala deviatisotykh godov 1902–1906. Po vospominaniiam, lichnym zapiskam i dokumentam'. Boris Bakhmeteff Archive, Columbia University.

Procurator's pre-trial statements the Lopukhin treason case (in Russian). Untitled MS, Nikolaevsky Collection.

Russia, MVD, Departament politsii. Po 2 deloproizvodstvu. *O preobrazovanii politsii v Imperii*, 1 Sentiabria 1913g. No. 20. 083, Sterling Memorial Library, Yale University.

Russia, MVD, Departament politsii, *Sbornik sekretnykh Tsirkuliarov obrashchennykh k Nachal'nikam gubernskikh zhandarmskikh upravlenii, Gubernatoram i pr. v techenie 1902–1907. New York Public Library. These circulars were apparently a file of the Nizhnii Novgorod Gendarme Directorate.*

Russiian, V.N. 'Rabota okhrannykh otdelenii v Rossii'. Moravsky Collection.

Schneiderman, Jeremiah. 'Sergei Zubatov and Revolutionary Marxism: The Struggle for the Working Class in Tsarist Russia'. MS loaned by the author.

Spiridovich, A.I. 'Evreiskii vopros v Rossii v Poslednee Tsarstvovanie'. Spiridovich Collection, Sterling Memorial Library, Yale University.

Spiridovich, A.I. 'Peter Ivanovich Rachkovskii'. Spiridovich Collection, Sterling Memorial Library, Yale University.

Spiridovich, A.I. 'Poslednie gody Tsarskosel'skogo Dvora'. 2 Vols. Spiridovich Collection, Sterling Memorial Library, Yale University.

Svatikov, S.G. 'Sozdanie "Sionskikh protokolov" po dannym ofitsial'nago sledstviia 1917 goda'. Nikolaevsky Collection.

Tennant Ellis [Edward Ellis Smith]. 'The Department of Police 1911–1912: From the Recollections of Nikolai Vladimirovich Veselago'. Hoover Institution.

(c) Doctoral Dissertations

Bennet, Hilju. 'The *Chin* System and the Raznochintsy in the Government of Alexander III, 1881–1894'. PhD diss., University of California, Berkeley, 1971.

Blakely, Allison. 'The Socialist Revolutionary Party, 1901–1907: The Populist Response to the Industrialization of Russia'. PhD diss., University of California, Berkeley, 1971.

Bohon, John W. 'Reactionary Politics in Russia 1905–1909'. PhD diss., University of North Carolina at Chapel Hill, 1967.

Calhoun, Arthur Fryer. 'The Politics of Internal Order: French Government and Revolutionary Labor, 1898–1914'. PhD diss., Princeton University, 1973.

Doctorow, Gilbert Steven. 'The Introduction of Parliamentary Institutions in Russia During the Revolution of 1905–1907'. PhD diss., Columbia University, 1975.

Dussel, Daniel, C. 'Russian Judicial Reforms and Counter-reforms 1864–1914'. PhD diss., University of Missouri, 1981.

Healy, Erickson, Ann K. 'The Russian Autocracy in Crisis: Tsarism and the Opposition from 1905 to 1907'. PhD diss., University of Wisconsin, 1972.

Johnson, Richard J. 'The Okhrana Abroad, 1885–1917; A Study of International Police Cooperation'. PhD diss., Columbia University, 1970.

Judge, Edward H. 'The Russia of Plehve : Programs and Policies of the Ministry of Internal Affairs, 1902–1904'. PhD diss., University of Michigan, 1975.

Kilcoyne, Martin. 'The Political Influence of Rasputin'. PhD diss., University of Washington, 1961.

McDaniel, Frank James. 'Political Assassination and Mass Execution: Terrorism in Revolutionary Russia, 1878–1938'. PhD diss., University of Michigan, 1976.

Prevo, Kathleen. 'The Revolution of 1905 in Voronezh: The Labor Movement and Political Consciousness in a Russian Provincial City'. PhD diss., Indiana University, 1979.

Santoni, Wayne D. 'P.N. Durnovo as Minister of Internal Affairs in the Witte Cabinet: A Study in Suppression'. PhD diss., University of Kansas, 1968.

Schaeffer, Mary E. 'The Political Policies of P.A. Stolypin'. PhD diss., Indiana University, 1964.

Schneiderman, Jeremiah. 'The Tsarist Government and the Labor Movement 1898–1903: The Zubatovshchina'. PhD diss., University of California, Berkeley, 1966.

Verner, Andrew Marshall. 'Nicholas II and the Role of the Autocrat During the First Russian Revolution, 1904–1907'. PhD diss., Columbia University, 1986.

Waxmonsky, Gary Richard. 'Police and Politics in Soviet Society, 1921–1929'. PhD diss., Princeton University, 1982.

Zuckerman, Fredric S. 'The Russian Political Police at Home and Abroad (1880–1917) : Its Structure, Functions, and Methods and Its Struggle with the Organized Opposition'. PhD diss., New York University, 1973.

II PUBLISHED SOURCES

(a) Books, Pamphlets and Government Documents

Afanas'eva, N.I., ed. *Sovremmenniki: Al'bom Biografii.* St Petersburg: 1909–1910.

Agafonov, V.K. *Zagranichnaia okhranka.* Petrograd: 1918.

Alekseev, I.V. *Istoriia odnogo provokatora: Obvinitel'noe zakliuchenie i materialy k protsessu A.E. Serebriakova.* Moscow: 1925.

—— *Provokator Anna Serebriakova.* Moscow: 1932.

Allison, Graham T. *Essence of Decision: Explaining the Cuban Missile Crisis.* Boston: Little, Brown and Co., 1971.

Amburger, Erik. *Geschichte der Behordenorganisation Russlands von Peter dem Grossen bis 1917*. Studien zur geschichte osteruropas, no. 10. Leiden: E.J. Brill, 1966.

Anan'ich, B.V., R. Sh. Ganelin, B.B. Dubentsov, V.S. Diakin, and S.I. Potolov. *Krizis samoderzhaviia v Rossii 1895–1917*. Leningrad: 1984.

Arutiunov, G.A. *Rabochee dvizhenie v Rossii v period novogo revoliutsionnogo pod"ema 1910–1914gg*. Moscow: 1975.

Ascher, Abraham. *The Revolution of 1905: Russia in Disarray*. Stanford: Stanford University Press, 1988.

Avrekh, A.IA. *Stolypin i Tret'ia duma*. Moscow: 1968.

—— *Tsarizm i IV Duma 1912–1914gg*. Moscow: 1981.

—— *Tsarizm nakanune sverzheniia*. Moscow: 1989.

Aziât [pseud.] *Russkie shpiony v Germanii*. Berlin: 1904.

Badayev, A. *The Bolsheviks in the Tsarist Duma*. New York: International Publishers, 1932.

Bakai, M. *O razoblachitel'iakh i razoblachitel'stve, pis'mo k V. Burtsevu*. New York, 1912.

Betskii, K., and P. Pavlov. *Russkii rokambol': Prikliucheniia I.F. Manasevich-Manuilova*. Leningrad: 1925.

Blau, Peter M. *Bureaucracy in Modern Society*. New York: Random House, 1956.

—— *The Dynamics of Bureaucracy: A Study of Interpersonal Relationships in Two Government Agencies*. Rev. ed. Chicago: Chicago University Press, 1963.

Bobrovskaya, C. *Provocateurs I Have Known*. London, [1931].

Boevye predpriiatiia sotsialistov-revoliutsionerov v osveshchenii okhranki. [1918].

Bogdanovich, A.V. *Tri poslednikh samoderzhtsa: Dnevnik A.V. Bogdanovich[a]*. Moscow: 1924.

Bonnell, Victoria E. *Roots of Rebellion: Workers' Politics and Organizations in St. Petersburg and Moscow, 1900–1914*. Berkeley and Los Angeles: University of California Press, 1983.

Bramstedt, E.K. *Dictatorship and Political Police: The Technique of Control by Fear*. New York: Oxford University Press, 1945.

Brokgaus, F.A., and I.A. Efron, eds. *Entsiklopedicheskii slovar'*. 41 volumes in 82. St Petersburg: 1890–1904.

Browder, Robert Paul, and Alexander F. Kerensky, eds *The Russian Provisional Government 1917: Documents*. 3 vols. Stanford: Stanford University Press, 1961.

Bukhbinder, N.A. *Zubatovshchina i rabochee dvizhenie v Rossii*. Moscow: 1926.

Burtsev, Vladimir. *Bor'ba za svobodnuiu Rossiiu: Moi vospominaniia (1882–1912g.)* Vol. 1. Berlin: 1912.

—— *Protokoly sionskikh mudretsov: Dokazannyi podlog*. Paris: 1938.

—— *Tsarskii listok*. Paris: 1909.

Bushnell, John. *Mutiny amid Repression: Russian Soldiers in the Revolution of 1905–1906*. Bloomington: Indiana University Press, 1985.

Chapman, Brian. *Police State*. London: Macmillan, 1970.

Chermenskii, E.D. *Burzhuaziia i tsarizm v pervoi russkoi revoliutsii*. Moscow: 1970.

Chernukha, V.G. *Vnutrenniaia politika tsarizma s serediny 50-x do nachala 80-x gg. XIX v*. Leningrad: 1978.

Chlenov, S.B. *Moskovskaia okhranka i ee sekretnye sotrudniki: Po dannym komissii po obespecheniiu novogo stroia*. Moscow: 1919.

Christopher, Andrew. *Theophile Delcassé and the Making of the Entente Cordiale: A Reappraisal of French Foreign Policy 1898–1905*. New York: Macmillan, 1968.

Cobb, Richard. *The Police and the People: French Popular Protest 1789–1820*. London: Oxford University Press, 1970.

Cohn, Norman. *Warrant for Genocide: The Myth of the Jewish World – Conspiracy and the Protocols of Zion*. London: Eyre and Spotteswoode, 1967.

Conroy, Mary Schaeffer. *Peter Arkad'evich Stolypin : Practical Politics in Late Tsarist Russia*. Boulder: Westview Press, 1976.

Crisp, Olga, and Linda Edmondson, eds. *Civil Rights in Imperial Russia*. Oxford: Clarendon Press, 1989.

Crozier, Michel. *The Bureaucratic Phenomenon*. Chicago: The University of Chicago Press, 1964.

Dan, Theodore. *The Origins of Bolshevism*. Edited and Translated by Joel Carmichael. London: Secker and Warburg, 1964.

Delevskii, IU. *Protokoly sionskikh mudretsov: Istoriia odnogo podloga*. Berlin: 1923.

Delo A.A. Lopukhina v osobom prisutsvii pravitel'stuiushchago senata: Stenograficheskii otchet. St Petersburg: 1910.

Diakin, V.S. *Russkaia burzhuaziia i tsarizm v gody pervoi mirovoi voiny, 1914–1917*. Leningrad: 1967.

Dillon, E.J. *The Eclipse of Russia*. New York: George H. Doran, 1918.

Downs, Anthony. *Inside Bureaucracy*. Boston: Little, Brown and Co., 1967.

Dubrovskii, S.M., comp. *Agrarnoe dvizhenie v 1905–1907gg.: Materialy departamenta politsii*. Vol. 1. Leningrad: 1925.

—— *Krest'ianskoe dvizhenie v Revoliutsii 1905–1907 gg*. Moscow: 1956

Dzerzhinsky, Felix. *Prison Diary and Letters*. Moscow: Foreign Language Publishing House, 1959.

Dziak, John J. *Chekisty: A History of the KGB*. New York: Ivy Books, 1989.

Eckstein, Harry, ed. *Internal Wars: Problems and Approaches*. London: The Free Press, 1969.

Eisenstadt, S.N. *The Political Systems of Empires: The Rise and Fall of the Historical Bureaucratic Societies*. New York: The Free Press, 1969.

Elwood, Ralph Carter. *Roman Malinovsky: A Life Without a Cause*. Russian Biography Series no. 2. Newton Mass.: Oriental Research Partners, 1977.

—— *Russian Social Democracy in the Underground: A Study of the R.S.D.R.P. in the Ukraine 1907–1914*. Publications on Social History, issued by the International Institute of Social History, no. 8. Assen: Van Gorcam and Comp., 1974.

Emmons, Terence. *The Formation of Political Parties and the First National Elections in Russia*. Cambridge: Harvard University Press, 1983.

Engelstein, Laura. *Moscow 1905: Working-class Organizations and Political Conflict*. Stanford: Stanford University Press, 1982.

Erenfel′d, B. *Tiazhelyi front: Iz istorii bor′by bol′shevikov s tsarskoi tainoi politsiei*. Moscow: 1983.

Eroshkin, N.P. *Istoriia gosudarstvennykh uchrezhdenii dorevoliutsionnoi Rossii*. 2d ed. Moscow: 1968.

—— *Ocherki istorii gosudarstvennykh uchrezhdenii dorevoliutsionnoi Rossii*. Moscow: 1960.

Etzioni, Amitai, ed. *A Sociological Reader on Complex Organizations*. 2d ed. New York: Holt, Rinehart and Winston, 1969.

Feoktistov, E.M. *Vospominaniia E.M. Feoktistova: Za kulisami politiki i literatury 1848–1896. Leningrad: 1929.*

Florinsky, Michael T. *The End of the Russian Empire*. New York: Collier Books, 1961.

—— *Russia: A History and An Interpretation*. 2 vols. New York: Macmillan, 1953.

Fosdick, Raymond. *European Police Systems*. New York: The Century Co., 1915.

Friedrich, Carl J. *Tradition and Authority*. London: Macmillan, 1972.

Fuller, William C. Jr, *Civil-Military Conflict in Imperial Russia 1881–1914*. Princeton: Princeton University Press, 1985.

Futrell, Michael. *Northern-Underground: Episodes of Russian Revolutionary Transport and Communications through Scandanavia and Finland 1863–1917*. London: Faber & Faber, 1963.

Galai, Shmuel. *The Liberation Movement in Russia*. Cambridge: Cambridge University Press, 1973.

Gapon, G. *Istoriia moei zhizni*. Ed. A.A. Shilov. Leningrad: 1925.

—— *The Story of My Life*. London: George Bell & Sons, 1905.

Gerasimov, A.V. *Na lezvii s terroristami*. Paris: YMCA Press, 1985.

Gerson, Lennard D. *The Secret Police in Lenin's Russia*. Philadelphia: Temple University Press, 1976.

Gerth, H.H., and C. Wright Mills, eds. *From Max Weber: Essays in Sociology*. Oxford: Oxford University Press, 1958.

Gessen, V.M. *Iskliuchitel′noe polozhenie*. St Petersburg: 1908.

Getzler, Israel. *Martov: A Political Biography of a Russian Social Democrat*. Cambridge: Cambridge University Press, 1967.

Ginev, V.N. *Bor′ba za krest′ianstvo i krizis russkogo neonarodnichestva, 1902–1914 gg*. Leningrad: 1983.

Ginger, John. *Portraits of Mean Men: A Short History of the Protocols of the Elders of Zion.* London: Cobden-Sanderson, 1938.

Golder, Frank A., ed. *Documents of Russian History 1914–1917.* Trans. Emanuel Aronsberg. New York: The Century Co., 1927.

Goriushkin, L.M., ed. *Ssylka i obshchestvenno-politicheskaia zhizn' v sibiri (xvii–nachalo xx v.).* Novosibirsk: 1978.

Grave, B.B., ed. *Burzhuaziia nakanune Fevral'skoi Revoliutsii.* Moscow: 1927.

—— *K istorii klassovoi bor'by v Rossii v gody imperialisticheskoi voiny: Iiul'1914g.-fevral'1917g.* Moscow: 1926.

Guerassimov, Aleksandr Vasil'evich. *Tsarisme et Terrorisme, souvenirs du général Guerissimov.* Paris: Plon, 1934.

Gurko, Vladimir I. *Features and Figures of the Past: Government and Opinion in the Reign of Nicholas II.* Translated by Laura Matveev. The Hoover Library on War, Revolution, and Peace Publication no. 14. Stanford: Stanford University Press, 1939.

Haimson, Leopold H. *The Russian Marxists and the Origins of Bolshevism.* Boston: Beacon Press, 1966.

Harcave, Sidney. *First Blood: The Russian Revolution of 1905.* New York: Macmillan, 1964.

Hasegawa, Tsuyoshi. *The February Revolution: Petrograd, 1917.* Seattle: University of Washington Press, 1981.

Hingley, Ronald. *The Russian Secret Police : Muscovite, Imperial Russian and Soviet Political Security Operations.* New York: Simon and Schuster, 1970.

Hosking, Geoffrey A. *The Russian Constitutional Experiment: Government and Duma, 1907–1914.* Cambridge: Cambridge University Press, 1973.

Ianzhul, I.I. *Vospominaniia I.I. Ianzhula o perezhitom i videnom v 1864–1909 gg.* Pt. 2. St Petersburg: 1911.

Ingraham, Barton L. *Political Crime in Europe: A Comparative Study of France, Germany and England.* Berkeley and Los Angeles: University of California Press, 1979.

Isvolsky, Alexander. *Recollections of a Foreign Minister (Memoirs of Alexander Isvolsky).* Trans. Louis Seeger. New York: Doubleday, Page and Co., 1921.

Izgoev, A.S. *Russkoe obshchestvo i revoliutsiia : Izdanie zhurnala 'Russkaia Mysl'* Moscow: 1910.

Izoblichennye provokatory. Petrograd, [1917].

Judge, Edward H. *Plehve: Repression and Reform in Imperial Russia 1902–1904.* Syracuse: Syracuse University Press, 1983.

Keep, J.L.H. *The Rise of Social Democracy in Russia.* Oxford: Oxford University Press, 1963.

Kennan, George Frost. *Siberia and the Exile System.* 2 vols 1891. Reprint. New York: Russell and Russell, 1970.

Kingston, Charles. *A Gallery of Rogues.* London: Stanley Paul and Co., 1924.

Kirchheimer, Otto. *Political Justice: The Use of Legal Procedure for Political Ends.* Princeton: Princeton University Press, 1961.

Kizevetter, A.A. *Na rubezhe dvukh stoletii. Vospominaniia (1881–1914).* Prague: 1929.

Knight, Amy W. *The KGB: Police and Politics in the Soviet Union.* Rev. ed. Boston: Unwin Hyman, 1990.

Koenker, Diane. *Moscow Workers and the 1917 Revolution.* Princeton: Princeton University Press, 1981.

—— and William Rosenberg. *Strikes and Revolution, 1917.* Princeton: Princeton University Press, 1989.

Kokovtsov, Vladimir Nikolaevich. *Out of My Past: The Memoirs of Count Kokovtsov.* Ed. H.H. Fisher. Trans. Laura Matveev. The Hoover Library on War, Revolution, and Peace Publication no. 6. Stanford: Stanford University Press, 1935.

Koz′min, B.P. *S.V. Zubatov i ego korrespondenty.* Moscow: 1928.

Krovavaia politika i Belostokskii pogrom. Moscow: 1906.

Krupskaya, Nadezhda K. *Memoirs of Lenin.* Trans. E. Vernay. New York: International Publishers, 1930.

Kurlov, P.G. *Gibel′ imperatorskoi Rossii.* Berlin: 1923.

Lane, David. *The Roots of Russian Communism: A Social and Historical Study of Russian Social-Democracy 1898–1907.* Publications on Social History, issued by the International Institute of Social History, no. 6. Assen: Van Gorcum, 1969.

La Palombara, Joseph, ed. *Bureaucracy and Political Development.* Princeton: Princeton University Press, 1963.

La Porte, Maurice. *Histoire de l′Okhrana la police secrète des tsars, 1880–1917.* Paris: Payot, 1935.

Leggett, George. *The Cheka: Lenin's Political Police.* Oxford: Clarendon Press, 1981.

Leiberov, I.P. *Na shturm samoderzhaviia: Petrogradskii proletariat v gody pervoi mirovoi voiny i Fevral′skoi revoliutsii (Iiul′ 1914– Mart 1917g.).* Moscow: 1979.

Leikina – Svirskaia V.P. *Intelligentsiia v Rossii vo vtoroi polovine XIX veka.* Moscow: 1971.

—— *Russia intelligentsiia v 1900–1917 godakh.* Moscow: 1981.

Liang, Hsi-Huey. *The Berlin Police Force in the Weimar Republic.* Berkeley: University of California Press, 1970.

Lincoln, W. Bruce. *In the Vanguard of Reform: Russia's Enlightened Bureaucrats 1825–1861.* DeKalb: Northern Illinois University Press, 1982.

—— *The Great Reforms: Autocracy, Bureaucracy, and the Politics of Change in Imperial Russia.* DeKalb: Northern Illinois University Press, 1990.

Longuet, Jean and George Silber. *Terroristy i Okhranka.* Moscow: 1924.

Lopukhin, A.A. *Dokladnaia zapiska: Direktora departamenta politsii Lopukhina, razsmotrennaia v komitete ministrov... ianvaria 1905.* Geneva: 1905.

—— *Nastoiashchee i budushchee russkoi politsii.* Moscow: 1907.

—— *Otryvki iz vospominanii (Po povodu 'Vospominanii gr. S.IU. Vitte').* Moscow: 1923.

Lowenthal, Max. *The Federal Bureau of Investigation.* New York: Harcourt Brace Jovanovich, 1950.

Lüdtke, Alf. *Police and State in Prussia, 1815–1850.* Trans. Pete Burgess. Cambridge: Cambridge University Press, 1989.

McDaniel, Tim. *Autocracy, Capitalism and Revolution in Russia.* Berkeley and Los Angeles: University of California Press, 1988.

Maiskii, S. *Chernyi Kabinet: Iz vospominanii byvshego tsensora.* Petrograd: 1918.

Makhnovets, V.P. *Kak derzhat′ sebia na doprosakh.* Geneva: 1902.

Mannheim, Karl. *Ideology and Utopia: An Introduction to the Sociology of Knowledge.* London: Routledge and Kegan Paul, 1960.

Manning, Roberta Thompson. *The Crisis of the Old Order in Russia: Gentry and Government.* Princeton: Princeton University Press, 1982.

Martov IU., P. Maslov and A Potresov, eds. *Obshchestvennoe dvizhenie v Rossii v nachale xx-go veka.* 4 vols. St Petersburg: 1909–1914.

Martynov, A.P. *Moia sluzhba v Otdel′nom korpuse zhandarmov: Vospominaniia.* Stanford: Hoover Institution Press, 1972.

Mayer, Arno I. *The Persistence of the Old Regime: Europe to the Great War.* New York: Pantheon Books, 1981.

Mehlinger, Howard, and John M. Thompson. *Count Witte and the Tsarist Government in the 1905 Revolution.* Bloomington: Indiana University Press, 1972.

Melancon, Michael. *The Socialist Revolutionaries and the Russian Anti-War Movement, 1914–1917.* Columbus: Ohio State University Press, 1990.

Men′shchikov, L.P. *Okhrana i revoliutsiia. K istorii tainykh politicheskikh organizatsii sushchestvovavshikh vo vremena samoderzhaviia.* 3 vols in 2. Moscow: 1925–1932.

—— ed. Russkii politicheskii sysk za granitsei. Pt 1. Paris: 1914.

Merton, Robert K., ed. *Reader in Bureaucracy.* Glencoe: The Free Press, 1962.

Miller, Forrestt A. *Dmitrii Miliutin and the Reform Era.* Nashville: Vanderbilt University Press, 1968.

Miller-Fülöp, René. *Rasputin: The Holy Devil.* Trans F.S. Flint and D.F. Tait. London: G.D. Putnam's Sons, 1928.

Mommsen Wolfgang, and Gerhard Herschfeld, eds. *Social Protest, Violence and Terror in Nineteenth-and Twentieth-century Europe.* New York: St Martin's Press, 1982.

Monas, Sidney. *The Third Section: Police and Society under Nicholas I.* Cambridge: Harvard University Press, 1961.

Moskovskoe okhrannoe otdelenie. (1917).

Mosse, George L., ed. *Police Forces in History.* London: Sage Publications, 1975.

Mossolov, A.A. *At the Court of the Last Tsar.* Trans. by E.W. Dickes. London: Methuen and Co., 1935.

Murashov, S.I., ed. *Partiia Bol'shevikov v gody pervoi mirovoi voiny i sverzhenie monarkhii v Rossii.* Moscow: 1963.

Mushin, A. *Dimitrii Bogrov i ubiistvo Stolypina.* Paris: 1914.

Naimark, Norman M. *Terrorists and Social Democrats: The Russian Revolutionary Movement under Alexander III.* Cambridge: Harvard University Press, 1983.

Naumov, A.N. *Iz Utselevshikh Vospominanii 1868–1917.* 2 vols. New York: 1954.

Nikolaejewsky, Boris. *Aseff the Spy: The Russian Terrorist and Police Stool.* New York: Doubleday, Doran and Co., 1934.

—— *Aseff the Spy: Russian Terrorist and Police Stool.* 1934. Reprint. The Russian series, vol. 14. Hattiesburg Miss.: Academic International, 1969.

Novitskii, V.D. *Iz vospominanii zhandarma.* Leningrad: 1929.

Ob"edinenie russko-evreiskoi intelligentsii. *Aleksandr Isaevich Braudo: 1864–1924.* Paris: 1937.

Orlovsky, Daniel T. *The Limits of Reform: The Ministry of Internal Affairs in Imperial Russia 1802–1881.* Cambridge: Harvard University Press, 1981.

Orzhekhovskii, I.V. *Iz istorii vnutrennei politiki samoderzhaviia v 60-70-x godakh XIX veka.* Gorkii: 1974.

—— *Samoderzhavie protiv Revoliutsionnoi Rossii.* Moscow: 1982.

Otkrytoe pis'mo P.A. Stolypinu, russkomu prem'er ministru. Paris: 1911.

Ovsiannikov, N.N., ed. *Dekabr'skoe vosstanie v Moskve 1905g: Materialy po istorii Proletarskoi Revoliutsii.* Collection no. 3. Moscow: 1920.

—— ed. *Na zare rabochego dvizheniia v Moskve: Materialy po istorii Proletarskoi Revoliutsii,* collection no. 2. Moscow: 1919.

Paléologue, Maurice. *The Turning Point: Three Critical Years, 1904–1906. Translated by F. Appleby Holt. London: L. Hutchinson and Co., 1935.*

Pamiati Viacheslava Konstantinovicha Pleve (Sbornik). St Petersburg: 1904.

Partiia bol'shevikov v gody mirovoi imperialisticheskoi voiny:,Vtoraia revoliutsiia v Rossii 1914 god -Fevral' 1917 goda. Moscow: 1963.

Pavlov, P. *Agenty, zhandarmy, palachi: Po dokumentam.* Petrograd: 1922.

Payne, Howard C. *The Police State of Napoleon Bonaparte 1851–1860.* Seattle: University of Washington Press, 1966.

Pearson, Raymond. *The Russian Moderates and the Crisis of Tsarism 1914–1917.* London: Macmillan, 1977.

Perrie, Maureen. *The Agrarian Policy of the Russian Socialist-Revolutionary Party: From its origins through the revolution of 1905–1907.* Cambridge: Cambridge University Press, 1976.

Pinchuk, Ben Cion. *The Octobrists in the Third Duma 1907–1912.* Seattle: University of Washington Press, 1974.

Pintner Walter M., and D.K. Rowney, eds. *Russian Officialdom: The Bureaucratization of Russian Society from the Seventeenth to the Twentieth Century* Chapel Hill: The University of North Carolina Press, 1980.

Pipes, Richard, *Russia Under the Old Regime.* London: Weidenfeld & Nicolson, 1974; Penguin Books, 1977.

Porter, Bernard. *Plots and Paranoia: A History of Political Espionage in Britain, 1790–1988.* London: Unwin Hyman, 1989.

—— *The Origins of the Vigilant State: The London Metropolitan Police Special Branch Before the First World War.* London: Weidenfeld & Nicolson, 1987.

Poslednii samoderzhets: Ocherki zhizni i tsarstvovaniia Imperatora Rossii Nikolaia II-go. Berlin: n.d.

Radkey, Oliver H. *The Agrarian Foes of Bolshevism: Promise and Default of the Russian Socialist Revolutionaries February to October 1917.* New York: Columbia University Press, 1958.

Raeff, Marc. *Understanding Imperial Russia: State and Society in the Old Regime.* New York: Columbia University Press, 1984.

—— *The Well-Ordered Police State: Social and Institutional Change through Law in the Germanies and Russia 1600–1800.* New Haven: Yale University Press, 1983.

Revoliutsionnoe dvizhenie v Rossii Vesnoi i Letom 1905 goda, Aprel'-Sentiabr'. Vol. 1. Leningrad: 1957.

Robinson, Geroid Tanquary. *Rural Russia under the Old Regime.* New York: Macmillan, 1932; University of California, 1967.

Rogger Hans. *Jewish and Right-Wing Politics in Imperial Russia.* Berkeley and Los Angeles: University of California, 1986.

—— *Russia in the Age of Modernization and Revolution 1881–1917.* London and New York: Longman, 1983.

Rowney, Don K. *Transition to Technocracy: The Structural Origins of the Soviet Administrative State.* Ithaca: Cornell University Press, 1989.

Rudé, George. *Ideology and Popular Protest.* London: Lawrence and Wisehart, 1980.

Russia. Chrezychainaia Sledstvennaia Komissiia. *Padenie Tsarskogo Rezhima: Stenograficheskie otchety doprosov i pokazanii dannykh v 1917g. v Chrezvychainoi Sledstvennoi Komissii Vremennogo Pravitel'stva.* 7 vols. Moscow-Leningrad: 1924–1927.

Russia. Departamenta politsii. *Zapiska po istorii revoliutsionnago dvizheniia v Rossii (do 1913 goda).* St Petersburg: 1913.

Russia. Glavnoe tiuremnoe upravlenie. *Ssylka v Sibir': Ocherk eia istorii i sovremennago polozheniia.* St Petersburg: 1900.

Russia. Gosudarstvennaia Duma 1st 1906. *Stenografichecheskie otchety.* Vol. 2. St Petersburg: 1906.

Russia. Gosudarstvennaia Duma 3d 1909. *Zapros ob Azefe v Gosudarstvennoi dume (zasedaniia 50 i 51 oe): Po stenograficheskomu otchetu.* St Petersburg: 1909.

Russia. Gosudarstvennyi Sovet. Pervyi departament. *Zhurnaly I departamenta Gosudarstvennago soveta*, no. 5 (20 March 1912); no. 13 (11 May 1912).

Russia. Inspektorskii Otdela Sobstvennoi E.I.V. Kantseliarii. *Spisok Grazhdanskim Chinam Chetvertago Klassa.* St Petersburg: 1906.

Russia. Inspektorskii Otdela Sobstvennoi E.I.V. Kantseliarii. *Spisok Grazhdanskim Chinam Pervykh Trekh Klassov.* St Petersburg: 1906.

Russia. MVD. *Spisok Vysshikh Chinov Tsentral'nykh i Mestnykh ustanovlenii Ministerstva Vnutrennikh Del.* Pt 1. St Petersburg: 1905.

Rutenberg, P.I. *Ubiistvo Gapona: Zapiska P.I. Rutenberga.* Leningrad: 1925.

Sablinsky, Walter. *The Road to Bloody Sunday: Father Gapon and the St Petersburg Massacre of 1905.* Princeton: Princeton University Press, 1976.

Savinkov, Boris. *Memoirs of a Terrorist.* Trans. Joseph Shaplen. New York: Albert and Charles Boni, 1931.

Schapiro, Leonard. *The Communist Party of the Soviet Union.* New York: Random House, 1960.

Schleifman, Nurit. *Undercover Agents in the Russian Revolutionary Movement: The SR Party 1902–1914.* Basingstoke: Macmillan, 1988.

Schneiderman, Jeremiah. *Sergei Zubatov and Revolutionary Marxism: The Struggle for the Working Class in Tsarist Russia.* Ithaca: Cornell University Press, 1976.

Schwarz Solomon M. *The Russian Revolution of 1905: The Workers' Movement and the Formation of Bolshevism and Menshevism.* Trans. Gertrude Vakar. Chicago: University of Chicago Press, 1967.

Selznick, Philip. *TVA and the Grass Roots: A Study in the Sociology of Formal Organizations.* Berkeley and Los Angeles: University of California Press, 1953.

Semennikov, V.P., ed. *Revoluitsiia 1905 goda i samoderzhavie.* Leningrad: 1928.

Semenoff, E.K. *The Russian Government and the Massacres.* London: John Murray, 1907.

Senn, Alfred Erich. *The Russian Revolution in Switzerland 1914–1917.* Madison: The University of Wisconsin Press, 1971.

Serebrennikov, A., comp. *Ubiistvo Stolypina: Sviditel'stva i dokumenty.* New York: Telex, 1986.

Serge, Victor. *Memoirs of a Revolutionary, 1901–1941.* Trans. Peter Sedgwick. New York: Oxford University Press, 1963.

Shchegolev, P.E., ed. *Provokator: Vospominaniia i dokumenty o razoblachenii Azefa.* Leningrad: 1929.

Shanin, Teodor. *Russia, 1905–07: Revolution as a Moment of Truth.* New Haven: Yale University Press, 1986.

Shatsillo, K.F. *1905-i god.* Moscow: 1980.

Shepelev, L.E. *Otmenennye istoriei chiny, zvaniia i tituly v rossiiskoi imperii.* Leningrad: 1977.

Shipov, D.N. *Vospominaniia i dumy o perezhitom.* Moscow: 1918.

Shuster, U.A. Peterburgskie rabochie v 1905–1907. Leningrad: 1976.

Simon, Herbert A. *Administrative Behavior: A Study in Decision-Making Processes in Administrative Organizations.* 2d. ed. New York: The Free Press, 1957.

—— and James G. March. *Organizations.* New York: John Wiley & Sons, 1958.

Sinel, Allen. *The Classroom and the Chancellery: State Educational Reform in Russia under Count Dmitry Tolstoi.* Cambridge: Harvard University Press, 1973.

Smith, Edward Ellis, comp. *The Okhrana, The Russian Department of Police: A Bibliography.* Hoover Institution Bibliographical Series, no. 33. Stanford: Hoover Institution Press, 1967.

Sovetskaia Istoricheskaia Entsiklopediia. Vol. 5. Moscow: 1964.

Spiridovich, A.I. *Istoriia bol'shevizma v Rossii: Ot vozniknoveniia do zakhvata vlasti 1883–1903–1917.* Paris: 1922.

—— *Les derniéres années de la cour de Tsarskoe-Sélo.* Trans. M. Jeanson. 2 vols. Paris: 1928–1929.

—— *Revoliutsionnoe dvizhenie v Rossii: Rossiiskaia Sotsial-Demokraticheskaia Rabochaia Partiia.* Pt. 1. St Petersburg: 1914.

—— *Revoliutsionnoe dvizhenie v Rossii: Partiia Sotsialistov-Revoliutsionerov i eia predshestvenniki.* Pt. 2. Petrograd: 1916.

Squire, P.S. *The Third Department: The Political Police in the Russia of Nicholas I.* Cambridge: Cambridge University Press, 1968.

Starr, S. Frederick. *Decentralization and Self-Government in Russia 1830–1870.* Princeton: Princeton University Press, 1972.

Stepniak [Kravchinskii, Sergei M.]. *Underground Russia.* New York: n.d.

Suvorin, A.S. *Dnevnik A.S. Suvorina.* Moscow: 1923.

Svod zakonov rossiiskoi imperii. 16 vols. St Petersburg: 1892.

Swain, Geoffrey. *Russian Social Democracy and the Legal Labour Movement, 1906–1914.* London: Macmillan, 1983.

Szeftel, Marc. *The Russian Constitution of April 23, 1906: Political Institutions of the Duma Monarchy.* Studies Presented to the International Commission for the History of Representation and Parliamentary Institutions, no. 61. Brussells: Librairie Encyclopédique, 1976.

Tekhnika bol'shevistskogo podpol'ia: Sbornik statei i vospominanii. 2d ed. Moscow: 1925.

Tikhomirov, L. *Vospominaniia L'va Tikhomirova.* Moscow: 1927.

Troitskii, N.A. *Bezumstvo khrabrykh: Russkie revoliutsionery i karatel'naia politika tsarizma, 1866–1882 gg.* Moscow: 1978.

—— *Tsarizm pod sudom progressivnoi obshchestvennosti, 1866–1895gg.* Moscow: 1979.

Tsiavlovskii, M.A., ed. *Bol'sheviki: Dokumenty po istorii bol'shevizma s 1903 po 1916 god. byvsh. Moskovskogo okhrannago otdeleniia. (Materialy po istorii obshchestvennago i revoliutsionnago dvizheniia v Rossii.* Vol. 1. Moscow: 1918.

Ular, Alexander. *Russia from Within.* London: W. Heinemann, 1905.

Urussov, Sergei D. *Memoirs of a Russian Governor.* Trans. Herman Rosenthal. London: Harper and Brothers, 1908.

Vasilyev, A.T. *The Ochrana: The Russian Secret Police*. Trans. René Fülöp-Miller. Philadelphia: J.P. Lipincott, 1930.

—— *The Okhrana: The Russian Secret Police*. Trans. René Fülöp-Miller. London: George G. Harrap, 1930.

Viktorov, V.P., ed. *Soiuz Russkogo Naroda: Po materialom chrezvychainoi sledstvennoi komissii vremennogo pravitel'stva 1917g*. Moscow-Leningrad: 1929.

Volkov, A. *Petrogradskoe okhrannoe otdelenie*. Petrograd: 1917.

Von Bock, Maria Petrovna. *Reminiscences of My Father, Peter A. Stolypin*. Ed. and Trans. by Margaret Potoski. Metheun, N.J.: The Scarecrow Press, 1970.

Von Laue, Theodore H. *Sergei Witte and the Industrialization of Russia*, New York: Atheneum, 1969.

Vserossiiskaia politicheskaia stachka v Oktiabre 1905 goda. Moscow: 1955.

Walkin, Jacob. *The Rise of Democracy in Pre-Revolutionary Russia: Political and Social Institutions Under the Last Three Tsars*. New York: Frederick A. Praeger, 1962.

Weissman, Neil B. *Reform in Tsarist Russia: The State Bureaucracy and Local Government, 1900–1914*. New Brunswick: Rutgers University Press, 1981.

Whelan, Heidi. *Alexander III and the State Council: Bureaucracy and Counter-Reform in Late Imperial Russia*. New Brunswick: Rutgers University Press, 1981.

Witte, Sergei IU. *Vospominaniia: Tsarstvovanie Nikolaia II*. 2 vols. Berlin: 1922.

—— *Vospominaniia*. 3 vols. Moscow: 1960.

Wolfe, Bertram D. *Three Who Made a Revolution*. 4th rev. ed. New York: Dell Publishing Co., 1964.

Wolin, Simon, and Robert Slusser. *The Soviet Secret Police*. New York: Frederick A. Praeger, 1957.

Wortman, Richard S. *The Development of a Russian Legal Consciousness*. Chicago: University of Chicago Press, 1976.

Yaney, George L. *The Systematization of Russian Government: Social Evolution in the Domestic Administration of Imperial Russia 1711–1905*. Urbana: University of Illinois, 1973.

Za kulisami okhrannago otdeleniia: S dnevnikom provokatora pis'mami okhrannikov, tainymi instruktsiiami. Berlin: 1910.

Zaionchkovskii, P.A. *Krizis samoderzhaviia na rubezhe 1870–1880 godov*. Moscow: 1964.

—— *Pravitel'stvennyi apparat samoderzhavnoi Rossii v XIXv*. Moscow: 1978.

—— *Rossiiskoe samoderzhavie v kontse XIX stoletiia, (politicheskaia reaktsiia 80-X – nachala 90-X godov)*. Moscow: 1970.

—— *Samoderzhavie i russkaia armiia na rubezhe XIX-XX stoletii*. Moscow: 1973.

Zavarzin, P.P. *Rabota tainoi politsii*. Paris: 1924.

—— *Zhandarmy i revoliutsionery: Vospominaniia*. Paris: 1930.

(b) Articles

A.P. 'Departament politsii v 1892–1908 (Iz vospominanii chinovnika)'. *Byloe*, n.s. nos 5/6 [27/28] (November/December 1917): 17–24.

'Agrarnoe dvizhenie v Smolenskoi gubernii v 1900 gg.' *Krasnyi Arkhiv* 74 (1936): 92–141.

Aleksandrov F.L., and L.M. Shalagnova. 'Den′ 9 Ianvaria v 1908–1917 (Obzor dokumentov TsGIAM'. *Istoricheskii Arkhiv* no. 1 (1958): 212–21.

'Arest dumskoi "piaterki" v 1914 g.. S predisloviem A. Badaeva'. *Krasnyi Arkhiv* 64 (1934): 37–51.

Armstrong, J. 'Old Regime Governors: Bureaucrats and Patrimonial Attributes'. *Comparative Studies in Society and History 14 (January 1972): 2–29.*

—— 'Tsarist and Soviet Elite Administrators'. *Slavic Review* 31 (March 1972): 1–28.

Asin, T. 'K statistike arestovannykh i ssyl′nykh'. *Russkoe Bogatstvo*, pt 2 (October, 1906): 1–37.

Avrekh A. IA. 'Dokumenty Departamenta politsii kak ustochnik po izucheniiu liberal′no – oppozitsionnogo dvizheniia v gody pervoi mirovoi voiny'. *Istoriia SSSR*, 1987, no. 6: 32–49.

Badaev, A. 'Dumskaia fraktsiia bol′shevikov – "piaterka" v russko – germanskuiu voinu: (Po vospominaniiam i arkhivnym dannym)'. *Krasnaia Letopis* no. 10 (1924): 86–101.

Bakai, M.E. 'Iz vospominanii M.E. Bakaia'. *Byloe*, Paris, nos 11/12 (1909): 162–7.

—— 'Iz vospominanii M.E. Bakaia: Provokatory i provokatsiia'. *Byloe*, Paris, no. 8 (1909): 99–136.

—— 'Iz vospominanii M.E. Bakaia: O chernykh kabinetakh v Rossii'. *Byloe*, Paris, no. 7 (1908): 119–33.

—— 'Iz zapisok M.E. Bakaia'. *Byloe*, Paris, nos 9/10 (1909): 191–211.

Bassow, Whitman. 'The Pre-Revolutionary *Pravda* and Tsarist Censorship'. *American Slavic and East European Review* 13 (1954): 47–65.

Bennet, Helju A. 'Evolution of the Meanings of *Chin*: An Introduction to the Russian Institution of Rank Ordering and Niche Assignment from the Time of Peter the Great's Table of Ranks to the Bolshevik Revolution'. *California Slavic Studies* 10 (1977): 1–43.

Blau Peter M. 'The Dynamics of Bureaucracy'. In *A Sociological Reader on Complex Organizations.* Edited by Amitai Etzioni, 387–97. 2d ed. New York: Holt, Rinehart and Winston, 1969.

Bobrovskaia, Tsetlina, and Osip Piatnitskii. 'Zagranichnyi sysk vokrug Lenina'. *Krasnaia Letopis′*, no. 13 (1925): 156–64.

Bonnell, Victoria E. 'Radical Politics and Organized Labor in Pre-Revolutionary Moscow 1905–1914'. *Journal of Social History* 12 (1978): 282–300.

'Bor'ba S.IU. Witte s agrarnoi revoliutsiei'. *Krasnyi Arkhiv* 31 (1928): 81–102.

'Bor'ba Tsarskogo pravitel'stva s "buistvom i svoevoliem krest'ian"'. *Rabochee Delo*, 1899, no. 1: 40–3.

Brovtsnova, E.P. 'Karatel'noe zakonodatel'stvo tsarizma v bor'ba s Revoliutsiei 1905–1907 godov'. *Istoriia SSSR*, 1975, no. 5: 110–17.

Burtsev, V. 'Kak Departament Politsii otpustil Lenina zagranitsu dlia bolshevitskoi [*sic!*] propagandy.' *Byloe*, Paris, n.s. no. 2 (1933): 85–92.

—— 'Lenine and Malinovsky'. *Struggling Russia* 1 (May 1919): 138–40.

Byrnes, Robert F., 'Pobedonostsev on the Instruments of Russian Government'. In *Continuity and Change in Russian and Soviet Thought.* Edited by Ernest J. Simmons, 113–28. Cambridge: Harvard University Press, 1955.

Cherkunov, A.N. 'Provokator Vladislav Feliksovich Gabel': (Iz vospominanii smolenskogo katorzhanina)'. *Katorga i Ssylka*, no. 22 (1926): 195–206.

Christian, David. 'The Supervisory Function in Russian and Soviet History'. *Slavic Review* 41 (1982): 73–90.

'D.F. Trepov v bor'be s obshchestvennost'iu'. *Russkoe Proshloe*, 1923, no. 4: 42–54.

'Departament politsii i vopros ob amnistii v 1913 godu'. *Katorga i Ssylka*, no. 89 (1932): 54–61.

Diakin V.S. 'The Leadership Crisis in Russia on the Eve of the February Revolution'. Translated by Michael S. Melanson. *Soviet Studies in History* 23 (Summer 1984): 10–37.

'Dnevnik Borisa Nikol'skogo (1905–1907)'. *Krasnyi Arkhiv* 63 (1934): 55–97.

'Dnevnik G.O. Raukha'. *Krasnyi Arkhiv* 19 (1926): 83–109.

'Doklad direktora departamenta politsii Lopukhina ministru vnutrennikh del o sobytiiakh 9-do ianvaria'. *Krasnaia Letopis'*, no. 1 (1922): 330–8.

'Doklad P. Rachkovskago Zavedyiushchego zagranichnoi agentury'. *Istoriko-Revoliutsionnyi Sbornik* 2 (1924): 191, 247–53.

'Doneseniia Evno Azefa (Perepiska Azefa s Rataevym v 1903–1905 gg.)'. *Byloe*, n.s. no. 1 [23] (July 1917): 196–228.

'Doneseniia iz Berlina S.S. Tatishcheva V.K. Pleve v 1904: Soobshchil E.V. Tarle'. *Krasnyi Arkhiv* 17 (1926): 186–92.

'Donosy tsariu o russkoi emigratsii.' *Byloe*, Paris, nos 11/12 (July/August 1909): 138–61.

Drabkina, F. 'Tsarskoe pravitel'stvo i "Pravda" '. *Istoricheskii Zhurnal* 7 (March/April 1937): 115–23.

'Dva dokumenta iz istorii zubatovshchiny'. *Krasnyi Arkhiv* 19 (1926): 210–11.

Eckstein, Harry. 'On the Etiology of Internal Wars'. *History and Theory* 4 (1965): 133–63.

Eisenstadt, S.N. 'Bureaucracy and Bureaucratization: A Trend Report'. *Current Sociology* 7 (1958): 99–164.

Elwood, Ralph Carter. 'Lenin and Pravda 1912–1914'. *Slavic Review* 31 (June 1972): 355–80.

'Epokha reaktsii (1908–1910)'. *Krasnyi Arkhiv* 62 (1934): 215–22.

Erenfel'd B.K. ' "Delo Malinovskogo" '. *Voprosy Istorii*, 1965, no. 7: 106–15.

'Evrei v Moskve: (Po neopublikovannym dokumentam)'. *Byloe*, St Petersburg, no. 9 [21] (September 1907): 153–68.

Falaev, N.I. Rossiia pod okhranoi'. *Byloe*, St Petersburg, no. 10 [22] (October 1907): 1–43.

Ferenczi, Caspar. 'Freedom of the Press under the Old Regime, 1905–1914'. In *Civil Rights in Imperial Russia.* Edited by Olga Crisp and Linda Edmondson, 191–214. Oxford: Clarendon Press, 1989.

'Fevral'skaia revoliutsiia i okhrannoe otdelenie'. *Byloe*, n.s. no. 1 [29] (January 1918): 158–76.

Fitzpatrick, Sheila. 'The Civil War as a Formative Experience'. In *Bolshevik Culture.* Edited by Abbot Gleason, Peter Kenez, and Richard Stites, 57–76. Bloomington: Indiana University Press, 1985.

—— 'The Legacy of the Civil War'. In *Party, State and Society in the Russian Civil War: Explorations in Social History.* Edited by Diane P. Koenker, William G. Rosenberg and Ronald Grigor Suny, 385–98. Bloomington: Indiana University Press, 1989.

'G.V. Plekhanov i shpionskie zabavy: Soobshchil S.N. Valk'. *Krasnyi Arkhiv* 5 (1924): 263–66.

'G.V. Plekhanov: Materialy sobrannye departamentom politsii'. *Byloe*, n.s. 3 [31] (March 1918): 229–36.

Gan, L. 'Ubiistvo P.A. Stolypina'. Parts 1, 2. *Istoricheskii Vestnik* 135 (January 1914): 960–97; 136 (April 1914): 192–215.

'Gapon i Graf Witte'. *Byloe*, n.s. no. 1 [29] (1925): 15–27.

'Gapon i okhrannoe otdelenie do 1905 goda'. *Byloe*, n.s. no. 1 [29] (1925): 28–45.

Geertz, Clifford. 'Thick Description: Toward an Interpretive Theory of Culture'. In *The Interpretation of Cultures. Selected Essays by Clifford Geertz*, 1–30. New York: Basic Books, 1973.

George, Mark. 'Liberal Opposition in Wartime Russia: A Case Study of the Town and Zemstvo Unions, 1914–1917'. *The Slavonic and East European Review* 65 (1987): 371–90.

Gerschenkron, Alexander, 'Soviet Marxism and Absolutism'. *Slavic Review* 30 (December 1971): 853–69.

Glinskii, B.B. 'Period tverdoi vlasti'. Parts 1–3. *Istoricheskii Vestnik* 127 (January–March 1912): 667–90; 129 (July–September 1912): 271–304, 659–93; 130 (October–December 1912): 297–322, 767–810, 1164–90.

Grekov, B.I., K.F. Shatsillo, and V.V. Shelokhaev 'Evoliutsiia politicheskoi struktury Rossii v kontse xix – nachale xx veka (1895–1913)'. *Istoriia SSSR*, 1988, no. 5: 36–53.

Haimson, Leopold, 'The Problem of Social Stability in Urban Russia 1905–1917'. Parts 1–2. *Slavic Review* 23 (December 1964): 619–42; 24 (March 1965): 1–22.

Hamm, Michael F. 'Liberal Politics in Wartime Russia: An Analysis of the Progressive Bloc'. *Slavic Review* 33 (1974): 453–68.

'Iz bumag D.F. Trepova'. *Krasnyi Arkhiv* 11–12 (1925): 448–66.

'Iz istorii inostrannogo kapitala v Rossii'. *Krasnyi Arkhiv* 25 (1927): 189–98.

'Iz istorii rabochego dvizheniia nakanune mirovoi voiny'. *Krasnyi Arkhiv* 64 (1934): 52–72.

'Iz istorii rabochego dvizheniia vo vremia mirovoi voiny'. *Krasnyi Arkhiv* 67 (1934): 5–27.

'Iz istorii Ural′skikh zavodov'. *Krasnyi Arkhiv* 74 (1936): 66–91.

'Iz pisem L.A. Rataeva: L.A. Rataev – N.P. Zuevu'. *Byloe*, n.s. no. 1 [23] (July 1917): 144–8.

'Iz proshlago russkoi politicheskoi politsii zagranitsei'. *Na Chuzhoi Storone* 10 (1925): 181–5.

K.D. 'Russkie shpiony pered sudom germanskago parlamenta'. *Osvobozhdenie*, nos. 39/40 (January 1904): 274–5.

'K istorii aresta i suda nad sotsial demokraticheskoi fraktsiei II Gosudarstvennoi Dumy'. *Kransyi Arkhiv* 16 (1926): 76–117.

'K istorii "Krovavogo voskresn′ia" v Peterburge : Doklady prokurora Peterburgkskoi sudebnoi palaty E.I. Vuicha ministru iustitsii'. *Krasnyi Arkhiv* 68 (1935): 39–64.

'K istorii "Sobranie Russkikh Fabrichno Zavodskikh Rabochikh g. s. Peterburga": Arkhivnye dokumenty'. *Krasnaia Letopis′* no. 1 (1922): 288–329.

'K istorii zubatovshchiny v Moskve: (Po neizdannym protokolam zubatovskikh soveshchanii)'. *Istoriia Proletariata SSSR*, Collection 2 (1930): 169–232.

'Kak gotovilsia pervyi s"ezd RS-DRP'. *Krasnaia Letopis′*, no. 25 (1928): 13–22.

'Kak "Iskra" zavoevala Peterburg (1901–1902 gg.)'. *Krasnaia Letopis′*, no. 45 (1925): 216–43.

Kantor R.M. 'Frantsuzkaia okhranka o russkikh emigrantakh' *Katorga i Ssylka*, no. 31 (1927): 81–7.

—— 'K istorii chernykh kabinetov'. *Katorga i Ssylka*, no. 37 (1927): 90–9.

'Kar′era P.I. Rachkovskago. Dokumenty'. *Byloe*, n.s. no. 2 [30] (February 1918): 78–87.

Keenan, Edward L. 'Muscovite Political Folkways'. *The Russian Review* 45 (April 1986): 115–81.

Keep, J.H. 'Light and Shade in the History of the Russian Adminstration'. *Canadian Slavic Studies* 6 (Spring 1972): 1–9.

—— 'Programming the Past : Imperial Russian Bureaucracy and Society Under the Scrutiny of Mr George Yaney'. *Canadian-American Slavic Studies* 8 (Winter 1974): 569–80.

Kenez, Peter. 'A Profile of the Pre-revolutionary Officer Corps'. *California Slavic Studies* 8 (1973): 121–58.

Kennan, George F., 'The Breakdown of the Tsarist Autocracy'. In *Revolutionary Russia.* Edited by Richard Pipes, 1–25. New York: Harvard University Press, 1968.

Khaziakhmetov, E.SH. 'Organizatsiia pobedov politcheskikh ssyl'nkh iz Sibiri v 1906–1917 godakh'. In *Ssylka i obshchestvenno-politicheskaia zhizn' v Sibiri (XVIII – nachalo XXv).* Edited by L.M. Goriushkin, 54–91. Novosibirsk: 1978.

Kimbal, Alan. 'The Harassment of Russian Revolutionaries Abroad : The London Trial of Vladimir Burtsev in 1898.' *Oxford Slavonic Papers*, n.s.. Vol. 6. Edited by Robert Auty and J.L.I. Fennell (New York: Oxford University Press, 1973), 48–64.

Kipp, Jacob W., and W. Bruce Lincoln. 'Autocracy and Reform: Bureaucratic Absolutism and Political Modernization in Nineteenth Century Russia'. *Russian History* 6 (1979): 1–21.

Koliari, Edoardo. 'Russkaia tainaia politsiia v Italii'. *Byloe*, n.s. no. 25 (1924): 130–54.

Korelin, A.P., 'Krakh Ideologii "Politseiskogo sotsializma" v Tsarskoi Rossii'. *Istoricheskie Zapiski* 92 (1973): 109–52.

—— 'Russkii "politseiskii sotsializma": (Zubatovshchina).' *Voprosy Istorii*, 1968, no. 10: 41–58.

Kozlovskii, Iv. 'Podpol'e i katorga: (Peterburg v gody imperialisticheskoi voiny)'. *Krasnaia Letopis'*, nos. 54/55 (1933): 184–93.

Koznov, A.P. 'Bor'ba bol'shevikov s podryvnoi agenturoi tsarizma v period reaktsii (1907–1910 g.g.)'. *Voprosy Istorii KPSS*, 1986, no. 12: 59–74.

'Krest'ianskoe dvizhenie 1905 goda: Dokladnaia zapiska departamenta politsii predsedatel'iu soveta ministrov S.IU. Vitte'. *Krasnyi Arkhiv* 9 (1925): 66–93.

'Krest'ianskoe dvizhenie v kontse XIXv (1881–1894 gg.)'. *Krasnyi Arkhiv* 89/90 (1938): 208–57.

Kulakov, A.A. 'O trekh predatel'iakh (El'ko, Ostroumov, Geier)'. *Katorga i Ssylka*, no. 67 (1930): 79–88.

Kuropatkin, A.N. 'Dnevnik A.N. Kuropatkina'. *Krasnyi Arkhiv*, 2 (1922): 5–112.

L.B. 'Franko-russkoe shpionstvo i franko-russkii soiuz'. *Byloe*, Paris, no. 8 (1908): 58–64.

La Palombara, Joseph. 'Alternative Strategies for Developing Administrative Capabilities in Emerging Nations'. In *Frontiers of Development Administration.* Edited by Fred W. Riggs, 171–226. Durham: Duke University Press, 1971.

Leggett, George H. 'Lenin, Terror and Political Police'. *Survey* 21 (1975): 157–87.

—— 'The Cheka and a Crisis of Communist Conscience'. *Survey* 25 (1980): 122–37.

Lemke, Mikhail, 'Nash zagranichnyi sysk 1881–1883'. *Krasnaia Letopis'*, no 5 (1922): 67–84.

Levin, Alfred. 'The Shornikova Affair'. *The Slavonic and East European Review* 21 (1943): 1–19.

Lewin, Moshe. 'The Civil War: Dynamics and Legacy'. In *Party, State, and Society in the Russian Civil War: Explorations in Social History.* Edited by Diane P. Koenker, William G. Rosenberg, and Ronald Grigor Suny, 399–423. Bloomington: Indiana University Press, 1989.

Lieven, Dominic, 'Bureaucratic Authoritarianism in Late Imperial Russia: The Personality, Career and Opinions of P.N. Durnovo'. *The Historical Journal* 26 (1983): 391–402.

Lieven, Dominic C.B. 'Russian Senior Officialdom under Nicholas II: Careers and Mentalities'. *Jarbücher für Geschichte Osteuropas* 32 (1984): 199–223.

Lieven, D.C.B. 'Stereotyping an Elite: The Appointed Members of the State Council, 1894–1914'. *The Slavonic and East European Review* 63 (April 1985): 244–72.

Lincoln, W.B. 'Russia's Enlightened Bureaucrats and the Problem of State Reform 1848–1856'. *Cahiers du monde Russe et Sovietique.* 12 (October–December 1971): 410–21.

—— 'The Circle of the Grand Duchess Yelena Pavlovna 1847–1861'. *Slavonic and East European Review*, no. 112 (July 1970): 373–87.

—— 'The Genesis of an Enlightened Bureaucracy in Russia 1825–1856'. *Järburcher für Geschichte Osteuropas* 20 (September 1972): 321–30.

—— 'The Ministers of Nicholas I: A Brief Inquiry Into Their Backgrounds and Service Careers'. *Russian Review* 34 (July 1975): 308–23.

Lipkhin, A. 'Nakanune protsessa bol′shevistskoi fraktsii IV Gosudarstvennoi dumy'. *Katorga i Ssylka*, no. 30 (1924): 49–67.

—— 'Provokator Nikulin-Mikulin'. *Katorga i Ssylka*, no. 23 (1926): 98–119.

Long, James William. 'Organized Protest Against the 1906 Russian Loan'. *Cahiers du monde russe et sovietique* 13 (January–March 1972): 23–39.

—— 'Russian Manipulation of the French Press 1904–1906'. *Slavic Review* 31 (June 1972): 343–54.

Liubimov, D.N. 'Gapon i 9 ianvaria'. Parts 1, 2. *Voprosy Istorii*, 1965, no. 8: 121–30; no. 9: 114–21.

McFarlin, H.A. 'Recruitment Norms for the Russian Civil Service in 1833 : The Chancery Clerkship'. *Sociatas: A Review of Social History* 3 (Winter 1973): 61–73.

—— 'The Extension of the Imperial Russian Civil Service to the Lowest Office Workers: The Creation of the Chancery Clerkship, 1827–1833'. *Russian History* 1 (1974): 1–17.

—— ' "The Overcoat" As a Civil Service Episode'. *Canadian-American Slavic Studies.* 13 (Fall 1979): 235–53.

Maiskii, B. Iu. 'Stolypinshchina i konets Stolypina'. Parts 1, 2. *Voprosy Istorii*, 1966, no. 1: 134–44; no. 2: 123–40.

Miroliubov, A.A. 'Dokumenty po istorii Departamenta politsii perioda pervoi mirovoi voiny'. *Sovetskie Arkhivy*, 1988, no. 3: 80–4.

'Mobilizatsiia reaktsii v 1906 g.'. *Krasnyi Arkhiv* 32 (1929), 158–82.

Monas, Sidney. 'The Political Police: The Dream of a Beautiful Autocracy'. In *The Transformation of Russian Society.* Edited by Cyril Black, 164–90. Cambridge: Harvard University Press, 1967.

'Moskovskaia okhranka v 1915 g.'. *Golos Minuvshago*, nos 1–3 (January–March 1918): 251–87.

Mosse, W.E. 'Aspects of the Tsarist Bureaucracy: the State Council in the late Nineteenth Century'. *The English Historical Review*, 95 (April 1980): 268–92.

—— 'Russian Bureaucracy at the End of the Ancien Regime : The Imperial State Council, 1897–1915'. *Slavic Review* 29 (December 1980): 616–32.

'Na zare 1905 goda: (Stranichka raboty Peterburgskoi organizatsii R.S. – D.R.P. po dannym departamenta politsii)'. *Krasnaia Letopis'*, no. 12 (1925): 157–70.

'Nalet P.I. Rachkovskago na narodovol'cheskuiu tipografiiu'. *Byloe*, n.s. no. 1 [23] (July 1917): 277–83.

'Nelegal'naia rabota bol'shevistskoi fraktsii IV Gosudarstvennoi dumy: (Po dokumenty departamenta politsii'. *Krasnyi Arkhiv* 77 (1936): 61–90.

'9 ianvera 1905g.: Soobshchil B.A. Romanov'. *Krasnyi Arkhiv* 11–12 (1925): 1–25.

Novikov, V.I. 'Leninskaia "Iskra" v bor'be s Zubatovshchinoi'. *Voprosy Istorii*, 1974, no. 8: 24–35.

'Novoe o zubatovshchine: Soobshchil S. Piontkovskii'. *Krasnyi Arkhiv* 1 (1922): 289–314.

'Novyi pod"em rabochego dvizheniia'. *Krasnyi Arkhiv* 62 (1934): 223–48.

'O tom kak s neterpeniem zhdal prikhoda russkikh voisk v Krakov: (Iz arkhiva departamenta politsii)'. *Krasnaia Letopis'*, no. 33 (1929): 5–7.

'Obshchee polozhenie k iiuliu 1916 g.: Zapiska departamenta politsii'. *Byloe*, n.s. no. 3 [31] (March 1918): 24–30.

'Obvinitel'nyi akt: Ob otstavnom deistvitel'nom statskom sovetnike Aleksee Aleksandroviche Lopukhine, obviniaemom v gosudarstvennom prestuplenii'. *Byloe*, Paris, nos 9/10 (1909): 218–36.

'Okhrannikh ob areste uchastnikov i marta 1887 goda'. *Krasnyi Arkhiv* 9 (1925): 297–9.

Orlovsky, Daniel T. 'Political Clientelism in Russia: The Historical Perspective'. In *Leadership Selection and Patron – Client Relations in the USSR and Yugoslavia.* Edited by T.H. Rigby and Bohdan Harasymiri, 174–99. London: George Allen and Unwin, 1983.

—— 'Recent Studies on the Russian Bureaucracy'. *Russian Review* 35 (October 1976): 448–67.

—— 'State Building in the Civil War Era: The Role of the Lower-Middle Strata'. In *Party, State, and Society in the Russian Civil War: Explorations in Social History.* Edited by Diane P. Koenker, William G. Rosenberg, and Ronald Grigor Suny, 180–209. Bloomington: Indiana University Press, 1989.

Or-vskii, V. 'Iz zapisok politseiskago ofitsera'. *Na Chuzhoi Storone*, no. 14 (1925): 143–52.

Orzhekhovskii, I.V. 'Tret'e otdelenie'. *Voprosy Istorii*, no. 2 (1972): 109–20.

Osorgin, M.A. 'Dekabr'skoe vozstanie 1905 g. v Moskve v opisanii zhandarma'. *Golos Minuvshago*, nos 7/8 (July/August 1917): 351–60.

P. Shch. 'K delu 1 marta 1881 goda: Neizdannye doklady grafa Loris-Melikova, V.K. Pleve, A.V. Komarova'. *Byloe*, n.s. nos 4/5 [32/33] (April/May 1918): 12–69.

Palat, Madhavan K. 'Police Socialism in Tsarist Russia, 1900–1905'. *Studies in History*, n.s. 2 (January–June 1986): 71–136.

Peregudova, Z.I. 'Istochnik izucheniia sotsial-demokraticheskogo dvizheniia v Rossii (materialy fonda departamenta politsii)'. *Voprosy Istorii KPSS*, 1988, no. 9: 88–100.

'Perepiska S.IU. Vitte, A.N. Kuropatkina v 1904–1905 gg.' *Krasnyi Arkhiv* 19 (1926): 64–82.

Perrie, Maureen. 'The Russian Peasant Movement of 1905–1907: Its Social Composition and Revolutionary Significance'. *Past and Present*, no. 52 (November 1972): 123–55.

Pintner, Walter. 'Social Characteristics of the Early Nineteenth Century Russian Bureaucracy'. *Slavic Review* 29 (September 1970): 429–43.

—— 'The Russian High Civil Service on the Eve of the "Great Reforms" '. *The Journal of Social History* 8 (Spring 1975): 55–68.

Pipes, Richard. 'Russian Conservatism in the Second Half of the Nineteenth Century'. *Slavic Review* 30 (March 1971): 121–8.

'Pis'ma Mednikova Spiridovichy'. *Krasnyi Arkhiv* 17 (1926): 192–219.

'Pis'ma N.K. Krupskoi E.D. Stasovoi'. *Istoricheskii Arkhiv*, 1957, no. 1: 2–27.

'Pis'ma S IU. Vitte k D.S. Sipiaginu (1900–1901)'. *Krasnyi Arkhiv* 18 (1926): 30–48.

'Pis'mo Gapona'. *Krasnyi Arkhiv* 9 (1925): 294–7.

'Pis'mo Gartinga k provokatoru'. *Byloe*, Paris, no. 8 (1908): 153–4.

'Pis'mo L.A. Rataeva – S.V. Zubatovu 1900–1903: Soobshchil S.P. Mel'gunov'. *Golos Minuvshago*, no. 1 (June 1922): 51–9.

'Pis'mo S.V. Zubatova [ot 7 avgusta 1916 g.]: A.I. Spiridovichu po povodu vykhoda v svet ego knigi "Partiia s.r. i ee predshestvenniki" '. *Krasnyi Arkhiv* 2 (1922): 280–3.

'Pis'mo V.K. Pleve k A.A. Kireevu: Soobshchil E.V. Tarle'. *Krasnyi Arkhiv* 18 (1926): 201–3.

Pogozhev, A. 'Iz vospominanii o V.K. von-Pleve'. *Vestnik Evropy* 7 (July 1911): 259–80.

'Politicheskoe polozhenie Rossii nakanune Fevral'skoi revoliutsii v zhandarmskom osveshchenii'. *Krasnyi Arkhiv* 17 (1926): 3–25.

Polovtsov, A.A. 'Dnevnik A.A. Polovtseva'. Parts 1, 2. *Krasnyi Arkhiv* 3 (1923): 75–172; 4 (1923): 63–128.

—— 'Iz dnevnika A.A. Polovtsova (1895–1900 gg.)'. *Krasnyi Arkhiv* 46 (1931): 110–32.

'Posle pervogo marta 1881 g.: Soobshchil S. Valk'. *Krasnyi Arkhiv* 45 (1931): 147–64.

'Prikliucheniia I.F. Manuilova: Po arkhivnym materialam'. *Byloe*, n.s. nos 5/6 [27/28] (December 1917): 236–88.

'Psikhologia predatel′stva: (Iz vospominani "sotrudnika")'. *Byloe*, n.s. nos 27/28 (December 1924): 225–37.

'Rabochee dvizhenie i zhandarmskaia politika'. Parts 1, 2. *Revoliutsionnaia Rossiia*, no. 4 (February 1902): 10–13; no. 5 (March, 1902): 5–7.

Raeff, Marc. 'The Bureaucratic Phenomena of Imperial Russia, 1700–1905'. *American Historical Review* 84 (April 1975): 399–411.

—— 'The Russian Autocracy and Its Officials'. *Harvard Slavic Studies* 4 (1957): 77–91.

'Rataev, L. 'Evno Azef. Istoriia ego predatel′stva'. *Byloe*, n.s. no. 2 [24] (August 1917): 187–210.

Rawson, Donald. 'The Death Penalty in Late Tsarist Russia: An Investigation of Judicial Procedures'. *Russian History* 11 (September 1984): 29–58.

'Razoblachennyi Azef'. *Byloe*, n.s. no. 2 [24] (August, 1917): 211–15.

Remington, Thomas. 'Institution Building in Bolshevik Russia: The Case of "State Kontrol"'. *Slavic Review* 41 (1982): 91–103.

'Revoliutsiia 1905–1907 gg.'. *Krasnyi Arkhiv* 62 (1934): 173–214.

Rieber, Alfred J. 'Bureaucratic Politics in Imperial Russia'. *Social Science History* 2 (Summer 1978): 399–413.

Rogger, Hans. 'Reflections on Russian Conservatism: 1861–1905'. Jarbücher für *Geschichte Osteuropas* 14 (1966): 195–212.

—— 'Russian Ministers and the Jewish Question 1881–1917'. *California Slavic Studies* 8 (1975): 15–76.

—— 'The Formation of the Russian Right, 1900–1906'. *California Slavic Studies* 3 (1964): 66–95.

—— 'The Jewish Policy of Late Tsarism: a Reappraisal'. *The Wiener Library Bulletin* 25, nos. 1 and 2 (1971): 42–51.

—— 'Was There a Russian Fascism? The Union of the Russian People'. *The Journal of Modern History* 36 (December 1964): 399–415.

'Rossiia pod nadzorom politsii'. *Osvobozhdenie.* Parts 1–5. nos. 20/21 (19 April 1903): 357–8; no. 29 (19 August 1903): 86–7; no. 30 (2 September 1903): 110–11; no. 33 (19 October 1903): 165; no. 35 (12 November 1903): 185–7.

Rothe, Guenther. 'Personal Rulership, Patrimonialism and Empire-Building in the New States'. In *State and Society: A Reader in Comparative Political Sociology.* Edited by Reinhard Bendix, 581–91. Berkeley and Los Angeles: University of California Press, 1968.

Rowney, D.K. 'Higher Civil Servants in the Russian Ministry of Internal Affairs: Some Demographic and Career Characteristics, 1905–1916'. *Slavic Review* 31 (March 1972): 101–10.

Rowney, Don Karl. 'The Study of the Imperial Ministry of Internal Affairs: The Application of Organization Theory'. In *The Behavioral Revolution and Communist Studies.* Edited by Roger Kanet, 209–31. New York: The Free Press, 1971.

'Russkii sysk v Shvetsii'. *Osvobozhdenie*, no. 57. (7 September 1904): 101–3.

'S. Peterburgskoe okhrannoe otdelenie v 1895–1901 gg. ("Trud" chinovnika Otdeleniia P. Statkovskogo)'. *Byloe*, n.s. no. 16 (1921): 108–36.

Schleifmann, Nurit. 'The Internal Agency: Linchpin of the Political Police in Russia'. *Cahiers du monde Russe et Sovietique* 24 (1983): 151–77.

Schneiderman, Jeremiah, 'From the Files of the Moscow Gendarme Corps: A Lecture on Combatting Revolution'. *Canadian Slavic Studies* 2 (Spring 1968): 86–99.

Scott, E.J. 'The Cheka'. *St. Antony's Papers*, 1956, no. 1: 1–23.

'Sekretnye sotrudniki v avtobiografiiakh'. *Byloe*, n.s. no. 2 [24] (August 1917): 232–61.

Senn, Alfred E., 'The Bolshevik Conference in Bern'. *Slavic Review* 25 (December, 1966): 676–8.

—— ed. 'Russian Emigré Funds in Switzerland 1916; An Okhrana Report'. *International Review of Social History* 13, pt 1 (1968): 76–84.

Seregny, Scott J. 'A Different Type of Peasant Movement: The Peasant Unions in the Russian Revolution of 1905'. *Slavic Review* 47 (Spring 1988): 51–67.

Shidlovskii, Georgii. 'Peterburgskii komitet bol′shevikov v kontse 1913 goda i v nachale 1914 goda: (Po vospominaniiam i arkhivnym dannym)'. *Krasnaia Letopis′*, no. 17 (1926): 119–39.

—— 'Razgrom "Trudovoi pravdy" v 1914 g.'. *Krasnaia Letopis′*, no. 21 (1926): 154–63.

'Shkola filerov'. *Byloe*, n.s. no. 3 [25] (September, 1917): 40–67.

Sidorov, A.L., ed. 'Dnevnik E.A. Sviatopolk-Mirskoi'. *Istoricheskie Zapiski* 77 (1965): 236–93.

Sinel, Allen A. 'The Socialization of the Russian Bureaucratic Elite, 1811–1917: Life at the Tsarskoe Selo Lyceum and the School of Jurisprudence'. *Russian History* 3, pt. 1 (1976): 1–31.

'Sinodik "Pravdy" [1912–1914 gg.]'. *Krasnaia Letopis′*, no. 35 (1930): 244–56.

Slukhotskii, L. 'Ocherk deiatel′nosti ministerstva iustitsii po bor′be s politicheskimi prestupleniiami'. *Istoriko-Revoliutsionnyi Sbornik* 3 (1926): 247–86.

'Soveshchanie gubernatorov v 1916 godu'. *Krasnyi Arkhiv* 33 (1929): 145–69.

Spiridovich, A.I. 'Pri tsarskom rezhime'. *Arkhiv Russkoi Revoliutsii* 15 (1924): 85–209.

'Spiridovich i ego "Istoriia revoliutsionnogo dvizheniia v Rossii"'. *Krasnyi Arkhiv* 26 (1928): 213–20.

Stefanovich, IA. V. 'Russkaia revoliutsionnaia emigratsiia: Zapiska IA. V. Stefanovicha'. *Byloe*, n.s. no. 16 (1921): 75–85.

Suborin, M. 'Iz nedavniago proshlago: Beseda s ministrom vnutrennikh del A.N. Khvostovym'. *Byloe*, n.s. no. 1 [23] (July 1917): 56–63.

Sukhomlin, V.I. 'Provokatorskaia zateia zhandarmskogo generala Seredy'. *Katorga i Ssylka*, nos 28/29 (1926): 148–57.

Suny, Ronald Grigor. 'Commentary: Administration and State Building'. In *Party, State, and Society in the Russian Civil War: Explorations in Social History*. Edited by Diane P. Koenker, William G. Rosenberg, and Ronald Grigor Suny, 232–5. Bloomington: Indiana University Press, 1989.

'Svod pravil vyrabotannykh v razvitie utverzhdennago Gospodinom Ministrom Vnutrennikh. Del 12 avgusta tekushchago goda [1902]: Polozheniia o Nachal'nikakh Rozysknykh Otdelenii'. *Byloe*, Paris, no. 8 (1908): 54–67.

Swain, G.R. 'Freedom of Association and the Trade Unions, 1906–14'. In *Civil Rights in Imperial Russia*. Edited by Olga Crisp and Linda Edmondson. Oxford: Clarendon Press, 1989.

Szeftel, Marc. 'The Form of Government of the Russian Empire Prior to the Constitutional Reforms of 1905–1906'. In *Essays in Russian and Soviet History*. Edited by John S. Curtiss, 107–19. Leiden: E.J. Brill, 1963.

—— 'Personal Inviolability in The Legislation of the Russian Absolute Monarchy'. *The American Slavic and East European Review* 17 (February 1958): 1–24.

'Tainyi doklad: I.d. Moskovskogo Ober-Politsmeistera (po okhrannomy otdeleniiu) 8 Aprelia 1898 g.'. *Rabochee Delo*, 1899, no. 1: 24–34.

Tidmarsh, Kyril. 'The Zubatov Idea'. *The American Slavic and East European Review* 19 (October 1960): 335–46.

Tikhomirov, L. '25 let nazad: Iz dnevnika L. Tikhomirova'. Parts 1, 2. *Krasnyi Arkhiv* 38 (1930): 20–69; 61 (1933): 82–128.

Tiutiunik, L.I. 'Istochniki po istorii Departamenta politsii (1880–1904 gg.)'. *Sovetskie Arkhivy*, 1984, no. 3: 50–4.

Torke, H.J. 'Continuity and Change in Relations between Bureaucracy and Society in Russia, 1613–1861'. *Canadian Slavic Studies* 5 (Winter 1971): 457–76.

'Trepovskii proekt rechi Nikolaiâ II k rabochim posle 9 ianvaria 1905 g.'. *Krasnyi Arkhiv* 20 (1927): 240–2.

'Tsarizm v bor'be s rabochim dvizheniem v gody pod"ema: S predisloviem M. Lur'e'. *Krasnyi Arkhiv* 74 (1936): 37–65.

'Tsarizm v bor'be s revoliutsionnoi pechat'iu 1905 g.: Vvodnaia stat'ia I. Kovaleva'. *Krasnyi Arkhiv* 105 (1941): 140–55.

'Tsarskaia okhranka o politicheskom polozhenii v strane v kontse 1916 g.'. *Istoricheskii arkhiv*, 1960, no. 1: 203–8.

'Tsarskoe pravitel'stvo i protsess Beilisa: S, predisloviem A.S. Tagera'. *Krasnyi Arkhiv* 54/55 (1932): 162–204.

Turnbill, Daniel. 'The Defeat of Popular Representation, December 1904: Prince Mirskii, Witte and the Imperial Family'. *Slavic Review* 48 (1989): 54–70.

'Uchet departamentom politsii opyta 1905 goda'. *Krasnyi Arkhiv* 18 (1926): 219–27.

'V.I. Lenin v gody imperialisticheskoi voiny: Vvodnaia stat'ia I. Iaroslavskogo'. *Krasnyi Arkhiv* 92 (1939): 39–69.

'V gody reaktsii'. *Krasnyi Arkhiv* 8 (1925): 242–3.

'V nachale 1916 goda: (Iz dokumentov)'. *Krasnaia Letopis'*, no. 7 (1923): 208–11.

'V Petrograde nakanune Fevral'skoi revoliutsii: (V osveshchenii petrogradskogo okhrannogo otdeleniia)'. *Krasnaia Letopis'*, no. 22 (1927): 39–47.

Ventin, A.B. 'Piatiletnie itogi (17 oktiabria 1905g.–17 oktiabria 1910g'. *Sovremennyi Mir* 7, no. 12 (1910): 81–9.

Von Laue, T.H. 'Count Witte and the Russian Revolution of 1905'. *The American Slavic and East European Review* 18 (February 1958): 25–47.

Walkin, Jacob. 'Government Controls over the Press in Russia, 1905–1914'. *Russian Review* 13 (July 1954): 203–9.

Wcislo, Francis W. 'Soslovie or Class? Bureaucratic Reformers and Provincial Gentry in Conflict, 1906–1908'. *Russian Review* 47 (1988): 1–24.

Weinberg, Robert. 'Workers, Pogroms and the 1905 Revolution in Odessa'. *The Russian Review* 46 (January 1987): 53–76.

Weissman, Neil. 'Regular Police in Tsarist Russia, 1900–1914'. *The Russian Review* 44 (January 1985): 45–68.

Wilcox, E.H. 'The Black Cabinet'. *The Fortnightly Review* 109 (February 1918): 248–58.

Yaney, George L. 'Bureaucracy and Freedom: N.M. Korkunov's Theory of the State'. *American Historical Review* 71 (January 1966): 468–86.

—— 'Bureaucracy as Culture: A Comment'. *Slavic Review* 41 (1982): 104–11.

—— 'Law, Society and the Domestic Regime in Russia in Historical Perspective'. *American Political Science Review* 59 (1965): 379–90.

—— 'Some Aspects of the Imperial Russian Government on the Eve of the First World War'. *Slavonic & East European Review* 43 (December 1964): 68–90.

Zaionchkovskii, P.A. 'Vysshaia biurokratiia nakanune Krymskoi voiny'. *Istoriia SSSR*, 1974, no. 4: 154–64.

Zakharova, L.G. 'Krizis samoderzhaviia nakanune revoliutsii 1905 goda'. *Voprosy Istorii*, 1972, no. 8: 119–40.

'Zapiska A.A. Lopukhina: O razvitii revoliutsionnago dvizheniia v Rossii (1904g.)'. *Byloe*, Paris, nos 9/10 (1909): 74–8.

'Zapiska direktora depart. pol. Lopukhina o stachkakh v iiule 1903 g. v Odesse, Kieve, Nikolaeve'. *Krasnaia Letopis'*, no. 4 (1922): 382–95.

'Zapiska Generala Novitskogo'. *Sotsial-Revoliutsioner*, Paris, no. 2 (1910): 53–113.

'Zapiska A.F. Redigera o 1905 g.'. *Krasnyi Arkhiv* 45 (1931): 86–111.

'Zhandarmy o "Pravde": (Zapiska okhranki ot 3 iiunia 1914 g.)'. *Proletarskaia Revoliutsiia*, no. 14 (1923): 454–68.

Zhilinskii, V. 'Organizatsiia i zhizn' okhrannago otdeleniia vo vremena tsarskoi vlasti'. *Golos Minuvshago*, nos 9/10 (September/October 1917): 246–306.

Zubatov, S.V. 'Iz nedavniago proshlago: g. Zubatov o Zubatovshchine'. *Vestnik Evropy* 3 (March, 1906): 432–6.

—— 'Zubatovshchina'. *Byloe*, n.s. no. 4 [26] (October, 1917): 157–78.

Zuckerman, Fredric S. 'Political police and Revolution: The Impact of the 1905 Revolution on the Tsarist Secret Police'. *Journal of Contemporary History* 27 (1992): 279–300.

—— 'Self-Imagery and the Art of Propaganda: V.K. von Plehve as Propagandist'. *The Australian Journal of Politics and History* 28 (1982): 68–82.

—— 'Vladimir Burtsev and the Tsarist Political Police in Conflict, 1907–14'. *Journal of Contemporary History* 12 (1977): 193–219.

OTHER NEWSPAPERS AND JOURNALS CONSULTED

Budushchee
Il'Lavoro
L'Eclair
Le Matin
Le Temps
Moskovskiia Vedomosti
Novoe Vremia
Obshchee Delo
Pravo
Rech
The Times (London)
Vechernee Vremia

Key to chain-of-command drawing

—— This line denotes the initial chain-of-command. Orders, instructions or information from the Special Section (which might have originated in the Department of Police or come from the minister of internal affairs himself) are passed on to subordinate branches of the political police administration.

---- This line reflects the reverse process (District Gendarme Directorates excluded); the funnelling of information collected, and various dispatches and requests (i.e. for funds or instructions) back to the Special Section and in turn to the Department of Police (its director), or perhaps to the minister of internal affairs. The District Gendarme Directorates funnelled their requests and intelligence to their provincial superiors.

•••• This line represents the control of the Ministry of Internal Affairs over the Separate Corps of Gendarmes (the Corps of Gendarmes being under the direction of an assistant minister of internal affairs).

=== This line indicates that the Provincial Gendarme Directorates and those of the Siberian and Warsaw regions reported directly to the Department of Police as well as to their immediate superior, the Corps' Chief of Staff, and to the Special Section.

═══ This line reveals that the Department of Police undercut the authority of the Separate Corps of Gendarmes by issuing orders of its own to the Gendarme Directorates. Note: the Special Section itself also undercut the Corps of Gendarmes' authority over Gendarme Directorates (see red line).

—— This line indicates all those bureaux which dispatched information to the OOs, and reveals that the OOs exchanged information among themselves and with the Investigation Stations.

--- This line reveals that the OOs shared their information and sometimes issued orders to the various Gendarme Directorates, often using the Investigation Stations as conveyors.

•••••• This line depicts the line of command between the Separate Corps of Gendarmes and its subordinate branches: the Gendarme Directorates, the Railway Gendarmes, the Gendarme Directorate of Shlusselburg Fortress, and the Border Gendarme Directorate.

oooooo This line denotes the flow of intelligence from Gendarme Directorates to the Separate Corps of Gendarmes.

-—— This line depicts the flow of instructions to the gendarme military units which occupied the lowest position within the bureaucratic structure of the Separate Corps of Gendarmes. These units controlled civil disorders usually at the request of the civil authorities.

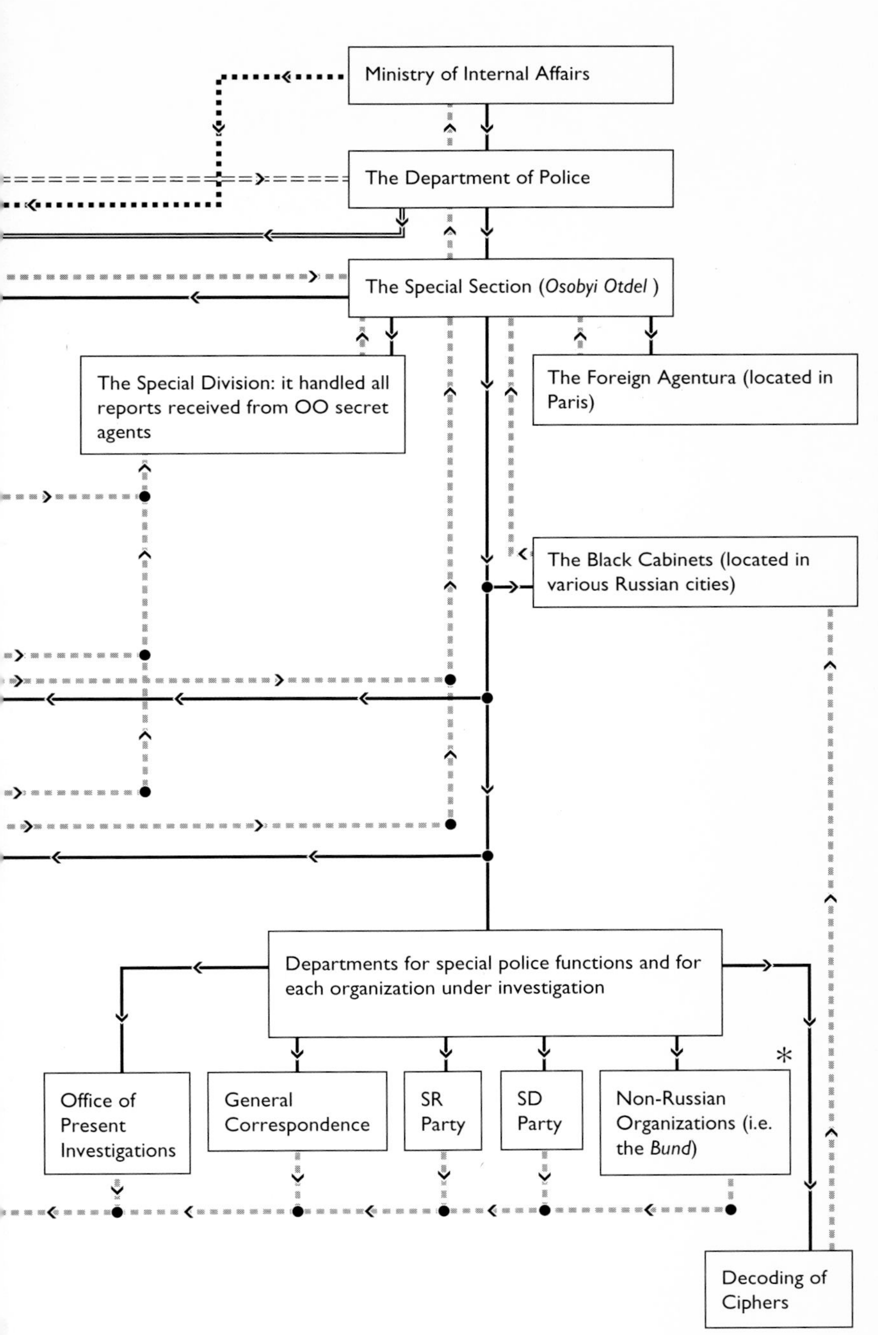

*As noted in the text, the number of these sections depended upon which groups, both legal and subversive, the Special Section thought best to keep under investigation.

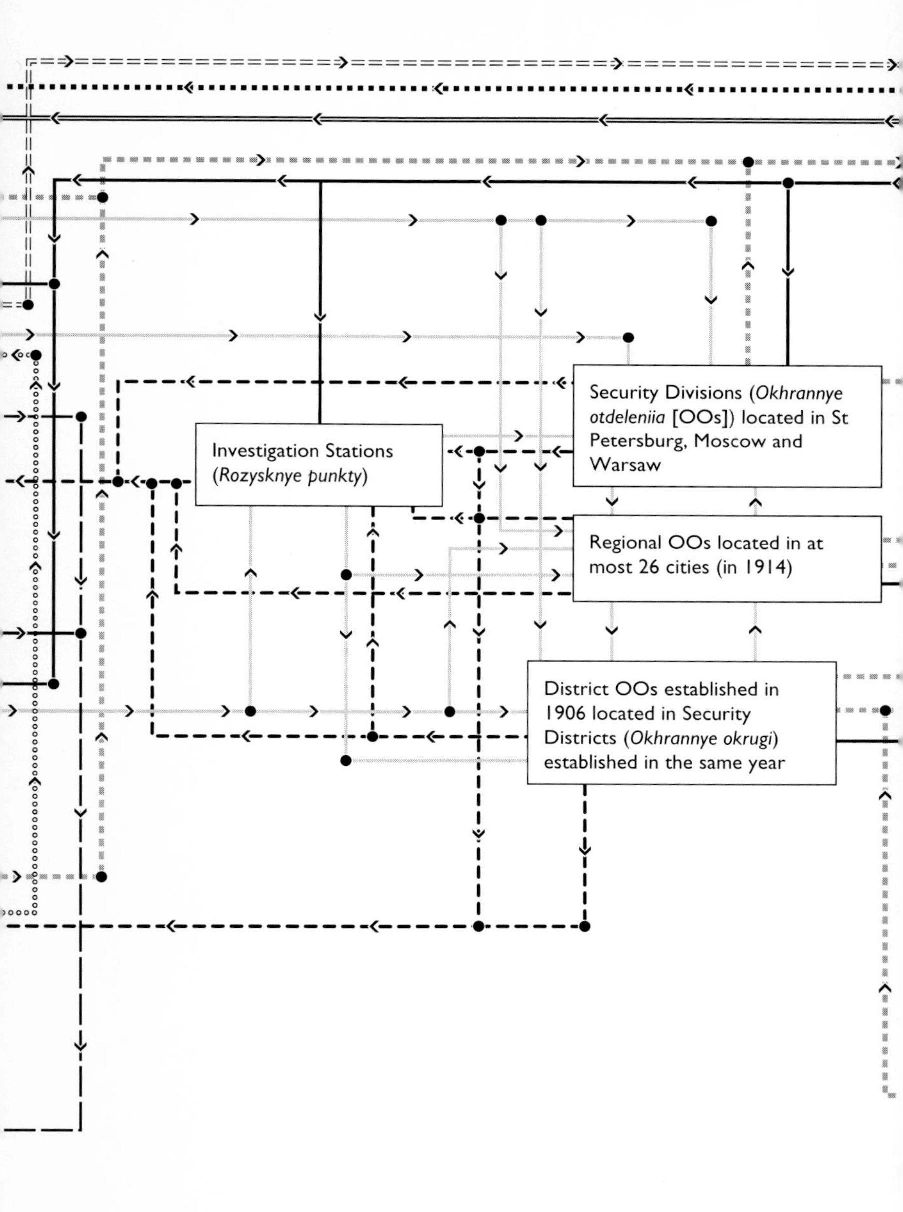
Security Divisions (*Okhrannye otdeleniia* [OOs]) located in St Petersburg, Moscow and Warsaw
Investigation Stations (*Rozysknye punkty*)
Regional OOs located in at most 26 cities (in 1914)
District OOs established in 1906 located in Security Districts (*Okhrannye okrugi*) established in the same year

A diagram of the chain-of-command of the Russian political police displaying the chain-of-command and diagramming the routes of information received on its way to the special section

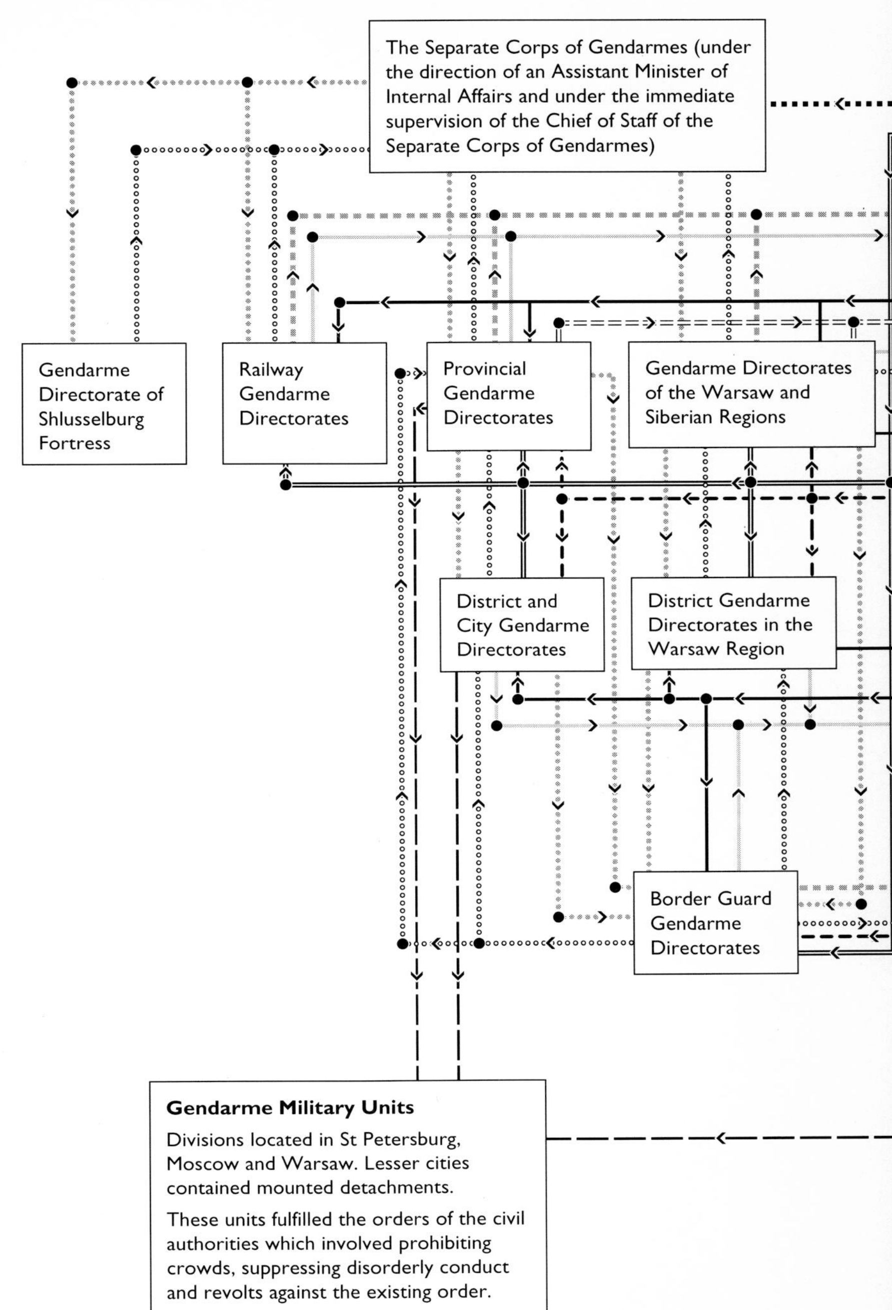

Index

Entries in this index in bold type indicate the location of a table.